Illustrations on the cover and cartoons throughout book created by Klaus Shmidheiser.

Copyright © 2009, 2010 by John Boyer
Copyright © 2006 by Kendall/Hunt Publishing Company
ISBN 978-0-7575-8292-9

Printed in the United States of America
10 9 8 7 6 5 4 3 2

Acknowledgments

Contributing Writers: Steven Rich, Flash Clark, Josette Torres, Amber Zoe Smith, Alexander Reniers, Nicholas Reinholtz, & Jason Hushour

Chief Editor and Zen Master of the Red Pen: Josette Torres, aka girlinblack

Editors: Josette Torres, Stacy Boyer, Chris Drake, Tacy Newell-Foutz & Amber Zoe Smith

Image Acquisitions: Katie Pritchard

Graphics Creation: Katie Pritchard

Film Critic: Steven Rich

Plaid Avenger's Transcription Team: Chris Drake, Renata L. Hafich & Steven Rich

Personal Assistant to the Plaid Avenger: Katie Pritchard

And a special thanks to the most awesome plaid artist on the planet:
Cartoonist: Klaus Shmidheiser

PART ONE
UNDERSTANDING THE PLAID PLANET

A Plaid World Intro

1

What is globalization?

How do the interconnections of the global economy and politics affect my life?

Why are some places rich while others are poor?

What does the future of the planet look like?

All great questions, fellow world watchers—questions that deserve great answers. Thoughtful, intuitive and well-researched answers contained in a well-ordered and glibly constructed textbook.

This is not that book.

Welcome to my world. The world of the Plaid Avenger, where seeking knowledge of our planet is imperative, where blissful ignorance is not accepted, and where truth and justice can only be achieved by those willing to learn . . . willing to work . . . willing to fight. It is not a place most are ready to enter yet. But you are here. Good. Read on.

In *The Plaid Avenger's World*, we will strip off the shallow window dressing in which you have been trained to see the world. We will lay it bare to see what is really happening around the planet. We do this in order to gain enough insight about the current state of the world to truly understand the how and why and where things are happening right now. In this world, no single government or press dictates our views; no single political party shapes our opinion; no single religion or ethnicity tints our not-so-rose-colored glasses. We will see the world in plaid: a mystical weaving of facts, figures, cultures and viewpoints from every corner of the planet, culminating into the fabric that is today.

Many, if not most, in our society would say, "Why bother?" Here's why:

AGE OF GLOBALIZATION

Globalization: what is it and what does it mean to me? Economically? Technologically? Politically? Socially? Morally?

We constantly hear about how the world is getting smaller—is it? Hell, the world is the same size it has always been . . . *but* it is becoming more connected and more interdependent than ever before. More information flows faster from even the most remote parts of the planet. For the first time ever we can travel to any part of the world virtually overnight. Corporations move capital and jobs from one country to the next in a matter of days. News of international significance is reported seconds after it happens. We can communicate in real time with any part of the globe. The world is now one system . . . mostly.

We are the first generation of humans who enjoy foreign travel as a casual part of life, who communicate by direct-dialing to any country on all continents, who receive instant news of world happenings, who expect to work overseas or work for a company that deals overseas. Let me reiterate that—expect; it is not an exception. This is a really important concept, especially to you—the first generation that is living in the postindustrial, highly interconnected age.

Many if not all of you will work for multinational companies whose business is all over the world. Many if not all of you will work and live outside of the US at some point in your careers. Businesses and jobs are internationalizing as we speak—almost all jobs, not just the fancy ones. You guys are the people who are going to be running the world. You guys are the decision makers—when all is said and done, I'm just a single superhero out thwarting international intrigue. But *you* will be the ones building the bridges, and electing leaders, and stabilizing governments, controlling monetary exchange rates; you may even be setting up all sorts of private or national or even international businesses/programs/projects that will shape the world and its population.

Make no mistake about it, the AIDS rate in Africa *does* affect you, the increasing coal consumption in China *does* affect you, an earthquake in Japan, and the price of cocaine in Colombia *does* affect you. (allocation of your tax dollars, your jobs, the price you pay for goods, the amount of goods we sell, etc.) Globalization is pretty much a one-way street. We are not going back to medieval times, no matter what isolationists say, do, or think. Ignore the rest of the world at your own peril—you won't be hurting anyone but yourself. How did this globalization happen anyway . . . and how has it shaped our planet?

A WEALTH OF -ATIONS

Of all the organisms hanging out on this blue marble we call Earth, us human-types have been the biggest modifiers, movers, shakers, benders and breakers of our fair planet. We grow food, we congregate in cities, we move around, we plan, we build machines, we communicate, we educate, we procreate . . . and we have done it faster and more thoroughly year after year after year at a larger and larger scale that has inevitably consumed the world. The idea that globalization is merely a modern phenomena is pure poppycock: all of human history can be seen as a relentless drive to expand our tribe to every nook and cranny of the planet, and to increase the non-stop interactivity between peoples, for better or for worse. Think about it. Civilization, migration, urbanization, industrialization, modernization, communication: all have served to organize, spread, and interconnect us. What a wealth of -ations that all feed into one grand scheme of globalization!

You probably have learned about a lot of these -ation terms in other classes and coursework, but I want you to think about them again for a few minutes in the context of this globalization concept. Without getting into too much tedious detail, I tell you that humans have been globalizing since the birth of the species (or since a naked dude and a naked dudette were plopped down in a garden, if you prefer). **Migration** of humans started when the first modern *Homo sapiens* started hauling ass out of Africa over 70,000 years ago . . . damn, did Africa suck even back then? Humans subsequently spread to all continents and all major islands, and this process of movement is still going strong today.

Humans used to migrate in order take advantage of new unpopulated lands, untapped resources, or to follow game; in today's world they migrate for jobs, for security, for a better life in a richer place. Wait a minute . . . is there a difference between those migration motivations? Maybe not. Did you really think that "illegal" Mexican migration to the US or African migration to Europe was some new thing? Ha! We've been on that route forever. But let's be civilized about this, which brings me to . . .

Civilization, a process that wildly impacted the human experience. See, we used to be the ever-expanding, ever-migrating, hunter-gatherer types living in small unconnected bands scattered across the planet, but around 10,000 years ago, some folks stumbled upon agriculture, and that was a game changer. All that extra food surplus as a result of growing plants in a predictable cycle led to folks settling down in permanent places, the domestication of animals, the creation of better tools,

Take a bite, and let's get this globalization ball rolling . . .

specialization of work, and complex societies which encouraged trade and cooperation. And not just trade within a single society, but between different ones in different places.

Aha! That was the evolution of intentional interconnections between populated areas in an effort to trade not just goods and services, but ideas and technologies and peoples themselves! Globalization on! They call this stuff "outsourcing" and "economic activity" and "'technology transfer" in today's world . . . but it's all the same stuff as way back when. Same shit, different millennium.

This civilization gig also transforms the geographic organization of human life: we go from small bands of folks out in the wild to hanging out with each other in bigger in bigger numbers in things called villages, then towns, then cities. The first major civilizations that popped up 6000 years ago in China, Indus Valley, Mesopotamia, Egypt, et al. began a perpetual process of population growth and **urbanization** that continues unabated to this day. Translation: humans have increasingly chosen to live in big population clusters in built-up areas that we call cities as opposed to hanging out in the sparsely-populated po-dunk rural areas we refer to as "the sticks." Humankind reached a milestone just back in 2009 when, for the first time in human history, over 50% of the world's population now lives in an urban area. And that percentage is growing bigger, faster than ever.

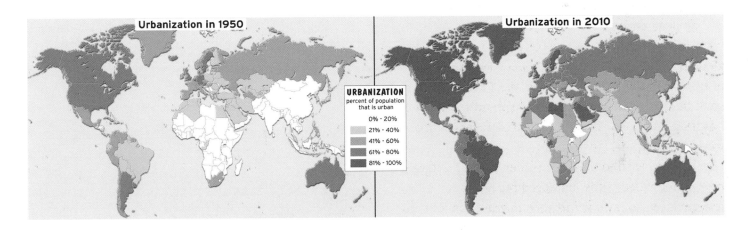

This urbanization has intensified human interaction exponentially over time; interaction which has accelerated the creation and transfer of ideas and technologies. New ideas, new inventions, new stuff! Which prompted **industrialization,** of course! Did you ever stop and wonder how it is possible for so many people to now cram themselves into cities, thus not being able to grow their own food or collect their own water or hunt their own bison? Because we invented machines to do the heavy lifting that used to require all our labor, and we discovered energy sources to fuel those machines. Bottom line: one dude on a tractor can grow enough food to feed a million people in the city; ten kids in a sweat shop can make all clothes for that million, and oil-powered big machines can build skyscrapers and sewer systems and water lines for that million people. What the hell is left for those city folks to do?

They have time to think. To interact. To create. To be inventors, doctors, artists, engineers, scientists, industrialists, priests, rock stars, and whatever else we come up with. That's how we got electricity, the polio vaccine, the Hoover Dam, mobile phones, and computers. Unfortunately, with so much free time and such diverse and bizarre human motivations, we also have nuclear weapons, mustard gas, lawyers, and Sham-Wow. Such is the yin and yang of life. But I digress. This urbanization/industrialization combo has served to link up the globe like never before: more humans compacted into bigger, concentrated urban areas has caused even more interaction within the city, but also increasingly between cities worldwide. Cities are both the engines and the nodes of globalizing forces; the conduit for transfers of ideas, money, technologies, and power, everywhere, all the time.

This "connectedness" is now happening at light speed, thanks to advances in transportation and ***communication***. Yep, our last -ation is really the power-booster icing on this globalizing cake. From smoke signals to the Pony Express to trans-oceanic telegraph cables, we humans have spent a lot of time and effort figuring out how to better transmit information to each other across the planet. Let me be the first to tell you, my brothers and sisters: we have almost reached the end-game on this one. With mobile phones, the Internet, and satellite TV/radio, we can pretty much transmit any type of information almost instantaneously to any part of the globe. It's totally insane if you think about it.

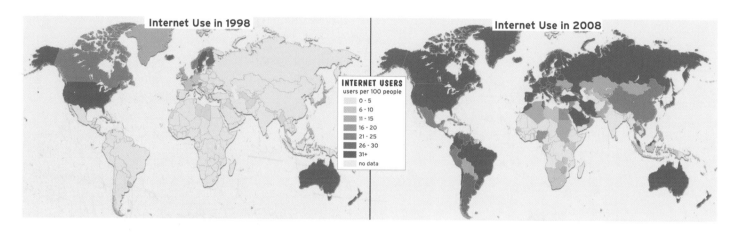

More ideas, more information, more interaction between more people than *ever* before. Twittering every second of our collective experience! And more folks are jumping into the system faster than ever before as well. Just look at the figure below to see the speed at which the world is hooking up on-line!

We have essentially set ourselves up as a single huge worldwide computer, wherein all the humans attached to this systems are interacting to solve problems, sell goods, provide news, and everything else! What is the Matrix? Hell, just look around! We can chat with friends in Uzbekistan, watch a live news report from Brazil, vacation at the Vatican, have business transactions with Singapore, and share research ideas via Skype with associates in Switzerland. That, my friends,

is global connection. That is globalization, made possible by all the other -ations of note in this section.

What does it all add up to? A more fully connected world in every sense of the word, in which the actions of any one person affects the lives of everyone. All of the aforementioned -ations have gone from local, isolated or internal concepts to completely planetary themes in scope and practice. In this increasingly populated and interconnected world, it is becoming clear that all "local" problems are actually "global" problems, from the movement of narcotics, to an outbreak of an infectious disease, to environmental pollution, to the existence of nuclear weapons, and so on.

However, the solutions lie within this connected framework as well. See, this globalization is neither bad nor good. It just is, and will continue to be. Will globalization result in a homogenization of culture? In a modernization of all societies? In a pacification of the planet? In a disintegration of the concept of the sovereign state? Oh, my oh my, what a delicious stew of other -ation possibilities that I will leave to you to debate . . .

For now, I just wanted to spill some of that crazy globalization knowledge on your skullcap to see the sparks fly.

Knowledge is power, or at least empowerment. The more you know about the globalizing world in which we live, the more power you have. It's good to have at least a minimal geographical understanding of our planet. What's that? You don't know what geography is?

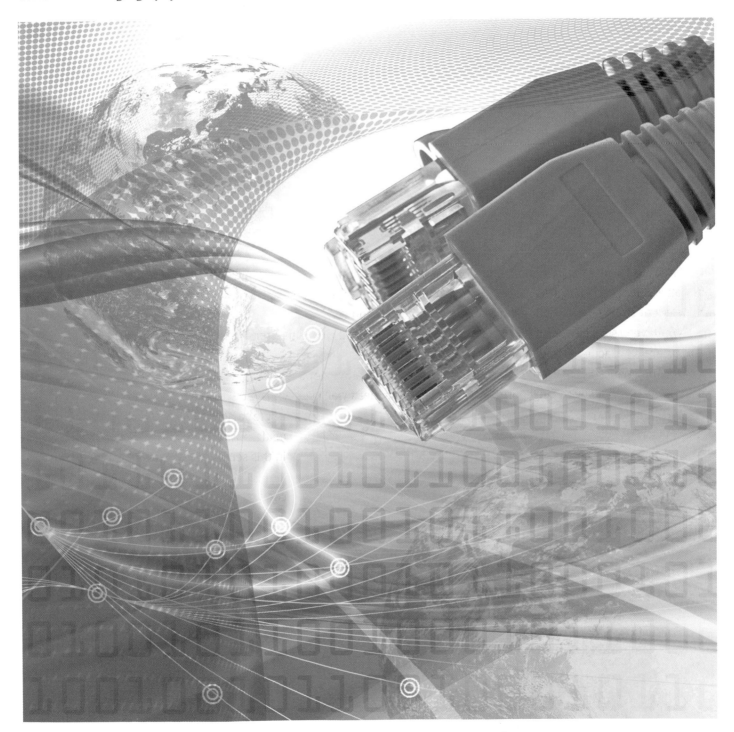

WHAT IS GEOGRAPHY?

Geography is one of those words, and subsequently one of those fields of study, which has become so generic that it seems to have lost its own definition in the modern world. The term is so truly holistic in meaning that many other social sciences, as well as a lot of the physical ones, are actually sub-branches of it, as opposed to geography's current designation as a sub-branch of one of them. What am I talking about? Consider for a moment the origin of the word and the discipline; *geography* has its roots in the ancient world, roughly translated as "describing the Earth," and every culture and society with a written record has done just that—described both physically and culturally the environment around them as they understood it.

Be it Greek philosophers calculating the size of the known world in the 2nd century BCE, Chinese diplomats considering trade ties with Southeast Asia in the 11th century, military strategists planning the Boer War in Africa, or American scientists assessing the impact of the loss of Brazilian rainforest on world climate in the 21st century—all are geographers in the sense that they are studying the physical and/or cultural components of their environments to gain understanding and make decisions—just as all of us do every day in our own lives. How do I get from here to there? Should I buy an American car to support the American economy, even though their fuel efficiency is worse than imported cars? What is the foreign policy of the political party I support? Should I donate money to alleviate hunger in Ethiopia? Is this neighborhood I'm in a high-crime area? Paper or plastic? All questions require us to consider economic, social, political, and environmental knowledge and repercussions of that knowledge on the world around us.

We are unique!

I am intentionally pointing out here that the world around us, every place on the planet no matter where you are, has both physical traits and cultural traits that make it unique. Every place has a certain climate, particular landforms, and some kind of soils, vegetation and animal life. These are its **physical** traits, much like every human has some natural hair color, skin color, a certain height and weight, and particular physical abilities—maybe to run fast or jump high. At the same time, every place has languages being spoken, religious practices, economic activities, political organizations, and human infrastructure like roads and buildings. These are the **cultural** traits of the place, just like a human has certain religious beliefs, spoken language, a job, a learned skill like archery, and a favorite flavored ice cream. Just like every human in the world, every place in the world is unique in its own right, kind of like snowflakes. Defining any place in the world, or any region of the world, involves looking at both of these aspects, as well as their interaction with each other.

Every place on the planet is unique in that even when many of these factors are identical—say between two small towns in the Midwest located only five miles apart—there will still be tangible differences. Each town has a different history. The weather may be pretty much the same, but one will get more rainfall than the other. The people may all be of the same religion, but there will be different churches that do things just slightly different. The economies may both be based on corn, but there will be different business names, and different storefronts. There will be at least one Chinese restaurant in both towns, but they will definitely have different tasting General Tso's chicken. Like human identical twins, no matter how much is the same, there are always distinguishable differences upon closer examination. To understand our world, we will look at the physical and cultural traits of regions of the planet, how these traits converge to form a distinct region, and perhaps more importantly for our assignment, how these regions interact with each other.

What the heck is a region?

WHAT IS A REGION?

The world is just too darn big and filled with a heck of a lot of things going on and way too many facts and figures and images and names and places for us to know and comprehend everything all of the time. You can't possibly even know all the facts and histories and physical variables of your own home town, much less your county, your state, or your planet. There's just too much, and the story is added to and updated daily. But don't give up hope! Don't become despondent! And for goodness sake, don't start drinking cheap Chardonnay. The human mind has a coping mechanism for this overflow of knowledge, which of course has gotten much worse with the advent of global communications and the 24-hour news cycle: We assess importance. We filter. We generalize. We are going to do the same geographically for the planet. By synthesizing and systematizing vast amounts of information from parts of the world and making pertinent generalizations, we create a unit of area called a *region.*

Regions are areas usually defined by one or more distinctive characteristics or features, which can be physical features or cultural features, or more often than not, a combination of both. We could identify a strictly physical region such as a pine forest, the Sahara Desert or the Mississippi drainage basin. Conversely, we could form up an area that we would identify culturally like the Bible Belt, a Wal-Mart store service area, or even Switzerland (defined by human-created political borders). However, since we have already pointed out that every part of the planet has both types of traits, most regions are identified as a combination of physical and cultural characteristics, such as the regions we refer to as the Midwestern US, tropical Africa, or Eastern Europe. These names typically make one think of both physical and cultural traits simultaneously, and may actually be meaningless in a context of just one or the other. This last type of world regional delineation is what we will mainly utilize in our journey.

That is a good jumping off point for what we will consider a region for our global guidebook. A region has three components:

1. Has to have some area.

2. Has to have some boundaries—although these boundaries are typically fuzzy, or imperfectly defined. Where does the Middle East stop and Africa start?

3. Has to have some homogeneous trait or traits that set it apart from surrounding areas. This is the most important thing to consider.

The user defines what trait is homogeneous. You can define any place on earth as being in an infinite number of regions, depending on what trait you pick. Your current exact position could be described as in a distinct political region like Charleston, California, or Canada. Or perhaps you're in a distinct physical region like the Everglades or the Appalachians or the Badlands. Simultaneously you may be in a distinct socially defined region like the Bible Belt, the Rust Belt, or the "The Beltway"—what region do you think you are in right now? Play this exciting "name your region" game with all your friends, and you will be the toast of the town. Or perhaps a big geek. But I digress.

Here is a quick breakdown of the world regions we will be examining:

FIGURE 1.1 WORLD REGIONS AS DEFINED BY THE PLAID AVENGER

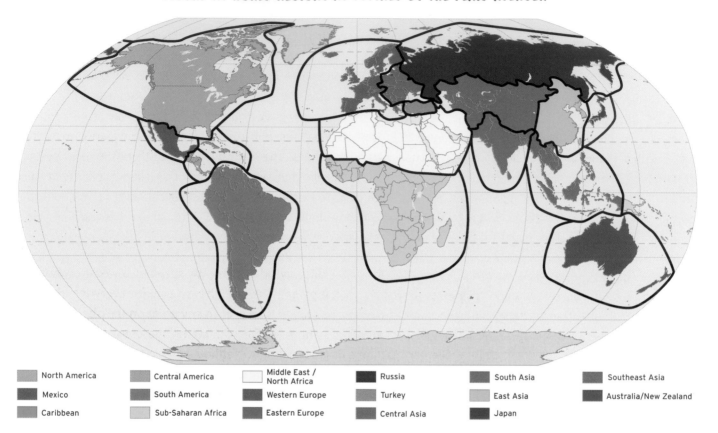

North America	Central America	Middle East / North Africa	Russia	South Asia	Southeast Asia
Mexico	South America	Western Europe	Turkey	East Asia	Australia/New Zealand
Caribbean	Sub-Saharan Africa	Eastern Europe	Central Asia	Japan	

Why these areas? Why these borders? Why these regions? Because they are defined by homogeneous traits as picked by me. These are the Plaid Avenger's world regions. The bulk of this book will be explaining these regions and their homogeneous traits. Your world regional map may be different than mine depending upon what traits you want to focus.

Don't like my regions? Write your own damn book.

A MATTER OF SCALE

When we are being geographers, or defining regions, or even just trying to get from point A to point B, we must always keep the *scale* of our endeavor in mind. How much area are we talking about? How far are point A and B from each other? Does this description of the environment in my hometown scale apply to a larger scaled area like my state or country? It rarely does. Thus we must always be wary about how far we can push our analysis. Changing scales typically calls for reassessment of the area being considered.

The other reason to pay attention to scale is because it plays an important component of our definition of regions. Since we have already expressed that regions have some sort of homogeneous factor that defines them, we must consider at what scale does this homogeneity apply—because the scale itself defines it. Let me give you an example.

Several presidential elections ago our country, by majority, elected Bill Clinton—a Democrat—to the presidency. Since more than half voted Democrat, we could say that the US, at the country scale, is a Democratic region, based on that singular homogeneous trait. However, if we looked at the state of Virginia, it voted predominately Republican—so at a smaller scale, we are in a Republican region. Fairfax County, a smaller region within Virginia, may have voted predominately

Democrat, thus, in that smaller region, we are back to a Democrat-defined area. Maybe most of the people on a certain city block in Fairfax County, a smaller region still, voted Republican, so at the block scale you are in Republican territory again. Thus, defining regions based on voting preferences *demands* that you state the scale of focus. Most importantly, the larger the region you define, the more exceptions to your homogeneous trait you will find within your region.

This is what generalizations are all about—we are going to discuss and define our regions with *generally homogeneous* traits within the region, knowing full well our generalization won't apply to everyone and every place. For example: by any definition, the Middle East region would be identified as an area dominated by Islam. Oops, except for a radical and extremely important exception—that of the Jewish state of Israel. For our travels, we will be pointing out and elaborating mostly on those homogeneous traits which define our regions, but will also include those glaring exceptions to the rule when they are of particular significance to today's headlines. The other main goal of this guide is to describe each of the world regions' interactions with each other, and their role in the world at large. This is a tall order to be sure, but a goal worthy of pursuit by the mightiest of global superheroes, the Plaid Avenger.

SO WHO THE HELL IS THE PLAID AVENGER?

Yes, it seems that everything is growing into a singular world system. We speak of a world economy in which goods and services and businesses move all over the planet; they even have a club for everyone: the WTO. We have a great global transportation network that can transport us faster than ever to any point on the planet. We have the United Nations: a world legislative body that sets standards and rules for conduct on the planet (and I've heard rumors that they are also supposedly peace-keeping enforcers of these rules . . . although I won't swear to this). Thanks to mass media and global telecommunications, we can even speak of movement towards a more homogeneous world culture—where in the world can you *not* talk on your mobile phone while you watch MTV and sip on a Guinness?

But wait, there seems to be something missing. Hmmm. . . . Global leadership . . . check. Global legislature . . . check. Global economy . . . check. Global judicial system . . . Global judicial system . . . Global justice??? Bueller . . . Bueller . . . Bueller? Where is it? I knew something was missing, dammit.

Just as the world continues to become more interconnected, and every event across the globe becomes more pertinent to our daily lives, we gain more knowledge about inequalities and unfairness around the planet. This comes at a time here at the dawn of the 21st century when conflict proliferates around the globe, multinational corporations grow unchecked and unhindered by law, diseases have the capacity to truly create an unprecedented planetary epidemic, and trade in guns, drugs, and people continue unabated. Yes, even the trade in people . . . you know, slavery. Global inequality may be reaching a new zenith; that is, the gulf between the rich and the poor widens as every day passes, and those poor folks are growing in numbers.

The Plaid Avenger is a product of this age. Somewhere at a major university on the Eastern Seaboard, a meek but smartly dressed college professor by day, he toils in an effort to educate the youth of America about the wider world, and their role in it. By night, he roams the planet fighting organized international crime, abusive multinational corporations, and corrupt governments, wherever they may be. He also has a penchant for fine wines and liquors from around the globe, but that is a different story. The Plaid Avenger: international equalizer and educator. A fighter for truth, global justice, and the international way, he also possesses an unstoppable urge to bring plaid back into fashion.

That brings us to your first assignment: Your first mission to become globally literate—that is, smart—and know the locations of the states of the world. In America, we call them "countries," but you should start calling them states now and just get over it. Look back to Figure 1.1, and get to work. The reason? While I'm not an advocate of memorizing every town, district, and province on the map, we do need to have a working vocabulary to discuss things intelligently. Not that you need to be able to draw a map from memory, but you will be amazed how much more intelligent you appear when you are in a discussion about a news event and you know with authority that Senegal is in western Africa, not in Central Asia. Trust me, chicks dig it.

Got them all down? Then look at the following figures. A straight-up matching game with some style. As the Plaid Avenger must often work undercover around the planet, he has an endless array of outfits to help him blend into the environs he is investigating. He also frequently meets up with local undercover escorts who "assist" him in his missions. Match the appropriate high-lighted country map to the outfit the Plaid Avenger would be wearing and the appropriate undercover agent he would be meeting there. Good luck, and see you in Chapter 2.

1

2

3

A

B

C

a

b

c

d

e

f

4

5

6

D

E

F

World Population Dynamics

2

BEFORE we get to the regions, we will focus on several topics that are better approached at the global scale; they involve traits that all regions possess equally, like people or religions, or that all regions participate in as a singular global unit, like the world economy or international organizations. Since people create, define, and operate all the cultural aspects of our planet, let's start with them.

INTRO TO PEOPLE AKA WORLD SEX ED 101

People, people, people, all over the world. Old ones, young ones, rich ones, poor ones, black ones, white ones, Asian ones, and even plaid ones. Some places got lots of people, some places got just a few. Are there too many people? Perhaps not enough in some places? Some states have growing populations, while other states actually have shrinking populations. What's this all about? Although there are great differences around the world in numbers of people as well as growth rates of populations, it is best to approach the subject by looking at it systematically. That is, we can look at how human population dynamics operate as a whole, because the rules are essentially the same anywhere you go on the planet. Let's get to know how it works, and then you can apply your knowledge to understand what's happening in any state or region of interest. Game on!

For starters, you should know that we are currently closing in on 7 billion people alive across the world right now. This has not always been the case. In fact, numbers this huge for human population are actually quite recent. Consider Figure 2.1.

As you can see, for most of humankind's existence, population totals have been relatively small. It took approximately one million years, from the beginning of time until about the year 1800, for the first billion humans to appear on the earth at the same time. From then, it's roughly

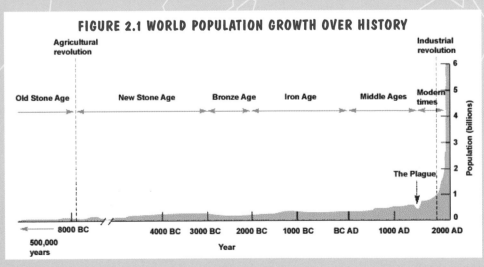

FIGURE 2.1 WORLD POPULATION GROWTH OVER HISTORY

Agricultural revolution

Industrial revolution

Old Stone Age | New Stone Age | Bronze Age | Iron Age | Middle Ages | Modern times

Population (billions)

The Plague

500,000 years | 8000 BC | 4000 BC | 3000 BC | 2000 BC | 1000 BC | BC AD | 1000 AD | 2000 AD

Year

→ 1927 that the second billion showed up

→ 1960 saw the crossing over to 3 billion

→ 1974 picked up number 4 billion

→ 1987 flipped the pop-odometer to 5 billion and

→ 1999 the predawn of the 21st century reached the 6 billion high-water mark. Or should I say, the high-broken-water mark.

What you may be detecting here is a radically accelerated population increase in the last forty years. The time it takes to add another billion people gets shorter every cycle, with the 7 billion mark quickly approaching. Why is this happening? Population growth is exponential, not mathematical. Adding ten more fertile females to the population pool doesn't equate to adding just ten more babies, but more like one hundred babies. Each woman has the potential to spawn many more offspring, who in turn can produce many more offspring themselves down the road. Get it? You can't blame it all on me either. I'm good, but not that damn good.

As a result of this exponential growth in the human population, many folks believe that the planet is already overpopulated. Is that true? I can't give you an answer for that, because it is a relative question. Where are we talking about? Siberia? It's certainly not overpopulated. Calcutta, India? Perhaps it certainly is overpopulated. Maybe. Many assume that Africa as a whole is overpopulated, but given the size of the place and its current population totals, it is actually quite sparsely populated, particularly if you compare it to a place like Western Europe. And if Western Europe is overpopulated, why do many of its governments encourage their citizens to have more babies? Hmmmm . . . things get complicated fast. Plaid Avenger rule of thumb: a place seems to be considered truly overpopulated only when not enough resources exist to supply the people who live there. Thus, the 70 million people in Ethiopia may all agree that their country is overpopulated, but the 80 million people in Germany would probably not consider themselves so, even given that Ethiopia is roughly three times the size of its schnitzel-eating friend.

But enough for now on the theme of over- or underpopulation. Let's look at where people are in the first place.

CHART 1 TOP 20 POPULOUS STATES
COUNTRIES RANKED BY POPULATION: 2008

Rank	Country	Population
1	China	1,323,775,000
2	India	1,131,750,000
3	United States	305,000,000
4	Indonesia	240,000,000
5	Brazil	189,000,000
6	Pakistan	165,000,000
7	Bangladesh	158,000,000
8	Nigeria	150,000,000
9	Russia	142,000,000
10	Japan	128,000,000
11	Mexico	108,000,000
12	Philippines	90,000,000
13	Vietnam	87,000,000
14	Germany	82,000,000
15	Ethiopia	79,000,000
16	Egypt	75,000,000
17	Iran	72,000,000
18	Turkey	71,000,000
19	France	65,000,000
20	Thailand	63,000,000

REGIONAL DIFFERENCES IN POPULATION

Where are people, and where are they not? In some parts of the world, harsh climates and terrains are too formidable for large numbers of humans to hang out in. The cold Arctic areas in Canada and Russia, the great desert and steppe regions in North Africa and Central Asia, and the high Andes and Himalayan ranges serve to keep population numbers low. Humans tend to proliferate in well-watered areas and along coastlines. Generally speaking, human settlements favor the mid-latitudes; there are far more people in Eurasia and North America than in tropical areas. Draw on your own experiences to figure out this trend. Would you like to live in a tropical rainforest, a desert, or a mountain top? Why or why not?

FIGURE 2.2 POPULATION DENSITY, MAJOR CENTERS

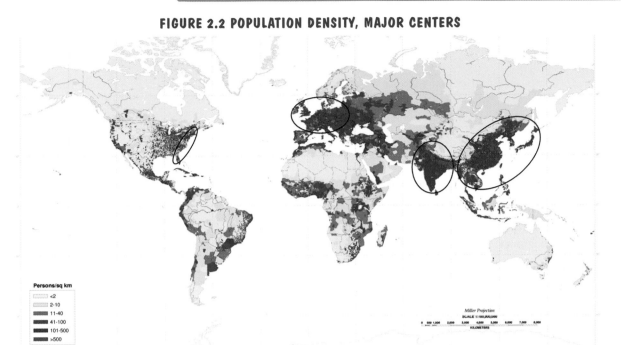

People have adapted to living in just about every extreme environment on our planet—just not in great numbers. What is the deal with the great numbers? It has a lot to do with history, culture and current population dynamics which we'll get to in just a second. First, a few points about the map in Figure 2.2. As you can see, I've circled the four biggest population clusters on the planet for our discussion.

Over half the world's population are found in Eurasia, particularly a people-packed arc from Japan to Eastern China, through Southeast Asia to South Asia. The common perception is that China is far and away the most populated place with over a billion people. But watch out! India has a billion people as well, and, more importantly, is growing at a faster rate than China, which means that it will certainly become the top slot within a couple of decades. Don't forget India's neighborhood—Pakistan and Bangladesh are both members of the top ten most populous states in the world as well.

The monstrous Asian population centers are, in large part, a product of history. People in these areas have been getting busy—in more ways than one—for thousands of years since the innovation of agriculture and the birth of civilization as we know it. They have existed as stable civilizations for long periods of time. They also happen to be in physically conducive environments—well-watered, mid-latitude lowlands. This also helps to explain why the cradle of Western Civilization—Mesopotamia, which is just as old—did not form huge populations over time. Its physical environment is arid and unable to support large numbers of people.

However, due to great leaps in technology during the Industrial Revolution, including lots of technologies that helped keep more humans alive longer, Europe's population boomed in the last several hundred years. They are another significant center for people-packing on the planet. By contrast, not a lot of folks have been in the Western Hemisphere for very long. When Europeans did arrive in the New World, they brought diseases that wiped out a vast number of people, thus leading to much lower numbers on our side of the planet. History, combined with the physical world, has a lot to do with where most people are today.

Two more global population points of interest: Africa, largely believed to be overpopulated, is a huge-ass place, but with half the population totals of South Asia or East Asia. My favorite population fact deals with Russia and the US, the two Cold War adversaries. Look again at the map, and realize this: these two regions account for less than 10 percent of the world's population, but have effectively shaped the political and economic fate of the other 90 percent during the last 50 years. Interesting, isn't it? Okay, maybe not, but it certainly was during the Cold War. Those commies produced some fine vodkas, which apparently diminished their child-producing capabilities because Russia is a state currently in population decline. Which brings us to our next point: where are populations growing, where are they shrinking, and why?

HOW POPULATION IS CHANGING

To complicate matters further, not just total population but also **population growth rates** are unevenly distributed around the world. Population growth rate refers to how fast or slow a group's population total is expanding . . . or shrinking, when referring to our Cossack friends. When you see a number like 3.5 for a population growth rate, it indicates that, by this time next year, the population total for that country will be 3.5% bigger than it is right now. A negative number is the inverse: population growth of −0.5 means that population total for next year will be 0.5% smaller than it is presently. See if you can detect any patterns in the map on page 27.

Saudi Arabia's population total is expanding very quickly, which means the country has a high growth rate. China's total population gets bigger every year, but not by much percentage-wise; the country has a moderate to slow growth rate. Belgium's population total remains the same every year—a stable or flat growth rate. Russia's population total is getting smaller every year—a negative growth rate. You may have also identified a major trend: the highest growth rates typically occur in states that we consider underdeveloped, a.k.a. the poor ones. Say again? You mean the poorest areas of the planet are where more people are being added faster than ever? That is correct. The developed, or richer, states all seem to have low growth rates. So the places that could afford to provide for more kids, have less kids? Yep, that's true as well. Why is this so? Good question. Answer: the Demographic Transition.

FIGURE 2.3 WORLD POPULATION GROWTH RATES

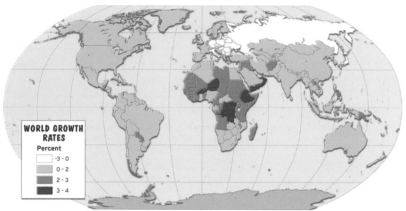

WORLD GROWTH RATES
Percent
-3 - 0
0 - 2
2 - 3
3 - 4

Source: CIA World Factbook 2009

HOW/WHY/WHERE POPULATION IS CHANGING: THE DEMOGRAPHIC TRANSITION

The Demographic Transition is a lovely little model that goes a long way in explaining lots of things about human population change around the world today. Be forewarned: it is just a theory, but damned if it doesn't make a whole lot of sense when applied to just about anywhere, just about anytime. It helps us understand why population is booming in the poorer parts of the world while it shrinks in richer areas, and even why women in Laos may have ten kids, when women reading this book here in America may not want to have kids at all.

The model is based on the experience of the richer, fully developed states, which underwent a population surge on a smaller scale beginning about 1700 in Europe, and then later stabilized. Other states—typically ex-colonies of Western European powers, such as the United States or Australia, or states in close proximity to Western European powers, such as Russia—followed suit in the last several hundred years. Every other place on the globe can be seen as somewhere in the transitional process that these states have gone through.

Generally speaking, this "transition cycle" begins with high birth rates and high death rates, passes into a high birth

FIGURE 2.4 BASE MAP, DEMOGRAPHIC TRANSITION

rate/lower death rate period for a variety of reasons, and ends with low birth rates and low death rates. The total population at the beginning and end of this cycle is stable or has a very low, perhaps even negative, growth rate. However, it is the massive increases in population during the middle phases that makes the model so compelling, and explains so much about what is happening in today's world. But I'm getting ahead of the story. Let's take it one step at a time.

For the rest of this discussion, **birth rate** refers to how many children are born every year per 1000 people. To give you some context, the birth rate in the US right now is about 14/1000 every year. **Death rate,** of course, refers to how many people kicked the bucket that year per 1000 people. The US death rate is currently around 8/1000. Now, on to the transition.

DEMOGRAPHIC TRANSITION STAGE ONE

This whole concept hinges on the idea that all societies want to go *from* premodern, hunter-gatherer, stick-collecting goobers *to* postmodern, latte-sipping, Vespa-driving goobers. It does seem to make sense. Given the option anywhere in the world, I think most folks would choose the latte; that is, most societies are striving to become industrialized, richer, and all-around better off. You don't have to buy my theory, because quite frankly, I'm not selling it. There are those that argue that we would all be a lot better off living in grass huts somewhere weaving baskets from giraffe hair, because that would be true sustainable development in harmony with Mother Earth. Good luck with that one. Give anyone a chance not to live on a dirt floor, and I'll bet they pack their bags, set the giraffes free, and head out to a better life for themselves and their kids. But I digress. Where were we? Ah! Stage One . . .

STAGE ONE of societal development finds us making baskets from giraffe hair. We typically associate this stage with premodern times; most folks are hunter-gatherers, living solely by collecting food naturally occurring out in, um . . . nature. This is pretty much the way things were for a great number of humans for a good long time in human history. Small groups of folks on the move, searching for food, waiting around for civilization to pop up. Of note for our model is that both the birth rates and the death rates are extremely high and erratic. Essentially you have a situation where lots of kids are born per 1000 people, and lots of people die per 1000 people, with some years being really good, and others being really bad. Why?

FIGURE 2.5 DEMOGRAPHIC TRANSITION STAGE ONE

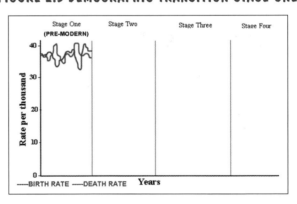

Why the high death rates? Because this lifestyle is hard, and it sucks! It's easy to die from just about anything: lack of health care, food shortages, poor food containment so things go bad fast, lack of regular clean water, lack of sewage disposal or worse yet, your sewage disposal plan involves your drinking water source, animals that want to eat you, animals that just want to kill you, animals just having fun with you, diseases of all sorts, simple infections you could contract from a hangnail . . . ew, this sounds like no fun at all. **Infant mortality,** the number of children that don't make it to their first birthday per 1000, is also high because of lack of immunizations and/or lack of adequate diet. **Life expectancy,** or the average age to which the population is expected to live, is low. Old people get sick more easily, can't pull their own weight out picking berries and therefore don't eat as much, and in general, are slow enough to get caught by the animals that want to eat them. Poor Granny. I really liked her. Now she is cheetah food.

Why are the birth rates high? For the same reasons that they are high in parts of today's underdeveloped world. For starters, it's a mindset; if you expect half your kids to die before they reach adulthood, then you should have twice as many. Makes sense. Also, children are often seen as a resource in these societies: maybe Junior starts picking berries at an early age to help out the fam. So more kids = more labor = more food = good. Plus, no health care = no health education = no sex education = no contraceptive usage. Well, I guess people could always just abstain from having sex . . . yeah, right.

Why are the rates so erratic? For the simple fact that some years are good, while others years are bad. A drought or a plague would cause births to drop and deaths to rise. A very good, wet season with lots of food available would cause the spikes to move in the opposite direction.

Because both birth and death rates are extremely high, they offset each other, equating to a total population that is low and a population growth rate that is slow or stable. Looking back at Figure 2.1, you can see that for most of human history, population growth rate has been very slow, or stable, right on up to the Industrial Revolution. Before we leave this rather boring phase, just a quick note: there really are no more societies like this left anywhere on the planet. You have to dig deep into the Amazon rainforest, the remote savannas of tropical Africa, or into the highlands of Papua New Guinea to find folks still living this lifestyle. Even then, they will be very small numbers of people in isolated pockets. No state on the planet today would be classified in Stage One.

STAGE TWO is the trickiest phase to consider, because we are going to pack a veritable smorgasbord of different human experiences under this single banner. They occur over long periods of time, but have this one big Stage Two result: the death rate declines while the birth rate remains high and stabilizes. Fewer people die; same amount of people being born. What happens to the total population numbers in such a situation?

FIGURE 2.6 DEMOGRAPHIC TRANSITION STAGE TWO

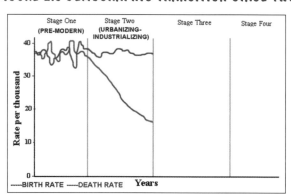

Before we answer that, let's define the stage a little more. I said it is fairly all-inclusive of the human development spectrum, and I meant it. Stage Two includes the transition of humans from hunter-gatherers to agriculturalist to factory workers. Yes, this is a long stretch of time that also entails the formation of what we call technical innovation, civilization, and urbanization. Essentially, dudes figure out that staying put in one place and growing food is more productive than hunting all the time—an agricultural revolution. With increases in technology, so much extra food is produced that not everybody has to be farmers. Some become blacksmiths, butchers, priests, and rock stars—that's specialization. This leads to the formation of villages, towns and eventually cities where larger and larger groups of dudes hang out—that's urbanization. Further technological advancements lead to the creation of machines to automate our work, which leads to the creation of machines that make stuff, and even make other machines. Yikes! The Matrix! Unplug me!

What's all this got to do with people having kids? During this part of the societal transition, death rates absolutely plummet. Why? Remember how I told you that everything sucked in Stage One? In Stage Two, everything gets way better. Increases in food production and increases in food storage technology allow for a steady, stable food supply. There are no more "bad" food years or, at the very least, not as frequent as they were in Stage One.

Technological advances in water resources, sewage treatment, and public health care, all based on growing scientific knowledge, serve to keep more people alive for longer periods of time. Child mortality drops and life expectancy rises. We have developed the shotgun to ensure that Granny is not eaten by the cheetah. More important, however, is the fact that more kids stay alive than ever before; young children become an increasingly bigger percentage of the total population. Education across the board, at all levels, also significantly increases quality of life and survivability.

During this vast sweep of progress, death rates drop and birth rates remain solidly high and even stabilize high. What is going on here? Basically, people are caught in a warp and old habits die hard. If Mom had ten kids, and her mom had ten kids, and her mom had ten kids, it is highly likely that you would be of the mindset to have ten kids as well. It's just what people do. The society as a whole, and certainly not the individuals within it, does not understand that it is going through a transition. The mentality that producing large numbers of kids is good because half of them are gong to die and the rest will work in the fields remains the same, even though conditions have changed. In a Stage Two society, half the kids are now not going to die; maybe only one or two of them will die, maybe none at all. Granny had ten kids and only five survived. Mom had ten kids and seven survived. I had ten kids and . . . dammit, all these little brats are still here!

FIGURE 2.7 CULTURAL LAG

This mind warp is called ***cultural lag.*** Conditions have changed, but the culture is lagging behind. Folks with Stage One mentality are thinking "Hell, this is just a good year," without realizing that it is a good year after a good year after a good year, and they are still having kids like it's a boom-and-bust cycle. Result: ***population explosion!*** More kids beget more kids, and people just don't die like they used to.

Stage Two main points: death rates decrease, birth rates remain the same, total population explodes, and the structure of the total population becomes more youthful. This last point is the most important for the rest of this story, as we have more potential baby-makers entering the scene. Many states in the world may fall into the later fringe of Stage Two, mostly in Africa, Central America and parts of Southeast Asia. These states are still heavily reliant on agricultural production as a main economic activity. They also may have their death rates drop more from foreign external aid, importation of life-saving technologies, and humanitarian relief than from true upward evolution of the society. An important note: since all of these things will help the death rate drop immediately, which means the period of cultural lag will likely be longer—significantly increasing total population overall. Angola and Guatemala are example of states in Stage Two.

FIGURE 2.8 DEMOGRAPHIC TRANSITION STAGE THREE

As we move to **STAGE THREE,** we approach more familiar ground. Stage Two ends with the beginning of the industrialization of the society. Stage Three takes us the rest of the way through it, ending with what we refer to as the "mature industrial phase." Most states on the planet are currently located here, with varying degrees of development that can be quite radically different, depending upon whether they are early Stage Three or late Stage Three.

A this time, the Stage Three state continues down the modern industrial path. This is marked particularly by a shift in what the majority of folks do for a living. It is at this point that the scale gets tipped; more people are working in the processing, manufacturing and service sectors than are working as farmers. This development is significant because this typically means that agricultural technology has superseded the need for vast amounts of human labor in the fields. This equates to less farmers, which equates to more people leaving the countryside and heading to the big city to get a job—increasing urbanization.

Even today, agriculture is still the number one job on the planet. However, states in which agriculture is not the predominant occupation are further down the development road. That is, they are typically richer than states that still rely heavily on the agricultural sector to employ people. Food for thought—pun intended.

We're just getting warmed up with the impacts of this age–to–industry and rural–to–urban shift. What happens to the ideas about having lots of kids when this shift occurs? Plenty! Life in the big city is more costly. Having more kids to feed costs more money. Plus, you've got to clothe them and house them and buy school books for them and throw birthday parties for them and eventually buy them cars. Wow! This is starting to suck as bad as Stage One. But it gets worse! The value of kids has changed as well. Junior used to be an asset picking berries and plowing the fields. Now Junior is an added cost who only picks his nose and plows the family car into the side of the garage. Little bastard! The cultural lag is over thanks to you, Junior! No more kids for us!

In addition to these changes, several other things of note are on the rise. Health care technology and accessibility continues to increase, and especially with regards to increasing knowledge about birth control and contraceptive use in general. Increasing education across the board helps more and more people, but I want you to think more specifically of the education of women and how that effects the whole equation: more educated women = more women entering the workforce = more contraceptive use = more women delaying family formation = fewer kids.

Educating the women of any society decreases ***fertility rate*** instantaneously. Okay, maybe instantaneously is a bit strong, but it's a HUGE factor in affecting the fertility rate in today's world.

FIGURE 2.9 WORLD FERTILITY RATES

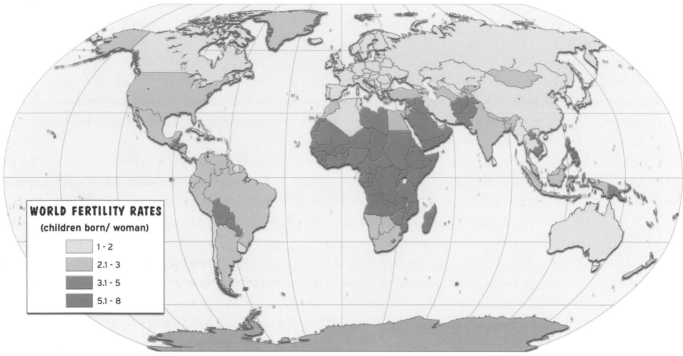

Source: CIA World Factbook 2009

Fertility rate is simply how many kids on average one woman will have in her lifetime in a particular state. The fertility rate of the US is about 2.1. In Italy, the fertility rate is about 1.3. But in Mali, the fertility rate is about 7.5. The average woman in Mali will have seven kids and one half, say from the waist down. In the US, a woman will have two kids and a leg. For our international readers, that is what we call a joke. Actually, the US figure is a quite important fertility rate; that number also happens to be something called the ***replacement level.*** A fertility rate of 2.1 is exactly what it takes to "replace" the current population. See, two people have to get together to create kids (at least still for now, thankfully) and if two people produce 2.1 kids, then when the parents die, there are still two humans they've created to take their place. Sweet! We'll return to this idea in a little bit.

Back to Stage Three. The result of increases in health care, technology, childcare and education serve to knock the death rates down even further. However, there is only so much that modern medicine can do, and eventually that line flattens out. Child mortality decreases and life expectancy increases a bit more, but we all have to die sooner or later, so we'll say goodbye to Granny once again.

Of a more radical impact, increasing urbanization due to the employment shift, re-evaluation of the cost and benefits of having children, increased education of women (and all that entails) combine to overcome cultural lag causing the birth rate to plummet and meet the death rate. People may still be getting busy, but they are not having the babies like they did previously. After several generations, the fertility rates sink down closer to 2.1, the percentage of young people in the society about equals the middle aged cohort, and the older people as well. Good examples of early Stage Three states would be India and Brazil; late Stage Three, China and Chile.

Now we are through the transition, approaching life as we know it here in the fully developed, postindustrial, mostly Western world. **STAGE FOUR** is characterized by population stability, where death rates and birth rates are both low and parallel each other nicely. The post-industrial world is one in which yet another economic shift has occurred; now most folks work in the service sector, not quite as many in the manufacturing sectors, and virtually no one works in agriculture. If these terms are confusing to you, just hang on; we will be delving into economics in the next chapter.

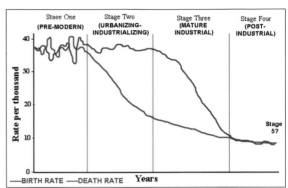

FIGURE 2.10 DEMOGRAPHIC TRANSITION STAGE FOUR

In this stage, the population age structure has become older overall. Technology and education may still be increasing, but only in minute detail can they lower death rates anymore. The population of a Stage Four state is overwhelmingly urban and educated; they use some form of birth control and spend way too much on coffee. The US, France, and Japan are all great examples of Stage Four states. As a result of expected higher standard of living and higher costs of living, many people will plan to have one or two children at most. Some people will decide not to have any children at all.

This leads us to a possible expansion of the Demographic Transition to a Stage Five, in which birth rates actually dip below death rates. The effect? Net population loss—the state's population shrinks every year, and unless supplemented by immigration, the state would eventually disappear. *Immigration* is when people not born in the state move into it. *Emigration* is just the opposite perspective: when people leave your state, they are emigrating out of it. These concepts are increasingly critical in today's world, because many Stage 4 and 5 states rely on immigrants to fill jobs, pay taxes and boost slumping population growth rates. The US is a prime example whose population is increasing primarily because of immigration; the locals just aren't having lots of kids. This is actually more pronounced in Europe where states may be fading away.

Of course, the disappearing state thing has never happened before, but there are several states that are currently in this Stage Five category. Russia, Sweden, Italy, and Japan are all losing people. Italy and Japan are both in dire straits, but for opposite reasons; both have declining fertility rates, but people are emigrating out of Italy like never before, while Japan refuses to allow any immigration into its pristine palace. We shall see how that works out in the long run. Serves them right for creating Pokemon.

POPULATION PYRAMIDS

A final tool for our consideration of population dynamics on the planet is called a population pyramid. Population pyramids are constructed to show the breakdown of the population for gender and age groups. The x-axis across the bottom displays either a percentage of total population or actual population numbers, and the y-axis shows age cohorts, typically in 5-year increments. The two sides of the pyramid are divided up with males on one side, females on the other. Kind of like your junior high prom dance floor. In the Figure 2.11, you can see that in the rainbow

FIGURE 2.11 A POPULATION PYRAMID

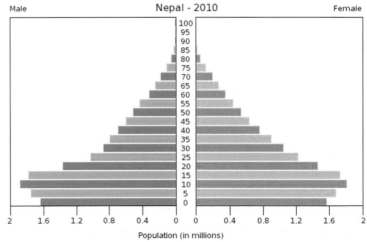

Source: U.S Census Bureau, International Data Base

of fruit flavors for Nepal in 2010, there are about 2 million males aged 0–4 years old, about 1.5 million females aged 10–14 years old, and about 0.5 million males aged 50–54.

Like I give a crap about how many Nepalese women are over 80 years old! What do these pyramids really tell us? They tell us all sorts of things about a state: current population, current economic conditions, and quite a bit about the standard of living as well. But that's not all! These pyramids tell us a whole lot about what the future will hold and you don't even need a crystal ball. Consider the three basic shapes that these pyramids can take a *classic pyramid,* a *column* shape, or an *inverted pyramid.*

FIGURE 2.12 THREE TYPES OF PYRAMIDS: CLASSIC, COLUMN, AND INVERTED

Source: U.S Census Bureau, International Data Base

THE CLASSIC PYRAMID

The classic pyramid shape is, um . . . shaped like a perfect pyramid. The wide bars at the bottom taper up gradually to smaller and smaller bars as age increases, displaying that there are more people in the younger brackets and the size of the group diminishes steadily with age. Broad-based pyramids, like this one, are characteristic of populations with high birth rates and low life expectancies. Why? You already know the answer! Look back at the Stage Two and Stage Three descriptions of the Demographic Transition.

Industrialization and agricultural innovations, as well as increases in technologies across the board, result in advances in food supply and public health overall. This results in recently reduced infant and childhood mortality rates and slightly increased life expectancy. However, they are definitely in the cultural lag mode, as fertility rates continue to be high. This results in high population growth rates and in many cases, outright population explosion. Each year, the bottom bracket of 0–5 year olds gets wider than the previous year. Of particular significance: the numbers of kids under the age of 15 is larger than the number of folks in the 15–35 brackets.

Why is this significant? Because the under 15 are dependents in the society; that is, they absorb resources. Typically, the 15–35 year olds are the biggest providers in the society, both in economic means as money-makers for the state (gross domestic product, or GDP) and as family sustainers of young people and the elderly. That is, they provide most of the resources. Perhaps now you are starting to see why countries with this type of pyramid are often poorer or less-developed; the dependents often vastly outnumber the providers. More often than not, Stage Two and early Stage Three societies exhibit the pyramid shape demographic. The best examples of this type are any African country.

But there is ever so much more we can say about a society with this type of pyramid. It is probably heavily reliant on agriculture or other primary industries for much of its economic earnings. Most people definitely grow some food, either as an occupation, for sustenance, or both. The society probably has lower literacy rates and little to no social safety nets like welfare, and also lacks adequate infrastructure, like good roads or sewer systems. Also, as pointed out earlier, many of the gains in health care, food availability, and life-sustaining technologies may be attributed to foreign aid and humanitarian aid programs. This adds a distinct 21st century dimension to the transition model; no one really knows what impacts this will have in the long run for less-developed countries.

THE COLUMN SHAPE

All columns are not created equal, and there can be radical variations on this shape, but the main thing to identify this type of population pyramid is the more overall fuller figure. No, I'm not talking about a full-figured gal—that's a different book altogether. The real distinguishing mark here is that the size of the 15–50 year cohorts are *roughly* the same size as the under-15 cohorts, giving the overall shape more of a cylindrical look. The older age brackets also grow slightly, and upwards, as more people stay alive longer, adding to the elongated shape.

When this is the case, we realize that the fertility rate must be much lower than in the true pyramid shape, usually hovering between 2.0–3.0. This means that those child-bearing folks (typically between 15–50 years old) are having just 2 or 3 kids each, roughly replacing themselves or maybe even just a bit more. Remember that term replacement level? Well, the closer a society gets to that 2.1 fertility rate, which constitutes the replacement level, the more perfect the column shape will become. Some examples of this are the US, Lebanon, Norway.

The operative words in these states is "stability." The population growth rate is low, or perhaps even zero, with the state adding just a few percentage points of population every year. What else can be said about these countries? They are fully developed industrialized or post-industrialized societies. The highs: GDP per capita, standards of living, health care quality and access, available social programs, life expectancy, education levels, technology levels, urbanization, use of birth control, service sector jobs, SUV ownership. The lows: fertility rate, infant mortality, illiteracy, farmers, miners, people who die from infectious disease.

INVERTED PYRAMID . . . YOU MEAN IT'S UPSIDE DOWN?

Indeed. This is an easy one to describe, because its essential ingredient is that the younger cohorts are smaller than the older ones, child-bearing peoples are creating less people than themselves, and total population is actually shrinking! Fertility rates are under 2.1 and thus the replacement level is not being reached, and ultimately, left unchecked, the population would shrink into nonexistence. This has never really happened before, and is not likely to ever come to its full conclusion either; to counter this effect, immigration is increased or some other government policy is put into place to encourage fertility rates to rise.

Why does this scenario happen? Perhaps due to several different reasons. The first and foremost explanation is due to the same processes at work which serve to end cultural lag in developing societies. Namely, the higher cost of living in highly urbanized areas coupled with the transition of children from asset to expenditure changes attitudes towards family size. Smaller is better in industrialized societies. They only have one or two kids, and invest heavily in them, as opposed to having lots of kids. In some places here in the 21st century, this has gone to an extreme; many people totally opt out of the family thing altogether; they have no children in order to maintain their own high standard of living. End result: fewer or no kids, replacement level for the state is not reached. The best examples of this today are Japan, Italy, and Sweden.

Another reason for declining populations in the world may be due to economic circumstances. Some countries, while considered part of the developed world, have gone through radical changes and economic collapse due to the end of the Soviet Empire. Russia, Belarus, and Ukraine are all in this inverted pyramid category due to lack of resources, jobs, health care, and many other services that the government used to supply. This is particularly evident in some of the measures of well-being for Russia, whose current life expectancy more approximates a poor, underdeveloped African country than a former world superpower. Hard times can also cause fertility rates, and a state's population, to decline as life becomes too difficult and large families too expensive to maintain.

IT'S HARD TO STOP HAVING BABIES

Many of you will look at these definitions and numbers and come up with some puzzling questions. You may wonder how China is the most populous state on the planet, a 1.5 billion people, yet their fertility rate is only 1.73. Or perhaps you may discover that projecting ahead in India, they will continue to grow their population rapidly for some time to come, and indeed will surpass China as the most populous state very soon, but their fertility rate is only 2.73. That's not very much more than replacement level! How is this possible?

Simple. **Population Momentum** is the answer you seek. Consider India for the next 50 years:

FIGURE 2.13 INDIA: THE SNOWBALL GROWS

What these three images from 2000, 2025, and 2050 in India are showing you is the Demographic Transition model in action. In 2000, India was early- to mid-Stage Three, as you can just detect the perfect pyramid starting to round away the edges of the bottom age cohorts in an obvious sign that cultural lag is wearing off and fertility rates are starting to sink from what were highs of 4 to 6 kids average per fertile female. We see that, in 2025, this has taken full effect; India is certainly in the column shape as its late Stage 3 or early Stage 4 industrialization has knocked down fertility rates to a precise 2.1, the replacement level. It's a perfect column. So how can population totals continue to expand after this?

Population momentum is like a snowball rolling down a steep hill. Even after fertility rate stabilization, the population pyramid will have to "fill out its figure," as you can see by projecting further ahead to 2050. Everyone may be only having 2.1 kids, but a much bigger number of them are doing it, as represented by those bottom age cohorts back in 2000, where the stabilization actually starts. By the time the snowball reaches the bottom of the hill, it is massive—as will India be by the time its population total flatlines.

SOME FINAL THOUGHTS ON PEOPLE . . .

They disgust me! No, I'm joking. I love the peoples, especially the ladies. . . . What can we say about the future of population on our plaid planet? It shouldn't be too hard to figure out some general trends. Most countries will continue down the development path, and thus we should be able to track what's happening in societies and within population dynamics through the lens of our Demographic Transition model. Everybody in the world wants a good job, a good standard of living, access to health care, a better life for their kids. It's just the human way.

Having said that, there is nothing to lead me to believe that poorer states won't continue to try and modernize and industrialize like the rich ones have. Is this possible? That's a whole other ballgame we won't get into yet. But what will this mean for the peoples of the planet? The world population total will continue to go up for some time to come, but we can be more specific than that:

→ The least-developed countries are the places where population will truly grow the fastest, and the most. Regions like sub-Saharan Africa, the Middle East, Central America, and most of Asia will continue to pile on the humans, even though they are the regions perhaps most ill-equipped to handle more.

→ Regions further down the development path, like China, India, Mexico, and South America, will continue to grow, albeit at a slower pace as fertility rates stabilize.

→ Fully developed regions, like Western Europe, US/Canada, and Australia are stabilized populations with no growth, but with the potential to grow bigger only through allowing immigration from other regions.

→ Regions that are currently shrinking in populations, like Russia, Eastern Europe, some parts of Western Europe, and Japan, will almost certainly not disappear—but most certainly will encourage folks to have more kids and allow more immigration as well.

→ However, we should never underestimate the power of culture to undo all our tidy demographic transition assessments! Some states in the Middle East and South America are maintaining their high birth rates even despite increased development and climbing costs of living. This is due primarily to powerful religious influences (Islam and Catholicism) which prize large family size. Also, there are folks bucking the trend in places like China, where the state-sponsored One-Child Policy predominated for decades, because the wealthy and growing middle class can now simply afford to have more kids and want to do so despite government penalties. Quite the opposite of anything the model would have predicted. These wacky humans can be so impulsive when it comes to procreation!

This is the current state of the plaid world. This is the future state of the plaid world. How many kids do you want? How many can the plaid world support? All of the factors explained in this chapter combine to create the world population of today. Check out the regional totals in Figure 2.14 to see how these things are reflected in today's world, and know these figures well.

FIGURE 2.14 WORLD REGIONAL MAP WITH POPULATION TOTALS

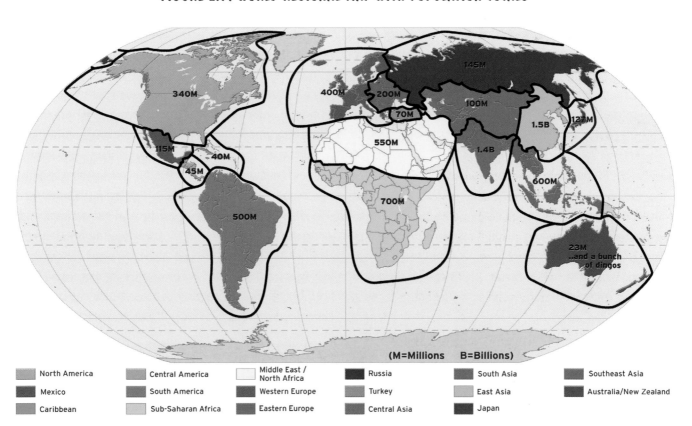

(M=Millions   B=Billions)

North America	Central America	Middle East / North Africa	Russia	South Asia	Southeast Asia
Mexico	South America	Western Europe	Turkey	East Asia	Australia/New Zealand
Caribbean	Sub-Saharan Africa	Eastern Europe	Central Asia	Japan	

Now let's see what you've learned about population dynamics, population pyramids, and fertility rates. Help the Plaid Avenger find his way home with his family. Match the Plaid Avenger fertility rate to the appropriate population pyramid and then to the country to which they belong. Be sure to notice the partial children!

Fertility Rate

Country of Origin

Population Pyramid

Source: U.S Census Bureau, International Data Base

Source: U.S Census Bureau, International Data Base

CHAPTER OUTLINE

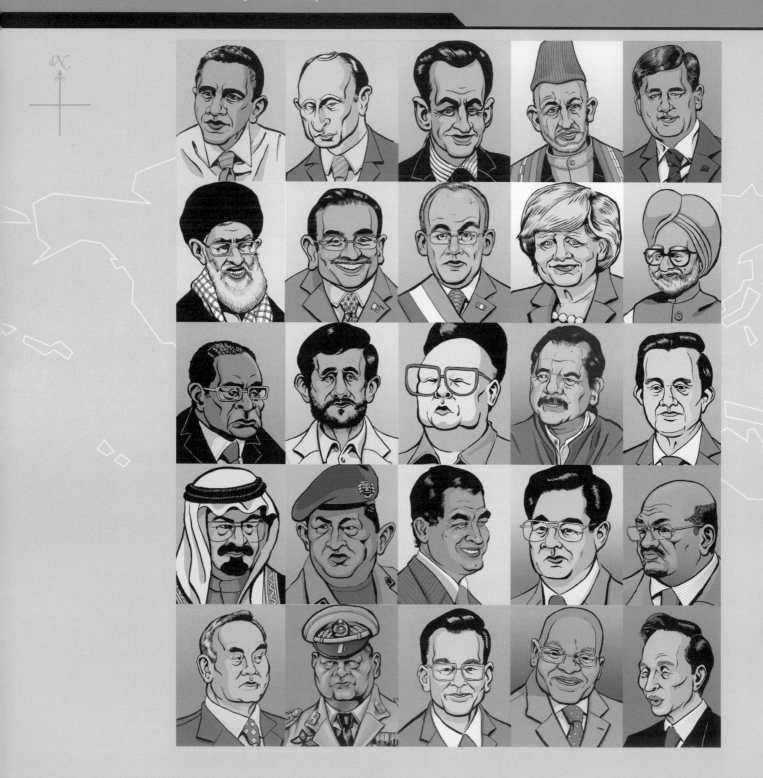

Know Your Heads of State

3

WE'VE talked about peoples in the world, we've talked about what people do for a living, their economy, maybe we've even talked about people's religions—where are they doing all this? Mostly they are doing it in some place we call a state. This textbook is all about the regions of the world, and indeed we're going to tackle 18 or 19 of those regions here in a little bit. That's first and foremost how the Plaid Avenger wants you to understand what's going on around the planet. But regions are user-defined, and even as good a user as I am, many edges around regions can be fuzzy. On the other hand, everybody is located in a legally and physically defined entity—a thing called a state. The borders of a state are not up for debate. What the hell's a state? What's that all about? Where did it come from? What's going on with it? Why is it important for understanding the world?

IDEA OF A STATE

The idea of a defined territory over which a political entity would rule is a fairly new concept. If you think back, for most of human history there have been kings, or rulers, or leaders of *peoples*, not of geographically defined political *spaces*. Think back to, let's say, the French. I know most of us try not to think about the French, but bear with me for a moment. Throughout most of history, the king or leader has been referred to as the *King of the Francs*, not the *King of France*. Only around the 16th and 17th centuries did the innovation of legally defining a space on Earth evolve— the idea that we're going to define a place on the planet in which those Francs cohabitate and call it France. In the 18th century, the concept spread to the European colonies and ex-colonies, and then on to the rest of the planet.

FIGURE 3.1 SOVEREIGN STATES BY AGE

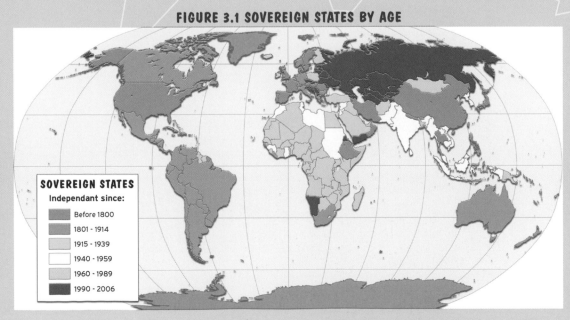

SOVEREIGN STATES
Independant since:

- Before 1800
- 1801 - 1914
- 1915 - 1939
- 1940 - 1959
- 1960 - 1989
- 1990 - 2006

There are some truly old states in the world. China and Persia (Iran), in particular, are ethnically distinct nations of folks who marked the borders of their empires for a good long time. While we can recognize this fact, the idea that these borders are recognized by all other states is the truly European addition to the idea; it is also why most European states are counted among the world's oldest, even though they may be relatively new in the real scheme of things. One has to look no further than the United States to see how new this concept is; the US is in the "oldest" category of states despite the fact it is truly one of the youngest countries on the planet! We've only been around for 200 years total, but we are one of the oldest sovereign states!

A 19th century wave of "new" states cropped up as European colonies started declaring independence: the countries of Latin America, South Africa, and Australia. Some others popped up as a result of disintegrating empires in Europe: Germany, Italy, Bulgaria, and Romania. Another wave cropped up as the Ottoman Empire, which controlled a large chunk of the Middle East, dissolved in the early 20th century. Sovereignty didn't really get to places like Africa and India and Asia, large chunks of which were European colonial holdings, until they became independent countries—that is, states—in the second half of the 20th century. If we look around the planet, most states in the world are fairly new.

A state, in its basic definition, is a politically defined area with people who are recognized across the planet. Most sovereign states on the planet are fairly new, having been reshaped or declared independent in the last fifty years or so. Maybe we should start defining these terms that the Plaid Avenger is throwing out here. What is a state? What is a nation? What is a nation-state? Before we even get to those, we have to tackle the critical issue of sovereignty, which is one of . . .

THE ESSENTIAL INGREDIENTS

What are we talking about? We hear these terms all the time, but what do they mean? Well, we kind of already hinted at it. A state has something to do with some defined boundaries. That's easy. A **state** is a legally defined and recognized political area on the planet. Lines are drawn like a deed, and all the neighbors agree to its parameters—at least for the most part.

But it's not just about a legal description, is it? When we think about the term "**the state,**" and if you ask people what was exactly needed to have a state, you would get a wide variety of answers. Many would say you need a government to head up the state, or a military to protect the state, or a fence around the state. Others would say you need an economy, or money, or an official currency, or jobs to have a state. Some might point out that you obviously need some area and some people and some stuff to have a state. Maybe you need roads and buildings and sewer systems and hospitals and McDonalds to have a state. Perhaps you need a constitution, or laws, or courts to have a real state. What do you think a state needs?

I'll give you the brief answer: you really only need two things to have yourself a state. Number One is sovereignty. The concept is so important, that the Number Two thing you need is also sovereignty. Yeah, I'm a goofball, but now you will always remember the two things you need to be a state: Sovereignty and sovereignty. If you have it, you don't even need all that other stuff to be a state.

What state am I in, when I'm in the United States?

By the way, the term *state* is what we use synonymously with *country* here in the United States of America. It gets confusing. Here in the US, we say we're in the state of Virginia, but we're not really. We're in the state of the USA. We just say *countries* because it makes it easier. Country equals state, state equals country; just use the term **state** when you're dealing with international politics. Everybody understands it better. What state of inebriation are you in right now as you are contemplating which state of the United States you are in, which of course is a state in its own right, right now. Right?

ALL YOU NEED IS LOVE . . . NO, I MEANT SOVEREIGNTY

What is *sovereignty*? Well, the concrete definition of sovereignty is really up for grabs nowadays. For the last few hundred years, it has been a concept that everybody has agreed on and understood. However, in the last couple of decades, there's been some serious debate about what it truly means. Times have changed, and it appears the idea of sovereignty is also changing. This redefinition is causing considerable consternation in the world, among big states, small states, and all states in-between—but I'm getting ahead of myself.

First, we want to find out what it truly means for an entity to have sovereignty, and thus be called a state. The Plaid Avenger's simple interpretation is this: holding the ultimate power over the people in your territory constitutes true sovereignty. No other state can have power over your territory or the people in it. How can you demonstrate that you hold ultimate power over your people? Kill them. Straight up. If you can legally get away with it, then you have sovereignty, and you are a sovereign state in the world.

What?

Let me say that again.

In the end game, does the political entity have the ultimate right to do the ultimate deed within its borders? And what is the ultimate deed? The ultimate, beat all, true test of power is the taking of life. When you think about it, everything else is quite trivial, isn't it? The right to tax, to boss around, to enact laws over, to make inferior products at crappy jobs, or sing crappy national anthems . . . that's all pretty tame stuff compared to death. If you can legally kill people within your state—that is, the leaders and government can kill their own citizens legally and nobody else in the world cares or can do anything else about it—then you're in something we call a state.

People want to say that sovereignty means a system, a government, some leadership, some people who vote, some walls . . . well, you'll have all of that. But if you want the real test of "Is this place a state?" then find out if they can kill their own citizens. Now that sounds extreme, and . . . it really is! Are we a sovereign state in the US? Can the US pass the ultimate sovereignty test? Absolutely. We kill people every day; it's called capital punishment. The death sentence.

So the government kills people. They put criminals to death. But that's too easy. That's something we understand. That's just baby stuff to the real issue I'm talking about here. Let's take it a step further: How about innocent people? What would happen if the government of this country, or any country, just decided to kill 10,000 of its own citizens? Let's say the FBI or the CIA bungled some information—like that's never happened before—decided the entire state of Delaware had to be eliminated by presidential directive, and then nuked it. Now, again, that's extreme. Nothing like that's going to happen . . . yet. But let's say it happened. What would France's response be? What would the United Kingdom do? What would China do? What would Angola do?

Save for giving the offender a great big collective hairy eyeball, the answer is . . . they would do nothing (*especially if it were France*). Even though it's an extreme event, and it may be of horrific consequence, the US is a sovereign state. They can legally kill their own citizens, as can all sovereign states. That is an agreed upon principle, and again, it's the extreme. If you can kill someone in your state, then you can pretty much do anything else: tax them, you tell them what to do, make some laws, all that stuff. If you can do the extreme, you can do all the lesser stuff, and that's the first big principle rule of sovereignty. The *Number One Rule of Sovereignty* is: Does the state have the ultimate right to do the ultimate deed to its citizens, without the interference of other states? If the answer is "yes," then you're in a sovereign state.

How do you get that status? What if I, The Plaid Avenger, created a Little Plaid Nation over here, and I said, "Well I'm giving myself the authority to kill all people who enter the royal domains of my backyard, which I have christened Plaidtopia." Obviously people would say, "No, you can't do that, man, you are crazy!" Even if Plaidtopia had a constitution, some laws, an economy, some area, a fence, a military, a police force, and a harem of women bodyguards who were trained to kill interlopers on my behalf, it still wouldn't be a sovereign state. The reason that *I* could not do it is because other political entities, namely the other sovereign states, wouldn't agree with it. That's the *Number Two Rule of Sovereignty*.

The *Number Two Rule of Sovereignty* is that all the other states in the sovereign state club recognize your sovereignty. You are in the "country" club, so to speak. Indeed, the United Nations is kind of the country club, and if all the other sovereign states say, "Yes, not only can you kill your own citizens, we respect your right to kill your own citizens," then you indeed possess sovereignty. If you are in a legally defined political territory, recognized by other sovereign states, and no other state has power over your territory—as ultimately tested by killing your own citizens—you are a sovereign state. Everything else is inconsequential.

BUT SOVEREIGNTY MAY BE REDEFINED

Why would I suggest that this concept is up for grabs? One of the reasons that today's world is so complicated is because the nature of the world has changed. For centuries everyone has said, "Yeah, you can kill your own citizens. As long as you're not attacking another sovereign state, no one's got a problem with it." That's been the agreed upon, core, central component to sovereignty. Part of the base principle here is reciprocity: we will not intervene in your state affairs when you mess with your own citizens. In return, we expect you to respect our ability to mess with our citizens as well. That's the way it all goes. Even today we say, "Hey, the US doesn't like what China's doing to its citizens; we think your human rights are atrocious." But we're not going to invade. No one's going to do anything about it, really. We might protest and say, "Hey! China! You suck for the way you treat people but . . . here . . . be the host of the Olympics anyway." At most, an official condemnation issued from a head of state or perhaps even a trade embargo would be the extent of any disapproval. No active military intervention is going to happen, because that's what it is to be a sovereign state. We respect their sovereignty so that they will respect ours. At least, that is the way it was . . .

I love cigars, and redefining sovereignty.

Why is it changing? It's actually the fault of United States! I'm actually referring to Bill Clinton.

In March of 1999, during the Clinton administration, the United States led NATO on a bombing campaign of Yugoslavia. Why did the United States and NATO start bombing Yugoslavia, a sovereign state?

Because Yugoslavia invaded the US? No.

Threatened US citizens? No.

Because Yugoslavia invaded another fellow NATO country? No. Threatened or invaded any other sovereign state? Ummm . . . no.

Because Clinton wanted to re-enact the movie *Wag the Dog*? Mmmm . . . good one, but no.

Does that attack seem important to you? Do you remember hearing anything about it? I doubt it. Let me be the first to educate you on how big a deal it was to sovereign states. Here's an excerpt from the British *Financial Times:* "The enormity of NATO launching its first attack against a sovereign state is not to be underestimated. Unlike Iraq, Belgrade has not invaded another country. Nor is the situation akin to Bosnia, where the legitimate government invited outside intervention. Nor, finally, has the United Nations Security Council specifically authorized NATO to bomb."

The thing that happened was that this crazy guy, Slobodan Milosevic, started killing his own citizens. The who or why or how is not important right this second. What is important is that killing your own citizens was one of the baseline agreements of sover-

Slobodan sez, "I can kill them if I want . . ."

eignty. States respect the authority of every other sovereign state to kill its own citizens. You may remember that from seven paragraphs ago. It's the cornerstone. In this circumstance, it was an ethnic cleansing situation, where Slobodan—then the leader of Yugoslavia, currently worm food pushing up daisies—may have been persecuting and encouraging his national army to outright kill members of a specific ethnic group. In hindsight, there is not much debate about it. Slobodan was actively pursuing genocide/ethnic cleansing . . . but only against his own citizens. He was the leader of a sovereign state. Should be no problem, but . . .

Apparently, it got to be too much to bear. There was a large outcry about the situation in Europe and indeed in the United States. Perhaps it was the memory of the Jewish Holocaust that occurred in Europe, or perhaps the instability in this region that had previously launched World War II, or even as some have pointed out, it was simply because there were white people being slaughtered. For whatever reasons, President Bill Clinton decided to enact a bombing campaign, coordinated with NATO, to stop the genocide. Long story short—the United States bombed Yugoslavia into submission for what it was doing to its own citizens.

Why am I telling this story? Because this changed the whole identification of a sovereign state. As we suggested, this whole "kill your citizens" thing used to be the standard. What a state did to its own people was not up for debate, but apparently this was the straw that broke the camel's back—and it's not an isolated incident. Since the 1999 bombing campaign on Serbia, the US and/or NATO have played an active role in Afghanistan, Bosnia, and Iraq under the umbrella of liberating the locals. Meanwhile, serious genocides have been occurring in Sudan and the Congo, for which many in the international community are calling for invasive action to remedy. Those are on the heels of the now infamous Rwandan genocide of 1994, which no state, international organization, or otherwise, stepped in to stop.

All of the listed above are actions, or inactions, based upon unacceptable sovereign state behavior in dealing with their own citizens. Again, it used to be the hallmark of what defined a sovereign state; now it's totally up for grabs. How much misbehavior will the international community allow before intervening even when that misbehavior is confined inside a single state?

This is causing a lot of consternation on the planet. If the golden rule for what defines a sovereign state is up for question, then what exactly is a sovereign state? Sorry, my friends, the Plaid Avenger doesn't have an answer for you right now, because nobody does.

With the current movement of UN troops around the planet, and unilateral actions by the United States in today's world, we don't really know. You can see this in today's news as a major point of contention particularly with the Chinese, and a lot of times with the Russians. Why those two? Just because they hate the United States? No, it's got nothing to do with that at all. These two countries, particularly the Chinese, are really big into the sovereignty thing because they want to cover their own asses. Remember, forever it's just been: don't invade other countries, respect everyone else's sovereignty, and you can get away with whatever you want in your own country. Well, that's up for grabs now. The Chinese and the Russians think, "We are not really keen with the US involvement in other countries because it is violating the sacred rights of sovereignty to which we've all agreed." Now we're rewriting the textbook and folks are a little troubled by it, particularly in countries where they might actively be doing stuff to their own citizens (e.g., Russia, China). We're not really sure which way it's going to work out, as it's all being redefined right this second.

Sparked by the US/NATO bombing campaign in Yugoslavia, sovereignty has also been called into question by human rights groups and lots of folks around the planet who say, "Okay, you're right. We're in the 21st century, we cannot allow acts of genocide to occur, even if it is in a sovereign state." While Yugoslavia was the test run for this, in terms of a trial flight on intervening into a sovereign state to protect its citizens, it will probably be used more. Indeed, the former Bush administration said, "One of the reasons we went to Iraq was to protect the Kurds and the Shi'ites there from what their own government was doing to them." There are folks around the world who are calling for more action from the UN and the world to stop genocide in other places. Right now, people are saying, "Hey! What's the deal? You guys bomb Serbia to protect *those* guys, and you're currently in Iraq protecting *those* people from their government, so how come you didn't interject in Rwanda? Why aren't you in Sudan right now?" This is a big debate on the world forum right now. It's another reason why, you'll see, that people hesitate big time in the UN to use the word "*genocide.*" Why is this?

What's the Deal with Genocide?

The deal with genocide is that, well, we all recognize what it is. It's when a government, or a group of people, kills or tries to completely exterminate another specific group of people, usually based on ethnicity or religion. The worst example of this in modern history occurred during World War II, when the Germans tried to exterminate all of the Jews out of German territory, actually out of all of Europe. This was such a horrific act that, after World War II, the world agreed that we would never allow this to happen again. All the states in the world passed a United Nations law making genocide an international crime. The *Convention on the Prevention and Punishment of the Crime of Genocide* says this: "Any of the following acts committed with intent to destroy, in whole or in part, a national, ethnic, racial or religious group, as such: Killing members of the group; Causing serious bodily or mental harm to members of the group; Deliberately inflicting on the group conditions of life calculated to bring about its physical destruction in whole or in part; Imposing measures intended to prevent births within the group; and forcibly transferring children of the group to another group."

But the old rules of sovereignty were still in play. Things floated along pretty well, until the appearance of possible genocide in Serbia/Yugoslavia, in Rwanda, and in Sudan. Now wait a minute. Didn't we all agree we were not going to let this happen again? Shouldn't we do something?

That is one of the calls on the world stage right now. The reason you did not hear Rwandan situation referred to as genocide, or the situation in Sudan today, is because the use of that particular word demands a call for action. In other words, as long as everybody in the UN is just saying, "Yeah, well, they've got a civil war," or "They have some sort of internal conflict," or perhaps "They may have isolated acts of ethnic cleansing," (which was said about Rwanda) then there is no need to act. Sovereignty takes precedence. They say these things very intentionally because everyone is scared to whisper, "It's genocide." If everyone in the UN agrees that genocide is occurring, then they have to act. It's their law.

That's the deal with genocide and why people gingerly dance around the term, particularly the UN. You also now know how genocide is calling into question the whole sovereignty theme. Plaid Avenger tip: Watch Sudan for the next big explosive test of sovereignty, and how far it can be pushed in relation to genocide.

NATION, STATE, OR NATION-STATE?

Now we've looked at what constitutes a state. Perhaps now you know more about what constitutes a state than you ever wanted to know. Yeah, me too. But it's my job. However, what about these other terms? What is a *nation*? Is it different from a *state*? If so, then what in the living hell is a *nation-state*? It's easy. Let's break it down.

A *state,* you now know, is a legally defined political unit that possesses *sovereignty.* Fair enough. I've beaten you over the head with that for several pages now.

A *nation,* straight up, has nothing to do with a state. You think it does, but it doesn't. A nation is about the people. Remember the intro paragraph of this chapter? This is what it *used* to mean in the world, a leader led a specific group of people. It's all about the peoples. A nation has much more to do with the people than any specific area. In fact, some peoples don't even have an area—but I get ahead of myself. A nation refers to a group of people who share a common culture, and who may even want to have their own government, and may want to rule themselves. Common culture could be just about anything, but often it is a combination of a lot of things: ethnicity, religion, historical background, diet, shared beliefs and customs, traditional attire, intoxicating beverages . . . whatever.

The number of nations is undefined. There could be thousands, hell, millions. It depends on what group of people and on what scale you're looking. Perhaps in every town there's a small nation of people who think that they're different; that they share a common culture, and perhaps would like to form their own country. Again, it's an undeterminable number, but it is all about the people. Let's think about some true examples on the planet that we can all agree are distinct groups of people who share a common culture. This is actually quite easy.

Distinct nations are all over the place . . . but are they in nation-states?

What common cultures are there around the world that are tied to people? How about the French? How about the Germans? Wow, this is getting easier; let's stay in Europe. How about the Italians? Think of all these guys. They all have distinct common cultures from each other; just think about cuisine if nothing else. Think alcoholic beverages: Germans drink beer, while the French drink wine. The Czechs, the Poles, the Russians are all distinct cultures and peoples. But it can get even more specific. We could look at the UK as a UK culture. Kind of, but there's definitely a Scottish culture within the UK, and an English culture, but we're stuck in the Old World. Is there a Saudi nation? Yes, I believe so. Is there an Argentinean one? That one gets a little fuzzier, but it's possible. Japanese? Yes, definitely. The Japanese are a nation, a distinct group of people and distinct common culture. The Chinese? Yes. The Vietnamese? Yes. Thai, Laotian, Indian, Kurds, the Turks, the Maasai tribesmen in Kenya? Sure. We could go all over the planet and see this common culture, and an idea of a group of people who share something in common who, may or may not, want to rule themselves, under their own government. That's a nation.

Let's get to the final definition here: what is a nation-state? Simple. Let's just add a nation to a state, and presto, you got a nation-state. A **nation-state** is a group of people who share a common culture, who want to have their own government

FIGURE 3.2 TYPICAL NATIONS WITH STATES

Turks in Turkey, Thais in Thailand. Yep, that's a nation-state!

FIGURE 3.3: SOME EXAMPLES OF NATIONS WITHOUT STATES

Nations sans statehood

and want to rule themselves—a nation—and do so in a defined and recognized political area—a state—which has sovereignty to boot. That is a nation-state. Let's give an example of a nation-state. We look around the world, and see a lot of the ones we've already talked about. Germany: perfect nation-state. This group of people with a common culture in a distinct area that we call Germany. The French: same deal. The Japanese: even better. The Koreans are the best example yet; a 100 percent ethnically homogeneous group of folks with a distinct Korean culture and cuisine. That's it; that's a nation-state.

The list can go on and on, all over the world. Most of the places in the world are close to what we call a nation-state. Of greater significance than listing all that are nation-states would be to look at those places in the world that are not.

Which brings up the question: can we have a **nation without a state**? Indeed, we certainly can, and this is one of the causes for conflict on the planet today. There are lots of groups of people with a shared common culture, and a desire to rule themselves in a legally defined territory, but they don't have that sovereign state status. A prime example is the Palestinians in a place called Palestine, which is not yet a state—it might be soon—but who are still largely under the control of Israel. Both parties are working on making the Palestinians a nation-state.

Let's get more complicated. Places like Chechnya—yeah, good one! A very distinct culture in a place that's called Chechnya, but it's not sovereign. They'd like to be sovereign; they would love to not be part of Russia, because they are not Russian.

Lama has no state.

What about Tibet? You've heard of them. The leader of the Tibetans, the Dalai Lama, is the spiritual leader of the Buddhist movement on the planet. Their spiritual and traditional homeland has been Tibet. Most of the people there share this Tibetan and Buddhist culture, but they are part of China. Thus, they are not a nation-state. It's one that's likely to *never* become a nation-state. That's a little Plaid insider tip for you. Sorry, Lama.

These are all very good examples of nations without states. Some of these are areas quite active in the world in the terms of conflict, with those people trying to become stand-alone nation-states, and full-fledged sovereign states at that.

HOW MANY STATES ARE THERE?

There are an unidentifiable number of nations. Groups of people that are self-defined, and at multiple scales, are all over the place. Every country will have small pockets or groups of folks that consider themselves culturally different. Like the Basque in Spain, the Scots in the UK, or the French in Canada—maybe we should just say the

French everywhere. It's impossible to determine the number of nations. Now nation-states, that's a little bit easier, but even that definition gets a little muddled if you think about it too much. Is the US a nation-state? What's our common culture? Besides a shared hatred of Céline Dion, do we share any unequivocal commonality?

However, the number of states we can identify with some confidence. Yes, we can look at some numbers. You'll hear this question a lot, and the number is growing, so you have to keep up with world events to stay ahead of the curve. How many states are there? The magic number we're using right now is 192. If you look at the number of countries in the UN, that number will be 191. What are we talking about again? We're talking about sovereign states in the "country" club. They all recognize each other, and they recognize each other's sovereignty.

Pope sez, "Hell no" to UN.

Let's get back to the numbers. There are 191 members of the United Nations. Why 191? Because the Vatican City, which is a sovereign state—though all the other 191 recognize it as a sovereign state—is not a member of the UN. That's why there's a little confusion here. The Pope and his buddies have said, "Nah, that's okay, the UN is cool, but we're kind of a religious people. We're going to keep to ourselves."

191 is the official ticker at the UN, and everybody recognizes the Vatican City, so that makes 192. Some folks would perhaps say there are 193 states. Where is this confusion arising from? The confusion is Taiwan. It is somewhere in the middle, at least for a little while longer. Is it a nation? Yes, probably. Is it a state? No, probably not. Most other states recognize this fact. Others do not. There are about 23 sovereign states in the world that say, "Yes, we actually do recognize Taiwanese sovereignty. We think they should be in the country club." The vast majority, the other 169, don't see it that way, so Taiwan is not considered a fully sovereign state. Not at the UN, not in the US, and not in most of the world. In the future, you will see that group of 23 who do recognize Taiwan as a sovereign state shrink away to non-existence. Our boys over in China are working hard on those countries that do recognize Taiwanese sovereignty to make sure that they soon won't.

However, there will soon be a 193, and we might see 194 coming up in the next several years as well. The first tag-along is East Timor. It was formerly a colony of the Portuguese—a situation that made it distinct from the rest of the Indonesian territory that was controlled by the Dutch. In the last decade, they had an independence movements and the Portuguese finally pulled out, the Timorese declared independence. Indonesia was not keen on that happening, so it turned into a bloody mess. We won't get into it here, but East Timor is now on the path to becoming a sovereign state. They have a few more hoops to jump through, but people at the UN say, "Yes, when it comes up for a vote, we will vote to recognize East Timor as a sovereign state."

Number 194 will probably be Palestine. This is a big "IF," since it's the Middle East, and you can't predict its future from one second to the next, much less year to year. For the last decade, there has been a general movement toward true Palestinian independence from the state of Israel. Indeed, given the track record of the last two years, it does seem, with a lot of trouble and turbulence, that they are heading toward that goal. We might be looking at two years out, we might be looking at ten years out, but certainly at some point, there will probably be 194.

Speaking of Israel and Palestine, it is also important to note that the recognition of a state is

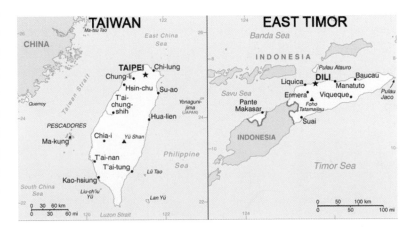

Future statehood? Taiwan out, Timor in!

not always a given, depending upon to whom you are asking the question. For instance, while Israel is certainly fully accepted as a state by most governments in the world and the UN, many Arab and Islamic countries continue to shun it;

in particular, Iran outright refuses to recognize it at all. North Korea refuses to recognize South Korea, and vice versa. Turkey refuses to recognize Cyprus. In what can only be called the most un-exciting recognition refusal of all time, Liechtenstein and the Czech Republic refute each other's existence because of some ancient WWII-era decree. What a bunch of boneheads.

The most current, hottest sovereignty showdown erupted in early 2008, when Kosovo declared independence from Serbia, and about 40 countries, including the US and most European Union states, immediately recognized it. This would perhaps be no big deal, like the Taiwan issue is not anymore, but for one small fact: this showdown is pitting major powers against each other. What do I mean? The US, UK, and France all recognize Kosovo, while China and Russia are firmly opposed. Hey, that's a major rift at the UN Permanent Security Council, a topic for later discussion.

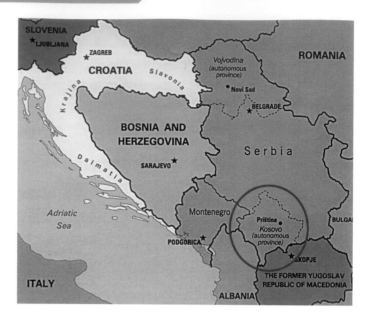

Kosovo causing consternation.

One more thing: let me point out a few places that are not states, but are often mistaken for states. Some of them are still colonies of other countries. For example, French Guiana, a fairly big place in South America, is a French colony; it's not a state. Greenland is still a Danish colony. There are some extenuating circumstances and also some strange ones, like Western Sahara, which Morocco is claiming and attempting to absorb legally and politically. It's in some nowhere land status in the middle. Bermuda is an overseas territory of the UK, not a sovereign state. Puerto Rico is not a state, not really an independent territory, and not really a colonial holding, either. It's just kind of associated with the United States. That's a bit of a muddled situation there as well.

On top of that, you have a lot of nations around the world *without* a state, which are sometimes mistaken for states. Places like Tibet in China we have referenced already, or like the Scots we think of Scotland, a political subdivision of the UK, not a state. It's a nation, a group of people who definitely think they're culturally distinct. You know, Scottish people, we'd all agree to that—the guys that wear kilts, play noisy instruments, and eat haggis. Damn, that is definitely a distinct culture—and let's make sure they stay that way. They are eating that stuff? The hell with them—give them the nation-state status! Of course, they produce that lovely beverage called Scotch which is distinct around the entire planet as well. But they are a sub-state, a province of the UK, for lack of a better word. They are not an independent state. There are 192 in the world right now that are true states; possibly 193 and 194 are coming up in the batter's circle.

Extreme Left
Anarchy . . .

Communism . . .

Direct Democracy . . .

Representative
Democracy . . .

One-Party State . . .

WHO CONTROLS THE STATE?

We talked about what was a state, what is a state, who is not a state, it's all about the state . . . but who controls the state? That's what the rest of this chapter is all about: World governments and world political systems,the guys in charge of these sovereign entities. Before we get to that, we have to throw out a few terms that we hear all the time. The Plaid Avenger is going to make sense of it for you, but boy, is it a mess. There are so many terms and they refer not to just politics, but sometimes economics and religions and social issues. They are terms like the **Left** versus the **Right, Liberal** versus **Conservative, Communism** versus **Capitalism.** We'll get to some of these terms in later chapters, but let's start with the **Left** versus the **Right.** Throughout this book, we're going to talk about leftist governments and rightist movements and we're going to deal with them politically right this second.

What does it mean to be the **Left** or the **Right** in the political spectrum? Often we've heard "lefty commies" and "extreme rightist" or "rightist fascist." What does this mean? Again, we're talking about the *world* political stage, not the politics within independent sovereign states. It's easy to get the terms mixed up; you might hear reference to "the liberal Left" or the "conservative Right" in America, but that stuff doesn't mean the same thing that we are talking about on the world stage.

Check out the world stage, the world political spectrum, from left to right as you can see across the bottom of these pages. Maybe you're starting to get a sense of what it means. Here's what I want you to know about it. On the extreme left would be government styles like communism or anarchy. These are ruling systems where there is little to no central government control. Another way to put it as you head to the left less government power, more power in the hands of the people. This is best displayed by anarchy, which we think of as a chaotic state, but indeed there are anarchists, political anarchists, and what they believe in is that there should be no government at all. Every single person within every single state in every single society should have the right to do anything they want. That's what anarchy really means. It's never existed anywhere, and probably never will, but the theory is that the people have *all* of the power. Never mind the bollocks, the government, or the rulers of the state, have no control over individual people. That's an extreme.

What's on the other side of the political spectrum, on the other extreme? That's on the total extreme right, which is just the reverse. All of the power is in government hands. Control of the country is in the hands of the few, the people in charge. Most of the population has zero or limited political voice on the extreme right. To think of it in perspective—and extremes are always good to clarify the perspectives—is that the power pyramid is upside down in anarchy. The people are on the top; they get everything, and can do anything they want. On the extreme right are fascists like Hitler, who actually said something along the lines of the following: "*I* am the state. An individual person. Me. I am the state. Everyone here in this state of Germany is here at my disposal at my will. *I am the state.* You work for *me.*" On the left, is just the reverse; the state works for *you.* The state as an apparatus that exists solely for the people. That's a huge difference to consider. That's what the real spectrum is all about. All of the political systems in the world fall somewhere between these two extremes, because—and here's a little insider tip—these extremes don't exist anywhere. In fact, some of these systems hardly exist anywhere at all. Let's go through them really quickly.

Theocracy . . .   Monarchy . . .   Military Government . . .   Dictatorship . . .   . . . Extreme Right Fascism

ANARCHY

He did it his way.

We'll start on the left. **Anarchy**, as I already suggested, is essentially no government at all. Maybe the Libertarian party in the United States is close to ideological anarchy in that they don't want any interjection or interference by anybody. Yeah, Ron Paul partying with Sid Vicious—now there's a good time! No superstructure, no hierarchy of folks that are in control of anything. In an anarchy state, there would be really no government to speak of, no national defense, no one taking care of roads, or any of that kind of stuff. You're starting to get the flavor of this; high schoolers with punk rock jackets may think that anarchy's really cool, but it doesn't sound too good when you really begin to define what's going on in this type of society. It's pretty much every man for himself. We already know in human society that this deteriorates fairly rapidly into people beating the living daylights out of each other for a cigarette. In a political spectrum, when we're just thinking about this abstract idea politically, it comes down to this: "It's the individual right to do anything he or she wants." Long story short, anarchy never happened anywhere, and anarchy will never happen anywhere. Are there any anarchy states anywhere in the world today? There is perhaps one, but it's not intentional, and that would be Somalia. It is a state that has fallen into chaos—and we typically consider anarchy and chaos synonymous—and indeed, that is the case for Somalia. But they aren't really an anarchy; they didn't intentionally become anarchic; they've just deteriorated into chaos. In the sense of an intentionally instituted system of anarchy, the whole concept humorously contradicts itself, much like Ron Paul running for president. Really, there aren't any true anarchic states in the world.

COMMUNISM

Communism is another hilarious system because it doesn't exist anywhere either. What a barrel of laughs. The Plaid Avenger wonders if it actually ever did exist anywhere. What are we talking about here then? Why are we talking about it at all if it doesn't exist? Because the ideology is powerful, and it has greatly shaped history, especially the last century. Communism as an idea is still a potent force that shapes judgments of decision makers around the planet. There are several confusing factors about Communism, and before I get to those confusing points, let's just say what it is.

Famous dead communist dudes.

Communism was a concept that had been around forever, but some folks in 19th century Europe, namely Karl Marx and Friedrich Engels, really put it into its modern interpretation. These guys were living in the environment of the Industrial Revolution. They were witnesses to flagrant excesses of capitalism, ruled by monarchs on the throne who controlled all political power, and rich factory owners who controlled the economy. Marx and his ilk looked around and said, "This really sucks. We have no power over our lives. We need more power to the people." So they wrote their manifestos and all that jazz, and long story short, came up with this: In a Communist political system there is a government, but the government is solely there (remember the inverted pyramid) to provide everything that the citizens need. To facilitate this provision of economic and political needs, the government would set up small **soviets**: that is, small groups of folks in cities of which every citizen is a member. Everybody is attached to a specific soviet, kind of like voting districts here in the US, but much much smaller. These soviets would debate on every issue that affects the people. In this manner, the government listens to the people directly and distributes resources or makes decisions based on the citizens' needs and requests.

How can a government afford to do that? In this society, there is no private property; the state controls it all. In other words, the government is kind of "by the people, for the people"—we think about that in democracy, but it's even beyond that. It exists solely to distribute everything as per the needs of the people in the society, and that means economic as well as political power. That's one of the reasons it's extremely confusing.

→ Confusing point #1: Communism is both a political and economic term, because it combines politics and economy into one system in which all ownership of property is communal and all resources are owned by the government; the entire economy and the political system is run by a singular government. It's the only kind of system that works that way. All of the other political systems we'll talk about are just politics, and the economy goes its own way and does its own thing. In true Communism, it's all one big happy family where the government, Big Brother, controls everything.

→ Confusing point #2: When we think about the manifestations of Communism in the world, we typically think of dictatorship. The big one, of course, is during the Russian commie experience: the USSR under Josef Stalin. Or even Chairman Mao. Communism in China turns into Maoist China, a singular leader that ends up being a dictator. Even when it's not a well-recognized singular leader, these systems tend to perpetuate a small group of people in charge of everything.

Indeed, that's exactly what has always happened. Politically, when Communism has tried to manifest itself, it never works because the whole thing is supposed to be a transition. What do I mean by that? During the Russian experience, Vladimir Lenin came to power in 1917 with his commie posse. They were attempting to implement a system that had never been tried before. To become politically Communist meant to be politically and economically Communist. Lenin said, "Well, okay, this has never been done before. We want to get to this utopian society where everybody's equal, and all decisions are made communally, and all property is held communally, and all resources are distributed communally—that's what we're shooting for. But we're not there yet. In fact, we're very far from it. We need to set up a small group of people in order to get from point A to point B. In other words, to get from where we are now to our perfect commie society, we basically have to become an oligarchy/dictatorship . . . just for a while." I'm paraphrasing here. That is not a quote from Lenin. He is not as good-looking as me, although the goatee is stylin'.

Main point: this is supposed to be a temporary thing, a transition, a transitory government. Here's the problem, folks: Of all of the societies that have tried to go down the Communist path, not one single one has actually finished the transition. In other words, they start the transition, and they want to get to this pure utopian society, but it always ends up as a power grab by few people, or typically one person, who we then call a dictator. Some good examples are in the Soviet system, where Josef Stalin became a singular dictator. In the Cuban system, Fidel Castro, who's still there, is a singular man in charge of everything. In China, Chairman Mao, and then his successors, were singular people. It never fully develops into equality for all. Plaid Avenger Tip: Communism will never, has never, and, did I mention, will never work the way it ideally should.

→ Confusing point #3: There are no Communist countries on the planet right now. They don't exist. Even if we look at places like today's China, or even today's Cuba, these are something closer to what we would call one-party systems, because *purely* political Communist states can't exist—remember, the system is a political and economic combination. It's like peanut butter and jelly or Batman and Robin: they got to happen together. Today, everybody pretty much now has some form of capitalist economies. In other words, the economies of even the Communist countries are not communist. Everybody's given up on that. Since Communism in its pure form is both politics and economy, it does not exist. We've got to re-classify everything that *was* categorized a commie in some other category.

Those are the three confusing points about Communism. Let's move onto something more sound, and that is . . . direct democracy.

DEMOCRACY

Now we're getting into familiar territory; this is the stuff that we all get and understand, because we live in it. **Democracy**: *ocracy* = "ruled by" and *demo* = "the people." We are still in this inverted pyramid in which the government is here mostly for the people, as a service for the people, and not the other way around. We are not here to serve the US government, it is here

No libation without representation!

to serve us. It protects us; it does things that are in our interest, not its own interest. That may be up for debate on some issues, but that is the system as it is in the abstract form. **Direct democracy** doesn't really exist anywhere; we don't even have it in the United States. Direct democracy says, "We think everybody's so equal that every single issue and every single person we vote for and every law we enact must be voted upon by every single person involved in democracy, that is, everyone in the state." You can probably figure out why there's not too many of these in the world—because it's impossible. In countries that have millions of people, you can't have millions of people trying to come to a common consensus on what's going on, even if it were something as simple as a dog-leash law. Direct democracy, that is, democracy that involves every single person, really only exists in one place, and these guys are screwed up on several fronts: Switzerland. I mean, even their cheese is full of holes, so you can't expect too much from the rest of the culture.

The Swiss have the closest manifestation of direct democracy on the planet. All citizens have to spend a large component of their time dealing with all the laws that have to be passed. Sounds like that **soviet** stuff described above, doesn't it? There is a much larger percentage of people who serve in some sort of elected office, like almost all of them. I won't say it's a chaotic system, but it's definitely a time-demanding system that most of the planet is not willing to ascribe. That's why most of the planet is a multiparty state/**representative democracy**.

This is exactly the same as a direct democracy, in terms of the government working for the people. But, instead of all of us voting on every damn thing, we just vote for a few people and say, "You guys go decide. We will elect you into positions of power, knowing that you are here for our good. If you piss us off, or you do something wrong, we will remove you from your positions by voting for somebody else." That's the way it works, but the main term here is "representative." That is, one person is going to represent our county, or district, or state, and we're giving him or her the power to decide what's best for us. Does that make sense? It should—it's not that complicated.

On a side note: Multiparty states and representative democracy are all the rage on the planet right now. It is the government option of choice for most, and one that is growing. In the last twenty years, since the demise of the Soviet Union, this is the one that all the cool kids do. It is the most accepted, and the most perpetuated by the UN, and by big states like the United States and various European countries. This one is heading up in the numbers column. Most of the planet is in this category already.

Before we go on to the other ones, I want to point out another thing under this representative democracy description. How could direct democracy and representative democracy be right next to communism on the political spectrum? This is confusing, and we've already pointed out why the term communism is so confusing. If we are not leftists here, then why are the two right beside each other on the left side of the spectrum? People in the US don't consider themselves to be leftists, but indeed, if you look at the whole spectrum, you are. That is, you're for the people, and that's more liberal, to the left. Liberate the people, freedom for the people, everything's for the people. In that sense, communism, on paper, is right beside democracy. There's just slightly different takes on how to go about getting power in the hands of the people. It's confusing, because communism has never worked. In theory, it's all about people, just like democracy. Now it gets a little simpler, as we're going to start heading to the right with one-party states.

ONE-PARTY STATES

One-party states are exactly what they imply. Something that looks like elections happen from time to time. Sometimes there are things that look like choices on the ballot, but there's only one real political party that always seems to win. There's only one political party that seems to be in charge. Some of these are in a transition zone from what used to be called communism, like China. Some of them are bordering on dictatorship, like Egypt, but have been wise enough to keep in the good graces of Team West by putting on the democracy window dressing. That is, they do have parliaments, and they do have groups of people come together who make laws, but it's pretty much only one group of people or one political party that's in charge. In other words, you can go vote at the polls, but there's only one group of folks for which you can vote. Egypt is another great example of this: They've had elections for thirty years, and the same guy has won every single time, and that is President Hosni

Hosni and Hu: The only ones to vote for.

Mubarak. Is he that popular? Do people love him that much? Well, perhaps, but maybe it's because he's the only person on the ballot. Even though he's a staunch ally of the United States, and we say, "Hey, that's kinda democracy," Hey, we know that it's kinda not. It's a one-party state. It would be the equivalent of having the current US system, but only having several candidates all from the Republican party on the ballot for every election. Just one party. Obama no like.

One-party states have the illusion of choice; some of them might have some choices for some of the legislature and parliamentary sections, but it's really one group of folks that kind of have most of the power. They do some things for the people—they are not necessarily completely top-down hard-core, but they are indeed not true democracies. It perhaps would only take a nudge to get them there, though. As opposed to theocracy.

THEOCRACY

We are holy, and we are in charge.

Now we're getting to real hard-core rightist politics. Here's where the pyramid now has tipped. Indeed, there are some people who rule the states, and they do it for their interest in what they consider the right way to do things with little to no input from the people. This will get worse as we progress rightward.

Theocracy is fairly straightforward. It's an *ocracy*, "ruled by," *theo*, "religion." Some sort of religion controls the state. Our best examples would be Iran and Vatican City. These are states which are not secular. There is no division between the church and the state; in fact, it is one singular unit. The church *is* the state. The person at the top—which in other places we would call the king, or the president, or the head cheese—is a religious person in a theocracy. Like the Pope: he is the head of the Catholic Church, and also the head of Vatican City. In Iran, you have the Ayatollah: a supreme religious leader. He is also the leader of the state; they are one in the same.

Now the Pope has been around for a while, hell, I don't know, like since biblical times I think. But the Iranian theocracy is something quite new on the world stage, and is a whole new take on how states should be managed. Indeed, most consider the Iranian Revolution of 1979 the last truly revolutionary idea of human history thus far. It's a big deal. The idea that a modern state can be recast and re-organized with religion as the central theme has not been tried lately, if ever. In the past we have had kings or queens or governments that are inherently tied to religion, or that even share power with religion. But this version of theocracy is totally unique in that ALL other power structures are subservient to the religion. It is a new idea, and one that has not totally figured itself out yet, even in the Iranian example, but the concept is finding fertile ground in many Islamic countries around the globe.

As you might expect within these states, religious law or biblical/religious text law is the state's law. This is of particular significance for Muslim states, as there are lots of folks around the planet in Muslim countries who would like to see their countries become theocracies. In doing so, they want to enact religious law as their state law. The Muslim manifestation of this is something called **sharia.** Sharia law is Koranic law: the laws and punishments described in the Islamic holy text, the Koran. The big problem with this, and why I'm pointing this out in this section, is because this is becoming a world issue. There are very few states in the world that have just Muslim people in them, or just *any* single ethnic group, or just *any* single religious group. To adopt the religious law as state law means to enforce that religious law on people who are not of that religion. In their defense, many proponents of sharia would argue that western democracies embarce biblical law as a major component of their legal systems, and that is a valid point. Thou shall not kill, and all that stuff, is the basis for western law, so what's the difference? We'll look at this in more detail when we look at the Middle East and sub-Saharan Africa, as this is a particular problem in Nigeria and Sudan. But we need to finish off our political systems. Let's go further right to . . .

MONARCHY

Royal goobers: A dying breed.

Now these are getting extremely easy. **Monarchies** are the royal families, who, by the blessing of God, are smarter and better than all the peasants within the country that they lead. To be honest, this has been the most important and utilized system of human rule for the better part of human history. The emperors of China, the Shahs of Iran, the Maharajahs of India, the Sultans of the Ottoman Empire: all family lineage positions of leadership. And don't forgot those wacky Euro-trashers! This used to be all the rage in Europe; everybody loved their monarchs in Europe. In fact, those chip-eating, goober British still love their monarchs so much that they still have them there, hanging out, even though they have no real power. If you want to get into a good fight in Australia, just make fun of the Queen of England. For whatever reason, there is a strong attachment to this idea, an idea that the Plaid Avenger not only finds preposterous, but quite frankly, revolting. The concept that, at birth, someone is better than me and has the power by the blessing of God to rule me, I find repugnant.

We don't have to describe the system any further; it's simple. The original royal family touched by the divine hand of the creator and papal decree begat some sons and daughters, creating the kings and queens who are far superior to us mortals. They get to rule until they beget more sons, who beget more sons; and pretty soon, they're all begetting each other, and that's why half of them are insane anyway. What is the power structure of the state? Why, it exists for the frolicking and pomp and circumstance of the crown-wearers, of course! By your leave, your majesty? Yeah, I'll leave you something of great majesty—my plaid boot in your hind-quarters!

There is one important point to make about this government type: it was repudiation and disgust with monarchy that led to the creation of most of those systems to the left of it on our spectrum. The concept of "divine" rights reserved for this elite group of people, particularly the rights to rule the rest of us, became so infuriating to so many on the planet that it became the catalyst for revolutionary thinking—thinking that created a lot of the other government types that we just talked about. Democracy (as we know it today), communism, Marxism, socialism, and probably a handful of other –isms on the left side came about because people were so ticked off and tired of the monarchy system which dominated Europe at the time.

Can anyone think of any examples of this? Oh, how about the United States of America? Yeah, they had a revolution and kicked those tea-sipping suckers out. Later on, the French took their fight one bloody step further than we did by outright killing their royals during the French Revolution. Vladimir Lenin and his commie crew assassinated the royal family as part of the Communist Revolution. Wrap your head around this idea in particular: many of the alternate systems of government around the world today are the rebellious progeny of former monarchies. Before we go any further, let's point out that democracy is an ancient concept; Socrates and the other philosophizing Greeks came up with this stuff long ago. However, democracy in its modern form, in its modern manifestation on the planet, was a result of aversion to monarchy, as was communism. Monarchy is top-down and a goofball concept all the way around, but there are some other political systems that leave a worse taste in the Plaid Avenger's mouth, like military governments.

MILITARY GOVERNMENTS

Military governments are exactly what they say they are: governments run by people with guns. Every country on the planet has a military, or something that looks extremely similar to a military. Maybe called a self-defense force, or an emergency reserve, or a ground self-defense force, or a national guard—places like Japan and Costa Rica don't have an "official" military. Whatever name it goes by, the military in most states is sub-servient to the central government. That is, it's there for national defense, maybe even to internally put down revolts, but it works for, or at the request of, the government. Typically, the head of the state is also the ultimate commander of the military, but is not active militarily. Typically.

My guns are bigger than the politicians!

However, in states run by a military government, the military has actually superseded the political leaders. Often a small group of military elites takes over effective, real control of the government, directly or indirectly, by military coup. The best examples of this on the planet today are places like Burma, Sudan, and Libya. In those states, people who are from a military background, or are still active in the military, have wiped out the government for whatever reasons—maybe the government was corrupt, maybe as a move for national security—and have taken control. Does this mean they control everything and everyone at gunpoint? Not necessarily, but the military is the true power in any country.

I know this is confusing. People in the United States might say, "No, not here," but just ask yourself this—if the entire military of the United States wanted to take over the country, could they? Well, obviously, but we have laws and stuff in place here that all of us, including the military, respect. Their role is to serve, and to uphold the law. In other parts of the world, that's gotten a little fuzzy. Governments are taken over by military dictatorships. The government may continue to run as a functional entity, and we would say, "Hey, they've got a senate or legislature; they have courts," but the real power is from a small group of people, and if it's a singular person, we typically refer to them as a military dictator. If it's a group of military people, we would typically refer to them as a *junta.* There are several of these around the world that are still quite active today. Of particular note in current events in Burma; a more crooked pot of scum and villainy you won't find anywhere else in the world. Those junta jackasses have been killing folks outright for years, and more recently refused to let the international community even come in to help out after the typhoon that killed thousands back in May 2008. Other folks like Muammar Qaddafi, the leader of Libya, may look like kindly old gentlemen, but check out his resumé. Yep, he's only had one job as leader of the military, and then later he picked up the "leader of the country" title. That makes it a military government. When military governments get particularly nasty, they can turn quickly into dictatorships.

DICTATORSHIP

Saddam and Mugabe: They held all the cards!

Dictatorships are typically, but not always, started as military governments, where the military has taken over for whatever reason. A central strong figure rises from the crop, and sometimes through cults of personality, sometimes through brute force, become the sole leader of the country. A true dictatorship exists when all decision making occurs at one individual's whim.

He has the final say on all laws, all actions, all everything. The state apparatus functions only through him. For example, Hitler said, "I am the state," and he meant it! He decided if they were going to invade another country, or what the tax system would look like, or what rights individuals had. It's usually implemented by force of the military, but that's not the defining feature—it's the singular person holding all the cards that sets it apart. It can be military, or it could be religious—these lines get fuzzy. We can say the Ayatollah kind of looks like a religious dictator, and perhaps that's kind of true, but even he has a group of religious folks who work for him that have to come to a consensus on certain things. That does not exist in a true dictatorship, where a single guy has all the power.

The best example of this in the modern world was Saddam Hussein, currently residing somewhere in Hell. He was a single dude, insulated by a cult of personality, who built up and protected his power through use of force. There are other active ones, like the president of Zimbabwe, Robert Mugabe. Mugabe—and again, all dictators are not active military, although he started as a military guy—was a rebel leader who helped fight off the colonial powers, helped liberate his country into independence, and originally was a hero. He was elected, assumed elected power, and then over the years and decades, he consolidated that power and just couldn't seem to get enough of it. After thirty years, he holds all the cards. One man, with all the power; that's a dictatorship. He has refused to give up power, as is often the case in these scenarios, particularly in Africa. Power seems to ultimately corrupt, and the longer you hold on to it, the greater the hunger for it, like crack, or "the one true ring" that Bilbo Baggins found. But I digress. Damn hobbits always get me off track!

The point here is that dictators can come from a variety of backgrounds, often military, but not necessarily. We might have the tendency to look at Fidel Castro as a dictator. This leads to some questions about a dictator vs. a fascist.

FASCISM

I am the State!

As has already been reflected in the extreme left, anarchy doesn't exist anywhere. **Fascism** doesn't really exist in today's world either. What separates fascism from dictatorship? A very thin line, I suppose. What the Plaid Avenger calls the manifestation of true fascism is that it *is* kind of a true dictatorship, but it's a dictatorship that's not necessarily perpetuated by the use of force. In other words, it's typically a cult of personality. It is a dictator—it is one person with all the cards—but one who has been put there because people like him so much. He's put there by popular mandate.

This is where your best examples are Adolf Hitler and Benito Mussolini, perhaps the only real examples in modern history. While we consider most of their dictatorial actions pretty bad in hindsight, at the time, they were very popular. They were rulers of the military, but they did not need the military to maintain control, nor to gain power originally. Hitler certainly was the leader of the military, and certainly using that military knocked the living crap out of Europe. But, in his rise to power, he did not hold the Germans under the sway of the gun and say, "I want you to agree to all these policies." Most people just said, "We think you're great, do whatever you want, this is awesome." Then Hitler got the smack-down, and that was pretty much that.

Let's face it: fascism blows on every level. On the one hand, you have a generally charismatic leader who is a few fruit loops short of a complete breakfast who rises to power by mesmerizing the hell out of some needy folks who are only looking for a solution to their miserable lives. On the other hand, you have a large population of people who more or less blindly allow their government to get away with ultimately controlling their lives while destroying the lives of others. And that story always seems to have a happy ending. Or not.

Famous fascists biting off more than they could chew.

ANOTHER PLAID AVENGER INSIDE TIP: Neither Hitler nor Stalin drank alcohol. Both were teetotalers in societies well-known for their drinking habits. Think about it. Have a drink.

SO WHO IS WHAT, AND WHERE?

Check out the map in Figure 3.4 of current political systems around the globe. Can we detect any patterns? Any problems? Regional variation? As you can see, we have some dominant political systems with some variations on theme region to region.

Look at the Americas. All of North America is staunchly democratic with a well-established government. Europe is also staunchly democratic with well-established governments—even the ones that still have kings and queens hanging around. We call them ***constitutional monarchies***, but the kings and queens have no real power, they are simply figure-heads; old habits die hard. Mexico and South America is also staunchly, long-term democratic. India is the largest democratic nation on the planet, and places like Japan and the UK are considered staunch democracies despite the continues presence of their figurehead monarchs. Don't forget about Turkey, easily the most die-hard democracy on the planet that happens to be totally composed of followers of Islam.

New or newly established democracies on the planet are found in Eastern Europe and Russia. Since the fall of the Soviet Union, they've embraced democracy, but they are still what we call in transition, only about ten to twenty years old. Most of Africa, both in the Middle Eastern sections and sub-Saharan Africa, is sort of in the democracy column, but they are kind of new as well. And if we want to summarize the rest of sub-Saharan Africa, there's a little bit of everything going on down there. There are some chaotic states, some military dictatorships, some new democracies, and a couple of old democracies; it's quite the patchwork quilt. The Middle East is characterized by a patchwork quilt of a different flavor: they have most of the theocracies and true monarchies on the planet. Iran is a theocracy, but Saudi Arabia, Yemen, and Morocco have some true old-school kings and queens still in charge.

FIGURE 3.4 POLITICAL SYSTEMS OF THE WORLD

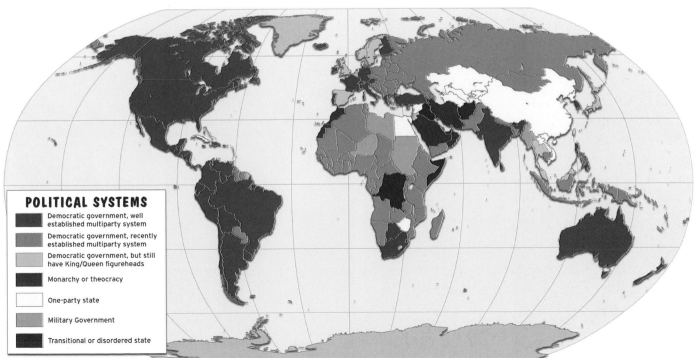

POLITICAL SYSTEMS

- Democratic government, well established multiparty system
- Democratic government, recently established multiparty system
- Democratic government, but still have King/Queen figureheads
- Monarchy or theocracy
- One-party state
- Military Government
- Transitional or disordered state

We get to Central Asia to find a real crapshoot. Some states have put up the new democracy façade, but it's too new and too close to call which way they are going. One of the themes we'll talk about in Central Asia is that they're kind of leaning back toward one-party states. Folks are getting in charge there and hemming up power and staying in control. Of course, we get around to places like Southeast Asia; they've got a little bit of everything. Some places are staunchly democratic, like the Philippines. Some places are staunchly not, like the military dictatorship in Burma, and then there's every place in between. Also, we've got some wanna-be commies in there. You've got a little bit of everything in Southeast Asia.

In East Asia, we have China, which is definitely a one-party state. I know that the Communist China label is confusing to a lot of people because politically, they have a party called the Communist Party, and that is the party that is in charge, but they are not an economically communist state. Therefore, it's better classified as a one-party state. North Korea is definitely a distinct crazy wacko one-party/dictator state, perhaps better described as a one-psycho state, and South Korea is just the opposite, a staunchly democratic place. That's just a quick summary of what's going on politically in the world. We'll go into more detail about this in each of our regions.

A FINAL WORD ON THE STATE OF STATES

A few general points to consider across the planet here in the dawn of the 21st century:

The number of states is actually growing. That's the first thing to consider. Why is that? The bigger entities are breaking down into smaller ones. Smaller entities perhaps better fit the people within (e.g., the demise of the Soviet Union, the breakdown of Yugoslavia). The best example of all is the division of Czechoslovakia into a Czech state and a Slovak state.

The other main trend to consider is the demise of communism in the global sphere, and the movement away from dictatorships and one-party states to democracies. That is, there is a growing trend of democratization across the planet, something the leaders of the United States are very happy about and promote, of course. You can see this particularly in places like Eastern Europe—the Ukrainian and the Georgian Revolutions, respectively referred to as the Orange and Rose Revolutions. Afghanistan and Iraq? Well, I suppose they are heading towards a democracy, even if it has to be implemented at gunpoint.

A minor trend of which you should also be aware: the Iranian experiment with theocracy is both new to the world stage, and being exported abroad. Other states with large Islamic populations may be gravitating towards this system of government. I should say the *people* in those states are interested in some form of theocracy, but certainly not the current governments of those states who like the power structure that has them in the driver's seat right now, thank you very much. One need only look to an extreme manifestation of theocracy, the Taliban in Afghanistan, to see that this idea is not just an Iranian thing. There are also numerous political parties in virtually all Muslim states, from Nigeria to Egypt to Saudi Arabia to Pakistan to Indonesia, which are pushing for a ruling system along the lines of the Iranian model.

The number of states and the number of democracies are on the rise, but we need to know a little more. The Plaid Avenger has put together a little high school yearbook of faces for you to identify, memorize, and be able to recognize if you pass them on the street. These are good people to know—not because they are necessarily good people, but because knowing them will make you a savvy global citizen. This yearbook is certainly not exhaustive, but contains particular faces that will be movers and shakers, newsmakers, and deal-breakers in the year to come. Know them well, my plaid friends, and join the ranks of those in the know, globally speaking. I've provided the names and places. You figure out who is who, and to which type of government they belong. I've provided some superlatives as clues to help you on your way. Good luck!

You simply must know your heads of state to be globally cool.

THE PLAID AVENGER WORLD YEARBOOK

Names	Places	Government Types
Kim Jong-il	Iran	Established Democracy
Benedict XVI	Australia	Young Democracy
Abdullah bin Abdul Aziz Al Saud	Russia	One-Party State
Angela Merkel	South Korea	Theocracy
Hu Jintao	Argentina	Monarchy
Recep Erdogan	Zimbabwe	Dictator
Hosni Mubarak	Israel	Anarchy
David Cameron	Afghanistan	Communism
Barack Obama	North Korea	Fascism
Dr. Manmohan Singh	Vatican City	State of Insanity
Lula da Silva	Saudi Arabia	
Hugo Chavez	Germany	
Nicolas Sarkozy	China	
Jacob Zuma	Turkey	
Viktor Yanukovych	Egypt	
Mahmoud Ahmadinejad	United Kingdom	
Julia Gillard	United States	
Vladimir Putin	India	
Lee Myung-Bak	Brazil	
Cristina Fernández de Kirchner	Venezuela	
Robert Mugabe	Japan	
Naoto Kan	France	
Hamid Karzai	Ukraine	
Benjamin Netanyahu	South Africa	

Most Likely to Fahrvergnügen

Chancellor _____

State: _____

Type of Gov't: _____

Chinese-iest

President _____

State: _____

Type of Gov't: _____

Most Likely to Never Lose an Election

President _____

State: _____

Type of Gov't: _____

Fish n' Chipiest

Prime Minister _____

State: _____

Type of Gov't: _____

The Other, Other White Meat

Prime Minister _____

State: _____

Type of Gov't: _____

The Most Popular Politician on the Planet

President _____

State: _____

Type of Gov't: _____

Best Turban Wrap

Prime Minister _____

State: _____

Type of Gov't: _____

Cleanest Linens

King _____

State: _____

Type of Gov't: _____

Most Likely to Lambada

Leaning-est Leftist & Most Winning Smile

Most Likely to Run Screaming from a Large Lizard Creature Who was Awakened from Its Underwater Slumber

Most Likely to Surrender

President _____

State: _____

Type of Gov't: _____

President _____

State: _____

Type of Gov't: _____

Prime Minister _____

State: _____

Type of Gov't: _____

President _____

State: _____

Type of Gov't: _____

Insane-ist

"Dear Leader" _____

State: _____

Type of Gov't: _____

Most Holiest Roliest

Bishop of Rome _____

State: _____

Type of Gov't: _____

Most Likely to Say "Nyet" to NATO

President _____

State: _____

Type of Gov't: _____

Most Likely to Eat Vegemite, Crikey!

Prime Minister _____

State: _____

Type of Gov't: _____

Most Likely to Stroke a Nuclear Missile in an Inappropriate Way, If He Had One

President _____

State: _____

Type of Gov't: _____

Baddest Ass

Prime Minister _____

State: _____

Type of Gov't: _____

Most Potent Polygamist (Has 20 Kids!)

President _____

State: _____

Type of Gov't: _____

Squintiest

Prime Minister _____

State: _____

Type of Gov't: _____

2010 World Prom Queen

President _____

State: _____

Type of Gov't: _____

Most Kosher

President _____

State: _____

Type of Gov't: _____

Biggest Bastard

Prime Minister _____

State: _____

Type of Gov't: _____

Most Likely to Not Survive Until the Next Edition of This Book

President _____

State: _____

Type of Gov't: _____

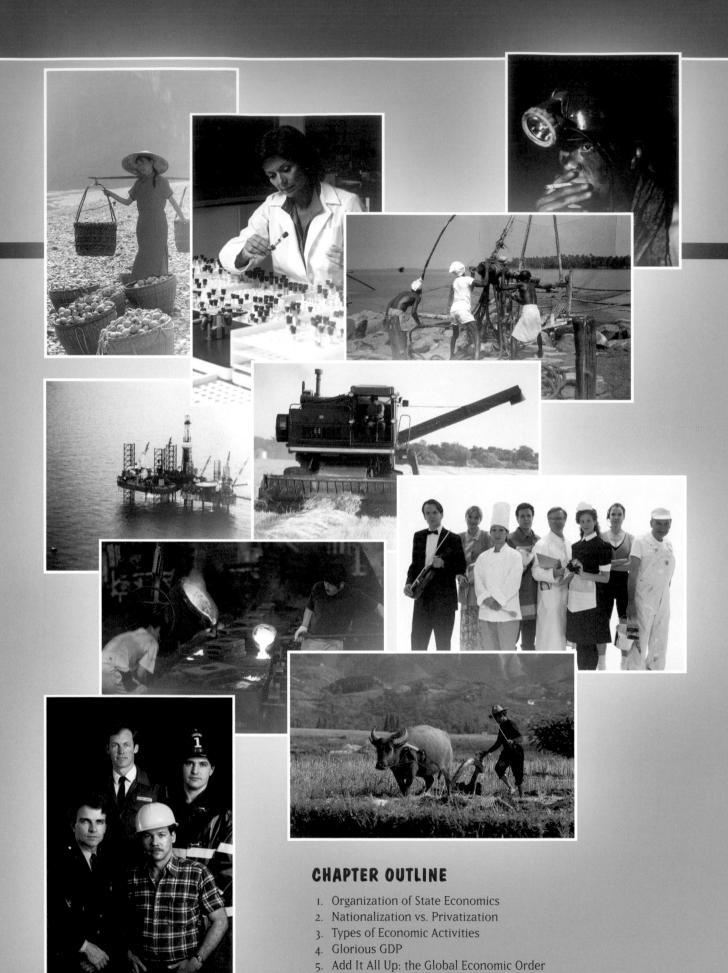

CHAPTER OUTLINE

1. Organization of State Economics
2. Nationalization vs. Privatization
3. Types of Economic Activities
4. Glorious GDP
5. Add It All Up: the Global Economic Order
6. Money! We Are Done with This Chapter!

The Plaid World Economy

4

OK we talked about people on the planet, where they are, how many there are, and how they procreate. We then looked where people live, the state, and how they are ruled within that state. Now let's look at what people do. People like to eat. People like to buy clothes. People like to buy cars. People like to buy stuff for the kids. People like to buy stuff for themselves. For all this stuff people want to buy on the planet, they have to have money to do it. All this buying and selling of stuff worldwide makes the economic world go round. So how do people make money in the world? Of course we don't want to look at each individual person; we want to look at the entire state. How does the state make money? What is going on in the global economy? Let's talk dollars and sense about world economic systems shall we?

ORGANIZATION OF ECONOMIES: HOW THEY SHAKE THEIR MONEY-MAKER

Now to start, we have to look at the overall organization of the economy within each state, and subsequently each region. We are going to revisit a theme we talked about last chapter, which is: the left versus the right. There's a left and a right in political systems and there's left and right in terms of social idealism; there's also a left and right spectrum when it comes to economies. What does it mean in the economic context when the media refers to the left versus right?

THE LEFT VERSUS THE RIGHT . . . ECON-STYLE

Often, you see terms such as communism versus capitalism related to the economic spectrum and indeed that's a good place to start. Think about the Cold War. Not only was it the "free" democracies versus the "evil" communist in terms of politics, but was also defined as "free market" capitalism versus communist "command economy."

Communism

Socialism

Capitalism

When we talked about the left versus the right politically, we defined things like communism as a system that was all about the individual, where their state was functioning in a capacity to serve the individual: the state exists only to serve the people. The opposite, right side of that spectrum was exemplified by a person or small group of people at the top of the government that had all the power and the state worked for them. We can kind of look at this similarly on the economic spectrum by discussing what systems exist and on what sides.

TYPES OF ECONOMIES

COMMUNISM

We'll start on the extreme left, just like the last chapter, which makes sense since communism is at once a political system and an economic system all rolled into one. In the economic sense, communism refers to a society where everything in the state is owned, possessed, controlled and operated by the government. What? I thought you just said that the left was all about the people having all the power? I know it is confusing, but dig this: the government in a true communist society simply controls all these things in the name of the people. The commie interpretation is that all the people in the state *are* the state, and thus are the true owners of everything. The government is simply composed of a small group of people that are passing all the stuff out to you, as you need it, because it's your stuff. Bottom line: all stuff is public stuff; no private ownership of anything allowed.

What stuff are we talking about here? All the goods, all of the services, all of the resources, all the factories, and all the means of production. Everything. Under resources, it's pretty obvious: all the oil, all the wheat, all the coal, all the gold, all the forest, all the land—which is an important one. Means of production include all the factories and processing plants, all the plants that make cars, and tanks, and refrigerators, and light bulbs. Everything is owned and controlled by the state.

Again, the state is doing this *for* the people; all the people truly own all the stuff. People, people, people. Why do I keep reiterating that the people own all this stuff in a communist system? Because it don't freakin' work, never has, never will. It's a farce; it's just an abstract idea on paper that this is the way that it should work. As we already referenced in the last chapter, communism has never manifested itself truly in this way—in fact, it has never even come close. Every attempt at it has gone awry. A small group of folks has gotten in charge in order to make the transition to this type of society but it has never worked, because money and power ultimately (and sometimes quickly) corrupt the small group of people in charge.

In addition, an entire economy—of even the smallest state—has way too many variables to try to control through a central administration, and winds up being more complicated than any small group can handle. The Russian description of this experience was **command economy,** and you can see just from the words themselves, that the government attempted to control and thus command all aspects of everything. A tall order for even the smartest and least corrupt.

So corruption and complication have combined to make pure communism pretty much an abject failure everywhere it has been attempted. True, pure economic communism is, on paper, possession of everything by everyone. In the real world, it's nonexistent.

Confusing commie points:

→ Communism is both a political and economic term because it combines politics and economics into one system in which ownership of all property is communal, and there is not supposed to be a strong central government.

→ You may think, and correctly so, that Russian communism's political and economic power was very concentrated in the hands of few. This was supposed to be a temporary position while they "fixed" the economy to a true communist utopia. As you know now, they never got it right.

→ But even in today's world you hear references to "Communist China," "Communist Cuba" or even "Communist Vietnam." Make no mistakes about it, my plaid friends, these countries' economies are much more capitalist in nature. Their political leadership may still be called communist, but not their economies.

CAPITALISM

Let's head right to the other extreme. On the other side of the spectrum is something of which we are much more familiar: *capitalism*. In capitalist society, all the resources, all the stuff, all the oil, all the land, all the fish, all the gold, and all the means of production, all the factories, all the car plants, all the refrigerators are all owned by private individuals. **Private ownership** is the key here in a purely capitalist society.

Where did this system come from? Capitalism is an amazingly popular and resilient system, mostly because it happens quite naturally. Humans naturally gravitate towards marking off territory and claiming stuff. There is also an inherent agreement that the harder you work and the more risks you take, the more money you should accrue, or at least deserve to accrue. Everybody takes care of themselves, and in doing so, the economy takes care of itself. What this equates to over time is ownership by the few—which reinforces why these systems are on opposite sides of the spectrum. In a communist society everybody owns everything; in a capitalist one, just a percentage of the population owns things.

Hard-core capitalists would argue for free trade, for free markets, and for minimal government intervention. "Let the market forces run their course" is a mantra of the capitalist. However, in a purely capitalist system in which the government plays no role, it would pretty much be every man for himself. Dog eat dog world. Only the strong, smart, and/or rich survive. Wealth would continue to be further and further concentrated into fewer and fewer hands. That would eventually equate to large segments of the society as destitute, impoverished, uneducated, and perhaps even unemployed. Is that a society that anyone wants? Probably not. Thus . . .

Just like communism, where does true capitalism exist? Nowhere. We live in a predominately capitalist world and capitalism is a popular system on the planet right now. But where does a purely capitalist or a pure communist state exist? Not anywhere, because virtually every place on the planet is in the middle. What is in the middle? Socialism. That's next.

Confusing capitalist points:

→ We think that all the rich countries, and many of the poor, are pure capitalist societies. Pure capitalism is an extreme in which the central government of the state plays absolutely no part in the economy. This is not true anywhere on the planet, not even in the US which is resoundingly the biggest proponent of capitalist expression on the globe.

→ Even hard-core capitalist countries end up having anti-monopoly laws for big businesses. Why? Because if businesses and capitalist entities are extremely successful, they will keep getting bigger and bigger and absorbing other businesses until their power becomes unchecked, and uncheckable. Isn't that what capitalism is all about? Indeed. But no state wants to become second fiddle to a corporation.

→ We like to think of the capitalist system as the "best" or most equal or even the most catering towards individual rights because everyone has an equal opportunity to own the stuff. However, having the same opportunity does not make for equal, or even fair, distribution of stuff. In the end, capitalism will concentrate wealth into fewer hands—many would say this is appropriately based on how smart you are, level of skill, your hard work, etc. Others say that concentration of wealth perpetuates stagnation in the masses, as idiot-savant kids inherit all the wealth from their rich mommies and daddies (sorry country-clubbers!) and opportunities to access that wealth by the masses becomes diminished. What do you think?

SOCIALISM

Now I know some of you ardent conservatives are saying to yourselves right now, "Blasphemy! There is no such thing as socialism in the US. We're not socialists here in this country; that's a bad word! They're just a shade off of those damn commies!" But I'm here to tell you that when we're looking at things economically on the planet, virtually everybody is somewhere in the socialist sphere. Having said that, there is a broad range of what it means to be socialist and it goes all the way from close to the extreme left to close to the extreme right. In other words, that's where everybody really is: in a shade of socialism. And there are many, many shades. They all have the root of the word in their interpretation: *social.* In other words, they look out for, or have some role in, the societies over which they rule; societies made up of people.

What is economic socialism? You might have figured this out already. It's somewhere between the extremes. That is, the government (i.e., the state), owns some stuff and controls some stuff, maybe some lands, maybe some industries, maybe some of the resources, maybe some oil. At the same time, private interests or private individuals own some stuff as well: some oil, some factories, some lands, some things, and indeed, that's pretty much where the world is. Let's flush this out in a little more detail.

Why would the state want to control any of this economic stuff? Short answer: to provide services for its peoples. Even the most ardent capitalist would agree that the state should provide things like an army to defend the country and maybe road systems or postal systems to facilitate economic growth. Others in a society think that the state should do a whole lot more, like provide social security, welfare systems, and unemployment checks, maybe even health care. Different states provide different amounts of these things.

In either case, how is the state going to pay for these things? The answer: by way of resource/industry control or taxation or some combination of both. Some states are very heavy-handed in this approach, perhaps controlling the most lucrative industry in its entirety, like in the state operated oil industries of Saudi Arabia or Venezuela. Other states like the US make some money off resources (mostly by selling the rights to drill to private companies) and some money off taxation. Other states, like Sweden, tax the living hell out of everybody to make money. Different states have different approaches to making money. Look at the graphic below to see what I'm talking about.

Confusing Socialist points:

→ Socialism comes in many packages; you may see references to democratic socialism, or mixed systems which are prevalent in Western Europe and increasingly prevalent in Latin America.

→ Socialism can refer to heavy state ownership and control of some industries—South American model. Socialism can also refer to states that generate revenue by heavy taxation in order to provide lots of services to citizens—the European model.

→ The term is often misused by the conservative right in the US who confuse regulation of certain aspects of the economy with government ownership of business—you will see this when any laws are passed which limit big businesses in any way; those on the right will say the US is drifting into Socialism. You may also have heard "socialism" used a lot when when the Obama administration was passing its health care legislation in 2010.

→ Even though the US and many other states control/own aspects of their economy, we still refer to them as "capitalist" simply because they are more toward the right side of this socialist spectrum. Conversely, places like Venezuela are openly referred to as "socialist" because they are much closer to the left side of the spectrum, as they control many more aspects of the economy. Well, that and the fact that they call themselves socialists.

Let's look at this spectrum from left to right again in terms of some active interpretations of this socialist sphere because really, the entire planet is somewhere in here—albeit in varying degrees.

If we think of all-the-way-left commies like Lenin, we see the attempted manifestation of true communism. He wanted the state to control everything in order to provide all stuff and all services to all the people all the time. He died. Didn't work out so well in the long-term. Or the short-term. Or really any term in between.

Castro is the modern-day Leninist attempt at communism. In Cuba's case, the state does control quite a bit; all of the resources in Cuba are owned supposedly by the people and are administered and controlled by the government for the people. But it's not working out so well, and there is a large underground free-market/black-market economy at work to supplement the services and stuff that is supposed to be supplied by the government, but is not—because they're broke.

King Abdullah and Hugo Chavez are slightly more to the right. Neither embraces communism, and indeed there are a lot of private businesses and private ownership in their countries. However, in both cases, the state controls the extremely lucrative

Extreme Left, Full State Control . . .   . . . increasing gov't control of the economy

oil industries and uses the profits generated from oil to provide all sorts of services to their people. Saudi Arabia happens to be a little bit better at it right this second, and everything from health care to education is provided to its citizens. Hugo is trying, and he openly embraces socialism full-on as the way to success for his country, but his rhetoric is bigger than his actions thus far. However, he is widely supported by the poor people because of this same propaganda, which promises more stuff to the masses.

Hu Jintao's China comes next, even though it is supposedly a communist state that one would assume should be on the extreme left side of this spectrum. Not so. China initiated capitalist reforms for the last three decades and privatization ensued, but the government does still play a heavy hand in many industries and policies. Next we see Vladimir "the man" Putin from Russia. What? Russia? They were the center of the commie sphere! How can they be right of center now? Because they fully embraced the capitalist way after the collapse of the USSR, and they did it with such a vengeance that it became a "wild west" of capitalism. Most things went into private ownership, and the government became so broke that it could not provide all those services that it once did. As a result, Russia has since re-taken control of its lucrative oil industry once more, leaning back towards the left side of the spectrum. More on that later. This is the classic example of how the world as a whole is firmly capitalist in outlook, even if the individual states exhibit varying characteristics of socialism.

We can go a little bit further to the right and we get perhaps a lot of European states like Sweden, France, and Norway that—while they don't control a lot of resources outright—heavily tax luxury items like cars in order to raise revenue to supply stuff to their citizens. In Sweden, (I'm picking on Sweden in particular because everybody likes those boxy Swedish cars, the Volvos) almost no one can own a Volvo because the government taxes the heck out of them. Why do they do this? It's considered a luxury good like alcohol or mink furs. They heavily tax those items to raise revenue, because they supply some serious services to their citizens. When a woman has a baby in Sweden, she gets like two years off—PAID—maternity leave. Two years? Paid? Wow. In the US, women get like two hours off after having a child. Then it's "Okay, it's out. Get cleaned up, and get back to work! And by the way, those sheets you messed up, yeah, we're gonna have to get five hundred bucks from ya for those. Thanks bunches."

Now we're on familiar ground. The US is certainly much closer to the purely capitalist camp, but through limited resource control and taxation does provide a lot of services to the people. Quite a bit, actually, but not as much as many European states or even Canada, which has free health care. None of the government activities of the developed countries would be considered resource re-allocation, as maybe we would define activities in Venezuela or Cuba, but a lot of stuff is provided to the citizens nonetheless.

It is always up for debate in the US between Republicans and Democrats as to how many of these services the government should supply. In fact, it's one of the main dividing lines between these two parties. Republicans are considered as favoring big business because they support free market, free trade, and privatization of perhaps all government services. Democrats are typically associated with wanting the government to provide these services, and maybe even more. You may have heard reference to this lately as President Obama has talked of a possible federal health care program. This of course comes on the heels of President Obama partially nationalizing some banks and even the US auto manufactureers as the economic meltdown has unfolded. Hmmm . . . tricky business for the undisputed champion of free market capitalism.

. . . decreasing gov't control of economy   . . . to the Right, Full Private Control

Adam Smith rounds out our line-up on the extreme capitalist right, and he is here intentionally as the symbol of pure capitalism—he is the dude that wrote *Wealth of Nations* in 1776, the handbook on how/why to keep governments out of the economy altogether. Because as I've already pointed out, pure capitalism doesn't exist anywhere. And Mr. Smith is long since dead, so he doesn't exist anywhere either. No state on the planet does nothing for its people—because that's actually a really good way to get your ass thrown out of office, chucked off the throne, and/or guillotined.

WHY SO MANY SYSTEMS?

Speaking of getting your ass chucked off the throne, where did these systems come from? Just like the concentration of political power in the hands of a few was the undoing of monarchy in Europe, there is the same type of impetus in the economic systems. This largely arose because of the Industrial Revolution. The Industrial Revolution, which occurred in the 17th, 18th, and 19th century European experience, enabled a vast concentration of wealth in the hands of the few industrialists— the factory owners—and simultaneously pathetic circumstances for the peasants, the peons—the factory workers.

Industrialization: Rise of the Machines.

During this societal evolution, there were not many laws; in fact, they were nonexistent for things like child labor or workplace safety or minimum wages. The industrialists were all for the 195 hour work week—hey, that sounds good. How about we only pay people a dime a day? That sounds good too! Five-year-olds working in the factory? Why not? Got to give the little people something to do!

What you had was unregulated growth and crappy working conditions that really tested the limits of what societies would tolerate. This really pissed off lots of people and got them thinking about possible alternative systems to unregulated capitalism. Marx and Engels, and then Lenin and others, thought, "Hey, this is unfair. These few factory owners have concentrated wealth and power. And we are powerless." This sentiment was not unlike the active aversion felt by peoples ruled under monarchies at the time as well. Result? Marxism, communism, socialism, and perhaps a few more —isms I don't even know about, were created to offer other options. These new economic systems evolved to offer alternatives to the unchecked power of capitalism—just like alternative government types evolved to counter unchecked power of monarchy at the time. And now, strangely enough, we have come full-circle. Whereas many of these systems originally evolved to check concentration of power and wealth in state systems, the states are now looked to by many to help counter wealth and power which has accumulated somewhere else . . . where would that be? Answer: the corporation!

Corporations are a significant thing to consider, if for no other reason then they've kind of replaced governments as the true holders of real power on the planet. You have to understand this; governments were seen as holding all the real power 200 years ago giving way to revolutions to unseat or redistribute that power (e.g., see American Revolution, French Revolution, Russian Revolution, etc.). In today's world, multinational corporations are seen as the real powers on the planet and thus we've had a kind of move from protesting against a government or saying, "Hey this government is unfair, we should change it or do

What Is the Deal with . . . MultiNational Corporations?

An executive with Dow Chemical recently said, "I have long dreamed of buying an island owned by no nation and of establishing the World Headquarters of the Dow Company on the truly neutral ground of such an island, beholden to no nation or society." Such is the story of multinational corporations. For most of history, the world economy has been controlled by nation-states. They made the rules, set taxes, and imposed regulations and corporations had to follow them. This is changing.

In today's world of globalization, multinationals have become the primary actors in the world economy. Free trade agreements are reducing the barriers for companies to operate in other countries and the global economy is becoming more interdependent. Many countries want multinational corporations to do business within their borders because they boost the local economy, bring jobs, and pay taxes. Therefore, countries, and even regions of the world, compete with each other to attract multinational corporations by offering tax breaks, lax environmental or labor standards, and improved infrastructure. Multinational corporations may have their headquarters in one country, but they do business in multiple countries of their choosing. In this way, the multinationals now make the rules.

Multinational corporations, which include Exxon, Microsoft, Pepsi, and Nintendo, have become very powerful; some of them have higher revenues than most poor countries. However, they also have their critics. Nationalists and patriots are suspicious of them because they think that all they care about is making money (corporations would never do that!) and taking advantage of the host country. Antiglobalization protesters claim that the great power the multinationals wield is forcing countries to bend over backwards to please them by doing things like looking the other way when they ruin the environment or take advantage of poor people. There have been arguments that multinationals ruin local culture (so you won't be able to tell Cairo from Tokyo in a few years) and that they destroy local businesses because they just can't compete with the big multinationals.

Fun Fact: Some consider the Dutch East India Company, founded in 1602, to be the first multinational company.

something about it" to "Hey, this multinational corporation has all the power; they've got more money than our government does and they work outside the laws of our government because they're operating in maybe ten or twelve different countries."

When you see protests against multinational corporations, or outcry against entities like the WTO, you are seeing a manifestation that true power is not held solely by governments anymore. These protesters feel that the new oppressing force on the planet is not any particular state or government, but these powerful economic entities. In their opinion, real threats to human rights and human pursuit of happiness are made primarily by corporations. Now it appears that these multinational corporations are bigger, badder and with more money than most states on the planet.

The result? People are turning to state governments to counter the unchecked power of multinational corporations. Confusingly enough, the liberal movement started as anti–big government, and now in most countries is credited with being very pro–big government. How did that happen? Part of that answer lies in how the world has changed in the last few hundred years; 200 years ago, governments were the primary sources of all power, with economic entities like corporations running a very distant second. Is that how it is in today's world? Not hardly. The multinational and even just the national companies in our world have become the major powers, with governments running a close second. In this atmosphere, the liberal attitude has shifted from "liberating" people from an oppressive government to attempting to "liberate" them from the economic powers of today's world. They attempt to do this by using the powers of government to counter those of big business.

NATIONALISM VERSUS PRIVATIZATION

We need to further define a couple of terms that we've been tossing around here while describing all of these economic systems. You will see these terms frequently, and they often cause consternation for folks on either side of the economic spectrum. These forces in action have oftentimes been the cause of public unrest, of strained international relations, and have even been the impetus for invading countries or assassinating leaders. What's the deal?

Nationalization is the state acquisition and operation of businesses previously owned and operated by private individuals or corporations. It is usually done in the name of social and economic equality, often as part of communist or socialist doctrine. Nationalization of foreign owned property, like the Suez Canal by Egypt in 1958 or the copper mining industry by Chile in 1971, typically attempts to end foreign control of an industry or the economy and poses complex problems for international law.

In other words, the state assumes control of an industry, kicks out owners/operators, and starts taking the profits to the state bank account. This seriously ticks off the corporations, who in turn usually get their home government to kick up a fuss, take the case to an international arbitrator like the WTO, embargo the nationalizing state, or maybe even invade the country outright to get their stuff back. Sound preposterous? It's happened plenty in the last hundred years. France and Great Britain invaded Egypt to try to regain the Suez Canal, and the US has destabilized or overthrown whole governments in Chile, Guatemala and Cuba to satisfy pressures by corporations who fell victim to nationalization.

As you might have guessed already, *privatization* is just the opposite. Selling of businesses to private ownership after they have been the property of the state is the process of privatizing. Since the collapse of the USSR, Russia and all of its former areas of control have been in a mad scramble to privatize industries. But they are not alone. India and China are fertilized fields for mass privatizations, and the trend is still occurring in the developed world. Western European countries and Japan, who just privatized their postal service, continue to push more government operations to the private business sphere. In the US, the term has often been broadly applied to the practice of outsourcing the management of public schools, prisons, airports, sanitation services, and a variety of other government-owned institutions. Sometimes this contracting of services does not entail the outright sale of the industry to private hands.

Why the persuasive theme of privatization in the world? The popular argument is that government-run business is like a monopoly—and lack of competition makes the business not-so-productive and noncompetitive and wasteful, and maybe even ripe for corruption. That is certainly a valid point. The other reality is that bigger and bigger corporations have much more leverage than ever before in the past to put pressure on states to privatize. Who funds lobbying groups to persuade congressmen to privatize? Who has money to fund big studies that show that government operations are wasteful? Who would have the money to buy the senator a Ferrari for his teenage daughter's graduation present? And then who would be wealthy enough to bid on the sale of government resources and services that were being auctioned off? Um, maybe massively rich multinational corporations? You can call the Plaid Avenger jaded, you can even call him a leftist, but he is merely a realist. It's the way the world works.

Privatization is the growing theme in the 21st century, but nationalization is far from extinct. Hardcore capitalists and businessmen and multinational corporations across the planet still shudder when they hear the word. Five years ago, I would have said that this idea and this concept were completely dead and that you wouldn't see this happening much anymore. However, it is making a slight resurgence particularly in the left-leaning South American region—I should say left-leaning Latin America because it rolls off the tongue much more glibly. You'll also see some of this happening perhaps in Africa in the very near future, but I digress.

NATIONALIZATION ADDENDUM!!! How right I was years ago to include the paragraph above concerning the resilience of nationalization! Since the global economic meltdown started in 2008, governments around the globe have been scrambling to nationalize key industries, even in the hardcore capitalist countries. Forget socialist Venezuela; one need look no further that the US which has partially or fully nationalized a bunch of banks and even the auto industry in an effort to stabilize the crashing economy. Russia and China are following suit, quickly leaning back towards more state control in all things economic in order to prevent the financial chaos which has ensued in the west. Adam Smith is rolling in his grave.

And that brings up a confounding question: why would states which advocate free-market capitalism ever stoop to the depths of nationalization? Several reasons crop up. In times of national emergency or war, states often nationalize critical industries like steel or energy in order to ensure national security (can't have disruptions in bomb and tank production during war time). It can also occur if a state deems the social benefits far outweigh the economic costs, such as running a postal or healthcare system. Sometimes it is done for purely economic reasons, i.e. gov't takeover of a business or industry about to fail, which would equate to lost jobs and lost revenue for the country.

Put all those reasons together into one big pot and stir, and you have the answer to why US President Barack Obama and many other European leaders are back in the nationalization game right this second. Partial or full government takeover of financial institutions and car companies is being done under the banner of "saving the economy/saving the country" from further collapse and preserving social benefits like jobs, while also alluding to a sense of maintaining national security which would inevitably be threatened if critical components of the economy like the whole banking system were to crash. Interesting stuff. We shall see how long it takes them to re-privatize these industries as the economy recovers. . . .

TYPES OF ECONOMIC ACTIVITY

No matter what the type of economy or how far to the left or right in the socialist world they may be or even if things are being nationalized or privatized, people on the ground are always doing something to make this thing called an economy go forward. What is it those guys are doing?

I'm not talking about economic structure at the state scale. I'm talking about what people do on the ground. In real life. What the heck do you do? You chop down trees for a living or do you make toothpicks? You raise kids? What do you do that makes money? I can certainly think of all the unsavory things that people do on the planet to make money because I've participated on both sides of the trade myself. Now we're on familiar ground here, and this chapter gets exceptionally easy because we can really classify all economic activity that happens in the world into four distinct types of activity.

Why are we doing this? Just so we can call out people and see what level they're on? To point and laugh? Hahahaha—your mama sells crack for a living in the service sector. No! We want to identify these things because it's important to understand what different states are doing and how many people are dedicated to certain activities within the state. This in turn tells us a lot about how the economy operates, why some places are richer than others, and how this is currently changing in different regions around the globe. And it is oh so simple. They all go in order and it is even numerical. Let us proceed with speed: Primary.

Primary economic activities is as simple as it gets. Literally. This level includes anything and everything that involves natural resource extraction from the earth. Just taking stuff from Momma Earth and then selling it is a primary activity. The list is actually short:

→ Agriculture production: Cucumbers, acorns, squash, cocoa leaves—I don't care what it is; it's a primary economic activity if it's just simple agriculture.

→ Timbering/logging: Chop down a tree and take it. That's extraction of a raw commodity.

→ Mining: Oil, coal, gold, diamonds—mining of everything. That's all simple extraction. Just pull it out of the ground and give it to me.

→ Fishing: Yep, just taking a fish out of the water. That's a primary economic activity, even if you use dynamite to do it.

Pretty straightforward, pretty simple stuff. Resource extraction is the key. And that is primary. Now the point to take home with you here, particularly when you hear things like gold or oil, you think, "Ooooooweee . . . that is worth a lot of money!" Here is what the Plaid Avenger wants you to know: No it really ain't.

Virtually all primary activities aren't worth squat in the long term. How can I say that? Oil is worth a lot of money, isn't it? Well, it's critical for everything; it's used for everything, it's . . . but it's worth less per gallon than homogenized milk, and that isn't worth much either, is it? Speaking of milk, what are all agricultural products worth per pound? Per boatload? How about wood? Quick question: would you rather have a business that grew oranges, or made orange juice concentrate? Why? Because one makes more money than the other due to processing of the product, which leads us to . . .

Secondary economic activities involve the processing of everything you got from the primary economic activities. All secondary activity consists of somehow manipulating, altering, refining, making better, doing something to the stuff you got from the primary activities—that is, the raw materials are modified in some way. Here's the main point: modified in such a way so it is worth more money.

You are adding value and that is something that will continue to happen as you go up this chain of economic activities. As I've suggested earlier, products of primary activity are not worth much. You can cut down a tree, and a tree lying down on the forest floor is worth something, but not a lot. How about if we take that tree, rip off the bark, cut it into planks and then further cut them into boards.

Now that's worth a lot more! Contractors and construction people will pay for boards, not for a tree.

Processing something of a big quantity to a smaller quantity is simple processing, but it still adds value. Then there is also refining. If we take oil out of the ground, it doesn't go straight in your gas tank. It has to be processed. It has to be cleaned up. Taking the oil out of the ground is our primary activity, processing it at a refinery is a secondary activity that adds a lot more value. Further manipulate it into gasoline and it's worth quite a bit more.

This can include a vast array of activities, which you don't often think about. Simple things like cleaning up coffee beans or roasting coffee beans. Are roasted coffee beans worth more than raw coffee beans? Indeed they are. How about mud? Mud? Mud is just mud—but form it into squares, let it dry out, and now you have bricks. You can't sell mud but you can sell bricks. You've processed it; you've added value. Processing of any raw material counts—including taking a fish and chopping out its guts. Is a gutless fish worth more than a fish with guts? Indeed it is. Ask anybody who wants to cook a fish. Any and all "basic manufacturing" items fall into this category: from textiles to furniture to cars to paper to toys. If it is modified or made, it's a manufactured item, and manufactured/factory goods are all secondary activity stuff.

Now let's get on with it; let's get to tertiary level activities. **Tertiary level activities** are also known as service sector activities, so stage three includes all services on the planet. Perhaps we're going to take some of the raw commodities, or even some finished commodities, and do something with them, maybe move them around, further manipulate them, or sell them—provide a service of some sort.

The service sector is what most of us in the developed world are used to. What most of us have done for a living; you really got to go out of your way to find agriculturalists or lumberjacks or people who work in mills anymore in the rich countries. But a service sector job? Yeah, we've all done those.

Every hamburger that gets fried, every surgery that gets performed, every used car that gets sold, every fire that gets put out—someone has provided a service. Even simple transportation is a service. Truck drivers are an excellent example of this: taking raw commodities from one place and simply moving to another place. I'm sorry, what have we done here? We've added value to the commodity! A bunch of lumber sitting in the middle of Saskatchewan Canada doesn't do a dang thing for us here in the United States—but if you put it on trucks and move it here, now you've added the value to it. We can use it; it's more accessible.

That's just one division of the service sector. We tend to think of everything from construction to police to doctors to teachers to army people, navy people, air force people, marine people as all providing a service. Perhaps the biggest one you think of is sales—service people at McDonalds, at the mall, at Wal-Mart, cashiers, wait staff; all these people are providing a service to you. They are moving around stuff from the first two activity levels and getting it to customers and/or increasing the value in some way, shape, or form.

Again, this process entails a ton of different activities, but its main feature is its tendency to increase the overall value of stuff from stages one and two in some discernible manner. Reconsider our hamburger: a cow that we killed in primary activity terms is ground into hamburger during secondary activity—worth more than the cow to be sure, but even raw hamburger is not valuable. Now take it to a restaurant and provide some services in the form of a cook and then maybe a maître d' that seats you at the table and maybe a waiter or waitress that brings you that hamburger. Now you've provided a bunch of services and

you will pay a lot more for that hamburger in a restaurant than you will for the raw hamburger at the store and even more than you'll pay for the dead cow somewhere out in the field.

You see, as we progress up this chain we keep providing more, adding more value to commodities. Providing services adds value to commodities. Here's another important thing to consider: how much more do people get paid in the service sector than, say, farmers or lumberjacks or even people who work in a mill? Well, sometimes we have comparative salaries between occupations, but oftentimes as we progress up this chain, people get paid more to do, in real terms, what is a little less. Every level adds value to the commodities themselves, as well as to the salaries of the people who are doing it.

So what's left? **Quaternary sector** is kind of a new one. Some analysts and economists don't even recognize this one yet, due mostly to the fact that these types of jobs have not been on the planet for very long, and don't constitute a big percentage of the labor force. But they are on the rise, and do

tell us some important things about the societies in which they occur. Quaternary sector provides something new. Not a natural resource, nor a processed commodity, and not really a service either. In essence, the quaternary sector deals with the creation and manipulation of intangibles—and the main intangible that I am thinking of here is information.

In the technologically advanced countries, an increasing number of people aren't dealing with hamburgers or trees or oil or services so much anymore as they are with the idea of information for information's sake. Computer programming, researchers, lab technicians, even astronauts are all in the realm of data creation, but don't necessarily "provide" a service to anyone. The results of their work may lead to a commodity that is mass produced, but their work in and of itself is neither a commodity nor a service.

To a certain extent, you can even say stock market people are in the quaternary sector because they are not really producing anything. Perhaps they are providing a service, but it's more likely that they are manipulating information and moving abstract things around to create or add value to them (i.e., stocks).

It's a fuzzy one to be sure, but the reason I like to point it out is because we can make some easy assumptions about any country that has folks working in this sector. It has to be developed, advanced, and rich if you have a significant presence of quaternary sector jobs filled in your state. No two ways around it. How much do those folks get paid? Bangin' bank, that's what. What are those products worth? Genetic code, computer programs, cures for diseases . . . are you kidding me? That's real money!

If you can critically examine what economic activities that different countries and regions focus on, you can go a long way to understanding why rich countries are rich, why poor countries are poor, and how the global economy is working. This insight, or should I say sight beyond sight, gives you the inside scoop on the real mechanics of money flow in the world. What? You don't have the sight beyond sight yet? Better call in Lion-O and proceed directly to. . . .

I WANT TO GO UP THE FOOD CHAIN . . . SECTOR EVOLUTION

We can look at any state on the planet, just in terms of their economic activities, to get a fuller picture of what's going on, how rich they really are, and indeed, what their future holds. It's not only about how much money they've got and how much money they are going to make but also what's going on in their society, how developed or developing they are, and lots of other things that we can typically tie to other demographic and cultural factors. And it's easy. Check it:

FIGURE 4.1 ECONOMIC SECTOR RATIOS

As you can see in the above graphic, the percentage of people within each state who work in each of these levels of economic activity tells us volumes about what's happening. We can define some obvious patterns between developed and developing countries, as well as explain anomalies to these patterns. First, the trends:

The fully developed countries, that is, the richer countries in the world, have a much greater percentage of their workforce in the tertiary/service sectors than in primary and secondary sectors. Check out Luxembourg, the UK, and Germany on the top of the chart. In fact, primary industries in the developed world account for almost nothing, but that should make sense to you now. Advanced technology and machinery in these countries equates to small percentages of folks needed to grow all the food and mine all the coal.

In the US, just 2 percent of the population is farmers, yet they supply the other 98 percent with food, and even export tons of food on top of that. They are all the way through the demographic transition; one big tractor in the US operated by one guy can do the work of 1,000 small farmers in Africa—hell, maybe more like the work of 10,000.

Secondary/manufacturing sector jobs are continuing to decrease in the developed world due primarily to the cost of labor. Developed countries have labor unions and health benefits and minimum wage laws; all of which serve to increase the cost of labor. Developing countries typically have none of these things, thus, labor is cheap. Manufacturing jobs of virtually all things—cars, toasters, toys, luggage, computers—have been migrating from developed countries to developing ones to take advantage of this cheaper labor. What does that leave for everyone to do? Service sector employment in an area emphasizing skilled labor coupled with an increasing commodity value. Good money for most. Of course some of the folks in these societies have the know-how and opportunity to create and manipulate information, leading the world in quaternary level activities. In developed regions, there is:

→ hardly anyone in the primary sectors,

→ typically less than a quarter in the secondary processing sector,

→ a majority of the workforce in the service sector,

→ and a significant number of people in the high-end quaternary sector.

Just the reverse is happening in the developing countries. To point out these major differences, let's start with some of the countries that are the least developed, and subsequently are the poorest parts of the planet. Check out the bottom brackets filled by the African countries. They are overwhelmingly primary industry based, very limited secondary and service sector employment; quaternary is out of the question. What can we say about a place that is almost exclusively agriculture or fishing or mining based? What are those products really worth? As pointed out earlier, not much. In the least-developed regions:

→ most folks are in primary—most of them are farmers,

→ less than a quarter are in manufacturing—sometimes much less than that,

→ Even fewer are in the service sector—none in quaternary.

Most states on the planet are somewhere in between. The trends do seem to indicate that the more developed a place becomes, the more tertiary and secondary will be gained at the expense of the primary sector. More service, more manufacturing, fewer farmers. End game: more money. We can see this reflected in the chart above. Costa Rica and Brazil are diversified across sectors more in tune with developed countries, and are doing pretty well. We wouldn't think of those countries as impoverished or undeveloped. India and Vietnam are hustling and transforming, but they are still overwhelmingly agricultural based societies, and as such, are not making the big bank money yet—not per capita anyway. China and Turkey are stable, prosperous societies that are perhaps the most balanced across the board in economic activities. Plaid Avenger inside tip: this balance and diversity will probably serve both these countries well in the future, and you may see other countries try to emulate this approach as opposed to stacking up solely in the tertiary category. Just a hypothesis. But I'm usually right. China has actually stated that they want to keep this diversity in order to maintain their competitive edge in manufacturing.

Confucius say: Keep farmer. Keep miners. Keep low wage to keep manufacturing sector; make China strong.

He could be onto something.

Now to look at an anomaly. What's the deal with Egypt up there? Looks pretty balanced, perhaps even more developed than Turkey or China. Are they really approaching full development as their economic activity breakdown suggests? Probably

not. We have to look at the real world in this case to decipher the truth; Egypt has a low percentage of folks in primary sector, not because it's an evolved economy, but because they don't have a lot of agricultural land to farm! It's a desert! Except along the Nile, of course. They have some oil to mine, but not very much, and it just doesn't create many jobs anyway. So low primary activities. Why high service sector, then? One of the money-makers for Egypt is tourism. You know, go see the pyramids. How much money are those tourism jobs worth? Again, not too much. We can make sense out of these economic activities on a case by case basis when some of these countries buck our trends.

But the trends do make sense. They do seem to support the concepts outlined in the Demographic Transition Model from Chapter 2. Most states are working toward increasing manufacturing and service sectors, and lessening dependence on primary sector, because that makes them more money. Currently, most of the value added to primary commodities happens in the developed world—to primary products shipped to them from the developing world. You should be able to see how this puts the poorer countries at a "permanent disadvantage"—they export low value stuff and have to import high value stuff. That's why the more successful countries in the 21st century are trying to

Confucius say: Show me the money!

catch up, not by producing even more cheap stuff, but by changing percentages in their economic activities sectors. China and India are changing fast and will be making big bucks. Saudi Arabia and Equatorial Guinea are making big bucks on primary sector stuff (oil) but not changing or diversifying internally. Who is going to win in the long term?

GOOD FOR YOU AND GOOD FOR ME: IT'S NOT JUST GROSS, IT'S GDP!

How does what all these folks do for a living in all these different states in the world affect real wealth—that is, real money and real dollars. That something is called GDP. **GDP** is Gross Domestic Product. You may have also heard of GNP, or Gross National Product. What's the difference between the two? Are you ready for this? Nothing; they are two terms which mean the same thing. GDP has been growing in popularity and GNP has been falling out of use. Okay, so what do they mean?

GDP is simply all the goods and all the services within any state that are created and sold in that year. What do I mean by all the goods and all the services? Well, everything. Every single thing that is bought and sold. Every transaction in terms of a final sale. Every hamburger that's sold, every car that's sold, every service that's provided, every employee salary at McDonalds, all of it. All of it added together for the year is the GDP.

You do have to put this in context of the *final sale of the commodity* and what that means. For GDP, we only count the final sale and not all the transactions that led up to that final sale. Example: a car. A car gets sold on a lot for $20,000. That $20,000 car transaction is the final sale because it is going to a consumer, who will then "consume" it. That $20,000 goes into the total for GDP for that year. Now the reason we say only the final sale counts is because you can't sell things twice or three times or five times in the case of commodity chains anywhere in the world. The car has tires on it when the guy sold it off the lot. Well, those tires were made somewhere, and then sold to a distributor, who then sold them to a retailer, and then the retailer maybe sold them to a car manufacturer and that's like three separate transactions, but you wouldn't count those other transactions because then you would be counting the same tires three times within one year. Only the last sale counts.

However, the car salesman's salary, the distributor's salary, the assembly-line worker's salary—all these services are a part of GDP for the year. The final sale and all worker salaries go into this equation. It doesn't matter if twenty people were involved in the movement, creation and distribution of that car; all their salaries go into GDP.

Now we know what GDP is, but what can we say about patterns of GDP on the planet? Keep your world regions in mind when analyzing the following map.

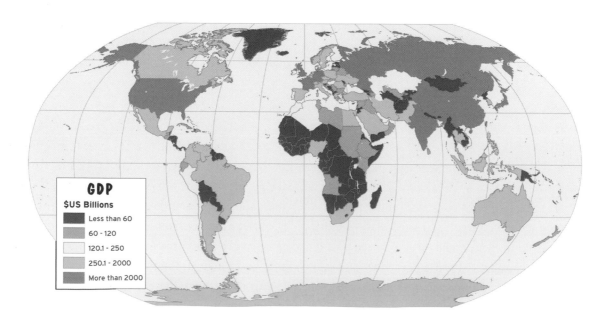

GDP

$US Billions

Less than 60

60 - 120

120.1 - 250

250.1 - 2000

More than 2000

If we look at the GDP planetary totals, we see that the heavyweights who make the most money on the planet are represented by the developed world, with the United States economy weighing in at number one in the world (for now). Second in line, Japan has the number two economy on the planet. The third is now China, who bumped Germany from that slot just last year. They all have GDP that total in the trillion-dollar range. That is a million million, or is it a billion million? I can't remember; it's a one with a hell-load of zeros behind it. Over a trillion dollars per year.

But this is where the lines are drawn and we have to stop making comparisons about what we consider to be the developed and developing world based on just GDP. Mainly because China really makes things interesting: China surpassed France and the UK in total GDP in 2008, then bumped the Germans in 2009, which I'm sure is really freaking out my Frenchie friends. Is China fully developed? Most would say not. I personally argue the affirmative, but we will get to this in the next chapter. They sure are making bank, though.

We see that most of the Western European states are still in the high GDP category, and most of Africa and Asia are in the low GDP category, with Latin America, South Asia, and East Asia falling somewhere in between.

I do want to point out a couple things as we look at these totals around the planet. Maybe you are thinking "Wow, the rich countries—they are really, really rich. The poor countries, they really stink. They don't make squat. I guess everybody's sitting around there not making any money. They're not providing any goods or services. They suck." Reality check: we have to throw in a disclaimer here. When examining GDP totals, in relations to a state's actual wealth we have to consider what is not included in GDP. Check out the little green box, yo!

I'd like to point out one example in particular. If we look at Afghanistan on the map above, we see that they are on one of the lower levels of GDP on the planet. Were you to include the heroin economy, they would instantaneously be in the top ten nations on the planet for GDP. Don't undervalue the stuff that's not being counted.

I bring this up because when we look at the poorest places on the planet, they're actually working pretty hard—but none of the stuff they do actually counts in the totals. GDP is a Western-derived definition of wealth, a Western-measured definition of wealth, and simply does not always adequately reflect reality. What do I mean by this? Well, when we look at Africa, it looks like nothing's going on there but indeed, let's face the facts; a whole heck of a lot of work goes on there to keep that place going; it's just not measured.

What Is Not Included in GDP?

We said all the goods and all the transactions of all the goods and all the services are included in GDP—that's everything, isn't it? What would this not include?

First, think of some things that don't have monetary value in an exchange sense, but are indeed actually work. This list would include housework, child rearing, any labor done in the home, food grown for home consumption, food gathering, food preparation, firewood gathering, the list goes on. Why would I point this out? Because that's what most of the people on the planet are doing. Every single day. Day in, day out. None of these activities are included in GDP.

Second: anything that the government doesn't know about. Any transaction that occurs between folks under the table. This can refer to anything as innocent as a flea market or a yard sale to items or services traded, bartered or sold between people that is untaxed and therefore not included in the tally. But this also includes anything illegal—stuff the government prohibits and therefore wouldn't be able to tax or know about, including all illicit narcotic production and trade, all moonshining, gunrunning, and human trafficking. All of these activities, which do generate large amounts of wealth, are not included in GDP.

In summary, anything that's done at home, for home, anything that happens between friends, any type of barter transactions, and any illegal, illicit activities are not counted as part of GDP. That would radically change the map of what's going on here. There's one more thing to consider: the comparison between GDP and GDP per capita.

GDP PER CAPITA

Total GDP we covered earlier. **GDP per capita** is simply the total GDP divided by the population total for the state. In other words, it tries to approximate how much wealth there is per person in the society; this is perhaps a much better indicator of how the average Joe is doing in the world. Looking at these two maps side by side offers a contrasting picture of what's happening on the planet in terms of levels of wealth and economic activity. As to be expected, the most developed countries maintain themselves in the highest brackets, and the most undeveloped countries maintain themselves in the lowest brackets of both maps, but look what happens to some interesting places in between.

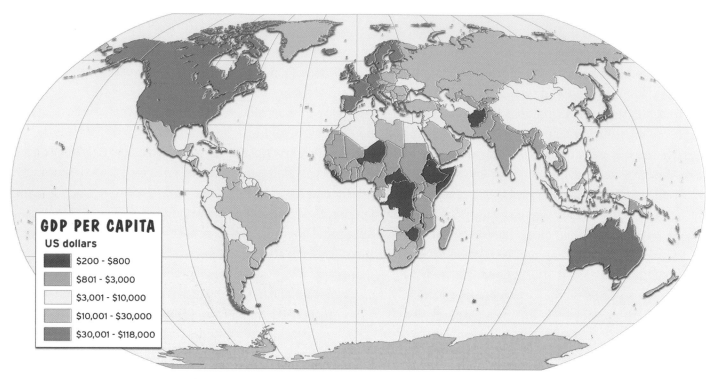

GDP PER CAPITA
US dollars
- $200 - $800
- $801 - $3,000
- $3,001 - $10,000
- $10,001 - $30,000
- $30,001 - $118,000

If we look at total activity, that is, the total GDP map on page 68, we see total wealth as a singular number that a society or state produces. All these numbers look really big and wow, would you look at that? China and India are right up there with the developed countries! So is Saudi Arabia! Sweet! They're making bank money! They're not doing too bad, right? Brazil, Argentina, they're doing pretty good as well. Everyone in Saudi Arabia is rich, aren't they? Um, how do I put this delicately for my Arab friends? . . . Does a chicken have lips? How do I know everyone there is not rich?

Well, let's check out a more realistic interpretation in the GDP per capita. What you see is a bit of a shakedown. India and China in particular have gone from the top classes of total GDP, to the lower classes of GDP per capita, a significant shift when broken down to the individual level. Why does this happen? Well, because they have big populations, and they're producing lots and lots of valuable stuff, *but* broken down to an individual level, it ain't really that much. **GDP per capita** is a much better gauge of what's happening in the society in terms of how well the place is really doing. A trillion dollars doesn't really make as much impact if everybody in the society is only getting a buck each.

This high GDP, low GDP per capita scenario possibly could be a very equal society, but unfortunately it never happens that way, at least not on this planet. The reality is a concentration of wealth in certain businesses and certain sectors and certain hands, with most people not really cutting much of a piece of the pie. This comparison becomes a much better measure of wealth disparity, and as such, is a much better indicator of how this society or state is really doing.

Sometimes these measures can be skewed radically. In other words, even if a state has a huge number in terms of GDP, and perhaps even when a state has a big number in the GDP per capita category, we still may not be getting the real picture. I'll pick on a few states in particular here. Places like Equatorial Guinea, Saudi Arabia, even Oman; what's happening in these places? High total GDP, high GDP per capita. Are they really so rich? Are they fully developed like the other rich, developed countries?

I think you already know the answers to these questions. Something doesn't add up. Equatorial Guinea, a rich place? Look how much money per person! On the books, they make $50,000 GDP per capita. That makes them one of the world leaders in that category . . . oh, except for the fact that most folks are starving to death under a thieving dictator.

Indeed, the majority possess squat and a handful of people own virtually everything. Wealth disparity is massive, but the figures remain high because of a double whammy; the GDP total is absolutely massive, and the total population is low, which equates to an exceptionally high GDP per capita.

That's when you have to take the sector breakdown of labor in conjunction with GDP and GDP per capita to get a real sense of what's happening in these states. The real deal that's happening is that these societies have high numbers based on one single thing: the export of oil. They export tons and tons and tons of oil which means they make tons and tons and tons of money, a big number. Even if you divide by the population, it is still a decent number, but all of the wealth is, in reality, in the hands of very, very few people.

Equatorial Guinea is a particularly nasty case where none of these numbers mean squat because most of the people there are impoverished beyond belief, while a single corrupt ruler and his cronies get 100% of the money from the sale of the state's resources. Saudi Arabia, Oman, Iran, and many other OPEC countries fall into similar situations, though not as bad as the Equatorial Guinea extreme. You have to consider other things—looking at the economic sector breakdown of a place in conjunction with its GDP per capita gives us a good sense of what's going on, as well as a good sense of development and standards of living.

A CORE/PERIPHERY EPIPHANY!

Let's add up all of the stuff we have learned so far in this chapter about economic activities and apply it to the singular global economy of which we are all now a part. What do I mean by that? Well, whether you want to accept it or not, the whole human world has been ever-slowly moving towards increased global connectivity, with economic activity being the most pervasive and successful system thus far.

The creation and movement, and buying and selling of stuff now happens across the entire globe as a single system. Oil from Kuwait is processed into gasoline in Burma and then fills the tanks of Toyotas in

Booting up the global economy!

Tokyo. Auto engines made with German parts are constructed in Romania and then shipped to Brazil to be installed in VW Jettas which are sold in Chile. Argentinean leather and Indonesian rubber is sent to southern China to be made into Nike shoes which end up on the shelves of the Wal-Marts of Wisconsin. That is just the easy to understand tangible stuff; there are also billions of dollars worth of services, stocks, investments, and currency exchanges which happen every single day among all the countries of the world. Which brings us to an interesting concept, appropriately named **world-systems** theory, which tries to make sense of the winners and losers of such a global economic scenario.

The development of the current world economy is the result of intensification of world trade, interconnections, and industrialization at a much higher level than in the past. For the last 500 years, the Europeans, and then the Americans (and maybe the Japanese, et al.), have dominated and shaped this global system, and many would argue to their ultimate advantage. Hey wait a minute! Europeans, Americans, and Japanese, that's the rich Team West! Damn skippy it is. Through past colonial/imperial activity, coupled with modern industrialization, the Team West core is certainly a huge beneficiary of this world economic situation. *Core* is a great term to use, because it is at the heart of world-systems theory.

KILLER CORE AND THE PATHETIC PERIPHERY

This dude named Immanuel Wallerstein formulated this functional flowchart back in the 1980s, and it continues to evolve even today. He characterizes the world-system as a set of mechanisms which redistributes wealth from the economic **periphery** to the **core**. Another word for periphery would be "edge" or "fringe". In other words, the core gets stuff from the periphery, either resources or money via economic exchanges; in this scenario, the core always gains and the periphery primarily loses, particularly in the long run. Typically, the core country buys the raw resource for cheap, let's say it's steel, from a periphery country. The core makes that steel into a car, and then can sell that car back to the periphery country for a much higher price. Core wins, core wins, core wins!

In Wallerstein's terminology, the core is the developed, advanced, industrialized, rich part of the world, while the periphery is the not-so-developed, raw materials-exporting, poorer part of the world. The free-market and financial systems are the means by which the core exploits the periphery. Maybe some of you think that this is the natural order of things, and that the word "exploit" is too harsh. That's cool. I'm not trying to make a political point here, I just want you to understand how the economy works, and this world-systems approach does do a good job explaining the current flows of wealth in the world, as well as why rich places get richer while poor places mostly get poorer. Pointing out the winners and losers makes the game easier to follow.

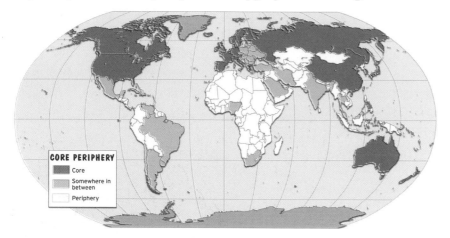

CORE PERIPHERY
■ Core
■ Somewhere in between
□ Periphery

Check out the map to the left, and then let's add some more descriptors to these elements to enlighten even further.

Core states have the maximum level of industrialization and technology, which of course makes them centers for innovation and creation . . . and manipulation of capital; you know, money and credit. Whether you dig this theory or think it's leftist propaganda, there is no disputing that for all of the modern era, the core countries have controlled global economic institutions like the IMF, World Bank, Inter-American Bank, the WTO and a host of others. The core runs the show, although that is now starting to change a bit (see G-20 in Chapter 6). The core has smarts and the industrial capacity to make raw resources into much more valuable commodities. The core also has the cash to reinvest in its own infrastructure and businesses continually in order to keep itself in the top slot. The core is all about keeping free-trade free and opening up new markets to the global system . . . because, of course, all these things benefit them tremendously!

The periphery is the total opposite. They are poorer countries that may lack industrial capacity, financial means, and/or technological savvy to process their resources into finished goods. But they do have natural resources and tons of workers ready to slave away for pennies a day. They end up selling raw resources/cheap labor, which are cheap, and then importing finished goods, which are expensive. You don't need to be a math major to figure out how this story ends. Also, most of the industrial capacity and resource extraction that happens in periphery countries is usually owned fully or partially by multinational corporations from the core, which means that the core countries sometimes benefit economically even from the raw resources too. Ouch! Double-whammy! Most of Sub-Saharan Africa would be the best examples of periphery.

Because they are on the losing side of this equation, periphery countries are often locked into a cycle of never having enough money to invest in their own education systems or businesses in order to break out of this gerbil-wheel. Epic economic fail! When the situation gets bad enough, or when a strong leader comes to power, in a periphery country is when you sometimes have things like **nationalization** occur. Remember that stuff from ten pages ago?

Of course, not every single state in the world falls nicely into one of these two categories. There are those countries that benefit more from their resources, like most of the Middle Eastern states which fully control their oil resources, and there are some places that have effectively nudged their way closer to the core via crafty economic policies and strategic political alignment. Which reminds me to get back to point:

LET'S GET TO THE CORE OF THIS ISSUE

Can a state get to the core if they are seemingly stuck in the periphery? Oh yes my friends! Things are changing very fast here in the 21st century! While Team West is currently the richest and certainly has an outstanding competitive edge in today's world, this was not always the case. In times past, both India and especially China would have been considered as the economic core of the global system, positions that they are working very hard at reclaiming in the modern era.

China has been strategically controlling its own resources, as well as acquiring cheap resources from other periphery states. They have used these resources along with their massive pool of cheap labor to become the manufacturing "workshop of the world," producing every imaginable industrial and commercial product. They are now core winners. India has taken a slightly different path: investing heavily in service and quaternary sector jobs like computer programming is what is currently pulling them out of the periphery realm.

They are not alone. Some other states have taken alternative paths in an effort to break out of the "poor/loser" category. South Africa, Turkey, UAE, and Brazil are a few examples of up-and-coming regional economic powers whose paths we will look at closer next chapter. Speaking of which, let's get to that. Someone . . .

SHOW ME THE MONEY!

In summary, what people do around the planet and how the economy of the state is structured, in large part, determines how well or how poorly the state is doing—and will be doing in the near future.

The periphery as the base floor of the wealth of the core!

We have to look at several more factors to determine the true level of development of a place. Numbers aren't always enough, but we can look around the planet and see some obvious trends. Some of the ones we've already pointed out:

→ The developed countries and regions are richer, have high GDP as well as high GDP per capita, and have more employment in service sector and quaternary sector activities than primary and secondary ones, such as North America, Western Europe, Japan, Australia

→ The developing countries and regions typically have lower GDP as well as lower GDP per capita. However, in some circumstances, even when GDP total is high, the GDP per capita will still come out on the lower end of the spectrum.

→ The developing countries and regions typically have more people employed in the primary and secondary activities than tertiary and quaternary, such as Sub-Saharan Africa, the Middle East, Central Asia, Central America, the Caribbean

→ The states and regions that are developing the fastest are changing this equation more successfully than other states who are still heavily reliant on primary activities, such as South America, East Asia, Turkey

→ Some states and regions are currently lagging in GDP not due to economic activity structure, but because of turbulence attributed to shifting economic systems. They are slowly rebounding. See Russia and Eastern Europe

There's a diverse mix of what's going on economically in the world. Know these factors and features and what people are doing around the world to get a better sense of what's happening in today's world and which way the states are heading. Who has got the money? Who will have the money? Who is developed? Who is developing?

Developed or developing? Hey, that's our next topic . . .

CHAPTER OUTLINE

Developed or Developing?

5

STINKING RICH places. Dirt POOR places. Some states are really well-off, and a whole lot more are struggling day to day to make ends meet. Why are some countries/regions rich, and others poor? As this manual has pointed out, it is not simply a matter of size of the country or the resources it contains. Reality, as always, is much more complicated than that. Before we can even identify traits of these developmental differences around the globe, we should first sort out some basic definitions and terms. Have you ever wondered. . . .

IF THERE IS A THIRD WORLD, WHERE ARE WORLDS ONE AND TWO?

In order to understand these crazy catch-phrases, let's start with a close-up of some other common conundrums. These words and descriptors are often tossed around to describe the state of states—that is, how well off they are, or inversely, how close to being in the global gutter they are.

A **developed country** is one that we would consider first and foremost . . . rich! Most texts, news articles and smart people somehow forget to speak the plain damn truth and call a spade a spade. They will describe lots of different variables that account for why a state is rich, without ever outright just saying it. The developed countries are the rich ones! Admit it! Have you heard of a fully developed country that's flat broke? I suppose it's possible, but I've not partied in one yet.

Developed also carries the connotation that these countries are matured, at the end of the cycle, and therefore stable. I think that's a very good way to put it. But what cycle are we talking about? We'll get to that in a bit. You might also hear developed countries called *industrialized countries, more economically developed countries* (MEDC), *fully developed countries,* or even the *First World.*

A **developing country** on the other hand, is perhaps not so rich. However, it may not necessarily be totally poor either, which could be indicated by such measures as GDP and GDP per capita. Most of the planet would be in this category (both numbers of states as well as numbers of people) and, as such, there is tremendous range in the spectrum of "developing-ness." Some states are close to being fully developed. Some are desperately poor and stagnant or not really "developing" at all.

Perhaps developing countries are best described as all the regions that are obviously not fully developed. Is that a nebulous enough description? Yes, but it kind of works. The operative word here is developing, which means that these countries are in transition, are changing, are developing into something newer, better, and richer. No state is actively trying to un-develop are they?

Synonyms for developing countries include *less-developed countries* (LDCs), *least economically developed countries* (LEDCs), *underdeveloped nations, undeveloped nations,* and the most popular term that everyone recognizes: *the Third World.*

The **Third World**. What a hilarious term. Everyone recognizes and uses it, but no one knows what it really means. And it really doesn't mean anything anymore. Here's the real deal. During the Cold War, there were two opposing camps: Team 1 was the capitalist democracies led by the US, aka "The West." Team 2 was the communist countries lead by the USSR, aka "The Soviet Bloc." They became known, respectively, as the **First World** and the **Second World**. All the other countries were encouraged to join one of these teams, and many did—or at least would allow themselves to be associated with Team 1 or Team 2.

However, there was a group of holdouts who refused to side up. They wanted nothing to do with the Cold War nonsense, and identified themselves as non-aligned. India, Egypt, Ethiopia, and Yugoslavia led this **Non-Aligned Movement (NAM)**. I point them out by name because their status then, as now, has a lot to do with how the term "the Third World" evolved. Many other similar states joined this movement, and as you might imagine, their poor, less-developed economies became an identifying mark . . . a mark that still sticks today. There is no more Cold War, and there are no more First and Second Worlds, but somehow the Third World is still out there batting. Can someone please tell them the game is over?

But seriously, why was it that these countries were so much poorer than the First and Seconds Worlds at the time? And why have they not changed much since the Cold War era, which is why the Third World terminology has stuck? Ah! I'm so glad you asked! To understand today's world of development, we must travel back in time just for a bit and pick up a theory we introduced at the end of the last chapter. . . .

A PITHY HISTORY OF THE PERIPHERY

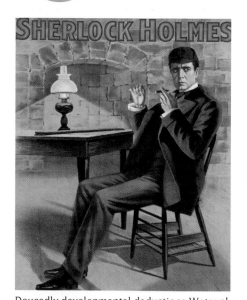
Deucedly developmental deductions Watson!

Think back to that Immanuel Wallerstein stuff I threw at you in chapter 4. Remember the **world-systems** approach I alluded to? It was that set of mechanisms which redistributes wealth from the economic **periphery** to the **core**. Time to dust it off and take a second look through a historical lens, so that we can more clearly see why places like India and Vietnam and Brazil came to be on the peripheral edges of the world economy prior to the Cold War as well as how the US and Europe were at the core.

In doing so, we can also elaborate on why these descriptions have persisted into the modern era, along with some examples of major changes which are currently underfoot. Ha! Watson, the game is afoot! And Sherlock Holmes' Britain is a great place to start the investigation. . . .

COLONIAL PERIOD

In terms of world history, the 1500's to the early years of the 1900's are really a European heyday. Prior to this age, neither European states individually nor the region as a whole made a significant impact on the rest of planet earth. They certainly were not anywhere near the 'core' of a global economy, nor a center of political power, nor a center of technical innovation. You would have had to go to India or China or the Middle East to get those things. Because Europe was a backwater; the US was as of yet "undiscovered"; and Japan was an samurai-infested, isolated state.

But what a difference a few hundred years makes! As the 1500's and 1600's unfolded, European traders, scientists, businessmen, sailors, and military men all increasingly adopted and refined technologies from other societies. Namely, Arab sailing technologies from the Middle East and gunpowder from the Chinese. As a major case in point, the Chinese had invented explosive powder, and employed it for . . . ready for this? . . . fireworks!

Chinese firework make big bang for Europeans!

The Europeans borrow this explosive powder stuff from China and they make . . . guns! I think you may be starting to see how the core/periphery tide was starting to turn already, but I digress. . . .

The Europeans take their newly modified and improved technologies and build grand navies and militaries which inevitably make them masters of the seas, both militarily and for trade. And with that mastery came colonization and imperial takeover. . . you know, the Europeans setting sail and taking over the rest of the planet. North America, South

America, Australia, and eventually Sub-Saharan Africa, South Asia, even parts of China et al, come under the direct control and exploitation of the Europeans. Raw resource wealth, wealth from any existing manufacturing, along with wealth created by trade itself, now flowed from the colonized areas back to Europe. Europe is quickly becoming the core.

Then starting in the 1700's the Europeans are the first to undergo this whole process we now call industrialization. Making machines to do stuff that humans and animals used to do . . . and doing it better, faster, cheaper! Virtually all aspects of agriculture, manufacturing, mining, and transportation are made way more productive and profitable. And this also means that Europe is now

Tools of the "trade"

the center of innovation and the technology leader . . . which of course makes them richer still. Europe sustains this revolution by fully mastering trade relationships around the globe: absorbing the raw resources of the planet, taking them back home to be processed (thus creating jobs and wealth at home) and then pushing their manufactured goods to their colonies.

Example: UK forces India to stop producing cloth by insisting that they instead sell the UK all their cotton. The UK takes the cheap cotton back to the textile mills in London, produces it into cloth, and then sells the finished goods back to India, at a higher price of course. Buy low, sell high. Europe is now the core and India has become part of the periphery. It is important to note that China undergoes a similar devolution at this time, having their core status severely eroded by European, Russian and even Japanese trade dominance during the 1800's . . . culminating in the catastrophic 1839 Opium Wars in which the UK totally dismantled Chinese authority altogether in their bid to forcibly sell opium under the banner of "free trade" to China. Wow. Put that in your pipe and smoke it, China. And they did.

Please keep in mind, in this scenario Europe's strong naval presence is perhaps more significant in its successful take-over of over global trade systems than it is for its takeover of physical territory itself. Because inevitably they will lose those colonies, but the trade dominance remains for some time after that. Here is an equation to consider:

Dominating world trade creates wealth at home = more taxes collected by government = stronger government = government invests more back into technology, infrastructure, military and businesses = stronger military and businesses = more power abroad to colonize and control trade = more wealth = go back and repeat equation. Repeat for centuries.

Not bad for a few hundred years work by folks who previously were groveling in the mud waiting for King Arthur to find the Grail. But changes are coming. . . .

Got Grail?

INTO THE MODERN ERA

Of course, the good old days don't last for the Europeans forever. Independence movements worldwide were kicked off by the American Revolution in 1776, but they didn't happen all at once. It took from 1800 right on up to the 1960's for those European imperialists to lose control of their overseas possessions, with many African states the last to shake off the colonial hangover. These movements coincide with the abolition of slavery and serfdom worldwide, and thus the end of free labor, which also put a crimp in the European wealth-generating machine.

In addition, some former colonies and others learned the lessons of European history very well . . . and then duplicated them! The United States in particular underwent its own industrial revolution and rise to global power, and thus entered the core arena itself by the 1900's. Russia and Japan modernized as well, and quickly became core players as well, albeit on rockier paths that we will investigate further in later chapters. Australia and Canada followed suit. Point is, the core expanded to include others now in competition with the European masters, and the periphery became even weaker as these new global power players had more economic strength than even imaginable in the past.

But hang on! Do not interpret this as the end of European economic dominance! Because as I suggested above, the trade patterns had been well-established for hundreds of years, and they proved to be a much more tenacious beast than simple ownership/control of colonies. Colonial labor may not have been free anymore, but let's face it: former-colony labor remained extremely cheap, as it does into today's world. Basic manufacturing has shifted from the core to the periphery in order to take advantage of this cheap labor, but the profit margins still go to the core. Same as it ever was.

In addition, while the UK or France or Spain may have officially left the colony of India or Algeria or Chile, they usually left behind multinational corporations under their sponsorship which still controlled and/or profited from the raw resource of the former colony. This is a situation that is still common today. Almost all of the biggest and richest multinational companies of the world originate in Europe or the US, and operate with huge competitive advantage in the "poorer" parts of the planet . . . you know, the periphery! Local yokel companies in Africa or Asia can't possibly compete with the likes of Wal-Mart or Exxon. Core wins!

End result: core countries still import cheap raw resources from the periphery and produce high-value commodities which they then export to the periphery. Core wins! Quite frankly, the equation has not changed much, and neither have the goods traded. The periphery exports cotton, tea, bananas, oil . . . and imports finished goods. The core imports raw stuff and basic manufactures, and exports guns, machines, finished goods, etc. Same as it ever was.

Let's be brutally honest here: the rich, core countries have absolutely no vested interest in changing the system. Why would they? No government or business is going to actively try to change the rules of the game that ensure their own victory. So is economic history finished? Is the system now set forever? Ha! Nothing stays the same forever, and even in the most structured system. . . .

ESCAPE IS POSSIBLE!

As you have now seen in this historical overview, these core/periphery labels are not stagnant statuses my friends! Oh no! China and India in particular used to be core, then were subverted to periphery during the rise of the Europeans, but now they are breaking out again. And speaking of the Europeans: for sure, they are still rich parts of the core . . . but they are starting to slip a bit, and no one here in the 21st century would label Western Europe as a center of innovation or technology anymore. Many analysts are now speculating that perhaps even the top-slotted USA is taking it on the chin from the rising Asian titans. Times are a-changing. However, it is difficult to be dethroned from the core once you are there, so there is no

Let's get the hell out of the periphery!

point to focus too much on the top dogs . . . they will maintain their monopoly for some time to come. More to the point, let's look at those entities that are climbing out of the periphery to join the kings of the core. . . .

ESCAPEES OF NOTE

There are a variety of countries in the world right now that don't fit nicely into the definite core or definite periphery categories. Some states do have significant control over their own resources, or have competitive local industries that do compete on the international stage, or do make more high-valued finished goods for export. Of note, Brazil, Argentina,

Chile, Turkey, South Africa, Bahrain, and the UAE could all be considered much further down the development path, and I even refer to them as power-players within their respective regions.

With no reservation though, China and India are the future core members to consider. How did they climb out of the core/periphery cycle? Well, both of these countries are unique in that they were previous core members, countries with huge populations, and countries with significant periods of technological innovation and know-how. It's not like they have had to start from scratch. The current rise of these Asian giants has more to do with throwing off the yoke of colonial powers and reasserting political, and then economic independence.

India chucked out the Brits in 1947; the Chinese started their modern era after the defeat of their Japanese oppressors in WW2, and a bloody civil war, which ended in 1949. Both states have used their massive pool of cheap labor to increase agricultural production, create a manufacturing sector, and invest in their infrastructure. As pointed out in previous chapters, China has really focused heavily on its manufacturing sector to make a myriad of products for cheaper than anyone else on the globe, and they have done this exceptionally well, to the point of now easily beating the core countries in the competition. Ever see *Made in China* on the tag of any products you own? Ha! You probably can't find anything you currently possess that was NOT made in China!

We take this back now.

With all the massive inflow of wealth, China has invested heavily in its infrastructure, technology and industries to make themselves even more competitive . . . hey! just like the core countries do! Yep. China is now in the core. India is not quite as far along, and is taking a slightly different path. Instead of focus on manufacturing, India has been specializing in service sector and high-end stuff like computer programming. Ever call your Dell computer 1-800 help line? Who did you talk to? Yeah, you know it! Someone in India! Their famous technical support centers are even featured in *Slumdog Millionaire*! Oh yeah! Citing Indian specialization reminds me to include this next section. . . .

ESCAPE ROUTES

I have now alluded to different strategies which India and China have taken in order to become more developed, and less peripheral. Let's go ahead and flush these things out totally so you can better assess the strategies that other countries have taken (or will be taking in the future) to attempt to better their situation. There are some major paths that have been followed by poorer peripheral states in order to bust out of the cycle.

1. **Nationalize** a particular resource in the country, focus on efficiency and technology for that one industry, become way more competitive globally for that one industry, and thus reap a bigger percentage of economic benefits. We've talked about this concept already. Middle Eastern countries, and almost all other OPEC members, did the nationalization thing with their oil. It sometimes results in alienation by the core countries, and less competitive and poorly run local industries. But no one would argue that Saudi Arabia, Venezuela, or even Russia is worse off for nationalizing their oil. It has reaped large profits in the modern era, and gained them some measure of control in the global economy. Other states have done it with other commodities as well, even into the modern era.

2. **Import substitution** has been experimented with ever since the Great Depression crunched the whole global system. This is a policy in which the government works with private industry to set up production of a variety of higher-valued manufactured goods like cars, washing machines or textiles. The point is not to export them, but sell them to their own citizens, thus decreasing the reliance on importing expensive finished goods from the core. These local goods are given an advantage by the government putting high taxes or **tariffs** on similar goods being imported from other countries, thus making the local goods cheaper and a better deal. More of a short-term fix than long-term solution, but has had mixed successes.

3. **Specialization** on a few commodities which, with government help, can become efficient enough to compete on the export market globally. China focused on making a literal boatload of manufactured commodities at cheap prices, and has done very well. But most other countries usually focus on just a handful of things: India is focusing on service sector jobs and computer programming, while Brazil focuses on an extremely competitive steel industry, as well as military computer applications.

Japan, Taiwan and South Korea all have made trillions focusing on consumer electronics and automobiles. Those country names are just synonymous with high quality products! When a country does something the best, everyone knows it, and everyone wants it . . . especially when they do it the best for the cheapest . . . then that state is making the money! And thus heading out of the periphery, which many of those Asian tigers have!

Make no bones about it; in all of the examples above, former peripheral states challenged and out-competed core states in these industries, which is why they can't be counted among the totally undeveloped, not-as-developed, or underdeveloped states in the world today. Egads! I have totally lost sight of the development of this chapter! We were supposed to be talking about the developed versus the developing world! Let's get back to topic. . . .

Consumer electronics: Asian Tiger escape route.

DIFFERING DEGREES OF DEVELOPMENT

What are some common measures of the fully developed state versus the fully undeveloped one? The richness versus poorness? Core versus periphery? People in a developed state typically enjoy a high standard of living—i.e., life is good. Food in the fridge, healthy children, bills paid, access to health care, good housing, good environment, and there's even some leisure time to party. Yeah, that sounds about right. And developing? Those folks are probably not eating as much as they should, maybe not getting access to health care, maybe not having clean water or electricity, and their leisure time is otherwise known as "too sick to work."

But we can do even better than that. Let's look systematically at some categories of human life to better compare and contrast the standards of living on our planet. Below is a brief outline of some of the contributing factors of current levels of development in the wider world. This list is not exhaustive, as we have not included all the historic factors that have influenced current state of affairs, or physical resources that these regions possess. However, I want you to think about the bigger developed/developing picture here—if we can understand the mechanics of what is going on in these places, we can better understand the present and better predict the future.

TECHNOLOGICALLY SPEAKING . . .

The fully developed state has the highest levels of technology across the board. I'm not just talking about computers here either. Agriculturally, they can grow more food with way fewer people; one big tractor can do the work of hundreds of humans. Industrially, they can produce more and better stuff with machines in factories that typically displace workers as well. Machines do the work; people run the machines. They

Nukes are high-tech!

are also the creators of information; they have the best military technology like nuclear weaponry; they do extreme stuff which requires extreme cash, like space exploration.

The newest and coolest stuff is created in the fully developed world. Infrastructure like roads, bridges, buildings, and communications are at the highest quality and highest safety levels. Emergency and medical services provide lightning response and insane possibilities of keeping people alive. You can reattach an arm? No way! The frontiers of science, medicine, and technology are pushed forward here. The developed world produces all the newest information, is responsible for 99% of new patents, new trademarks, and new copyrights. Meanwhile, *Grand Theft Auto IV* offers mind boggling graphics to thousands of glassy-eyed users.

The developing state does not have all of these technological advances, and some states may have little to none of these things. Agriculture and industry are still labor-intensive, and typically not as productive. Infrastructure is not as good; roads and communication systems may be lacking. When an earthquake or flood occurs, sub-standard buildings crumble. Buildings and sewer systems and electric grids may be not as safe or efficient as possible; blackouts and back-ups occur regularly. They may possibly be at minimum standards, which means they don't function as well, or for as long. Life-saving technologies and services operate at less than favorable standards. There is no 911. You will lose the arm.

INDUSTRIALLY SPEAKING . . .

The developed state uses more machine labor than human labor. As such, they have higher **labor productivity**, which means one human can do a crap-load of work. One guy on a tractor can plow a thousand acres. One guy in a semi can move twenty tons of cargo a thousand miles in a day. Because of this, they get a hell of a lot more work done per person, but the developed world is also much higher in energy consumption per person; just think of all the energy you use in one day for electricity in your home, at the office, driving your car around, and in making your skinny, half caff, sugar free, mocha lattes. In addition, most of the energy produced in the developed world is based on fossil fuels. As a result, there is a high fossil fuel dependency in the developed world: Iraq will have to be invaded . . . hahahahaha I'm joking! (maybe)

The fully undeveloped world can vary greatly in the amount of machine versus human labor. In places where development is low, there is a greater percentage of human labor involved, thereby reducing the rate of productivity in total work done. How many humans does it take to plow that same thousand acres? And how much longer does it take them? Just using elbow grease, the energy consumption per person is significantly lower. Even the type of fuel used changes in the developing world; fossil fuels are too costly, so less efficient fuel sources like coal, wood, and even dried dung are used more often.

There is a plus side, though: a lower dependency on fossil fuels, and dried feces is cheap, as it should be. However, those fuels are not very efficient in outputting energy and are overly efficient in outputting pollution. But do realize this little known fact: many oil-exporting countries actually don't use a lot of oil themselves . . . it is too expensive for them! They

What a load of . . . inefficient fuel.

make too much money exporting the stuff to actually want to burn it! That's why places like Iran are investing in nuclear energy, even though they are a major exporter of oil. How bizarre!

Looking broadly at the economies of each of these societies, we have to point out the the fully developed world has not only already undergone a full industrial revolution in their society . . . but most of them have now long since left the industrial economy behind. They took full advantage of the technological advances and profits from their industrial/manufacturing era, and are now onto the service and quaternary sector activities. Totally undeveloped states may have yet to undergo this revolution, or perhaps only done it in patches . . . mostly due in part to foreign multinational corporations setting up industrial capacity for specific manufacturing purposes. In that scenario, the true benefits of an industrial revolution are never realized. They just get the crappy jobs and the pollution.

ECONOMICALLY SPEAKING . . .

Speaking of those crappy jobs, how do we differentiate the developed and developing states economically? Well, the easy descriptors include what people do for a living; the stuff we covered in the previous chapter. It never hurts to summarize again, though.

In the developed state, higher technology and industrial capacity equate to increased labor productivity, which in turn equates to higher salaries. The economy is more diversified. There are more desirable types of labor, more choices of occupations, of typically safer types of labor. You can get a job just using your brain. What a novel idea. More of the economy is focused in the service sector, with some in the quaternary sector as well. Primary and secondary jobs are available, but are not the primary earners of GDP for the state.

More importantly, GDP per capita is high. Corporate earnings are higher. The developed state produces value added products which makes them more expensive. Processed goods and high-skilled services are apparent: computers, cars, lawyers, investment bankers. Exported high-value goods equate to a positive trade balance for the state; it sells more stuff than it buys every year. It has a surplus at the bank. All of these factors lead to increased investments that are funneled back into the economy and infrastructure, perpetuating the positive cycle.

In the developing state, lower labor productivity usually leads to limited options for everyone economically. Most of the economy is focused in the primary and secondary sectors. Lots of agriculture and basic manufacturing exists, which produces goods of less value. Harder labor, and laxer environmental and safety laws mean more unhealthy/dangerous working conditions. It should also be noted that many developing countries have a very large chunk of their GDP based on a single commodity, like oil or diamonds or copper. This is an extremely risky situation for the state. What happens when the price of oil on the world market plummets . . . sometimes overnight? Yep, that's right: that state is screwed. Very volatile economics for the developing state.

Lower salaries, lower corporate earnings, and a special twist—many of the companies operating in the developing states are foreign multinationals, so most profit exits the state and goes back to the multinationals' country of origin. Low value goods are exported, high value goods are imported, resulting in an overall negative trade balance. Put it all together and it spells out a lower investment in the infrastructure and economy, less personal wealth, usually less GDP, and almost always less GDP per capita almost always—although we have seen some exceptions to this rule as well.

DEMOGRAPHICALLY SPEAKING . . .

Just to reinforce some concepts from chapter 2, we should also highlight some obvious differences in the demographic makeup of a state based on its level of development. Fully developed states have fully undergone the demographic transition, and both their fertility rates and their population growth rates are relatively low. Fertility rates usually hover around the 2.1 replacement level, and the overall population total is either stable or perhaps even shrinking, in the case of Japan, Russia, and many Western European states. The column or inverted pyramid shape of the population pyramid indicates that there are typically a smaller number of folks under the age of 15 (dependents) as there are working age cohorts 15 to 55 (the suppliers of labor and wealth).

By contrast, less developed states are somewhere in late Stage 2 or Stage 3 of the demographic transition, as indicated their classic pyramid shape suggests that they are currently in a cultural lag/population explosion scenario. The later in Stage 3 they are, the more rounded the pyramid will appear, especially in the younger age cohorts. Fertility rates

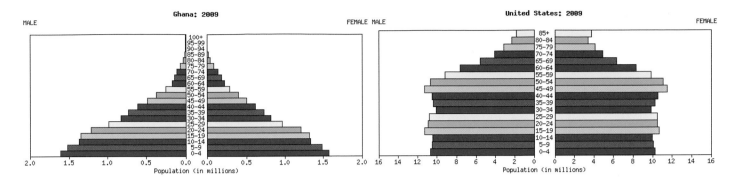

Ghana: 2009

MALE   FEMALE

| 100+ |
| 95-99 |
| 90-94 |
| 85-89 |
| 80-84 |
| 75-79 |
| 70-74 |
| 65-69 |
| 60-64 |
| 55-59 |
| 50-54 |
| 45-49 |
| 40-44 |
| 35-39 |
| 30-34 |
| 25-29 |
| 20-24 |
| 15-19 |
| 10-14 |
| 5-9 |
| 0-4 |

2.0   1.5   1.0   0.5   0.0 0.0   0.5   1.0   1.5   2.0
Population (in millions)

United States: 2009

MALE   FEMALE

| 85+ |
| 80-84 |
| 75-79 |
| 70-74 |
| 65-69 |
| 60-64 |
| 55-59 |
| 50-54 |
| 45-49 |
| 40-44 |
| 35-39 |
| 30-34 |
| 25-29 |
| 20-24 |
| 15-19 |
| 10-14 |
| 5-9 |
| 0-4 |

16 14 12 10   8   6   4   2   0 0   2   4   6   8   10 12 14 16
Population (in millions)

remain well above the 2.1 replacement level, usually in the 2.5 to 4 range . . . and the higher the number, the more explosive the overall population growth. Of particular note, the classic pyramid shape indicates that there are way many more folks under the age of 15 (dependents) than in the working class/provider brackets.

What does this mean in real life, for real families? In the developed world, people have just one or two kids, invest a lot of time and money into keeping those kids alive, healthy, educated, and happy . . . and then eventually pass all their remaining wealth to the kid once mommy and daddy kick the bucket. This type of high investment per kid equates to a huge competitive advantage for children of the developed world. How can they fail?

In the undeveloped world? Large family size means less investment per kid, less resources per kid, and much less wealth to pass on after death. And they don't have that much to pass around to begin with. As total population continues to swell year after year, there are less and less resources to divide up among an ever increasing number of folks. For even an exceptionally smart or gifted child, the climb out of poverty is fraught with major challenges.

SOCIALLY SPEAKING . . .

In the developed state people make decent money. Those folks have higher salaries, which equates to more disposable income, which equates to higher consumption rates of everything and higher rates of saving. It also means people can invest in their own future, as well as provide better health care and education to the next generation. That is crucial. Literacy rates are high. Developed countries heavily invest in education—each generation gets smarter, richer, better, and more cognizant of the Plaid Avenger's World.

The developed world also has higher mobility and social safety nets, like welfare, which increase risk-taking and increase opportunities. You can risk quitting your job to start a new business or go back to school without your family starving

We ain't so fully developed. This sucks.

to death. This increases your opportunities for employment and income-making potential. It also makes the country a center of innovation and wealth, as these risk-taking entrepreneurs become successful. Think about it: Could Bill Gates the kid have become Bill Gates the trillionaire had he been born in Uzbekistan or Ethiopia? Doubtful. Infrastructure and education provide a tremendous amount of opportunities that allow the citizenry of the developing world to make their dreams come true.

By contrast in developing countries, less expendable income means less food on the table, less overall consumption, less investment in the future generation, less education, and generally lower literacy rates. Lack of social safety nets leads to less risk-taking, fewer opportunities in employment, and in life. Availability and quality of infrastructure and educational opportunities are generally much lower, thus locking in the cycle of poverty from generation to generation. Focus is on survival, not upward social mobility.

HOW IS YOUR HEALTH?

In the developed state, people are pretty damn healthy overall. Increased education, increased access to health care, and increased public hygiene equate to decreased infant mortality, increased longevity, and decreased susceptibility to epidemic outbreaks. You will live longer in the developed world, but what will it eventually get you?

Due to changes in work types, increased consumption, and wider variety of dietary choices, a distinct health shift occurs as a state becomes fully developed. People become more sedentary as they use their brains instead of their brawn to work. They have stress from using their brains too much. People over-consume in caloric intake. In diet, they move from whole grains and fruits and vegetables to processed foods with a radical increase in sugars, fats, and meat. Result? Around 75 percent of people in a developed world die from diseases of the circulatory system (heart disease, stroke) and cancers.

Poorer people eat more grains and veggies. The richer you get, the more your diet sucks!

poor →——— rich

In the developing world people are not as healthy. Less education, less access to health care, poor public sanitation and hygiene, and even little or no access to immunizations equate to high infant mortality and lower life expectancy. Epidemics can be catastrophic. Diets consist of basic grains and fruits and vegetables, which is really good, but their caloric intake may not be sufficient for optimal health. Result? 50 to 60 percent of the people will die of an infectious or parasitic disease, or in childbirth. The infectious diseases are easily preventable and curable.

PLAID AVENGER SURE-FIRE WEIGHT LOSS PROGRAM: Move to a developing country

HOW BIG IS YOUR MIDDLE?

No, I'm not talking about your waistline . . . we will get to that in a few paragraphs . . . I'm referring to the size of the middle class. I want you to think critically about this concept, because it ends up being a core component of how most of us now classify the levels of development around the planet . . . especially for those states that do not easily fall into either the full-on developed nor the totally un-developed categories.

In fully developed states, there is much less wealth disparity. That is, there is a roughly equal distribution of wealth across the society. Now, every society and every state has some wealth concentration in the hands of a few rich folks: the upper class, or aristocracy. And every society and state has a lower, poorer class of folks with not much wealth at all. That is true the world over. However, the percentage of the haves to the have-nots differs wildly from state to state, and I'm suggesting here that fully developed states have a lower percentage of wealth concentration in the hands of the few, with greater distribution of that wealth across the whole society. That's where the middle comes into play.

Poor classes exist even in rich states, as do the ultra-rich. But in the fully developed states, the middle class constitutes the biggest group overall. You know, it's the folks that have a good job, a nice house, a decent car, can go on vacations, and can send their kids to college, and can eventually do this awesome thing called "retire." The ability for a majority of folks in the state to achieve adequate levels of wealth is an extremely powerful stabilizing factor, and one that may be the the the newest, best indicator of how developed a state is here in the 21st century. Because as you have seen in previous chapters, a state like Equatorial Guinea has a huge GDP, and even a big GDP per capita figure. BUT, the wealth is totally concentrated in the hands the state dictator and his family . . . while the masses are starving. Therefore, there is no middle class at all. Speaking of which. . . .

In the developing world, there are much greater differences between the haves and have-nots . . . in some societies it may be best described as the few have-all's versus the masses of have-nothing's. Wealth disparity is huge. Wealth is overwhelmingly concentrated in the hands of a few, who then, of course, have the power and influence to make sure it stays that way! The impoverished masses have no real competitive avenues to accumulate wealth, and for them "vacation" is another word for unemployed, and "retirement" occurs only at death. Kind of like killing a *Replicant* in movie *Blade Runner.* This makes for an unstable economic and political situation in the state as a whole, which brings us to. . . .

GOVERNMENTALLY SPEAKING

In the developed states, democracy is the undisputed champion. All the fully developed states on the planet are democracies. The political/economic structure may have varying degrees of socialist policy, but all are staunchly democratic. These systems are more dynamic, more open to change, and they prove it by rotating out leadership in a timely and regulated manner. In addition to their dynamic demeanor, developed states are politically stable, leading to stable economies which actively participate in global trade and investment. This stability is one of the primary reasons that international investment is typically higher in developed countries: because your money and your investment are safe in a stable environment.

In the developing world, most other types of governments can be found. Military dictatorship, theocracy, monarchy, one-party states, and chaotic states abound. It should be noted that many developing states are also democracies, but usually not well-established with long track records. Why is this important to note? Aside from the newer democracies, these systems are more static, or closed to change; some exhibit no possibilities for change at all. The more closed a system is,

Power to the few = revolution overdue.

the more opportunity arises for corruption. This creates an unstable situation in the long term because underlying tensions and forces usually manifest themselves in violent upheaval, civil war, or outright implosion of the state.

Unstable governments can often lead to unstable economies, and unstable economies are not where international investors put their money. These states are often insular, protecting their industries or economic interest above all, which discourages global trade and investment. As alluded to in the middle class section above, impoverished masses themselves are always a potential flashpoint for total chaos within a state: when conditions get horrific enough, and people have nothing left to lose, they sometimes band together and topple governments. Check out the Haitian or Russian Revolutions for details.

MILITARILY SPEAKING . . .

There's one last category that most people don't really look at to assess development status, but the Plaid Avenger does lots of things that other people don't. I think it's a keen insight into what's happening in the society . . .

In the developed world, military technology is at the maximum. Nuclear capabilities are either possessed or easily acquired. Like in industry and agriculture, most manual labor is done with machines. Soldiers operate big machines and the "death-wielding labor productivity" is very high. Developed states prefer to use their military technology as opposed to large numbers of humans on the ground. Human casualties and injuries are minimized at all costs. A major final point: while total expenditures on the military may be high, in a developed state this expenditure is a fairly low percentage of their GDP total. Check out the box to the right to see what I'm sayin'. (And holy hand-grenades! Be sure to note how many Middle Eastern states are on this astounding arming agenda! We will follow up on that issue in chapter 18.)

In the developing state, military technology can be advanced, but typically is not. They usually buy hand-me-down weapons and last year's camouflage fashion from the developed states, and to be sure, the fully developed states never sell them the top-of-the-line gear. Some states, like India, Pakistan, and China, have nuclear capability, but they are pretty much alone in the developing world in this respect. Lots of other states may want it, but will have to try and buy it, since they lack the infrastructure to develop it themselves.

In developing countries, manpower is still the primary component of the military, and most real action will be dudes on foot, firing guns. China has the largest free-standing army on the planet right now. The last major point: while total expenditures on military expenses may be lower in the developing world, it's a fairly high percentage of GDP and/or the government's budget. Yep. You got it. The less money a state has, the more it usually spends on guns.

THE BOTTOM LINE: WHO IS DEVELOPED? WHO IS DEVELOPING? WHO IS SOMEWHERE IN BETWEEN?

Let's get this chapter wrapped up already! Given the terminology, the historical precedent, and the specific categories of comparison, can we now officially point out exactly who the developed and developing countries are? Well, why not? Let's give it a go! Below are a few different systems for classifying these levels of development, and we might as well start is out with the best one . . . namely, mine!

PLAID AVENGER DEVELOPMENTAL RULE OF THUMB

The rich countries are easy to see, so let's not dally on those developed dudes; the rest of the planet is much more interesting to consider. You won't find this theory in a textbook anywhere, besides this one, because it's a Plaid Avenger original. Lots of different states have lots of the developed world features, but still don't seem to be in the fully developed category. Like who?

MILITARY EXPENDITURES AS A PERCENT OF TOTAL GDP (THIS IS NOT AN EXHAUSTIVE LIST)

Country	Percent
North Korea	23%
Oman	13%
Qatar	10%
Saudi Arabia	10%
Iraq	9%
Jordan	9%
Israel	7.5%
Yemen	6.6%
Armenia	6.5%
Eritrea	6.3%
Burundi	5.9%
Syria	5.9%
Angola	5.7%
Mauritania	5.5%
Kuwait	5.3%
El Salvador	5%
Morocco	5%
Bosnia	4.5%
China	4.3%
United States	4%
Russia	3.9%
France	2.6%
United Kingdom	2.4%

Pakistan has advanced weaponry and nuclear bombs, but is not fully developed economically or demographically. India has nuclear bombs and is a well-established democracy, but is not fully developed. Saudi Arabia has a huge GDP and free health care, but is not fully developed. China is getting rich as Midas, has high technology, has nuclear bombs, a stable population growth rate, a diversified economy, and even put a man in space . . . maybe they are getting really close, but even they don't seem to be in the fully developed column yet. Okay, maybe they are. Its a close call at this point. So what makes the Plaid Avenger difference?

For me, it's all about how the average Joe is doing. How are most people doing in the society? How much health care or good jobs or education do the majority of folks have access to? What is the real GDP per capita of the bulk of the workers? It kind of gets back to that theme I've hit you with about the middle class. There will always be a small percentage of excessively rich folks, and there will always be a lot of poor folks. But how are folks doing in the *middle*? Any country can have any amount of any of the factors listed above, but if it's not accessible to the majority of folks, then I classify the state as still developing. The fully developed states are always marked by the majority of people doing well and having access to all of those great things.

Make sense? That's why places like India may be booming economically right now, may be focused on quaternary computer jobs, have a space program, be a democracy, have a strong military and a huge GDP . . . but most people in India still live on a buck or two a day. And most of a billion people is a lot of damn heads. India may have lots and lots of trappings of the developed world, but how can you call them fully developed when half a billion people don't have access to health care, or lack a proper diet?

My answer: I don't.

HDI: A UN TAKE ON HOW FOLKS ARE DOING

I think the good folks at the UN agree with the Plaid Avenger on this one, too. Here is their take on things:

The UN Human Development Index (HDI) is some sort of complex mathematical formula that takes into account poverty, literacy rates, education, life expectancy, fertility rates, and a host of other factors. It has become a standard means of measuring overall human well-being. The index was developed in 1990 by a Pakistani economist, which gives it more credibility in the Plaid Avenger's book, and is used by the United Nations Development Program in its annual Human Development Report.

FIGURE 5.1 MAP HDI

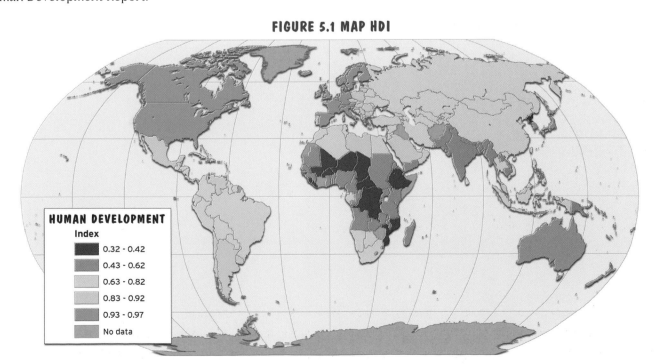

HUMAN DEVELOPMENT
Index
- 0.32 - 0.42
- 0.43 - 0.62
- 0.63 - 0.82
- 0.83 - 0.92
- 0.93 - 0.97
- No data

As you can see from the map, the closer you are to a perfect score of 1, the better off the humans are in that state. Take what you like from the map, but I just wanted to point out a few trends. Obviously, the developed, richer countries stand out near the top of the spectrum in North America, Europe, Australia and Japan. South America is not in bad shape by this measure, especially the southern states on the continent. Eastern Europe and Russia have slipped; they probably used to be in higher brackets, but factors such as life expectancy in some of these places has plummeted, as has their HDI. China and some parts of the Middle East and Southeast Asia come next, perhaps rising in the ranks. All of South Asia—India included.

WORLD AT NIGHT: ANOTHER FUN PLAID AVENGER MEASURE OF HOW THE WORLD IS DOING

There's a final image to consider. It can show you a lot about the levels of development on the planet. Plus, it's just so awesomely cool.

FIGURE 5.2 EARTH AT NIGHT

From the Visible Earth: A catalogue of NASA images and animations of our home planet:
This image of Earth's city lights was created with data from the Defense Meteorological Satellite Program (DMSP) Operational Linescan System (OLS). Originally designed to view clouds by moonlight, the OLS is also used to map the locations of permanent lights on the Earth's surface. The brightest areas of the Earth are the most urbanized, but not necessarily the most populated. (Compare western Europe with China and India.) Cities tend to grow along coastlines and transportation networks. Even without the underlying map, the outlines of many continents would still be visible. The United States interstate highway system appears as a lattice connecting the brighter dots of city centers. In Russia, the Trans-Siberian railroad is a thin line stretching from Moscow through the center of Asia to Vladivostok. The Nile River, from the Aswan Dam to the Mediterranean Sea, is another bright thread through an otherwise dark region. Even more than 100 years after the invention of the electric light, some regions remain thinly populated and unlit. Antarctica is entirely dark. The interior jungles of Africa and South America are mostly dark, but lights are beginning to appear there. Deserts in Africa, Arabia, Australia, Mongolia, and the United States are poorly lit as well (except along the coast), along with the boreal forests of Canada and Russia, and the great mountains of the Himalayas.

Credit: Data courtesy Marc Imhoff of NASA GSFC and Christopher Elvidge of NOAA NGDC.

AVENGER ASSESSMENT OF STATES STATUSES

So tell us, Plaid Avenger: who is developed? Who is developing? Who is disorganized? Who is damn near deceased? Name the names! Alright then, since you have been so patient and asked so nicely, let's wrap this bad boy up. Here's a final word from the UN about development statuses:

> There is no established convention for the designation of "developed" and "developing" countries or areas in the United Nations system. In common practice, Japan in Asia, Canada and the United States in northern America, Australia and New Zealand in Oceania and Europe are considered "developed" regions or areas. In international trade statistics, the Southern African Customs Union is also treated as developed region and Israel as a developed country; countries emerging from the former Yugoslavia are treated as developing countries; and countries of eastern Europe and the former USSR countries in Europe are not included under either developed or developing regions.

Well, that's nice, I guess. And totally safe. But I'm all about the real deal. Many textbooks and news sources and academics simply lack the spine to actually point things out for what they are. But you know that I've got balls-a-plenty, and I'll tell you the shades of developmental plaid that I view the world in. Consider the following map, as created by yours truly:

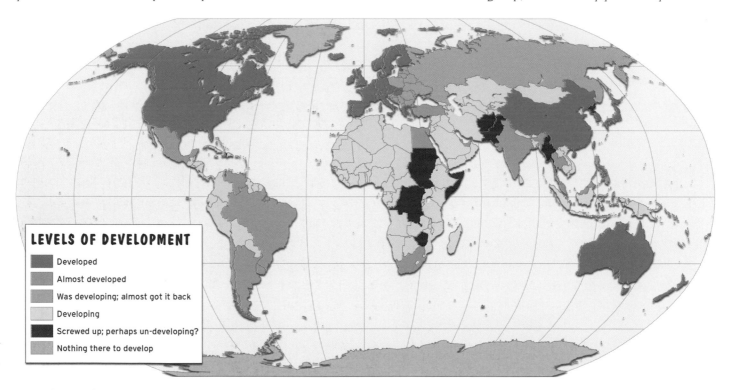

LEVELS OF DEVELOPMENT

- Developed
- Almost developed
- Was developing; almost got it back
- Developing
- Screwed up; perhaps un-developing?
- Nothing there to develop

Here's the Plaid interpretation:

Full-on Developed: The easy category. We've beaten these guys down enough this chapter. North American region (US and Canada), Western Europe region, Australia-New Zealand region, Israel, and Japan are the pedal to the metal, full-on fully developed regions/countries. One wildcard from Southeast Asia: Singapore. Fully developed. No doubts.

You know what? I'm going to go ahead and go out on a limb. Let's pull the tooth and add China to the fully developed category. I know, I know, I know! Most other analysts and books are not ready to do this yet. That's why I'm ahead of my time. China is booming; and Macau, Hong Kong, and Taiwan are already considered fully developed, and are being reintegrated back into China proper. The Chinese have also pulled something on the order of 400 million people above the poverty line since 1980. Nothing suggests that these trends won't continue. High levels of technology, man in space, huge GDP, internal infrastructure investments, growing middle class . . . the hell with it! Smells like fully developed to me!

Almost developed: This can be a bit tricky, but you can handle it given all you have learned in this chapter. Many South American countries are getting close, like Brazil, Argentina, and Chile. Mexico wavers back and forth—sometimes closer to full development, sometimes falling back to developing status. Check it year to year to see how it's doing. South Africa, Egypt, UAE and Turkey are beating down the door of full development as well. They have most of the features, but their GDP per capita is still fairly low and their middle class still thin in comparison to other developed places. India is booming, but with a much longer way to go, and a much bigger gap to close. The Philippines, Thailand, and Malaysia are our best Asian examples that are rounding out those countries getting close to developed status.

Was developed, almost got it back: Eastern Europe and Russia are the only players in this category. And a distinct category it is. We don't really consider any place becoming "undeveloped," particularly when those places are nuclear powers and former world superpowers. However, the economic and political meltdown caused by the dissolution of the USSR in 1991 has left many of these countries with GDP numbers and life expectancy numbers more similar to impoverished African nations than European states. But they have the know-how, they have the technology . . . and like the six-million-dollar-man . . . they can rebuild it. The Plaid Avenger is assuming that they will: go for it, former commies! Russia could easily jump back to fully developed status soon, especially if they can encourage their declining population to get busy and grow the middle class some more.

Developing: This category still includes a whole lot of countries with a whole lot of people. Comprising big areas of sub-Saharan Africa, the Middle East, Central Asia, South Asia, Southeast Asia and South America, there can be tremendous variability on how far down the path of development they are. Or aren't.

Despite their high per capita GDP, places like Brunei and the Middle Eastern states of Bahrain, Kuwait, Oman, Qatar, and Saudi Arabia are generally not considered developed countries because their economies depend overwhelmingly on oil production and export. This lack of economic diversity is compounded by lack of political diversity; most are old school monarchies and theocracies. However, some of these countries, especially Bahrain, have begun to diversify their economies and democratize. Similarly, the Bahamas, Barbados, Antigua and Barbuda, Trinidad and Tobago, and Saint Kitts and Nevis enjoy a high per capita GDP, but these economies depend overwhelmingly on the tourist industry.

Many other countries—particularly in sub-Saharan Africa, Central Asia, Central America, the Caribbean, and Southeast Asia—have a patchy record of development at best. Most indicators of progress discussed in this chapter would be on the lower end of the development spectrum. Many have a hell of a long way to go, and are not currently traveling that fast on the footpath.

Screwed up; perhaps un-developing? This category is comprised of countries with long-term civil wars, large-scale breakdown of rule of law, or leaders who are totally insane. All could be described as nondevelopment-oriented economies or just outright chaotic systems. You may also see some of them referred to as "failed states." Best examples: Haiti, Somalia, Sudan, Burma, Democratic Republic of Congo, and North Korea. Zimbabwe may be joining them soon if Mugabe continues his dictator antics. I hate to have to do this, but my friends in Pakistan are currently on a serious rocky road which may end catastrophically for them, so they get bumped to this category. Pakistan is not so much focused on developing so much as simple survival right now! Good luck, guys!

I'M DEVELOPMENTALLY SPENT . . .

There it is. That's the Plaid round-up. Hope you now understand the true differences in what is going on in the world in terms of levels of development, and that you have a better handle on how the world will be changing in the coming decades. I know I do.

QUICK REFERENCE ROUND-UP

	Developed	Developing
Technology	• Highest levels of technology • Machines work faster and better • Extensively developed infrastructure • Effective emergency response	• Little to no technology • Without machines, people work harder and accomplish less • Unsafe or inefficient infrastructure • Poor emergency response
Industry	• More machine than human labor • High productivity • High energy consumption • Dependent on expensive, efficient fossil fuels	• More human than machine labor • Low productivity • Low energy consumption • Dependent on cheap, inefficient alternative fuels
Economics	• High salaries, high GDP per capita • Diverse economy • Large service sector, some quaternary • Value-added goods and services • Positive trade balance for state	• Low salaries, low GDP per capita • Limited economic options • Large primary and secondary sectors, no quaternary • Low value primary goods • Negative trade balance for state
Society	• Majority of population in middle class • Widespread investment in health care and education; high consumption • Can afford to take risks • Column or inverted population pyramid; fertility rate around 2.1 • Each generation gets better	• Majority of people in lower classes; middle class might exist • Little money to invest in health care, education, or consumption • Can't afford to take risks • True pyramid-shape population; high fertility rates (variable) • Each generation gets more screwed

	Developed	Developing
Health	• Decreased infant mortality, increased longevity • Access to effective health care • Sedentary work with mental stress • More processed foods • Most people die from circulatory disease or cancer	• Increased infant mortality and lower life expectancy • Susceptible to epidemics • Physical work with physical stress • Healthy food but insufficient calories • Most people die from preventable and curable disease
Government	• Solid democracy • Politically stable • Open to change protected against corruption • Participation in global trade and investment	• All forms of government found • Politically unstable • Closed to change susceptible to corruption • Insular economies; absent from global trade and investment
Cultural Cues	• Lots of fat people • They eat animals • People go to specific areas named "gyms" in order to stay lean • People have extra time to "recreate" "vacation", and "chill" at malls, parks, beaches, and foreign countries • Some people are so bored that they take drugs for fun • People do this cool thing called "retire" after they have worked for most of their lives	• Mostly skinny people • Animals eat them • People bust ass trying to stay alive 24/7 to stay lean. It's called life • People generally "hang out" only with their families at home or in the village. Most never leave their local area, much less their state • Some people grow drugs for the bored rich people in order to earn money so they can eat • People do this thing called "die" after they work their entire life
Military	• Maximum military technology • Actual or possible nuclear power • Weapons preferred to standing army • Casualties minimized • High military spending is low percentage of GDP	• Typically limited military technology • Nuclear power impossible (with some exceptions) • Standing army is main military power • Higher casualties • Low military spending is high percentage of GDP
Plaid Rule	• Most people are doing pretty well	• No matter what the stats say, most people aren't doing that well
HDI	• Close to score of one	• Close to score of zero
Night View	• Lit up like a Christmas tree!	• Lights out

International Organizations

6

AND now we get to a chapter that is more of an introduction than anything else; an introduction to the trendiest world trend of globalization. This chapter consists of brief explanations of some entities that fall outside, or rather across, state boundaries—global players in a global age. We call them **supranationalist** organizations. Above and beyond the national level, these organizations play an increasingly important role in what is happening across our planet. But who are they? Where did they come from? How are we supposed to know this stuff? I don't know, friends. If the Plaid Avenger doesn't tell you these things, who will?

Supranationalist organizations are groups of states working together to achieve a common, or outlined, objective. This is another fairly new concept in human history, as states or nations have spent most of their time doing the opposite: beating the hell out of each other or undercutting each other at every available opportunity. So why do countries now work together? The Plaid Avenger sees order in the universe; we can classify cooperation into three main classes: economic, defensive, and cultural.

I'll introduce you to the more important and happening entities here, but by no means is the list exhaustive. This chapter will also serve as a functioning reference for you as you progress through the rest of the book; come back often to refresh your memory when you see these acronyms appear in the regional chapters.

ECONOMIC ENTITIES—SHOW ME THE MONEY

Money. Who doesn't want it? Not any of the states of the world, that's for sure. A great way to make more money, if you are a country, is to make some trade deals with other countries. I'll buy all my bananas from you if you buy all of your wheat from me—sound good? On top of that, I won't put an import tax on your bananas, but if any other countries try to sell bananas here, I'll tax the hell out of them. Deal? This is the essence of **trade blocks** which are, as you might have guessed, quite a bit more powerful than the individual countries that are in them.

Many economists believe that "free trade" between countries increases competition, which decreases prices, which in turn increase consumption of products . . . which ultimately benefits producers and consumers alike! Get governments out of the way, and let the market rule! For this reason, both the United States and the European Union are trying their hardest to promote "trade blocs" or "free trade zones" with neighboring countries, so that they can improve economic performance and increase sales. Even countries in Latin America, Africa and Asia have caught the bug.

However, there is a tug-of-war going on. Independent nation-states naturally want to protect their economies, so they are reluctant to sign up for free trade when they think that their industries will not be competitive. For example, if Chinese shoe companies make cheaper and better shoes than French shoe companies, France is not going to want free trade in shoes with China. Everybody in France would obviously want to buy the less expensive Chinese shoes, so the French shoe companies would go out of business. Historically, the cheaper imported products are hit with a **tariff,** an import tax, which subsequently makes the price of the product more expensive, and thus the local products can compete better.

Many times, poor countries accuse rich countries of trying to take advantage of them by using free trade agreements. These poor countries argue that free trade isn't beneficial for both sides; it's only beneficial for the industrialized country because their companies are more competitive. Furthermore, they accuse developed countries of cheating, and they point to agricultural **subsidies** in these rich countries as an example. Farmers in Europe and America produce crap tons of food using lots of big equipment and fertilizers, thus their costs are high, and subsequently the food they make costs more. Farmers in poor countries don't use that expensive stuff and have cheaper labor, therefore their food should cost much less, giving them a competitive advantage in the world market. However, the rich farmers still "win" on the international market because Europe and America give their farmers huge subsidies to offset the higher costs of production they face. Uncle Sam gives American farmers money just to be farmers, and the farmers can turn around and sell their food for cheaper prices and still make money. You dig? And if you dig a lot, maybe you should become a farmer.

Poor countries argue that the only reason that rich countries became rich in the first place is by protecting their domestic industries using things like tariffs and not signing up for free trade agreements. Also, it can be argued that fully developed rich-ass companies from rich-ass countries are so technologically superior that they have a competitive advantage that can never be overcome . . . meaning that the less developed states will always be stuck buying finished goods and selling primary level commodities, thus always losing money. On the other hand, free trade usually does mean more trade, so the less developed countries do stand to sell much more oil or lima beans or flip-flops or beef lips. Poorer countries are torn as to whether or not it is in their best interest to join these trade blocks with the fully developed states.

Perhaps it's on these grounds that we are seeing many new trade blocks springing up that are comprised solely of states in developing status, with no "rich kids" invited to the party. It certainly is the reason for the foot-dragging with the FTAA, but once again, I have gotten ahead of the story.

Check out these economic entities that you will be hearing a hell of a lot more about, as they will play an increasingly larger role in the way the global economy operates:

NAFTA

Members: United States, Canada, and Mexico

Summary: NAFTA, which stands for North American Free Trade Agreement, is a free trade agreement between the United States, Mexico, and Canada. This agreement is meant to gradually eliminate all duties and tariffs between these three countries. However, the three nations are resisting lowering barriers that would hurt their economies. For example, the United States and Canada have been bickering because the United States imposes a duty on Canadian lumber that goes to the United States. The Canadians are accusing the Americans of not sticking to the treaty and are considering imposing duties on American goods to retaliate.

NAFTA has been very controversial in other ways. Generally, transnational corporations support it because lower tariffs mean higher profits for them. Labor unions in the United States and Canada have opposed it because they believe that jobs will go from the United States and Canada to Mexico because of lower wages there. They were all correct: manufacturing jobs, particularly from the auto industry, migrated rapidly south of the border where wages were significantly lower, but this did make the costs of products cheaper to the consumer as well. American jobs were lost, but Americans pay lower prices for goods. Also, farmers in Mexico oppose it because agricultural subsidies in the United States have forced them to lower the prices on their goods. There has even been an increase in illegal immigration from Mexico to the United States because Mexican farmers have gone bankrupt.

Fun Plaid Fact: Chapter 11 of the NAFTA treaty allows private corporations to sue federal governments in the NAFTA region if they feel like that government is adversely affecting their investments.

DR-CAFTA

Members: United States, Costa Rica, Dominican Republic, El Salvador, Guatemala, Honduras, Nicaragua. Currently, the US Administration is pushing hard to get Colombia and Panama into this club as well.

Summary: DR-CAFTA stands for Dominican Republic—Central America Free Trade Agreement and is an international treaty to increase free trade. It was ratified by the Senate of the United States in 2005. Like NAFTA, its goal is to privatize public services, eliminate barriers to investment, protect intellectual property rights, and eliminate tariffs between the participating nations. Many people see DR-CAFTA as a stepping stone to the larger, more ambitious, FTAA (Free Trade Agreement of the Americas).

The controversy regarding DR-CAFTA is very much like the controversy regarding NAFTA. Many people are concerned about America losing jobs to poorer countries where the minimum wage is lower and environmental laws are more lax. Also, some people are concerned that regional trade blocs like DR-CAFTA undermine the project of creating a worldwide free trade zone using organizations like the WTO.

Fun Plaid Fact: Many Washington insiders see DR-CAFTA as a way of reducing the influence of China in Central America.

CAFTA members

FTAA (PROPOSED ONLY!)

Members: *PROPOSED* All of the nations in North and South America, except Cuba. 'Cause the US hates commies. Damn commies.

Summary: The FTAA, which stands for Free Trade Area of the Americas, is a proposed agreement to end trade barriers between all of the countries in North and South America. It hasn't been ratified yet, because there are some issues that need to be worked out by the participating countries. The developed (rich) countries, such as the United States, want more free trade and increased intellectual property rights. The developing (poorer) countries, such as Brazil, want an end to US/Canadian agricultural subsidies and more free trade in agricultural goods.

The key issue here for poor countries is agricultural subsidies. Farmers in the United States, and in rich countries generally, produce agricultural goods at a higher price than poor countries do. However, to keep their goods cheap, and thus competitive on the world market, the government of the United States pays their farmers subsidies. These subsidies make developing countries very angry because they believe subsidies give American farmers an unfair advantage. For this reason, some Latin American leaders have stalled the agreement. Venezuelan President Hugo Chavez called the agreement "a tool of imperialism" and proposed an alternative agreement called the Bolivarian Alternative for the Americas.

Proposed FTAA members

For rich countries, the issue is intellectual property rights, which is best exemplified by copyright laws. Less developed countries sometimes oppose these rights because they believe that if they are enacted, they will stifle scientific research in Latin America and widen the gap between the rich and poor countries in the Americas.

It should be noted, as of this writing in 2010, that this tentative agreement has been totally stalled by the leftist alliance of Castro, Chavez, and the Bolivian president Evo Morales. The "leftward swing" of Latin America, that we'll talk about in a later chapter, has seriously squashed the US administration's agenda on this issue.

Fun Plaid Fact: The only country that would not be included in the FTAA is Cuba, because the United States has an economic embargo that prohibits all trade with the communist regime. For this reason, Cuba more fully supports the Bolivarian alternative for the Americas, which is MERCOSUR . . . we will get to that on the next page.

EU

Members: Belgium, Bulgaria, France, Germany, Italy, Luxembourg, The Netherlands, Denmark, Ireland, United Kingdom, Greece, Portugal, Spain, Austria, Finland, Sweden, Cyprus, Czech Republic, Estonia, Hungary, Latvia, Lithuania, Malta, Poland, Romania, Slovakia, Slovenia

Summary: For years, European philosophers and political observers have recognized that the best way to ensure peace on the European continent while also increasing trade is to politically and economically integrate the nations. After the destruction and loss of life caused by World War II, European nations finally began taking small steps toward interdependence. They started by integrating their coal and steel industries in the ECSC (European Coal and Steel Community). What a long way they have come since then! Currently, the European Union, which has 27 member states, has a common market, a common European currency (the euro), a European Commis-

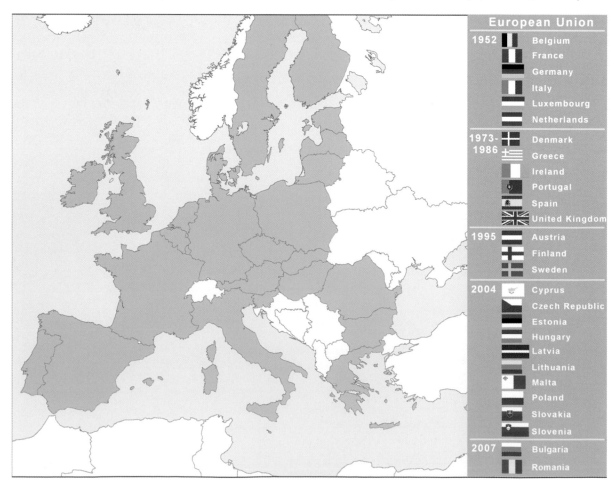

sion, a European Parliament, and a European Court of Justice. The nations of the EU have also negotiated treaties to have common agricultural, fishing, and security policies. More so than any other free trade agreement, the European Union covers way more areas other than just trade.

Consequently, the EU is the most evolved supranationalist organization the world has ever seen—perhaps a "United States of Europe." Free movement of people across international borders of the member states makes it unique in the trade block category. Of greater importance is an evolving EU armed force, a single environmental policy, and increasingly, a single foreign policy voice. That is a very big deal!

However, there has been some resistance to integration within European countries. Some countries, like Norway and Switzerland, have refused to join, and others, like the United Kingdom, have refused to fully adopt the euro: the Brits do use the euro, but maintain their traditional pound as well. Also, in 2005, a constitution for the European Union was rejected by French and Dutch voters, putting the future of European integration into question. Many Europeans simply don't care about the European Union and others see it as a secretive, undemocratic organization that is taking away power from their home countries. Some of the richer countries in Europe are afraid that adding nations with weaker economies will take away money from them and give it to the poor.

But make no bones about it, the EU unification and expansion has made Europe a global power once again. Individually, these European countries are rich places, but none could compete on their own with the likes of the US or even China. However, as a unit, the EU has the largest GDP on the planet. After a serious growth spurt in the last decade, it appears that the expansionism may be played out. Future candidates include Croatia, Bosnia, Macedonia, Albania, and possibly Turkey . . . but Ukraine and Georgia are now seen as too hot to handle for the EU given Russian resurgence of influence in these areas. Russia itself is usually invited to big EU talks as kind of an associate member already, although the idea of Russian ascension into the EU will never happen. Not everybody likes it, but the EU makes Europe a player in the world economy and world political terms. Divided, they are not much. United, Europe still has a big voice.

MERCOSUR

Members: Brazil, Argentina, Uruguay, Paraguay, with the newest addition: Venezuela!

Associate Members: Bolivia, Chile, Colombia, Ecuador, Peru

Summary: MERCOSUR is a free trade agreement between several South American countries that was created in 1991 by the Treaty of Asuncion. Like other free trade agreements, its purpose is to promote free trade and the fluid movement of goods and currency between the member countries. Venezuela was accepted as a member in 2006, much to the glee of anti-FTAA and US-basher Hugo Chavez. But he is not alone. Many people see MERCOSUR as a counterweight to other global economic powers such as the European Union and the United States.

MERCOSUR faces several challenges. For one, its countries are generally much poorer than those of the United States and Europe. Its combined GDP is only 1/12 of the United States', standing at 1 trillion dollars. MERCOSUR was also greatly weakened by the collapse of Argentina's economy in 2002. In addition, two of its biggest members,

MERCOSUR (MERCOSUL)

■ Member states
■ Associate members

Brazil and Argentina, have been locked in trade disputes. However, keep an eye on this one as leftist events unfold in Latin America. It could become a viable force.

Fun Plaid Fact: Israel is currently the only non-South American free trade partner of Mercosur. WTF? Oy! Why ask why?

ASEAN

ASEAN

Members: Brunei, Cambodia, Indonesia, Laos, Malaysia, Burma, Philippines, Singapore, Thailand, Vietnam

Summary: ASEAN, which stands for Association of Southeast Asian Nations, is a free trade bloc of Southeast Asian countries. Like the European Union, ASEAN may possibly evolve into more than just a free-trade zone; it aims for political, cultural, and economic integration. It was formed in 1967 as a show of solidarity against expansion of Communist Vietnam and insurgency within their own borders. During that time, many countries around Vietnam were turning communist, and capitalist governments were extremely worried that communism might infect them as well. However, even Vietnam has joined ASEAN since then.

ASEAN is significant because of the heterogenous nature of its constituent countries. ASEAN countries are culturally diverse, including Muslims, Buddhists, and other religions. Governments in ASEAN range from democracy to autocracy. The economies of ASEAN countries are also very diverse, but they mainly focus on electronics, oil, and wood.

These guys are increasingly modeling themselves after the EU experiment, too. Even though they remain much more nationalistic than the European countries, the ASEAN group has much bigger goals than to simply be trade block. A common electric grid across the member countries has been proposed; an "open-sky" arrangement is soon taking effect (free movement of all aircraft among member states); and common environmental policies are being adopted across the region. The most interesting ASEAN prospect is now focused on, of all things, human rights! They actually wrote and adopted a legitimate constitution/charter which mentions the idea of protection of equal rights for all. This from a club which has the dictatorship of Burma as a member! Interesting Asian times ahead for the ASEAN.

Fun Plaid Fact: During annual ASEAN meetings, the three ASEAN Dialogue Partners (China, Japan, and South Korea) meet with ASEAN leaders. India hangs with the cool kids now. Say what? China, Japan, South Korea and India? Dudes! That's like four of the largest economies on planet earth under one umbrella!

PLAID ALERT!
Holy trade tips! Keep your eyes on this one as well. This could turn into the largest, richest, baddest block on the planet in your lifetime. Booming economies in most member states with more growth in the future. Bigger deal than that: China, South Korea, Japan and India as "associates" members? Are you kidding me? That's like over half of the entire planet's population under one economic umbrella. Watch out! They are going to be hot!

APEC
VIET NAM 2006

APEC

Members: Australia, Brunei, Canada, Chile, China, Indonesia, Japan, Korea, Malaysia, Mexico, New Zealand, Papua New Guinea, Peru, Philippines, Russia, Singapore, Taiwan, Thailand, United States, Vietnam—pretty much all the guys with Pacific coastline.

Summary: The Asia-Pacific Economic Cooperation trade bloc is a group of Pacific Rim countries that meets with the aim of improving economic and political ties. Like most free-trade blocs, the goal of APEC is to eventually reduce tariffs to nothing. Also, like many free trade agreements, agricultural subsidies have become a point of controversy. The leaders of all APEC countries meet annually in a summit called "APEC Economic Leaders' Meeting" which meets in a different location every year. The first of these meetings was in 1993 and was organized by US president Bill Clinton.

The countries in APEC are responsible for the production of about 80 percent of the world's computer and high-tech components. The countries in many of the Pacific Rim are also significant because the population in many of these countries is increasing dramatically. This trade bloc could possibly become a huge force in the global economy in the near future.

OECD

Members: Austria, Belgium, Canada, Denmark, France, Germany, Greece, Iceland, Ireland, Italy, Luxembourg, Netherlands, Norway, Portugal, Spain, Sweden, Switzerland, Turkey, United Kingdom, United States, Japan, Finland, Australia, New Zealand, Mexico, Czech Republic, Hungary, South Korea, Poland, Slovakia

Summary: The Organisation for Economic Co-operation and Development (OECD) is an international organization of countries that accept the principles of democracy and free markets. After World War II, when Europe was in ruins, the United States gave European countries aid in the form of **the Marshall Plan** to rebuild the continent and repair the economy, while also ensuring that European countries remain democracies. The Organisation for European Economic Co-operation (OEEC) was formed in 1948 to help administer the Marshall Plan. In 1961, membership was extended to non-European countries and renamed the OECD. Because it contains most of the richer, more developed states around the world which are all democracies to boot, the OECD is really kind of the core of what I refer to as "Team West" throughout this text.

Like many trade agreements, the purpose of the OECD is to promote free trade, economic development, and coordinate policies. The OECD also does a lot of research on trade, environment, agriculture, technology, taxation, and other areas. Since the OECD publishes its research, it has become one of the world's best sources for information and statistics about the world.

Fun Plaid Fact: The Republic of China (Taiwan) has observer status on two OECD committees, but since many countries do not recognize Taiwan as an independent country, it is not a formal member.

DEFENSE

Why should countries get together defensively? If they are all on the same team, then they won't fight—right? Well, that's the emphasis of the UN. But perhaps more pertinent are regional defense blocks that have cropped up between countries throughout history. Their thinking is more along the lines of: "I'll help you if you get attacked by an outsider, if you help me if I'm attacked by an outsider." If this sounds like trivial schoolyard thinking, don't laugh; the basis for World War I was a whole host of such pacts between European countries—once one country was attacked, virtually

every other country was immediately pulled in as a consequence of defense agreements. Here are the big three that are pertinent in today's world—even though one of them is now gone.

THE UNITED NATIONS

Members: All the sovereign states in the world except Vatican City. There are currently 192 of them. Even the Swiss finally joined a few years ago.

UN Secretary General Ban Ki-Moon

Summary: The United Nations, or UN, was founded in 1945 as a successor to the League of Nations. Like the League, the goal of the UN is to maintain global peace. Unlike the League, no major world wars have happened on the UN's watch. This is not to say that the United Nations has achieved global peace. In fact, UN "peacekeepers" have been on hand to witness some of the most egregious violations of human rights in recent history.

The UN is made up of several bodies, the most important of which is the Security Council (see Security Council section). The second most important body in the UN is the General Assembly where each of the 192 member nations has a representative and a vote. The General Assembly has produced gems such as the *Universal Declaration of Human Rights* and the lesser known *International Convention on the Protection of the Rights of All Migrant Workers and Members of Their Families*. The General Assembly is clearly the home of utopian thinkers but not of any real international power. This leaves the United States free to ignore everything that the General Assembly says, without even having to waste the time vetoing it.

The UN also includes hundreds of sub-agencies that you've heard of before, such as the World Health Organization (WHO) and UNICEF. The WHO is in charge of coordinating efforts in international public health. UNICEF (The United Nation's Children Fund) provides health, educational, and structural assistance to children in developing nations. Both agencies are supported by member nations and private donors. UNICEF also receives millions of pennies collected each year by children on Halloween.

Critics often charge the UN with being ineffective. This is largely true, but the United Nations was never really intended to be a global government. The best way to view the UN is a forum in which nations can communicate and work together. The UN is ill-equipped to punish any strong member for violations. If a member is especially naughty, a strongly worded UN resolution might recommend voluntary diplomatic or economic sanctions. Perhaps after World War III, the United Nations will be once again renamed and given stronger international authority. If there is anything left of us.

THE REAL POWER AT THE UN: THE UN PERMANENT SECURITY COUNCIL

Members: US, UK, Russia, China, and France

The Security Council is composed of five permanent members (the United States, the United Kingdom, Russia, China, and France) and ten other elected members serving rotating two year terms. The Security Council is charged with responding to threats to peace and acts of aggression. Basically, for anything to get done, the Security Council has to do it. But things rarely get done because each of the five permanent members has the power to veto and prevent any resolution that they do not like. A single veto from any one of the permanent members kills the resolution

on the spot. This group of rag-tag veto-wielding pranksters is currently the ultimate source in interpreting international law. Most of the Cold War saw little to no consensus on anything, as Team US/UK faced off against Team Russia/China. Whatever one team tried to push, the other team generally would veto. The Frenchies vetoed according to mood and lighting of the room. Even today, votes tend to fall along these same alliance lines.

The other ten rotating members of the Council do not have veto power, but are often used as a coalition building tool to get things done. During the build-up to the current war in Iraq, the US worked very hard to get as many members of the Council as possible to back the resolution to invade Iraq, knowing full well that China and Russia would veto it. This was a strategic move to show broad support for the war, even though the US accepted up front that the resolution would not be passed.

There is currently speculation that new members may be added to the UN Permanent Security Council. The prime candidates are Germany and Japan. The United States supports their candidacies; maybe because we have over 270,000 military personnel (including dependents of military) in Germany and Japan combined, and they are staunch US allies. There is also talk of including Brazil or India, or even more remotely, an "Islamic member" or an "African member." But seriously, what incentive does the Security Council have to dilute their powers? Remember, all five would have to agree to let a new member in, so while the United States would certainly support the incorporation of Japan, China would be more likely to tell Japan to go piss up a rope. However, the four most likely members (Japan, Germany, Brazil, and India) have released a joint statement saying that they will all support the others entries. The best argument for enlargement is that Japan and Germany are the second and third largest contributors to the UN general fund, and thus deserve more power. Regardless, don't count on the Security Council getting any bigger unless serious global strife starts going down, which it will, sooner or later.

NATO

Members: Bulgaria, Estonia, Latvia, Lithuania, Romania, Slovakia, Slovenia, the United States of America, France, the United Kingdom, Iceland, Spain, Portugal, Germany, Italy, Belgium, Switzerland, Luxembourg, Finland, Poland, the Czech Republic, Hungary, Greece, Turkey, Norway, the Netherlands, Denmark, and Canada. New members inducted in 2009: Albania and Croatia!

NATO, which stands for the North Atlantic Treaty Organization, is a military alliance between certain European countries, Canada, and America. It was originally created in 1949 to serve as a barrier to a possible attack from the Soviet Union (which never occurred). The most important part of NATO is Article V of the NATO Treaty, which states, *"The Parties agree that an armed attack against one or more of them in Europe or North America shall be considered an attack against them all. . . ."* This is called a mutual defense clause and basically means that the United States must treat an attack on Latvia the same as it would treat an attack on Tennessee.

Although NATO is a multilateral organization, the United States is clearly the captain of the ship. As a rule, US troops are never under the command of a foreign general. NEVER. Because of this, NATO troops (mainly American) are ALWAYS under American command. The United States also uses NATO countries to base its own troops and station nuclear weapons. Many historians blame the United States for provoking the Cuban Missile Crisis, saying that the Russians only wanted to put nukes in Cuba because the United States had recently stationed nukes in Turkey (a NATO nation).

Since the Cold War, NATO has been looking for a new role in the world. Many of the former Soviet republics have since been admitted to NATO—which, by the way, really pisses off Russia. NATO expansion was promoted as an expansion of democracy and freedom into Eastern Europe. More likely, it was to make sure Russia would never be able to regain the territory. NATO has also been increasingly active in international police work, although there is no real justification for this in the NATO Treaty. NATO forces were heavily involved

NATO Secretary General Fogh Rasmussen. Don't make him angry. You wouldn't like NATO when he's angry.

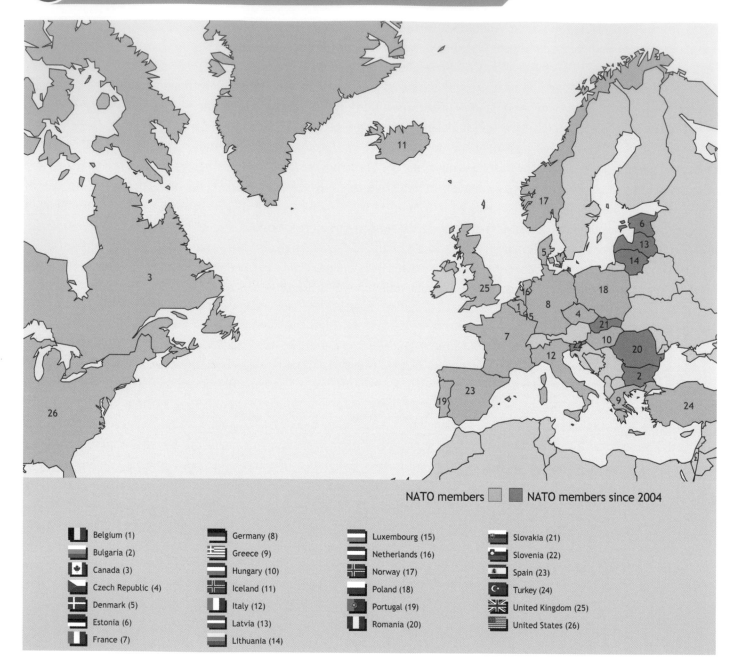

NATO members ☐ ■ NATO members since 2004

Belgium (1)	Germany (8)	Luxembourg (15)	Slovakia (21)
Bulgaria (2)	Greece (9)	Netherlands (16)	Slovenia (22)
Canada (3)	Hungary (10)	Norway (17)	Spain (23)
Czech Republic (4)	Iceland (11)	Poland (18)	Turkey (24)
Denmark (5)	Italy (12)	Portugal (19)	United Kingdom (25)
Estonia (6)	Latvia (13)	Romania (20)	United States (26)
France (7)	Lithuania (14)		

in the Bosnia conflict in 1994 and the Yugoslavia conflict in 1999, although in reality these were just American troops under a multinational flag. After September 11th, NATO has also become involved in the anti-terrorism game, even invoking Article V for the first time with regard to Afghanistan. Remember, the war in Afghanistan is a NATO mission, not a US mission. But let's be honest here; the US does most of the heavy lifting, as usual.

Fun Plaid Fact: The only country in NATO without a military force is Iceland. The Icelandic Defense Force is an American military contingent stationed permanently on the island.

WARSAW PACT—DEFUNCT!

PAST Members: Soviet Union (club president), Albania (until 1968), Bulgaria, Czechoslovakia, East Germany (1956–1990), Hungary, Poland, and Romania.

The Warsaw Pact, or if you prefer the more Orwellian Soviet name—the "Treaty of Friendship, Co-operation and Mutual Assistance," was the alliance formed by the Soviet Union to counter the perceived threat of NATO. The Warsaw Pact was established in 1955 (six years after NATO) and lasted *officially* until 1991 (two years post-Berlin Wall). Much like the Bizarro-Superman to the United State's real Superman, the Warsaw Pact never had the teeth or the organizational strength of NATO. Perhaps this is because many of the members actually hated the dominance of the Soviet Union. Two countries, Hungary (1956) and Czechoslovakia (1961), tried to assert political independence and were subsequently crushed by Soviet military forces in exercises that would make Tiananmen Square look like an after school special.

The main idea behind the Warsaw Pact was mutual protection. If the United States attempted to invade any of the Warsaw members, it would guarantee a Soviet response. In this way, the Warsaw countries acted like a tripwire against the expansion of Western-style capitalism and democracy, firmly establishing the location of the Iron Curtain. Shortly after the Cold War, most Warsaw Pact countries either ceased to exist or defected to NATO.

Fun Plaid Fact: The Soviet Union despised American acronyms. Instead of taking the first letter from each word, the Soviets preferred taking the entire first sound. For example, Communist International was "Comintern."

 NEW KIDS ON THE BLOC

SCO

Members: China, Russia, Kazakhstan, Kyrgyzstan, Tajikistan, and Uzbekistan

Observer States: India, Pakistan, Mongolia, and Iran

Goodbye, Warsaw Pact! Hello, SCO! Watch this new BLOC! It is evolving fast, with gigantic repercussions for international relations and world balance of power in the future of Asia!

Summary: The Shanghai Cooperation Organization grouping was originally created by 5 member states in 1996 with the signing of the *Treaty on Deepening Military Trust in Border Regions* . . . however with the addition of Uzbekistan in 2001, which brought them up to 6 members, they can't use that wicked cool nickname of "Shanghai 5" anymore. Too bad. But they are are the hottest defense block to keep an eye on, as they are the newest on the scene; so new, in fact, that they have not exactly quite figured out what they are yet. Part military, part economic, part cultural . . . but 100% important to know. Let's just focus on military aspects for now.

SHANGHAI COOPERATION ORGANISATION

■ Member States ■ Observer States ■ Dialogue Partners

Created with that *Deepening Military Trust* issue, they have also agreed to a *Treaty on Reduction of Military Forces in Border Regions* in 1997 and in July 2001, Russia and China, the organization's two leading nations, signed the *Treaty of Good-Neighborliness and Friendly Cooperation* . . . wow, could they get any more sickening sweet with the descriptors? What an Eurasian love-fest. The SCO is primarily centred on its member nations' security-related concerns, often citing its main threats/focuses as: terrorism, separatism, and extremism. You can easily read into this as a great vehicle for all these governments to help each other crack down on any internal political dissidents.

They work together thwarting terrorism and stuff, but they are also quickly absorbing other avenues of cooperation like domestic security, crime, and drug trafficking. Over the past few years, the organization's activities have expanded to include increased military cooperation, intelligence sharing, and counterterrorism. Of significant note: there have been a number of SCO joint military exercises, and while it is very early to think that the SCO is a serious strategic military power, please keep in mind that the group is still very young and has a long way to go and to grow. We may just be seeing the beginning of their military prowess. Dig this: both Russia and China are nuke powers, Russia has shit-ton of weaponry, and China has the largest standing army on Earth.

Is this thing sizing up to be a counterbalance to US power or as an overt anti-NATO? Perhaps. But one thing is for sure: its six full members account for 60% of the land mass of Eurasia and its population is a third of the world's . . . and if you include the observer state, they collectively account for half of the human race. The SCO has now initiated over two dozen large-scale projects related to transportation, energy and telecommunications and held regular meetings of security, military, defense, foreign affairs, economic, cultural, banking and other officials from its member states. No multinational organization with such far-ranging and comprehensive mutual interests and activities has ever existed on this scale before. A combo EU/NATO of Eurasia for this century? Could be! So you gotsta' know the SCO! They are fast becoming a playa'!

CULTURAL ORGANIZATIONS

Some supranationalist organizations form out of a desire to maintain a cultural coherence with like countries or to promote certain aspects of their culture among their member states. In other words, monetary gain is not the driving force behind the organization, although economics usually sneaks in there as well. Here are three very different such organizations to compare and contrast.

ARAB LEAGUE

Members: Egypt, Iraq, Jordan, Lebanon, Saudi Arabia, Syria, Yemen, Libya, Sudan, Morocco, Tunisia, Kuwait, Algeria, United Arab Emirates, Bahrain, Qatar, Oman, Mauritania, Somalia, Palestine, Djibouti, Comoros

The Arab League is an organization designed to strengthen ties among member states, coordinate their policies, and promote their common interests. The league is involved in various political, economic, cultural, and social programs, including literacy campaigns and programs dealing with labor issues. The common bond between the countries in the Arab League is that they speak a common language, Arabic, and practice a common religion, Islam. The Charter of the Arab League also forbids member states from resorting to force against each other. In many ways, the Arab League can be seen as a regional UN. It was formed in 1945.

However, the Arab League is better known for their lack of coherence and in-fighting more so than any unifying activities they have had so far to date. In fact, Libyan leader Muammar Qaddafi threatened to withdraw from the League in 2002, because of "Arab incapacity" in resolving the crises between the United States and Iraq and the Israeli-Palestinian conflict. If the Arab League ever gets its act together, it could be a powerful force in the world. Right now, it is not.

Fun Fact: Egypt was suspended from the Arab League from 1979 to 1989 for signing a peace treaty with Israel. Libya has sporadically quit and re-joined the group multiple times depending on how Muammar Qaddafi was feeling at the time. (see more on that in the AU section on next page.)

Let's get this Arab party started!

OAS

Members: Argentina, Bolivia, Brazil, Chile, Colombia, Costa Rica, Cuba, Dominican Republic, Ecuador, El Salvador, Guatemala, Haiti, Honduras, Mexico, Nicaragua, Panama, Paraguay, Peru, United States, Uruguay, Venezuela, Barbados, Trinidad and Tobago, Jamaica, Grenada, Suriname, Dominica, Saint Lucia, Antigua and Barbuda, Saint Vincent and the Grenadines, Bahamas, Saint Kitts and Nevis, Canada, Belize, Guyana

Summary: The OAS, which stands for Organization of American States, is an international organization headquartered in Washington, DC. According to Article 1 of its Charter, the goal of the member nations in creating the OAS was "to achieve an order of peace and justice, to promote their solidarity, to strengthen their collaboration, and to defend their sovereignty, their territorial integrity, and their independence." Other goals include economic growth, democracy, security, the eradication of poverty, and a means to resolve disputes. Historically, the first meeting to promote solidarity and cooperation was held in 1889 and was called the First International Conference of American States. Since then, the OAS has grown, through a number of small steps, to become the organization it is today. Like the Arab League, this organization is a kind of regional UN.

Unlike free-trade blocs, the OAS encompasses many areas other than just trade. For example, it oversees elections in all of its member countries—of particular note, they declared the last election in Peru as illegal, and the last election in Mexico as the first verifiably legal. However, it has been criticized as a means for America to control the countries in Latin America. For example, when America wanted Cuba kicked out of the OAS, the organization quickly did so. However, many dictatorships that America has supported have remained within the OAS.

But this "US as imperialist" attitude is changing fast in the OAS. US President Barack Obama personally addressed the group in April 2009, pledging to bring more unity to the hemisphere and even hinting at thawing relations with the Cubans. Hell, Obama even shook hands with legendary US-hating Venezuelan President Hugo Chavez! The OAS may actually be gaining ground as a legit forum for problem-solving in the Americas. As of this writing, Cuba is being reconsidered for membership, and it appears that things are moving forward rapidly.

Fun Plaid Fact: Even though Cuba is again a member state, the current regime is denied the right of representation and attendance at meetings and of participation in activities.

AU: AFRICAN UNION

African military problems to be increasingly solved by African troops. How novel!

Members: Algeria, Angola, Benin, Botswana, Burkina Faso, Burundi, Cameroon, Cape Verde, Central African Republic, Chad, Comoros, Democratic Republic of the Congo, Republic of the Congo, Côte d'Ivoire, Djibouti, Egypt, Equatorial Guinea, Eritrea, Ethiopia, Gabon, Gambia, Ghana, Guinea, Guinea-Bissau, Kenya, Lesotho, Liberia, Libya, Madagascar, Malawi, Mali, Mauritius, Mozambique, Namibia, Niger, Nigeria, Rwanda, & Zimbabwe.

Suspended Members: Mauritania

"Up yours, Arab League. I'm African now!"

Summary: The Organization of African Unity was established in 1963 at Addis Ababa, Ethiopia, by 37 independent African nations to promote unity and development; defend the sovereignty and territorial integrity of members; eradicate all forms of colonialism and promote international cooperation. This organization changed its name to the African Union in 2002. Institutionally, the AU is very much like the EU with a parliament, a commission, a court of justice, and a chairmanship which rotates between the member countries. The AU is also beginning to deploy peacekeepers, and it has sent over 2500 soldiers to the Darfur region of the Sudan. Every country in Africa is a member of the AU except for Morocco, which withdrew in 1985. Also, Mauritania was suspended in 2005 after a coup d'etat occurred and a military government took power. The new government has promised to hold elections within two years, but many observers are doubtful that it will.

There are many problems facing Africa such as civil war, disease, undemocratic regimes, and poverty. However, the biggest problem facing the AU is the spread of HIV, the virus that leads to AIDS, on the African continent. It is expected that millions of people will die in the coming years, and these events will probably destabilize the African continent. The AU has many challenges to face in the coming years. However, its most successful component to date is the military wing of the AU. Major powers from around the globe have hailed the common AU military as the most awesome thing the continent could do, and have supported it whole-heartedly. Why? Because the AU military can thus be tasked with solving African conflicts, without the outside powers becoming directly involved. After the US debacle in Somalia (go watch *Blackhawk Down*) no one wants to send actual troops to stop African conflicts, such as the Rwandan genocide; the AU has become the choice d'jour for outside support to deal with these issues. While the AU may not get outside support for anything else, look for the military to be bolstered with funding and training from the US, the EU and maybe even China and Russia, in lieu of actual participation in conflicts on the ground.

Fun Fact: The idea of an African Union separate from the OAU came from Muammar Qaddafi, who wanted to see a "United States of Africa." He was sick of developments in the Arab world and publicly gave up on being an Arab.

INTERNATIONAL ODDBALLS

In addition to these, other entities have been formed at the international level for specific functions as well as for the supposed good of all humanity. Many of these organizations are frequently in the news, so I feel a brief introduction to them is merited. Haven't you ever wondered who the heck is the G7, the G8, the IMF, the World Bank, or the WTO, and what is an NGO?

G-7 GROUP OF SEVEN

Members: Canada, France, Germany, Italy, Japan, UK, and the United States

The Group of Seven (or G-7) is the country club of international relations. It's a place where the richest industrialized nations go to talk about being rich, form strategies for staying rich, and—like any other country club—figure out how to keep everyone else poor. The leaders from G-7 countries meet each year for a summit. The summits are often widely protested for reasons such as global warming, poverty in Africa, unfair trade policies, unfair medical patent laws, and basically, for a general sense of arrogance. Protesters, mark your calendars; the summit returns to the USA in 2012 (location TBD).

Originally, the group was called the G-6, which was the G-7 minus Canada. They formed out of the Library Group because rich countries were pissed about the 1973 oil crisis. Then Canada joined the group in 1976, making it the G-7. Even though this group has since evolved into the G-8, the G-7 group still meets annually to discuss financial issues.

G-8 GROUP OF EIGHT

Members: G-7 plus Russia

Same as above, with Russia in attendance. Russia is still a nuclear power, still the largest territorial state on the planet, and perhaps most significantly a major energy resource provider to the world—especially to the G-7 countries. They have to invite the big boy to the party every now and again, or the big boy might get too pissed and go play with China. The G-7 doesn't want that. They need their energy! Like we said in the G-7 section, the G-8 group grew out of the G-7. In 1991, Russia was given a special membership, creating the P-8 or G 7+1. In 1998, they did their math, and renamed it the G-8. Who knows how much longer the G-7 or G-8 will even last given the rapidly changing face of our planet. What do I mean? Well, in our day and age, what point is there to having a meeting of the "biggest" world economies that doesn't include China? Or India? It's getting to be kind of outdated and pathetically sad for all the old white-boy countries to get together to chat about world affairs without these other up-and-coming-non-white states having input, so we are probably witnessing the end of days of both the G-7 and G-8, although old traditions die hard and they will survive for a bit longer. At least you now know the reality of things.

G-20 GROUP OF TWENTY

PLAID ALERT!!!

Great googly global groups! We have a new international organization titan in our midst, my friends! The G-20 (formally, the Group of Twenty Finance Ministers and Central Bank Governors).

Members: Technically, it is comprised of the finance ministers and central bank governors of the G7, 12 other key countries, and the European Union Presidency (if not a G7 member). Also at the meetings are the heads of the European Central Bank, the IMF, and the World Bank.

The literal translation: the G-8 rich states + Argentina, Australia, Brazil, China, India, Indonesia, Mexico, Korea, Saudi Arabia, South Africa, Turkey + all those aforementioned bank heads. Collectively, the G-20 economies comprise 85% of global GDP, 80% of world trade and two-thirds of the world population. Damn! That's all the money!

Summary: The G-20 is a forum for cooperation and consultation on matters pertaining to the international financial system which was created in 1999. It studies, reviews, and promotes discussion among key industrial and emerging market countries of policy issues pertaining to the promotion of international financial stability, and seeks to address issues that go beyond the responsibilities of any one organization. The key here is to "promote international financial stability," but I'm thinking they are quickly turning into a whole hell of a lot more. Why would I think that?

Because all the prime ministers and presidents are now showing up for these meetings! A Washington, D.C. summit was held in November 2008 and a London summit in April 2009, which were attended by all the heads of the respective states. Barack was there baby, chillin' with Gordon Brown! And these folks are truly transforming the power structure of the planet: the G-8 guys realize that they can't fix nothing without the cooperation of titans like China and India. In London, the G-20 adopted a collective approach to solving the global recession, but also are reorganizing the IMF and World Bank to incorporate other non-G8 voices, which have dominated global financial institutions for years. This is exciting stuff!

I truly believe this G-20 unit has now fully superseded the G-7, the G-8, and any other G's as the premier problem-solving institute on earth. The UN is too big and bureaucratic, and the G-7 too white and too exclusive, but the 20 seems to be a great balance of peoples and powers from across the planet. I would speculate that this much more representative and simultaneously streamlined group will be where all sorts of international treaties and agreements will have their foundation stones set; from economic crises to global warming issues to nuclear proliferation problems, look for the talking points to be brought up at these G-20 pow-wows.

This star is new, but shining already. And its future is bright indeed!

Fun Plaid Fact: There actually has been another G-20 gang comprised of an array of developing nations from Africa, Latin America and Asia. Their primary goal has been fighting for trade rights, particularly in the agricultural sector. You probably won't hear much from that group anymore, but just be aware in case you do . . . they are the poor G-20, not this huge rich G-20 described above.

BRIC

Members: Brazil, China, India & Russia

The Avenger has his plaid panties in a bunch about this unofficial "group" because it represents a serious global shift that has started in the last several years: a move to more representative economic and political power on the world stage. You can possibly look at the BRIC as an alternative center of power to the "Team West" rich countries that have run the global show for a century. It is a new, dynamic, and growing coalition which you will hear a lot more about in the future . . . . just as you will increasingly hear less and less about the G-7 or G-8. So what is this BRIC house all about?

An acronym for the states of Brazil, Russia, India and China combined, BRIC was first coined in 2003 by a financial analyst at Goldman Sachs who speculated that by 2050, these four economies would be wealthier than most of the current major economic powers put together. For sure, China and India will become the world's biggest suppliers of manufactured goods and services, with Russia and

Brazil becoming some of the biggest suppliers of natural resources. All four are developing and industrializing rapidly and making bank. Because of their emerging statuses, their increasingly educated populations, and their lower labor costs, the BRIC has also become a magnet for foreign investment, outsourcing, and development of R&D centers.

But this thing has already grown well beyond a simple classification of future rich countries, and this is the deal I really want you to know. It is consistently pointed out that these four countries have not formed a structured political alliance like the EU, NAFTA or NATO . . . . . yet! I'm telling you friends, these guys are thinking about it! They started having face-to-face summits in 2009, and are increasingly agreeing on a whole lot of economic AND foreign policy issues which they then announce to the world under a common voice. Craziness!

What am I spouting about? At the last meeting of the G-20, the BRIC countries demanded, and received, more voting power in global financial institutions like the IMF and World Bank (which they should, since they are increasingly funding them). And what is certainly the boldest and most telling strategic political initiative they have taken to date, all four BRIC countries have jointly declared that they do not support harsh sanctions against Iran and that they support Iran's right to develop nuclear power. What's that got to do with economic policy? Nothing! But it certainly does fly in the face of Team West's opinion of Iran, and that is why I think its important that you know that the BRIC is fast evolving into something much more than a simple economic group . . . . they are becoming a global entity on par with Team West. It's not official, it's not on paper, it's not heavily coordinated yet, but for sure the BRIC is going to be a significant entity of the 21st century. Get hip to the BRIC!

Fun Plaid Fact: Think the BRIC will have some clout in the 21st century? The four countries, combined, currently account for more than a quarter of the world's land area and more than 40% of the world's population, and with little reservations analysts assume that all the BRIC countries will be richer than the G-7 countries (except the US) within 20 years. Expect the top five economies for the rest of your life to be the US followed by the BRIC.

WTO

WORLD TRADE ORGANIZATION
ORGANISATION MONDIALE DU COMMERCE
ORGANIZACIÓN MUNDIAL DEL COMERCIO

Dudes In Club—150 total members

Dudes Observing the Club—Iran, Iraq, Sudan, Vietnam, Vatican City . . .

Dudes NOT In the Club—Palestine, Somalia, North Korea . . .

The World Trade Organization (WTO) is an international, multilateral organization that makes the rules for the global trading system and resolves disputes between its member states. The stated mission of the WTO is to increase trade by promoting lower trade barriers and providing a platform for the negotiation of trade. In principle, each member of the WTO is a privileged trading partner with every other member. This means that if one member gives another a special deal, he's got to give it to everyone else—like in elementary school if you were caught with candy.

Things that make the WTO sigh in delight are "open markets," "tariff reductions," and "long walks on the beach at sunset." The WTO is basically the application of capitalism on a global scale. The key idea is that competition creates efficiency and growth. *Any* country should be able to sell *any*thing it can, *any*where it wants, at *any* price that *any*one will pay. The WTO can boast some successes in growing international trade, but these have also been accompanied by increased wealth disparity between rich and poor nations AND between the rich and poor within nations.

Formally established in 1995, the WTO is structured around about 30 different trade agreements, which have the status of international legal texts. Member countries must ratify all WTO agreements to join the club. Many of the agreements are highly criticized including the Agreement on Agriculture, which reduces tariffs hurting small farms in developing countries. One of the most famous antiglobalization protests occurred around the 1999 WTO meeting in Seattle. Also, the Man loves the WTO.

Fun Plaid Fact—The Kingdom of Tonga became the 150th member in 2005. The oldest animal ever recorded, a tortoise named Tu'i Malila, died in Tonga in 1965. Okay, this has nothing to do with the WTO, but turtles are cool.

IMF

Members: Everyone. Seriously. Okay, you got me! Everyone except North Korea, Cuba, Liechtenstein, Andorra, Monaco, Tuvalu and Nauru.

The primary responsibility of the International Monetary Fund (IMF) is to monitor the global financial system. The IMF works at stabilizing currency exchange rates. Doing this, they provide security to overseas investors and help promote international trade. The IMF's policies are also aimed at reducing the phenomenon of "boom and bust," where economies grow rapidly, then stagnate, then grow rapidly, then stagnate, then grow rapidly, et cetera. The main tool of the IMF is "financial assistance" (aka loans), which they provide to countries with "balance of payment problems" (aka big time debt). As a condition of the loans, the IMF mandates "structural adjustment programs." These programs are designed to turn a cash profit, allowing the borrowing country to repay its debt to the IMF. Here is a short glossary of "structural adjustment" terms and how they are interpreted by the locals:

IMF sez . . .	Locals sez it means . . .
Austerity	cutting social programs
User Fees	charging for stuff like education and health care and water
Resource Extraction	selling stuff out of the ground that rich countries want
Privatization	selling state owned stuff to rich companies (usually foreigners)
Deregulation	removing domestic control over stuff
Trade liberalization	allowing foreigners to open sweatshops and exporting stuff made in sweatshops

Much like the WTO and World Bank, the IMF is often congratulated for growth in the global trade and production and simultaneously scorned for increasing the poverty gaps within countries and between countries.

THE WORLD BANK

Similar to the IMF, the mission of the World Bank (actually the World Bank Group) is to encourage and safeguard international investment. All the while, the World Bank attempts to help reduce poverty and spawn economic development. The World Bank works primarily with "developing countries" helping them develop in a Westerly fashion. Also, like the IMF, the World Bank loans are contingent on adopting "structural adjustments." While the IMF deals primarily with currency stabilization, the World Bank is primarily like a real bank, loaning countries money for very specific development projects like a hydropower plant or a disease-eradication program.

Unlike the IMF, which is headquartered in Switzerland, the World Bank Group is headquartered in Washington, D.C. and the US plays a very heavy hand in both its leadership and loaning activities.

It should be noted that the World Bank is breaking new ground on the redefinition of the sovereignty issue that we covered in chapter 3. Due to government corruption in many states, particularly Africa, the World Bank is now putting further stipulations and oversight on all the loans it makes to countries. They are going in and making sure that the money they give a country to build an AIDS clinic doesn't end up getting used to buy weaponry for the state. The Plaid Avenger is proud as punch at such a bold move, but many states are hopping mad that this type of intense oversight, which is now mandatory before the Bank hands over any money, violates their sovereignty. I'm with the World Bank on this one. Suck it up, sovereign states. If you want the jack, prove it's going to be used responsibly.

Watch for this issue to gain world attention soon. As of this writing, it's causing consternation in Chad as we speak . . . .

NGOS

NGOs are Nongovernmental Organizations. These are basically every organization that is not directly affiliated with the government, from Amnesty International to Greenpeace. We are talking about the growing number of highly influential international groups that are playing an ever important role in transnational politics. These groups transcend borders and unite common interests. NGOs are set up to represent a diverse array of special interests (environmental protection, human rights, et cetera). Here are a few examples of influential NGOs:

→ Human Rights Watch—With a budget of ~$20 million a year, this NGO aims to document violations of international humanitarian law by sponsoring fact-finding research. HRW recently waged a successful campaign against the use of land-mines, which the U.S. government opposed.

→ Freedom House—This NGO supports research for democracy promotion. Also, each year FH ranks countries on a scale from "Free" to "Not Free." Luckily, as of 2009, the United States is still "Free."

→ Greenpeace As the name suggests, this NGO hopes to achieve greenness using peaceful means. Greenpeace is also the only NGO to own a ship (*The Rainbow Warrior*) that the French government intentionally sunk. Funny story, actually; google it and find out. The greatest French military victory since the Napoleonic era.

→ Amnesty International—This NGO is committed to protecting the human rights enshrined in the Universal Declaration of Human Rights.

→ International Red Cross (and Red Crescent)—The sole function of the Red Cross is to protect the life and dignity of victims in armed conflict. The Red Cross is independent, neutral, and all that other crap. They help anyone and everyone.

We will discuss some of these NGOs in more detail in later chapters. Party on.

THE NUKE GROUP

Members: US, Russia, UK, France, China, India, Pakistan, Israel

Questionable Members: North Korea, Iran

Last, but certainly not least, is a most important gang of states on planet earth with this homogenous trait: they got nuclear bombs! While not an "official" entity in the spirit of the other groups discussed in this chapter, I would be remiss without sticking this information in some-where . . . . and what better place than a chapter on clubs, as this particular club has enough firepower to blow up all of the other clubs on the planet? The club with the biggest clubs! But it's much more important than that if you want to understand how the world works and how geopolitical power is actually wielded in real life in our day and age. What do I mean?

Well, who is in the club? Let's start with the original declared nuclear powers: US, Russia, UK, France, and China. Hey! Wait a minute! That's the exact same group that as the UN Permanent Security Council! How true, my quick-witted friends, and that is no coincidence! These 5 countries were the first to develop, test, and therefore prove that they possessed nuclear weapons. The face that they admitted this to the world means that they have "declared" their status. Kind of like coming out of the nuclear closet. Because of their "first-ness" and openness, these nuke powers have the veto powers at the UN, as per their permanent status on the security council.

Soon after the development of nuclear weapons, most everyone agreed it would be a horrible idea for all countries on earth to have access to these weapons, so a movement to limit them emerged, culminating in the 1970 **Nuclear Non-Proliferation Treaty** (or **NPT**). This treaty has been signed by 189 countries, including the aforementioned big 5 declared nuke powers . . . only four countries are not signed up for it (more on that in a sec). The treaty has three basic pillars it strives to deal with:

1. non-proliferation, or non-spread of nuclear weapons and/or nuclear weapon information;

2. disarmament, or getting rid of existing nuclear weapons; and

3. the right to peacefully use nuclear technology, which means all signers of the treaty are allowed to have nuclear energy, but not nuclear bombs.

As you can see, this treaty is mostly to ensure that nobody is making nuke weapons, but nuke power technology is allowed by the NPT, which makes enforcement of it tricky and a hot potato in current events. But before we get to that, what about the other nuke powers not yet named? Which would be India, Pakistan, and Israel. Ah! Yes! Those would be the exact four countries that have not signed the NPT. What a coincidence! Not! Here is the deal:

India developed and tested its nuclear weapons in 1974, and not to be outdone, Pakistan followed suit in the late 1990's. Why would these countries need nuclear weapons? Because they hate each other and have already fought three wars so far, with more to come. Once India became nuclear, Pakistan could not rest until it got the bomb as well. That's the way rivalries work. The tension between these two countries is so great, that neither will give up their right to possess, and even create more, nuclear weapons, which is why both countries have refused to sign the NPT. But they have declared and proven that they have bombs, so they make the list of nuke powers, even though they cannot legally pursue nuclear energy industries since all that stuff is also regulated by the NPT.

Who is left? Israel, of course! With no reservations, everyone on the planet knows that Israel is also a nuclear power, but they have never tested, proven, or declared it. The US and many others never want them to declare it either, for fear it would spark a regional arms race. Israel has probably been a nuclear power since the 1960's, and it wants to have that nuclear edge mostly in order to ensure its survival, were it to ever be attacked by surrounding states again (see chapter 20). Because of this "secret" status, Israel has refused to sign the NPT, because to do so would mean it would have to open up for inspections and declare their stockpile . . . which, again, might cause a regional arms race.

Finally, there are those who might be trying to get into this nuclear club, but aren't quite there yet. North Korea originally signed the NPT but has subsequently quit, mostly because having the elusive illusion of possibly having nuclear material is the only bargaining chip they have left to play to get international attention as their state nears collapse. The koo-koo North Koreans actually exploded something underground a few years back and claimed it was a nuclear device, but no one is really quite sure what the hell they actually have. Including themselves. And I'm sure you have heard plenty about Iran recently too . . . they actually are a signatory of the NPT, which gives the the right to develop nuclear energy. Which they are, while claiming peaceful intent. But Iran's semi-crazy leaders have already made reference to themselves as a "nuclear power," which of course they are technically not. Yet. Maybe. Damn, this is confusing! Why am I throwing you all this info on the Nuke Group? Well, unless you have been hiding out in an underground nuclear bunker since the 1950's, you know that the issue of nuclear energy/nuclear weapons has become an extremely hot topic in today's world. Like radioactive hot. Like 1.21 gigawatts hot. Crazy North Korea may be developing something which it then may use to blow up a neighbor. And there is great fear of terrorist organizations obtaining nuclear material and doing something nasty with it. But most of all, the world is currently at arms with itself over what to do with Iran: half the world thinks Iran is just developing nuclear power, the other half think Iran is trying to get nuclear weapons . . . it is possibly the most divisive issue of current times, and may result in war. That's why the UN permanent Security Council is debating these issues non-stop, why Team West is at odds with the BRIC, and why current US President Barack Obama held the first-ever "Nuclear Security Summit" in Washington DC in 2010, at which all these issues and more were debated. No state currently with nuclear weapons, and the lion's share of states that don't, wants to see more states go nuclear; these things are dangerous and deadly and could spell the end of humanity! Dudes! I've seen *The Road Warrior* and *The Matrix!* It's scary! At the same time, there are those states that want nuclear weapons. With no question, nukes are the absolute best deterrent that would prevent your country from being attacked. Who wouldn't want a nuke? I mean, let's be honest here: the main reason that the Cold War never turned into a hot war was because both sides had nuclear weapons; therefore, neither

side could attack without suffering the same nuclear annihilation itself. Would the US have dropped atomic weapons on Japan in World War II if Japan was equally armed? Would the US administration be openly talking about invading/bombing Iran if Iran was already a nuclear power? Having a nuclear weapon is a game-changer.

This brief section was only to alert you to the nuclear status of our planet, not to fully explain and engage all the complicated topics surrounding these weapons of ultimate destruction. Hopefully, you now at least have a handle on the hotness and how it plays out in current events and the world regions. Regions? Oh yeah! That's what this book is about! Let's get to the regions now!

CHAPTER OUTLINE

North America

7

NOW that we've discussed all the preliminary stuff, we can get to the real meat and potatoes. Let's start with the biggest meat and potato eaters—the North American region.

This region consists of two major countries: the United States and their redheaded stepchild to the north, Canada. But damn, what an incredible impact on the rest of the world this region makes. Of course, I'm referring mostly to the powerhouse of the planet, the United States of America. For most of the following discussion, I'll be talking about the United States, but always keep in mind that our chilly Canadian cohorts are generally on board for all things North American, even our foreign policy. So is their population; 90% of Canadians live within 100 miles of the US/Canadian border. Hell, I'm not even sure why it's a separate country at all sometimes. I think the only real difference between these states is the bacon. But I digress.

Canadian Prime Minister Stephen Harper: "Don't forget about us, eh!"

WHY IS THIS A REGION?

Why is this a region at all? We learned earlier exactly what is a region. A region takes up space, of which North America has plenty. A region must also have some borders, which may be fuzzy. The region's borders are actually very clear cut; it's everything north of the US-Mexican border. Also necessary for a region is homogeneity. It must have some traits that are roughly the same throughout the region in order to unify the countries.

This is one of the most homogenous regions on the planet due to several main characteristics. It has a high standard of living; it is one of the wealthiest regions in the world. If we head south of the border, we see that Mexico is distinctly different economically, which is one reason why it is not included in this region.

Another factor is language. There is, for the most part, a single language that dominates. Although there are many people who speak Spanish in the US—and of course there are also those wacky French Canadians—primarily both countries are English-speaking. Canada and the US also share historical and cultural backgrounds. Both countries were British colonies at one time. This cultural baggage, which includes religion and the aforementioned trait of language, also solidifies these two countries into a region. The fact that the US and Canada are the oldest and most stable democracies is also important. Human rights, the belief in individual freedoms, and similar governmental structures also make this a solid region.

THE GREATEST REGION ON EARTH!

Wow, that's a bold claim that the Plaid Avenger's making. Why would I suggest that the United States and Canada, combined into our North American region, would be the greatest on the planet? That does come with some caveats, of course. The greatest at many things, and simultaneously the not-so-greatest at others. Two sides of a very particular coin here in the 21st century world. Let's talk about what the hell I'm getting at here. We'll start with "the greatest."

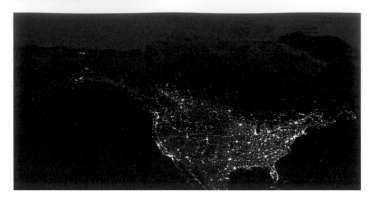

Canadian lights not too far from the border.

+THE RICHEST

Why would I say that the United States and Canada is the greatest region on Earth? For starters: they're the richest. There's no getting around that. My plaid friends, I think you all accept this, as do most, that the United States is the richest country on the planet. We forget their Canadian cohorts to the north, though. The Canucks are also pretty well off in terms of per capita GDP. Why, and in what respect, are they together two of the richest countries on the planet? Let's break this down.

PHYSICAL RESOURCES

One: physical resources. These two countries are the second and fourth largest countries on the planet in terms of size. Lots of land in which to move around and lots of space to grow. Space and land is a valuable commodity in and of itself for future potential growth of a country, and both these big boys have it. The US and Canada contain tons of natural resources . . . and I mean everything across the board. These countries produce tremendous amounts of food, be it grain or grapes or bananas or corn or any damn thing else. They have tremendous amounts of water resources. H_2O is an oft overlooked resource when people think about a place's richness, but hey, you've got to face it, friends—if you don't have water, you have nothing. The US and Canada have lots of food and lots of water . . . but also lots of the other natural resources. North America is virtually saturated with almost every type of resource possible: coal, oil, tobacco, lumber, copper, steel, gold, fertile croplands, and almost anything else. You use it, you want it—North America has it.

PHYSICAL DISTANCE

This North American region also has a strategic advantage in that it is far from other places. What's so special about that? Why would that make them rich? If for no other reason, you have to consider the fact that while the US and Canada have been involved in virtually every major world conflict of the last century, the fights have never occurred on their own soil. To my recollection, Pearl Harbor and the September 11, 2001 attacks are the only times that anyone for a century has even made it to North American shores for a strike. While those were horrific events to be sure, they were pinpricks in comparison to the larger wars of which they were a component. Having two great oceans separate this region from the rest of the planet is a big plus, indeed.

Specific example: After World War II, Europe was destroyed. China was decimated. Parts of Russia were blasted. Japan was completely leveled. The United States and Canada? Sitting pretty and virtually untouched. Besides Pearl Harbor, nothing happened on the soil of this region during those wartime eras.

Also, consider terrorism in the modern world: for those with malicious intent, it is very difficult to get to North America from other parts of the world. This is one of the reasons why the 9/11 attacks were a really big deal in the North

American region. People just couldn't believe it. Folks around the rest of the world are used to bombings, terrorist attacks, uprisings, but it's very unique in the North American region—it just doesn't happen. Terrorist attacks occur in Europe, Asia, the Middle East, and across Africa all the time, but not in North America. After 9/11, people in the United States were freaking out. Quite frankly, terrorist attacks happen across the globe all of the time.

Why do they happen in other places and not here? Distance! People that may be upset with the United States and Canada are very far away. North America is not an easy place to get to if you're a disgruntled Afghan. You can hate the US all you want, but you're not going to get there to do anything about it unless you are well-funded and organized, which rules out most of the people on the planet.

The US and Canada have chosen to get involved in world affairs when it suits them. Very few other places have this convenience. The result? Untouched for virtually all global wars and confrontations of the last 200 years, and even now in the 21st century, they have a wide safety buffer from the rest of the world's problems. Their distance is a key feature.

EVOLUTION OF AN ECONOMIC POWERHOUSE

The North American region has experienced 200 years of continuous growth. That's not something that any other region can brag about. Look through the rest of this damn book. There is no other place on the planet that has essentially gotten richer decade after decade, century after century, like the US and Canada have for 200 years straight.

The formation of the United States and Canada in this region, of course, goes back to the colonial era when the British, the Spaniards, and the French rolled across the Atlantic in boats—though it's doubtful any of them yelled, "I'm on a boat!" while doing so—and staked claims on the next continent. From this nice little nest egg of an area, they proceeded to invest heavily into infrastructure and developing industries. It was a beautiful little place to get a start-up country going—a nice little fixer-upper.

The physical geography of the region ties in here because of the Appalachian Mountains. European settlers were all over the few hundred miles of land from the shores of the Atlantic to the mountains, the location of the 13 colonies. This became a perfect little incubator for the embryonic United States. It set the colonies away from Amerindians, who were on one side. The protection that the mountains provided allowed the colonists to gain control of the region and build up resources and population which, in turn, set up the right conditions for westward expansion.

This is where distance begins to tie in to the US history. As the colonies began to develop their own ideas about government, freedom, and self sufficiency, they realized that they didn't need the British overseeing them anymore.

During a little thing called the American Revolution, though the British had superior firepower and numbers, the distance was still too great to effectively fight a prolonged war. Distance helped win the war, and also kept foreign powers at bay while the fledgling country strengthened itself in the early years.

No other country in the history of the world has had such a large amount of growth continuously sustained for 200 years than the United States. This place has gone steadily upwards since its inception.

From that point forward, 200 years ago, the United States grew westward, as did Canada, adding more resources, more water, more fields to grow more food, more coal, more oil, more gold, expanding all the way to the west

The east coast womb.

coast of the continent. The US and Canada had essentially 100 years of continuous physical and economic growth; gaining more stuff, more resources, more land. It was manifest destiny at its best, and mo' money, mo' money, mo' money. Running out of land or opportunity in Virginia? Then move to Indiana or Saskatchewan and then on to California or the Yukon!

Did this mean economic expansion stopped? No way, dude! It just took a new direction. In the late 1800s, early 1900s, the American Industrial Revolution began to kick off. Luckily, the Americans had witnessed a similar revolution in Britain almost a hundred years earlier, when they were the top dog.

The Americans took all the best things from the European industrial revolution, and eliminated all the worst. While Europe was very destructive during theirs, the Americans were able to avoid a lot of the pitfalls, and

"You all have little girly economies."

By the way, a Plaid Avenger note: if you broke off California from the rest of the continental US and made it its own sovereign state, it would have the 8th largest economy on the entire planet. Also, Gov. Arnold Schwarzenegger himself would be the 18th largest landmass.

go straight for the goods. The US shifted from an *agricultural* based economy to an *industrial* one. After the land and resource grabs, they exploded industrially.

In the 1960s and 1970s, there was another change. When other countries also began to industrialize, they could produce things cheaper than the US, due primarily to their lower labor costs. Things like automobile, textile, and steel production shifted to developing countries. Was this the end of American economic expansion? Are you kidding me? The US once again shifted gears and changed to a *service sector economy* with an emphasis on *technology*. You know: computers and what not. Nowadays, the next wave of transformation has the US as a leader of the *information age* . . . in which the economic focus is on manipulation and creation of computer programs and new medical breakthroughs and patenting DNA codes. Instead of making cars and textiles, the US now produces information as one of its key resources. This region is truly the first to undergo this technological transformation.

Long story short: 200 years of growth in various ways, either increasing land or resources, then increasing to an industrial capacity, and then increasing into the service sector, and now transforming the world as the leader of the technological and information age. Of course, you have the Great Depression in there, we don't want to forget that little tidbit; that was a real blemish on a basically 200 year perfect record of economic growth. Even now, here at the outset of the 21st century, the North American region has the biggest total GDP on the planet, with no close second. If money talks, then this region has a lot to say.

BIRTHPLACE OF IDEAS; TECHNOLOGY TITAN

Why is the North American region the greatest and richest region on Earth? It has do with what we just talked about: this is a birthplace of ideas. The North American region is the place that came up with things like the telephone, the computer, and the Internet (sadly, not actually invented by Al Gore). This region has the freedom to do

The Boilermaker

1 shot Kentucky bourbon

1 cold beer

This is an old-school drink that is awesome for stumping bartenders—because it's so damn easy. It also demonstrates a great economic point about the US. The drink is named for blue-collar workers who would order a shot and a beer after their shift. Blue-collar as in steel, textile, and automobile production workers. Also: boilermakers. Why don't young bartenders know the drink? Because secondary economic activities have largely disappeared from the US; thus, boilers are made elsewhere. Most of those jobs are gone, and the culture surrounding them disappeared as well. I always order the Boilermaker to honor those manufacturing sector folks that made this country great.

USA GDP =

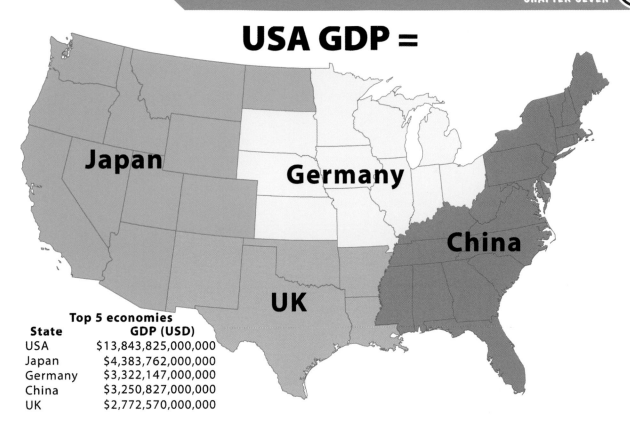

Japan
Germany
China
UK

Top 5 economies	
State	**GDP (USD)**
USA	$13,843,825,000,000
Japan	$4,383,762,000,000
Germany	$3,322,147,000,000
China	$3,250,827,000,000
UK	$2,772,570,000,000

lots of things and grow industrially and technologically, and it comes up with all kinds of new crazy great stuff. This region has the highest levels of technology because it is always on the forefront of innovation. Japan makes cool stuff cooler, and China is growing fast, and India is becoming a software hub, but North America is still the top dog when it comes to the forefronts of science, engineering, and computer innovation. However, the competition is getting tougher.

Since World War II, the United States has been not only an industrial leader but on the forefront of science and technology in all capacities: the Internet, the computer, the telephone, the microwave, nuclear bombs. Put a damn man on the moon? You betcha! This region did it. That is one of the things that makes the US really rich. People come from around the world to invest here, go to school here, and they do all these things because this is the place to do it. Also, it has the highest levels of technology across the board in fields such as science, math, computers, military and nuclear capabilities, right on up to the upcoming space race. The US, because it is a technology leader, is still the only country that has made it to the moon. It will be joined soon by China, but that's for another chapter.

BIG REGION; SMALL POP

The North American region actually has a fairly small population given its size; this equates to a very high GDP per capita. Both of these countries are fully industrialized and developed, and there's not that many people here. This may be argued by folks in the United States right this second who have problems with immigration: "We've got too many people here! Wah wah wah!" Whatevs.

The original—and equally unsuccessful—anti-immigration faction. Not pictured: Lou Dobbs.

There's around 310 million people in the United States, while Canada has about 30 million; it's the biggest population that they have ever had in its history. About 340 million people total live in two of the biggest countries on Earth. There's a lot of space in this place and not really that many people in it, relatively speaking. There's tremendous room for growth. Even if growth does not occur, you're looking at tons of resources and a huge economy, both in the US and Canada, that's divided up amongst not that many folks on the global stage. If you're looking out at China, they've got a billion and a half people. India is working on 1.2 billion people; Sub-Saharan Africa has three-quarters of a billion, and even rich-ass Europe has over half a billion residents. The North American region? Ha! A fraction of that, especially given the space.

In conclusion: lots of space, lots of room, and lots of stuff per person makes the North American region fairly well off. The United States has the biggest GDP total on the planet. Canada is in the top ten as well; both countries have some of the highest GDP's per capitas, and that's not likely to change anytime soon. Yes, China and India are growing fast, but neither will ever have the amount of richness per person that the United States and Canada enjoy right this second, if ever.

+THE STRONGEST

We just talked about why North America is the richest. Now let's talk about why it's the strongest.

MILITARY POWERHOUSE

The North Americans are the best and the strongest when it comes to military stuff. You can talk about whether you like the US or not, you can talk about whether you agree with its policies or not, but that's of no consequence to the Plaid Avenger. I'm just trying to explain why this is one of

Team America on patrol.

the richest regions on the globe, or the greatest region on the globe. Militarily speaking, you cannot dispute that the US has the strongest single military power on the planet. This is not by size, by the way. We all know size matters, but in this case, the US does not have the largest standing military, meaning troops on the ground. China holds the top slot with 2.5 million people in their military. The United States and Canada don't need to have the largest amount of people in the military because—technologically speaking, of course—we all know they are the best.

The North American region has the most weapons per capita on the planet. We're not just talking about handguns. We're talking about shotguns, right on up to intercontinental ballistic missiles, tanks, and warships. The United States has the most aircraft carriers on the planet and this is a very real projection of power. Militarily speaking, no country can compete with the United States, not even Russia, their old Cold War adversary. In terms of military spending, no one else is even in the US ballpark. Yearly military expenditures for the US now top half a trillion dollars. Wow. That's ten times what China spends, and roughly half the world total. There is no contest when it comes to who's the strongest or most technologically advanced military on the planet. That's the North American region, particularly the United States.

PROJECTION OF POWER ABROAD

WOPR asks: Shall we play a game?

However, it's not just numbers and budgets. It's also about the ability for the Americans to project this power abroad. This is what makes them the strongest. Aircraft carriers are a great item to consider. With an aircraft carrier, you can push your power to all points on the globe, and this is what the United States is perhaps better at than anyone on the planet right this second and perhaps even throughout history. Sure, the British had their fleet that did a pretty damn good job, and the Spaniards had their Armada before that, but that was centuries ago. The United States has the technological capacity to annihilate so many more humans than the British did that no comparison can really be made. With a carrier, you can essentially "move" your country anywhere in the world on the water to set up an island to launch a strike. That is some serious global power. Fun fact: the US has 12 aircraft carriers—more than the rest of the planet combined!

Country	Military Expenditures 2008 (USD)
United States	$583,283,000,000
European Union Total	$311,920,000,000
France	$74,690,470,000
United Kingdom	$68,911,000,000
China	$59,000,000,000
Germany	$45,930,000,000
Japan	$41,750,000,000
Russia	$40,000,000,000
Italy	$32,600,000,000
Saudi Arabia	$31,050,000,000
South Korea	$28,940,000,000
India	$26,500,000,000
World Total	$1,200,000,000,000

The American region is the absolute best at moving troops, people, guns, and missiles anywhere on the planet. That is real ultimate power. One need look no further than current conflicts in which the American region is involved in Afghanistan and Iraq, which are on the other side of the planet from the region.

The aircraft carrier: Carrying war straight to your door!

If you start to look at American military stationed abroad, it's mind boggling. The US has active troops, dudes and dudettes with guns, in about fifty countries. That's astounding if you think about it. That you would have military people stationed all over the planet, even in countries where there is not an active conflict, is quite amazing and a real projection of power. This region is certainly the most powerful when you consider the current active conflicts and military deployments, and consider that the United States is a natural leader of NATO (re-read chapter 6 if you forgot about NATO). The Plaid

Maverick! Goose! Take to the skies!

Avenger argues that NATO is easily the most successful defensive organization of all time. I stand by that claim, and the United States is at the core of it.

The United States has the most intercontinental ballistic and nuclear missiles. As I suggested earlier, the US is the only country that has landed men on the moon. I won't say the US dominates space, but it has the strongest presence in space. Also, factor in the fact that the US is a big proponent of some sort of anti-missile defense shield, which will certainly, if it ever comes to fruition, make the United States even more powerful. Think back to the Ronald Reagan era when he wanted to put lasers in space to shoot down other countries' missiles. This is a real projection of how great the US is to even consider such a plan and then to put resources toward actually making it happen. I keep harping on space because that is the next frontier; the US is promising to build a moon base and perhaps a missile defense shield in space, and lots of other things in space as well. That just takes tremendous resources, and you've got to be great to pull off those kind of things.

By the way: I keep talking about the United States, but Canada is right beside the US in every single conflict in which it has been involved. All of them. Therefore, we can logically speak of this as a singular North American venture.

MULTINATIONAL CORPORATIONS

Think about North American corporations in the world, both US and Canadian. These are some of the biggest, richest entities on the planet. I'm speaking of multinational corporations which operate globally. Every multinational corporation needs to have a home base somewhere, for many, this base is North America. Of the top 2000 largest corporations on the planet right now, over one-third call North America home (that is down from over half a decade ago). Exxon, Wal-Mart, General Motors: these are some of the richest entities on the planet, and with that wealth comes power. These folks have a lot of power to do the things they want to do in other parts of the world.

Consider an entity like Exxon. Sure, it's just a company, not a government, and it doesn't have political power like the US. Well . . . yes and no. Exxon makes a quadrillion dollars a year; if it wants to look for oil in Namibia, it is going to get what it wants, regardless of Namibian opinion. Let's face it, the company makes ten million times more money than the country of Namibia; with that money

2008 TOP SALES OF MULTINATIONAL COMPANIES

Company	Home Base	Sales (USD)
Wal-Mart Stores	USA	378.00 billion
ExxonMobil	USA	358.60 billion
Royal Dutch Shell	Netherlands	355.78 billion
BP	UK	281.03 billion
Chevron	USA	203.97 billion
Toyota Motor	Japan	203.80 billion
Total	France	199.74 billion
ING Group	Netherlands	197.93 billion
General Motors	USA	181.12 billion
General Electric	USA	172.74 billion
Ford Motor	USA	172.46 billion
ConocoPhillips	USA	171.50 billion
Citigroup	USA	159.23 billion

From Special Report: The World's Biggest Companies, edited by Scott DeCarlo 04.02.08, Forbes.com comes tremendous weight to throw around. Whether through open economic pressure or illegal backroom bribery of officials, huge corporations can get their way.

Some of these North American companies are the biggest and the richest in the world, and many are getting richer and more powerful by the day. At this writing, Exxon just captured a world record by earning the highest profits in a single economic quarter ever—thank $150 a barrel for oil for that one! Folks are starting to openly debate whether or not multinational corporations are stronger than governments. The answer: of course! Uber-rich corporations are stronger and more powerful than small countries and weak governments. There's no doubt about that, and it's a situation that's likely to increase in the future. To restate: a lot of those companies are US or Canadian in origin. But let's shift to another topic, and the final subsection of why this region is the greatest.

+THE FREE-EST

OLD MAN DEMOCRACY

Both the United States and Canada are two of the oldest democracies on the planet. This is an entire region that prides itself in a somewhat egalitarian light; everybody is equal regardless of race, sex, creed, religion, or anything else, and everyone has an equal voice. That is one of the cornerstones of this entire region. They are the free-est. There are other countries around the world that are democracies, but the North American ones have been around the longest and have been the most successful for the longest stretch. In fact, these countries, mostly the US—sorry Canada, I have to poke a little fun at you—were so determined about democracy that they had a little revolution and kicked the Europeans out. They said: "Hey, Europeans, that's cool, we're glad you came here and set up shop for us, sent us some immigrants, set up some industries, but you guys can all go home now because you're not being fair enough to us."

Maybe you've heard of it: the American Revolution. Why am I making fun of the Canadians? They kissed some British monarchy ass for quite a bit longer, like another hundred or so years, before they threw off the yoke of the Common-

wealth. Even during their Queen-kiss-up years, Canada was pretty much into the democracy thing. To restate, North America is the home of two of the oldest, strongest, longest lasting democracies on the planet.

In fact, these guys have really set the trend for everyone else. You can look at Europe and say that they are also rich, developed democracies with a long track record. Yeah, that's true, dudes. But starting when? Was it before the American Revolution or after? That's right—it was after. The American experience was kind of the impetus for the French Revolution. The French Revolution then begat other revolutions across Europe, which eventually led to all of them becoming something closer to democracy. If you look at it as a chain of events, the Americans started things up. George Washington, Thomas Jefferson and Benjamin Franklin kick so much ass. Nice job, guys!

Teabagging, American Revolution style.

FOCUS ON INDIVIDUAL LIBERTIES

A focus on individual liberties is also a cornerstone of this region from its inception. This is something quite distinct from democracy itself. Democracy is a ruling system in which the people have a say in who's ruling them. On top of that, civil rights and individual liberties are extremely important to this region. Maybe this is confusing to you, but I just want to point this out: there are other democracies in the world, pseudo-democracies or real democracies, where they don't have this focus on individual liberties as much.

Places like Egypt or other parliamentary systems in the Middle East are sort of a democracy. They vote, they elect people, but there is nothing in their constitution that says that they believe every single person is exactly equal, and that

"We come for individual freedoms—and native babes."

the state is there to protect their individual rights. Look at Iran, which has a semi-democracy. People vote; in fact, their voter turn-out shames most US election participation. They do elect many of their leaders, but they definitely don't have the focus on individual liberties. The government still controls ultimately what people can read or say, and even the way they can dress. Perhaps making comparisons to Iran or Egypt is too extreme, because they aren't developed and rich like the US. Okay, how about Singapore or Russia? Both countries are rich and developed, but done so at the expense of individual liberties. They are tightly controlled democracies where too much individual expression may be detrimental to your business.

Only in the North American region do they say first and foremost, "We have a democracy, but it's based on individuals having liberties." By the way, if you think about how the United States came to be, it's because people were fleeing from places that weren't giving them true liberty. Those Pilgrim cats who went to Plymouth Rock were fleeing religious persecution back in Europe. They wanted more freedoms to individually do their own thing here in North America. That's how the thirteen original colonies started, and quite frankly, it's still going on today. People flock from around the world to head to the North American region because they know when they get there, they have individual liberties to live the way they want. This is not the case across the entire planet, even in established democracies.

I'm not suggesting all these liberties have been there since the beginning. Freedom of thought, religion, and speech were there early on. More recently, civil rights and liberties regarding race and sex were fought for and won by activists and concerned citizens. And the US not only sets the world standard for freedoms, but continues to be on the front lines of battles over civil liberties and rights: look at the fight for gay rights or the rights of an unborn child for examples of how passionate this region gets about individual liberty.

The reason this is because the North Americans, quite frankly, don't give a damn. Wait, what?

PERSONALLY THEY DON'T GIVE A DAMN

This region doesn't give a damn about you individually. That sounds a little backwards. What does this mean exactly? We can make fun of North America for being a region of imperial power, of gun-loving nuts, and of isolationism. But if you get there—when you are actually in house—it's really freakin' cool. North Americans just generally don't give a damn who you are or where you are from on a personal basis. They are laid back. Do what you like! It's cool. Just don't ruin any of my stuff. This is a phenomenally great component of North American society.

If you look around the planet at the history of human society around the world, we have a pretty consistent record of kicking the living daylights out of each other. Why do we do this? It has a lot to do with intolerance of differences between people. Sometimes we kill each other over resources or land or whatever. However, conflict mostly arises between people of different religions, ethnicities, races, or nationalities—and sometimes it escalates to some pretty nasty business. Think of the atrocities of Nazi Germany or the Rwandan genocide or the implosion of Yugoslavia. The list goes on and on.

This is a common theme across the planet, except in North America. By no means are all Americans sitting around eating s'mores and singing "Kumbayah" together. Of course, there are people here who don't like other people, but this is at nearly the absolute minimum in the history of the world. Americans don't care where you're from, what color you are,

Britney Spears: a symbol of a tolerant America. We even give K-Fed a pass!

how smart or stupid you are, what god you pray to, or even what you do with your leisure time. Quite frankly, American tolerance toward their fellow man may be the best example the rest of the world should follow.

In real life in America, not caring equates to everyone being pretty much equal. Some people call it a meritocracy, meaning you only advance by doing good stuff—by earning your way. Your position in society is not, or isn't supposed to be, based on your religion or skin color; they don't have organized ethnic or religious clashes. Many people from around the world emigrate to this region to escape those very issues.

Let me elaborate on why I'm saying this is a positive thing. In most other parts of the planet—and this is today's world, not historically—people don't have the luxury of not giving a damn, meaning that there is serious ethnic, religious, and racial strife all around the world. If you are in the minority, practice a religion that's not fashionable, or are from the wrong ethnicity, you may not have equal rights at all. Even if the country pretends you do, you may be discriminated against on a daily basis. You might be thrown out of the country or you could be caught up in ethnic genocide or civil war or religious persecution, which happens all the time across the planet.

That doesn't happen in North America because individuals are doing their own thing. They don't give a damn about the guy sitting next to them on the bus. They just don't, and that's a very powerful thing. I can't stress it enough: it's one of the reasons why folks from around the world say, "Damn. If I could just make it to North America, then I truly am free. Nobody cares that I'm from a Hmong ethnicity. Nobody cares that I'm a Zoroastrian. Nobody cares if I tattoo my face, dye my hair blue, and watch Pauly Shore movies. I can do what I want to when I get to those shores." By and large, that is true and that is one of its real benefits. It is one of the free-est places on the planet. Okay, maybe they should pass a law against Pauly Shore movies, but for now it is still protected behavior.

PLATFORM FOR SUCCESS

What this sets up, essentially, is that the North American region is a kind of platform for success. People know that once they make it to North America, all other factors are equal. You work hard, you pay your dues, you put your nose to the grindstone, then you can be successful. No, the streets aren't paved with gold in North America, as the old saying goes. They are paved with opportunity, because immigrants don't have to worry about things that they'd have to worry about in their home countries. The North American region is a real platform for success. That sets up a situation in the world known as **brain drain**.

What's the Deal with Brain Drain?

Any person given a free plane ticket from their Third World country to any other destination in the world will most likely choose the North American region.

The type of people that actually make it here are smart, educated people with options. Also, wealthy people who want to become wealthier figure out ways to come to the North American region.

This is actually a problem, because the elites of other societies are leaving their native regions to emigrate to wealthy regions in order to become successful. There are all sorts of political, religious, and economic reasons to flee native lands and set up shop in North America. When the political problems arise, people leave. When people are afraid of losing their assets or afraid of religious persecution, they will go to a place that accepts them and allows them to continue growing. For a hundred years, the destination of choice has been the United States.

Brain Drain has been a fantastically successful concept in the development of North America. Whenever bad things happens around the globe, the US and Canada stand to gain.

Political crackdown in Iran? Economic meltdown in Thailand? Religious persecution in Sudan? North America gains in refugee and immigrant populations.

For example, after World War II, the Russians took half of Germany's rocket scientists and America got the other half. That's why both the US and Russia started space programs. Brilliant inventors come here, and they use the US as a platform for success. There are other great platforms, but the US has been a very important one for the last 100 years.

This has a lot to do with immigration. People want to come here to express themselves. It has become a self-perpetuating cycle; the US is so rich and doing so well that people all over the globe want to come here with their ideas. People want to start businesses with the highest probability for success—and that is in the US. Success breeds success, and more people want to come. American success is a strong magnet in the world. Rich and poor alike have a strong attraction to the North American region for all of its opportunities. It's an extremely competitive place, but it does seem to work for the vast majority of its inhabitants. Poverty numbers are very low; opportunities exist for even the most destitute.

If you live in an impoverished society, one with no welfare program or unemployment benefits, you cannot take risks. New things come about by taking risks, and environments like that do not enable people to take risks. America will take care of you if you or your idea fails. You can afford to work hard, save money, start your own business. No wonder people think the streets are paved with gold—golden opportunities, am I right?

Another great thing about this region is its **hypermobility**. The size of the region allowed for the interstate system, developed by US President Dwight Eisenhower, whereas other countries that are smaller rely more heavily on public

We Like Ike! What's the Deal with the Interstate System?

The formal name of the United States interstate system is the "Dwight D. Eisenhower National System of Interstate and Defense Highways." The US interstate system was created by the Federal-Aid Highway Act of 1956, which, as the name suggests, was championed by Eisenhower. The US interstate system was built for both civilian and military purposes. Some of you might be thinking, "Yeah! One in every five miles of road must be straight so that military aircraft can land and take off on them!" Well, maybe. The true military aspects of the interstate system are primarily to facilitate troop movement and to allow for the evacuation of major cities in the event of nuclear war.

The civilian aspects of the Interstate Highway System have helped shape American culture in more ways than we can possibly imagine. Most US interstates pass through the center of cities, which allows people to live outside the city and commute in for work, which has also played a huge role in the creation of suburbs and urban sprawl. The highway system also gives the federal government power over state governments. The US government can withhold interstate highway funds, which are huge amounts of money, from uncooperative state governments. The US government used this tactic to increase the national drinking age to 21 and to lower the blood alcohol level for intoxication to 0.08%. According to the Constitution, both of these issues should be decided by states. However, if they choose to disobey, they don't get their highway money.

Also, the US highway system allows high speed transportation of consumer products. This makes the prices of everything, from bananas to concrete, cheaper. The result: the US is an automobile culture heavily reliant on fossil fuels for the movement of everything and for virtually all aspects of our lives. Americans are quite unique in this respect. It's also why they are the best stock car racers in the world. Who else has NASCAR? Who is more worried that the price of oil is reaching $150 a barrel?

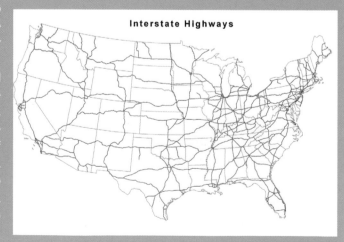

Interstate Highways

transportation. People can go anywhere and do anything, anytime they want. They even have four-wheel drive vehicles to take them places where roads are nonexistent.

Mobility allows people to take advantage of opportunity and expands individual choice. Any job, any opportunity, any time, any place. Not all folks in other countries have this convenience. There is an exactly proportional relationship between mobility and choice. The more mobile you are, the more choices you have; as a result, the US is more successful.

Living in the North American region furnishes infinite choices and provides opportunity to take risks; this is unprecedented anywhere else on the planet. If you have a great idea and you could have any choice of where to cast the dice to really make it work for you, it's a no-brainer for you to come to North America. It just makes sense. The odds are stacked in your favor. Not true in Europe for immigrants, not true in Asia or Africa as a whole—but particularly true in North America.

CORE OF TEAM WEST

To wrap up this free-est section, all of these factors put together are what make the North American region the true core of what I will refer to as Team West. This is a concept we'll come back to later in the book. North America, along with Europe and Australia, form a common block of ideology that sets them apart from other cultures in the world. You know what? Let's throw Japan in there as well. Even though they're way out in the east, they more closely follow the western tradition.

What are the identifiable traits of this team? As exemplified by North America, Team West has a basis in the western civilization tradition that values democracy in their governments, a focus on individual rights in their societies, and are strident free-market capitalists when it comes to their economies. This team consists of regions and states that are fully developed, largely rich, technologically superior, and focused on service sector and information age types of employment. Other attributes include rampant materialism, an obsession with pop culture, and unproportional power and leverage over the rest of the globe—but those are more negative attributes.

How appropriate, because it's time to get negative on the team leader right about now!

THE WORST PART OF BEING THE GREATEST

We're going to shift gears and see the underbelly of the greatest region on Earth. I've told you about how awesome the North American region is and why it's the greatest and the leader in terms of richness and power and free-ness. Now let's take a look at why it's perhaps not so great. What's the worst part of being the greatest region? It's an easy schemata, because we're just going to follow the same outline we did before. We'll start with number one.

-THE RICHEST

Wait a minute! I thought I just said that being rich was great? Everybody thinks being rich is great, but the bad side of being the richest region on the planet is that US and Canadian policies, of course, favor their own companies.

UNSPORTSMANLIKE CORPORATE CONDUCT

In other words, they take care of their own. Why wouldn't they? Every country has its own interest as the number one priority . . . that is completely natural. US foreign policy is no exception: be it intervention into another country or manipulating the World Trade Organization or some sort of other pressures on other countries in order to help their own multinational corporations succeed. It happens. I'm not making fun of anyone, but I'm trying to get you to understand why other folks around the world may have discontent about American power. All regions have self-interest, but being the richest most powerful region means you can achieve those self-interests better than anyone else can! The cards are stacked in your favor!

The United States and Canada have some of the biggest, richest multinational corporations in the world. Simultaneously, the US and Canada are two of the richest countries in the world. Therefore, it's almost a set of unprecedented power players that have really never occurred before—that the richest country can help out the richest multinational corporation.

This gives those corporations quite a bit of leverage and power in the world. Power to do what? Well, most free-marketers would say to do what business does: go out and acquire resources, produce products, and sell those products. That's true, but they also have a lot of power to screw with other people or governments, if they so choose. They have the power to ignore other countries' environmental regulations or to bend the rules to favor themselves as frequently as possible. There is no way that a local company in a less-developed country could possibly compete with a Wal-Mart or an Exxon; these big boys can pretty much take what they want, when they want it.

This does present a problem. It is a situation where there is a fairly lopsided trade balance around the world where multinational corporations have the power to take a lot more from poor countries and give a lot less back. It's just simply the way it is. It's not good. It's not bad. In my book, that's just the way it is. US and Canadian policy favors their corporations, which are already excessively rich. This helps them perhaps take advantage of other countries. Also, the North American's global policy typically ignores the rest of the globe to maintain its own richness. Let me put in a disclaimer: every country does that. China certainly is going to try to favor Chinese policy. The French look out for France. But the North Americans are so powerful and so rich that, here in the dawn of the 21st century, their attitudes toward the globe are now looked upon with some animosity by others on the planet.

SELECTIVE SELF-SERVING SELF-RIGHTEOUSNESS

Let me give you some examples, and there are many to choose from. The idea of free trade may be the most blaring example of North America not practicing what it preaches. The US and Canada are fervent supporters of this concept, which essentially equates to trade based on the unrestricted international exchange of goods. This means no tariffs (taxes) should be levied on other countries' goods that are coming into your country, and no helping out industries within your country to make their goods more competitive than imported goods. North America regularly touts, praises, and leads the charge for free trade to the rest of the planet. In particular, the US wants a free trade area for the entire Western Hemisphere (FTAA, see Chapter 13) and it pushes hard to beat down the countries of Latin America to support the idea. Also, the US is the unrivaled leader in bringing up lawsuits against other countries at the WTO for infractions of the world trade rules.

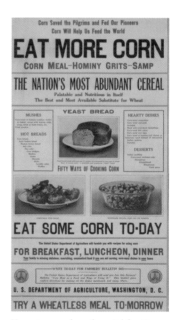

Your taxes already paid for it, so eat it, just eat it!

But get this—the US and Canada regularly cheat on free trade all the time! Both countries support agricultural subsidies for their farmers, which essentially equates to paying farmers money every year in order to make them more profitable. Farmers can then charge less money for the food they produce, making it cheaper than food imports from Africa or Asia. Both countries also fairly regularly slap tariffs on imported steel or textiles in order to kiss the ass of political lobby groups and voting constituencies at home, especially in election years.

Another example of this selective support on issues: US policy on global warming. Sure, it's changing now, but it took a long time for the US to come around. For around two decades, most of the other countries on the planet have been saying, "Hey! This warming is a global thing, part of a global commons, and we need to look after the globe by all working together to reduce carbon dioxide emissions." The US and Canada have basically been very frank by saying, "No, we're not doing a damn thing. We refuse to do anything because it's going to hurt our companies. It's going to hurt our richness. We don't want to change our consumption patterns. We don't want to change how much money we have, and therefore, we don't give a damn about reducing CO_2 emissions. The rest of y'all can go do whatever you want. We're going to keep doing our own thing."

It's also important to point out that the North American region is the highest user of world resources per capita. People in the US and Canada use more oil, more food, more plastic, more everything per person than any other folks on the planet. Whatever! It's a free market economy and people can do whatever they want, right? But other folks on the planet, and there are quite a few of them, kind of look at this and say, "Dudes. You guys are really selfish. You use the most, but you don't want to help out with any global problems." Being the richest has come at some cost, mostly at a cost to the reputation of the region, which is increasingly not seen as a real world leader on world issues.

-THE STRONGEST

What's wrong with being the strongest? Somebody's got to be the strongest, right? When it comes to North America, and I'll mostly pick on the United States right here, there is a perceived or real threat of US imperialism by many folks across the planet. That is, as I suggested earlier, the US is the undisputed, strongest country on the planet; because of this, people think, "Damn. They are unstoppable!" The US is so powerful, it appears that it could do anything it wanted. You know what? Quite frankly, that's true. If the US wants to bomb Uzbekistan tomorrow, it has the capacity to do it, and current events have shown that sometimes it does.

It is a very real consideration that people around the world say, "The US scares me. They have absolute power. Nobody could stop them if they want to do something." That is true. Who would stop them? Russia? China? The UN? Give me a break! The UN . . . that's a good one.

We need look no further than the current Iraq war. Most folks around the world said, "Hey! We think it's a bad idea." Most countries of the UN said, "No, we're not going along with that. We're not doing it." The US said, "Well, we're doing it anyway." Again, I'm not making fun of them, I'm not trashing the Iraq war or the Bush administration. I'm just saying, think about the perceived light of imperialism that most folks around the world now view the United States bathed in. It does cause more than a bit of consternation and concern for both enemies and friends of North America alike.

DOESN'T PLAY WELL WITH OTHERS

The current Iraq war is worthy of further consideration for a moment more. This story gets at a larger point . . .

There is a particular disdain of the United Nations by the US. Let me put it more bluntly: the US as a whole totally hates the UN. Why? Because the US is so powerful and resourceful on its own, that the only thing the UN does for it is to get in the way of US objectives. Does that make sense? The US has a certain opinion about things in the world, and it wants to act on its opinion to fulfill its own self-interests. Many in America would argue that indeed this is exactly the job of their government: to look out after their own self-interests, the rest of the world be damned. Since the US *can* do anything it wants, it *should* do anything it wants to benefit itself. Following this train of thought, what exactly is the point of asking the UN for permission, advice, or for any damn thing else?

You almost can't blame it either. The US did save Western Europe's butt from Hitler without asking permission from anybody. Other folks don't like this unchecked influence, even if it is supposed to be for good. This is something that people in the US just don't get. They don't get it because they see themselves as good: "We are the good guys! We help people! We helped the French and Brits in World War II! We saved the Koreans and Kuwaitis and Kurds! We have always helped to defeat bad guys around the planet!"

By and large, that is true. The US seems to be fighting the good fight, but that's not always the perception around the world, particularly in this day and age. Back in World War II, everybody understood that the Germans were the bad guys, and recognized the US as fighting the good fight. In the current War on Terror, however, the enemies and objectives are not so well-defined. This unchecked ability of the United States to make judgment calls on all these issues bothers many people.

Another example involves nukes. Even though the Cold War is now over, and the US is busy fighting terrorism and not communism, the United States still maintains the **nuclear hit list option**. What is that? During the Cold War, all of the countries that had nuclear capabilities had lists of who they would blow up first. Number one on the US list was Russia, then maybe China because they are dirty communists, then maybe France just for good measure, etc. All countries with nuclear capabilities had these lists during the Cold War.

US Nuclear Hit List still in play.

Recently, most countries have said, "Now that the Cold War is over, we'll get rid of the hit list and start to disarm our nuclear warheads. We're not going to point them at anybody." All the countries got together, particularly Russia, and said, "Hey, let's all do this! It'll be a good thing!" The United States said, in essence, "You guys are so cute! You should do that! Thanks guys, but we are going to hang on to our nuclear hit list option."

At a time when many states want to ratchet down the nuclear issue, the US stands alone in its opinion. That has increasingly been the case for the last two decades. The US maintains its hit list, is not a full player in UN procedures, and openly refuses to sign treaties that the vast majority of countries in the world support. Things like the Law of the Sea Convention, which defines territorial rights of the ocean, or the Kyoto Protocol to reduce greenhouse gases, even legislation banning the production of land-mines. In all of these circumstances and many more, the US stands virtually alone in its non-participation.

Is the Plaid Avenger trying to indoctrinate you into thinking the US is bad, or too powerful, or too pompous? Not at all. I'm trying to educate you on perhaps why the US has a bit of a bad rap on the world stage right now. Sometimes standing alone is a sign of strength; sometimes it is a sign of selfish stubbornness. You have to decide for yourself, as will the rest of the world.

POWERFUL POWER PROJECTIONS

The overwhelming strength of North America has also brought a sense of helplessness and outright fear to some parts of the globe. Specifically, the US has a basically open, identifiable, and (some folks would say) scary projection of real power as evidenced by the active wars in Iraq and Afghanistan. These active wars are possible, and proceed rapidly, because of the active US military presence around the globe. Whether for good or bad, it's not a judgment call here; there are North Americans with guns all over the planet.

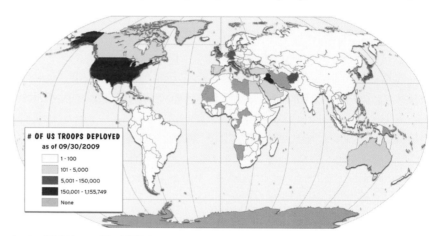

Active US Military World Wide

More often than not, you see US soldiers more than you see any other country's soldiers. You can see UN soldiers, NATO soldiers, and EU soldiers sometimes, but those are groups, associations of countries, not single countries like the US. US soldiers are the only ones from a specific country that you can find all over the planet. This military presence is perceived as unchecked strategic military power. In a very real sense, you can't find Chinese soldiers in Iraq, or Afghanistan, or in the United States. Can you even conceive of having foreign soldiers on US soil? The thought is almost comical. Other countries accept that there are US troops around the world, on foreign soil in Europe, Asia, South America, just about everywhere. It is a reality elsewhere, but inconceivable in North America.

There are no other countries that have that type of real power evidenced around the entire planet, not just the active wars, but in deployment of troops. Factor in the largest nuclear arsenal on the planet, the most sophisticated and largest air force, and more aircraft carriers than the rest of the world combined, and you have the basis for other countries soiling themselves at the thought of US intervention.

CULTURAL IMPERIALISM

Finally, under the strongest category is something that you probably have never thought of before critically: cultural imperialism. With no doubt, North America is the most successful, if you can call it that, at this thing called cultural imperialism. Whether the US and Canada are true imperial powers is debatable. However, it isn't really up for debate that the culture of the US is the most successful thing being spread around the planet. What am I talking about here?

We just discussed power-driven imperialism, including an actual military presence, so what is this cultural imperialism thing? Imperialism usually means that people step in with guns and take over saying, "We are an imperial power; your stuff is now ours." Think about Darth Vader and the imperial storm troopers. They are taking over and ruling by force.

However, cultural imperialism is much more subtle. There are no guns, there is no iron-fisted dark lord, and there are no storm troopers. Cultural imperialism simply means that people begin adopting your culture. Think about pop culture. This is the one that most often springs to mind. People around the world from France to South Korea to Australia to South Africa like watching crappy American movies, listening to crappy American pop songs, and watching ridiculously crappy TV shows like *American Idol*. Think about the title: it's *American* Idol and it's watched and *idolized* by people all over the planet! How crazy is that?

The secret weapon of American imperialism: cheerleaders!

Cultural imperialism is much more subtle, because nobody has a gun to anybody's head telling them to do this or that. For some strange reason, people just like it. There have been millions of movies made in America that have been exported to every other country on the planet, so many of which you'll never see because they suck so bad that nobody in this country will watch them—but people in other countries will, just because they're American. People are attracted to that successful vibrant American pop culture. You can go to Tibet and watch *Titanic*, you can go to Russia and listen to Run DMC (sorry, the Plaid Avenger's old school), or you can go to Burma and see an episode of *Baywatch*.

A lot of countries in today's world are passing laws to try to limit the amount of American pop culture that enters their countries. France is a good example, because every few years they attempt to ban the importation of American-made films. It never lasts long, but they try. Middle Eastern countries try to keep all that American pop music and porn out. Even China tries to tightly control Internet action so that none of those American democratic-human-rights-and-freedoms ideas can seep into their culture, which brings us to another point to consider. Pop culture is the main component of cultural imperialism that you know of, but here's one that is much more intriguing to the Plaid Avenger.

America's fifth column: Team Ocean.

Cultural imperialism from an *ideological* standpoint is much more important to acknowledge, especially considering how world events are going down right this second. I'm talking about the ideologies of capitalism and democracy being spread. As you know from current events, unless you have been living under a rock, the United States has an active military presence in Iraq and Afghanistan and perhaps will occupy some other places in the very near future. They don't necessarily import Britney Spears at the end of a gun, but what is happening is that they are heavily influencing the societies to become like the US in terms of adopting democracy, individual liberties, and capitalist culture.

The capitalist part is not that difficult, since every country makes money in some way or another on capitalism. However, some people in the world tend to have a problem with the democracy part. These are ideas Uncle Sam pushes across the planet quite openly. The US says, "Hey! We're going into Iraq because we want a democracy here. We're going to help them have a democracy. We're going to manipulate or push or try our best to get other countries to embrace capitalism because it benefits us and we think it benefits the world. We're going to try to get everyone to do it." Indeed, the US and Canada in most of their endeavors say, "Yes, and we believe that all people are equal and that we think individual rights and civil liberties should be the norm across the planet."

You're not gonna stand there and let Lady Liberty take it, are you? Of course not!

This is not something up for dispute. You can see this every day when the US government says, "Hey! We think China has horrific human rights abuses and we're going to complain about it at the UN." The US may complain about the Chinese treatment of the Tibetans and say that their human rights suck. That is essentially saying, "We believe that our system is right and yours is wrong," and that's something to consider.

Let the Plaid Avenger go on record as stating that I uphold the idea of democracy in the world and think human rights are the most basic necessity for every human being on Earth. I'm a bit biased since I'm from this region. I have this ideal myself. However, not everyone in the world does, and I'm willing to recognize that. I may not accept it, but I at least recognize that another point of view exists.

The US planting seeds of democracy in the Middle East is of great consequence in today's world. It's the reason that your tax dollars are going to support troops who will continue to prop up governments and establish democracies in places that have no history or background in such cultural phenomena. Lots of people in the Middle East and other places in the world have no experience with democracy and don't necessarily want it. They do, however, feel as if the world power, i.e. the United States, may be pushing them toward it.

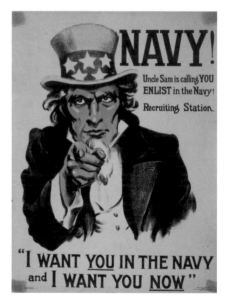

Now you know where the Village People got the idea for "In the Navy."

I don't think it's an exaggeration to describe it that way, and I think that's a fair assessment. It's up to you as American and world citizens to decide if that's kosher. However, I just want you to understand that democracy is a major part of your culture that you accept as right and good and proper. Other people in other places may not share that sentiment. Food for thought.

-THE FREE-EST

What would be the worst part about being the free-est? The first thing I want to point out is the freedom to be clueless. North Americans as a whole, and we do have to pick on the Americans more than the Canadians in this respect, are completely clueless about what's going on in the world.

FREE TO BE CLUELESS

Most Americans have no idea where Tibet even is on a map, much less what human rights abuses are happening there. It is part of the North American society in that yes, they're semi-isolated. They're far away from other regions; therefore, they're not as heavily impacted, even in this global interconnected world. North Americans focus on their own thing. I won't call them isolationists, but they have a tendency to focus on themselves at the cost of simply just not caring about the rest of the world.

To sum this up: internationally, they don't give a damn.

It seems bizarre for the Plaid Avenger to say because this entire chapter so far has been spent explaining how the US is a central key player, deeply involved in the world's political and economic systems. But by and large, American citizens don't give a damn about other countries. Many around the world would say that American politicians, whose job it is to care about foreign affairs, don't give a damn either.

As the Plaid Avenger has traveled around the planet and talked to lots of people everywhere, a common theme reveals itself: many people perceive America as an unchecked power, and around the world people feel that America doesn't care about them. Perhaps they are too small or not enough like the United States, or they have no economic resources that the United States cares about, and so their perception is that the United States doesn't care about them. Perhaps they're right.

In this interconnected and globalized world where everyone knows everything all the time, citizens of the United States, by and large, know the least about what's going on in the world. If that's a radical statement to you, then stop looking at Facebook and open your eyes.

If people in Sudan can get to the Internet, they know everything that's happening in the world and they pay attention to what's happening in global movements of ideas and people. Of course, they especially know the details of the relationship between the US and Sudan, and what the UN Security Council is doing about Sudan. If you ask anyone in the United States, they won't have an utter clue. Sudan? Security Council? Huh? Is *American Idol* on yet?

That bothers a lot of people around the world. They say, "Wow, this is the richest group of people who have the most influence on the entire planet, and they don't give a damn because they don't know. How could they not care enough to know, for instance, that this genocide is going on?" Isolation is a dual edged sword. We say the US is great because it has been isolated, but at the same time, that allows its people to be lazy. The general US population does not know what's going on, and that really burns people's

I have no joke here, I just like saying, "Get your hoe ready!"

asses around the planet simply because citizens of the United States have so much power individually. They could easily change some things if they wanted, but they don't because either they don't know and/or they don't care.

EXPORTER OF FREENESS . . . BY FORCE

As I suggested just above, this region is also a huge exporter of democracy and capitalism and individual civil liberties and rights or at least the concepts of them. That sounds like a pretty good deal, and the Plaid Avenger is all about individual liberties and justice, so I'm all for it. Let's get this game on! Mostly, the North American region exports these themes in its literature, ideas, technology, and pop culture. However, we can't overlook the fact that sometimes these good ideas—democracy, capitalism, and individual rights—are also exported by force if necessary. That can be a little problematic.

Sure, it's awesome that you want people to have a democracy, but perhaps not so awesome that you go there and kill them in order to make them one. Current events are playing out right now to determine how successful forced democracy is going to work out in the Middle East, and it doesn't look too good so far for the forces of freedom. In terms of freedom, can it be forced upon a society? Can it be given, or can it only be earned? We shall see, unfortunately, at the expense of many lives.

North America is the free-est, with lofty and admirable goals for others, but being blinded by ambition has led to a big fat negative for North America. Which leads us to the next theme . . .

HUBRIS AND HYPOCRISY

For some of you reading this book, don't bother writing letters saying that the Plaid Avenger is some blatant tree-hugging bunny kissing liberal wannabe commie who's just making fun of the US. I'm not, okay? I'm trying to get you to understand what what's going on here!

It is problematic around the globe right this second that the United States and Canada say, "Hey! We're all about democracy. We're all about individuals. We're egalitarian. We think democracy is great." They do. I truly believe that. However, when you have things like the Abu Ghraib prison scandal in Iraq, as well as increasing civilian death counts there, and then you have people being held in Guantanamo Bay without individual rights forever, you start to get a bad rap. The world, not the Plaid Avenger, is looking upon this and saying, "Wait a minute. You guys are talking this mean game about equality and democracy, but you're not even doing it yourselves." Given current events, in the modern context in the 21st century, there's a bit of a problem with being the free-est when you're not living up to it.

Well, maybe not in the Middle East . . .

FREENESS ENVY

Finally, there might be something going on that I like to call "freeness envy." Oh, man, am I good or what? Freeness Envy . . . ha! And that is something that other cultures don't necessarily dig. Freeness in the United States/Canadian definition. What am I talking about here? The North America region is all about the freeness, man. Equality, democracy, freedom of speech, religion, choice, peace, love, dirty hippies, whatever. It's all about equal rights. Everybody's equal. Everybody's cool. Yeah, man, pass the greenery Snoop Dogg . . . . oops, I digress . . .

However, don't assume that the rest of the world holds these ideals as highly as the North Americans do. Let me give you some examples. The Saudi Arabian government and most of the Saudi Arabian population is not necessarily in favor of equal rights for women. The idea that women are completely equal in all aspects doesn't really play there. Let's go with something else like gay people. You know, in North America, everybody's equal, but that doesn't play in Africa, man. In Sub-Saharan Africa, and parts of the Caribbean, gays are persecuted heavily; most folks in those societies would say, "No. We are not about those people being as free as we are." You can go around the world and look at different societies—and this is the people I'm talking about here, not just the governments—and lots of folks would say, "No, we're not about that type of freedom." China isn't really into freedom of the press. Countries in the Caribbean aren't really into gay rights. The Vatican isn't really into freedom of choice. The Middle East may not be really into sexual equality or freedom to draw cartoons.

Freeness envy may be happening around the globe. The Plaid Avenger is all about individual liberties, so I am a big proponent of it. But when I go into other cultures, I don't assume that everybody around the entire planet wants democracy. Well, I think they should have it, but that doesn't mean they all want it. I think that all women should be equal, because in the Plaid Avenger's world, all women are equal in my eyes, but I don't assume that all cultures necessarily accept that, either. You have to keep this in context. Freeness Envy, huh? Great term.

UNCLE SAM WRAP-UP

Let's wrap this thing up. We've looked at the good side of the greatness of North America. We've looked at the negative side of the greatness of North America. Uncle Sam is really a bipolar fellow here lately. Sammy, my man, has a real Jekyll and Hyde complex going down.

You know Dr. Sammy Jekyll, the good doctor. He's out there doing good, fighting the good fight, standing up for the impoverished, the people who don't have democracy or with no rights. Yes, Uncle Sam does quite a bit; even though he's taken a bad rap in today's world, the United States and Canada continue to be the biggest foreign aid donors, the biggest funders of the UN, and also do a hell of a lot for the planet. Even though they're sometimes a bit heavy handed about it, they think they're doing it for good reasons. Who's to dispute that?

There is of course, the seedier Mr. Hyde that comes out every now and again. Sometimes this region does bad things abroad in the world, even when supposedly done for a good cause. However, there are other times that this region is quite openly selfish in terms of looking after its own interests. Since it's the most powerful region, it can do it in the most aggressive manner across the globe. Again, no judgement call here, that's just the way it is. The US and Canada are going to look out for their own corporate and economic interests. If that means telling people to kiss their ass on the Kyoto Protocol, then that's what they're going to do. That's typically, what they've done.

Nice Uncle Sammy always picking up the ladies . . .

Dude, you are scaring me.

The bigger issue to think about: we are in the midst of big changes in the world power structure that will most greatly affect the North American region more than any other. Why? Because the United States has been used to being the sole superpower for twenty or thirty years now. Ever since the Soviet Union went away, and the US won the Cold War, the North American region has been uncontested for power on the planet. It has the most political, military, and economic power, as I pointed out earlier.

But times are a-changing, Sammy: China and India are on the rise, the EU has tightened up as a unit, Russia is back and bolder than ever, and other international players like Iran, Team Arab, and the Latin Leftists are all making regional impacts on the balance of power as well. The planet is morphing into a multi-polar world, a place with more than one superpower. This isn't up for debate, nor a future prediction—this is happening now. The world of the future is a place where the US is not the only primary actor making global decisions. The question then becomes, how is Sammy going to deal with this new world, this up-and-coming, changing world right now in the 21st century?

Will Sammy go lightly into this world? Will he see the changes that are coming and work with other big powers and other big countries to get the job done and still push his own agenda? Or is it going to be more of a rougher road, where the United States has a tough time giving up its top slot and is perhaps bound and determined to have its way at all costs? This could result in potential conflict, war, stonewalling economically or in other ways, or becoming isolationist and just putting up a big wall and looking inward to try to focus on itself only.

That is the big question, the $20,000 question to which no one has the answer yet. But this is a region of greatness and the US/Canadian team is not going to go away anytime soon, meaning it's going to maintain its powerful position as a major player in planetary affairs for some time to come. But will it be a bigger force for good or more of an internally-looking isolationist state? Only time will tell.

As the insightful Uncle Ben once told Peter Parker, "With great power comes great responsibility." Good advice for Spiderman, and probably for North America as well.

What next, Sammy?

BARACK ATTACK: THE OBAMIFICATION OF THE NATION!

I would be remiss without adding in at least a paragraph of pontification about the current US administration. Obviously, President Obama must have perused these plaid pages before inauguration, because a definite foreign policy shift had occurred, and I mean shift like at the plate-tectonic-scale.

This is a book about the whole world, so I won't dally with dreary domestic decisions, but I do want you to be very aware of the major swing in diplomatic style. Team Obama is out and about in the world re-casting US ties in a much more embracing and engaging manner.

By that, I mean there is a lot more talking and asking as opposed to demanding and invading, both to their allies and their enemies. They want to reset relations with Russia, chill out with China, and even engage world Islam in a much bigger way than ever before. Be it pulling out forces from Iraq, possibly re-establishing a dialogue with Iran, and even ending the 60-year-old Cuban embargo, this Obamification of foreign policy approach is fascinating to say the least, and will certainly initiate some changes in attitudes of the US. For better . . . or worse.

"Hold on, General, let's talk to them before we drop the bombs . . ."

That's right. It won't always work, and I don't own it so I'm not trying to sell it to you. . . . I just want you to be down with this debate as we try to deduce the impacts of this daring new diplomacy. Some people think that engaging in discussions with adversaries is a welcome approach. Others think it is a sign of weakness and a waste of time. What do you think?

NORTH AMERICAN RUNDOWN & RESOURCES

View additional Plaid Avenger resources for this region at http://plaid.at/na

 BIG PLUSES

- → Biggest economy in the world
- → Most powerful military in the world
- → Leader of technological innovation in most fields
- → Leader of democracy and human rights promotion worldwide
- → One of the most solid infrastructures in the world
- → Great educational system, decent social safety nets
- → High standards of living, high degree of personal freedoms
- → Multi-cultural, multi-ethnic, multi-religious region where everybody pretty much gets along
- → Politically stable, solid rule of law

BIG PROBLEMS

- → Overzealous focus on materialism has made region the biggest consumer of everything on the planet and a giant polluter
- → Overzealous focus on materialism has made region's citizens fattest on planet and increasingly disillusioned
- → Economic, political, and foreign policies typically focus solely on short-term solutions
- → Two-party system has become entrenched, unresponsive, corrupt and grid-locked; citizen apathy is reaching all-time high
- → Has a tendency towards over-doing it on the global stage, or alternatively intense isolationism
- → Chronic dependence on fossil fuels and illegal narcotics imported from other regions; you decide which one of those is worse

DEAD DUDES OF NOTE:

George Washington: Father of the US, first US President, dollar-bill guy, refused to be appointed King in favor of establishing the democracy, warned against two-party system.

John A Macdonald: Father of Canada, first Prime Minister, Canadian ten-dollar bill guy, helped forge the 2nd largest nation on the planet, thus ensuring it wouldn't be absorbed by the US.

Ronald Reagan: Commie-hater extraordinaire; claimed by some to have single-handedly won the entire Cold War. A demi-god to the conservative right.

PLAID CINEMA SELECTION:

Atanarjuat aka *Fast Runner* (2001) The first feature film to be written directed and featuring only actors using the language Inuktitut, used by the Canadian Inuit population. Excellent look at some of the indigenous people of Canada from their perspective rather than that of outsiders. And assuredly, it is the only film you can see a naked man running across icebergs and insane Arctic landscapes for over two hours.

Bon Cop, Bad Cop (2006) Archetypal buddy cop film which pairs two policemen from Quebec and Ontario who are nothing alike. Film shows great contrast of real cultural differences between these two provinces as well as examples of both Francophone and Anglophone humor. Second highest grossing Canadian film behind *Porky's*.

The Corporation (2003) Full-on documentary only for those serious about understanding how the business world works. Be forewarned: it does not paint a pretty pro-corporate picture, but is a worthwhile watch even for the future board members among you. While corporations are not an exclusive American phenomenon, this film pieces together their rise in the modern world, which has been extremely US-influenced and defined.

Roger & Me (1989) You've heard all the hype about the ultra-liberal Michael Moore, but so few have actually ever checked out his first, and easily best, docu-drama. Like him or hate him, this film is an excellent look at a by-gone era of American manufacturing culture, and will help you understand why the US car market crashed and burned, and also how the "Rust-Belt" formed in the now abounded post-industrial northeastern US.

Smoke Signals (1998) Atypical buddy/road-trip movie that features great insight into current Native American reservation culture, with fantastic diverse biome shots of western and northwestern US.

Super Size Me (2004) Documentary/comedy on eating patterns of Americans, and the real-life consequences when the nastiness is pushed too far. Features an attempt at an all-fast food diet!

LIVE LEADERS YOU SHOULD KNOW:

Barack Obama: US President— yeah, the head honcho of the world's sole superpower.

Stephen Harper: Canadian Prime Minister—huge US ally and head honcho of that other country just north of the US.

Hillary Clinton: US Secretary of State—top US diplomat who has to deal with all that international relations stuff.

Robert Gates: US Secretary of Defense—after all, he does control the largest war machine on the planet.

CHAPTER OUTLINE

Western Europe

8

WORLD MAKER, SHAKER, AND BREAKER

What the heck's that supposed to mean? Well just this—while the United States and the North American region in general may enjoy prominent status in today's world, it's Western Europe that really has shaped the current cultural, social, economic, and political world in which we live today. They've been at it for about 500 years longer than the US, and have been a tremendous impact worldwide in determining what's happening right now.

Let's face it—English is an international language not because of America, but because of the British, and their influence. Soccer is the world sport, not American football, for the same reasons. When we look at today's world, Western Europe may not be the world leader anymore, but it certainly was the maker and shaker. What about the breaker?

Well as you know, Western Europeans spent a lotta time in the last thousand years, and particularly the last hundred, beating the living crap out of each other. WWI, WWII. . . need I say more?! But today's world is very much different for Western Europe for it is united as never before—making, and shaking, without breaking, in the 21st century. Let's get to it!

WHO IS IN THE REGION . . . AND WHY?

Everybody knows and understands that Western Europe is a region. It is the western side of the Eurasian landmass. But being a Plaid Avenger world region is not solely based on just the physical geography, so what is it that makes this a homogenous region? We need to back up before we ask that question and ask who, what, and where is this region? What states? All the western European states? Which ones are those? All those cool ones that we take vacations to visit. Places like Norway, Sweden, Iceland, UK, Ireland, Germany, Belgium, Luxembourg, Switzerland, Austria, France, Spain, Portugal, Italy, Greece. Oh, wait, and Greece . . . Greece? But it's on the eastern side of Europe!

Look at the map here on the opposing page. All of those that are connected somehow are all Western Europe, but Greece is disconnected; it's over on the side by itself. Indeed, I think all of us would say, "Yes of course. That is definitely part of Western Europe." That gets at the heart of what it is to be Western Europe, of what it is to be in this region, and the homogeneous traits therein.

What characteristics do these countries share that categorize them as a region? What could possibly be the same about all of these countries?

What we have is a set of extremely distinct nation states. In fact, all of these countries are exceptionally different from one another. When we look back at the US and Canada, we said they share a common culture and language and background. When we get over to Western Europe, we have Spain; with Spanish people who speak their own language that is much warmer in the winter and a little cooler in the summer than other places at equal latitudes. As we move into the continent towards Eastern Europe and Russia, we are going to see the places at the same latitudes get quite a bit colder. Western Europe is pretty moderate. What's so great about that? As we saw in America, a well-watered, moderate climate is conducive to human settlement and population growth. While a few thousand years ago nobody was hanging out in Western Europe, in the last couple thousand it has become increasingly populated, and has become one of the cores of population on the planet because, physically speaking, the situation is right.

PLAID AVENGER'S HISTORY OF WESTERN EUROPE

We don't need to waste too much time talking about European history, as you have probably already had a thousand classes on it in during your scholastic career, but the Plaid Avenger can summarize the last couple thousand years for you very quickly. The big pluses: the agricultural revolution (they learn to produce a lot of food), the age of colonization (they learn to take over the world and get a lot of stuff) and the industrial revolution (they learn to invent machines to make a lot more stuff). Put it all together, and it's a rich region.

It should be noted for the record that the transformation of this region into the dominant world leader is really only a product of the last 500 years. Yes, I know the Greek and Roman Empires were really hip in their day . . . but they were also very local . . . and then they went away and Europe was completely ass-backward until the Renaissance. The region was NOT a global leader, and it was NOT a global force, prior to 1500AD. Other civilizations around the globe made Western Europe look like a backwater of buffoons. And it was.

But then those Europeans got savvy after their Dark Ages. They learned about sailing and navigation and shipbuilding from Muslim traders. They learned about the global trade network from Asian merchants. They learned about gunpowder from the Chinese. The Europeans took all this information and applied it in new and exciting ways which subsequently made them masters of the seas, masters of the global economy, and especially masters of military. China made fireworks with their gunpowder. Europeans made guns. You can figure out the rest from there.

If these guys were taking over the world by storm, then what were the negatives? In a word: competition. All these different ethnic groups, religious groups, and different nationalistic groups have spent a whole lot of time in the last couple centuries beating the living hell out of each other. You have probably heard of war after war after war that you had to memorize in high school; all of them occurred on European soil. The last couple of biggies were the World Wars of the 20th century, but there were hundreds of other confrontations before those.

Virtually all of these contests were based on competition between these European states for more power, money and influence on both the European and the world stage. The states of this region, as a whole, have spent a good deal of their time figuring out how to out-maneuver, out-flank, and generally beat up their nation-state neighbors. Why is that? How did it get to be this way? How has it radically changed in the last 50 years? These are the important questions that you need to consider. The whole concept of a nation-state was formed in Western Europe. How did this concept form here if they have spent all this time fighting?

There are groups of people identifying themselves as distinct cultures, like the French, the Italians, the Swiss. Those terms mean something to us. It means something to them as well. The idea that you would have a distinct group of people and that you would outline a political area in which you reside is a Western European phenomenon, just like all the "-isms" and philosophies we talked about. Unique, competitive cultures sitting side-by-side in the little chessboard of Europe. Yep. That's how conflict started.

I should also reiterate that there are people who begat people who begat people to make Western Europe one of the most populous regions on the planet, especially in the last 500 years. People are all over Europe. The coastlines and river sys-

Land and latitude comparison: US and Europe.

tems are packed to the point that Europe as a whole is about half the size of the United States with about twice the population. We talked about the North American region having tons of space that fostered the evolution of the automobile, interstate system, suburbs, and individual transport systems; Europe is the reverse. You don't have all that space. You have double the population in half the space. We can see the physical manifestation of this with public transportation. People use trains and buses; not everybody owns vehicles there. It's quite a different society just from the standpoint of land and how little of it there is.

I said something about colonies a second ago, which has everything to do with everything. You already know from the Plaid Avenger History that the North American region is the number one region in terms of military, economy, wealth, and all that stuff. But that only came about in the last 100 years. Who used to be there? Western Europe did, and they had their day in the sun for a good 500 years. From Columbus right on down until about World War I, Western European countries had the tiger by the tail and controlled most of the world.

What does the Plaid Avenger mean by "controlled most of the world?" You mean like cultural imperialism from the United States? No. I mean *direct imperial control*. Because of the physical geography we talked about, Western Europe was full of maritime nations, and because of the certain situation at that time in their history, they started going out and exploring the world. Their technology increased and surpassed the technology available in other places on the planet. Thus, their exploration potential increased.

These guys, at the exact right time in history, went out and bumped into the New World. They took over all the New World and colonized it. They said, "Hey, look! North America! That's ours! South America! We'll take that too! Divvy that up between Spain and Portugal! North America? We'll divvy that up between the French and the British!" That's not all. Throughout the last 500 years, a tiny handful of states from Western Europe controlled the rest of the planet.

As you can see from the graphic to the right, eight nations—UK, Germany, France, Spain, Portugal, Italy, Netherlands, and Belgium—controlled all the countries in pink. This is a massive territorial holding. Again, the Plaid Avenger is trying to get you to understand how it is that Western Europe has some of the richest countries in the world right now. Look at this chart again. For 500 years, these guys siphoned the material wealth off the rest of the planet.

Let's think about a place like the Netherlands. There isn't anything there, my friends. It's flat. They grow tulips! How are they, of all countries, one of the richest in the

Western European Imperialism
- Colonizing countries of Western Europe
- Past and present colonies and other territories of Western European Countries

Colonial masters of disaster!

world? You have to understand this much about history: it's because they controlled massive territorial holdings, many of which were exclusively economically exploited colonies. The Dutch just siphoned off wealth.

Think about the Spanish Armada, which controlled all of South America, Mexico, Central America, and the Caribbean. They brought back gold and silver bouillon . . . the booty! It was all there in the New World, my friends. What did the Spaniards do with it? Did they dig it up in Mexico and redistribute to the natives? Hell no! They took everything of value and brought it back to Western Europe. All of it. Meanwhile, the British were busy bringing back all the tobacco they could smoke up, as much cotton as they could weave into fabric, and as much rum as they could pull out of the Caribbean and disperse to their sailors.

All of this stuff occurred to the benefit of these Western European countries. This is not the case with Eastern Europe. You do not see Eastern European or Russian colonies in the world. There is a small enclave in Western Europe of material wealth, which controlled the rest of the planet. This is significant to note, to learn, to learn, to love. It has been largely overlooked in textbooks, for whatever reason. All of the world's wealth went floating back to a small group of countries. That may sound pretty negative. Maybe it is. I think if I were somewhere in sub-Saharan Africa and had been a colonial holding for the last 500 years, which left me and my people poor while those countries are rich as Midas, I might be a little bitter. Fortunately, the Plaid Avenger grew up in the United States, where we kicked those Brits out before they exploited us for too long. The United States is in a much different situation than many other ex-colonies in the world.

Let's not beat up our European brothers anymore right now. Let's think about some of their other impacts on the world. What are the other things to consider when we look at the Western European region that had such a tremendous influence on the planet? What's the number 1 sport in India? Cricket. Brazil? Soccer. What language do they speak in Pakistan? What language do they speak in Chile? What religion do they follow in Mexico? What are the religious practices in the Philippines? What types of government do all the countries of the world follow? What are the major philosophies that most people in Africa ascribe to? These questions all have answers of Western European origin.

All the types of government in place across the globe, many modes of thought, major religions, major languages were all spread throughout the world via the conquests of Western Europe. People in Brazil speak Portuguese because it used to be a colony of Portugal. A lot of people in India speak English because the British used to colonize those dudes. All sorts of little things, including dietary habits, holidays, and particularly the world's sports that people love for unknown reasons, have their origins in Western Europe.

Why are significant portions of the populations of North America, South America, and Australia white? In addition to the movement of ideas and culture, you also have the mass movement of peoples. You have English and French and German and Italian and Irish and Scottish enclaves all over the damn planet. As a result of this movement, nearly all of European thought and culture is accepted as part of today's world culture all over the globe. You need to know the good and the bad. Why is Western Europe rich? It has something to do with them exploiting the rest of the world. Why can you communicate using English all over the world? Same reason.

If you are a pilot that flies between countries, you must speak English. It's an international standard. Why? It's not because America is so great, but because Western Europe, Britain in particular, has had so much influence on the planet over the last 500 years. America was just the heir to the throne of global power and influence that was created by the period of Western European colonial imperialism.

This colonial period is really the most important in European history, probably in world history. It led to the amalgamation of wealth that essentially made Western Europe the rulers of the world. We can debate whether the United States is an imperial power, but there's no debate about Western Europe. They were a hegemonic imperial power that controlled the entire known world and amassed incredible wealth from it. They don't have that position anymore, of course. The US has that top slot. What are some of the reasons for this? They lost their colonial holdings and ran out of land. They cannot continually expand as the United States has done over the last 200 years. They don't have any more resources because they have been using those resources for generations upon generations. Europe is like a geriatric version of the US. It ran out of its room to grow and is a young buck no longer.

THE BEGINNING OF THE END: THE 20th CENTURY

That's enough history to set the stage. Western Europe is not number one today. Why is that? It is still very rich. It still has a lot of influence in the world, though what we are seeing in the 21st century is that European power is actually on the decline. How did it go from top banana to just another in the bunch? Europeans may not like to hear the Plaid Avenger say that, but it's true. They are slipping. They have a very unique solution on how to stop that slip, by the way, and we'll discuss that in the last part of this chapter. But back to the slip . . . wait a minute. Banana . . . slip. Am I good or what? But I digress . . .

As we already pointed out, they were on top of the world for quite a while, but the 20th century was unkind to not only Western Europe, but Europe as a whole. Just as America was exploding onto the world scene, Europe decided to beat the living hell out of itself for 50 years solid—and did a good job of it. These nation-states with their independent cultures and separate identities smashed themselves not once, but twice, in World Wars I and II. The Cold War settled in after that, and that didn't help matters at all. The same 100 years that Europe was destroying itself, it was losing its colonial holdings. They had already lost America long ago, but in the 19th and 20th centuries, they lost all the rest. Canada went away, South America went away, a lot of Africa went away, Australia went away. And the few colonies that they retained to the bitter end were giving the Europeans nothing but a headache too: India for the British, French Indochina for the French, the Middle East for everybody. These places broke out into independence wars, civil disobedience, and catastrophe in general. So little by little, as we approach the modern era, the Europeans lost these territories that, for a long time, gave them their wealth accumulation and serious competitive edge.

As the Plaid Avenger suggested already, America has continuously expanded economically because of its incredible amount of resources and territory. You have that with the Western European powers as well, but this reversed in the last 100 years. They lost all their territory. They lost the unfettered access to the resources of those places as well. This reversal of fortunes happened at the same time they battled each other in wars, destroying their entire infrastructure. Make no bones about it: World War II was the most destructive thing that could have happened to any region as a whole. There was total devastation across the entire continent. Factories, roads, and bridges were entirely wiped out. Again, this plays back into why America is so great, because none of this happened in America.

Massive WWII destruction in Europe.

So, the first half of the 20th century was not kind to Europe. It lost colonies and destroyed themselves to the point of collapse. At the end of this destruction, people woke up and realized they needed to do something different. They couldn't continue to beat each other up. Some very wise people figured out that Western Europe couldn't compete on the world stage. These thinkers dreamt up a new way to get back into the game. What they thought up was something entirely new.

THE EU

THE RISE OF THE EU

The EU is the salvation of Western Europe and the only real reason it is still a global player, period. What do I mean by that? Well, after the destruction of World War II, some smart dudes—incredibly, they were French—said, "We've got to stop killing each other. We need to economically integrate ourselves so that we are not competing with each other anymore."

They thought that part of the problem was that the Germans hated the French and the French hated the British and the British hated everybody because they were in competition with each other. And they were right. The Western Europeans were once the masters of the universe, but those days are gone. To continue to compete with each other, just within the continent, was disastrous, as they already found out. So they said, "We should work together, we can all get a little bit richer if we all try and work together better. Let's start rebuilding from WWII by pooling our coal and steel industries."

That's how the EU started. Everybody needed coal and steel to rebuild stuff, and all of Western Europe had to be rebuilt. The smart guys who thought this up knew it would evolve into something else. They said, "We'll do this as a start, and it will tie us to each other so much that we won't be able to afford to attack each other. If we make this into a common industry, Germany won't be able to attack France, because it would be hurting its own economic needs." You can't beat up the people you're actively trading with because you will lose their trade. It was an interdependence that they formed in the coal and steel industries, but they wanted to make it something else. They wanted it to reach farther.

This is where we have the real rise of supranationalism in Europe following WWII. The EU grew and it said, "Well, let's not stop here; let's continue to make things more and more solid as every day passes so we can't compete anymore. We are so far behind now; we are so wiped out. America is totally whipping our butt, and we lost our colonies. How can we effectively compete on the world stage?" The answer was to expand the coal and steel thing into a free trade zone thing—a free trade block.

What does this have to do with world trade? Can Belgium compete with the United States' economy? No. Can Italy? No. How about Ireland? Not a chance—they are all too busy drinking Guinness. How about Germany, the number three economy on the planet, can they

What's the Deal with . . . Coal and Steel?
In 1951, six European countries—France, Belgium, West Germany, Italy, the Netherlands, and Luxembourg—signed the Treaty of Paris establishing the European Coal and Steel Community (ECSC). The ECSC created a common market, free of trade barriers, for steel and coal. These two commodities were especially important, because both were key resources for industrialization and rebuilding after WWII. Trading coal and steel freely was the first move to quell European power rivalries by establishing this economic unity and interdependence. The ECSC is often credited with creating a community between former World War II enemies. In fact, the European Union can directly trace it roots to the ECSC. The ECSC member countries soon after established the European Economic Community, which was renamed the European Community; this became the first, and most important, "pillar" of the European Union in 1992.

compete? Nope. Bidding on a contract or trying to make some sort of international tie or trade tie with another country, the United States will win every time. These countries got together and said, "Wait a minute! What if we all act under a common umbrella? Can all of our countries together as a unit effectively compete against the United States?" Yes, and they can compete with lots of other trade blocks around the world as well.

The EU evolved into a **trade block,** and, as you read about in chapter 6, trade blocks are all about decreasing tariffs and taxes between states to encourage trade. The French said, "Hey, Germany, we won't tax your sausages if you don't tax our wine!" They all agreed not to tax each other's stuff and therefore, people were able to afford to buy more of it. People bought more, people sold more. Mo' money. Once that got going and they got back on their feet during the last 50 years, the EU expanded into something that the world has never seen. That's why I am going to spend the rest of this chapter just talking about what's so cool about the EU.

WHAT'S SO COOL ABOUT THE EU?

Why is it of such great significance? Thanks to the EU, Europe is turning from a bunch of nation-states that competed with each other for a thousand years into the **United States of Europe.** What does that mean? The independent sovereign nation-states of Europe are becoming much more like substates of the United States than independent countries, in terms of free movement of peoples and elimination of borders. Borders are still there, but they don't really mean anything. If you walked in a straight line across Europe twenty years ago, you would get your passport checked twenty different times according to how many countries you crossed.

That policy is largely disappearing. In fact, the number one thing for you to remember about what's different from the EU and all other trade blocks, or even supranationalist organizations around the planet, is the *free movement of peoples.* Nowhere else on the planet do you have a coalition of countries in which the people in your country can move anywhere within all the countries of the club without having their passport checked. This free movement of people is a big, big deal. A 2009 note: This free movement of people is being seriously re-evaluated right now, especially for the most recent EU inductees, but it is still a critical and revolutionary idea within a trade block.

Compare this to NAFTA, the free trade union between the US, Canada, and Mexico. Do we have a free movement of people? No! You can go back and forth between Canada and the US and they will check your passport, but you can't just do anything you want. Can you move back and forth from Mexico to the United States? Oh, no way! The US has a huge wall that it is, in fact, trying to make bigger. The unique factor about the EU is free movement of people. Because of this

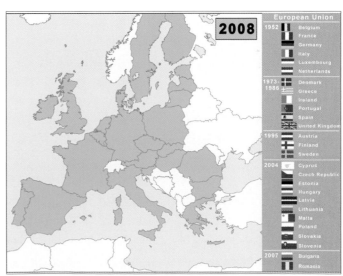

fact, they have to have a common law system as well. They are building a common judicial system, and a common legislative system. Thus, the EU is becoming a United States of Europe.

Before I go any further, does everybody in Europe think this is the most awesome idea ever, with everybody standing around the campfire singing Kumbaya? Oh, no. Political leaders think a United States of Europe would be totally sweet, particularly leaders whose countries participated in the wars. Businesses and a lot of other people like the idea. However, not everybody does, and the reason for the animosity lies in that cultural imperialism thing that we talked about in the last chapter.

What does that have to do with the EU? People in Italy are Italians and they have their Italian heritage. A lot of the French are fiercely defensive of French culture. Those Brits will defend the Queen and teatime with their lives. Because EU dudes are nation-states with independent cultures, there are lots of folks within them that see the EU as a threat to the survival of their culture. Sometimes you'll see a McDonalds restaurant being set on fire in protest of the EU. You can interpret any sort of anti-conglomeration or anti-homogenization attack on a multinational organization as a protest against the EU. The anti-EU opposition is losing the battle, but they are there. They will tell you, "This EU thing sucks! I don't want to be in the United States of Europe! I want to be Italian!" . . . or Swiss, or whatever nationality they are.

The EU is definitely continuing despite the small amount of dissent, but where's it going? Well, it's got a common defense system, which is a huge stride. Each country, for the most part, has its own little army, but the EU also has a common defense army. You can hear about the EU forces being sent into places like Yugoslavia, or EU forces being requested in Iraq. The idea of a unified army for these countries is a massive change in a region that has spent a thousand years beating itself up. They now have a common defense force, which pretty much eliminates the possibility of any future conflict. You can't fight wars with each other if you have the same army.

POWER STRUGGLES & POWER STRUCTURE OF EUROPE

The EU is growing because most member countries think that for their organization to compete better on the world stage, their numbers need to be higher. Those members think the EU should become bigger. The bigger the club, the more world power it has, and the more power they have as individual countries. That is the common perception in the EU, so they are expanding into Eastern Europe. This means places like Poland, the Czech Republic, and Latvia are now in the EU. Places as far east as Ukraine may be members of the EU soon. This block is expanding eastward, unifying Europe more than it's ever been.

This has set up some internal power struggles within the EU. There is something the Plaid Avenger calls **Europe's Continental Divide of Power.** These internal struggles for power within the EU have a lot to do with how the system is set up. It's a lot like the United States in that there is a legislature, a judiciary system, and something similar to a House of Representatives in which each nation-state has a say according to the size of its population. The EU also has something like a Senate, in which each nation-state has a single representative. We can obvi-

> Here in the Plaid Avenger's book, we have been talking about Western Europe and Eastern Europe in separate chapters, but in another five or ten years there may be no difference; it may just be Europe. We will save the remaining differences for the next chapter, but for now, we will leave it at that.

ously tell who has the power by looking at populations. Who's got the power? Big surprise: France and Germany. They're the big power players in population and economics within Europe, so they have much more say in what the EU does. A lot of smaller states within the EU say, "Hey wait a minute, we are not getting as much of a voice! This is unfair! We don't like this! I'm Liechtenstein! Hear me roar!"

While the French and the Germans have battled each other throughout history, they are actually a team now. And what a team! It's the **Franco-German Alliance,** if you want to have some really cool terminology to throw around at dinner parties. These guys are also on the continent, so I call them **the continentals.** Germany is the number three economy on the planet, and France is number six. This makes them a huge power core of the EU. These two states, while they have historically agreed on nothing, pretty much agree on everything nowadays. They are big pro-EU states quite frankly because they are power players in it. A lot of the EU's smaller states complain that if France and Germany don't like a proposal or idea, then it's not going to happen. There is definitely some truth in that. If France and Germany are against an idea, it can get stymied easily. This causes a true power divide between big states and small states.

The EU's number two power core is the UK. Perhaps you never thought of the UK this way, but it is kind of distinct from the rest of Europe. "Say what? Plaid Avenger, I thought you just said the UK was *part* of Western Europe?" It is physically; it's there off the coast of the Eurasian continent, and all of its history is European history. However, the British have, for quite some time, been elitist. Snobbish. Tea-sippers, with the pinky in the air. Remember the old British blue-blooded aristocracy—the same ones who still think the Queen is the bomb. A bit of snobbery remains, and the British have seen themselves as distinct from the rest of Europe proper throughout history.

As I said before, the British were the predecessors to American power on the planet. They were on the world throne for a very long time, but not anymore. Here's a Plaid Avenger interpretation: the attitude of the British is that they are still number one. They would still very much like to be the singular world power. If you *can't* be the world power, what should you do? *Hang out* with the world power! If you're not the biggest kid on the block, *hang out* with the biggest kid on the block and make him your buddy. So the British actually have much more in common with, and are much more eager to hang out with the United States in world politics than they are with the Franco-German alliance on their own continent, in their own trade block.

Big states and small states argue over constitutional power structures and representation. The older EU states argue with the newest EU states over immigration policies. And the Franco-German axis may argue with the British over economic and foreign policy. But the times are a'changin' on this front as well, which brings us to . . .

TODAY'S EU

Western Europe's going through some fairly radical changes here in the dawn of the 21st century. The first that's already been alluded to, and that's the EU. It's regeneration. It's the butterfly coming out of the chrysalis as a brand new creature that is really flying high in more ways than one. Let's elaborate a bit more on the EU in today's world, because it really has become the face of Western Europe and Europe as a whole, led by Western Europe, though.

The EU, if taken as a singular entity, is the largest economy on the planet. It has the largest GDP. Yes, indeed, a Gross Domestic Product bigger than that of even the United States. Now again, that's putting all the member countries of the EU together into a single block, but that's of course, what they are. And although it perhaps started as trade, perhaps morphed a little bit into politics, it is something entirely new on the world landscape, and it's becoming more powerful every day.

What's so new? What am I talking about here? Well, the EU has been working hard to frame a constitution for itself, an endeavor which has not met with ultimate success—so far. But it's quite important to consider, if for nothing else, that when it does get passed eventually, and it will, it's going to dawn an entire new age for Europe. It really will lay the foundations of Europe being the United States of Europe, a different beast altogether than anything that has come before in continental Europe. And they're doing a whole lot of things to cement this idea that this is a very different beast.

A constitution, and also a unified judicial system, which is becoming stronger every day. They have unified, singular environmental policies. They've already unified their monetary system. The borders between the original EU states are fairly solvent, meaning you can move around within them—free movement of people. We've already talked about that. With the introduction of lots of new states in Eastern Europe, from Eastern Europe, the free movement of people is changing a bit, but we'll get to that in just a second.

The thing I want to finish on, relating to the EU and its future in the world, is that it also has a common defense. This appears to be growing rapidly here very recently, as well. They want to have a defense structure—essentially an army—an EU army, that behaves and acts independently of the United States and even of NATO, of which most EU countries are a member.

To finish, the big point: foreign policy. Increasingly, and this is bizarre, the EU is more and more speaking with a single voice when it comes to foreign policy. That's important because here lately, the EU foreign policy line does not agree with, or contradicts, the US foreign policy line. This is, again, quite important to understand what's going on in the world. Meaning that the EU, a singular entity, puts out political statements about its attitude about things that are happening on the planet. It's not always completely unified, but the fact that they are doing it is what's important. Maybe a few examples are warranted here.

When Robert Mugabe's trashing Zimbabwe here lately, the EU steps forward with a statement and says, "We do not condone this behavior. We are going to have sanctions against Zimbabwe." That "we" being the entire EU. We're seeing that increasingly the EU is acting as a singular entity to make statements about, say, Chinese human rights, or other issues that are occurring around the planet. This, combined with this singular EU national defense, are the most important points that are being developed rapidly here at the dawn of the 21st century, and are what's making the EU a real political, as well as economic, force in the world.

Why would they do this? Just like with the economic stuff, no singular European nation can compete with the US or increasingly can even compete with China, or Japan, or many other places in the world. So they got together, and as a singular economic unit, they can compete quite well as one of the biggest economic units on the planet.

Now the same thing has happened with politics. They realize that, yes, while the UK has a big voice in the world, by itself it can't do as much, and certainly Belgium can't, and there's no way Poland can. But as a singular unit, politically their voice is much, much stronger. But they don't agree on everything.

PROBLEMS: IMMIGRATION AND CULTURE FRICTION

Western Europe also has some big problems ahead of it. The main BIG issue that it's currently confronted with is people. What? Why are people a problem? People are a double-edged sword in Western Europe because the populations of most Western European countries are stagnant, which means they're not growing, or actually declining—they're getting smaller. Therefore, to keep their economies going, moving forward and growing, you have to have people. You have to have people filling jobs—working on farms, working in restaurants, washing dishes, putting down the beds at the hotels. Western Europe with its declining local populations, has had to rely on immigration from other regions in order to fill those jobs. It has to happen. That's a fact. But how is it happening?

We talked about distance being one of the United States' great physical attributes; it is far away from most other places in the world, and only borders one other distinctly different region. On the other side of the spectrum, Europe is very close to every place else. Western Europe can almost be considered the epicenter of every place nearby, in that it is infused with people from Eastern Europe, Russia, the Middle East, Africa, and pretty much anybody else that can very easily get to Europe. Europe, like the US, is extremely rich. The Middle East, and Africa, and Russia could be put in the poorer column. Maybe even the *extremely* poor column. This results in a great movement, a great migration wave, of people that are hitting Europe, and causing tremendous problems. Europe has generally welcomed them, but it is reaching a kind of critical breaking point now.

The French in particular have always had a sort of an open-door immigration policy with all of the citizens of its former colonies, particularly in Africa. "You were French citizens when you were a colony, so we are going to consider you French citizens if you want to come here." Well, that's all fine and dandy, except that the French state is now going broke! A more lefty, socialist state which provides a lot of government benefits is starting to feel the economic strain as its population continues to swell with Arab and African immigrants. In addition, *collisions of culture* are starting to ferment.

CULTURE FRICTION

Cultural collision—what does that mean? That sounds a bit strong. Perhaps cultural friction is better. A lot of people are getting quite worried across Europe right now, that they're losing their Europe-ness. That perhaps the Belgians are losing their Belgian-ness, that the French are losing their French-ness. Why? Because the larger and larger numbers of immigrants from other places are bringing their cultures and languages and religions into the European homeland, and in more deeply integrated ways than ever in the past. Let's consider this for just a moment more.

A big debacle in worldwide news in September of 2005 was the Danish cartoon of the prophet Mohammad that originated in Western Europe. Why was *that* such a big deal? Because so many immigrants are of Middle Eastern Muslim and African Muslim background, both of which constitute growing percentages of the population in Western Europe. But cartoons are only the tip of the iceberg when contemplating the current European friction with Muslim culture.

Why would I pick on those folks in particular? Well, what these both black African and Arab Middle Easterners that are of Muslim religion have brought to Europe is a whole new kind of layer of different culture into the European experience. There are mosques being built all over Europe. There are folks who dress differently being incorporated into Europe. There are folks with different ideas about, say, individual liberties and rights that are being incorporated all over Europe. Liberties like the value of freedom of speech to draw a cartoon of a religious figure.

Result? An anti-immigration backlash has started to creep into European society. There has been a rise of more ultra-conservative rightist political factions across Europe—in places like Austria, Germany, and even France in particular. Those political parties are gaining popularity by saying, "We're losing our Austrian-ness, we're losing our German-ness. And we wanna kick out all the foreigners or at least limit them coming in to prevent this."

Legislation has been passed in Switzerland and in Austria banning the construction of new mosques. In France, laws banning Muslim headscarves have been passed, and the French and Dutch are debating about banning the burqa altogether. Speaking of the Dutch, a politician from the Netherlands now has 24-hour a day protection for life since he released an anti-Islamic film in 2008 mostly as an ultra-rightist political stunt, a stunt which resulted in Muslim countries around the world boycotting Dutch goods. Starting to see the problem here?

Burqa high fashion not hip in Holland.

To make a long story short, Western Europe is torn right now. Its governments (being part of Team West, the core of Western Civilization) say, "Hey, we protect individual rights to do crazy stuff like offending Muslims by drawing a cartoon of the prophet Mohammed." However, they also have larger and larger Muslim constituencies, which is causing real conflict and clash in different parts of Europe who find offense in some of these things.

This cultural friction is not limited to the Muslims either. Let me give you another example, and we'll even stick with our Dutch wooden-shoe-wearing-tulip-growing friends. The Netherlands is also having problems with Catholic Christians from Poland! What? What is that all about? Well the Netherlands is . . . I won't say an atheist state, but it's not really a fervently religious group of folks. In fact, most of Western Europe is fairly blasé when it comes to attending church or being very religious, but the Poles sure are! Staunch Catholics, that bunch! As lots of Polish folks have migrated to western Europe seeking better economic conditions, their numbers are starting to tip the balance on societal views of everything from drug use to abortion rights.

That's a good topic to pick on. Catholic Poles are staunchly anti-abortion. Well, the Netherlands is known as being staunchly whatever-you-wanna-do! "Hey, we have a Red Light District—go have a hooker! It's all legal. Smoke some hemp! We don't care! You wanna have an abortion? Have three." Well, wait a minute. Now you have a big constituency of Catholic Poles in the Netherlands saying, "No, we don't agree with that." The Dutch government has to consider these things. So the Dutch may be losing their Dutch-ness to Catholic Poles now, as well as Muslims from North Africa. At least, that is the perception of some.

IMMIGRATION

One last point on the whole immigration and cultural friction issue that you should be aware of is that immigration is not equal across all of Western Europe, and that means immigration problems are not equal across all of Western Europe. I just wanted to point out this spatial feature of who's the most concerned about immigration within the greater EU. As might be evident, the closer a state is to, say, North Africa or the Middle East, the more concerned it is with immigration, because that's the most used and easiest traveled avenue to get into Europe.

Key Migrant Routes from Africa to Europe

Meaning, if you want to migrate from North Africa to Western Europe, you go through the countries that are closest to you, namely Spain, Italy, and Southern France. As fate would have it, the countries that are most concerned with immigration, most worried about it, raise up the most fuss about it at the EU, are Spain, Italy, and France. Surprise! The further that European countries are from other world regions, the less likely they are to be complaining about any immigration problems, because the less likely they are to have any. Again, let's start with the evident. Norway, Sweden, Finland—these places are *far* away. They're also a lot colder. Who wants to go from North Africa to Finland? And Iceland? Don't even get me started! Like those guys would ever have an immigration problem. Even Leif Ericson hauled ass out of there.

You should be aware that there's also internal tribulations when the EU gets together and meets. Because states like France and Spain say, "Hey, we have a real immigration problem and we need to pass more stringent, strict laws to control this." Other places say, "Well, no, we don't really think it's that big an issue." It has become enough here in 2010 that the EU is now working on a singular, collective immigration policy for the entire block. Look for it to be passed by 2011, and I'm willing to wager it's going to make getting into Europe a lot more difficult for potential immigrants.

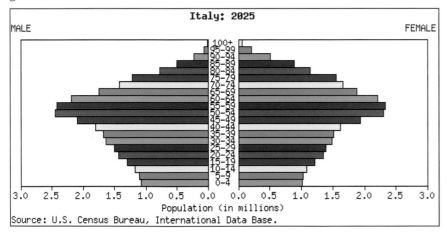

Bye-bye Italians! Hello immigrants!

Of course, the complicating factor here is that Europe is *dependent* on at least some immigration. European population dynamics, as we discussed in chapter 2, indicate that population is declining in Western Europe. In Italy, the population is declining because people aren't having enough babies. In Sweden, the population is going down perhaps due to too much movie watching.

Now lots of folks are saying, "Isn't that good? Less people means more stuff for the people there, right?" Not necessarily . . . who's going to work at the factories that prop up the country's GDP? Who's going to make money for the economy? Who's going to work in the service sector? Population is completely stable or declining in all of these countries in Western Europe, which means they actually need immigrants to come in and keep things moving forward economically. That's the rub. They cannot possibly stop immigration, and at the same time, it's causing tremendous conflicts both culturally and with the movement of jobs and people. *This is Western Europe's biggest problem.* Think I'm making it up? The conflict over the anti-Muslim film in the Netherlands, the rise of skinhead movements in Germany, full-on race riots targeting Africans in southern Italy, and even anti-Semitic crime in France have all been major headlines in the last years.

NEW FACES, NEW DIRECTIONS

To sum up and finish up our tour, we just need to talk about the power structure of what's happening in Western Europe right now as new folks have arrived—no, not the immigrants, but the fresh faces on the political scene. Leadership has rolled over all across Europe in the last few years, but let's just focus on the folks that make the biggest impact worldwide, and for the US in particular. Before we go any further, please, please, please remem-

Sammy needs you, baby!

ber this political fact about Western Europe: it is currently undergoing a significant shift to center-right all across the continent, especially in leadership. There are many reasons for this shift, such as economic recession, immigration issues, and cultural frictions; reasons which typically make people get all conservative and traditional, and vote for like-minded leaders. It could also be that all politics is cyclical, and its just time for the other team to have a go at it. Europe is definitely moving to right of center politically, and possibly socially.

There has also been a resurgence in extreme-right groups like skinheads in Germany, anti-immigration hate-groups in France, and borderline-fascist groups in Austria; many of these groups have been gaining support by playing up the immigration and cultural friction fears discussed in the previous sections. But those are just the extremes.

Whatever the logic, more conservative, center-right (and sometimes far-right) politicians are getting elected almost everywhere in the region. What I want you to know about for this section are the main conservative center-right folks that have been swept into power in that all-important EU-3. In UK, France, and Germany, leadership has flipped from left to right in the last few years. Let's look at these playas and how this shift is playing out.

First, the way it was: As we have previously discussed, the US and the UK are tight allies, and the UK has typically, in the last hundred years, gone along with all things the US desires, more so than they have with the folks in their own neighborhood, namely the rest of continental Europe. This staunchly close US-UK situation has been referred to for a century as the **Special Relationship**. You could see this highlighted at its best most recently as the US was ramping up for the current Iraq War, and came to the EU and said, "Hey, we're all buddies, we're all in NATO, hey EU countries, help us out. Support us for our Iraq invasion." The British, of course, said, "Absolutely! We're lap dogs of the US foreign policy, we'll do anything you want. Yes sir, yes ma'am, sure thing Uncle Sam."

However, the Franco-German alliance said, "No, absolutely not. We're not on board with that policy at all." Indeed, most of the rest of Western Europe went along with the Franco-German alliance on that. That's very typical of the way things have been for the last 10 to 20 years, maybe even more like fifty years. Yes, the Europeans *in general* are US allies and friends, but when it comes to global issues and foreign policy, the US has only been able to rely on the UK year in and year out. And it could generally count on the French to oppose it year in and year out. But this equation is changing; we can pretty much put that relationship on its head here in 2010. What do I mean?

UK first: The Brits just put conservative David Cameron into the Prime Minister position in May 2010, the first center-right (Tory party) guy to hold the post for nearly 14 years!

New kid Cameron in charge of the UK, and quite possibly the sexiest prime minister since Margaret Thatcher.

Of course, he is still a huge US ally, no getting around that, but Cameron will be much more reserved and will make the UK much more independent on the foreign policy front than the previous government. How do I know this? Well, Cameron is center-right while US President Obama is center-left, so they are ideologically not on the same page. And the Tory Party of UK will certainly support the war on terrorism, but historically it pulls Britain to a more independent route in the international sphere. Look for them to become more critical of US policies, but also more anti-EU and definitely anti-Euro given the financial debacle that Greece has caused the EU. They're still an ally, but not as staunch, and certainly will not be on board for everything the United States wants.

"New-School" Nick Sarkozy. Bonjour!

Let's shift to the continent: France and Germany—the biggest states, populations, and economies in the EU. Together they form a significant power center, and to restate, one that is typically not always in agreement with all things British, or American. What of our Franco-German friends? Strangely enough, they have completely flip-flopped as well!

Both Angela Merkel and Nicolas Sarkozy, the leaders of Germany and France respectively, took over for folks who were more liberal, more on the "left" spectrum of things. Both of them are more conservative and closer to the "right" side of the spectrum. As such, both have become much stronger advocates of the United States in world affairs, but they will have the same issues with the Obama administration that Cameron of the UK does. Okay, strong may be too powerful a descriptor for Merkel, but not strong enough for Sarkozy! Nicolas Sarkozy used to visit with George W. Bush. Merkel doesn't like Bush personally (dudes, google "Bush-Merkel back rub" to see what I mean—but Germany is now a much greater friend of the United States, as is France.

The proof? Both countries, the French in particular, have recently pledged more troops to the US-led NATO endeavor in Afghanistan. As soon as Sarkozy came into office, he said, "No, no, I'm gonna help out the US-led NATO endeavor in Afghanistan. We're gonna dedicate more French troops." But hold the phone: Sarkozy is also calling for French participation in Iraq via the UN. Wow. That's crazy! As I already suggested earlier, France and Germany refused to even support the initial endeavor into Iraq.

It's a full turnaround—Sarkozy being very assertive on the foreign policy stage. He is trying to bring France back into the limelight of world affairs. He wants to get France back into the command leadership of NATO, and he is talking about making new French army bases around the world, to perhaps even mimic the US, but certainly going to be much more proactive in world affairs than any of his predecessors since before World War II. (The most famous French leader since WWII was Charles de Gaulle: a guy who intentionally pulled his country out of NATO command and distanced France from the US and UK, because he wanted to re-establish France as a major power in its own right. Does that help explain why the US and France have not gotten along very well for decades, why they treat US tourists like crap, and why we mock them mercilessly?)

As for Angela Merkel, nobody is taking the Teutonic titan of a Chancellor for granted either. Merkel has had much success in the last couple of years swinging the Germans back to the conservative side of the spectrum. Her predecessor Chancellor Gerhard Schroeder was much more liberal and much more anti-US. Germany's first woman leader has strengthened its economy, pulled in the reigns of immigration, and become a serious force in world affairs in her own right. When she talks, people listen. Merkel is more of a supporter of US policy, although not enough to get involved in the Iraq thing, as most Germans on the street are still vehemently opposed to it. But do remember this, my plaid friends: increasingly Germany has been invited to sit in on the workings of the UN Permanent Security

She's Merkel-icious!

Council. Even though it does not have an official vote, the German voice is becoming of greater significance on the world political stage by affecting UN policy decisions.

So, big changes going on. New faces, new directions. These leaders taken collectively carry a lot of weight in Europe, and in fact their countries together are often referred to as the *EU-3*. All three of these leaders are much more comfortable with the US, and cozier with each other. Am I suggesting this is some big love fest between these three? Absolutely not. They're still competitive to a certain degree, but these three countries and these three leaders are friendlier to each other than any of their predecessors of the recent past. Given their loosely shared ideology, look for more conservative measures to pass in each of their countries, but also in the EU as a whole. I have only hit the big 3; there are also center-right leaders in Italy, Austria, and Switzerland. Not to belabor the point, but limiting immigration and "cultural preservation" legislation, like banning burqas, will almost certainly be percolating through the EU in the very near future. You heard it here first.

SUMMARY—WESTERN EUROPE

Increasingly, Western Europe and Eastern Europe are simply becoming Europe. However, we can still tease out enough stuff in today's world to make some finishing remarks about this Western Europe region. It is one of the richest regions in the world. It is one of the most politically powerful regions in the world. Along with the United States, it is the foundation stone of Team West: one of the most important economic, political, and even cultural forces on the planet. While the US certainly leads Team West in the world today, Western Europe is where Team West started, thus the term Western Europe . . . . Team West: go figure!

It does have some new faces, some new attitudes, but the main big theme in today's world is the EU becoming somewhat of a United States of Europe. What that means for the future in terms of not just a Constitution, but defense and foreign policy, are important points to consider. Following that with these new faces in today's world, we're seeing a Western Europe that is being increasingly supportive of the United States, but still quite independent in its own right.

However, I must now be brutally honest with you, my plaid friends . . . this region has passed its prime, and its not likely to return to the glory days anytime soon. Yes, Western Europe is rich. Yes, Western Europe is a core component of the powerful and potent Team West.

Keep us in the game, coach!

Yes, Western Europe is probably one of the most awesome places to party on the planet. BUT, Western Europe is no longer a center of innovation and creation; not for technology, not for business, and not even for demographics! They can't even crank out enough kids to keep up with replacement level! Which is, of course, why immigration is both a necessity and a problem for their region.

Western Europe is great, but mired in bureaucracy and tradition that simply does not facilitate it as a revolutionary center of activity anymore. Given its imperialistic phase and its centuries of conflict, this may not necessarily be a bad thing. Either way, these Europeans will continue to focus on EU evolvement to keep themselves in the global game as a serious player, knowing full well that its better to still be on the sidelines as the seasoned second-stringer than out of the ballpark altogether. At the core of the EU, the IMF, NATO, World Bank, UN, and Team West, this region has still got game, even if it gets winded easily.

WESTERN EUROPE RUNDOWN & RESOURCES

View additional Plaid Avenger resources for this region at http://plaid.at/we

 BIG PLUSES

→ Biggest economy in the world

→ The EU is the most highly organized and successful political organization of all time

→ Interstate armed conflict is virtually impossible; very stable place

→ The EU as a singular entity is the biggest economy on the planet

→ Western Europe has some of the highest standards of living on the planet

→ Multi-ethnic, diverse societies that generally get along with each other

→ Fantastic regional rail transportation network which interconnects the region and runs extremely efficiently (except for Italy)

 BIG PROBLEMS

→ Rough EU roads ahead as the richer economies (Germany, France) have to continue to take care of the poorer economies (Greece, Portugal)

→ Move to conservative center-right will certainly exacerbate anti-immigration friction that is starting to rear its head across the region

→ Aging populations, over-extension of state benefits, and high costs of living will make economic growth extremely challenging in the future

→ Western Europe will continue to lose its once overwhelmingly-predominate position as a major center of technological innovation, finance, and investment . . . mostly to Asia

→ Cultural friction will continue to grow as folks feel they are losing their cultural identity to a monolithic EU and/or foreign immigration

DEAD DUDES OF NOTE:

Winston Churchill: The British Prime Minister guy that held the UK and Allied powers together during WWII. Great statesman, orator, historian, artist, and drinker by all accounts. Coined the phrase Iron Curtain and fostered the tight Special Relationship with the US

Adolf Hitler: Great public speaker and snappy dresser that tried to take over the world and kill everyone that wasn't white and German. His idiocy transformed Europe and became the impetus for forming the EU, the UN, and the UN convention against genocide.

Charles de Gaulle: National hero and dominant political leader of France during and after WWII, he was one of the few Frenchies who didn't surrender. Charismatic and proudly nationalistic, he pursued an independent path from both Europe and the US, which is why France was not a major payer in NATO, or great friends with the UK or US for decades.

Margaret Thatcher: Conservative Prime Minister of UK from 1975–90, was nicknamed the "Iron Lady" for her aggressive stance towards commies. She was the "Ronald Reagan of the UK" in that the two were identical in political and economic ideology. Oh, and she's not quite dead yet.

PLAID CINEMA SELECTION:

(Look, I know there are ten million awesome classic films from Europe that are probably way better than this list. I'm just giving you a handful of more modern picks that will intrigue the younger generations a bit more. Frankly, I usually can't stand anything labeled as a "classic" of cinema.)

GoodBye, Lenin! (2003) Fantastic drama-comedy that takes place in Germany as the Iron Curtain falls, and the soviet economy/culture of East Berlin is replaced by western materialism/consumerism. A crowd pleaser.

Trainspotting (1996) Scottish cult heroine film, made Ewan McGregor famous pre-Obi Wan Kenobi. Great look at blue collar life in UK and drug culture. "Toilet scene" is classic insanity you won't forget.

Pan's Labyrinth (2006) Bizarre whacked-out insane fantasy film set in Franco's fascist Spain in the 1940's. Gives some insight into Spain's fascist period, and will cause hours of sleeplessness.

Gomorra (2008) A contemporary mob drama set in Naples that exposes Italy's criminal underbelly by telling five stories of individuals who think they can make their own compact with Camorra, the area's Mafia. Oh, and the Camorra actually exist in real life.

Amélie (2001) Wildly popular, clever, unconventional, light-hearted comedy from France. Nothing too serious, but a pleasant look at modern French life, and will make you not hate the French so much.

Run Lola Run (1998) Awesome action/adventure/time warp film that perhaps has no great geographic utility, but is a great high energy MTV-style flick that I use to introduce hesitant students to foreign film. They love it, despite the subtitles.

Volver (2006) Director Pedro Almodóvar is in love with the entire country of Spain, including its women, and it shows in this comedy of errors involving murder and family secrets. If you don't find the gorgeous Spanish scenery compelling— and why not?—then the gorgeous live-action Spanish scenery that is Penélope Cruz will keep you entertained.

Ocean's Twelve (2004) Okay, it's just a guilty pleasure, but damn I love watching this heist film which jumps across Western Europe. No great learning material here, although it does feature Interpol and a variety of excellent landscapes across the continent. And most people despise the "trick ending," which makes me like it even more.

LIVE LEADERS YOU SHOULD KNOW:

Nicolas Sarkozy: center-right President of France, 5th largest economy, EU power player, married a supermodel, wears lifts in his shoes.

Angela Merkel: center-right Chancellor of Germany, 4th largest economy, EU power player, routinely voted the most powerful woman on the planet.

David Cameron: newly-elected, center-right Prime Minister of UK, 6th largest economy. Huge ally of the US, and all that will entail. Probably likes fish n'chips, but too soon for me to call it.

Jose Zapatero: center-left President of Spain, 10th largest economy, the country most likely to go broke this year after Greece and Portugal. And he is a dead ringer for "Mr. Bean."

Silvio Berlusconi: Prime Minister of Italy, 7th largest economy, and proof that not all horribly corrupt and tasteless leaders are in 3rd world countries. Once referred to Barack Obama as "a very tanned fellow." Oh wait, he didn't do that once, he did it three times.

CHAPTER OUTLINE

Eastern Europe

THE BOOKENDED REGION

We just wrapped up Western Europe. We now know of its extremely rich and multifaceted world influence. And we are aware of how it destroyed itself in the 20th century. Let's move on to Eastern Europe. It has slightly different physical geography, slightly different cultural geography, and it's a place that has been radically different from Western Europe in the past. But things are changing . . .

Eastern Europe is the *bookended* region, as the Plaid Avenger refers to it, and bookended in a variety of ways. The bookend reference means there is something in the middle being held up, propped up, or pinched between two bigger sides. In this respect, physically, Eastern Europe is between the giant Russia to its east, and those Western European states to its west. (Western Europe—the region we just covered.) Ideologically, it's also in the pinch in the middle. Eastern Europe has been a buffer zone between these two same giants—Russian culture to the East, Western European ideas to its west. Because of this, it has essentially been the battleground between these two teams, and therefore a fuse to the pow- derkeg of big conflicts. Where did the major transgressions of the 20th century start? World War I, World War II, the Cold War? Yep . . . all got launched in Eastern Europe.

This region had been marked for a very long time by **devolution**, or shattering apart; big political entities breaking down into smaller units. This region is also distinct because it has been a **buffer zone** and a battleground of ideologies throughout the 20th century. It was a buffer between Russia and Western Europe, and as such, was a battleground for the Cold War. Commies in Russia thought one way, dude-ocracies in Western Europe thought another way, and everyone in Eastern Europe was caught in the middle. The book getting squished by the bookends.

On top of that, we're going to see that there are a lot of historical influences that have permeated Eastern Europe proper, making it extremely diverse in every aspect you can imagine: linguistically, ideologically, religiously, ethnically, cul- turally . . . It's all here. This diversity is one of the reasons Eastern Europe has historically yanked itself in lots of different directions and shattered apart. That's why it's a region, and just one of the many reasons why it's distinct from surrounding regions. Russia is Russia, Western Europe is Western Europe, and Eastern Europe is something in-between right now.

But that was then and this is now. If you want a key word, a single word that keeps coming up in the discussion of Eastern Europe, the Plaid Avenger has one: **transition**. This is a region in transition. Of course, every place on the planet is changing and moving around, but this is an entire region in which just about all facets of life are on the shift: with an obvious place they came from, and with an obvious place they're going. All the states in this part of the world are going through this process of transition. What sort of transition, Plaid man? A transition from what to what? We'll talk about that in more detail as we go along.

THE PHYSICAL MIDDLE GROUND

When we think of Eastern Europe as I just suggested, we think of that region that's sandwiched between two much bigger and more powerful other world regions. But if we just look at it physically, just physically for a minute, it's also kind of a buffer zone in a very natural sense, in a variety of different ways.

CLIMATE

The temperature and precipitation patterns of Eastern Europe are more **continental** in character than areas to its west. Being further and further away from the Atlantic Ocean, and particularly its most moderating Gulf Stream effect, makes these states more prone to increased temperature disparity: that is, it can get much cooler in the winters and perhaps even more hotter in the summers. As we progress further into the continent and away from large bodies of water, this continentality effect becomes even more pronounced. We'll see this played out to the extreme when we get into Russia, deep in the continent's interior, where it's way colder still. Nothing is quite like Russia, where the only thing that's not frozen is the vodka. The Plaid Avenger's beard froze up in that place multiple times on secret subversive missions. When we think of the inverse, we think about the coastlines of Western Europe. We think of a more moderated climate. It's not too bad there; it rarely freezes, even in places as far north as Great Britain.

Eastern Europe is in between, in that it's not quite as bad, not quite as extreme as Russia but not quite as moderated as the West. As you progress from Western Europe inward, into the continent, you get more continentality—meaning less moderation, more temperature extremes during the year, and certainly cooler, if not downright colder, in the wintertime. Climatically, they're in a zone of transition, as well, from the West to Russia. But don't let me mislead you: this place does have some nice climates, and in fact some areas are exceptionally rich in natural resources and soils. In fact, Eastern Europe actually produces a lot of food. The Ukraine has classically been one of the breadbaskets of all of Europe, and it continues to be. There is a lot going on here physically, but it's just not quite as pleasant, not quite as moderated as its Western European counterpart.

LAND SITUATION

The bigger, physical feature to consider with Eastern Europe is that big sections of these countries are landlocked. When we think of Western Europe, we think of maritime powers—all of them have sea access, all of them have coastlines, and, therefore, they all have big navies and armadas, and they're all big traders and were all big colonizers. Not so much so for the Eastern European, if at all. Yes, there is some coastline along the Black Sea for some countries like Bulgaria and Romania. Yes, some of them have Med access like Albania and Croatia. And yes, some have Baltic Sea frontage like Poland and Estonia. But none of these states in what we're considering Eastern Europe were ever big maritime powers, and they're still not. Unlike their Western European counterparts, none of these states were big colonial forces in the world. They didn't have the advantages we talked about in Western Europe of sapping off the resources and riches of the planet by controlling vast areas outside of Europe proper. Eastern Europe is quite distinctive in that history answers us quite clearly when we ask, "Why are they poorer?" Answer: They were never maritime powers!

CULTURE CLUB SANDWICHED

The last big physical thing to consider is that they were physically in the middle of some very big powers, that have very different cultures. What do I mean by this? Well, Eastern Europeans have their own culture, obviously. There are Polish people there and therewith Polish history and Polish culture. There are Ukrainian people there with their own Ukrainian history and culture. Those folks are sandwiched between entities that have *bigger* histories, *bigger* cultures, and are *bigger* powers. By bigger, don't misinterpret, I'm not talking about "bigger is better." In some cases that's true, but

I'm just suggesting here that they're *bigger* in terms of having more of an impact within their regions, but also beyond their regions as well. A main one to consider is Mother Russia: a very distinct culture, language, religion, and ideology that by its very size and strength has dominated areas close to its Moscow core.

Order up! Who wanted the Turkey, Polish sausage with Russian dressing on rye?

But they're not the only ones. Team West and its cultures influenced the region, as has North Africa. You also have the former Ottoman Turk Empire down south. The Ottoman Empire is long since gone but Turkey took its place, and so there's a Turkish culture that abuts them. An important part of that Turkish culture is the fact that they are Muslim, and the Ottomans brought Islam into the region in general. That's important to note, by the way, because perhaps unlike any other world region or other part of the world, you have a variety of world religions that come together in one place, albeit, not always on friendly terms. You do have Islam which did penetrate into Christian Europe via Eastern Europe. But even before you get to that, you have to think about the divisions of Christianity. Of course, there's Old School Christianity that got divided into Eastern Orthodox; hey, that's in Eastern Europe. That then got divided into Catholicism; hey, that's in Eastern Europe, too. And then Catholicism was further branched into Protestantism, and that's in Eastern Europe as well.

A quick summary here: Eastern Europe in the middle of major world cultures—Russian versus Western versus, say, Arab Islamic. Also, it's the middle ground of major world religions—Christianity, Judaism, Islam, and all the divisions of Christianity itself, as well. These divisions all coming together—different ethnicities, different people, different religions, different cultures, different histories—has served to play out within Eastern Europe, more often than not, as a battlefield of all these differences. This leads us to the concept of Eastern Europe as, not just a battleground, but a shatter belt . . . a zone of breaking down, breaking apart bigger entities to smaller and smaller ones. Perhaps I'm getting ahead of myself. Before we get to this idea of a shatter belt and a breaking down, a.k.a. **devolution** (another great word), let's back up the history boat for just a second and take these things one at a time as they proceeded throughout history.

IDEOLOGICAL MIDDLE GROUND

As pointed out above, Eastern Europe is in the middle of lots of different cultures, different religions, and different ethnicities who have battled it out across the plains of Eastern Europe over the centuries. I'm not going to bore you with all the details; we don't need to get into a lot of this stuff. I'll just set the stage so you understand the modern era, how some of these outside influences came to cohabitate within this region over time, and why perhaps it's still causing some conflicts today.

HISTORICALLY

TEAM WEST VS. RUSSIA VS. THE OTTOMANS

Historically speaking, and I'm only going back a few hundred years, Eastern Europe was kind of a battleground of big empires. We have some of the Team Western players like the Austrian empire, the Prussian empire (which evolved into the Germans), the Russians, and the Ottoman Empire. Four big entities which virtually controlled all of what we consider now Eastern Europe. Just so you know the Russians and the Ottomans fought it out for

1815: Four main players.

1915: Goodbye, Ottoman Empire!

long periods of time vying for control of these territories. The Russians and the Austrians did the same thing, as did the Prussians and the Russians.

These empires have radically different cultures as well, in things like language, ethnicity, economies, politics, and religions. Differences which sow the seeds of conflict for generations. Consider only the religious differences for a moment more. The Germans and Austrians were mostly Protestants and Catholics; the Russians were staunchly Christian Orthodox; the Ottomans were Islamic. They are all vying for cultural and political influence in this region. Are you starting to get a sense of the confluence of conflicting ideas in this area? Empires trying to expand, fighting each other, in this fringe zone we're going to call Eastern Europe, as we get a little further along.

Now that's the background set-up. We need to get into the modern era, and in the modern era there are some major devolutions that occur. Evolution has the connotation of growth, of building into something bigger and more complex. **Devolution** is just the opposite: a term that simply means breaking down—devolving into smaller, simpler pieces. Devolution in a political sense involves a big empire or a big country breaking down into smaller countries; that's a real big theme for Eastern Europe historically and perhaps even into today's world.

WORLD WAR I

The starting phase of devolution in the modern era was with the Ottoman Empire. The Ottoman Empire, which was a Turkish-Islamic empire, introduced Islam into southeastern Europe. Places like Bosnia, Albania, and Kosovo are still predominately Muslim today as a result of the cultural influences that the Ottomans brought in. You have to remember, the Ottomans were actually knocking on the door of Austria for a very long time in a bid to expand their empire into Europe, but they were weakened considerably and were on the brink of collapse by the time the 20th century rolled around. Let's fast forward: this declining empire most unwisely allied themselves with the Germans during the lead up to World War I (you can read more about that in the chapter on Turkey). But the Germans lost that war, which resulted in the carving up of the Ottoman territory. By 1915,

there was no such thing as the Ottoman Empire. It's subdivided, as you see in the map into a variety of new states already—places like Romania, Yugoslavia, and Bulgaria.

The Austria-Hungarian Empire, which kind of started World War I—or at least the assassination of their leader Franz Ferdinand started it off—they lost the war as well, and the Austria-Hungarian Empire was the next shatter zone. Ottomans shattered first, then the Austria-Hungarian Empire shattered next, which created several more countries—individual entities which declared independence.

We also have to point out that Russia was pulled into World War I, and was decimated by the Germans. World War I was just so hilarious. Everybody declared war on everybody simultaneously. We had multiple fronts of people fighting and then losing. The Russians got pulled into it, while dissent and revolution were fermenting back home, by the way, and they proceeded to lose horribly on the battle front. The result of which was that when our main Commie friend, Vladimir Lenin came to power in Russia in 1917, he essentially said, "Hey, we want out! We're out of

1919: Goodbye Austro-Hungarians!

World War I. We surrender. Germany can have all the territory that we have ceded thus far. They can have it. Take it! We're done!" This was actually a very popular policy back home in Russia, which was on its way to becoming the USSR.

Even after the Russian withdrawal, Germany didn't really win the war either, and therefore, they lost that Russian territory, as well as some of their own. The result of which was a bunch of new countries that popped up around 1920—places like Estonia, Latvia, Lithuania, Poland, even parts of Ukraine. They all declared independence. They were in this middle zone, again, this Eastern European middle zone between these major battling powers. A whole bunch of new countries popped up then, but they ain't gonna last . . .

1945

Goodbye, Germans!

WORLD WAR II

Because, of course, Russia then became the Soviet Union under Lenin's tutelage and, as the USSR grew in power, it wanted its Eastern European territories back. That brings us up to World War II, because the Germans were still over there hopping mad under Hitler and they wanted more territory back as well. Under "der Fuehrer," they decided to have a re-conquest of Eastern Europe and, what the heck, they'll take over Western Europe. To ensure they could pull this off, Hitler got together with Stalin—what a fun party that must have been—and together these two signed what is called the **Pact of Non-Aggression.** Basically, Hitler said, "Uhh, okay, I'm gonna take over the world, but hey Stalin, you seem cool enough to me. Yeah, we won't attack you as long as you don't get in the way of us wiping out Western Europe. And we know you want some of these Eastern European territories back, so you can have those and we'll take everything else." Stalin, in all his wisdom, said, "Yeah, that sounds cool to me. Cheers!"

However, about halfway through the war, Hitler reneged and decided to attack the Soviet Union, pulling them into the war. Why would he have done that? That's right: because he was an insane megalomaniac. You know the end of the story: Since Hitler attacked the USSR, the Soviet Union sided up with the US and Western Europe to beat the Nazis. During this Nazi smack-down, the Soviet Union swept in from the East, the US and allies swept in from the West, and the Nazi smack-down finished up with everyone high-five-ing right square in the middle of Eastern Europe.

Amazingly, if you look at the line where the Allies met, it's right in the middle of what we call Europe today. The troops met and high-fived each other when they finished killing all the Germans, or at least the completely crazy ones who continued to fight, then that was it. World War II was over. Peace! Peace out!

Well, kind of. It was great, for all of five minutes, before it became a face-off, again, but with new players . . .

THE COLD WAR

After the success of the allied powers with the Soviet Union at the end of World War II, you essentially have what happens for the next 60 years—this ideological face-off. You've got the Soviets controlling Eastern Europe, where they swept in and cleaned

As Borat would say: "Aaah-High-Five" in Europe.

out the Nazis, and the West who swept in from the West and cleaned out the rest of the Nazis. Although they were playing for the same side during World War II, where they met became the new face-off of major powers. This is more familiar ground we're getting into—the modern era. You, of course, know that this is the Commie world squaring off against Team West—the freedom-loving democratic capitalists in Western Europe. But how did this go down? How did this happen since they were all allies during the War?

SOVIETS TAKE OVER

Well, as I suggested, we had the Soviets, who were buddies of Team West at the time and helped wipe out the German threat. When it was over the Soviets said, "Well, you know what, you guys over in Western Europe are kind of crazy. We keep getting invaded by you. This Hitler guy was just the most recent one; the German Kaiser Wilhelm before that, and even Napoleon did it before him! You people are nuts!"

A PLAID AVENGER TIP ON WHAT NOT TO DO: Never invade Russia. No one has ever successfully invaded Russia. Everyone who invades Russia loses. Always. Period. Napoleon. Yep. Hitler. Yep. They sucked at it. If megalomaniacs can't pull it off, who can?

The Soviets said, "Hey, you know what you guys, crazy people over in Western Europe keep invading us, so we're going to stay here in Eastern Europe, for a couple of different reasons." One: they wanted to reclaim a lot of these territories they lost in World War I. That is Estonia, Latvia, Lithuania, parts of Poland and Ukraine were pulled back into Mother Russia—the Soviet Union. Two: Russia very openly said, "We're going to stay in Eastern Europe to create a buffer zone so that there are no further intrusions from the West." Now the way this turned into essentially a Soviet takeover to make this Soviet buffer zone, but it was done in such a way that it wasn't as imperialistic-looking as it truly was.

Here's how they did it. Just as the Americans, French and British hung around Western Europe to help with reconstruction, the Soviets claimed they were following the same playbook by chilling out in Eastern Europe to mop up and clean up. The Soviet official line was, "Okay, we're here helping out. We'll stay in Poland. We'll stay in Estonia. We're going to stay here in Hungary. We're going to help clean things up and help rebuild just like you guys are going to do in the West. And ya know what? We'll even help them run elections. This'll be great!" Lo and behold, every Soviet-overseen election that occurred in Eastern Europe resulted in a landslide victory for Communist candidates. What a surprise! Go figure. The Communist party just went through the roof of popularity!

Now was any of this real? I don't know, perhaps. I wasn't there. I was busy deep undercover protecting the Champagne stocks in the underground vaults of France. In the east, the Russians really were liberators of many of these places during the war, so perhaps there was some sympathy, some empathy, and some popularity of communism at the time, but certainly not as much as would have swept a tide of elections across all of these countries. Basically what I'm saying is, this was all farce. Soviets held up these elections and said, "Well, they all elected Soviet leaders, they all elected Communist leaders, so they're just under our umbrella now. We're just here helping out. Isn't that great?" It was, indeed, a Soviet takeover to create this Soviet buffer zone.

People in the Western European realm, and the US as well, were exceptionally unhappy about these developments. Maybe you younger generations today might think, "Why didn't they just go in and get the Commies then? Get those commies outta there?" You have to remember that they were the allies during World War II; they were on our team, and we could not have won without them. World War II had just finished. Nobody wanted to fight a new war. Nobody wanted to then declare war on the USSR and have to do all that fighting all over again.

No one was really that happy about what the Soviets were doing, but it happened anyway. This happened when Team West was busy rebuilding the west—rebuilding and restructuring: laying the foundations for the EU to rebuild Western Europe. It happened when the eastern side was being rebuilt and reoccupied by the Soviet Union. Where these two teams met during the war, of course, became the division between these two forces . . . and is where something called the Iron Curtain then fell. See map below for Iron Curtain.

When all this action was going down, all of those countries in Eastern Europe fell into one of several different categories of which I want you to be familiar. First, some of this territory of Eastern Europe was simply absorbed back into the Soviet Union and became part of other entities and simply just went away. Parts of Poland were worked back into the Lithuania SSR and the Ukrainian SSR. So *absorption* was one option. But what is an SSR?

Ah! That's the second option: some of these briefly independent states became *republics* of the USSR. See, USSR stands for the Union of Soviet Socialist *Republics*. Kind of like states of the United States of America, like Wisconsin is a political component of the USA.

What's the Deal with . . . the "Iron Curtain"?
In 1946, British Prime Minister Winston Churchill delivered his "Sinews of Peace" address in Fulton, Missouri. The most famous excerpt:

From Stettin in the Baltic to Trieste in the Adriatic an "iron curtain" has descended across the Continent. Behind that line lie all the capitals of the ancient states of Central and Eastern Europe. Warsaw, Berlin, Prague, Vienna, Budapest, Belgrade, Bucharest and Sofia; all these famous cities and the populations around them lie in what I must call the Soviet sphere, and all are subject, in one form or another, not only to Soviet influence but to a very high and in some cases increasing measure of control from Moscow.

This speech introduced the term "iron curtain" to refer to the border between democratic and communist (soviet controlled) states. Because of this—and because most Americans have no clue what a "sinew" is—Churchill's address is commonly called the "Iron Curtain Speech."

The "Iron Curtain Speech" was received extremely well by President Harry Truman, but much of the American public was skeptical. Throughout the speech Churchill's tone was very aggressive towards the Soviet Union. Many Americans and Europeans felt that this was unnecessary and that peaceful coexistence could be achieved. The United States had recently considered the USSR an ally. In fact, Stalin, whom the American press had dubbed "Uncle Joe" to boost his popularity during WWII, was probably the most pissed about the speech, feeling he was betrayed by his allies. The "Iron Curtain Speech," besides coining an important Cold War term, set the tone for the next 50 years of US-Russian relations—which is ironic, considering it was given by a damn Brit.

The Iron Curtain Falls
- Iron Curtain Line
- Communist Sphere
- Democratic Capitalist
- Commie, but not Soviet

STETTIN
POLAND
BERLIN
EAST GERMANY
WEST GERMANY
PRAGUE
PILSEN
CZECHOSLOVAKIA
VIENNA
AUSTRIA*
HUNGARY
TRIESTE
YUGOSLAVIA

*Austria remained occupied by Allied powers until 1955, at which time it became independent upon condition of neutrality.

Iron Curtain. But which side was Iron Maiden on?

Some of these entities in Eastern Europe actually went from being an independent sovereign state, to becoming a republic of the USSR. I'm thinking specifically of Moldova, Estonia, Latvia, and Lithuania. They ceased to be sovereign states, and became a part of the USSR.

The third and final possibility, and perhaps the most important option, was that some of these sovereign states actually retained their sovereign state status but became **Soviet satellites.** Mainly, I'm thinking of Poland, Romania, Bulgaria, Hungary, Czechoslovakia, and East Germany. These were countries. They were sovereign states. They had a seat at the UN. However, they didn't really have control over their own countries, and everybody knew it. Everybody knew the Soviets were pulling the strings of the Polish government, of the

Romanian government, of the Czech government. *Everybody* knew it. They did have seats at the UN, they were supposedly sovereign states, but the Soviet Union really did control them, because the USSR had their patsy commie officials running the show in the governments of these places. Does that make sense?

That's the scenario as it was for about fifty years during the Cold War. The Soviets either controlled directly or indirectly (due to their massive influence) every place that is now called Eastern Europe. Team West was on the other side of the curtain: the democracies, the free market capitalist economies that were supported by the US. Those are your two teams during the Cold War. Eastern Europe was close enough to see all the fancy stuff going on in the democratic countries, while they were getting paid visits by the KGB to make sure they still loved being Commies. Now you see how Eastern Europe is a battleground in the middle of this most recent ideological game.

Soviet territory regained, and soviet satellites acquired after WW II.

MARSHALL REJECTED

The other term I want you to think about as well, or at least understand and know, is that the Soviet satellite states did not accept the **Marshall Plan:** a US-sponsored program of aid, loans, and material support to rebuild Europe. The United States, in its infinite wisdom, said, "You guys are screwed over there! The whole damn continent's blown up!" Some smart folks in the United States government said, "We should help them out." In particular, Secretary of State George Marshall said, "Look, we gotta help these dudes out. We need to get them back on their feet, because if we don't, their economy will get worse, collapse and then turn into complete chaos, and if we don't help Western Europe out, the Soviets—who we are already worried about—are right next door. The Soviets will sweep all the way through if we don't do something!"

Probably a fair statement. That Marshall was a smart cookie.

More on the M-Plan: this aid package was offered to all of Europe. The US went to every single one of these countries and said, "Here, we'll give you a ton of money to help you out with industrial capacity and infrastructure to get you back on your feet economically." It was even offered to the Soviet Union. The countries in yellow text on the map accepted the Marshall Plan and took the aid, the sweet cash. Can you see what's happening here? Lo and behold, these are the richest countries in Europe right now. The countries labeled in white refused the Marshall Plan, and those are the poorer countries of Europe right now. While we certainly can't pin everything in the modern era on a singular aid package from the US, it certainly had its impacts back in the day.

If you look at this map of who accepted the Marshall Plan and who didn't, you'll see our same Iron Curtain division between Eastern and Western Europe again demonstrated perfectly. We know that one reason why Eastern Europe is poorer is because the Soviet Union eventually lost the Cold War, mostly because their economy sucked so bad. The second reason is they were stymied out of the gate because they were influenced by Russia to decline the Marshall Plan.

We've already talked about what a Soviet satellite was, and the Soviet influence in Eastern Europe. Make no bones about it; Poland would have probably loved the Marshall Plan. The citizens of the Czech Republic would have loved the Marshall Plan, but they were under Soviet influence, and they were talked into declining it. Maybe there was stricter coercion than just talk going on. Who knows? That's why Eastern Europe is, generally speaking, poorer than Western Europe even today, but they are trying to catch up quickly.

NATO VS. THE WARSAW PACT

Back to the story. Once those Soviet states and Soviet puppet states did not accept the Marshall Plan, the writing is really on the wall at this point. The lines are drawn. The Iron Curtain has fallen, and this is most evident by this nice Cold War relic map shown below of the formation of NATO versus the Warsaw Pact. NATO was formed by the US and all of those Western European states who were looking over at the USSR and Eastern Europe saying, "Oh, we feel threatened by them. They might invade us. They might come and kill us. Therefore, we're going to form up NATO, which says if any of you peo-

ple attack any Western European state, the US is going to come to our aid—all the NATO countries will come to their aid." That's why NATO was formed, on one side of that Iron Curtain.

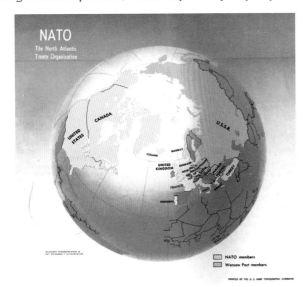

The USSR, not to be outdone, said, "Oh yeah? You guys have your own NATO club? Fine! We have our own club. We're calling it the Warsaw Pact." The **Warsaw Pact** was essentially an anti-NATO device based on the same premise that an attack on one constituted an attack on all. Of course, everyone knows it's bunk, since the participating countries were simply puppets of the USSR anyway. But the Soviets said, "Oh, no, no, no. Everybody's free around here. So we asked Poland if they wanted to join, and they said yes. We asked Romania, and they said yes too." The goofball Soviets even went out of their way to name it the Warsaw Pact to try and demonstrate that it was the Poles who had thought it up. Yeah, right.

This is a sweet Cold War relic!

What you had was an entrenchment of ideas—NATO on one side, Warsaw Pact on the other. Free western democracies on one side, the Communist Commies on the other. Why am I talking about this in detail? Because that's what Eastern Europe has been through for the last sixty years. Now you know the end of the story, though. It won't last for too much longer as we approach the modern era . . .

THE THAWING

What's happening today? What we've had since around 1988 is that the Soviet Union began to **devolve**. There's that word again! The Soviet Union fully collapsed in 1990. They finally figured out, "We can't do it anymore. We give up." During this entire Cold War, the Soviets kept insisting that the Eastern European states were voluntarily part of their sphere of influence, and specifically told the states themselves, "If you guys don't want to be part of the Soviet Union, just have a vote and we'll let you out." Basically, that was a bluff. Occasionally, the peoples of some of these countries would take them up on it, and have street demonstrations and stuff like that. Every time that happened, the Soviet Union sent in the tanks and shut it all down. Everyone knew the Soviets were lying. They'd say, "No, really, you guys are sovereign states. Really!" Wink wink, nudge nudge.

As 1989 approached, when the Soviet Union started to collapse, this notion crept back up again. You may have heard of this Mikhail Gorbachev guy. He was floating around saying, "The Soviet Union's in trouble for lots of different reasons. However, if you guys over in Poland want self-determination, maybe we'll *think* about letting you guys go again. If you really want self-determination, go ahead and have yourselves a vote." This caused an explosion. Once a little bit of the leash was let out, everybody ran. What you had was an instantaneous devolution, where Eastern Europe pulled away as rapidly as possible from the Soviet Union. You see here in this independence dates map is that the USSR, a single political entity, had turned into fifteen different countries virtually overnight.

Independence dates post-USSR

Became Independent in: ■ 1990 ■ 1991 ▨ 1992 ▨ 1993 2006

Free at last!

Czechoslovakia, Poland, Hungary and lots of other places said, "Yeah! The Soviet Union is going to let us out! Good, we vote to be out, we're out! We're truly sovereign again, we're free!" Places like Estonia, Latvia, and Lithuania said, "We want out too!" Romania, Bulgaria, Ukraine, "We're out!" Everyone wanted out. But it didn't stop there! Even after all these states are out, places like Czechoslovakia said, "Uhh, we're already out, and we want to devolve further into the Czech Republic and Slovakia for lots of different reasons." (See **What's the Deal with . . . the Velvet Revolution?** box on page 176.) There is another, separate wave of devolution in what was Yugoslavia, which all occurs at roughly the same time, but for different reasons, but we will get to that later.

FLIGHT OF FANCY

This flight from Soviet influence didn't end with declarations of independence. Oh no! That was just the beginning of their run for the border! Let's take a closer look at three states in particular that set the trend for what was to happen next: Poland, Czechoslovakia, and Hungary. These three states crystallize all of the stuff we've been talking about. During the Soviet occupation and the era of Soviet influence, every time the Soviets bluffed about possible independence, people in these three countries took to the streets to challenge it. As you can see from the map, the biggest street protests and riots in the last 45 years of the Cold War era took place in Poland, the Czech Republic, and Hungary. These countries were never entirely happy with being under Soviet influence. In fact, after World War II, they initially were like, "Yay! We're free! We can be just like Western Europe now!" It's hard to be free when the Soviets set up a puppet government for you.

Now, guess which three countries pushed to get out immediately after the devolution process began in the early 1990's? Guess which three countries wanted in NATO immediately? Guess which three countries petitioned to be in the EU immediately? That's right, kids! It's the same three countries: Poland, Czech Republic, and Hungary. As soon as it was possible, they immediately voted themselves out of Soviet influence. They were the first out of the blocks. But that wasn't enough for them. The peoples within these countries had been so pissed off being under the Soviet yoke for over 50 years that they wanted to ensure that it didn't happen again. All three countries immediately petitioned to join NATO.

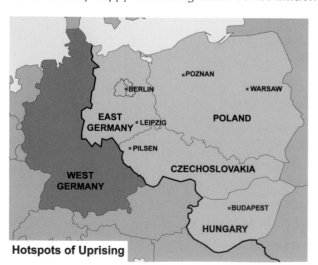

Hotspots of Uprising

We talked about NATO in previous chapters, so you know about the impacts of being a NATO member. They wanted to become NATO members immediately to ensure no further Russian influence. I say again, *ensuring no further Russian influence*. These guys did not want to be anywhere near the Soviets; they wanted to be a part of Western Europe as fast as they could run to it! You know that NATO Article 5 says, "Hey, anybody that's in our club gets attacked, then we take that as an act of war against all of us." Poland, Czech Republic, and Hungary said, "Sweet! We're in the NATO club! Russia can't touch us. We're like the UK, France . . . we might as well be Canada! Russia can't do anything to us!" That was exactly the case. All these countries also immediately petitioned to get into the EU. Eastern Europe, being under Soviet sway, was just as broke as the Soviets. They had not done well during the Cold War. They started with a blank slate in the early '90s—broke, ideologically bankrupt, embracing the west, embracing NATO, wanting out of Soviet influence, and particularly wanting into the EU as quickly as possible for the sake of their economies.

RE-ALIGNMENT WHILE RUSSIA IS WEAK

As you probably already picked up from some of the details in this chapter, we are in an era of transition for this Eastern Europe region. And now it becomes quite obvious what they are transitioning from and to—from that Soviet era of occupation and control, they are mostly realigning and transitioning to become adopted into the capitalist democracies of the west. This happened at a brisk pace after 1991 when the Soviet Union officially voted itself out of existence, and the entity broke from one huge power into fifteen sovereign states, as already pointed out.

We also already pointed out, many of the states, Czech Republic, Hungary, and Poland, were quick to embrace the West; Estonia, Latvia, and Lithuania were right on their heels, by the way. Because, as you now have learned in this chapter, they used to be independent sovereign states in between World War I and the end of World War II, but then were reabsorbed by the Soviets. Those guys were always chafing under Soviet rule, so Estonia, Latvia, and Lithuania were the second round of states that jumped ship into the arms of the West. Many others have since followed. All of this realignment and transitioning of these countries of Eastern Europe was occurring right after the Soviet crash . . . quite frankly, when Russia (and Russia became a new country, as well, at this time) was excessively weak. I mean, they just lost the Cold War, and they mostly lost the Cold War because they were freaking broke. You'll read more about that in the next chapter. Their economy was in shambles, their power structure was shattered, and their government was in chaos. It was precisely in this period of Russian weakness that so many of these Eastern European countries just *ran* to the west.

This transition, of course, happened in a couple of distinct ways by some distinct entities we've talked about many, many, many times already in this great text. Number one was the EU—the European Union. Most, if not all, of these countries *immediately* applied for EU entry status. Many of them were soon granted it. As you can see by the maps to the right, there has been a progressive wave of Eastern European countries entering the EU since the very beginning of their "freedom" from Soviet domination.

As already suggested, Hungary, Poland, and the Czech Republic were the first three that jumped in. They were

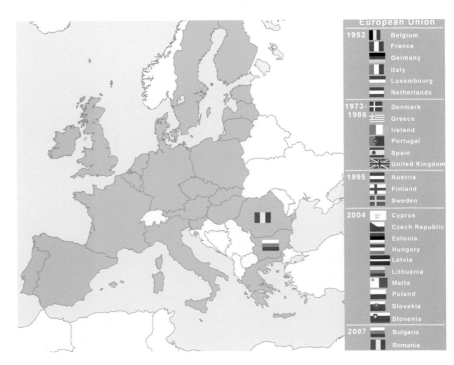

What's the Deal with . . . the Velvet Revolution?

What's up with Czechoslovakia? Why did it split into two, the Czech Republic and Slovakia? Were there two different ethnic groups that wanted their own self-determination and their own countries? Not really. While there are ethnic Slovaks and ethnic Czechs, neither group had much of an idea that a partition was even occurring. They couldn't have cared less. There was no animosity between these ethnic groups. So what's the deal? Why did they do it if there wasn't a problem? Why did they split?

They split because the western side of Czechoslovakia, where the Czech Republic is now, was much more like the West. It bordered Germany; it had the industrialized sector, and was richer, with a higher GDP. Slovakia, the eastern side of the state, was much more Russian/Soviet influenced. It was poorer and more agricultural. Folks in the Czech Republic, as the Soviet Union was collapsing, said, "Hey, we want to get into the EU. Help us out, Plaid Avenger! What should we do?"

I said, "Well, let's look at this strategically. To get into the EU, your economy has to be decent and it has to be stable. As a whole, your economy is neither. But if you were to lop off the poor bastards on the eastern side of your state, your GDP per capita would go up! All your averages would go way up!" Indeed, that's exactly what happened. People in what is now the Czech Republic said, "Hey, we'd be better off on our own without Slovakia dragging us down!" Czechoslovakia underwent a transition called **The Velvet Revolution** in 1993. This revolution was like velvet, nice and smooth. There were no shots fired. From the stroke of a pen, one country became two.

followed by a whole host of countries that jumped in by 2004, and the fun's not over yet. Romania and Bulgaria just entered in 2007, and there are multiple potential candidates. Most of the countries that constituted the prior Yugoslavia have asked for entry. It's quite important to note that Ukraine, a huge country and a former part of Russia historically, has applied multiple times and debates within the country are determining just how hard and fast they should push for EU entry. We'll come back to Ukraine in a bit.

Perhaps the most telling tale to tell about the push for the EU in Eastern Europe is Czechoslovakia, a country that used to be one, that's now two—another shattering within Eastern Europe—simply to get into the European Union. That sounds bizarre—you've got to bust up your country just to join a supranationalist organization! Indeed, it is a bit bizarre, and you should know why, when, and where that happened. It was called the Velvet Revolution.

That brings us to the other avenue for the Team West love embrace by these newly independent Eastern European countries in the 1990s, and that was NATO. No surprises here. In fact, you can essentially look at the story told by those maps of EU entry and see that the NATO entry tells the same tale. As already suggested, Czech Republic, Hungary, and Poland were quick to escape the Soviets and jump under the NATO security blanket. Estonia, Latvia, and Lithuania right on their heels—just like with the EU. Many of the other countries who joined the EU are also now NATO members.

Where did it go?

NATO Core
Joined NATO 1999
Joined NATO 2004

This has been miffing Russia a bit as they have watched the continued eastward expansion of these western clubs to their Russian borders. And that, my friends, is worthy of an entire new section . . . .

RE-INVIGORATED RUSSIA CAUSING NEW CONSTERNATIONS

What's all that about? Well, this eastward expansion of western institutions, like EU and NATO, is now being slowed, stalled, or stopped, depending upon your point of view. What am I talking about? Hey, I'm talking about Russia, man. These guys are back. As I already pointed out, all of these Eastern European countries hauled ass for the west when Russia was weak—right after the Soviet Union crashed, when Russia was down and out, when they were poor, when they were politically bankrupt. But that time has passed. They're back and they're flexing their muscles in more ways than one. And by that, I am thinking specifically of Vladimir Putin. Have you seen this dude topless? Watch out, the man is a menace! But seriously . . . okay, seriously, he is ripped . . . Russia as a great power is back on the world stage, and is no longer allowing encroachment into their arena of influence. We can look at some current events to underscore this Russian resurgence.

ISSUE 1: UKRAINE YEARNING: THE ORANGE REVOLUTION

Like the Velvet in Czechoslovakia, the Orange Revolution in Ukraine was defined by the east/west differences of folks within the state, although unlike the Velvet, it did not end with the permanent division of the state into two new states. Yet. While the Velvet Revolution occurred seventeen years ago, the Orange one just happened in 2004–2005. Russia has exerted influence and/or control over Ukraine off and on throughout most of its history. Russian influence is very strong in areas physically closer to it, like eastern Ukraine with whom it shares a border. Back in 2004, Ukraine had a big move towards true democracy. The scenario included two dudes. The first was Victor Yushchenko: the pro-democracy, pro-EU, pro-NATO candidate. A real poster child for the west. The EU supported him, and the United States thought he was awesome. They loved this dude!

His opponent was Victor Yanukovych: an old-schooler, very conservative, more Russian influenced, and in fact, he's the candidate that Vladimir Putin from Russia came over and campaigned for. To try to help lock up the election before it even was held, former elements of the KGB even unsuccessfully poisoned Yushchenko! Talk about a street fight!

How hilarious is this? I can almost hear the boxing announcer: "In the red, white and blue trunks, fighting for Team West, hailing from western Ukraine, it's Victor Yush! And his opponent, in the red trunks, representing the red Russians, from eastern Ukraine, its Victor Yanu!" Hahahaha dudes, could you make this stuff up? Victor vs. Victor—I wonder who will be the victor?

Why's the Plaid Avenger bringing up this election in Ukraine of all places? Because it exemplifies what's still happening in Eastern Europe, which is this battle between the West and Russia; it's a battle that's not so much for outright control as it

Bush

Yushchenko

Yanukovych

Putin

Bush supported Victor Y. while Victor Y. was backed by Putin. Y ask Y?

is for *influence* within this region. Russia still has serious economic and security interests in this area, and still likes to think of it as within Russia's sphere of influence. When this election went down, the pro-Russian candidate won, and everyone in the world said it was a fraudulent election. There were massive street protests, and this ultimately turned into the 2004/05 **Orange Revolution**. So much heat got put on the Ukrainian government, they threw out the election results, re-ran it, and then the pro-western Yushchenko won. We can see this as part of an ongoing battle for influence in Ukraine, which is representative of the broader battle for influence in the region as whole.

The Russian candidate was downed because the pro-western candidate won—down, but not out. In the Post-Orange Revolution Ukraine, there are still a lot of pro-Russian people. There's a pro-Russian political party, and in March of 2006, the same party gained enough seats to win back control of the Congress. The Plaid Avenger knows that those in the US think democracy's great, that the good guys won, and that's that. Not so! This is an ongoing battle for control. It's not over! Most other countries have gone the way of the west, but it's definitely not over yet for the Ukrainians.

And the country is about evenly split between the western pro-West and the eastern pro-Russia, as you can clearly see from the results of the 2006 election cycle in the map below. Could the divisions in this country be any geographically clearer?

Because of the pro-Russian political party gaining the majority of seats in their Congress, they got to choose the Prime Minister position . . . . which promptly went to Yanukovych! (The President is voted in by direct election, Prime Minister appointed by majority of Congress.) So after the 2006 election, you had this bizarre situation where President Yushchenko was pro-West, and Prime Minister Yanukovych was pro-East! Talk about a country with a split personality!

Official Breakdown of Ukraine's Pro-Western vs. Pro-Russian Districts (as per the 2006 presidential election)

won by Victor Yushchenko
won by Victor Yanukovych

This internal division EXACTLY symbolized the fight for influence in Eastern Europe between Team West and Russia. Yushchenko continued to push for EU and NATO entry; Yanukovych actually announced that no way in hell his country would join NATO. The US sent aid to Yuschchenko and his allies; the Russians sent aid to Yanukovych and his party. The Russians and pro-west Ukrainians even had several economic battles over Russian supplies of oil and natural gas to the country.

Meanwhile, the entire country's economy has tanked and they are more reliant on outside aid than ever to keep themselves afloat, which means this pitched battle for influence has gotten even more important. Are you Yanuk-ed out yet? I hope not because the story gets crazier as we play it forward to the present, as the truth is always stranger than fiction. Dig this . . .

The Ukrainians went back to the presidential polls in 2010, and take a wild stab who won. Victor Yanukovych, of course! Seriously? Yep, seriously, and apparently legitimately this time. So is the Orange Revolution dead? Umm . . . .

Second time's the charm for now-President Yanukovych

kind of, I guess. I mean, Ukraine is still a democracy, and they did have a free and fair election, but unfortunately for those revolutionaries, the same pro-Russian guy they had the revolution against is now the guy who won and is in power.

The first order of business for Yanukovych was to solidly state there would be no NATO in Ukraine's future, which coincided with Russia giving a huge price break to Ukraine on oil/gas contracts and promising them a bunch of foreign aid as well. Isn't it funny how coincidences like that happen? Yanukovych also immediately extended leases on critical Russian naval bases located on the Crimean Peninsula, a move which infuriated pro-Western politicians who retaliated by throwing eggs at the Speaker of the House when the bill was passed.

In particular, there is a serious fight brewing over the future of Ukraine's southernmost province otherwise known as the Crimean Peninsula, but we will save that story for world hotspots in chapter 25. By all means, flip to it now if you can't wait to find out more!

ISSUE 2: RUSSIAN PETRO POWER

By this, I mean that Russia possesses vast amounts of natural gas and oil, something we will cover in more detail in the next chapter. For now, know this: Russia provides something on the order of about one-third of all European demands for energy. That's a lot, dudes. By Europe, I mean Eastern and Western Europe depend on Russia for about one-third of its energy needs. What's that got to do with current events? What's that got to do with a reinvigorated Russia? Just this: they have petro power now. To reassert their strength and influence in Eastern Europe, they are playing the fuel card. Meaning, when those Eastern European states get a little too uppity, when they do things Russia doesn't like—for example, if

Caption: Russia keeps laying the pipe.

the Ukraine says they want to join NATO—Russia says, "Ho, ho, ho. Hold on there comrades. You get your oil from us. You piss us off—and the price of your heating fuel might double overnight. You piss us off a lot—and you get no oil. You dig that? It gets cold there in the winter too, don't it? How do you like them apples?"

Does this sound like fiction? It shouldn't, my friends; it's already been occurring. Russia has raised prices at various points in the last couple of years to essentially punish states that are doing stuff that they don't want them to do. They did it to Ukraine and Belarus in 1994 and again in 2006 when they doubled the prices to their Belarusian brothers. They completely dried up shipments to Latvia in 2004–06 to pressure the Latvians into a port deal. Most recently, the Russians shut down a section of pipeline that supplied a Lithuanian refinery under the guise that the infrastructure was just too old and needed to be replaced. I'm sure that was totally unrelated to the fact that Lithuania was threatening to veto an EU-Russian economic pact. Total coincidence, I'm sure.

Even though the price of oil has dropped drastically since its historic highs of $150/barrel back in 2008, Russia has made trillions over the last decade, with more rubles to come . . . but it's not just about that. Yes, they get rich from it, but more importantly, it has given them political power due to the economic leverage that controlling that commodity brings. Russia is like the crack dealer to Eastern Europe in particular: they've got the stuff that those Europeans need. If you piss off the dealer, you might not get your energy fix. That's not a situation the Eastern Europeans are happy about. The Russian influence is back. That's not all that Russia is doing to flex its muscles in this region.

ISSUE 3: NYET! TO NUKE SHIELD

Another thing that's extremely topical—and we haven't seen the end of this story yet, either—is the proposed missile

defense shield system that is being pushed hard by the United States to be implemented specifically in the Eastern European countries that are NATO members. Specifically right this second, we are talking about the Czech Republic and Poland. This is seriously pissing off the Russians.

Maybe I should back up—what is this *missile defense shield* nonsense about? This is a concept the United States has been toying with for 60 odd years. It has never really come to fruition. But the idea is, you set up a bunch of missiles and a radar system which can detect if any missiles are coming into Europe. Then, you launch your missile to blow up the incoming missile before it lands. Again, it's never worked; out of perhaps ten million tests maybe they've done it once successfully, but that's not the point of this rant right this second.

It's the fact that these new NATO members in Eastern Europe have said, "Uhh, okay, yeah, we'll do it since we still support the US." At a NATO summit which occurred in February of 2008, all the NATO countries—all of them—agreed to go forward with the US plan for the

Early version of European Missile Defense Shield.

missile defense shield. And just to kind of wrap this up, Russia is seriously *pissed* off about it. They have been pounding their fists on the table, saying, "Nyet, this is not going down. This is seriously aggravating us and we are going to use economic leverage and political leverage to intimidate the Eastern European countries that are going along with this."

What do they mean by that? Well, they've already made the fuel threat. When the Ukraine said they wanted to join NATO, Russia said, "Yeah, that's fine. You join NATO and we will re-target nuclear missiles at you." This is something that Russia has also promised to do to any of the states that jump into the missile defense shield program. This is serious stuff, man. Again, this story is still ongoing. The United States says, "Hey, look Russia. Come on, dudes. The Cold War's over. We're not enemies anymore. This is mostly a defense system against . . . Iran, ooh, Iran. Yeah. Iran's going to send a missile somewhere, so this is about that. Or other terrorists might bomb our NATO allies."

But Russia says (and you've got to empathize with them a little bit here), "Uh, yeah right. Come on. NATO's been encroaching to Russian borders for the last ten years. Now you're putting up this big missile defense system. It's an obvious attempt to neutralize or marginalize Russian power in this region and in the world."

The Russians are still pissed about that game.

The Plaid Avenger's take on this mess is that the United States is probably telling the truth, but Russia sees it in a very different light . . . and, again, I always try to empathize. Not sympathize, not agree with, but empathize. The Russians do have a long history of being screwed with by folks over in Western Europe, from Napoleon, to Hitler, right on up through the 1980 US hockey team's miracle victory over the Soviets at the Winter Olympics. So in no way, shape, or form, or any time soon, are they going to be okay with an encroaching military technology that is set up on their borders. And they're really pissed off about it. Vlad "the man" Putin has been saying, "No, we're going to do everything we can in our power to make sure that does not happen, including veiled threats about missiles and open threats about energy issues." As always, sucks to be in the middle of the mess, but Eastern Europe seems to have a historical niche for it. **2010 Update!!!** Since US President Barack Obama and his team took power, they have been doing everything possible to "reset" relations with Russia and calm the big bear down. This has resulted in the US officially canceling (or putting on hold) the entire missile defense mission in Eastern Europe. In other words, missile defense shield is now a dud scud, at least for now. The Russian pressure has won the day on this issue, and the Americans are certainly hoping that this means that the Ruskies will now help them out on a host of other concerns, namely containing Iran. We shall see.

ISSUE 4: YUGO-SLOB-IAN MESS: KOSOVO CHAOS

Finally, for the current events underlying what's happening in Eastern Europe with this reinvigorated Russia, comes the latest chapter in the disintegration of what was Yugoslavia. I've intentionally kept the mess out of the chapter up until this point because it's a debacle that muddies the Eastern European waters a little too much to tackle it up front. But now that you understand the rest of the region, I am confident that you can now figure out this confounding coalition of convoluted crap with the greatest of ease. Well, we at least have to give it the old college try, since events here are once more crystallizing the fight between the West and the East. Let's do it.

The Plaid Avenger said earlier that Yugoslavia was different than the Soviet Union. Let's revisit them so you'll understand what's happening in today's former-Yugoslavia. They were never part of the Soviet umbrella. They were commies, but not Soviet. It was a communist state under

What's the Deal with Slobodan?

We all know this guy! He was arrested for war crimes, and died in The Hague before he even got through his trial. What did Slobodan do that was so important that the Plaid Avenger has to tell you about it? We know from Chapter 3 that the ultimate test of sovereignty is that you can kill citizens in your own country with no international repercussions. The government can do anything it wants to in its country if they are a sovereign state; it's their right.

"I'm dead, and I'm still pissed off."

So what's the deal with Slobodan? He's another strong-armed guy like his predecessor pal Tito. Except when he came to power, his state was disintegrating. He helped perpetuate the conflict that led to the breakdown of Yugoslavia. During that period, he essentially allowed genocide to occur. He was an Orthodox Serb, which was the majority ethnic and religious group. He allowed the Serbian people to start picking on and beating the hell out of the ethnic Albanian-Muslim minorities in the Kosovo region, which were perhaps petitioning for independence. He not only allowed violence; he promoted it.

This started to spiral out of control in the early 1990s to the point that people in the outside world—particularly Billy-boy Clinton from the United States and lots of folks from the UN—began debating the limits of sovereignty. The rest you know from our talk on sovereignty back in chapter 3. After the US/NATO intervention, Slobodan was eventually arrested for war crimes and died while on trial in 2006. He made it onto our "Bastards of the Region" list because of his genocidal policies. Oddly enough, when his body was brought back to Yugoslavia, lots of people were cheering him. He's considered a war criminal by most of the world, yet lots of Serbs have him held up as a hero. That's typically a bad sign. We'll talk more about that later.

Tito double vision: Josip or Jackson?

the tutelage of **Marshall Joseph Tito**. "Marshall" is really just a nicer sounding title than "oppressive dictator extraordinaire." The Plaid Avenger suggested earlier, as we were talking about the historical background of this region, that perhaps no other singular country has more different ethnicities and religions and cultures as did the former Yugoslavia. Emphasis on *did*.

They had Slovenes there, Croats, Bosnians, Herzegovenians, Serbians, Montenegrins; I don't even know what half these terms mean! On top of that, you have Christian Serbs, Muslim Serbs, also Christian Bosnians, a group that encompasses Orthodox and Catholic Bosnians, Muslim Bosnians . . . It's confusing! It was a multi-ethnic, multi-religious, multi-media mess.

Why has there only been serious conflict and devolution there in the past ten years? It's all because of Joseph Tito; not the Tito of the Jackson family, the other Tito, the dictator. Tito was a strong-armed dictator, like Stalin and lots of other folks in the communist realm. When ethnic or religious tension reared its ugly head in what was Yugoslavia, he sent in the army and crushed any uprising or disturbance with the iron boot. Through force, Tito held together this state full of all these different ethnicities and religions. Tito was the only reason it didn't devolve years ago. However, he died in 1980. Since

Yugoslavia was essentially a military state, it was able to perpetuate itself for about another decade, until it fell apart under Slobodan Milosevic.

Look at the time frame and do the math. Tito died in 1980; it held on for about ten years. That brings us to about 1990, the same time that all the other parts of Eastern Europe were devolving, splitting, splintering, fracturing, shattering into separate countries because of the implosion of the USSR. It all hit the fan in Yugoslavia as well. Without the strong-armed dictator there, it finally collapsed. It went into full-on civil war, with all of these groups that I've just suggested, and probably thirty more, all fighting it out for separate pieces of territory. Long story short, Eastern Europe in the last 15 years saw the USSR devolve from one entity to fifteen sovereign states, Czechoslovakia devolve from one country to two, Yugoslavia devolve from one country to five in the 1990's. In 2006, Montenegro became #6. And the fat lady has not sung yet, my friends, which brings us up to current events . . .

As you can see, the Yugoslavians have had kind of their own tale that's a bit separate from the USSR, but of course related, and that brings us full circle to today's world. And the shattering may not be over yet! Slippery #7

may be on its way, but this time it won't be without a fight. Kosovo may be the next to go. It is being widely disputed in today's world. In February of 2008, Kosovo declared independence. Immediately, a bunch of Western European states and the US recognized their independence, which, of course, *infuriated* both Serbia and Russia. Russia is not very happy about this. NOTE: Not all Western European states recognized Kosovo, and therefore, the EU as a singular entity did not recognize it either. The big boys like the UK and France did, but many other minor European powers did not, for reasons we shall get to in a minute.

We have this situation that, again, crystallizes this new power struggle within Eastern Europe that's related to the old power struggle. Russian influence versus Western influence. The Russians, their historic ally Serbia (that is, what's left of Yugoslavia), and other entities around the world said, "You can't recognize Kosovo. You guys were promising all along you wouldn't." Because, of course, the United States and NATO intervened in Kosovo, kicked out Slobodan, and protected the Kosovars. But they always claimed that they were merely preventing genocide, and not carving out a new state. Russia argued, "Hey, all along when you guys did that intervention thing, you said that you weren't setting up a new state, that you weren't going to let them have independence, that you were just going to stop the civil war, and basically you're liars."

Russia is not alone on this issue either. China, as well as many European countries, have refused to support Kosovar independence because they think it sets a bad precedent. If there's one small, little group of people that are pissed off at a country and you're going to allow them to declare independence, then there's going to be a whole lot more shattering going on, and not just in Eastern Europe. You're setting a precedent for other folks to do it around the world. Russia don't want the Chechans declaring independence; China don't want Tibetans declaring independence either. It's interesting to note that places like Spain did not support Kosovo independence because they said, "Hey look, we have a small group of radicals who want an independent Basque country, so no way. There's no way we're going to support that, because then the Basque people will say, 'We're going to be independent too.'" You see how complicated this issue has become.

Back to the point: this is all about Russian influence here. The Russians are supporting their old Serb allies, saying, "No, this is BS. We ain't recognizing Kosovo and nobody else should either." And the West is saying, "Oh, but, you know, they want to be a democracy, and peace-loving and all that stuff. We are going to support 'em.'" Yep. Eastern Europe right back in the middle again. I guess old habits die hard in the end.

The point of this last section is that Russia is back. They are re-flexing their muscles. They are reasserting influence, not control, but influence over their old Eastern European sphere of influence, and the West is still pushing in as well.

CONCLUSION: THE TRANSITION IS ALMOST FINISHED!?

A new era, a new time, and it seems like the Eastern European transition is almost done. Most of these states have joined the western block institutions, with perhaps just a few more to go. Most countries are in the EU. Most are in NATO. They are Europe now. Most are part of Team West. Most.

But Eastern Europe has historically been in a vice and perhaps it may be ready to explode again. This region does have a strange history of being under the influence of these greater powers to its east and its west, thus why I started the chapter calling it bookended. Somehow, Eastern Europe is the one that sparks all the trouble between the sides. Seriously, think about it. Go back to World War I. It was started in what is now Yugoslavia, when Archduke Franz Ferdinand (it's not just a band) was assassinated there by some Serbian radical. World War II started when Hitler invaded Poland. Then the Cold War battle lines were drawn in Eastern Europe, with most of the missiles either deployed on it, or pointed at it.

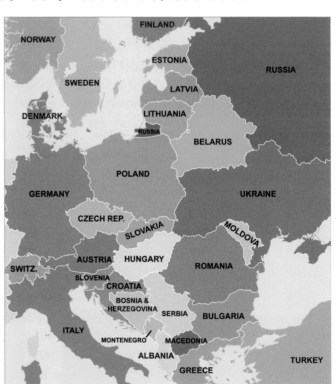

Eastern Europe today . . . at least for now.

Why list all these transgressions again? To stress a not-so-obvious point: all major conflicts of the last century were sparked in this bookended region. Hmmm . . . that certainly is food for thought, isn't it? Major players seem to get sucked into confrontation over this swath of land between Russia and Western Europe. Sucked in, and then life really sucks for all involved.

The disintegration of Yugoslavia also started here in Eastern Europe—go figure, because it's located there—and it's not done yet. That's why I bring up this Kosovo situation, which is once again pitting an east versus west, a Russia versus Team West. The Kosovo situation is promising to polarize these sides unlike really anything else that's going on here at the dawn of the 21st century. I know what you're thinking: "Hahahahaha what a load of bull, like a major war is going to start over some insignificant little hole in the wall like Kosovo?" Yeah, you're probably right. My bad. How stupid am I being? I mean, the odds of that happening are about as likely as a global war being started over the assassination of an unknown Austrian Archduke while motor-cading through Belgrade. Ummm . . . oops. Bad example.

The question is, when will these people quit? How many more subdivisions can occur? How much more shattering before it's over? Quite frankly, the answer is perhaps never, because it's outside forces which seem to promote, antagonize, and continue to push in this battleground buffer zone that we call Eastern Europe. As alluded to earlier, and elaborated much more on in chapter 25, Ukraine is now the country to watch as the next chapter of Eastern European devolution, and it promises to be the most exciting, action-packed episode yet! And never, ever discount the possibility of Bosnia or Serbia or Croatia blowing back up again; tensions continue to simmer under the lid of the former Yugoslavia. But that's all for now. We keep talking about Russia being involved as one of the players in this battleground of ideologies in Eastern Europe, so perhaps we should now turn our attention to the Bear. Oh Vlad . . . are you out there . . .

EASTERN EUROPE RUNDOWN & RESOURCES

View additional Plaid Avenger resources for this region at http://plaid.at/ee

 BIG PLUSES

→ Due to lower wages and overhead, Eastern Europe is attracting lots of foreign investment and jobs from Western Europe

→ Eastern Europe produces a lot of agricultural products and is becoming a manufacturing hub for Western Europe

→ Incorporation into the EU promises to help raise standards of living and the economy for most Eastern European states to eventually reach Western European standards

→ Incorporation into NATO promises to ensure political and military stability for its Eastern European members

 BIG PROBLEMS

→ Many states of the region have a long way to go to achieve western-style standards of living

→ Possibility of ethnic/religious/nationalist conflict rearing its head again is highly likely, particularly in the Balkans

→ Non-NATO states in the region (Ukraine, Belarus) and even some NATO members (Poland, the Baltic states) will continue to be torn between their western allies and having to suck up to Russia

→ Many Eastern European states are heavily reliant on energy supplies from Russia

DEAD DUDES OF NOTE:

Archduke Franz Ferdinand: Leader of Austria-Hungarian Empire who was assassinated by a radical Serbian nationalist in 1914; the Empire then declared war on Serbia, which triggered all of Europe to declare war against each other, thus World War I.

Marshall Josip Tito: The communist strong-armed dictator that held together Yugoslavia for decades, despite the wildly diverse ethnic/religious mix of the state. And when he died, it all came unraveled. He was Serbian and an ally of the Russians, but never a part of the USSR.

Slobodan Milošević: Former Serb President of Yugoslavia, this is the dude whose encouragement of Serbs to persecute Muslim Albanians in Kosovo resulted in the US/NATO bombing of his country into submission. He died in jail during his war crimes trial at the Hague. Still is looked upon as a nationalist hero by some Serbs.

PLAID CINEMA SELECTION:

Everything is Illuminated (2005) A freaky Jewish-American man (played by hobbit Frodo Baggins aka Elijah Wood) road trips to find the woman who saved his grandfather from Nazis during WWII in a Ukrainian village. Bizarre and intriguing, and great landscapes shot on location in Ukraine and Czech Republic.

No Man's Land (2001) Set in war-torn Bosnia-Herzogovina in 1993, a Serb and a Croat are caught in a catch-22 situation in a trench between opposing armies' with a guy laying on a live land mine. Also features: ineffective UN, physical scenery of Slovenia, and realistic rendition of how confusing this war is to outsiders and insiders alike.

Before the Rain (1994) Time twisting tale in 3 parts that shows the internal political turbulence of Macedonia as it pulled away from war-torn Yugoslavia and became independent. Shot on location in Macedonia, builds on the futility of the cyclical nature of violence endemic in this region, pitting families against each other, and their neighbors. After you watch it, retrace the timeline, and also figure out who actually killed who.

4 Months, 3 Weeks and 2 Days (2007) Set in 1987, on of the last years of the communist/dictatorship Ceausescu era, in Bucharest, Romania, this film documents the struggles of two adolescent girls, as one goes through an illegal abortion. At times, mildly disturbing, the power of cinema is evident throughout the entire film.

I Served the King of England (2006) Filmmakers from both the Czech Republic and Slovakia joined to create this film depicting Czechoslovakia during the 1940s. Nice historical sweep of the area from pre-war to German occupation to soviet occupation , and an excellent look at a variety of landscapes in Eastern Europe and Germany.

Katyn (2007) War torn Poland during WWII and the events leading up to and eventually culminating in the Katyn Massacre, where the soviets murdered 15,000 Polish POW officers and citizens. Includes actual German and Soviet newsreels from the time. This is as topical as it gets: did you hear about the Polish President dying in a plane crash in April 2010? He was heading to a Katyn memorial service at the time. Freaky!

Force 10 from Navarone (1978) Awesomely cheesy, action WWII film set in Yugoslavia and other parts of Eastern Europe. Shows little-known Nazi action in the Balkan Peninsula and actually filmed in parts of Yugoslavia and Montenegro. Stars a young Harrison Ford, as he shot it at the same time Star Wars was being made. Sorry, it's a plaid guilty pleasure.

LIVE LEADERS YOU SHOULD KNOW:

Boris Tadić: centrist, well-educated, and very level-headed current President of Serbia that is doing a pretty good job holding his fragile country together and re-incorporating it back into the European economy.

Viktor Yanukovych: His fraudulent election was the cause of Orange Revolution and, amazingly enough, is now the newly-elected President of Ukraine. Very pro-Russian, and therefore not so pro-western, in outlook and strategic alliance.

Viktor Yushchenko: previous pro-West president of Ukraine that surfed to power on the Orange Revolution wave. Tried unsuccessfully to incorporate his country into EU and NATO, but political stagnation and inefficiency got his ass tossed out of office. Oh, and he's the dude that got poisoned by ex-KGB during his run at the presidency.

Yulia Tymoshenko: International political hottie extraordinaire and previous Ukrainian Prime minister. Has her own pro-Yulia party, and is adept at playing both sides of the pro-West and pro-Russia sides of the game to her advantage. You will see her rise again in Ukrainian politics.

CHAPTER OUTLINE

Russia

10

THE BEAR IS BACK

Russia is the largest country on the planet. They were the Cold War adversary of the US; you know, the bad guys. We refer to Russia as the Bear, and this wild woolly bear seems to change focus and direction every semester that passes, just as a wild bear hunts in the woods. I'm scared! Not really, but it is a region that is in transition, much like Eastern Europe; in this regard, it is changing every day. However, unlike Eastern Europe which has a very distinct direction of change, Russia is what the Plaid Avenger calls a fence-straddler—that is, it is playing the field in terms of with whom it does business, with whom it has a political alliance, and with whom it will throw in its future.

Time to bear all!

Russia has been a distinct culture, a world power player, a part of the Soviet Union, and a major shaper of world history and events of the 20th century. But in today's world, it doesn't have as much significance as it once did. It has experienced tremendous political and economic upheavals and can almost be considered behind the times here in the 21st century. How did this region go from a global power to a globally broken basket-case? More importantly for our understanding of today's world, how is it successfully getting back into the game? All of these things and more, we will explore as we tell the story of the Bear.

One big bear. US/Russia size comparison.

HAIR OF THE BEAR

We always start our regional tour with a breakdown of what's happening in the physical world. When we think of Russia, several words typically come to mind: big, cold, and vodka. There's some truth in this. Russia is a cold place, a big place, and those Russians do love their vodka. But kids, just say "no" to that . . . unless you are in Russia, of course, and then you say, "Nyet."

Russia is the largest state on the planet, twice as big as Canada, the second largest. Does size matter? Do I even need to ask? Of course it does! Size matters in most aspects of life. This huge country crosses eleven time zones, spanning almost half of the globe. When the sun is setting on one side of Russia, it is rising on the other side! Just think of all the problems associated with infrastructure and communications in a state this big. Think of all the problems associated with just trying to keep all of your people within your country aware of what's going on at any given second, much less having to move things around in it, like military equipment.

Don't even try to think about having to defend its vast borders. Your head will explode. Russia has a top slot in terms of how many different countries it borders, which I believe is now fourteen in all. But it's not all bad. This massive territory contains loads of stuff—what stuff? All kinds of stuff: oil and gold, coal and trees, water and uranium and lots and lots of land. What do lots of people do with lots of land? They typically can grow lots of food, but that's not always the case in Russia because of its second physical feature—it's cold.

Help! I've fallen in Siberia and I can't get up!

Maybe that's why the bear has such a thick coat. Virtually all of Russia lies north of the latitude of the US-Canadian border. This high latitude equates to the cooler climates found on our planet; indeed, some of Russia lies north of the Arctic Circle, which means most of its northern coast remains frozen year round. To compound matters, Russia

Siberia! The Spring Break destination of the Soviets!

lies at the heart of the Eurasian continent; because of this fact, it has perhaps the greatest extremes of continentality expressed by its extreme temperature ranges, both season to season and also day to day. There are some parts of Russia in which the temperature within a 24-hour period may change 100 degrees—that is, it could be 60 degrees Fahrenheit at 3:00 in the afternoon and 12 hours later it might be −40 degrees Fahrenheit. That's extreme. Maybe this tough climate has something to do with Russian attitudes, their outlook on life in general. A tough place with a tough history which brings us to our last physical descriptor: vodka.

Russia is the greatest consumer of vodka on the planet. Both in terms of total quantity and per capita consumption, no one can touch the Russians when it comes to drinking vodka. Perhaps it's the bleak and challenging climate that makes the Russian life so hard and vodka consumption a necessity to deal with the challenge. Perhaps this is why vodka is such an integral part of Russian history. Did someone say Russian history?

FROM CUB TO GRIZZLY

How did the Russian state get to be the largest country on the planet? How did it get so much stuff? Where did these guys come from? What does it mean to be Russian? The "original Russians" were actually Swedish Vikings who moved into the area around modern day Moscow to Kiev, probably around 1200 to 1000 B.C.E. Thus Russians look European and share many of their cultural traits.

HISTORIC GROWTH

Looking at the maps across the bottom of the page, we can see that Russia, in 1300, was more like a kingdom than an empire; indeed, it was not a huge territory. It was a small enclave of folks that called themselves ethnically Russian but were politically subservient to the real power brokers of that era: the Mongols. **The Golden Horde** was a political sub-unit of the Mongol Empire that controlled parts of Russia and Eastern Europe at the time. It was not until 1480, under the leadership of Ivan the 3rd, a.k.a. **Ivan the Great,** that Russia stood up to the Mongols, threw off the yoke of Mongol oppression, and began its growth into the land juggernaut we know today.

Ivan united his people, kicked some Mongol butt, and expanded the empire. His son, Ivan the 4th, a.k.a. **Ivan the Terrible,** continued this trend by feeding the Bear and expanding the empire further. Ivan the Terrible earned his name by having an incredibly nasty temper, eventually murdering his son and heir apparent with an iron rod. Nice guy. Good family man.

Soon after the Ivans created this empire called Russia, an imperial family line was put into place that lasted uninterrupted up until the 20th century. They were the Romanovs, to whom you've probably heard references before. I'm not going to go into great detail on all of them, but just to put a few into perspective, let's list some of the more famous names. **Peter the Great** popped up around 1700 and was known for many things, notably creating and building the town of St. Petersburg. I wonder where he got the name?

Why is this significant? Because it shows what Peter was all about, and that was embracing Europe. Even back then, Russia lagged significantly behind its European counterparts in terms of industrialization, technology, military, and economy. Peter was all about catching the Bear up. St. Petersburg was often called "a window to the West" because the city

Russia in 1300   Russia in 1462   Russia in 1584

embraced Western technology and architecture and there was a real sense that it was opening Russia to interaction with the rest of Europe. Here's another example of how Russia is tied historically to the West: the term "Czar" in Russia was taken from the Roman Empire's "Caesar." In addition, Moscow was often referred to as "the third Rome" throughout history, as it viewed itself as the protector of true Christianity, in its distinctive Eastern Orthodox tradition. (Rome #1 was Rome; after the Roman Empire collapsed, then Rome #2 was Constantinople; after the Byzantine Empire crashed, then Rome #3 was Moscow). Russia has embraced and associated itself with the West in many ways over the years, although in most cases, it lagged behind.

Peter expanded the empire in all directions. This brings us to an interesting component of the Russian Empire's growth: Why expand? Many historians have speculated that there has been an inherent drive to expand the state in an effort to gain coastline. All major European nations with world dominance during this era had a lot of coastline and were maritime powers. Because of Russia's position on the continent, it is conceivable that most of its growth occurred in part to open up the coast in order to become a world power as well. This is speculative to be sure, but it does make some common sense.

A Tit Bit for a Russian Ambassador !!!!

Russian ambassador dealing with Napoleon.

One resource that's certainly driven Russian continental expansion was **fur.** Given the climate of this part of the world and the way people dressed, it certainly is the case that the trading of fur—that is, stripping the exterior of live animals and making coats out of it—was the main economic engine behind the continued growth of the land empire. Cold climate = animals with lots of fur = animals we want to kill for their fur = fur coats worth lots of money = more land = more furry animals to continue driving the economy. Speaking of continued land growth, we come to another familiar name in history, **Catherine the Great.** She radically expanded the empire across the continent, was a familiar face in European politics, and helped propel the Russian state into serious power player status on the continent during the 1760s and 1770s.

The last face to consider during our old school Russian tour is that of **Napoleon.** Wait a minute! He's not Russian! True, but he did invade Russia in 1812 in one of the many great blunders in history. Napoleon was doing pretty well conquering Europe until he invaded Russia. Here's a little Plaid Avenger tip from me to you: don't invade Russia. Don't ever invade Russia. No one has ever successfully invaded Russia. As Napoleon—and later, Adolf Hitler—found out, it's easy to get *into* Russia, but it's impossible to get *out.* As the French forces advanced to Moscow and eventually took over the city, they did so in the middle of a horrifically cold Russian winter, and because of their dwindling supplies, were forced to retreat. They were attacked continuously on their way out. Bad call, Napoleon. You silly short dead dude! Russian Trix are for kids!

Russia in 1800   Russia in 1867   Russia in 1955

Ivan the Great: Mangled the Mongolians.

Ivan the Terrible: Skewered his son.

Peter the Great: Wanted to be Western.

Catherine the Great: had fun with horses?

I bring this up to reiterate a common theme in Russian history: Russia always seems to come out stronger at the end of extreme turmoil. After Napoleon's invasion, it comes out sitting pretty as the world's largest territorial empire. We will see this theme again after World War II.

SERF'S UP, DUDES!

I've painted a pretty picture with lots of faces and names that you've heard before, but don't let me suggest that life and times in Russian history were good. Mostly they really sucked, for the lower classes in particular. During the imperial reign I've described thus far, life was fine for the royal court, but life as a commoner was brutal. We have a sort of a feudal system in Russia for most of its history. Serfdom in this country really turns into something more equivalent to slavery than traditional serfdom. What we're talking about here is a typical feudal structure where there is a lord who owns the land and under him, the mass of people in the country are tied to that land. As such, they have no rights to hold landed notes, no human rights, and are basically workers or slaves of the landholder. In combination with the fantastic climate of Russia, one can see how living here for most folks was not a fun time. Chronic food shortages and mass starvations were common occurrences as particularly brutal winters, bad crop harvests, and repressive taxation systems kept the peasants in a perpetual state of misery.

Why talk about the plight of Russian peasantry? Because the dissatisfaction among a vast majority is soon going to culminate in a revolution; a revolution the likes of which the world has never seen. It wasn't like the aristocracy didn't see it coming, either.

In an attempt to placate the masses, Tsar Alexander II passed the sweeping Emancipation Reform of 1861, which was supposed to end this miserable peasant situation. WTF? Emancipation didn't occur until 1861? That's late in the game! That's the same year that the US started their Civil War in order to emancipate slaves! Unfortunately for Russia, this proclamation on paper didn't amount to much in real life, and the crappy peasant existence continued. By the turn of the century, freed slaves in the US had more rights than supposedly freed peasants in Russia, not to mention that the vast majority of Europe as a whole had long since abolished both slavery and feudalism.

As we progressed toward the year 1900, many Russian folks were still essentially slaves of the land. This was a time when the rest of Europe was industrializing and getting more connected. Europe had political revolutions, which created states that emphasized equality for individuals, even the lowest classes. People in Russia knew what was going on in the rest of Europe. They heard about the French Revolution and Britain's change to a constitutional monarchy. If you look at a political map of Europe's changes over time, you'll see that things started in the West, and these changes took a long time to make their way to Russia. Indeed, economic and political revolution reached there last, but when it did come, it came big.

As changes were enacted in Europe, as common folk in Europe gained more and more rights and perhaps even more and more wealth, Russia was stagnant. Russia was falling behind yet again. Dissatisfaction was also on the rise, and things in the 20th century made it quite a bumpy ride for the Russian Bear, particularly for its royal line.

RUSSIAN PEASANTS   4157-10

Dimitri! Where's the party, dude? All the ladies are in the house!

THE BEAR TAKES A BEATING

The 20th century, taken as a whole, was not kind to Russia. It started the century on a downward slide. As Russia fell farther and farther behind the times and as popular dissent increased, the imperial government did the worst thing possible: it lost a war. One of the things that kept peasants in line was the concept of a strong central government, even though it may not be popular or even good. Citizens wanted a government to protect them from foreign powers, invasion or destruction from invaders. Even though the monarchy was not popular, at least they maintained a strong military presence to guard their citizens and territory. When they failed to do that, full failure of the state was not far behind, and Japan provided the first kink in the armor of the Romanov line.

GODZILLA ATTACKS

In 1905, the Japanese declared war on Russia. The Japanese, having risen in power for the last fifty years up to that point, began encroaching on Russian lands in the east. This came to a head when the Japanese took over part of mainland Asia claimed by Russia. **Tsar Nicholas II** deemed it necessary to go to war to reclaim this land and to put the Japanese in their place. Easier said than done. The Russians sent their entire fleet from Europe to take on the Japanese in the Sea of Japan. After this extensive voyage, the Russian fleet arrived to be beaten down by the Japanese fleet in a matter of minutes. It was the most one-sided naval battle in history. The entire Russian fleet was obliterated. Back home in Moscow, popular dissent turned into popular hatred after this stunning defeat. The **Russo-Japanese War** was costly and unpopular and served to really get people thinking about replacing the monarchy with a whole new system altogether. But the fun had only just begun!

Back home in Russia, the peasants and workers alike had about enough. Later in 1905, a general strike was enacted empire-wide to protest the slow pace of reform and general discontent with the aristocracy. The system was broken, and the people knew it. This protest was met with an iron fist by the government, and things turned nasty, fast. The 1905 Russian Revolution is best remembered for the legendary Bloody Sunday massacre; cross-toting, hymn singing protesters were slaughtered by government troops as they marched to the Tsar's Winter Palace. Brutal! The Romanovs had restored order, but not for much longer.

WORLD WAR I

The Russo-Japanese War may have been damaging and unpopular, but at least it was far away. However, the next phase of fun happened closer to home, when Archduke Franz Ferdinand of Austria was assassinated in what later became Yugoslavia. This was the spark that ignited World War I and everybody declared war on each other. Russia had diplomatic ties with Serbia, who was pulled into the war immediately, so the Ruskies had to jump in as well. As we pointed out, this came on the heels of a loss to the Japanese on the other side of the Russian empire. From the onset, World War I was extremely unpopular because people at home were saying, "Hey, you already lost to the Japanese! Life here is sucking! Things are going down hill fast and

Nicholas II rides to the front lines of WWI: "The Monk made me do it!"

now we are in a war? Nobody even knows what we are in it for! Serbia? Serbia who? What are you thinking?"

World War I was fought on Russia's front doorstep; for three long years, there was a catastrophic death toll on the Russian side. The Germans made huge gains into Russian territory and snapped up large parts of the front. Meanwhile, back at the bear cave, popular dissent was growing wildly, fueled in part by the shenanigans of yet another famous Russian, Rasputin. "The Mad Monk" as he was referred to by many Russians, was a shaman/con-man who worked himself and his magic into the inner circles of aristocratic power, including being a direct advisor to the royal family themselves. In point of fact, Tsar Nicholas II was strongly advised by Rasputin to personally lead the charge on the front lines of WWI, even though everybody knew good old Nick was not up for the challenge. Chaos then ensued both on the war front, but more importantly, back home as well. (check out inset box on Rasputin, next page).

Archduke Franz Ferdinand

My death started WWI. Sorry!

Tsar Nicholas II

My death made the Revolution irreversible. Sorry!

Vladimir Lenin

My death launched Stalin into power. Sorry!

The Mad Monk, Rasputin

I'm still not dead. Someone get me the hell out of this coffin!

196

The Regions

PART TWO

I don't need to get too much more into World War I history after this, because the Russians didn't have a lot to do with it. About halfway through the war, internal dissent within Russia reached an all time high. The Bear reeked of revolt.

THAT'S REVOLTING!
COMMIES TAKE COMMAND

The revolt occurred in February of 1917 and Tsar Nicholas II abdicated, meaning he quit before he got fired. When the Tsar, who had been out fighting in the battlefield during World War I, returned to Russia, he discovered his people were in open revolt. He abdicated, and put his brother on the throne. Faster than you can say, "I hereby resign from the throne," his brother abdicated as well. A temporary government was set up, but in terms of who is really going to take power, nobody could tell.

"Let's redistribute some damn wealth, people!"

On October 25, 1917, this culminated in an event that people all over the world know, **the Bolshevik or Communist revolution,** led by our good friend, Vladimir Lenin. Communism was not something that everybody in Russia were just jumping up and down about. In fact, most people had never even heard of it. Karl Marx and Friedrich Engels wrote about the concept in Germany and Austria; they weren't Russians. Lenin was a revolutionary even in his youth, and came in contact with a lot of these ideals during his college years. His older brother, who was executed because of his socialist activism, also influenced him. Lenin became a lawyer, but was eventually exiled to Siberia because of his radical revolutionary activities.

In Siberia, he wrote and published a lot of socialist literature, and became a prominent figure in the revolutionary movement. He eventually fled to Finland, and later Switzerland. While there, Lenin made appearances and speeches to other socialist groups in Europe. When the open revolt in Russia started to happen, Vladimir and other revolutionaries boarded a train and headed

What's the Deal with Rasputin?

The biography of Grigori Rasputin, a.k.a. the Mad Monk, is often fortified with folklore, which is fine by the Plaid Avenger because the folklore that surrounds Rasputin is hilarious. What is clear is that Rasputin practiced some sort of Christian-like religion and gained favor with Tsar Nicholas II by helping to medically treat his son through prayer. The Russian Orthodox Church didn't like Rasputin—mainly because churches never like competing ideology, but also because Rasputin loved

Big City Russian Pimpin'.

sinning. Much of this sinning involved prostitutes.

During World War I, Rasputin advised Tsar Nicholas II to seize command of the Russian military. This turned out poorly for two reasons: (1) Tsar Nicholas II wasn't a good army commander and (2) while Tsar was away, Rasputin gained considerable control of the Russian government and helped screw up the Russian economy. Needless to say, a lot of people were not happy with him. In December of 1916, a group set out to assassinate the Mad Monk. First, they attempted to poison him. The would-be assassins loaded two bottles of wine with poison, which Rasputin drank in their entirety. The assassins waited and waited, but Rasputin continued to display lively behavior. In a panic, they shot him point-blank in the back. When they came back later to deal with the body, Rasputin jumped up, briefly strangled his attempted killer, and then took off running. The group of assassins gave chase, shot Rasputin AGAIN—this time in the head with a large caliber bullet, and then beat him with both blunt and sharp objects. Finally, they wrapped his body in a carpet and threw it off a bridge into the Neva River, but, the river was frozen over, so Rasputin's body just smashed into the layer of ice. The assassins climbed down to the frozen river and broke the ice under Rasputin so his body would sink into the water. They eventually succeeded and Rasputin disappeared into the freezing depths. Three days later, authorities found Rasputin's body and performed an autopsy. The autopsy revealed that Rasputin had died from drowning and, in fact, his arms were frozen in a position that suggested he died while trying to claw his way through the ice and out of the river.

Me-oww! That cat was a freaky-freak. And his lives ran out. Maybe . . .

back into Russia after a long absence from their homeland. Once Lenin returned, he became a prominent figure in the Bolshevik party and leader of the Soviet revolution.

One of his ideas that gained popular support was not necessarily that communism was the greatest thing ever, but instead, "We need to get the hell out of World War I!" He received popular support for his Soviet ideas because monarchy, peasantry, and Russian life in general sucked. The power structure was completely unfair. What also gained popularity was the promise to get Russia out of the war in exchange for the support of his cause. Long story short, the Communist revolution became an internal power struggle, and the Bolsheviks came out on top. "Bolshevik" means "majority," but in reality, the movement was anything but a majority. The Bolsheviks had many political rivals in the struggle to control Russia. The commies were actually a very small group of people who enacted this revolution and took over the whole nation.

True to their word, as soon as the Bolsheviks took over the government at the end of 1917, they immediately bailed out of the war. They agreed to let the Germans have any invaded territory and signed a peace treaty. As you can see from this map, there were huge territorial losses as a result of this. The Russians lost territories that later became Estonia, Latvia, Lithuania, Moldova, and large parts of Poland. I am telling you this specifically because it is going to become Russian territory again after World War II.

Now as I just suggested, not everybody in Russia immediately embraced communism. In fact, there were many holdouts. As you might expect, there were conservative people in the aristocracy and the military who thought that

the monarchy, the old established way, should return and things should revert back to the way they were.

As soon as the Bolsheviks took power, one of the first things Lenin did was put the entire royal family under house arrest. Shortly thereafter, a civil war broke out; from 1918 to about 1920, there was open fighting throughout the country. The Russian Civil War was fought between the new party in charge, the Communists, and the old conservative holdouts and much of the military. The parties who fought the Russian Civil War referred to it as "the Reds versus the Whites." Obviously, the Reds were the communists and the Whites, the loyalists. The Red Russians versus the White Russians!

Again, our story here is that the 20th century was not very kind to Russia. It had a disastrous World War I and then an internal revolution which turned into a civil war. The civil war is eventually and bloodily won by the Reds. By the way, once the civil war broke out, Lenin ordered the assassination of the entire

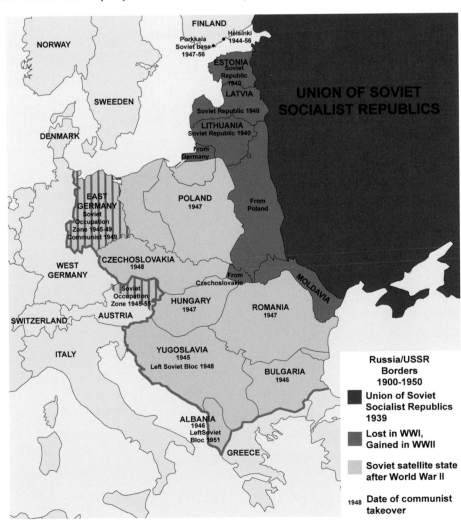

Check out the Russian losses in WWI.

royal family. Why did Lenin do this? I thought he was a nice commie. The reason Lenin did this was because he believed that in order to succeed, Communist Russia had to sever all ties with the past: "You people are fighting for a monarchy? You want to restore an imperial royal line? Well, we will fix that! They can't be restored to the throne if they're all dead!"

This made the statement that no matter who won the war, there would be no return to monarchy because there were no more monarchs. The Romanov line ended with the assassination of Nicholas II, his wife, and five children including Anastasia; rumors suggesting Anastasia escaped execution circulated for decades (see inset box on right). The civil war was finished by 1920, and the Communists had power over the government and the country. Unfortunately, fate was still not smiling on Mother Russia, as the country saw back to back famines in 1921–23 as the result of horrific winter weather—like the weather is even good in the good years? However, by the mid-1920's, the worst seemed to be over and it was time to get that commie transition on!

What's the Deal with Anastasia?
Anastasia was born the Grand Duchess of Russia in 1901. When the Bolsheviks took power in Russia, Anastasia's entire family was executed because of their links to the Romanov dynasty. However, legend is that Anastasia and her brother Alexei might have survived

Dead? Yep.

the execution. This legend is supported by the fact that Anastasia and Alexei were not buried in the family grave. Several women came forward in the 20th Century claiming to be Anastasia, but guess what: she's dead. Regardless of the intrigue and the crappy animated kid's movie, The Plaid Avenger is certain that Anastasia died of lead poisoning with the rest of her family. Lead poisoning induced by bullets. Lots of bullets.

THE BEAR BATTLES BACK

The next event of great significance happened in 1924, when Lenin died. For vehement anticommunists, that was a day of celebration; for Russians, it was not a day of celebration, because Lenin was the founder of the party, a rallying post, and a popular leader of the communist movement in Russia. He had the grand designs about where society was going, the ideal of equality where everyone shared the wealth, and the whole utopian society thing. Why was his death titanic? Well, because after he died, who would succeed him? The answer was Joseph Stalin.

STYLIN' WITH STALIN

From 1924 to 1953, Joseph Stalin, one of the biggest bastards history has ever known, was in power of what was now called the Union of Soviet Socialist Republics (USSR), the post–civil war title for Russia.

Stalin's ascension to power was tricky for several reasons. One: he was crazy. After he gained power, he was psychotic and became more psychotic as every year of his reign passed. He consolidated all power to the center under himself, basically as a dictator, and that's what he was. He set up the infamous secret police force, the KGB, who sent out spies amongst the people, and conducted assassinations of all political rivals, their families, their cats, their dogs, and their neighbors. Anyone who spoke ill of Stalin ended up in a grave with a tombstone over his head. No, I take that back. They ended up in a mass grave with dirt over their heads. He was a nasty guy in a tough place in an extremely gut-kicking century for Russian history. But our story is not over yet, kids—the fun is still not done!

Before I go any further, I should say there is always a bright side to every individual. Smokin' Joe Stalin's bright side was that part of the commie plan was to consolidate agricultural lands and speed industrialization. The Reds wanted to catch the country up with the rest of the modern world economically, technologically, and militarily. As much as I hate to admit it, that is exactly what occurred during the Stalin era.

Essentially Stalin oversaw a "crash course" of modernization, industrialization, and collectivization. These hugely ambitious goals could not have been achieved just by planning, though; the Russian people themselves have to be given a large share of the credit to have pulled this off. Perhaps Stalin's biggest contribution to these gains was not just organization and planning, but he somehow instilled a die-hard sense of uber-patriotic nationalism in the people that made for explosive societal gains. Specifically, the Russian people were convinced to work harder, work longer, make more out of less, consume less, and totally work hard for the country, not for themselves.

Of course, Stalin used all sorts of coercion and open force to achieve these aims when necessary. And again, he was nuts. But if we are going to credit Stalin with anything besides being the biggest bastard of the 20th century, we can credit him with the Soviet infrastructure moving forward at breakneck speed, and they indeed caught up in a matter of a few decades. They created the atomic bomb shortly after the US did, and even beat the US into space with the launch of the Sputnik satellite. Fifty years earlier, they were all beet farmers. That is some fast progress!

THE BEAR ENTERS WORLD WAR II

By World War II, the USSR was starting to be a major world force. Before the war began in 1939, Joseph Stalin and Adolf Hitler met and signed a nonaggression pact. The meeting went down like this, brought to you Plaid Avenger style: Germany said, "We are going to take over the world, but here's the deal: we won't attack you as long as you don't attack us." Smokin' Joe Stalin, in all of his wisdom, said, "Okay, go ahead and take over Western Europe and the rest of the world. That sounds good to us. They were always kind of bothersome anyway. Also, we won't attack you as long as you don't attack us. Deal!" The war officially kicked off in 1941, when Germany attacked everybody. Hitler later made the fantastically idiotic mistake, after taking over most of Europe, of reneging on the nonaggression pact. In other words, he attacked the USSR anyway.

As discussed before about Napoleon, one of the greatest historical blunders for anybody is to invade

Joseph Stalin: Biggest Bastard of the 20th Century
Unfortunately, the award for "Biggest Bastard" is highly competitive. There's Hitler, Pol Pot, Mussolini, Idi Amin, Pinochet, Margaret Thatcher, and many more. But the Plaid Avenger is fairly certain that Joe Stalin is the nastiest of them all. Stalin was one of the Bolshevik leaders who brought communism to Russia in 1918. When Vladimir Lenin, who was the original leader of the Bolsheviks, unexpectedly died in 1924, Stalin slowly assumed power. In 1936, Stalin initiated The Great Purge which lasted for two years. During this time, "dissenters" were shipped off to Gulag labor camps and often executed. Most "dissenters" were actually just normal folks who had been wrongly accused by other normal folks who were being tortured at a Gulag labor camp. As you can see, this was a self-perpetuating cycle. If everyone had to sell out eight friends to stop getting tortured, and each friend had to sell out eight friends, pretty soon you would have a ton of political "dissenters." It's like an incredibly violent email pyramid scam. Anyway, The Great Purge resulted in the death of approximately 20 million Russians.

While The Great Purge was probably Stalin's sentinel work of bastard-dom, it was far from his last. Stalin organized a giant farm collectivization which left millions homeless and millions more hungry. He also continued purging dissenters until he died in 1953. Historians estimate over 45 million Russians died directly from Stalin's actions (this figure does not include the estimated 20 million Russians that died during WWII). What a psycho.

Russian soldiers line up for their daily vodka ration—of three liters.

Russia. No one's ever done it successfully, and Hitler was one in a long line of idiots who tried. After he attacked the USSR, the USSR was then obliged to defend itself and was pulled into World War II. This is of great importance: the USSR was the real winner of the war in Europe. Once the Germans declare war on the United States, who joined the rest of the Allies, it became the Germans versus the world. The Germans were really in a pinch as they were attacked on all flanks, the Allies on one side and the Russians on the other. While I am certainly not going to devalue the role of the Allies in the west, Russia really took out a lot of Germans and caused them to divert resources and men to the Russian front, which is the reason why World War II was won by the good guys.

Had the Russo-German nonaggression pact been upheld by Germany, it would be hard to tell what the map of Europe would look like today. It certainly wouldn't look like it does now, because the Russian death toll was astronomical. There were almost 9 million Russian military deaths, and at least 20 million civilian casualties—29 million people total! Take 29 and multiply it by a thousand, then take that and multiply it by another thousand! The Plaid Avenger's not trying to insult your intelligence. I just want you to take a second and think about how many folks died in this thing.

This was some of the most brutal fighting on the entire continent. The Russian front was bloody, nasty, and deadly, and when all was said and done, the Russians beat the crap out of Germany. It was part of the main reason the Germans had to surrender in the end. I really want to stress the Russian losses. 29 million killed. We think about just the US's role in World War II, which was great by the way, but the US suffered maybe half a million to Russia's nearly 30 million deaths! As a result of WWII, Russia experienced an epic loss and made a major impact on the European theater of war. The war ended in 1945, the end of which set up the scenario for the next fifty years.

IS IT GETTING CHILLY IN HERE? THE COLD WAR

At the conclusion of the war, the Allies came in from the west and the Russians were mopping up in the east and they met halfway through Europe. They all did high fives and then they split Germany in half. Hitler was dead in the bunker, and there was a line where the Allies met after the war. The Allies were the United States, Britain, France, and the USSR. That's right! Smokin' Joe Stalin was on our team! Where the two forces met, as you see on this map, is halfway through Europe. That line quickly became known as **The Iron Curtain.**

What does this mean? Well, the Russians came in as a mop-up campaign; after the war was over and everyone finished celebrating, the Soviets said, "Maybe we will just stay here for a little while. We'll make sure everything has settled down. We'll help rebuild this side of Europe." The United States, under the **Marshall Plan,** was building up Western Europe. The Soviets were playing kind of the same role in Eastern Europe. Both parties occupied Germany to make sure it wouldn't start up trouble again—thus we had an East Germany and a West Germany, which reflected events happening in Europe as a whole.

In their effort to do this, the Soviets were pretty sinister. Under Soviet tutelage, "elections" were held all over, in places like Poland, Czechoslovakia, Hungary, Yugoslavia, and parts of Austria. We all know the outcome: lo and behold, the Communist party won resounding victories in every single place they held a vote! Everyone in the West knew this was a farce, but

The Iron Curtain Falls

⟍ Iron Curtain Line

■ Communist Sphere

▨ Democratic Capitalist

▨ Commie, but not Soviet

*Austria remained occupied by Allied powers until 1955, at which time it became independent upon condition of neutrality.

The metallic drapes were drawn.

nobody wanted to start another war. Remember, they were allies at the time, and they helped defeat the Germans together. The United States just wanted to get the hell out of there. They were not about to start a new war with Russia. The Western governments hesitantly went along with these newly "converted" communist states.

This set up a scenario where puppet governments replaced the previous governments. There's a term for this you should already know called **soviet satellites.** Some examples were sovereign states like Poland, Czech Republic, and Hungary that actually had seats at the UN—but everybody knew that the Soviets had the real control. These were puppet governments, to give the illusion of being expressive governments of their people. The situation simply evolved into Soviet occupation and control at this point. One of the reasons Western Europe and the United States allowed this to happen is that the Soviets very adeptly pointed out that they were staying in these Eastern European nations to make them a buffer zone because countries in Western Europe historically kept attacking them. That was true (e.g., Napoleon's France, Hitler's Germany).

These Eastern European states behind the curtain, that ended up being Soviet satellites, were actually parts of the territory that the Soviets had lost at the end of WWI, so the Soviets regained that loss. I like to point this out because it plays into what is happening in today's world. Whole countries that were sovereign states for a while between World War I and World War II, like Estonia, Latvia, Lithuania, Belarus, and the Ukraine, were totally reabsorbed by the Soviet Empire. These places declared independence after World War I, and then suddenly found themselves no longer sovereign states but republics or substates of the Soviet Union. That's why the map of Eastern Europe changed so rapidly. Places came and went as sovereign states were reabsorbed.

COMMIE ECON 101

The first half of the 20th century was fairly repressive, brutal, chaotic, and completely violent for Russia, but things stabilized during the Cold War. We have already set the stage in Europe for East versus West, which is going to turn into a global phenomenon that has shaped virtually every aspect of every region that we talk about in this book. What's the deal with the USSR as full-fledged commies after World War II?

As I have suggested previously, they had massive growth during Stalin's regime. He died shortly after World War II, but a lot of the industrialization which was radically successful under him continued on. Many of the programs, while oppressive and brutal, made the state a stronger world power. Indeed, it was the rise of the USSR which created the bipolar world that defined the Cold War. Stalin did a lot to get them up in the big leagues, and then checked out. He brought about massive industrialization, particularly in the weapons sector, which continued after his death.

What happened under the Soviet experiment post–World War II? What did they do? What did it look like there? What did they make? What did they produce? How would that be part of their eventual undoing? During the Soviet era one of the primary goals, even under Lenin, was to catch up industrially. They did this by centralizing everything. That's what communism is known for. The state runs everything, all aspects of politics—of course that's easy, it's what all governments do—but also all aspects of the economy—and that's typically not what the governments do. That is the communist way—full political and economical control of the entire country.

This is called **central economic planning,** and it entails the government's approval of where every 7-Eleven is located, where every ounce of grain is grown, where railroad tracks are laid down, where coal will be mined, where whole cities will be built to support something like an automotive industry. Every single aspect of life that we take for granted in a capitalist system was controlled in the Soviet sphere. This was done very early in the Soviet Empire to accomplish specific goals, one of which was called **forced collectivization.** Russia had been a peasant society, land based, rural, farmers digging around in the dirt, for hundreds of years. It couldn't do that in the 20th century if it was going to catch up and become a world power; it needed to get people off the land and into the cities. Why the cities? To work in the big factories that were industrializing and creating stuff.

Goal number one was forced collectivization. Pool all the land together, because it now belonged to the state: "You used to have rights to it and a deed on it, Dimitri, and

Tanks for the memories, commies!

maybe you used to grow tomatoes on it, but those days are gone now, comrade! You've got two options: go to a city or get in a collective, government regulated, growing commune." The state controlled all the land and agricultural production, because the state had one huge tractor to do the work of 1,000 men, and it had pesticides and fertilizers, which made huge monoculture crops. This new system produced tons more food. Whereas 1,000 dudes had to farm a piece of land before, now just ten can get the job done. 990 dudes headed to the city to accomplish the next goal: **rapid industrialization.**

To achieve rapid industrialization, the Soviet government needed to get everybody in and around the city into big factories. What were the factories going to produce? All of the things the West has that the Soviets needed to catch up on. Things like tanks, petrochemicals, big guns, rifles, maybe some big fur coats every now and again because it's cold there, aircraft carriers, missiles, bulldozers, heavy machinery, etc. The question you need to ask yourself at the same time is: what were they not making? The big difference between the communist expression and the capitalist expression in the 20th century comes down to this question. The answer is that the Soviets didn't make the items that normal people buy. Instead, they made huge stuff that only countries used. Like I told you earlier, the Soviet system stressed more work and *less consumption* by the individual, so that the state can become stronger.

You have to remember, the Soviet way was not focused on individual citizens or individual rights. The Soviet government didn't care about personal expression or fashion statements or if you liked building model airplanes. For them, the Soviet Union was an awesome state and an awesome idea and its citizens should be ardent nationalists and do everything for their state. By and large, people were pretty cool with that; at least most of them were, because to not be cool with that meant the KGB would run you down in the middle of the night and shoot you. People accepted it. Lots of them even liked it.

What wasn't produced in the Soviet economy? Consumer goods like cool clothes, sunglasses, lawn chairs, microwave ovens, refrigerators, independent-use vehicles. Anything that you'd go to a mall to buy today did not exist in the Soviet world. Knick-knacks did not serve the greater goal of the government, which was to catch up with the capitalists. That's just the way it was.

As much as the Plaid Avenger likes to make fun of knick-knacks and other crap you don't need, it played a role in why the Soviet Union unraveled—but that's for the next section. They did indeed catch up and became a world power under this system. One of the other things the Soviets did with the big things like tractors and bulldozers and weapons was to export them abroad. These are items that the Soviet Union is still known for. Russia is, to this day, a huge manufacturer and exporter of arms. Example: the Russian made AK-47 is easily the most popular and most widely distributed rifle on the planet.

Russia also exported a lot of this stuff at cut rates to other countries around the world. Why would you export a bunch of missiles to Cuba? That's right, for the Cuban Missile Crisis! You also want to send around machinery and petrochemicals and similar items that you produce to make money and recoup costs, but more importantly, to promote your influence in the world. That is what the Cold War was all about: coaxing other countries to join your side by providing them with things they really need, building bridges, selling them weapons and chemicals, and maybe even lending money. Anything to get people on your side. The United States and the Soviet Union both did this all over the place.

Only in a few places does this battle of ideology turn hot and people start shooting at each other. Two places of note where this occurred were in Korea, resulting in the Korean War and in Vietnam, resulting in the Vietnam War. We might even go as far to say as this also happened in Central America for all the Central American wars, during which both these two giants funneled in weapons so that the locals could fight it out between their opposing ideologies. The commies versus the capitalists in all these places was really what the wars were all about, and the two giants funded their respective sides.

CATASTROPHIC COMMIE IMPLOSION

How did the Cold War end for the Soviets? Why did I suggest that knick-knacks on the shelf may have been the saving grace of the United States, when all is said and done?

RUBLE RUPTURE

Buy now! These things are flying off the shelves!

The Soviet Union, from the 1960s through the 1980s, simply overextended itself. The United States and Western Europe's economies were based on producing a little bit of everything: tanks, aircraft, and petro-chemicals, but also consumer goods like cars, washing machines, toys, and Slap-Chops.

When you have stuff that individual citizens can buy and sell, you don't have to solely rely on big ticket items to fuel the economy. How many bulldozers can you sell in one season? I mean, The US system ended up championing in the end, because people buy consumer goods all the time. People like to buy refrigerators and new cars and blow dryers and pet rocks; but the US also made and sold bulldozers and missiles too. Long story short; US/Team West got richer, Soviets got poorer.

Russia's economy stank because it was based on flawed principles and was focused solely on items that eventually made it unsustainable. But there were other reasons these guys were going broke. Namely, they liked to give lots of money and support to their commie allies worldwide. During this expansion of Soviet influence across the planet, they really started to overextend themselves. They were giving stuff to Angola and the Congo in Africa, buying sugar from Cuba that they didn't even need, just so Cuba would be their ally, and lending money to places in Southeast Asia. By the 1980s, they were going broke while their economy was also stumbling.

Another ruble-draining effort was being stupid enough to get involved in a war in Afghanistan. Geez! Who would be dumb enough to get bogged down in an unwinnable war in Afghanistan? Oh, ummm, sorry US and NATO, I forgot about current events for a second. You guys should have really learned more from the Soviet experience, which was an . . .

AFGHAN BODY SLAM

Let's go into more detail on this mess, because it does play into current events more than most want to admit. Ever since the USSR came into existence, it crept further and further into control of Central Asia. eventually absorbing all of those -stan countries and making them into Soviet republics. All except one: Afghanistan. The USSR stayed very cozy with the leadership of the country, though, and gave them lots of foreign aid to ensure that they stayed under the commie sphere of influence.

However, there were other forces within Afghanistan that didn't like the Soviets and, for that matter, their own leaders. A group of Muslim fighters we'll call the **mujahideen** decided to wage a war to overthrow the Afghan government. The government feared a greater coup was at hand, so it invited the USSR to invade them to help out. Sounds good so far, huh? Yeah, right. This was a huge freakin' mistake for the Soviets.

In 1979, the Soviets invaded Afghanistan, and started a decade-long war which will serve to demoralize and humiliate them. Remember, this was during the Cold War, so the US CIA—under orders from the government—funneled tons of weapons and training to the mujahideen to keep the Soviets pinned down. It worked like a charm. In fact, it worked too well! After the mujahideen eventually repelled the Soviets, they then proceeded to have a civil war, and the winners of that civil war became the Taliban. Damn. Any of this starting to ring a bell yet? The Taliban are buddies with and shelter al-Qaeda, and after 9/11, the US declared war on both groups. Now the US finds itself fighting against forces it helped arm and train back in the 1970s. Oops.

But that is a tale for another time; back to our soviet story. The Soviet/Afghan campaign of 1979-89 was a devastating war for Russia, comparable to the Vietnam War for America. The active conflict in Afghanistan started to siphon away resources at a rapid rate. At the end of ten years of fighting, many Russian lives were lost, many Russian rubles were spent, and all for nothing; they were forced to walk away from the whole mess with their tail between their legs. Check out an awesome new flick which shows how this went down: *Charlie Wilson's War* starring Tom Hanks. As a bonus, it has male rear nudity—of Hanks, even!

THE GREAT COMMUNICATOR SAYS, "I HATE COMMIES"

Once the 1980s rolled around, a new component is introduced: the Reagan Factor. Ronald Reagan was the most hilarious US president ever, in the Plaid Avenger's opinion, and was certainly one of the reasons for the demise of the USSR. He is often credited as being the entire reason, which is preposterous, but his administration did a lot to accelerate the processes in play regarding Russia's economic decline. The drive for military buildup during the Cold War was all fine and dandy when the Soviet Union was expanding and growing industrially and economically, but this started to take its toll on them in the stagnant 1970s and 1980s. The Americans developed a new type of missile, so the Russians also developed a similar one in order to stay competitive. Then the Americans built a new type of tank, so the Russians built one as well. It was a "keeping up with the Joneses" sort of situation. You have to be as cool as your neighbors by having the same stuff, the newest and coolest stuff. That had been happening since the 1950s. The Space Race was a classic example of that competitiveness. Then in 1980, Ronald Reagan was elected president of the United States, and hilarity ensued.

"I hate commies."

Reagan hated commies. If you learn one thing about Reagan, it's that Reagan hated commies. He hated commies when he was a Hollywood actor and ratted out a bunch of other actors as communists during the McCarthy hearings. He hated commies when he was the governor of California, and he really hated commies when he became the president of the United States. He hated them so much that he was willing to send money and arms to anybody on the planet under the guise that they were fighting commies. In conclusion: Ronald Reagan hated commies. Have I made that clear yet? When he came in power in 1980, he had to deal with domestic issues because the US economy sucked. One of the primary things that he and his administration did very early on was accelerate military spending. This was a very clever move because it did a few things at once: It helped the American economy by creating jobs building more bombs, and also, Reagan knew that the Soviets were trying to keep up militarily, so he is made them spend more money as well.

This spending craze happened during the entire decade of the 1980s, just as internal dissent became more prevalent within the Soviet Union. Rioting broke out in places like Czechoslovakia, Poland, and Hungary, and as the economy continued to worsen in the Soviet Union, people began to starve to death. The US media showed scenes of people in long bread lines in the Soviet Union. These guys weren't just broke; they were going hungry at the same time they were spending millions, if not billions, on weaponry to keep up with the US. It was a crafty move that paid off huge dividends for the US. When the final Soviet leader came to power, Communist Party Secretary General Mikhail Gorbachev, he inherited a state that was broken and riddled with holes. Gorbachev came to power and knew his administration was screwed. The comrades continued to lie to themselves and used the KGB to scare everyone so they wouldn't utter it out loud, but the people at the top knew that the party is over.

20TH CENTURY COMMIE COUNTDOWN

Lenin: 20th century premier commie and snappy dresser.

Stalin: 20th century premier bastard with a serious 'stache.

Krushchev: Placed missiles in Cuba. Nice job, laughing boy.

Brezhnev: Patented the Unibrow, kin to Herman Munster.

Andropov: He "dropped ovv" after only 16 months in office.

Chernenko: Not to be outdone, he croaked after only 13 months.

Gorbachev: "Damn, this place is falling apart."

HOLY GLASNOST, THIS IS DRIVING ME MAD! PASS THE SALT, PERESTROIKA

What Gorbachev did was enact three things. Two of them are words you should know. One is **glasnost,** which means "openness." The second is **perestroika,** which means "restructuring." The third thing he did was try and limit military funding. Glasnost meant Gorbachev was tired of the secrecy of the Soviet government. He didn't want to lie to people any more, and he wanted to stop the KGB from terrorizing people. He wanted citizens to be more open with the government so it could improve. Places in Eastern Europe such as Poland, who wanted their own votes and no longer wanted to be a part of the Soviet Union, were let out. Under perestroika, Gorbachev knew they had to restructure the economy and reel in military spending. They also needed to cut off subsidies to countries they could no longer afford to prop up. This all leads to number three: not being able to spend any more money on the military.

This third enactment led to the **SALT,** first in the early 1970s and then again late in the decade. The **Strategic Arms Limitation Talks** were about curbing weapons production—not stopping weapons production altogether, not getting rid of weapons—just slowing down the speed at which they were being made. What you have to understand about the Cold War is that, if humans survive for another 1000 years, it will be looked on with hilarity and humor; the whole reason that we haven't killed each other yet is because there are so many bombs on the planet between the Soviets and the USA. There was a principle that basically sustained our life on earth, known as **MAD. MAD** stood for **Mutually Assured Destruction,** which essentially meant if anybody lobs a bomb, then the other side will throw a bomb, in which case both sides will throw all their bombs and everyone will die. Who is going to do that? MAD is the most hilarious thing ever in human history, because it stopped us from attacking each other, but it made us continue to make more bombs. We were already to the point where we'd annihilate each other off the face of the planet, but we kept making better bombs. The US would say, "We have 1000 bombs that can each destroy five countries at once!" Then the Soviet Union would build 1001. That's where you get into these astronomical numbers of bombs, a bomb for every damn person on the planet. Why? I can't really answer that, because it makes no sense. But I digress. I get a little agitated thinking about MAD; how fitting.

Back to our story: this equated to Gorbachev realizing that they had to stop doing this. During the SALT talks, they agreed, "Let's not build this type or class of bomb anymore, or build half as many as you were going to and we will build half as many. Also, how about we eliminate this type of submarine, and you guys eliminate that type of submarine." When these talks started, there was some capitulation, but for the really big thing, Gorbachev would say, "Let's not build these big intercontinental ballistic missiles," but Reagan, because he hated commies so much, built more of those missiles because he knew the Soviets were going broke. Indeed, not only did he *not* agree to weapons elimination, but accelerated production and built more. In the same year, Reagan appeared in front of the US Congress during the State of the Union address and said that the USSR was an "evil empire" and that we must do everything in our power to combat evil. He was really throwing all the cards down on the table—what a huge bluff in the global game of poker. It was hilarious, but indeed that was exactly what did it.

Here is the bluff that won the game: Somebody made mention to Reagan of how cool it would be if we put missiles in space; when the Soviets shot nuclear weapons at anyone, we could shoot their bombs out of the sky with our space missiles. This missile system would be a space laser to shoot out bombs and was called **SDI,** the Strategic Defense Initiative, given the nickname **Star Wars.** The Plaid Avenger is convinced this whole concept evolved at a Georgetown cocktail party courtesy of some dudes who had way too many drinks.

When this idea came out it was merely that: an idea. Then some people started throwing around some funds for this idea, which was most likely sketched on a cocktail napkin. Somehow Reagan got his hands on this cocktail napkin and started to circulate it around. Anybody heard about this Star Wars thing? It sounds pretty good. When news of this reached Gorbachev in the Soviet Union, the comrades said, "Oh, crap! They are going to have an orbiting missile defense system! In space! We are going to have to spend millions and billions of research dollars to figure out how to get one of these too and we are already broke. We can't do it!"

THE END

Gorbachev went to Reagan and said, "We will stop making these bombs, guns, and tanks, just don't do this Star Wars thing!" Reagan, in all of his wisdom, said, "Sorry, we can't; it is already built. We are too far along and can't stop now." This was a complete line of bull. There was nothing in space. Nothing was even tested. This huge bluff paid off because Gorbachev decided to throw up his hands and said, "Well, that's it then; we can't keep up. If we can't have a missile defense, that means you guys win. You could nuke us, so we quit. MAD is over and so are we!" This was when the USSR really fell down, around 1988 1989.

Several things collide here. The Soviet economy was in trouble, they had overextended themselves with their propaganda around the world and with Soviet aid in other countries. They had a war in Afghanistan with active fighting for 10 years, from 1979 to 1989, which proved

"We're not MAD anymore; we're broke!"

to be disastrous. It took a huge toll in not only millions of dollars of equipment, but also the death of 25,000 Russian soldiers. When all was said and done, they had not done anything there for 10 years. They failed to control Afghanistan, so they had to walk out of it. Glasnost and Perestroika are starting to be interpreted literally by Eastern Europeans and the Soviet people themselves, who were now calling for revolution and independence. In 1989, the Soviet Union had to throw in the towel: "Poland, you want out? Go ahead. Estonia, Latvia, Lithuania, you want out? I guess you guys are out as well. Central Asian republics, you guys are out." It all disintegrated in very short order, and all those countries declared independence.

Fifteen new sovereign states emerged from the ashes of the USSR. The strings of the Soviet satellites' puppet governments were cut. The map was redrawn in one fell swoop. In 1990, they adopted economic and democratic reforms into what is left of the USSR, which became the United Federation of Russia. In 1991, Boris Yeltzin was elected president of Russia. He recognized the independence of all the countries that had declared it. In that same year, the newly formed Congress voted for the official and permanent dissolution of the USSR. It was no more. From 1991 forward, it was called Russia.

RADICAL RUSSIAN TRANSITION

By the 1990s, the commie threat was gone and the USSR was dismembered, so everything in Russia should be all hearts and flowers, right? Unfortunately, everything still sucked for Russia. It has gotten a lot better in the last few years, but we are going to carry it forward from 1991, when all this becomes official in today's world. That first decade of post-Soviet independence for the Ruskies sucked as bad as the decade before it. The pain of a radical transition had to be suffered through as they approached the 21st century. What kind of transition, and what kind of pain?

ECONOMY TAKES A DUMP

As we pointed out during the final decades of the Soviet Union, their economy was in bad shape, and changing their name doesn't change the facts. Now it's the Russian economy that sucked. Their industries were still in Cold War mindset and only produced big stuff like tanks and missiles that didn't have much use in today's world. You could still sell such items, but not nearly enough to rebuild an economy. They had tremendous problems with shifting their entire industrial sector to more capitalist-centered stuff, normal consumer goods. Capitalism was still a new concept for them, and they were still breaking in their capitalist cowboy boots. The transition from commie to capitalist was full of pitfalls and road bumps and full-on collisions, which made for an extremely rocky economic road to recovery.

The Bear gets skinned.

On top of that, Russia lost its international status. They used to be "the other world power" but in the 1990s nobody would give them the time of day, much less a bank loan. This has changed in the last few years, but right after 1991, no one was willing to help Russia. Russia used to be a somebody, but now it was a nobody. It's also important to note that the USSR went from a singular sovereign entity to fifteen separate ones. It lost tremendous amounts of territory. Those other fourteen countries that weren't Russia were plots of land it no longer owned and there was the agriculture produced on that land, and mineral and energy resources under it, and the people who live on it were a workforce. Those are the basic foundations of economies. This territorial/resource was a tremendous blow to the Russian economy, an economy that was already hurting.

On top of this, you have to think about the Soviet era, during which the Soviets used a lot of resources from these countries. For example, most of the food production for the Soviet Union came from the Ukraine and Kazakhstan, which became separate countries. A lot of oil and natural gas came from Central Asia, and not only was Russia no longer profiting from these resources, it had to buy them back. It was a double-edged sword with both edges toward Russia. They were getting sliced and diced. Finally, most of the nuclear and weapons stockpiles were in what was the Ukraine and Belarus, and there were a lot of expensive complications involved in destroying and/or relocating those weapons.

The second problem with the economy was the influence of organized crime: the Russian Mafia. Crime is everywhere, so organized crime is everywhere as well. It is really strong in Russia. In fact, if you have ever seen adventure movies or international crime dramas, there is always a Russian mafia somewhere. They have always had a presence, even back in the days of communism when they created the Russian black market, which moved untaxed alcohol, weapons, and hardcore drugs. Indeed, they are still doing a tremendous job trafficking drugs and weapons internationally. They're also trafficking people. Yes, I did say people. A lot of the Russian mafia deals with the movement of women and children for sexual exploitation purposes. It's a fairly nasty business, but I guess that's what mafias do.

During the confusion and transformation of the Russian economy in the 1990's, these illegal criminal elements had a complete field day. The Soviet system was fairly corrupt internally to begin with, and that was perpetuated under free market capitalism where there are not a lot of rules. In addition, the government was broke and couldn't pay federal employees, such as the military and police. In such circumstances, corruption becomes endemic and easy to do at all levels. People do what they have to do to stay alive. The influence of organized crime is a major function of what is happening, even in today's Russia. Vladimir Putin himself came to power on a platform of being tough on crime, and in fact, nobody would be elected who is not.

This powerful criminal element in Russia not only stymies local business, but has negatively influenced international investment as well. But the open and outright blue-collar criminals were not alone in the 1990s. A new dimension of white-collar crime arose to give the underworld a run for their money (ha! Pun intended!): **the Oligarchs**.

OLIGARCHS OVER-DO IT

The oligarchs were white-collar criminals who, during the transition period of communism to democracy and capitalism in the 1990s, worked for the government or had insider ties with the government and bought whole industries and businesses under the table before they would go to auction. In communism, everything is owned by the state—all the oil, land, timber, energy production, everything. In capitalism, individuals own everything and the state owns virtually nothing. When a government goes from communism to capitalism, it starts selling everything. Ideally, this process would allow any individual the opportunity to buy former state industries at fair market prices. However, in Russia, this did not happen; most purchases were made by government insiders at rock bottom prices.

Here's an example: Yukos was Russia's oil company, a government owned oil company that was going to privatize. If you knew some government officials when it was going up for sale and could get the price, and you knew people who worked at a bank, here is what you would do. You find out the day before the sale occurs and go to your friend at the bank and say, "Lend me half a billion dollars," with the promise that you will personally give him 100 million bucks as a bonus after repaying the loan. He smiles and you take the check for 500 million bucks from the bank over to the natural resources department to your buddy who is overseeing the sale of the oil company. You hand him the check for 500 million; he stamps it sold and hands you

Top Five Russian Oligarchs			
Who?	What did he steal from the people?	How much? (USD)	Where is he now?
Roman Abramovich	Oil (Sibneft)	$14.7 Billion	In England, owns big-time soccer team Chelsea FC. Also owns four giant yachts and is building a fifth.
Vladimir Lisin	Aluminum and Steel	$7 Billion	Most likely sleeping in a pile of hundred dollar bills.
Viktor Vekselberg	Oil (Tyumen)	$6.1 Billion	Buying Faberge Eggs. Seriously, he digs them.
Oleg Deripaska	Aluminum (RUSAL)	$5.8 Billion	Hanging out with good friend Vladimir Putin.
Mikhail Fridman	Conglomeration of Valuable Things (Alfa Group)	$5.8 Billion	Lost much of his wealth in Russian tort suit—for stealing from the people, probably not enough evidence for criminal case.

the deed to the oil company. You and your conspirators walk out together the next day as owners of this oil company, and sell it for 2 or 3 billion dollars, its true value, and then you go back and settle up your loan for 500 million with your banking friend and you split the rest. Congratulations! You have joined the ranks of the oligarchs! This was a really seedy big business tactic in the wild west of capitalism where there are no rules. These guys became ultra-millionaires and billionaires overnight.

What is the big deal with this? What's the problem? The Russian people got screwed, that's what. You have state owned resources whose sale should have contributed to the economic growth of an entire country, which instead turned into a billion dollars in a Swiss bank account under one man's name overnight. It was a legal transaction, apparently, but also a massive loss to the government.

In his rise to power, Vlad "the Bad" Putin brought some of these crooks to justice—including Yukos head Mikhail Khodorkovsky, formerly the second richest Russian—although his motivation for doing so is questionable. It was likely a move designed to consolidate power more than a move to achieve justice.

Another platform in Vladimir Putin's campaign was, "I'm going after those Oligarchs! Going after crime and those chumps that robbed the Russian people!" That is one of the reasons he's such a popular leader. He is seen as a strong anticrime, pro-government force, and he's backed it up because the owner of Yukos is now sitting in jail. As a result, Putin helped Russia stabilize itself a little more.

PURGIN POPULATION

Another issue that is extremely problematic for Russia is the population itself. What's happening to the people in Russia? Russia's population is one of the classic examples, if not the classic example, of a population in decline: negative fertility rates and dropping birth rates. The population total is declining with only about 150 million people in Russia; that number keeps getting smaller every year. People have been leaving in droves, which doesn't do much for Russia's economy. You need working people to keep things moving. A lot of things are going on that can account for Russia's demographic decline. It is hard to pinpoint a single factor, but nevertheless, the population is shrinking. Shrinkage is just the start of problems.

If we looked at some of the social indicators for what's happening in Russia, you would swear that you were looking at an African nation. The life expectancy for males is around 47 years, a little more than half that of the United States. You might guess this life expectancy for sub-Saharan Africa or Central Asia, but you typically would not think of Russia. Several things may be contributing to Russia's decline. One is *lack of health care*. Because of the collapse of the economy and the corruption associated with it, health care has become a huge

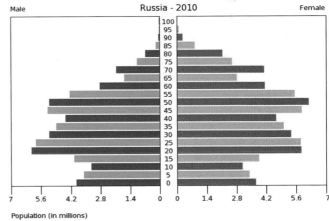

Numbers are going down.

issue. Access to good health care is almost nonexistent, but again, this may be changing. People aren't as healthy as they should be and don't have access to certain operations or preventive care. Drinking an average of 30 liters of vodka a year probably isn't helping matters either. Other unhealthy attributes include . . .

ENVIRONMENT ENDANGERED

In its rapid industrialization, forced collectivization, and striving to catch up with the West to be a global power phase, the Soviet system completely ignored the environment. There was no limit to the amount of toxic spilling and dumping, or atomic weapons testing. Anything the Soviets could do to get ahead was done with the thought that once they won, they'd go back and clean everything up. Oops, they lost, and it's all still sitting there. Parts of the Kara Sea glow green sometimes from all of the accumulated toxic waste dumped into the river systems. Also, be sure to check out the Aral Sea as soon as you can, because it is disappearing due to misuse and pollution during the Soviet era. There are no less than fifty sites in Russia with pollution of catastrophic proportions. Don't forget to include all of the old nuclear weapons silos that are sitting around, deteriorating. There is impending environmental disaster on a large scale here, just based on past pollutions and degrading weapons. Russia has dealt with this huge problem during the last fifteen years, with some international help from the United States and several others.

STOLEN SPHERE OF INFLUENCE: THE REALIGNMENT

The last thing you should be aware of in Russia right now is that a lot of its ex-territories and ex-states in its sphere of influence have now disappeared under radical realignment—much to the chagrin of Russia, because it still sees itself as a world player. What am I talking about? Eastern Europe is now desperately trying to become Western Europe by realigning with the West. Russia is losing its sphere of influence all over the place, though it's desperately trying to hold on. It is still actively courting Central Asia politically because there is a lot of oil and natural gas there. They are also courting China and want to keep good strategic ties there. It is really losing influence over Eastern Europe, and what's happening now only rubs it in their face.

That NATO stuff we talked about last chapter is still troubling the Russians. Something quite radical, that would have been unthinkable a decade ago, has happened. Places like Poland, Hungary, and the Czech Republic joined NATO very quickly after they declared independence in 1991, mostly to ensure no further Russian influence. The next wave of folks was 2004 when Estonia, Latvia, Lithuania, Romania, and Bulgaria, places that were once firmly in Soviet control, joined NATO. Russia now finds that its former territories, which it sometimes harshly subjugated, are sovereign political entities that want nothing to do with it. They are NATO members and could theoretically have NATO weaponry pointed at Russia. This is a big loss of status and influence for Russia. Think about this in an abstract context. The Baltic States go from being owned by Russia, to ten years later being sovereign states with weapons pointed at Russia. That's a fairly big change. But the scales are starting to tip back to the Russian side.

NATO creeps ever closer to the Ruskies.

RESURGENT RUSSIA: THE BAD BOYS ARE BACK!

Watch out! Things continue to change fairly rapidly for Russia, and it is the understatement of the century to say that things are looking up. Yes, I've talked about how crappy its economy has been. Yes, I've told you all about its people problems, its environmental problems, its crime problems, its international status problems. But what a difference one man can make, and the Russian man of the century is, with no doubt, Vladimir Putin. Putin, along with petroleum, has brought the Russians from the brink of the abyss back to world power status in less than a decade. There are a few other factors at play here as well that are serving to bring the Russian region back to a starring role on the world stage. Let's wrap up this chapter looking at this incredible reversal of Russian fortune.

"I can snap your neck with my bare hand. Enjoy your dinner."

PRES TO PRIME: PUTIN POWER!

This guy is unstoppable! So rarely in life can you truly credit a single individual with changing the course of history but, for better or for worse, that is an apt description for our main man Vlad. It's no wonder that Time magazine voted him Man of the Year for 2007—he really has made that big of a difference in his country, and in the world. Vladimir Putin is also easily the baddest leader on the planet: as a former KGB agent and judo blackbelt, he could handily whip any elected official on this side of the Milky Way. And the people love him! Putin held 60 to 80% approval ratings his entire eight years in office, and stepped down as President with closer to 90% love from the Russians. Stalin would have killed for that kind of popular support—oh, wait a minute, he did kill to get that kind of support. But I digress. Why all the love?

Putin is only the second president Russia has had. He was the hand-picked successor to Boris Yeltsin, a fairly popular leader in his own right. In his eight year run from 2000-2008, Putin oversaw the stabilization of the economic transition process that had thrown Russia into chaos for its first decade. He was tough on the oligarchs, and tough on crime, which helped stimulate international investment. He also took a fairly pro-active government role in helping Russian businesses, especially those businesses dealing with petroleum and natural gas. More on that in a minute. GDP has grown six-fold, and propelled Russia from the 22nd largest economy up to the number ten slot. The economy grew 6-8% on average every year he was in office. Investment grew, industry grew, agricultural output grew, construction grew, salaries grew; pretty much every economic indicator you could look at has gone up during his tenure.

President? Prime Minister? It's all Putin to me!

Unlike most world leaders, Putin was very savvy with this cash flow. He paid off all Russian debts. Imagine that: Russian National Debt = 0. Damn. That's legit. Putin also stashed billions, if not trillions, in a Russian "rainy day fund" that is set aside for any future hard times. How refreshing! Most leaders usually stash that extra cash in their personal Swiss bank accounts. No wonder Russians love him!

However, the love is not just based on economics. Vladimir Putin re-instilled a great sense of nationalism in his citizens. After the demise of the USSR, Russia was a second rate power with even less prestige, at the mercy of international business and

Back off, NATO! Putin is protectin' his 'hood!

banking and stronger world powers like the US, the EU, and NATO. Russia pretty much just had to go with the flow, even when events were inherently against their own national interest, like the growth of NATO, for example. Putin brought them back politically to a position of strength. He played hardball in international affairs, and re-invigorated a Russian national pride that has long laid dormant.

Of course, this has come at a cost: Putin achieved a lot of this by consolidating power around his position, controlling a lot of state industries, cracking down on freedom of the press and free speech, and manipulating power structures of the government. In fact, he stepped down from the presidency in May 2008, and stepped immediately into the Prime Minister position the same day, maintaining a lot of command and control of the system simultaneously. That crafty fox! He is increasingly reviled and even hated by Team West because people see him as leaning back towards totalitarianism, but also because he increasingly clashes with western foreign policy on the international stage.

But hold the phone! I keep talking about Putin, and have completely dissed the actual current president of Russia. Let's remedy that right now! Russian President Dmitry Medvedev was the hand-picked successor to Putin, and is one cool customer in his own right. He has pretty much followed and even strengthened virtually all of Putin's policies, and is therefore considered by many in the west as a mere Putin puppet. There could be some truth to that. However, he does have the popular support

My main man Medvedev.

of the Russian population, and why on earth would he stray too far off of the successful path that Putin had paved? Answer: he won't. What he has done since taking office is start a massive military makeover which seeks to revamp and remodel the Russian armed services into a state-of-the-art ultra-modern military that will certainly be causing consternation for the US and Team West in the future.

Look at these freaking Russian politicians.

And Medvedev is increasingly formulating his own strong policies which are certainly not an extension of his powerful Prime Minister's positions.

Namely, Medvedev's last state of the nation address specifically urged his fellow Russians to basically change or die! He said the country needed to reign in corruption and crime way more, strengthen its democratic institutions, and embrace foreign ideas to modernize its economy. Tough talk!

Dig this: there is already speculation that the Russian constitution will be amended to allow Putin to run for president again, in essence, scrapping their term limits. Given the rabid popularity of both men, I think their policies are here to stay for some time. Or perhaps forever.

In conclusion, Putin power is not to be underestimated. Since he can hold the Prime Minister position indefinitely either way, he will be around for some time to come. The Russians love him for making them strong, and making them rich. Let's look at some specifics of how he pulled this off and the implications for the future.

PETRO POWER!

Putin is awesome. On that point we are clear. However, we do have to at least partially, if not fully, credit his great success in turning the Bear around on this one single commodity: petroleum. Dudes! Russia has made total bank on oil and natural gas in the last decade. To understand the importance of oil for Russia, one need only consider this: when the USSR crashed in 1991, the price of a barrel of oil was about $10. In 2008, the price of a barrel of oil approached $150. The price may have dropped radically here in 2009, but oil is still the preferred energy source of choice for the entire planet. My friends, you should know this: Russia has a ton of oil! Look at the map! You do the math!

Increasingly, Russia has also reeled in all control of the petro industries to the state. They privatized a lot of those industries back in the 1990s, but they have been busy **nationalizing** a lot of them back since 2000. Remember those terms

Russian Oil and Natural Gas at a Glance

Oil	2006	Natural Gas	2006
Oil reserves	80 billion barrels	Gas reserves	48 trillion cubic meters
Oil reserves, as percentage of world	7 percent	Gas reserves, as percentage of world	26 percent
Saudi Arabian reserves	264 billion barrels	Iranian reserves	28 trillion cubic meters
US reserves	30 billion barrels	US reserves	6 trillion cubic meters
Oil production	10 million barrels per day	Gas production	612 billion cubic meters
Oil production, as percentage of world	12 percent	Gas production, as percentage of world	21 percent
US oil production	7 million barrels per day	US gas production	524 billion cubic meters
Oil exports	7 million barrels per day	Gas exports	263 billion cubic meters
Oil exporter, rank	2	Gas exporter, rank	1
Oil exports, to US	370,000 barrels per day	Gas exports, to Europe	151 billion cubic meters

Sometimes having a lot of gas is a very good thing: Russia may become the center of a natural gas OPEC-like cartel!

from Chapter 4? Russia sure does. It now has controlling interest in virtually all the oil and natural gas businesses in the country, which even more of the profits swing back directly to the state.

To reiterate a few points from this chapter and the last: oil is power for Russia. Not only have they paid off their foreign debt with oil money, they have re-invested that oil money back into their economy, and also set up their rainy day fund with oil dollars. Since the Russians supply one third of European energy demand, this gives them all sorts of economic and political leverage over their Eurasian neighbors. Mess with Putin, and you might not have heating oil next winter. But the Europeans aren't the only ones who need oil. Look eastward and you see Japan and China both vying for petro resources. Russia is really sitting pretty right now. Energy master of the continent!

GLOBAL WARMING? NO SWEAT!

I can't get out of this section without referencing the global warming situation. While the rest of the planet may be wringing their hands in a collective tizzy about rising temperatures, melting polar ice caps, and rising sea levels, let me assure you that Russia is not sweating the situation at all. Ha! Not sweating the warming—am I good or what?

Seriously though, think of the strategic benefits that are being bestowed upon Russia as the thermometer continues to creep upward every year. Russia has forever been a land empire due to its lack of accessible and navigable coastlines. Additionally, almost all of its river systems empty into the ice-locked Arctic Ocean, making them essentially useless for transportation and exporting commodities. But just wait! As the permanent ice cap covering the North Pole disappears, Russia will become more open to the world like never before in recorded human history!

You may not be paying attention to any of this, but the Russians sure are. In preparations for its ice-free northern coastlines of the future, Russia is staking a claim to the entire Arctic sea east of the North Pole. Seriously, I'm not making this up. The race for the Arctic has begun! Russia stands to be the biggest beneficiary as well. Not only will it open up their territory for greater sea and land access, and greater export power, but it is widely believed that there are massive oil reserves in the Arctic basin, reserves which will become accessible once the ice is gone. Russia is all about the global warming! Let's get this party started! No, actually let's end it with. . . .

"Comrades, the North Pole is ours now. Bye-bye, Santa!"

GEOPOLITICAL JUMP START

You got your Putin, and you got your petroleum, and you add to that a huge dose of nationalistic pride. Bake for twenty minutes, and you end up with an extremely resurgent and resilient Russia on the world political table. These guys are playa's once again. Their huge economy, their huge oil reserves, and their huge potential for the future is fast becoming the envy of the world. They can afford to play the fence when suitors come calling. What do I mean by that?

Russia has been invited to become a strategic partner state of the EU— not a full-fledged member, mind you, but a partner. Europe realizes that the Russian economy and Russian energy is such an integral part of their own lives, that to not have Russia at the table for major decisions would be folly. Russia has a real impact on some EU policy. The same can be said of NATO. While Russia is not a member, the group realizes that almost all major decision-making should involve the Russians since they play such an increasingly important role in Eurasian affairs. Russia is typically invited to major NATO summits now. Why doesn't Russia just join the EU and NATO fully?

Because the Russians are forging economic and strategic political ties to their east as well, mostly with China. They are at a historical east/west pivot point right now; they are straddling the fence about which relationships to make or break. I think they're being extremely savvy and are going to avoid taking sides in anything. Could Russia join the EU? It's already a strategic partner of the EU. I bet it will be invited to join as a full-fledged member, but I also bet it will decline.

Why? It is also strategic partners with China, the other huge economy on the other side of the continent. Russia will not be stymied economically by joining a club that can possibly limit their economic options. The Bear is also still a major player in Central Asia, an area with tons of natural gas and oil that has to be moved out of Central Asia to the rest of the world that wants it. That oil and natural gas usually moves out through Russian territory, supplying most of the fuel for Eastern and Western Europe, in addition to increasingly supplying fuel for Japan, China and India.

Beyond the geopolitical ramifications of energy and economics, Russia is back in full action militarily speaking! Big time! You do know that, in August 2008, Russia invaded the Georgian regions of South Ossetia and Abkhazia, right? It currently still occupies these areas, and has gone as far as to recognize their declared independence, which is infuriating the US and Team West as a whole.

You will have to turn to chapter 25 to get all the details of this conflict and its future ramifications, but I just want you to know this for now: Russia is back! The Russian–Georgian War did not change the balance of power in this region, it simply was an announcement that the shift in the balance of power had already occurred!

Russia is now openly and powerfully reasserting its influence in its own backyard, and that is a big deal. Russia now feels that it has regained a position of strength to not only stand up to what it sees as threatening Team West expansion to its borders, but to stop that advance with force if necessary. With guns! This open, bold, and even proud use of force by the Russians has changed the whole attitude of the US, NATO, and even the EU when it comes to political maneuvers near the Russian border. The bear has lashed out! The result? The US and NATO have now scrapped plans for that missile defence shield in Eastern Europe that was pissing off the Ruskies, and the push to get Ukraine and Georgia into NATO has also been tabled for now, if not forever.

At the risk of redundant repetition, what supranationalist organizations are the Russians all about if they don't really want to play with the EU and NATO? Well, remember the BRIC? They dig that one, and it should be notes that BRIC is specifically not a "Western" institution. Of even greater significance is the SCO. Flip back to chapter 6 or ahead to the Central Asia chapter to get the full run-down on this group, but just let me tease you for now by telling you this much: the SCO is going to be a bizarre cross between an Asian version of NATO and a Russian version of OPEC, and Russia has every intention of being the leader of this grand experiment. Stalin would be proud.

GHOST OF STALIN RETURNS

Which is a good jumping off point. I guess any mention of Joseph Stalin is a good point to get the hell out of Dodge. I want to leave you with this: the memory of Smokin' Joe Stalin is actually being softened in today's Russia, and that is a very telling sign of what's happening in the society. Some folks in Russia are looking back with pride at what most of us consider one of the biggest bastards in history. Why? This vibrant and growing economy, this resurgent world role, and this overall restored sense of Russian greatness has not been felt since the Stalin era, and quite frankly, the Russians are quite proud to be Russian again.

Add in trillions of petro dollars, increasing empire due to global warming, and a renewed sense of global political power, and you got yourself a region that will be shaping world events of the future. Growl! The Bear is back!

WRESTLING FOR WEALTH.

Team West taught the Russians too well!

RUSSIAN RUNDOWN & RESOURCES

View additional Plaid Avenger resources for this region at http://plaid.at/ru

 BIG PLUSES

→ Biggest state by land area, one that is extremely rich in virtually all natural resources

→ Specifically, a huge oil and natural gas producer: energy resources critical to world economy

→ Virtually no national debt

→ Regained sense of national pride and political world leadership

→ Has veto power at the UN Permanent Security Council

→ Has as many nuclear bombs as the US, if not more, as well as a serious military, second only to the US.

→ Is a founding member of some of the most promising future international coalitions like BRIC and SCO

→ Is still considered quite important to the EU and NATO too, enough to get invited to the meetings.

→ Global warming? No problem for Russia! Will increase usable land area and resource base

BIG PROBLEMS

→ Gi-normous size problematic for infrastructure, defense, and cultural cohesiveness.

→ Economy and social structures, like health care, still not fully recovered from Soviet era crash

→ Male longevity rates are lower than most African countries; alcoholism rates among the highest in the world

→ Population overall is shrinking.

→ Organized crime, rampant corruption, and tax evasion have seriously stymied international investment and hinder internal development

→ Economy still heavily reliant on exporting natural resources, mostly energy.

→ Has some of the worst environmental disaster areas on the planet

→ Anti-immigrant, anti-foreigner, and flat out racism are significant issues in Russia

DEAD DUDES OF NOTE:

Tsar Nicholas II: Last of the royal Romanov line, and last monarch of Russia, who was assassinated along with his whole family in 1918. His piss poor rule transformed Russia into an economic and military disaster which helped fuel the revolution which left the commies in charge.

Rasputin: The un-kill-able "Mad Monk" who recommended that Tsar Nicholas get Russia involved in World War I. He didn't instigate the royal family's demise, but he sure as hell accelerated it. May still be alive somewhere in hell.

Vladimir Lenin: "Father of the USSR" Passionate organizer, orator, and propagandist who led the Russian Revolution of 1917, in which he implemented the first ever communist experiment at the state scale. Then he died.

Joseph Stalin: The semi-psychotic who took over control of the USSR after Lenin's death. Formed the KGB, purged out all political adversaries, and may have been responsible for the deaths of 30 million Russians. But, he also oversaw the industrialization and expansion of the USSR into a world power, and helped kill the Nazis in WWII. So it's a mixed bag.

Nikita Khrushchev: Leader of the USSR at what was perhaps the height of the Cold War. Was the bonehead that decided to put Soviet missiles in Cuba pointed at Florida, which brought the world to the brink of nuclear war aka the Cuban Missile Crisis of 1962.

PLAID CINEMA SELECTION:

Prisoner of the Mountains (1996) Set in the Caucus Mountains with incredible scenery, this quiet "war film" is set during the First Chechen War . . . while the war itself was still happening! Themes to watch for: cultural differences in the region and the piss-poor state of the Russian military in the early 90's. Still topical, as tensions with Chechnya are still part of current events.

Tale in the Darkness (2009) A Russian independent film, which strives to explore the life of a female police officer in Far East Russia. This drama reaches a sort of "Men are from Mars, women are from Venus" conclusion.

Burnt by the Sun (1994) Set in USSR circa 1936, this film shows the effects of Stalin's insane political purges of his own peoples, even those loyal to him. A Soviet war hero on summer retreat at his dacha with his family becomes the target of KGB investigation and elimination.

Siberiade (1979) A film about the small village of Yelan hidden in the backwoods of Siberia. This epic, four part film shows the evolution of the small village until at the end of the film, it is no longer remote, as oil has been found in the village. Show realistic evolution of Russian culture as well as providing an early reflection of the processes of globalization.

Newsmakers (2009) A crime drama set in Moscow whose plot involves a savvy female detective setting up a real-life reality TV show as a ruse to flush out a criminal gang that got the better of the cops in a live shoot-out.

Oligarkh aka *Tycoon* (2002) Not a great film, but does chronicle the conversion of soviet command economy to full-on unrestrained capitalism that occurred as the USSR imploded. Greed, corruption, and cronyism via a personal storyline.

Brat aka *Brother* (1997) Hardcore bleak and gritty realistic gangster film in St. Petersburg that epitomizes the way it works at the local level in Russia. No big money or flash here, just desperate people who do desperate things. Spawned a whole culture of glorifying young gangsters in films, often called "keelers," much like gangsta' rap did in the US.

Nochnoy dozor aka *Night Watch* (2004) Okay this one is just for fun, and to throw a monkey-wrench into the film mix. This is a Russian vampire/wizard/good vs. evil/horror film that is now one of the highest grossing films in their history. It's *The Matrix* of Moscow.

LIVE LEADERS YOU SHOULD KNOW:

Mikhail Gorbachev: Oversaw the collapse of the USSR, implemented the glasnost and perestroika policies, and helped bring the Cold War to a peaceful end. Is a hero to the West and won the Nobel Peace Prize, but looked upon almost as a traitor in Russia.

Vladimir Putin: Now this dude is a hero to the Russians! President from 2000–2008 and currently Prime Minister, got Russia's mo-jo back, got them rich, and got them powerful again on the world stage. Look for him to be in Russian politics indefinitely.

Dmitry Medvedev: Current President of Russia, the Putin hand-picked successor. Many think he is merely a Putin puppet, but has so far shown himself to be an adept and strong leader in his own right who is continuing the successful Putin policy legacy.

Sergey Lavrov: Current Russian Foreign Minister, which is the equivalent of the US Secretary of State, the head diplomat of the country. This dude is wickedly smart, savvy, and has been behind the scenes making sure Russia regains its power status on the world stage.

THE BATTLE FOR TOKYO IS ON

Japan

KONNICHIWA!

Welcome to the islands! A most unique set of islands they are—so unique, in fact, that we will classify Japan not just as an independent state, but as an entirely unique region of the world as well. One of the classic mistakes that all text-books make, and that a lot of people in the West make, is overgeneralizing Asia. They look at this place and say, "Oh well, you know, it's just Asian people there and six of one, half dozen of the other. Japanese, Chinese, Koreans—whatever." This couldn't be further from the truth when we are talking about Japan and mainland Asia. Japan has an extremely distinct culture from all the countries around it, as do the Chinese, the Kore-ans, and the Vietnamese, but unlike the others, Japan has followed a more western trajectory in the last century that has set them quite apart from even their closest neighbors. They are the most western of the eastern cultures. Huh? Hang on. We'll get to that in a bit.

Just know this for now, we are coming up on the Clash of the Titans of the 21st Century: The

Clash of the Asian Titans. The titans are, of course, Japan and China, two states with huge economies, two states shaping global events, and two states with a long history of animosity between them.

One of the most critical relationships that will be affecting 21st century events is how these two Asian giants will deal with each other as China rises to full superpower status. But I am getting ahead of the story, as usual. Let's get some background on Japan itself, and then look at its evolution into the modern era, and finally finish with that all important relationship with China. Ready? Then Godzilla game on!

PHYSICAL

Japan is a group of four main islands: Hokkaido, Honshu, Shikoku, and Kyushu, from north to south. Japan was created by three or four different tectonic plates coming together in this area. Because of this, Japan is volcanic in origin. Another feature that goes along with this is its mountainous terrain. There are very few flatlands, and this equates to very little agricultural land. Due to plate tectonics, Japan is also earthquake prone. We've heard this before and we've seen some titanic earthquake events in the last hundred years in Japan. It is a cyclical thing and it will not go away anytime soon. It is not a question of *if* Japan is going to be hit by another major earthquake; it's only a matter of *when*.

Why should you care about this? Well, Tokyo's stock exchange, and Japan as a whole, holds tremendous amounts of foreign investment, foreign currency, and bank reserves. When the day comes that a major earthquake shuts them down, depending on the scale of the disaster itself, it could plunge the entire world into recession almost instantaneously. If it is a tremendously bad earthquake, it could plunge the world into a depression in the long term. It's another instance of globalization at its worst in that a big hit here from the physical world could equate to disaster for the entire planet. However the Plaid Avenger doesn't want to scare anybody; it's just a matter of when, so we'll see how it goes.

Ahhh! Most honorable Mt. Fuji!

"Honey, I think this section of the interstate is closed."

The other physical thing to consider with Japan is climate. Climatologically speaking, this is an easy one for the Plaid Avenger to describe to you; you could superimpose Japan, keeping latitude constant, on to the eastern seaboard of the United States (see image below). As you can see, latitude and size being held constant in this image, the climate of Japan is identical to the eastern seaboard of the United States. Hokkaido is around the upstate New York area and they get a lot of snow up there. Southern Honshu, as well as Shikoku and Kyushu, reach down into the southern United States and indeed, there are actually smaller islands that go down to what would be tropical Florida. Every place else is similar to some place else in between. For

instance, Tokyo is roughly the latitude of Washington, D.C. These two regions, though on opposite sides of the planet, have very similar climates.

One disclaimer here is that Japan is an island nation. As an island, it is surrounded by water, and water is a major modifier of climate. As such, it has a similar climate to the east coast of the United States, though somewhat moderated due to the influence of the surrounding water.

Lastly, physically speaking, Japan is lacking in natural resources. I just suggested that Japan is mostly mountainous, which means it does not have a lot of agricultural resources. The

Japan/US: size and latitude comparison.

Japanese have found ways throughout the centuries of getting around that by terracing rice paddies and fishing. There is still no way it can supply itself with its own food needs at this point due to its lack of agricultural resources, and lack of arable land. More importantly, it lacks just about everything else.

Japan is a real conundrum in that it is the second largest economy on the planet that, at the same time, lacks virtually everything that most countries with powerhouse economies have. Japan has to import most of its metals, ores, and virtually all of its energy resources. Japan is entirely dependent on the rest of the planet for all of these things. That has something to do with its history.

SAMURAI TO JACK

What about natural resources, Plaid Avenger? Not having any has something to do with Japan in the modern world. I'm going to go through the early history of Japan in fairly short order to point out one thing in particular: In terms of unique Asian cultures and unique ethnic groups, Japan is really a laggard. It's the latecomer. It's the last one to show up on the world scene.

Chinese civilization has been around for 5,000 years. The Koreans have been around for 3,000–4,000 years. Lots of people from Central Asia and Southeast Asia, like the Thais, the Vietnamese,

Bring on the bamboo.

and other ethnic groups with distinct cultures, have been around for a while. If you search hard, you will find that Japan's culture cannot really be called a distinct culture until about 1400–1500 years ago, and even at that point, wasn't anything closing in on what we consider a nation-state.

Japan started as a small group of people that migrated from mainland China and through the Korean Peninsula over the course of the previous thousand years. They did not become a unique entity themselves until comparatively late in the Common Era. The Plaid Avenger points this out not because I'm that concerned about you learning the history of every place in the world, but because this history plays into the modern world. In what way?

Virtually all of Japanese society is borrowed from other societies. All of the writing systems, religious systems, and philosophical systems all have roots over in mainland Asia. However, if you read Japanese literature or government propaganda over the last 100 years, it's all reversed. The Japanese are fiercely proud of their independence and their distinct culture, so given that they have been a powerhouse over the past fifty years, they have rewritten history to make it look like as if they were there first and everybody else gleaned stuff from them. This couldn't be further from the truth.

What we have is this group of folks that started up in 500–700 CE, and it was only at this point that they formed into something vaguely resembling a state. They started to have a head of state, a prince. They started a royal/imperial line, which actually stays in place to the current day. For those of you saying, "What? They still have a royal family there?" Yes, there is still an Emperor and there is still an Empress. They have the longest standing monarchy/royal family in world history, and it continues. You can trace it back to 600–700 CE,

Move over, UK! Japan has inbred snobs as well!

same family, same dudes. The faces change, but the DNA remains the same. It is very much like Great Britain and its constitutional monarchy—the idea of royals hanging out. They don't have any real power but they are still there.

Let's get back to history. We can fast forward very quickly because Japan turned into, for the next thousand years, something very similar to a feudal state in medieval Europe. That is, there was the Emperor on top, there were Dukes underneath him, there were Lords underneath the Dukes, and eventually, we get to the peasants that were essentially tied to the lands controlled by the Lords. There are different names and faces in Japan. They are Asians, not Europeans. They have sweet Samurai outfits and swords, instead of long shafts and jousts, but was all essentially the same system playing out on opposite sides of Eurasia.

The peasants lived on the lands and were essentially owned by the Lords, who paid tribute to the Dukes, who had one master, the Emperor. The easy reference is to what we call **Shoguns,** essentially militaristic governors which were the Dukes and the Lords. Just like in Europe, they competed for lands and ownership of things to gain political influence. They still recognized the Emperor as the main dude, but they all fought for places right below him on the totem pole.

Why was this so great? Nothing was really great about it, unless you're the Emperor. He allowed this feudal system to continue because, as all of his subordinates are fighting each other, no one was ever actually threatening him. That's the point. The kings of Europe did the same exact thing. The point of feudalism was to keep people beating the crap out of each other so they can't mess with you. This became standard operating procedure in Japan fairly early on, and it continued for most of Japanese history, which began pretty late in the Asian game.

We can tie some dates to this age of the Shogun, this really entrenched take on the feudal system. From around 1000 to 1580 CE, they had multiple competing shogunates all vying for power and influence. After 1580, one group rose to the top. They were called the Tokugawa Shogunate. The Tokugawa Shogunate unified the whole country under their single command from about 1600 to 1800. A single Duke or Lord from this line of shoguns became so powerful that they actually stopped all the infighting. Japan had a period of stability and peace where everybody was under the same blanket because of those Tokugawa guys. Here's the big thing: they unified the whole country, united all the smaller armies battling each other into a singular army, but most importantly, they plunged the whole country into global isolation.

What do you mean, Plaid Avenger? Well, these guys were tough. You've seen the movies! You've seen these guys. They were so awesome that they repelled a Mongol invasion in 1274—no one else pulled that off! They had their own little world going on and they were not interested at all in the outside world. They cut ties with everybody—not that they ever had a lot of contact. Historically speaking, they had always been a subservient state, or **tribute state** to the Chinese, though the Chinese never took them over physically. Japan knew that China was the big power, and therefore, kept itself on the fringe. This has all been fine and dandy throughout history. The Japanese have escaped takeover by all other entities.

What was happening in the rest of the world from 1600 to 1800? Europe was colonizing the world, was taking over other big parts of the planet and seeing the beginnings of its industrialization period. You had a foreign influence making its way over to the Far East, even into Japan. With industrialization occurring, these European guys had better weapons, better ships, and better navigation. By the 1800s, Europe virtually controlled three-quarters of the planet and finally arrived in Japan. Europeans started making in-roads to establish trade with Japan.

During the Tokugawa Shogunate in 1600–1800, missionaries started showing up at Japan's doorstep. The Shogunate said, "What are you peddling? What are you trying to convert us to? Really? Christianity? That sounds great. And now we'll chop your head off! Get out of our country! We are not interested in your beliefs. We are isolating ourselves! We are the Shoguns, we are the Samurais! We don't need your stuff, so go away! If you don't go away when we tell you to, then we'll kill you!" That was the way it went for a good long time, but it was only going to be perpetuated for so long.

We know this story already. This story is told again and again when we go through the rest of the regions on the planet. As Europe's technology and military hardware became more advanced, they could only be put off for so long. Through its self-isolation, Japan got behind the times technologically. It came to the realization that it couldn't compete with the rest of the outside world. The Japanese were still fighting with swords, fighting dudes with guns. Their isolated world came to a quick halt. The Plaid Avenger is not big on dates, but this is a good one to note: 1853. This is not long ago. In 1853, a dude named Commodore Matthew Perry showed up on the scene. Commodore Perry wanted to open up trade so he pulled his ironclad battle-ship into Tokyo Harbor and came ashore. He said, "Let's meet with the local head-honchos, these Samurai guys with their swords." Perry said, "Hey, we want to establish trade."

Commodore Perry, official Japan-opener.

For the previous 250 years, the Shogunate answered that with, "Get back on your ship and get out of here or we'll chop your head off!" Perry said, "Hold on, fellows, hold on. Take a look out in the harbor. Do you see that? That's an ironclad vessel. See those things poking out of it? Those are cannons. We can blow up you and all of your people right now and you are completely defenseless." Remember, these Samurai fought mostly with swords; now they were stacked up against modern military hardware. The Samurai figured out pretty quickly that this was going to be a one-sided affair. In one fell swoop, in 1853, Commodore Matthew Perry forcibly opened up trade with Japan. They kind of said, "Yeah, those guns probably do better than our swords. We probably are not going to be able to survive this."

What the . . . ? Commodore Perry, stop this Sumo madness!

It is important to note which country the Commodore hailed from: the United States of America. It's actually the United States that forcibly opened up trade in Japan and not a colonizing power. It is historically significant that it was *not* the Europeans who went over to Japan to take it over, but the Americans who went over there to establish a trade relationship. This was the beginning of one of the most amazing occurrences in modern history, as far as the Plaid Avenger is concerned.

When a country is confronted with an outside world in which they are severely behind, they can take one of two roads. All other regions faced this exact same choice as the onslaught of European colonization of the world occurred. Road One: "We can fight it out! Let's try to kick them out! Let's have protests and shoot guns at them and do whatever we have to do to kick out the European powers!" Most countries went that way. Road Two, which only the Japanese seem to have found: "Let's embrace the West! Let's do it way better than they do!" This precipitates a fascinating time in *world* history, not just Japanese history. This is what makes the difference between Japan and China in today's world. This is the crossroads. The Plaid Avenger is telling you, it's rare that you can say, "This is a definitive turning point. Everything is different after this!" The Plaid Avenger is telling you: **this is it.**

MEIJI

Meiji Makeover: Rickshaw to Railways.

In 1868, the Japanese decided to undergo something now referred to as **The Meiji Restoration,** named for the Emperor at the time, the Head Honcho Meiji as he came to power. He was known as being a fairly savvy guy, but it was probably the collaborative effort of his counselors and the people around him that, once they saw the world unfold around them, understood how far ahead the Europeans and the Americans were. They made this radical decision, saying, "Wipe the slate clean. Let's redo everything, EVERYTHING, in light of what we know about the outside world." They embarked on this fantastic restoration.

They sent what would be the equivalent of college students, learned men, as well as government workers, all over the planet. They sent thousands of them to Europe, to America, to the Middle East, everywhere there were centers of learning, centers of technology, centers of industry. Their mission was to find out every single thing they could. They not only learned stuff at universities and through businesses, they brought stuff back. They brought back military hardware, guns, tanks, whole steam engines, railroad equipment. They shipped it back to Japan, and teams of smart dudes ripped the stuff apart to figure out each individual component. They started the individual industries to make the pieces, the wheels, steam engines, and everything else on their own, from the ground up. This was a massive innovation, rejuvenation, a catching-up period, for technology in particular, but also for government and military.

The Japanese did this fantastically well. Think about what Japan does today. It's still like this, isn't it? They don't really make anything—they make everything better! They started this tradition way back during the Meiji Restoration. They are reverse engineers and efficiency experts. They did this in very short order, in around ten years. In two or three decades, they caught up from a lifetime of technological stagnation. It's insane! It's crazy! It's the Meiji Restoration!

At the same time, they modified a lot of things internally. You can see great movies about this, such as *The Last Samurai* with Tom Cruise. Scientology aside, it's a pretty decent movie. The film shows the extremely turbulent times in Japan when everything changed. Not just the technology stuff we talked about, that's easy enough. The social restructuring was the big thing. They actually got rid of the Samurai. They reinvented their society in the likeness of Western Europe and America. They banned the Samurai, which is what *The Last Samurai* is all about. They wanted to rid themselves of the old ways. They said, "No, we're going to rejuvenate! This is the restoration! We are doing everything to catch our military up, which means we're getting rid of the old Shogun ways. We're going to consolidate into a bureaucratic government, just like all these other places. We're going to restructure our banking system. We're going to redo EVERYTHING!" And they did it, in the image of the West.

This is why Japan is a very Western looking nation, as opposed to its neighbors. The Meiji Restoration was the critical turning point in history. Japan became Western-like. Every place else in Asia did not. Japan currently has the number two economy in the world. Every place else in Asia isn't even close, with the exception of China (number four), who has stepped up in the last few decades. But watch out! South Korea just broke into the top ten as well. This region has three economies in the top ten. That is a fact worth remembering.

TERRIBLE LIZARD

Back to the story. The Meiji Restoration was the complete, inside-out do-over of Japanese society on all levels, and it was extremely successful. Like I already suggested, they caught up within a few decades. Japan went from the 1850s, where the Samurais were in charge and fighting dudes with swords, to 1895 when, having been a subservient vassal state of China for their entire history, they attacked China. Why? Because once the beast awakened, it was hungry! The beast must be fed! What does it want? Resources! The Japanese adopted another very Western concept in order to get these resources: imperialism!

GODZILLA IS BORN

In 1895, during the Sino-Japanese War, the Japanese went into parts of modern-day Korea and Manchuria and started conquering. They attacked China, its colossal power-house neighbor, *and they won.* In 1905, ten years later, they attacked Russia, the largest state on the planet, *and they won.*

What were they doing this for? They were taking parts of Russian territory on the east coast of Asia. The Russians sent their entire naval fleet around to sink the Japanese fleet because they said, "Hey, we're Russia, we've been around for like 500 years. We're the biggest state in the world! We're European; we know what's going on." They sent their entire fleet around the entire continent, and it was sunk in five minutes. To put this in perspective: forty years earlier, the Japanese were fighting with swords. They sunk the entire Russian fleet in 1905 in five minutes, the biggest one-sided naval defeat in all of history! The **Battle of Tsushima** was an embarrassment for the Russians, and established the arrival of Japan in the modern world. Japan goes on to advance further into Korea, and in 1910 it took over all of modern-day Korea. In 1917, it annexed more of Russia, while the Russians were busy in their communist revolution.

Minute 1: battle begun. Minute 5: no Russians alive.

We can stop for a second and ask, "What were they doing all this for? Why were they taking all this land, inciting fights with their neighbors?" This gets back to what I was talking about in the physical section. This place had no resources. To become a world power, you need resources. To build railroad cars and tanks and airplanes and industries, you need resources. To build an army, you need resources. What Japan did, as it started to come into power, was acquire resources. Take them from other places. Take over lands. Japan becomes really the only Asian colonizing power in modern history. They were the only Asian imperial power in the Western European sense of the word (i.e., by forcibly taking over other parts of the world). Once the beast is awakened, he must feed. An insatiable hunger develops which inevitably leads to . . .

GODZILLA ATTACKS!

With Japan's acquisition of all this territory and all these resources in mainland Asia, you might say, "That's enough. You've got enough now, Japan." But once Godzilla is awake, he's not going back to sleep very easily! The Japanese continued to meet with

success after success. In 1914, before World War I was over, Japan strategically joined the Allies against Germany, though they played no real part in the war. As a result of their maneuver, they gained control of German territories in China and German-controlled islands in the Pacific. Without doing anything, they gained more territory at the end of World War I. We already said they started to pull out more pieces of Russia during Russia's civil war. After Russia got decimated in World War I, the Japanese took over some more of their territory in the interim period.

In 1931, the Japanese took over all of what is now Manchuria, the entire Northeastern part of China, and during the rest of the 1930s, they established more footholds in China and virtually every other Southeast Asian nation. In each new place, they set up shops and military camps.

In this period between World War I and World War II, all the Europeans were worried about themselves. No one was paying much attention to Japan, except the United States. The United States was very worried about Japanese movement and the growth of their Empire. Even before the war was officially launched, there was animosity between these two powerhouses, Japan and the United States.

The United States, being an anti-imperial and anti-colonial force, was looking over the Pacific and saying, "That doesn't look good. How could this end well? This isn't good for us or anybody!" Indeed, they were right. A lot of folks said, "Whoa, we're really surprised that Japan attacked Pearl Harbor." Nothing could be further from the truth. These countries may not have declared war at the time, but they weren't on friendly terms. In fact, the United States already had an oil embargo against Japan. That's one of the reasons Japan said it attacked the United States. Let's get to this attack

In 1941, the Empire continued to expand, taking over mainland China and places in Southeast Asia such as Vietnam, Cambodia, Laos, Thailand, Burma, Indonesia. Japan continued to expand its Pacific Island holdings as well. In 1941, it became so big that it decided to attack the United States over in Hawaii. Why didn't it attack mainland United States? That's anybody's

guess. In hindsight, it may have been a better idea, but who knows why any of this occurred? What if the Japanese had not attacked the United States? Maybe the United States wouldn't have done anything to them and there would still be a huge Japanese Empire in what is China today. It's hard to tell.

The Plaid Avenger's take on Pearl Harbor is that it was a warning signal. Japan was setting up a fence around its territory. Japan wasn't trying to take Hawaii over; it was establishing where the fence was. The Japanese said, "Okay, America, you're a powerhouse; we're also a powerhouse now. We can bomb you in Hawaii, so don't come on our side of the fence. This stuff over here, this is ours. This is our imperial holding over here, so just stay on your side." Japan apparently didn't reckon that would be a failure. We know the ultimate end to this. Maybe we've talked about World War II too much already in this book. But in the official war years, 1940–1945, Japan invaded every other nation in Southeast Asia and the Pacific.

The expansion, and then deflation, of an empire.

Here's a little known fact that the Plaid Avenger wants you to understand and know: Japan also had designs to invade India and Australia. When I said they had designs, I don't mean some sketches on a cocktail napkin. We're talking about war plans. They had their little Risk board marked with the movements of soldiers, and their troops were in place for this to become reality. It was only a matter of time. They already had small landing parties in Australia, who were camping and scoping things out on reconnaissance.

The other concrete item that still exists in the world today as evidence of Japan's dream to take over all of Asia is the Burma Railway, nicknamed "Death Railway" because 16,000 Allied POWs (mostly British, Australian, Dutch, and American) and over 100,000 Asian laborers died making it. It is the subject of a movie, *The Bridge on the River Kwai*. The laborers were forced to build this railroad system as a supply line for the planned Japanese invasion of India. It ran from Thailand, through Burma, right up to the Indian border.

ANIMOSITY IN ASIA

In these ambitious Japanese plans were a few more details we should flush out in order to understand today's world a little better. How was it that such a small state with a small army ended up rolling over all of Asia in the first place?

Before all the war crimes and atrocities, Japanese forces were often welcomed to intervene in internal affairs of many of these places. The Japanese Army in the 1930s didn't have to fight tooth and nail to take over many of these countries. Why? By and large, the Japanese came in under something called **The Greater East Asia Co-Prosperity Sphere.** The Japanese used this concept to say, "Hey, we're not here to take over; we're here to free you from your Western European colonizers! These guys are jerks! They're white men! Look at us! We look like you, man; we're Asians! We are here to liberate

The Asian Liberators?

you!" Japan was often welcomed, particularly by French Indochina, where Vietnam, Laos and Cambodia are today.

Japan went into these places and threw off the yoke of European colonialism. However, they simply replaced the colonizers, without any real liberation effort. It was all a big sham. This made a lot of folks within Asia pretty pissed off because the Japanese ended up being, during the war years, very brutal. The Plaid Avenger can tell you, war is brutal, and war sucks for everybody involved. Everybody knows that nowadays. However, the Japanese in WWII had a particularly nasty style of warfare and the war crimes and atrocities that were committed against a whole lot of Asian people by the Japanese has not been, and will not be, forgotten.

A horrific example is the Rape of Nanking in China from 1937 to 1938. The Japanese took over a city with millions of people, and since they didn't really feel like having a prison camp, they just killed everybody. They took their bayonets and chopped people's heads off. They lined people up in a row so one bullet would go through more than one of them. For several weeks, the Japanese slaughtered everybody. This is something the Chinese will never forget. It is still mentioned in popular context, in terms of why we should hate the Japanese. See the Japanese War Atrocities (inset box).

Let's not forget about our friends in the middle, the Koreans. Many still hate the Japanese with a passion as well. Japan took over and extracted all of the resources out of Korean mines. How did they do that? They enslaved the Koreans! The whole country essentially became a work camp for Japan. Everyone in Korea was also forced to change their names to Japanese names. Every single person in the country! This was an incredibly difficult time for the Koreans. Trust me, they have not forgotten about it.

The occupation was also pretty nasty for the Chinese and the Koreans, in that some of the worst documented use of biological warfare took place. The Japanese said, "Let's poison a water supply in a town of five million and see how long it takes to kill everybody!" Here's one of the Plaid Avenger's personal anti-favorites: "Let's get a bunch of plague-infested

What's the Deal with Japanese War Atrocities?
Bataan Death March

Approximately 75,000 Filipino and US soldiers, commanded by Major General Edward P. King, Jr., formally surrendered to the Japanese under General Masaharu Homma, on April 9, 1942, which forced Japan to accept emaciated captives outnumbering its army. Captives were forced to make a weeklong journey, beginning the next day, about 160 kilometers to the north, to Camp O'Donnell, a prison camp. Most of the distance was done marching, a smaller distance was a ride packed into railroad cars. Prisoners of war were beaten randomly, and then were denied food and water for several days. The Japanese tortured them to death.

Marching to nowhere . . .

Those who fell behind were executed through various means: shot, beheaded, or bayoneted. Over 10,000 of the 75,000 POWs died. Check out the old-school films *Bataan* (1943) and *Back to Bataan* (1945) with John Wayne.

Bridge on the River Kwai

Great freaking movie, you have to check it out. Based loosely on these real life events: In 1943, the Japanese used POWs to build a railroad across Burma (this is against the Geneva Convention on treatment of prisoners). This was part of a project to link existing Thai and Burmese railway lines to create a route from Bangkok, Thailand to Rangoon, Burma (now Myanmar) to support the Japanese occupation of Burma. The railway was going to be a critical connection and supply line for the planned invasion of India. About 100,000 conscripted Asian laborers and 16,000 prisoners of war died on the whole project. And the guy who played Obi Wan Kenobi in *Star Wars* is in the movie. That helps.

The Rape of Nanking

The Nanking Massacre, commonly known as **The Rape of Nanking,** refers to the most infamous of the war crimes committed by the Japanese military during World War II—acts carried out by Japanese troops in and around Nanjing (then known in English as Nanking), China, after it fell to the Imperial Japanese Army on December 13, 1937. The duration of the massacre is not clearly defined, although the period of carnage lasted well into the next six weeks, until early February 1938.

During the occupation of Nanjing, the Japanese army committed numerous atrocities, such as rape, looting, arson, and the execution of prisoners of war and civilians. Although the executions began under the pretext of eliminating Chinese soldiers disguised as civilians, a large number of innocent men were wrongfully identified as enemy combatants and killed. A large number of women and children were also killed as rape and murder became more widespread. Final toll: 10,000 to 80,000 raped; 5,000 to 20,000 slaughtered.

Want to know why there is animosity between the Chinese and Japanese to this day? Look no further.

rats, put them in a bomber, and drop them over the countryside to see how the disease progresses through the country!" They also did some other "little" things like mustard-gassing whole towns. This was pretty nasty business.

Now you know why many Asian countries view Japan with extreme suspicion, apprehension, and/or outright hatred. The Chinese government and some other governments still want more **war retributions,** monetary payments from the Japanese for the atrocities they committed during World War II.

The Plaid Avenger had to elaborate on this animosity that exists to this day between Japan and many other Asian countries, particularly China and Korea, because it continues to play a part of politics in today's world. Every year when the Japanese educational systems releases their history textbooks for the K-12 schools, Korean and Chinese people protest. Why would Koreans care about what school kids in Tokyo read? Just this: the Japanese textbooks continue to gloss completely over the war years, thus marginalizing all the bad stuff that was perpetrated on the other Asians groups. War crimes, biological warfare, and Japanese sex slave operations in Korea are all conveniently missing from the history books in Japan, and that really pisses off a lot of folks.

This animosity also bubbles to the surface whenever the Japanese prime minister visits a war shrine located in Tokyo: The Yasukuni Shrine. Why do you need to know this? It will continue to be a point of friction between these two countries who will be the two big power players of the 21st century. It's good to know why they hate each other and this is a great example. The shrine commemorates all of the Japanese soldiers who died fighting for, or in service of, the Emperor, no matter what the circumstances.

You have to know about these bad things in order to get the attitudes that these countries and their peoples have about each other. From the Japanese standpoint, you need to think about how big this goal of dominating Asia proper really was. From the Asian standpoint, think about how far the Japanese demonstrated that they were willing to go to achieve it. This isn't a trivial thing. This gets into why Japan is viewed with suspicion, animosity and sometimes hatred by parts of Asia to this day. The Plaid Avenger started off this chapter by saying China vs. Japan, Japan vs. China for a reason. These are places that do not like each other at all.

I'm sure you think that all this stuff is ancient history and that it really doesn't affect today's world at all. There hasn't been an official heads of state meeting between China and Japan for almost a decade because of the Yasukuni Shrine business. Trade deals have been blocked between the countries when tensions rise. Lawsuits between the countries on war reparations are still active. Is that real enough for you? Let's go ahead and get past the war years and bring it on home into the modern era.

I don't think America was happy about Pearl Harbor. Do you?

GODZILLA IS DEAD

After the Germans were defeated in Europe, Uncle Sam then turned all his attention to finishing the job in the Pacific theater of war. And it was brutal. Island by island, enclave by enclave, the Japanese were beaten back by the Americans, but at a horrific cost of human lives on both sides. The US was pressing Japan for total, unconditional surrender, something that was not going to come at an easy price.

What's the Deal with the Yasukuni Shrine?
Yasukuni Shrine (literally "peaceful nation shrine") is a controversial Shinto shrine, located in Tokyo, that is dedicated to the spirits of soldiers who died fighting on behalf of the Japanese emperor.

So what's the problem? Every country honors its war dead, don't they? The Yasukuni Shrine also honors a total of 1,068 convicted Japanese war criminals, including 14 executed Class A war criminals, a fact that has engendered protests in a number of neighboring countries who believe their presence indicates a failure on the part of Japan to fully atone for its military past. President Koizumi regularly visits the shrine, which serves to seriously piss off China and South Korea and perhaps even North Korea, but who knows since they are totally insane.

Yasukuni.

It's the equivalent of the Germans visiting a war shrine to pay respects to Hitler and the other Nazi war dead. Sound extreme? Yep. I call 'em like I see 'em.

What of their US big brother? Well, the balancing act continues. There is actually a large percentage of popular opinion in Japan that favors keeping the anti-military clause in the constitution, and this same group is adamantly opposed to the Self-Defense Forces being abroad. In February of 2008, the National Diet of Japan (the equivalent of Congress) refused to fund the Forces' mission of re-supplying US ships for the War on Terror. This was a big blow to the US at the time, although the funding has since resumed. However with the center-left Hatoyama now in charge, it is unclear how much longer will back the US in terms of active mission work. The Self-Defense Forces future status is far from resolved, as is Japan's direction in future foreign policy.

Luckily for the pro-military faction within Japan, the totally whacked-out Kim Jong-Il is rapidly changing the equation here in 2010. The increased nuclear activity and missile launching and saber-rattling by the North Koreans is starting to severely swing public support to change that constitutional clause before it's too late! Those asinine antics of the kooky Koreans may be what totally tips the scales and causes Japan to officially re-arm with a pro-active military. The Japanese government has been all for the change; the US government is for this as well. And now, maybe the Japanese public. Look for this to be hotly debated this year . . . or until the North Koreans attack.

SAYONARA!

With no doubts we can say that Japan will have considerable impact on world affairs for some time to come. As an economic leader in the world and in its neighborhood, it has set the example that other Asian economies are rapidly living up to. That role as an economic powerhouse will hold for a while longer, and it has company coming to dinner! Japan is the number two economy. China is the number four economy and soon will be number three, South Korea is number eleven soon to be number ten. Wow. Three top ten economies all within spitting distance of each other. This 'hood is hot!

Japan is also staunchly in the Team West camp as well, and one need look no further than the spill-over in commercial and popular culture to see how intimately tied they are to the west. Ninjas, karate, **Atari**, judo, manga, sushi bars, sake shots, Panasonic, Nintendo, Sony, Honda, Toyota, Kawasaki, Speed Racer, Samurai Jack, Tamagotchi, Totoro, Akira, the Matrix, Kill Bill, 4chan, Pocky, J-Pop, and the godforsaken Pokemon—there was a damn Pikachu blimp floating in the Macy's Thanksgiving Day parade right beside Snoopy, for pete's sake. Japan not only adopted western institutions and technologies, but has the unique ability to morph the Eastern and Western traditions together to come out with interesting products that appeal to consumers in both cultures. They do it like no other.

As they improve relations in Asia, and continue their strong relations with the US, the EU, and other rich entities on the planet, Japan will certainly have a unique perspective on the events of the 21st century. A shaper of the global economy, global politics, and most importantly, global culture, our Pokemon playing friends have a critical role to play.

Now, only if we can get them to un-invent karaoke. . . .

一條治卽忠棋
能光守教種

Don't be fooled by the dress: Samurai fighting techniques were unstoppable.

JAPAN RUNDOWN & RESOURCES

View additional Plaid Avenger resources for this region at http://plaid.at/ja

BIG PLUSES

→ Ninjas
→ Samurai
→ 2nd largest economy in the world
→ Center of technological innovation in electronics, auto industry, robotics, etc.
→ Some of the highest standards of living on the planet; highest longevity rates
→ One of the most solid infrastructures in the world
→ Environmentally awesome; 70% of the country is essentially a forested national park
→ Politically stable, solid rule of law
→ Huge US ally, and would certainly have the entire US military as back-up if they ever get into trouble

BIG PROBLEMS

→ Earthquakes
→ Population shrinking, and immigration not really accepted
→ Very high cost of living and high wages causing industry/job movement to Asia
→ Heavily dependent on natural resources, fossil fuels and energy in general imported from other regions.
→ Has been economically/financially stagnant for decades; little to no economic growth
→ Has been politically gridlocked and governmentally ineffective for several years
→ Friction still exists between Japan and Asia; particularly China and Korea. This has stymied closer economic/political integration with its nearest neighbors. (Both of which are huge economies)
→ Would likely be the #1 target of a missile if/when North Korea goes completely nuts

DEAD DUDES OF NOTE:

Commodore Matthew Perry: Commodore of the United States Navy that forcibly opened Japanese ports/trade to the West with the Treaty of Kanagawa in 1954, ending centuries of self-imposed isolation under the Shogun.

Emperor Meiji: The main man in charge of Japan during its revolutionary overhaul to western ways, which then set the stage for its imperial rise to world power. Thus, his name is attributed to the entire time period of his rule, and the 'Restoration' itself.

Hideki Tōjō: General in the Japanese Imperial Army and Prime Minister of Japan during most of WWII, Tojo is held responsible for the bombing of Pearl Harbor which pulled the US into the war. Tojo was later tried for war crimes and executed.

General Douglas MacArthur: General of the US Army, played a mjor role in the Pacific Thater of WWII, officially accepted Japan's full surrender at the end of the war, and oversaw the US occupation of Japan from 1941 to '45. As the effective ruler of Japan, he implemented radical economic, political, and social changes to the country. That's why they are kind of like the US!

PLAID CINEMA SELECTION:

Note: Japanese cinema tradition is as rich, diverse and numerous as American and European industries, so there is no real hope of selecting just a handful to represent. Instead, here is the plaid amalgam of picks from across the board.

Caterpillar (2010) A critique of the right-wing militarist nationalism that guided Japan during the Sino-Japanese War and into WWII. This bizarre story has a limbless war hero returning from the front lines of Japan's invasion of China, and depicts the ultra-nationalistic and militaristic attitudes of the country at the time.

Godzilla (1954) Documentary on the effects of giant lizards and their impact on a major city. Includes an indictment of use of weapons of mass destruction by the United States during World War II. 2004 US re-release is considered by some to be a cinematic masterpiece.

Lost in Translation (2003) A movie star with a sense of emptiness, and a neglected newlywed meet up as strangers in Tokyo, Japan and form an unlikely bond. Great quirky look at modern Japanese culture through the eyes of foreigners. And Bill Murray—total awesomeness.

Seven Samurai (1954) A film about a village of farmers who hire seven masterless samurais to help protect their farms from bandits. Considered the greatest film of Akira Kurosawa, arguably the greatest film director in Japanese history, and one of the best in the world. Influenced Western cinema for several decades after its release.

Shall We Dance? (1996) Another fantastic insight into the prim and properness of Japanese societal norms, this time in Toyko, and all about ballroom dancing. I know, sounds boring, right? But it will make you laugh out loud in parts, and is great at portraying the distinctly Japanese take on family life, work life, and even household life. Yes, this is the original that the idiots in Hollywood remade with Richard Gere, which does not work at all outside the Japanese cultural context.

Twilight Samurai (2002) Set only a few years before the Meiji Restoration, the film follows the life of a low-ranking samurai who is employed as a bureaucrat. Paints an accurate portrait of the life of a subordinate samurai at the end of the Tokugawa Shogunate. Set in same time period as Tom Cruise's *The Last Samurai,* and a million times better.

Udon (2006) A simple story of noodles. But man oh man, it's a great subtle comedy that shows so much more. Fantastic insight into today's Japanese culture. Shot on location all around Kagawa Prefecture on Shikoku. Long, but a student crowd pleaser, and will make you hungry.

LIVE LEADERS YOU SHOULD KNOW:

Junichiro Koizumi: Extremely popular former Prime Minister of Japan from 2001-06. Was "the Ronald Reagan of Japan": conservative, pro-business, pro-US, and had a penchant for wild hair and Elvis. Even visited Graceland. Sent Japanese Self-Defense Forces abroad for the first time in its history to help the US in Iraq.

Naoto Kan: Current Prime Minister of Japan, and the polar opposite of Koizumi. Center-left liberal who is more focused on establishing stronger ties with Asia, and possibly not following US foreign policy so adamantly. Is supposed to be a economic whiz-kid that may be able to put Japan's economy back on track; he is the 5th Prime Minister Japan has had in 5 years, so who knows how long he will last?

CHAPTER OUTLINE

Australia and New Zealand

G'DAY, MATES!

We're heading south from Japan to our friends in the Australia and New Zealand region. When the Plaid Avenger is traveling around the world and can't make it back home to America, I just stop off in Australia, or as I like to call it, the **Mini-America of the southern hemisphere**. If you ever want to piss off people from Australia, just pass that along. It infuriates them for some reason. They tell the Plaid Avenger that they're distinctly Australian and unique in their own way. Yeah, right! You dudes and dudettes are exactly the same as us, just an European and American 20th century cultural amalgamation rip-off!

The Plaid Avenger is always straight shooting, so I am not going to lie to you; this region is not one of tremendous significance on the world stage. But like Japan, it does play its part to effect current events. Its primary role right now is as a platform of European culture and US foreign policy in the southern hemisphere. Even that is changing quickly of late as the mates from "down under" are shifting their political and economic focus to be more in tune with their Asian 'hood. But I am getting ahead of myself. Let's first focus our attention on the physical traits of the region.

LET'S GO FOR A WALKABOUT

Physically, Australia and New Zealand are two island countries, even though Australia is classified as a continent. If you look at it, it's really just a big island. They are two islands of extremes. In Australia, the vast majority of the interior is desert and steppe. It's very similar to the American Midwest. There's a bunch of cattle ranching going on; it's

Area comparison.

Lights out in the middle!

the outback, after all, but there aren't too many people there. In fact, a massive percentage of the interior of Australia is so dry, it has caused a primarily coastal settlement pattern. Everybody's hanging out on the coast and the vast majority of Australia's population is located on these coastal margins, particularly the southeastern coastal margin.

As you can see from the lights at night, virtually everybody is on the east coast of Australia. Before we go any further, let me begin pointing out the parallels between Australia and America. Here is one outlined for you on the map: population primarily in coastal areas, particularly the eastern seaboard. In New Zealand, we have the same pattern, but for different reasons. New Zealand, much like Japan, is a mountainous country. In fact, Japan and New Zealand are almost identical. They are both island nations, made of several different islands, and both are on the borders of major continental plates; both are volcanic in origin, so the interior of the country is very mountainous. The terrain makes it a no-brainer for most people to live on the coast, especially those little hobbits which seem to be over-running the country here lately. Gandalf, help us!

Climatically speaking, these two countries are opposites. New Zealand is cooler and wetter, with a climate more like the Pacific Northwest section of the US, or even like the UK. Australia has some Mediterranean style climates on the southern coastlines, and even a little tropic savanna-type areas in the north, but the interior is largely steppe and desert; a dry area with limited rainfall, few trees, and scrub and short grass vegetation. What are those climates good for? Cattle and sheep production. There is a lot of grazing action going on in Australia. Big exports of wool, lamb, and beef.

One last physical note: what Australia lacks climatically, it more than makes up for in physical resources. They have tons of coal, iron, copper, opal, zinc, and uranium. Put that together with the agricultural commodities, and you have a serious export base to work with. Think about that for a second; what types of countries mainly export primary products? Hold that thought, we'll be back to it soon enough.

AMERICA, JUNIOR

Why does the Plaid Avenger refer to this region as the mini-America of the south? Where do many people from America who like to travel abroad want to go? Australia! Why? Because it's just like home! People want to see the same stuff, eat the same stuff, and speak the same language as in the US, because they are more comfortable in that setting. It's far enough away that you think you're actually being adventurous! There's actually something to the idea of Australia just being a transplanted southern piece of America or Europe, but just "down under." Down under the equator, that is.

Australia is quite unique in the southern hemisphere of this planet for a few reasons. For one, it's the only region in the southern hemisphere that is habitated primarily by white people. It's also the only region south of the equator that is totally rich and developed. It has standards of living and material wealth on par with that of Western Europe, Japan, and the US, and no other region south of the equator can say that. The standard of living thing is another reason why Australia is the Mini-America of the south. But oh, there's so much more.

BACKGROUND

Why is Australia white? Because it was colonized by the white man, of course! Both the US and Australia were originally British **convict colonies.** In the UK back in the day, in the 1600's and 1700's, one of the subsidiary purposes of Britain's colonies was to get rid of British criminals. Britain was getting overpopulated, and laws were very strict. The historical anecdote that explains this fairly well is the establishment of the **baker's dozen.** The baker's dozen is 13 instead of 12. Why? There was actually a law that stated if a baker shorted you a donut, he could be put in jail. So the baker's dozen was born. Throw in an extra one, because who the hell wants to go to jail over a donut?

This was a pretty legally strict society where lots of people got tossed into jail for sometimes menial offenses. Among the options given to convicts were the gallows or a boat ride to a colony. Guess which one people chose? You know there is a criminal element to America's background, and the same goes for Australia. Here's the funny part: the British used to ship their convicts to their American colony, so when did they start shipping them to Australia? Right around the 1780s. Why is that? In 1776, America had a revolution, and we kicked those British prisoner-exporters out, eliminating their felon-absorbing resource. The British, who were floating around the world, figured out that they had claimed a huge chunk of land down in the southern hemisphere. Look at that, a place to send convicts! Australia was established in 1788 as a convict colony, because the British couldn't send them to America anymore.

SOCIETAL STRUCTURE

How is Australia like America? Let me count the ways. If we look at virtually any facet of life in this part of the world, we can look at America and see that it's pretty much the same. Let's start listing them off, shall we? Australia consists of a highly **urbanized** society. There are roughly identical urbanization rates between Australia and the US. This point is of significance because everybody has the opposite impression about Australia. Everybody thinks they're all about the outback, the Crocodile Hunter, and Crocodile Dundee. There are all these wild and crazy guys down there! However, if you ask any Australian how much time they spend in the outback, "You've got to be kidding me, mate," is a likely response.

Why is that? Quite simply, the outback sucks. It's crazy that anybody would want to go to the outback. It has all kinds of dangerous creatures in it, spiders that will jump onto your face, the top ten poisonous snakes in the world, and so on. Nobody wants to go out in "the bush." It is a classic mythology of Australia. It sounds cool, makes them seem all brave and manly, but nobody hangs out in the interior of Australia. Most people live in cities and suburbs, which you are all probably familiar with. They are all content to stay out of the outback, and have the nice little picket fence around their manicured suburban lawns. There is no difference between the levels of urbanization in the US and Australia.

That is due to the standard of living. This is a very rich place. Per capita, it is on par with the US and Western Europe and any other rich place. Standards of living, levels of technology, material wealth: there's no difference. People live there just like they live here, and have all of the same creature comforts. This reiterates why nobody is out in the wild, because rich people go and see the wild when they're on vacation, and then they get the hell out of there because the wild sucks.

One of the reasons why they have a high standard of living: there are not a whole lot of people living in Australia, and therefore, less need to split the resources. Australia and New Zealand populations are extremely low, only about 23 million folks across this entire region. Most major metropolitan areas of the world have more people than that. Look at the population pyramid! As stable as stable gets. Only through immigration will the population of the region increase, much like the US. But there's more!

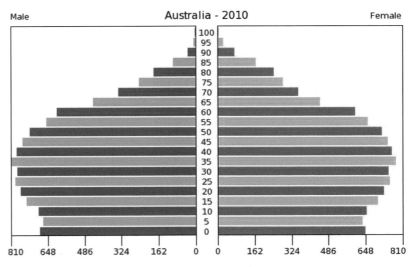

Population (in thousands)

Australia also has similar dietary habits, which ties back in with standards of living. They are big meat consumers, just like in the US. The only big difference is that the Americans like to slay the cows and eat hamburgers, but the Australians are all about lamb. They love the chops.

Lambs! How cute.

And how delicious!

They are also big beer and wine drinkers, like the US. In most places that were colonized by Western Europeans, the beer and wine tradition still exists. Australia is one of the booming wine regions now, soon to be the number one wine exporter on the planet. Also, what kind of beer do you think of when you think of Australia? That's right, Foster's!

Perhaps the Plaid Avenger is getting too shallow, talking about standards of living and beer and meat consumption. What other parallels are there?

This may just seem like a funny side note, but this may play a part in why the two nations are so similar today. Both countries have a criminal background, a criminal profile; remember, they started as convict colonies. How has that played into today's society? This is a stretch, but stay with me. What do people like to do in both of these societies? We've already pointed out the beer drinking thing, which seems like a nice criminal element. Both beer drinking societies, both like to party. What else do they like to do while consuming alcoholic beverages? I don't know—watch brutal sports? Yes! The Americans have their football, Australians have rugby. And the Aussies are even more hardcore than the US: they take the pads off and beat the crap out of each other, while everyone who isn't playing drinks beer and watches.

On a more serious note, each country has a rugged, individualistic archetypal character. The Americans have the Marlboro man, a lone, rugged warrior out on the plains, wrangling cows and looking out for coyotes. That's part of the common symbology, the perception of what it is to be an American. He embodies individualistic pride. They've got the same stuff down in Australia, except they wrangle crocs and look out for dingoes. Do these types of characters represent the majority of either place? No, but these characters are popular symbols in this society. There really aren't these archetypal figures anywhere else in the world. It may be partially due to the fact that both places have large expanses of land with low population density. They have frontiers, and there has to be the rugged individual to explore those frontiers.

Here's another similarity between Australia and the US: the settling convicts exterminated nearly the entirety of their respective native populations. There is a history of repression of native peoples in both places. In the US, it was the Native Americans, the Amerindians. In Australia they had the Aborigines. Both of those peoples suffered immensely in the onslaught of British colonization in exactly the same ways. In fact, it was particularly bad in Australia.

In Tasmania, an island off of the south coast, there were some indigenous people called the Tasmanians who were openly hunted during a period of the settlement of Australia. The government

American Cowboy.

Australian Cowboy.

See the difference?

essentially said, "Hey, settlers, want some free land? Go down to Tasmania! If the natives give you any trouble, don't feel bad about killing them." It became a sport to go out and hunt the indigenous Tasmanians. This was done so efficiently that they killed almost all of them. That's the criminal background manifesting itself in one of the nastier ways in history.

Another historical consideration of why both societies evolved out this frontiersman mythology has to do with how both countries grew. Both started on the eastern seaboard of a large uncharted land mass, and proceeded to expand and conquer the continents in a continuous westward expansion. Interesting, isn't it? Australia even underwent a western "Gold Rush" at almost the exact same time as the famous Californian rush of the same name, but with one slight difference: theirs was more profitable!

Brutal sports, slaughter of indigenous populations, mostly white, cowboy image, and an affinity for beer all play into this criminal background in Australia. This is why the Plaid Avenger refers to it as the Mini-America of the south.

Put all these historical, physical, and cultural factors together and you are starting to get a sense of why the Plaid Avenger draws so many parallels between the US and Australians region. But you don't have to take my word for it! There is proof a'plenty that these two states have a tight relationship: let's just take a look at their foreign policies for a minute.

AWESOME ALLY

When it comes to Team West foreign policy, one could not find a better friend than those Aussie mates. They have been there year in and year out for their western allies, for every single international conflict and conflagration. We can be even more specific: first, Australia has always supported every endeavor of the old British motherland, and then later came on board for all things American . This bunch really sticks together.

I'm not talking about supporting them on paper, or in a UN vote, or economically. I'm talking about Australians participating side by side with their English-speaking brothers-in-arms in World War I, World War II,

The 'Roo Brigade will always be ready to serve freedom!

the Korean War, the Vietnam War, the Cold War, the War on Terror, which has spawned the two newest Aussie supported wars: the campaign in Afghanistan and the war in Iraq. Every conflict, every time, they are there for the West. Check out one of Mel Gibson's first starring roles in a movie named *Gallipoli*, about Aussie troops fighting the Turks in WWI.

Being a small country with a small population, the numbers of Australian forces that have participated in these conflicts is not a huge number, but it's the thought that counts, especially when the thought is a bunch of dudes with submachine guns. But I digress. Point is, that they have regularly been looked to as a vote of support for western ideology worldwide; most currently, counting themselves as one of the "Coalition of the Willing" in the lead up to the Iraq War. They are the only folks south of the equator you can say that about.

So historically strong are the Australian/American ties that the Plaid Avenger counts them among the three most reliable, solid platforms of US foreign policy in the world. The UK, Japan, and Australia can be counted on to support US endeavors, almost with no questions asked. In the past, this essentially made these countries the American lapdogs in terms of foreign policy, but times do change.

While I stand by the description of Australia as a loyal ally of the US, modern times have forced them to be more pragmatic. Sometimes, being a loyal ally has to be pulled back due to popular opinion. Most Australians were opposed to the US-led invasion of Iraq, and the government did take a popularity hit for its staunch participation. It perhaps was part of the reason that the old government was thrown out in the most recent elections. Time to introduce you to someone new.

Prime Minister Kevin Rudd: "Sorry America, but we are getting out."

In a sign of the times, the Prime Minister Kevin Rudd has already announced Australian troop withdrawal from Iraq. He is the equivalent of a Democrat in the American political spectrum, and a fairly liberal one at that. In office since Dec. 2007, Rudd immediately signed the Kyoto Protocol on limiting greenhouse gas emission, an international treaty that both the US and Australia had jointly been stonewalling. Suddenly, it seems that the US is standing alone a bit more on the international stage. Don't be fooled by this slight change in support: Australia is still a big component of US and Team West foreign policy, and will stand by their boys for some time to come. LAST MINUTE 2010 UPDATE!!! Kevin Rudd has just been forced to resign by his own political party, and replaced by Julia Gillard . . . which makes her Australia's first woman Prime Minister!

A WORD ON THEIR WEIRD WAY TO WEALTH

This is where things get a bit trickier, so the Plaid Avenger is going to have to sort a few things out for you. We've made it expressly clear that the US is the powerhouse economy of the planet, but China, at number four, is catching up. Japan is at the number two slot and Germany's at number three. Where's Australia? It's in fifteenth place. In terms of total GDP, how rich is this place? Not very. However, in levels of material wealth per person, they're not in bad shape. How could this be? How could they have a standard of living identical to ours? They just sit around drinking beer and grilling shrimps on the **barbie.** That's a pretty good life. How can they be that way if they're not in the top ten economies? It is a strange circumstance, and perhaps a unique circumstance to Australia, that when we think of features that make it the most unique, it's not an exceptionally wealthy place as a total.

Australian number one export. Money!

What do they produce? What do they really do? What do you buy from there? Do they make computers? Cars? Linens? VCRs? Software? Video games? I don't think so. What have you ever bought that said, "Made in Australia"? Here's the quick answer: didgeridoos and boomerangs. That's not much of an export economy to put them among some of the wealthiest countries in the world. Well, that's not what has made them wealthy.

Australia is perhaps the only country in the fully developed world that has gotten rich from the export of *primary products.* That's pretty much what they do. Remember that primary products are things extracted from the earth like coal, oil, minerals, diamonds, uranium, wool, cattle, and meat. What is all this stuff worth? When it comes right down to it, not worth much. They are a bunch of unprocessed materials. How can the Aussies be rich if they are doing stuff that poor countries do? There are only 20 million people in the entire country, and it's the size of the US. They export so many goods because of the resource-rich land, and the wealth generated from that is spread between so few that they are rich overall.

"Plaid Avenger? Agent Aussie here. We need help diversifying my portfolio."

Don't let the Plaid Avenger lead you too far astray. If you look at the numbers, over 60% of the workforce is in the service sector, but who are they serving? Pretty much just themselves. Seriously, no innuendo implied. They work in malls and mailrooms and telemarketing centers. They produce computers and cars, but the manufacturing facilities are owned and operated by multinational companies, and the products are only built to be consumed in Australia. In other words, they make Apple computers there, because people there want Apple computers. They are not exported out of Australia. There are no cars or refrigerators exported from Australia. That's because they are too busy making serious bank on exports of primary commodities. Their internal economy has enough juice to keep them going and growing, but it is a matter of low population and lots of primary resource wealth that makes for such high GDP per capita. They are the only place on the planet that I know of that has gotten away with that. Bottom line: they may have 65% of the people in the service sector, but they make 65% of their total GDP on exports of primary products.

You'll often see information about sheep and lamb being a huge export to places like the Middle East, since they consume more lamb than they do things like beef and chicken. You'll also see information about the coal and oil that Australia has being exported to places like China and Japan, both of which are hungry for those things. Australia also signed a uranium deal with China on April 4, 2006, to export raw uranium to be processed and used. No other "rich" country on the planet is exporting raw commodities at this scale. Everybody else processes things, because that's where the money is. It's fascinating that their primary source of income is from raw products. They are definitely the economic black sheep of the world.

PACIFIC SHIFT

What is in Australia's future? To answer that we might ask ourselves what's changing, because while we've been saying that this is the mini-America of the south, things are definitely on the move.

Throw him on the barbie, I dare you.

ECONOMICALLY

As China increases in world power and wealth and requiring more resources, Australia is reorienting its economic focus to nearby countries in Asia—instead of trading primarily with other white English-speaking countries like the US and Great Britain. In the past, these two countries were the primary trading partners with Australia. Seriously, what a pain it is to ship exports that far. It's a long commute for meetings and it's difficult to maintain trading relationships with their white, English-speaking allies. What a joke. That's on the other side of the planet! Nothing, other than fine Australian wine, can be shipped economically all the way across the world anymore.

Also, consider what impact longitude has on trade relationships. If you are at the same longitude, you are in the same time zone. Now, Australia is doing business in real time, during their business day, instead of having to deal with the massive time difference between it and other trading partners like the US and Europe. It's a tremendous complication to be awake when your trading partners are asleep.

They have reoriented their trade relationships to more local areas like China and Japan. "Why continue trading with the white people that look like us, when we can make lot more money trading with the yellow people that don't look like us?" Money talks. This is the way it is.

In conclusion: Aussie economic future lies in Asia. Over the next few years, look for the portion of Australia exports of raw goods to Asian countries to increase, and dramatically. Raw material exports are not the only thing on the menu, my friends. Many Australian businesses, like so many others across the planet, are moving manufacturing facilities as well as research and development operations to Asian locations to take advantage of both cheap labor and the large local talent pool. I suppose the future of the continent may be as a giant national park serving tourists from around the world serving shrimp and Foster's on tap. Besides primary product production, what else will they be doing?

Even more so than America, Australia's future is tied closely with Asia. Asia is a booming region on the planet, a place where a lot of things are going on economically, and Australia is right there to help them along and make some profit at the same time. As we will see in the Mexico chapter, it is good to be next to a gigantic economic engine, and Australia's proximity to China, who will be the largest consumer of raw goods on the planet in the coming century, will enable Australia to turn huge profits. Former Prime Minister John Howard of Australia has been quoted in the past about Australia refocusing their efforts and economy to better compliment China's rising power. He has called Australia "an anchor of stability" in this region. He also said, "When we think about the world, we inevitably think of a world where China will play a much larger role." That's a real quote from the man, not a Plaid Avenger paraphrasing. Hey,

Former Prime Minister John Howard: "How can we as Australians kiss China's ass more?"

and dig this: the former Prime Minister Kevin Rudd not only speaks dingo English, but flawless Mandarin Chinese as well. Seriously, do I need to say anything else about shifting the strategies of the Aussies? That fact truly does express it all.

POLITICALLY

Let's stay with Former Prime Minister John Howard for just a minute more, so I can explain to you how Australia's role in the vicinity is changing politically as well. To do this, I must elaborate on the most hilarious "story of the sheriff" which ruffled many feathers. It goes a little something like this:

Several years ago, Former US President George W. Bush *complimented* Former Prime Minister Howard during a press release by referring to Australia's status as the "sheriff of Asia." What the hell is that supposed to mean? Most Asian countries interpreted this as "the white dudes in the area are in charge," that the long arm of the US law was being stretched through Australia to keep them down. This seriously pissed off all of Australia's neighbors. Malaysia, which is a hilarious state in its own right, nearly declared war over it. To paraphrase the Malaysian prime minister, "Think that all you want, but if you ever set foot on our soil we will declare war on you instantaneously, no matter what the US says about it."

Even John Howard was a little miffed. He was probably thinking, "Thanks for the compliment, Mr. Bush, but try not to ever say anything about me in public again." This was a problem especially since Australia is reorienting itself toward Asia. These are the guys with whom they are trying to buddy up! The last thing they need is negativity about their foreign policy ties to the US. They still want to be allied with the US, but they don't want to be throwing it in people's faces. This is a big stress factor for Australia in their part of the world.

The Plaid Avenger suggested in an earlier chapter that Europeans are slightly apprehensive to support US foreign policy, as there is a more likely possibility of terrorist threats due to their proximity to the Middle East. Australia is in the same boat. They're closer to other regions that may be slightly hostile to the US foreign policy. Australia is right there beside Southeast Asia, parts of which are known hotspots for extremism and terrorism. There are some seriously extreme fundamentalist Muslims in this area; even my Muslim friends would concur. Terrorist cells are known to exist in lots of places in Southeast Asia (e.g., Indonesia, the Philippines, or Malaysia).

This is why John Howard was quick to offer a modification of Bush's comment, because there is a real threat nearby. The US is far enough away to be safe from imminent threat, but it's not hard for terrorists to make it from Southeast Asia to Australia. Because Australia is seen as the face of American foreign policy in the area, it is very surprising that Australia has not seen any terrorist activity on their soil already. However, there have been several foiled terrorist plots in recent history and this situation is not likely to let up anytime soon. The Aussies remain ever vigilant.

Bush was quoted as saying that he didn't think of Australia as a deputy sheriff, "but as a full sheriff." In fact, Australia does supply soldiers in most UN activities in the countries surrounding them. In many cases, they are actually doing patrols and peacekeeping directly for the UN in places like the Solomon Islands, Indonesia, and other hotspots where the UN needs to send soldiers. The idea of them as sheriff does have some weight, and is going to cause them some problems in the future. Many countries in the 'hood remain perpetually pissed that the white man is on their soil at all, even as peacekeepers.

To end this rant, know this: this is changing fast. Former Prime Minister Kevin Rudd was a bit more liberal and conciliatory than his conservative predecessor, and he made moves to soften the Australian image in this part of the world. As I suggested above, he decided to pull Aussie troops from Iraq, and was much more engaged with local Asian countries' leaders to head-off any friction that might arise due to Australian presence, as UN representatives or otherwise. Oh yeah, I already told you he speaks Chinese, and not just to order from a take-out menu either. Given his liberal nature, I suppose it's no surprise what he did during his first month in office, but that has to be in the next section. His replacement, current Prime Minister Julia Gillard, will be maintaining these popular policies of the Rudd years . . . even though she don't speak no Chinese. Maybe she can call back Kevin to help her order the take-out: there is rumor that Rudd will soon become a top diplomat to China.

DEMOGRAPHICALLY

Because Australia is doing a lot of business with China, Japan, Indonesia, etc, they will become more like those countries culturally. This is changing very rapidly just in the modern era, because quite frankly it was not allowed to happen any earlier. How so, Plaid Avenger?

At the expense of pissing off my Aussie brothers, I will have to tell you that a racist streak has run through the society since its inception—a bad habit that they probably inherited from the Brits. Perhaps racist is too harsh, but certainly they had a superiority complex when it came to other peoples in their neighborhood. The Australian treatment of the Aboriginals was bad from the get go, mostly treating them as third rate citizens at best. There was also an official state policy from 1870 to 1970 which made it perfectly legal for the state to take Aboriginal children from their parents to re-educate and civilize them in white families. These folks are now referred to as the Stolen Generation.

Dude, does this really say the "finest traditions of our race"?

I guess that is better than what the Aussies did to the Tasmanians, which was to kill them all in an open hunting season. That sucks. On top of that, Australia had a white-only immigration policy in place for most of its history. What? Yeah, I'm afraid it's true. If you were of European or American background, then you had an open door to the country; the door was firmly shut for Asians of any stripe. Pretty nasty business.

To be fair to our friends "down under," they have made great strides in the last few decades to make amends. Much has been done to alleviate the impoverished plight of many Aboriginal communities, and even more has been done to overcome the negative attitude and stereotypes of the group. In fact, Aus-

Aborigines: Not held in high regard.

DISTRIBUTING SHIP CARGO OF STANDARD BUGGIES COAST OF AUSTRALIA

What is this madness? No wonder Rudd apologized.

tralia picked an Aboriginal woman to carry the flag into the introductory ceremonies for the 2000 Olympics. That brings me back to what former Prime Minister Kevin Rudd did his first month in office: in February 2008, he made an official government apology to the Aborigines for all past reprehensible deeds of the Australian government, specifically citing the Stolen Generation. This was big news, and perhaps a critical turning point for the society.

Back to the story: Since 1976, when their historically strict immigration laws became more relaxed, the country's Asian population has increased. Surprise, surprise. More people that are close by, from regions adjacent to Australia, are coming there because it is a rich place where there is more opportunity to succeed than there may be in their home countries. Again, it's America, Jr.! All of the poorer people nearby want to get there so they can set up shop. Australia may not be full-on encouraging it, but at least they are allowing it. They are changing direction, changing focus, and becoming more Asian. When you visit Sydney now, you can bump into a very vibrant and growing Chinatown for the first time in forever. These changes are occurring nationwide.

Who else have we talked about that is becoming more Asian due to increasing immigration from Asian states?

That's right: America, Sr.!

NO WORRIES

This is a region that plays a dual role as a US foreign policy anchor and as an economic player with China. This might put them in a tricky position, but a position perhaps enviable by nearby countries. They have a lot of natural resources and stable population growth. There is still the terrorist threat, however; we'll just have to see how they balance their security against their economic interest.

Australia would like to be a power broker between China and the US. This is promising; they have far fewer complications to worry about when dealing with China, as opposed to Japan, which has loads of historical emotional baggage. Japan may be a little more abrasive than Australia when dealing with Asian relations in general, and this gets the Aussies ahead.

Australia is going to have a leg up dealing with China and all the other Asian economic giants, because of proximity as well as the fact that they don't carry a lot of cultural baggage. What do I mean by that? They haven't pissed anyone off. They haven't invaded anyone. They never colonized anyone. They are pretty antiseptic all the way around. That is a big plus in today's world, particularly for any state wanting to get in on the action in Asia, which is, of course, everyone.

Uncle Sam's little brother down south is still a staunch ally of the US. Luckily, they remain just distant enough to dodge a lot of the negative press associated with such a role. Of course, the Aussies are distancing themselves slightly from US foreign policy of the last decade . . . but damn, who isn't? Australia is a pretty chill place all the way around: politically, economically, socially. That's why we like to go vacation there, because Australia is a laid back sort of place. Throw a shrimp on the barbie, have a beer, and enjoy the prosperous future, America Junior.

FIND AUSTRALIA'S LARGEST EXPORT

Here's a great game that all you kids will enjoy playing. Look around this page and see if you can identify Australia's largest export. Do you see any really large Australian exports? I mean, this sucker is large! Which of the following is Australia's largest export by volume, by weight, AND by dollars earned from it? If you just can't seem to find Australia's largest export, then check the answer at bottom of page. Good luck, and think large!

Coal is the answer! Coal is by far Australia's largest export. And Foster's Lager is brewed in Canada, so it doesn't even count anymore!

AUSTRALIA RUNDOWN & RESOURCES

View additional Plaid Avenger resources for this region at http://plaid.at/aus

 BIG PLUSES

→ Koala bears and kangaroos and hobbits. Who doesn't love them?

→ Small population that is about evenly balanced with resource/industrial base

→ Location, location, location! In the neighborhood of the hottest, fastest growing Asian economies, to which Australia sells tons of goods

→ 13th largest economy; very high standards of living

→ Resource/agricultural product rich

→ Stable democratic government

→ No real enemies on the planet; no international conflicts with anyone

 BIG PROBLEMS

→ Crocodiles, the Sydney funnel-web spider, 9 of the top 10 most deadliest snakes in the world. Crikey!

→ National legacy of racism: still has friction with its Aboriginal groups, and immigration is becoming a hot button issue much like it is in US

→ Economy not very diversified; heavily dependent on natural resource exports

→ By mere association with Team West, combined with its proximity to SE Asia, Australia is a high-risk target for international terrorism

LIVE LEADERS YOU SHOULD KNOW:

John Howard: Popular former Prime Minister of Australia from 1996–2007. Kind of the "Ronald Reagan of Australia": Center-right conser-vative, pro-business, pro-US, and presided over a period of strong economic growth and prosperity. Strongly supported US in Iraq and Afghanistan. Mostly lost in 2007 simply because voters were bored.

Kevin Rudd: Prime Minister of Australia from 2007–10, and the polar opposite of Howard. Center-left liberal who was more focused on establishing stronger ties with Asia, and possibly not following US foreign policy so adamantly. Speaks Mandarin Chinese fluently, supports Kyoto Protocol, made official apology to Aboriginals, and pulled troops out of Iraq.

Julia Gillard: Current Prime Minister, and first woman in Australia to hold the title. In an internal political party coup, Rudd was tossed and replaced by Gillard in 2010; since she is of the same party, there are no major policy shifts from the Rudd administration, although she is seen as more 'business-friendly.'

PLAID CINEMA SELECTION:

Australia (2008) Australian cowboy version of *Gone With the Wind*. At nearly three hours in length, this epic is based on real life events that occurred in Northern Australia during World War II. Shows, at length, much of the northern territory of Australia during wartime, including several aspects of Aboriginal life, and the national legacy of racism to boot.

"Crocodile" Dundee (1986) Probably the most well known Australian film of all time. Has two versions, an Australian version and an international version. The Australian version features more regional slang and extended scenes. Despite its comedic aspect, the film shows a lot of great examples of the outback, including both scenery and wildlife.

Matariki (2010) Complex film tells the plot through five interweaving stories, all in the days leading up to Matariki, the Maori New Year. The film shows a wonderful view of the landscape in South Auckland, New Zealand. Funded completely by the New Zealand Film Commission.

The Piano (1993) Dramatic film about a mute pianist and her daughter living during the mid-19th century in New Zealand. This wonderful film covers many aspects of language, as three languages are spoken in the film if you include sign language. Great scenery as the purples and greens of New Zealand capture the eye and don't let go.

Rabbit-Proof Fence (2002) Closely based on real events, a real fence, real people, and real national racist policies of the time. The story of three girls who are forcibly taken from their home and put in a camp because it was believed that the Aboriginals were a danger to themselves and should be bred out of existence. Shows struggles of Aboriginals in western Australia during the 1930s.

Romper Stomper (1992) Drama about a group of bored Neo-Nazi skinheads clashing with Vietnamese immigrants in a Melbourne, Australia suburb. Inspired by actual events, this film stars a young Russell Crowe in his pre-Gladiator days. The violent closing scenes take place within the natural beauty of Victoria's Twelve Apostles rock outcroppings (of which there are not actually twelve).

Walkabout (1971) Artsy-fartsy piece with little dialogue and loads of symbolism, this film was extremely controversial when released due to its overt sexual themes and nude scenes with a minor. But it is just awesome at showing the physical beauty and bizarreness of Australia, Aboriginal culture, and the disconnect between the "modern" human life and the "uncivilized" human experience. Not for those who need explanation and closure in films.

CHAPTER OUTLINE

Latin America

A SINGLE REGION?

Latin America is a region with a question mark after it. The Plaid Avenger has never really considered it a region in the past, mainly because a regional definition involves some sort of homogeneous singular trait that you can apply to the geographic space in question. I've said for years this place is too big. You can't apply singular homogeneous traits across all of Latin America because it encompasses everything from the south of the US-Mexican border all the way to Tierra del Fuego, the tip of South America, which is almost in the Antarctic. It's too damn big. You can't see any singular thing that applies across all of those regions! Except maybe . . .

What's the Deal with . . . the Latins in Mexico?

What happened was this freaky-freak Napoleon III—not Napoleon the short, dead dude we all know, but one of his later kin—sent over this other French dude named Maximilian to sit on the Mexican throne in a feeble effort to reestablish France's presence in the New World in 1862. The French were actually invited to do this by an elite rightist core of Mexican aristocracy who wanted to dismantle the leftist movements occurring in what was independent, sovereign Mexico at the time. So this French dude Maximilian was

Maximilian being executed.

in charge, and when he was out scouting around he said, "What the hell? We're French, we're not even Spanish. What rallying point can we possibly use to generate empathy that we should be in charge here?"

What our brilliant French brethren came up with was that the Spanish, Portuguese, and the French languages are all linguistically tied. They are all part of the Romance, or Latin-derived languages. In a fit of what must have been desperation at the time, Napoleon III told ol' Maxi to say, "Look, I may be just the French guy here in Mexico, but we are all brothers under the Latin language, so we're all family here in *Latin America*." Again, a totally bogus, politically made-up term, but somehow it stuck. The Mexicans deposed Maximilian's ass fairly quickly, but the term stayed—in fact, kicking out the French is what the Cinco de Mayo holiday is all about; it's not Mexican Independence Day.

That is what's Latin about Latin America. How bizarre. Now we associate "Latin" with scantily clad women shaking their booties to Ricky Martin songs. Caesar would be proud.

Cinco de Mayo festivities.

After thinking about the French fool Maximilian's antics for a while, the Plaid Avenger has realized that, indeed, there are a lot of traits that can be recognized across the whole of Latin America. We're going to look at some of those traits in this introduction pre-chapter to the subregions of Latin America.

WHAT IS LATIN AMERICA?

As pointed out in the previous box, Latin America is a *hilarious* term because it doesn't mean jack. It's a term that everybody understands, everybody gets, you know where it is, but it's based on a word that is completely and utterly meaningless: Latin. Do all of these people speak Latin south of our border? Hell no. Latin is a damn dead language. Nobody on the planet speaks that Caesar-ized stuff anymore. In fact, there are really only two predominate languages spoken: Spanish and Portuguese.

How did we get this term Latin America: are they all of Latin or Greek ancestry? Obviously not. As with many things on the planet, we can blame the French.

Geographically, the term means everything south of the US border. That's common knowledge across the planet. Mexico, which we teased out for obvious reasons earlier, is not part of the US/Canadian region. There are too many differences, including its Latin-based language, levels of development, poverty, and lots of other issues which distinguish Mexico from the United States. One reason Mexico is thrown in with Latin America is that there are a lot of similarities across countries south of the US/Mexican border. Before we get to those similarities, let's identify frequently referenced regions in this part of the planet.

LATIN LOCATIONS

There are a few terms that the Plaid Avenger wants you to know before we get into these subsequent chapters. These definitions will help us understand a lot of terminology used on the global stage. We already talked about Latin America encompassing every single damn country south of the US border, in the entire western hemisphere. Easy enough. Now let's break down some more specific regions within Latin America.

SOUTH AMERICA

The first one is easy enough. South America is both a continent and a region. The South American continent is that other big-ass continent in our hemisphere. That one is pretty solid. It starts with Colombia and then heads east to Venezuela, Guyana, Suriname, French Guyana, and then turns down south to Brazil. South of Colombia is Ecuador, Peru, Chile, Bolivia, Paraguay, Uruguay, and Argentina. It is important to note that most all of the countries of South America are fairly good sized; Brazil itself is a monster country, being the fifth largest in the world. This makes South American states quite territorially, physically, and economically distinct from the slew of much smaller micro-states to their immediate north. Food for thought, and I'm not talking about salsa either.

+ + =

MIDDLE AMERICA

The term **Middle America** is everything between the southern border of the United States and the South American continent. It's a fairly generic definition that usually only gets play in high school and college level textbooks anymore, but I suppose it doesn't hurt to know the reference when you see it pop up. For this magnificent treatise of learning, I will further break this area down to more manageable and meaningful subregions, described below. Study the Middle America map equation above to be cartographically clever.

MEXICO

The first subdivision is Mexico. Mexico is a country, a state in its own right, but it's also radically different from all the states around it, including the US, and it's also different from the Central American and Caribbean states. Mexico is its own subregion that we're going to define in the next chapter. In respect to size, resources, economy, population and level of development, Mexico stands apart from all its neighbors.

THE CARIBBEAN

The Caribbean is a group of island states that comprise the Greater Antilles and the Lesser Antilles. The Caribbean, when we think about it, calls to mind a distinct culture in terms of . . . everything. Cuisine, language, stuff they drink, how they party—it's all different. Caribbean means something to us, and it means something that's different than Mexico. We all understand that. We go to a Caribbean restaurant or a Mexican restaurant, but we never really see the two put together. (Note to self: that might be a good idea. Instead of Tex-Mex cuisine, how about Car-Mex cuisine—or is that a lip balm?) The island nations in the Caribbean Sea, south of the United States, are a distinct subdivision.

CENTRAL AMERICA

The last sub-region of Middle America is **Central America.** This is the one that causes the most confusion for younger students of the world. It is everything between Mexico and South America, noninclusive. Mexico and South America are the bookends. There are seven distinct countries in what is widely accepted as Central America: Belize, Guatemala, El Salvador, Honduras, Nicaragua, Costa Rica, and Panama. You may hear reference to Central American civil wars or Central American gangs; this group of countries is the origin for that descriptor. Yeah, good times.

We've got a bunch of Americas here, and Central America is quite distinct in that it has nothing to do with Mexico, the Caribbean, or even South America.

It has a lot going on, particularly in terms of the violence that we will talk about in much more detail when we get to the Central America chapter. It's a distinct place; a bunch of small states that bridge both North and South America, but they are all quite distinct, even from each other, in all other aspects.

South America plus the three regions of Middle America—Mexico, Central America, and the Caribbean—that's Latin America all the way around. Now that we know where it is and where the definition comes from, let's talk a little bit more about what Latin America *is*. What homogeneous traits can we use to define this region?

WHAT IS LATIN ABOUT LATIN AMERICA?

COMMON CULTURE

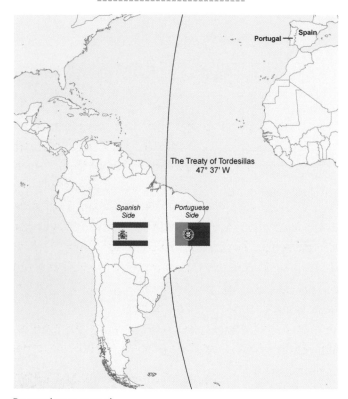

Portugal got screwed.

First, we can point out some distinct elements so we don't have to keep repeating ourselves in subsequent chapters. Number one is culture. There is a common culture south of the US/Mexican border, be it in the Caribbean, Central America, Chile, Argentina, or Brazil; there are some things that do remain the same. One of the kind-of-the-same things that we already pointed out is language. While Latin America is a joke term in and of itself, they do primarily speak Spanish, and the only other really big language is Portuguese.

How did this come about? Easy enough. It came about because of colonial endeavors in this region that date as far back as 1492 when Columbus sailed the ocean blue, came over here and bumped into the Caribbean. After his great discovery, the big naval powers at the time, Spain and Portugal, started floating over here in fairly short order as well. (Great Britain didn't come along until later. It wasn't as big of a naval power as the Spanish at the time, so it was a latecomer. It therefore had to head north for colonial expansion which is why it gets the leftovers—North America.)

Let's get back to our story here. Why do we have these two main languages, Spanish and Portuguese? Columbus came over in 1492. Two years later, a fairly important event occurred which I want you to understand and know about: **The Treaty of Tordesillas.** The Treaty of Tordesillas occurred in 1494 when these European countries were bumping into the New World, colonizing, taking over, and staking claim to places. Of course, there was friction between the countries. They had been beating the hell out of each other for hundreds of years at home anyway; now they were just taking the fight abroad. Much of the friction was between Portugal and Spain, two of the main colonizing powers in this part of the world. There was claim staking, and there were people getting pissed off about which country owned what. Both these countries, being predominantly Catholic—which is another common cultural tie we'll see more about in just a second—would listen to the papa, the **Pope,** the main man in the Vatican. The Pope said, "Hey guys, come on now, we're all civilized colonial imperial masters here. Let's all get on the same page, get around the same table here, let's work together! We don't need to fight! We're going to settle this fair and square. Papa is going to just draw a line on the map and everything on one side we'll give to the Spanish and

Pope responsible for Tordesillas . . . and Catholicism in Latin America.

everything on the other side we'll give to the Portuguese. Now you guys be good!" The line happened to be 45 degrees western longitude. Check out the map on the previous page. And the caption.

As you can see from the map, the Portuguese look like they got screwed pretty damn good on this deal. They only got the tip of what is now known as Brazil. Why is this? Did the Pope just want to shaft the Portuguese? No. This was during early exploration in 1494, only a few years after Columbus got there. They didn't even know what was there yet. They were just bumping around the coastline; with no comprehension about the actual size the continent is . . . neither North nor South America, quite frankly. What they thought was a good deal was based on known circumstances at the time, which really wasn't much. As we

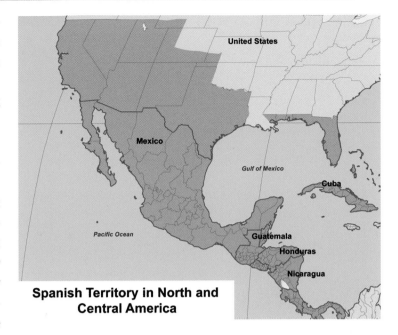

Spanish Territory in North and Central America

all now know, this is a pretty big place. South America is the fourth largest continent on the planet. As discovery continued and the true scope of the land's magnitude unfolded, the Portuguese did pick up what is now modern-day Brazil. Its boundaries naturally fell back to the Andes—a nice, easily defined natural border. Anyway, the Treaty of Tordesillas is the cornerstone of why the Spaniards ended up controlling so much of the New World—basically, all the rest of it outside Brazil.

First of all, they controlled Mexico. We think of today's Mexico as down south, but Mexico in its days as part of the Spanish Empire included all of western North America, as well. It was everything that's now California up to Washington State, to Utah, to New Mexico, to Texas. Spanish territory also included Mexico, all of Central America, most of the Caribbean, Florida, and all the way down the western seaboard of South America. Check it out on the map above. That is why today these territories are Spanish-speaking. I guess in today's world the Spanish-speaking territories might even include California, Florida, New Mexico, and Arizona, but that's a separate issue in immigration that we'll get to later.

This all means that those old colonial ties formed this common culture that's still in place today. It's a common culture primarily based on language, but also on one other thing I mentioned earlier: Catholicism. Two primarily Catholic countries colonized virtually all of South America. You can still see the deep, deep-seated Catholicism throughout Latin America today. There are no countries in Latin America that are *not* Catholic. When the Plaid Avenger travels down there, he can see some freaky-freaky crap that doesn't look like Catholicism. You can see some stuff down there that could make the Pope soil his robes, no doubt. You'd say, "That's not Catholicism! What is this voodoo hoo-ha? What are people doing with voodoo dolls and holding up bloody chickens saying Hail Marys?" Then there's this crazy stuff that's going on down in Brazil; they have these big parties that don't look like traditional Catholicism: the "Carnival." But what you have is indeed the basis of Catholicism mixed in within indigenous culture, local culture, and imported African culture. We're going to see in a little bit that a theme of South America and the Caribbean is the importation of folks from Africa.

Catholicism reaches across Latin America. It's all over the place; you can't miss it, but sometimes it's morphed into something that looks a bit strange to the white dudes in Europe who light candles and incense and stuff like that. Culture is our number one element of "What is Latin about Latin America."

Latins love the Savior.

URBANIZATION

Urbanization is a primary feature that is consistent across every place in Latin America, and I do mean *every place.* I've never even thought about this until recently, but this region is one of the most urbanized on the planet. When we usually think of urbanization, we think it means that most people don't live in the countryside; most people live in cities. We typically associate this with fully developed countries like the US, Canada, and Western Europe. That's where you *typically* have people who are all jammed in the cities, and hardly anyone out in the country. For some reasons that we will get into in a minute, Latin America is more urbanized than even fully developed places. This means everyone in virtually all of these countries is jammed into something called an urban area, typically a very big city.

Latins packed into the cities.

On average, upwards of 80–85 percent, sometimes upwards of 90 percent, of the population of a Latin American country is located in just a few major cities. This is highlighted best by Mexico City, which will probably soon be the world's most populated city with over 20 million inhabitants—a full one-third of Mexico's total population.

Why do people go to the city? It is suggested that in the developed world people go to the city for all the reasons we already talked about back in chapter 2. That's where jobs are. Jobs are concentrated in urban areas. People want to go to urban areas because there's health care, doctors, clean water, sewer systems, electricity, movie theaters, good restaurants. The reason everybody wants to move to a big city or urban area is because good stuff is there. The standard of living is higher and that's where your jobs are.

Is that true of Latin America? In most cases, it's not. It is a kind of conundrum in Latin America. In most urbanized places in the Latin world, all of the **pull factors** that we just mentioned—the good things that pull people to the city—are simply not available for the masses that come. There is the *perception* that all these great things are in the city and the *perception* that all these jobs are available, but it is simply not true for most folks who end up going to the city.

Now those are the pull factors, but there are also some **push factors,** or the not-so-good things that push people from rural areas to the city. One of the main push factors, a major theme across Latin America that we'll discuss at length, is **landlessness.** Because most people do not have access to land, or resources on the land, they are pushed away from it. Owning no land in title or having no serious claim to the land is just another reason to go to the city. There are a lot of pull and push factors that make Latin America one of the most urbanized places on the planet . . . and still growing.

One last note: An interesting phenomenon in Latin American cities that most Americans don't get is that they are set up in a kind of "economically reversed" scenario from the way we live. What the heck am I talking about? In America, what's found deep in the inner city? In fact, what is the connotation of the term "inner city"? I'll tell you what it connotes: slums, projects, poverty, ghettos. That's not where people want to be. As a result, most people who have money don't live in the inner city in America. They've got money, so what do they do? They move *away* from the city and into the "burbs," which we talked about back in the North America chapter.

Squatters got squat.

In Latin America, the situation is just the reverse. The city center is still the prime real estate, so the rich people concentrate themselves and their businesses in the true city center. Where do all these impoverished masses go that I have been suggesting flood into the cities? They make a ring around it. They get as close to the city as they can, usually in ramshackle, shanty-like town dwellings they put together out of corrugated-cardboard and any damn other thing they can pull out of a landfill. These shantytowns get very big and grow into almost permanent fixtures in rings around the cities. Whole shantytowns are a phenomenon that's very easy to spot in any major Latin American city. Just drive straight into or out of the city and notice how the poverty line fluctuates one way or the other. It's a distinct characteristic that has something to do with urbanization. It also has something to do with . . .

WEALTH DISPARITY/LANDLESSNESS

Perhaps there is no other region that we will talk about in this book or that you can go visit on the planet that has wealth disparity as extreme as Latin America. What is **wealth disparity?** Disparity is the difference between highest and the lowest, the difference between the greatest and the least. In terms of wealth, no place in the world is like Latin America in that so few people have so much of the wealth. I'm just going to guess-timate some numbers here. These are Plaid Avenger Figures that vary from country to country, but on average, the extreme amounts of wealth are held by the upper 5 percent of the population. The richest 5 percent typically own something like 80 percent of all the stuff. That's all the land, all the factories, all the businesses, everything. Maybe you think that's

not bad—perhaps that's the way it is in America as well. Not really. Because the other part of the equation is that 95 percent of people have got to split up that other 20% of the stuff. Of course, there is always a significant, or at least partial, middle class; some people have got to own some stuff, but there's always a significant majority of people in these countries that own nothing. No title to their land, no title to their house, no other economic means except their labor to sell. That is a kind of common feature across Latin America from Mexico down to the tip of Tierra del Fuego, and is particularly nasty in Brazil and lots of other places where people kill each other over land.

Times haven't changed much economically.

The George Washington of America: Simón Bolívar.

What's the Deal with Landlessness in Brazil?

Unofficial stats in Brazil refer to 1.6 percent of the landowners control roughly half (46.8 percent) of the land on which crops could be grown. Just 3 percent of the population owns two-thirds of all arable lands. The Brazilian constitution requires that land serve a social function. [Article 5, Section XXIII.] As such, the constitution requires the Brazilian government "expropriate for the purpose of agrarian reform, rural property that is not performing its social function." [Article 184.]

This is a big deal for everybody. It concerns politicians, business people, and the landless poor. In Brazil, they have a law on the books that basically says, "If you can successfully squat on a piece of land, cultivate it, and make it produce something for one year, then you have a legal stake to it. You can take it! It's yours! Here's the deed in your name!" You may say, "Hey, that sounds like a pretty good policy," and maybe it is.

However, the scenario develops a lot of squatter settlements: large groups of people who are squatting on owned land that is typically owned by some rich businessperson or some rich urban dweller who is not out there in the countryside. If they find out that people are squatting on their land, they send in henchmen to go clear them out. When the landless poor fight back or try to continue their stay on the land to finish out the year so they can have legal claim to it, the situation can turn violent.

This situation has also led to the formation of the Landless Workers' Movement, or in Portuguese, Movimento dos Trabalhadores Rurais Sem Terra (MST). This is the largest social movement in Latin America with an estimated 1.5 million landless members organized in 23 out of 27 states. And they can get violent as well.

This is still an issue that is alive today in Brazil and all across Latin America where hired gunmen are going and literally cleaning out villages and killing everybody on site. Because it is private property, the owners, ranchers, and other types of folks can just say "This is legally mine and these people wouldn't leave, so I killed them." This is a very hot issue. How hot? Brazil's current President Lula da Silva promised land reform and government action on the urban poor issue, which he is currently trying to make good on, and the poor are putting his feet to the fire . . .

Get on it, Lula!

This brings us to the issue of **landlessness.** Because of this lopsided scenario of so few people owning so much, including the land, people can't stake a claim to anything. In such societies where people don't have anything, their options are very limited. Mostly they go to cities, as already suggested. They can also try to work on someone else's land without their consent. This is a very unstable situation because the owner can show up at any time and kick them off. This is a particularly resonate issue in Brazil where landlessness has turned into an occupational hazard.

This problem of wealth disparity and landlessness is a common theme across Latin America, and a pervasive theme throughout history. You can look at the history of any country from independence (these movements in Latin America began in the 1820s–30s) and onward. This dude named Simón Bolívar headed up many of these egalitarian independence movements, and is viewed historically as the George Washington of Latin America. Wealth disparity/economic equality was one of his central themes to rally folks to fight. But the issue wasn't resolved at state inception, and it has plagued Latin America ever since. Just one example for now: The Mexican Revolution in 1910 was fought over land. Too many people got pissed off about landlessness, so they had a revolution. One of the core parts of their new constitution included equal rights for people and access to land. All politicians of any stripe have had to deal with this issue historically, and still do today.

Pancho Villa and his crew fought in the Mexican revolution for land reform. But even 100 years later, Mexican President Felipe Calderón, who by all definitions is conservative and could be compared to George W. Bush in political stance, had to include land reform in his platform. If you're going to run for office at all in Mexico, you have to

Pancho, Calderón, Lula, Castro and Hugo: Brothers for land reform?

address the land issue. The main opposition party in Mexico is called the PRI. It's a land reform party—go figure. It was founded to redistribute land and work out ways to give people access to land. We already referred to Lula in Brazil (see page 262)—he got into office as a land reformer. We're also talking about people like Hugo Chavez in Venezuela who is all about equal economic rights in a country with increasing wealth disparity, and other historic figures like Castro, who had his Cuban revolution to basically reclaim land and businesses from the rich and redistribute them to the poor in an old-school communist-style revolution. This issue of wealth disparity and landlessness is a prevalent theme whether you arc in Brazil, Mcxico, Cuba, or Chilc.

IN-"DOCTRINE"-ATION: A HISTORY OF US INVOLVEMENT

The Plaid Avenger has talked to many folks from Mexico all the way down to Argentina, and can tell you with no reservation that people respect the United States. Nobody hates any specific person in the United States, but taken as a whole, Latin America's historical relationship with the US in today's world is largely seen as negative. That may seem like a bold statement, and certainly there are those that still support US policies, but I can tell you who those people are. They are the rich people in Latin America. If life is good, you've got no reason to have qualms with the United States. Unfortunately, as we've already pointed out, that's not the majority by any stretch. Most people see the United States with a bit of an imperial taint, or in a bit of a **hegemonic** light. Certainly, given the US's involvement in virtually every country in Latin America, it's not hard to see why they have kind of a bad taste in their mouth when it comes to historical intervention by the US.

"Don't mess in our hemisphere, bitches!"

To what is the Plaid Avenger referring? You've got to know this, because it still applies in today's world. The number one thing you've got to remember from the US's history of influence is **The Monroe Doctrine.** It's this goofy, antiquated, 200-year-old statement that was made in 1823 by President James Monroe. It was a foreign policy statement that said in essence *(Disclaimer: Plaid Avenger Interpretation),* "If any European power messes in any place in this hemisphere, the US will consider it an act of aggression against the United States." In essence, if Spain were to go try to retake Mexico or Chile, if the Portuguese were to try to retake Brazil, if the British try to take back Jamaica—the US would consider it an attack on US soil. Hell, it doesn't even have to be a full-on takeover; any intervention at all would be considered an act of aggression. "If you mess with anyone down there, we will consider it as you screwing with us." It's extremely similar to NATO article 5 in saying, "If anybody here gets messed with, it's an attack on all of us."

Now why the hell would we say that? It seems kind of silly. I mean, in 1823, what sort of position is James Monroe in? The US was a new country that had only been around about 30 or 40 years. It had only expanded *slightly* over the 13 original colonies and was certainly not a world power. They did a great job shooting the British from behind trees,

KEEP OFF!
The Monroe doctrine must be respected.

Uncle Sam ready to whip some imperialistic Eurotrash back in the day.

but other than that, they weren't capable of fighting anybody. They could take care of their soil, but weren't up for fighting anybody else on foreign soil. This was largely a toothless threat. Maybe you are thinking, "Why is the Plaid Avenger telling us that this is important?" Here's why: This statement became a cornerstone that remains relevant in US/Latin American policy TO THIS DAY.

It didn't mean anything at the time when Monroe said it, but it has come to mean *everything*. Why did Monroe make it at that particular time in 1823? Mexico declared independence in 1820. The Central Americas seceded and most of the South American countries were declaring independence at or around this time. It was seen largely as a supportive gesture. The US was basically thinking, "Yes, our Latin brothers, kick all Spanish and other colonial powers out. We just did it in America so we will encourage everyone else to do it. We're the good guys and we're helping the other good guys, so it's all good!" Again, it was largely toothless and didn't mean anything at the time: the US literally could not take on the Spanish Armada at that time. Forget about it. No contest.

The Monroe Doctrine led to a bunch of other things, such as the **Roosevelt Corollary.** The Roosevelt Corollary was issued in 1904, about a hundred years later, and at that point, the US was quite a bit more powerful than it was during Monroe's tenure. The US was also under a very powerful president at the time, President "Rough Rider" Teddy Roosevelt. What was Teddy known for? What was one of his most popular sayings during that time? "Speak softly and carry a big stick." Indeed, that saying can be applied directly to what became known as the Roosevelt Corollary, which was the foreign policy towards Latin America at the time. Teddy said, "I like the Monroe Doctrine's policy that if anyone messes around in our backyard we'll consider it an act of aggression against us. That's good, but let's take it a step further. If there is any flagrant wrongdoing by a Latin American state *ITSELF*, then the US has the right to intervene."

"Speak softly, and carry a big stick. And a can of whup ass."

In other words, if any Latin American countries south of the US border attack each other, then the US has the right to intervene. More than that, if they just screw up internally, the US was giving itself the right to intervene as well. This had serious repercussions for what sovereignty meant at the time. Of course, I can't go back in time to hear their exact thoughts, but there is no doubt that it was not held in high esteem by Latin American states that were considered sovereign then.

In other words, you had the United States saying, "Sure, you guys are sovereign, as long as we agree with your sovereignty. Otherwise, we give ourselves the right to intervene." This became kind of a big deal because Teddy was carrying that big stick, and he was not afraid to smack people, or entire Latin American countries, down with it.

Under Roosevelt's corollary, relations deteriorated slightly between these regions. However, a bright spot in US/Latin American relations under the Good Neighbor Policy was just around the corner . . . maybe.

The **Good Neighbor Policy** was a popular name for foreign policy at the time of the next Roosevelt—Franklin D., that is—in the 1930s. In a marked departure from the heavy-handed foreign policies up to this point, FDR said, "You know, we're good guys, we're your buddies. We don't need to come down there and beat you with a big stick. My fifth cousin Teddy was a funny guy, but we don't really need to be that heavy-handed. We'll throw out that Roosevelt Corollary and we'll just be here to help if any leader needs us."

FDR sez: "Sup. We gonna chill over here. If y'all need us, holla."

That sounded pretty good, and it was certainly an improvement over the Roosevelt Corollary. But under the Good Neighbor Policy, we had a scenario where US troops were sent down at the request of "leaders" that sometimes could also be referred to as, oh, I don't know, let's call them *military dictators*, who happened to be touting US foreign policy at the time. Even though it sounded better, there were still slight implications that perhaps things were not completely on the up and up. That brings us to the last part of the US's history of involvement.

COLD WAR EFFECTS

After WWII, we had the Cold War. The Cold War has already been referred to several times in this book; you may be thinking, "Ah I'm tired of freakin' history; I don't need to know any of this stuff," but you can't understand the world unless you understand the historical and political movements of at least the last hundred years. Nothing has affected the world more than the Cold War and its politics. Even Latin America was affected.

We might think of Latin America and say, "What? There was no hot war down there, much less a cold war! There are no Commies down there; there's nothing." Not so! Latin America was actually quite radically impacted by the Cold War because of US anti-communist policies that were applied across the planet. That's the reason we got involved in Vietnam, Korea, and damn near everything else that was active at the time. We even supported leaders with questionable character, just as long as they didn't associate with the Soviets. This became of great consequence in Latin America.

When we think of the Cold War and Latin America, the first thing that pops into mind is Cuba and Fidel: that flagrant flaming Commie that the US still hates to this day. There have been lots of repercussions between the US and Cuba (i.e. why Cuba's pretty impoverished today), but all of the other Latin American countries were impacted as well. Some of them had much more violence with a much greater death toll than Cuba ever did.

What I'm talking about is a renewed distrust of the US as a result of its Cold War activities. The American government was so rabidly anti-communist that any movement towards the political left by any Latin American country was almost viewed as a hostile act. And so it became ingrained in US foreign policy for the last 50–60 years that it was absolutely intolerable for anybody to be left-leaning.

If you think back to our chapter on global politics and governments, not every single system on the left is Commie—but all forms of socialism were viewed as being a slippery slope. The US government believed that any form of socialism, however mild, would lead to communism or would lead to an opening for the USSR to make inroads. It really was battled at any cost. No cost was too high; no moral too low to violate in order to ensure that Latin America stayed firmly in the US's backyard of influence.

Sole Western Hemisphere Commie.

Now that we've gone through the grandiose two paragraphs about what the hell was going on, we can get into some specifics.

What did the US do in this all-out barrage to stop communism in Latin America? Be forewarned: This is going to hurt for the uninitiated. It's a little hard for many proud Americans to hear, but we did some pretty nasty things, quite frankly. While we are the champion of democracy on the planet, at the time of the Cold War, the USSR was seen as such a threat that we said, "Well, we're all about democracy, and it would be great if we had democracies there, but we can't allow anybody to go near the left. So it would be better to support someone on the extreme right as opposed to anybody that might be even the slightest bit Commie."

What this equated to was US support for people who might be considered brutal dictators at worst, and elitist dudes of questionable ethics and character at best. During the Reagan years in the 1980s, the threat of communist infiltration by arms sales in places like Nicaragua was interpreted as an immediate hostile threat. In response, support for dictators was sometimes pitched to the US Congress as basically, "We're about to get freakin' *invaded* by the Commies. They're going to get into Central America and they're going to sweep through Mexico and then they'll be knocking down Texas's door!"

In hindsight, we find this preposterous. To be fair to the Reaganites and their ilk, we do have to consider that at the time, the Soviets were as aggressive as the US was, had as many nukes as the US did, and had previously tried to hide missiles in Cuba. At least that was the argument. There was a very real fear of global domination by the Soviets.

You can listen to speeches by Henry Kissinger and the like that say, "You young people just don't understand that we had to do these horrible things because if we didn't, you'd all be wearing red right now." The Plaid Avenger is not here to speak on whether that's true or not, because I'd be wearing plaid no matter if it were commie plaid or otherwise. But what this equated to in the Reagan era was not only supporting extreme dictatorships but also plots to overthrow—and sometimes assassinate—democratically elected leaders. This also equated to supporting extremist rightist factions and rebel groups. Nicaragua comes to mind, as does Guatemala and El Salvador. We supported *anybody* as long as they weren't left-leaning and weren't socialists and didn't support any of those other ideologies, especially communism.

A lot of these groups ended up slaughtering thousands, and tens of thousands, of their own people. Many just ended up as bands of guerillas running around the countryside slaughtering folks. The end result of all these anti-communist policies in Latin America, particularly Central America, was civil war. These excessively destructive civil wars were supported in part by movements of US funds or arms or funds for arms. One of the more famous ones is the Iran/Contra scandal, during the Reagan era, when arms and guns were floated into Nicaragua in support of anti-leftist movements to overthrow the democratically elected leftist regime, which we'll discuss more in the Central America chapter.

All these things together, in terms of US intervention or involvement in Latin American affairs, bring up a term that's often used for Latin America: **the US's backyard.** You'll see this term used even in modern political science magazines and international news. It really summarizes the way the US has felt about Latin America, which is, "It's not really our house, but it's our backyard. We're not really cleaning it up or taking care of it *unless* someone starts coming around and messing around in it." The US doesn't want anybody messing around in its backyard; that's why it's been heavy-handed at times throughout history.

DRUGS

Oh yeah, I almost forgot about drugs! That is the hot new thing with US intervention in Latin America. The Cold War is over. We don't really have a Good Neighbor Policy or Roosevelt Corollary going on. Nobody is invading—that we know of—and we're not going to do anything about it if they invade each other. The current and active deal with US intervention in Latin America is all

Coke a dope! Just say 'no'!

centered on **drugs.** What the Plaid Avenger already knows from personal travels is that Latin America produces the bulk of the world's cocaine . . . and the United States *consumes* the bulk of the world's cocaine.

This creates a situation where the US government, armed with an anti-drug policy named "The War on Drugs," facilitates or makes it an imperative for us to intervene in other countries to stop drug production all over the world. The Plaid Avenger won't get into a big debate about the pure insanity of such an endeavor. I'll leave it to you students of the world to figure out if it's a good method to stop drug use or not, but certainly it is the US policy: "We don't really care so much that people are hooked on drugs up here; we just want to make sure they don't produce them down there." That will somehow solve the problem? Yeah, good luck with that one!.

This brings up one particular aspect of US foreign policy today called **Plan Colombia** (read box to the right).

US direct intervention right now is mostly focused on Colombia, Ecuador, Peru, and Bolivia: the big drug-producing

What is the Deal with Plan Colombia?

Plan Colombia is a program supported by the United States to eradicate coca production in Colombia. It may sound good, but Plan Colombia has become extremely controversial for several reasons. For one, although the coca plant is used to manufacture cocaine, it has also been used by indigenous peoples in the area for thousands of years for health reasons. Many of these people depend on coca to make a living. Furthermore, some of the methods that the United States uses to eradicate coca, such as aerial fumigation and the application of deadly fungi, pose severe health problems for people exposed to it.

Plan Colombia is also controversial because Colombia is undergoing a civil war right now. Many people claim that the goal of Plan Colombia isn't really to stop drugs, but to help the Colombian government fight the Marxist rebel group FARC, which gains much of its funding through the drug trade. When Plan Colombia was first introduced by the president of Colombia in 1998, its main focus was to make peace with the rebels and revitalize the economy of Colombia. However, policymakers from the United States revised it, and the focus became more about military aid to fight the rebels and the elimination of drug trafficking. Human rights organizations are indignant at Plan Colombia because they see it as a way of strengthening right-wing paramilitary groups in Colombia that are committing atrocities against peasants who are speaking out for equal rights and economic reform.

It's your tax dollars, so you should know: the US government has spent close to four billion dollars on Plan Colombia since the year 2000. In 2006, it was reported that coca production actually increased in the last three years. Hmmmmm . . . I'm no mathematician, but something don't add up here. . . .

Fun Plaid Fact: After Plan Colombia was revised by the Americans, the first formal draft was written in English, and a version in Spanish wasn't created until months after the English copy was available. In related news, many Colombians have accused Colombian pop star Shakira of being a language sellout for releasing an album in English.

and exporting countries. Plan Colombia, in particular, has equated to around 5 billion US tax dollars in an effort to stop Colombia from producing drugs. Money well spent! (Did you read the inset box yet?) Some governments, like Colombia, go along with US policy. However some others, like Bolivia, are increasingly not. That brings us to a related topic . . .

LEFTWARD LEANING

This is the most fun, exciting, new, and current part of "What's Latin about Latin America." Through a combination of virtually all the above reasons that Latin America is Latin, this notion is the one that pulls it all together. As we've already cited, particularly during the Cold War era, the US was very troubled by and directly intervened in leftist or left-leaning countries in Latin America. God forbid they embrace some sort of socialism, and certainly not communism. Nonetheless, some people went left anyway. Castro springs to mind. Cuba has been communist and certainly in the "lefty" column for this entire time.

By and large, he has been alone in the hemisphere until very recently. What we've seen in the last decade—perhaps because of the wealth disparity or landlessness or poverty in Latin America—is a general bad taste in Latino mouths about the US's history of intervention. This has really culminated in a lot of countries heading back towards the left column. One that springs to mind is Venezuela in South America. A rabidly left country (some might even say it's already communist), Venezuela boasts a new brand of socialism that strives for social equality and redistribution of wealth to a limited degree through social programs. But even its leader is not alone. President Evo Morales of Bolivia has recently joined the ranks of hard-core leftist, and has been busy nationalizing industries and moving his country in a fully socialist direction. The US government can look at Castro, Chavez, and Morales and hate them. They are easy men for the US to hate because they send the hate right back, or at least they have in the past.

Current US President Barack Obama is an overwhelmingly popular figure across all of Latin America, so the sniping from Castro and Chavez is now not in vogue. Obama has been actively trying to reach out to restore diplomatic street cred in Latin America, and has spoken openly about thawing relations with Cuba . . . and even shook hands with Chavez at an OAS meeting in April 2009! Change may be coming, and these historical animosities may be softening!

It's not just the bold and brash loud-mouths in Latin America who are embracing the left. Brazil has a left-leaning president as well. Last year, Argentina elected a left-leaning government. Chile just elected its first female president, and she's left leaning. Ecuador, Nicaragua, Haiti, and Peru have headed that way as well. As you can see from the map on the following page, the future of Latin America does seem to be in the left-leaning categories. Let's explore why that is.

Why is the left progressing and gaining popularity? Many people in the world are starting to look at Latin America as a singular entity—one of the reasons I decided to do this chapter—that perhaps may become a new axis of power on the planet. What the hell am I talking about? Well, as a group of disparate countries that didn't have a lot of common economic or political goals, now they do. As they have this leftward move, we can look at this entire region as representing that single ideology. There is no other region like that on the planet at this second. We can look at most of the planet which has progressively over the last 50–100 years been going toward something that's more on the right, more strictly capitalist, democratic systems. While certainly these are all democracies down there, they are going more left in terms of social and cultural issues, becoming much more openly liberal. In other words, the overwhelming focus in Latin America is to remedy the very wealth disparity that we talked about earlier.

Why is this happening here? Doesn't everyone want social justice and equality for people across the planet? Well yeah, lots of people do. But as I already suggested, this is the place on the planet that has the greatest wealth disparity. The landless, impoverished masses make this a perfect lab setting for this kind of experiment to evolve. Why is it here? Why is it right now? You have to understand that when you have any state, country, or place where most people are incredibly poor, you are asking for a revolution. When most people have nothing to live for, no stake in the land, no claims—it's all fine as long as the majority, who has the power and wealth, can keep them down. When it becomes too lopsided, it becomes tougher and tougher for the elite to keep a lid on it, and things will eventually boil over.

Societies like this are always on the brink of revolution (see Mexican Revolution, Communist Revolution, Bolivarian Revolution), and Latin America is rocketing back to that point today. It is because of this inequality that people are voting for the left, voting for parties whose *primary goal* is to alleviate wealth disparity. They want to make things more equal. They are striving to improve infrastructure like roads and schools as part of their primary goal. I'm not saying that this isn't a goal of the other parties, but this is the *primary goal* of leftist parties.

The primary leftist agenda involves things like human rights, investment in education and healthcare, and equal access to land for the impoverished masses. That is the main unspoken priority, and that is why the leftist agenda is so popular. In democratic countries, where nobody has jack to their name, the leftist candidates are extremely appealing because they are telling the people, "Hey, we are trying to make this better for you or more equal for you." Thus, it should not be a radical surprise that there is a big movement towards the left across the region that has the greatest wealth disparity on the planet. That's why people are voting for the leftist candidates.

Why are they not voting anymore for the rightist candidates? It's got a lot to do with the US's historic involvement and where we are in today's world. These are all established democracies, and in the 21st century, it is increasingly hard for a military dictatorship or for a government supported by an exterior government like the US, to hold power because issues are getting clearer and fewer people are being influenced to vote against their interests. The blatant corruption is getting easier to identify, so it's very difficult for extreme rightists to hold power anymore.

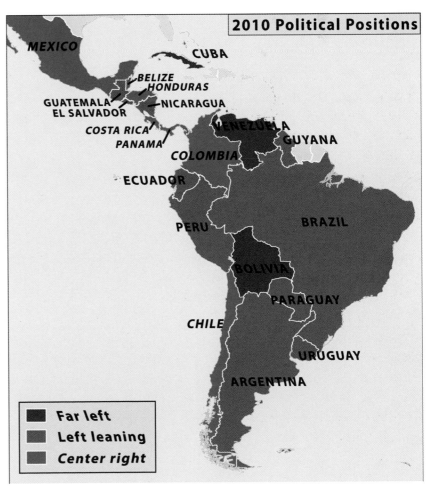

Just look at all that leaning!

2010 Leftist Latin Update: the trend described above still holds true generally speaking, but there has been some political shifting as of late which is countering the overwhelmingly leftist creep of the last decade. Center-right political parties are starting to regain ground in Argentina and Uruguay, Chile just voted in a center-right guy as President, and Honduras had a coup which tossed out the leftist leader and replaced him with a center-right guy until legit elections are held. This is no tidal wave of leftist takeover by any stretch of the imagination; as with all things in life, things change.

What's the Deal with the US Hatred of Venezuela?

Why does the US despise Hugo Chavez so much?

Venezuela has the means to produce over 3 billion barrels of oil per day, 60 percent of which is bought by the United States. Using this revenue, Venezuela has started to pick up some serious military hardware in recent years. President Hugo Chavez has worked hard to secure arms deals with countries such as Brazil, China, Russia, and Spain. Take these newly acquired MiG jets, attack helicopters, AK-47s and Scud missiles, put them into the hands of two million well-trained Venezuelans and you've got yourself a bit of a hemispheric headache. While Venezuela may not have this strength right now, these are the plans being set in motion by Chavez, convinced of a coming invasion by the United States.

Number One on the US Hate List.

Why in the world would Chavez believe that the big bad US is going to march into little Venezuela? Maybe it was the name-calling by Condoleezza Rice when she accused Venezuela of being a "sidekick" to Iran. Perhaps Chavez was offended when Donald Rumsfeld compared him to Hitler. Or maybe Chavez took it personally when evangelist Pat Robertson called for his assassination. In any case, Chavez certainly became suspicious of his neighbors to the north after the US refused to denounce an unconstitutional, and extremely undemocratic, 2002 coup which would overthrow his democratically elected self, even though it only lasted a few days. Virtually all countries denounced the coup within hours, but the US stayed mysteriously quiet. Oops. Probably a bad call on the US's part.

The US continues to criticize the policies of democratically elected Chavez as being "undemocratic," and in heated response he has vowed to cut every drop of oil exports and to mount an all-out guerilla war should the US step foot in Venezuela. And, given the former Bush's administration's doctrine of preemptive war, a simple cry of "terrorist!" could drive hundreds of thousands of US troops to South America. Sound crazy? Yeah, I guess. But that's probably what people in Afghanistan and Iraq thought as well.

Hang on! Don't be misled by the Avenger's rap on this dude; I'm not promoting the pronouncements of this proud peacock. He is certainly leftist, certainly socialist, and certainly legally democratically elected, but that doesn't mean he is doing a particularly good job. The dude apparently enjoys the international limelight he gets bashing the US slightly more than he enjoys actually getting anything done back home. While billions have been made from oil revenues in his tenure as president, Hugo has not been quite so successful at actually rebuilding his economy or pulling the masses out of poverty. He won't be around too much longer, even despite fostering a constitutional amendment in 2008 which allows him to run for office indefinitely.

Given that Hugo can no longer bash the US because everyone loves Barack, coupled with huge loss of revenues (due to low oil prices), his fellow countrymen may abandon him soon if he doesn't start producing some real results.

LOSING THE LATINS: US UNDONE

Why the US is *really, really* worried about this: The US is troubled by this leftist lean because it is largely seen across the planet like this: "The US has screwed up their foreign policy so bad that they have lost control and influence in their own backyard." This may be an extreme statement, but it is a fair statement, nonetheless. Part of the reason they have done that, and part of the reason rightist regimes have lost power, is that they have been perhaps a little too heavy-handed over time. Most of the US involvement and incursions into the region were for reasons previously mentioned, such as anticommunist intervention, but even through the Cold War and to the present day, another reason for US involvement is to protect US economic interests. This is seen as extremely problematic for locals, who are as poor as hell.

In situations when the US has invaded places like Nicaragua or Belize, or has helped assassinate a democratically elected leader in Chile, it was because of this fear that in lefty/commie countries, a redistribution of land and resources was going to occur—you remember: **nationalization.** That was unacceptable to the US, largely because there were US corporations down there yelling, "Hey, that land you poor people are taking is US property!" This was argued during the Cold War era, about Chile, in fact. A company said, "Hey! US government! You can't let commies take over Chile. They will nationalize our company (which means the commies will take it over and make the profit), and this is US property." A lot of US involvement has been due to protecting these US corporate interests. We'll examine this more in future chapters.

AND THE NEW KID IN TOWN . . .

The perception of US involvement as self serving, coupled with massive wealth disparity, in part explains why much of Latin America is going to the left. A lot of leftist candidates, particularly Chavez, Castro, and Evo Morales in Bolivia are saying, "We're not even pretending to do the neoliberal capitalist policies. To be a free market with free and open trade works for the United States, and it looks good on paper, but it isn't working for us."

A lot of these leaders are saying, "We're not anti-US, we're just anti-free trade." The current president of Bolivia says, "We've done it. We've tried to do free trade, and we're still poor as squat! We won't do it anymore! We're not going to give priority to American corporations, and we're not going to give tax breaks to American anything!" Why is that? Because there's a new kid in town that many countries may give incentives to: China. It is making huge inroads into Latin America right now. That's another reason America fears a loss of influence in Latin America.

To be honest, you can't really blame the Latins for taking advantage of the Chinese interest in their region. The Chinese are courting countries around the world, making sweet trade deals with them, in order to feed the Chinese economy's ever-increasing hunger for natural resources. Chinese foreign trade/foreign aid deals are even sweeter because they come with no strings attached, unlike deals from the US. On top of that—and this is critical—in the last decade, the Chinese President Hu Jintao and/or Chinese Premier Wen Jiabao have personally visited virtually every single Latin state, and multiple times, on multiple visits, in multiple years. US President Bush only managed to head south of the border twice in eight years. Starting to get the picture here?

But hold the phone! US President Barack Obama has already turned on the charm offensive on Latin America, having given the keynote address at the April 2009 meeting of the OAS . . . you know, the Organization of American States (OAS). He made it a point to head south of the border in his first 100 days in office, man! This dude ain't playin' . . . he's a playa'! Obama wants the US to be not just a leader but a friend of the all the states of this entire region, including the formerly alluded to hardcore lefties like Hugo and Evo. He will probably continue to use the diplomatic tact and his personal power of celebrity in order to woo the Latin sphere back into the US camp, thereby down-playing hemispheric intruders like China, et al. It is too early to see if this new "21st century Good Neighbor Policy Revamp" will work, because those Latin lefties do have a bit of momentum on their own course right now.

NAFTA members   **CAFTA members**   **Proposed FTAA members**

Now I have spent a lot of time explaining the viewpoint of the Latin Lefties, but I don't want to exclude the ideas of the other side of the political/economic spectrum. About people on the political right: I don't want to suggest that they only want to make money and they don't give a damn about people; that's not the case. Even these people on the opposite side of the spectrum (real anti-socialists) would argue, "No, we want to make these countries richer, too. We want their citizens to have more stuff and not be poor, but we don't think social programs are the way to do it. We think the way to make people richer in Brazil and Colombia and Mexico is to have free trade." Free trade is the typical conservative approach to alleviating poverty. I don't want to deify anyone that is socialist because there are people on the other side who also want good things. They just don't think leftist methods will work: "You can't just give them a welfare check! That's not going to solve anything! Then nobody will be rich! What we need is free trade." Thus . . .

The **Free Trade Area of the Americas** (FTAA) already is and will be a hot issue for this hemisphere over the next decade. It's going to be a rallying point for anti-globalization as well as globalization powers. There are going to be big revolts over it; there are going to be heavy stones thrown over it. It's already a big, big deal that's just going to get bigger as the adversaries of capitalism (and/or the US) use it as fodder for their fire.

"Oh, Plaid Avenger . . . please love my latin-ness . . ."

I bring this up because free-traders say, "Oh, we want Brazilians to be happy, but the way to accomplish that is a free trade union." **NAFTA** is a free-trade union between Canada, Mexico, and the United States. **CAFTA** is an ever-growing free trade area between the US and a handful of Caribbean and Central American countries with the inevitable goal of being the FTAA. The **FTAA** is a proposed free-trade area of every single country in the Americas. The United States, of course having an edge in all of this, is a big fan and proponent of the FTAA. It thinks the FTAA will make it richer, for one, but it also thinks it will help it to reestablish influence in the Latin American region as a leader of the FTAA. Anti-US, anti-globalization forces and leftist politicians in Latin America say, "No. We've been playing that game for a hundred years and we're still poor. We don't like it. We don't buy it."

We shall see how the battle for free trade pans out in the coming decades.

Chapter closer: These pervasive themes are not only historical, but they play into today's Latin America. Now let's take a look into some of Latin America's subregions to provide more specific details, so you can understand how each one works into today's and tomorrow's world.

LATIN AMERICA RUNDOWN & RESOURCES

View additional Plaid Avenger resources for this region at http://plaid.at/latin

 BIG PLUSES

→ Sizable chunk of real estate on planet earth with a hell load of resources

→ Has never invaded or pissed off any other country or region

→ Not a target of international terrorism at all. Who else can brag about that?

→ Becoming a serious place of interest and investment for China and other rising powers

BIG PROBLEMS

→ Biggest wealth disparity on the planet

→ Political instability chronic in some areas, possible just about anywhere

→ History of outside political and economic domination has left many residents with an inferiority complex

→ Heavily dependent on exports of natural resources and basic manufactures

→ Environmental degradation becoming rampant in exchange for economic growth

DEAD DUDES OF NOTE:

Simón Bolívar: The '"George Washington of South America": hero, visionary, revolutionary and liberator . . . he led Bolivia, Colombia, Ecuador, Panama, Peru and Venezuela to independence and instilled democracy as the foundations of all Latin American ideology.

James Monroe: 5th President of the US and important for this chapter for his **Monroe Doctrine** which became the cornerstone for US foreign policy in the entire hemisphere, right on up to the present. The Doctrine pretty much sez: any foreign power which messes with Latin America, will also be messing with the US.

Theodore Roosevelt: 26th President of US, and "Rough Rider" that helped invade Cuba in his spare time prior to becoming a politician. His **Roosevelt Corollary** was an amendment to the Monroe Doctrine which asserted the right of the US to even intervene in the internal affairs of Latin American states to "stabilize" them if necessary.

Franklin Delano Roosevelt: 32nd President of the US and creator of **Good Neighbor Policy** which sought to soften the apparent US hegemony over Latin America by renouncing the US right to intervene unilaterally.

PLAID CINEMA SELECTION:

We will cover the film selections in the respective sub-regional chapters to follow.

LIVE LEADERS YOU SHOULD KNOW:

We will cover these guys in the respective sub-regional chapters to follow.

The map shows Mexico with the following labeled locations: Tijuana, Ciudad Juarez, Chihuahua, Monterrey, Guadalajara, Mexico City ★, Puebla, Mérida. Bodies of water labeled: Gulf of California, North Pacific Ocean, Gulf of Mexico, Bay of Campeche. Lines: Tropic of Cancer, 20, 100. **MEXICO**

CHAPTER OUTLINE

Mexico

MEXICO!

The centerpiece; the central holding; the command center of the Spanish empire while it was conquering the New World. As such, it was a regional power center and a resource center, with a significant population and a more than significant native civilization. When we hear about all the gold and silver bullion that was heading back to the Old World on Spanish ships, Mexico is primarily where all this stuff came from. For a variety of reasons, Mexico has been the center of things in Latin America as the launching pad of Spanish expeditions.

But that was then, and this is now.

"NEW" MEXICO?

When we think about the term Middle America, which I gave to you in the last chapter, Mexico holds roughly 75 percent of Middle America's land. Mexico is a big place, and it used to be a lot bigger. It also has roughly 60 percent of Middle America's population, so by any account, it's the real powerhouse of Middle America. It is the giant among the smaller countries in the neighborhood. On another note, we can distinguish between Mexico and all of the other countries of Middle America and even South America, because it shares a border with the US. Being next to the colossus of the US, which is of course the one power on the planet militarily and economically, opens Mexico up to a lot more opportunities than its Middle American neighbors. It's in "The Good Neighborhood" so to speak. In this chapter, we'll go back and look at how it got to this point.

Perhaps an appropriate title for this chapter would be **Mexico: The *Next* Developed Region.** One of the distinguishing characteristics that caused us to tease Mexico out of the North American region is that it's not like Canada and America in levels of development. A point that I will try to make that I want you to know and understand before you finish reading this chapter is that Mexico should be rich! It should be wealthy! It should be in the "fully developed country" category for lots and lots and lots of different reasons! It's still the powerhouse of Middle America population-wise, even economics-wise, but it's not on par with the US and Canada. The Plaid Avenger here is suggesting that perhaps it should be. We need to figure out why.

PHYSICAL

Speaking physically for Mexico, this is an interesting country because it's got two major mountain chains running through it from north to south that are a continuation of the Rockies from the US, except in Mexico they call them the

¿Qué?

It all comes from south of the border, baby!

You have to remember that Mexico's a member of NAFTA (the North American Free Trade Agreement) along with the US and Canada. US = number one economy on the planet. Canada = number one trading partner with the US. Mexico = number two trading partner with the US. NUMBER TWO! How can they not be rich? It's incredible! Almost astounding! It flies in the face of everything that would be expected, everything that makes sense, to be trading partners with the biggest be-yatch with the most money on the planet and not be rich yourself!

Almost all of the things that are produced in Mexico end up in the US, and that's one of the reasons why so many businesses have relocated to Mexico. Car manufacturing, TV manufacturing, really all major-market products, are compiled and assembled in Mexico and end up in the US. They are adding value to a product, which means they should be getting something out of that. It's much better than just producing vegetables, which we already know that they do, as well. But the main commodity of significance produced in Mexico, though they can never produce enough of it, is oil.

Oil is one of the main things Mexico produces, of which the US is the biggest consumer. In other words, no matter how much Mexico produces, every single fluid ounce of it is *already* sold to the US. It's a guaranteed market. That's a really, really big deal. The economic nucleus to the north is of extreme importance in regard to why Mexico should be rich.

Consider stuff that's hard to deliver, hard to sell—things like drugs. It takes serious planning and coordination of efforts to move and sell drugs, but Mexico does it. Very well, I might add. Why is Mexico a huge producer and trafficker of drugs? It's obviously because America consumes copious amounts of drugs. Even something that's illegal, for which you can get thrown in jail or shot at and killed—even this stuff moving from Mexico into the US in huge volume every single day. Mexico should be rich solely off what it can do under the table for its northern neighbor.

Slightly more challenging imports.

LOCATION AND MILITARY: ¡DON'T MESS WITH ME, ESE!

Not only is Mexico in the perfect location geographically to really reap the benefits of an economic powerhouse, but on top of that, its geography also provides a military advantage. What does the Plaid Avenger mean by this? Mexico has not had to invest in a military for decades. Most countries on the planet have to defend their territory: they have to buy tanks, develop serious weaponry, and do a lot of expensive things that take money away from developing infrastructure in other ways. Mexico's relative location has again given it the prime spot because it doesn't have to do any of that. It's not a member of NATO because it doesn't have to be. Mexico is not a military power because it doesn't have to be. Why? With the US sitting right there, who in the hell is going to invade or attack Mexico? Nobody. Not even Russia at the height of the Cold War considered invading Mexico. Would China do it? Not a chance.

Even though Mexico is not protected by any specific treaty, nobody is going to mess around in the US's backyard. Think back to the Monroe Doctrine: touch the backyard and your ass is grass. It's just not going to happen. Not spending millions on a military is a tremendous boon for the Mexican economy. They could take that money and do something else with it. For some reason they haven't quite gotten there, which we will get back to in a second.

Relative location is key. There is no better location on the planet. Mexico and Canada are in the catbird seats. Canada has advanced, but Mexico has not. Being a NAFTA member with close ties to the economic powerhouse of the world, and already benefiting from its relationship with the US in terms of defense, Mexico should be rolling in the pesos.

¡RECURSOS! = RESOURCES!

The second major reason why Mexico should be rich: it is resource-rich. It has tremendous amounts of everything. I already pointed out agriculture, and that Mexico has guaranteed markets for its agricultural products in the US. Bananas, avocados, other fruits and vegetables come up from Mexico. We already talked about primary products and how they're not worth as much as others. Mexico's primary products are no exception. That's why relative location is important, because they have a pretty much guaranteed market for their agricultural products. Mexico also has things like tin, copper, iron, lead, zinc, magnesium—the list goes on and on, and they can sell every bit of it to manufacturers in the US. Guaranteed. The US can't get enough of that stuff. The one resource of particular consequence, referred to earlier, is oil.

A brief word about oil: Mexico is not a *major* producer of oil on the planet, but it is in our neighborhood. What's so great about that? Main reason why it's so great: the US is the biggest consumer of oil on the planet, both in terms of total volume and per capita. What better resource to have right beside the US than the one resource it uses the most? But it's a double-edged sword. Why? It has been a blessing because there's a guaranteed market for it in the US, every drop they produce can be sold, but it's been a curse because of the history lesson to follow . . .

1973 OIL EMBARGO

This is a major event in US history, even world history, because it has shaped economic and political relationships between the US and several different countries. Since we'll discuss it in more detail later, I'm going to keep this pretty simple. The US supported Israel in the Yom Kippur War in 1973. All of the Arab nations got seriously pissed off as a result, and they decided, since they are the lion's share of the members of OPEC, to enact an embargo against the US and Western Europe. They stopped selling oil to the US. The spigot got turned off.

We'll use some hypothetical prices to easily demonstrate how this affected the US and Mexico. Let's say oil was 10 dollars a barrel before the embargo. In a matter of weeks, it skyrocketed to 40 dollars a barrel. Prices quadrupled almost overnight, causing tremendous shortages. You probably don't remember this, but your parents might remember, and your grandparents certainly do. The shortages resulted in rationing, which was a huge deal. Unprecedented.

How does this relate back to Mexico? Mexico had oil, mostly offshore, but it wasn't worth a lot. It was of lower quality than Middle Eastern oil. There was much more refining that had to be done to Mexico's oil. Saudi Arabia could suck its oil out of the ground with a straw, dump it into a barrel, and let it go for 10 bucks. Mexico had to pull it out of the ground, clean it up, filter it, process it a bit, ultimately costing, let's say, about 15 dollars a barrel just to get it out the door. With these hypothetical prices, it is losing 5 bucks per barrel. Needless to say, Mexico wasn't in a rush to lose money quenching the US's thirst, so it wasn't a big oil producer. However, when the price of oil blew up to 40 dollars a barrel—now there's a profit of 25 bucks on the oil that our friend Pepe just refined for 15! It's worth it now!

At this point, Mexico developed its oil industry as fast as it could and, go figure, the US was thrilled to see another source of non-Arab oil pop up. The US lent Mexico millions and millions of dollars to invest in its oil industry's infrastructure to grease the wheels, and everything looked peachy for a few years . . . until oil prices stabilized. After the embargo ended and the price of oil dropped back down, Mexico was still producing, but not nearly at the profit margin when it was 40 dollars a barrel. Having diminishing profits and millions in loans to pay back to the US resulted in a big economic crunch for Mexico—which came to a head about 15 years ago during the Clinton administration when Mexico was essentially going broke. Therefore, oil is a mixed blessing for Mexico: it has been good overall, but it put the country in tremendous short-term debt, from which it is still trying to recover.

Mexico is resource-rich and can provide tons of raw materials. It also adds value to a lot of these things and sends them over in the form of TVs and cars, which are gobbled up in the US, their guaranteed market. It has one huge bonus for being next to the largest oil-consuming nation on the planet. Oil! So Mexico *should* be rich, but . . .

MEXICO SHOULD BE RICH . . . BUT THEY'RE NOT!

Why? What happened? They have some prime real estate with great economic and military support, and they've got tons of resources . . . so what's the problem?

ANOTHER PLAID AVENGER INSIDE TIP: Every time the price of oil goes higher on the planet, watch the US president go and visit three different countries to discuss increasing oil production. The first is Mexico. The president will go down and get it to produce more, which will help resaturate the market and bring prices down. He'll also visit Norway and Russia. These are three big oil producing and exporting countries that are non-OPEC members. This means that they are not tied to the rules and regulations that govern prices or limits of production. They don't care, and the US loves them for it.

The Big Non-OPEC 3.

NUMBER ONE ¡LA GENTE!

They have too many people. You know about the demographic transition; you know what a developed country looks like. Take a look at Mexico's pyramid and you see something much more like Africa, Central Asia, and the Middle East. This is a population that is still *exploding*. It's a perfect pyramid; there's a high fertility rate, and people still have lots and lots of kids. While Mexico's economy has expanded and diversified and it has actually gotten richer, it has also added way more people. When you look at total amounts of economic gain in terms of GDP, it's grown. But the people have grown more, at a way higher rate than their economy. As a result, their per capita numbers have gone down. This is still a place that we consider kind of poor.

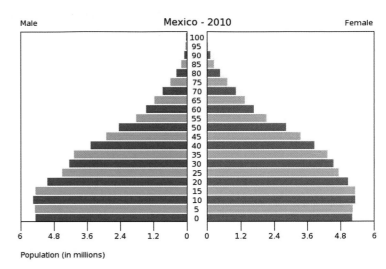

Damn! This pyramid looks like it's out of Africa!

This seems to be currently tapering off, stabilizing somewhat. But it has a long way to go. The current population is about 110 million. That is a huge number. It is the population leader in Middle America with a population that is almost exactly one-third of the current US population. This is funny because it's about one-third of the land size of the US. However, the economy is not even 1/300 of the US economy! That's where they've fallen down. So people are a big problem, and as the Plaid Avenger pointed out when we talked about Latin America, this is a place with massive amounts of urbanization. Most people live in the city. There is a draw, the idea that you are going to get a job in the city, which is often not the case.

Mexico City is now one of the largest cities on the planet, population-wise. It will probably approach the number one spot in the next five to ten years. There just aren't enough jobs for all those folks there. There are burgeoning urban populations, and on top of that, there is one other place where the Mexican population is increasing. Where? Along its border with the US. This leads to the number two reason why Mexico is not rich . . .

NUMBER TWO ¡MAQUILADORAS!

Maquiladoras are towns along the Mexico side of its border with the US, built around factories that are owned by foreign companies. There are some that have been there for a while, but many new border towns started popping up steadily after NAFTA was set up. NAFTA allows free movement of capital and business across the borders of its constituent states.

The companies build factories just over the border to take advantage of cheap Mexican labor. Many unemployed Mexicans flock to these towns for jobs.

In the last 20 years, the situation has developed such that companies in the US, or another place, manufacture the individual parts, ship them to their maquiladoras just across the border where Mexicans working for less money assemble the parts into the retail version of whatever product the company sells. It allows the companies to pay some guy a nickel an hour or whatever to put your TV or your car or your stereo or your car stereo together. The labor is so cheap that it makes it worthwhile for the company to

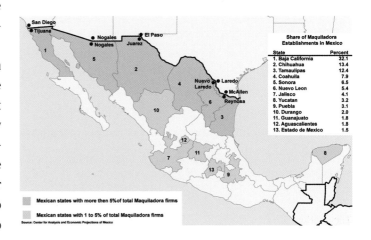

import the raw materials to make the parts and ship the parts down to be assembled in Mexico and then ship the finished product all over the US to be sold at a profit. Just for comparison, in 2000 the American minimum wage was about $5.25 per hour; the Mexican minimum wage was $3.50 *per day!* Know maquiladoras. Even though their growth has slowed, they still contain a large concentration of the Mexican population. The other big chunk of the Mexican population, as mentioned, is in Mexico City proper where the population is around 20 million and growing. This growth is based on the hope that people will find jobs.

This scenario is another double-edged sword for Mexico, like oil. Lots of folks down there would say, "Hey, don't complain; they're creating jobs and that's a good thing. We had nothing before, but now at least we have jobs, even though they don't pay squat." Many other folks would also point out the obvious; not only are the workers in the maquiladoras getting paid jack, but all the true value of the product is made by taking advantage of the impoverished Mexicans working for wages so small they're practically slaves. From the Plaid perspective, there is something to be said for both sides of the argument.

SOME MAQUILADORA COMPANIES YOU MAY KNOW

• 3 Day Blinds	• Honda
• 20th Century Plastics	• Honeywell, Inc.
• Acer Peripherals	• Hughes Aircraft
• Bali Company, Inc.	• Hyundai Precision America
• Bayer Corp./Medsep	• IBM
• BMW	• Matsushita
• Canon Business Machines	• Mattel
• Casio Manufacturing	• Maxell Corporation
• Chrysler	• Mercedes Benz
• Daewoo	• Mitsubishi Electronics Corp.
• Eastman Kodak/Verbatim	• Motorola
• Eberhard-Faber	• Nissan
• Eli Lilly Corporation	• Philips
• Ericsson	• Pioneer Speakers
• Fisher Price	• Samsonite Corporation
• Ford	• Samsung
• Foster Grant Corporation	• Sanyo North America
• General Electric Company	• Sony Electronics
• JVC	• Tiffany
• GM	• Toshiba
• Hasbro	• VW
• Hewlett Packard	• Xerox
• Hitachi Home Electronics	• Zenith

Here's the real kicker: even though these "sweatshops" may suck, the loss of them may suck more. As labor becomes cheaper in China and Asia altogether, companies are starting to move out of Mexico because the labor is too expensive. Too expensive? Damn, that's wrong!

NUMBER THREE ¡VIVA LA TIERRA!

Here's one thing that we already know occurs all across Latin America, and it's the number three reason why Mexico is not rich: wealth disparity and landlessness. This means that the top tier of citizens, the elite, own a disproportionate amount of the land. A very small percentage of the people own virtually everything. This means that the great majority of people own nothing, not even the land they live on. Landlessness is a big issue across Latin America as a whole, and Mexico is a great example.

Mexico's history is replete with the important issue of land reform. What am I talking about here? Just in the last 100 years, we have something called the **Mexican Revolution.** It seems like every major country has some sort of revolution. We talked about the Communist Revolution in Russia, the Meiji Restoration in Japan.

Mexico had its revolution in 1910. What was it about? It was about human rights and lots of other things, but its central concern was over land. When wealth disparity gets large enough, and wealth and power are concentrated in the hands of the few, the political system becomes unstable. When this happens, people typically get pissed off until revolution rears its ugly head. The tinder keg gets lit and they're off. The two revolutionary leaders you see pictured here are classic examples of what happened in Mexico when wealth accumulated too much into too few hands. In the

Pancho Villa (with his men).

north, there was Pancho Villa, who was a rebel/revolutionary leader, essentially a bandit type with sort of a bad reputation. He took up arms against the government as things became too corrupt and land was controlled by too few in the early 20th century.

Villa's counterpart in the south was Emilio Zapata. A poor farmer, all around good guy, a charismatic hero, Zapata took up the cause and got the word out to people that the government was screwing them over. "Look at us, amigos, we are poor as hell. None of us have land! We need to overthrow the government and make this a

better place!" There were two guys on both geographical extremes of Mexico, who ended up overthrowing the government. The central point is that it was all over land, all about the issue of landlessness. Zapata was a real foundation of this, since he was a farmer himself. It wasn't a political thing where he wanted to rule or be president; he just wanted land for everyone so they could all support themselves and each other. He wanted it to be fairly distributed. Why is this important? Land is *still* a major theme in Mexican government and politics today.

How did land ownership in prerevolution Mexican society get so top-heavy? Under the Aztec system, society was strictly hierarchical, a sort of military dictatorship almost. All the power was concentrated around the top. The head Aztec honcho basically owned and controlled everything; all land and all wealth was subject to his will. It was an ancient tradition. When the conquistadors arrived, under Cortés' leadership, they had an easy time taking over because they just lopped off Montezuma's head and put themselves in his place at the top. The system didn't get altered much when it changed hands from the indigenous rulers to the Spanish. Even when Mexico had its revolution and kicked out the Spanish, they kept an oligarchic system where there were a few ex-Spaniards that had control and maintained power over large amounts of the country. The wealthy hung on to all their resources and the poor got nothing. This arrangement stayed in place until the revolution.

Emilio Zapata.

The Mexican Revolution was a pretty big deal. It happened in 1910, and when it was successful, they wrote such an awesome constitution that almost shamed the US's. It was an extremely thorough document all about human rights, access to land, and many other important issues. But in many ways, this has been an unrealized dream in Mexico because some of the great stuff in the constitution never really came to be. It's a far-reaching document, and its promises are still being pursued in today's world.

Like I said, this land thing is not just a historical remnant. All political parties in Mexico today have to deal with the land issue. You can't get away from it. Both ends of the political spectrum in Mexico use land reform as a major element of their campaign platforms. Even though strides have been made, land is still a major concern in Mexican politics.

¡REBELS!

There are still rebels, and they are still pissed about land reform. They are fighting actively for the same things as 100 years ago. Subcomandante Marcos leads the Zapatistas, named after Emilio Zapata. These guys are in the southern Mexican state of Chiapas, which is in the tropical jungle highlands near the border of Guatemala. This revolutionary movement has been going on for two decades. What are these dudes still fighting for? You guessed it! Land Reform!

Interesting to note, the Zapatistas are one of *the* first, if not the first, revolutionary movement to have an official website: Zapatistarevolution.com. This link is actually a website posted by a trial lawyer in Texas who is sympathetic to the Zapatista cause, and who visited with them during a trip to Mexico. He wrote a fictionalized novel based on the facts of a 1994 Zapatista uprising. The site isn't maintained by the Zapatistas themselves, though a lot of their plight is described on it. They are a truly unique rebel/terrorist organization in this respect—the first online rebels.

We know Mexico is not rich for a few key reasons: wealth disparity, land issues, the double-edged sword of oil, the mixed blessing of maquiladoras, and population dynamics. What about their future?

¡EL FUTURO DE MEXICO!

The Plaid Avenger used to say that things are liberalizing, opening up, that perhaps NAFTA is going to be further entrenched and that Mexico will become a truer part of the North American region in terms of movement of people and economic activity. That was the case up until the US's War on Terror began, which has served to stymie movement between the US and Mexico as they try to catch potential terrorists. It has recently been compounded even more as illegal immigration has become a hot button election issue in the US. The current political mood in the US right now is to build an even bigger wall between these countries/regions. One complication has arisen because of the fact that the US needs immigration, and everybody knows it. Business people in the US know this: They need immigration for economic growth to continue. Immigrants fill many service sector and manufacturing jobs that some Americans either won't or don't want to do.

Mexican President Felipe Calderón (and even his predecessor Vicente Fox) is the political party equivalent of a Republican in the US. As such, he was a pretty staunch supporter of President George W. Bush, agreeing with Bush on all policies minus one: immigration. Calderón and others have expressed many reservations at the idea of building a wall between the countries. Mexico is more of the European frame of mind, which is essentially, "Aren't we in a free trade block? Aren't we allies? Aren't we friends? Why do we even have a fence at all?" Mexico is working towards further economic integration with the US, including a "worker passport" system that would indeed allow for more open movement of folks across the entire continent. However, opening trade borders that allow the free flow of goods and people can also allow the free flow of lots of other things . . . like drugs.

And holy hot tamale, be forewarned about this drug situation, my friends! This is the hottest—and by far most serious—cause for concern for Mexico, the US, and everybody in between. Drugs, drug crime, and gang-related crime,

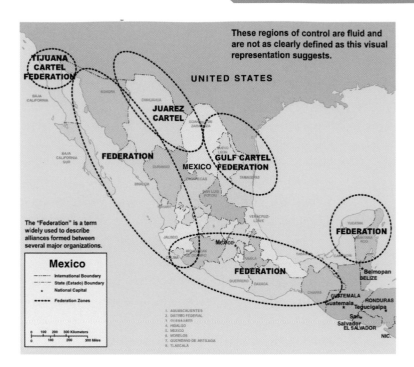

These regions of control are fluid and are not as clearly defined as this visual representation suggests.

The "Federation" is a term widely used to describe alliances formed between several major organizations.

Source: U.S. Drug Enforcement Administration, adapted by CRS (P. McGrath 3/2/2007)

all of which have been infiltrating the border region, have simply exploded in the last several years, in the worst ways possible. The volume and value of all that coke, dope, and amphetamines crossing into the US through Mexico has become so huge that organized crime has taken over, but the competition is so fierce that multiple syndicates/gangs are fighting to the death in turf wars all up and down the border.

We're talking about some nasty business here, my friends. Gangland kidnappings and assassinations of Mexican police, politicians and even army soldiers. Whole villages of innocents being slaughtered in turf wars. Mass graves being found. Human heads being thrown into high school prom dances to terrorize towns. I wish I were exaggerating here. These criminal gangs have grown so powerful that they don't run from the police: they stand and fight them. And they fight the army. And the DEA. The Mexican cartels of the 21st century are being compared to the old Colombian cartels of the 1980's in terms of power, wealth, organization and bloodlust. It is getting scary.

Go out and research it yourself to see the current situation. Just know this for now: this insane gang violence being brought directly to the doorstep of the US will probably be the straw that breaks the camel's back. Add the new drug wars to the already festering illegal immigration issue, and you can easily predict that more calls will be made for a "Great Wall of China" to be built on the border. President Calderón, being a conservative law-and-order guy himself, is working hard to fix this mess. He is working diligently alongside the US to restore order to the region. That means more cops, more army, more border patrol, more DEA involvement. Good luck to the boys in blue down on the border. They are going to need it.

Felipe fighting to fix border fiasco.

Here at the onset of the 21st century, these two countries are strong allies by all standards, but they are divided on the issue of free movement of people between them. Will Mexico ever be fully developed? It is entirely possible once the population stabilizes, its economy becomes a bit more robust, and they reclaim their northern territory form the criminal syndicates. However, new competition from elsewhere in the world is also threatening Mexico's dominance of cheap labor for US businesses. Like outsourcing from the US, Mexico has lost international business investment to East and Southeast Asia, who have even cheaper labor than Mexico can offer. What a twist they are in, as are all regions and states close to developed status. They typically get richer by offering cheap labor, which brings in investment dollars. Then, as they become successful and richer, labor rates rise. This causes the businesses to pick up and move elsewhere. Damn! Caught in a vice on that one, due to the preeminent rise of the Asian economies and their huge, cheap labor pools. Well, at least Mexico will never be invaded by anyone—except the coke dealers. It appears that the Conquistadors have returned, albeit in a new and more lethal disguise.

MEXICO RUNDOWN & RESOURCES

View additional Plaid Avenger resources for this region at http://plaid.at/mex

 BIG PLUSES

→ Next door neighbors with the largest economy on the planet
→ Gigantic US market buys every single thing Mexico produces; an assured market
→ Significant producer of oil, agricultural commodities, and basic manufactured goods

 BIG PROBLEMS

→ Ballooning population
→ Serious wealth disparity, and landlessness remain chronic political issues
→ Significant producer and transportation corridor of illegal narcotics
→ Has several drug cartels which are possibly more powerful than the government
→ A next door neighbor (the US) which increasingly doesn't want them to come visit as immigration tensions mount
→ Losing jobs/industries to even cheaper labor market in Asia.
→ Cultural inferiority complex permeates the state

DEAD DUDES OF NOTE:

Montezuma: Last head honcho and ruler of the mighty Aztec Empire; the empire reached its maximum size and power under his reign from 1502–1520. Unfortunately, the Spanish conquistadors showed up and destroyed him and the Empire. Now you can get nasty cheap tequila appropriately named Montezuma's Revenge . . . he is getting the white man back, one shot-glass at a time.

Hernándo Cortés: The white dude the led the Spanish conquistadors into Mexico to level the Aztec Empire in just a couple of years, and was the first wave of colonizers to lay claim to vast areas of the entire hemisphere in the name of the Spanish crown.

Pancho Villa: Originally a bandit on the run from the law for years (and even eluding US troops), Villa eventually became famous as one of the leading generals in the Mexican Revolution of 1910. He led the campaign in the north to overthrow the autocracy, redistribute land, and fight for human rights. A "Robin Hood" of northern Mexico.

Emiliano Zapata: Revolutionary leader of southern Mexico during the Mexican Revolution, his battle cry was "Tierra y Libertad" (Land and Liberty). Fought for land reform and emancipation of peasants. Zapata is considered one of the outstanding national heroes to this day. Even has a modern day rebel/terrorist group named for him: the "Zapatistans" of Chiapas state.

PLAID CINEMA SELECTION:

Battle in Heaven (2005) Film about a working class man in Mexico who, along with his wife, kidnap a baby to hold for ransom, which accidentally dies. Follows man's journey through the Mexican countryside, providing many beautiful examples of Mexico's landscape. If you like overly sexual movies, this is a film you should make time to see.

Tijuana Makes Me Happy (2006) An independent film, shot almost entirely in Tijuana, with a few scenes in San Diego. Takes an interesting look at the seedy world of cockfighting, and its ability to consume the lives of its participants through the filter of a little boy who aspires to purchase his own cockfighting rooster.

Y tu Mamá También (2001) One of the more well-known Mexican films of all time, has drawn the ire of many for its depiction of sexuality. Follows two adolescent boys as they take a road trip through the modern-day Mexican countryside with a woman in her mid-twenties. Provides an outstanding cross section of landscape and Mexican social classes in a modern context. Warning: explicit sex scenes!

Frida (2002) For the artistic types out there, this is a biography of Mexican artist Frida Kahlo, who channeled the pain of a crippling injury and her tempestuous marriage to Diego Rivera (another famous Mexican artist) into her work. Features depiction of Mexico City in early 20th century, has the famous commie Leon Trotsky as a character, and stars Salma Hayek. What more do you need?

Apocalypto (2006) Against my better anti-Mel Gibson judgment, let's throw in one that pre-dates Mexico in its entirety. An instant Mayan Empire classic! Well, at least it has killer landscape/biome backgrounds, as it is shot on location in southern Mexico in the states of Veracruz and Oaxaca.

Viva Zapata! (1957) Yeah, I know this is an ancient movie, but it does star a young Marlon Brando long before he got fattened up for the Godfather role. And if you want to understand Mexico, you gotsta know Zapata. The story of Mexican revolutionary Emiliano Zapata, who led a rebellion against the corrupt, oppressive dictatorship of president Porfirio Diaz in the early 20th century.

The WIld Bunch (1969) Okay, this one is a stretch, but I love it: an aging group of outlaws as they escape to Mexico looking for one last big score as the "traditional" American West is disappearing around them. Filmed entirely in Durango and Coahuíla in central Mexico, and set during the Mexican Revolution, so historical clues abound. Was the bloodiest, most violent film ever made when it was released. One of the best Westerns of all time.

LIVE LEADERS YOU SHOULD KNOW:

Felipe Calderón: Current President of Mexico, center-right, well-educated, conservative, strong-willed, pro-US leader who is up to his armpits trying to diminish the power of the drug cartels that have turned the US/Mexican border into a bloodbath.

CHAPTER OUTLINE

Central America

15

CENTRAL America is part of Middle America, as we've pointed out in an earlier chapter. It's an easily defined place because it can be distinguished by just looking at political borders. It goes from the Mexican-Guatemalan border all the way down to the Panamanian-Columbian border and encompasses the countries of Guatemala, Belize, Honduras, El Salvador, Costa Rica, Nicaragua, and Panama: the Central American seven. The Plaid Avenger can best summarize this region, unlike any other region on the planet, in a single word: **VIOLENCE.** This is an incredibly violent arena, in pretty much every way imaginable.

Central America is a place that, while not that far from the economic powerhouse of the US, is one of the poorer regions on the planet. Poverty is, of course, one reason for all the violence, but not the only one. There is a lot going on here, but not a lot to be happy about, quite frankly. The Plaid Avenger is fairly sure that most people in Central America would agree. Why is it such a violent region?

PHYSICALLY VIOLENT

To start, the physical world of Central America contains massive amounts of violence. If you look at a map of plate tectonics, you see several plates coming together in Central America causing a zone of geologic activity. The Cocos plate is ramming against the North American and Caribbean plates. It's actually getting shoved under the Caribbean plate, causing hell-load of volcanic and seismic activity all over the Central American isthmus. Earthquakes and volcanic activity abound. Central America has always been and probably will remain this way for the rest of human history, at least. We can project ahead and look at the Caribbean islands, and we can see that they have also been formed because of plate borders activity, but that's a story for the next chapter.

The isthmus here is a really violent arena, simply considering its geology. Does that have anything to do with why it's poor? Or why it's a hotspot? It does! We like to think that the physical world doesn't affect people's lives too much, but as we have seen with the other regions we've talked about, that's simply not the case. It's hard for people and businesses to move, adapt, or build structures to withstand frequent earthquakes and hurricanes. And these countries definitely don't have the resources to control the climate or the physical environment around them. The Plaid Position on Central America is that nature really rules the people here more than any other region. This cycle of physical violence from the natural world has shaped this region forever, and will continue to do so!

Let's get to some specifics. Here's an interesting story about the Panama Canal, which was originally supposed to go through Nicaragua. Some senators from the US were planning to build a canal 100 years ago, but they didn't know where just yet. Where was the US going to invest its money? Plans to build in Nicaragua were already drawn up, and they were nearly ready to mobilize. But some senator's business interest paid him off to lobby for their plans to go through Panama. It's tough to scrap plans that are in their final phases of development, but the senator pulled it off by using a postage stamp from Nicaragua with a picture of a volcano on it. He made copies and passed it around the senate, and said, "Check this out, chaps, we'd be fools to invest in a place full of volcanoes!" It's the Panama Canal now, not the Nicaraguan, thanks to a savvy, stamp-holding senator.

That may be just a cheese side story, but on top of the seismic and volcanic violence in this region, there is also the weather to contend with. The tropical climate of this region, bordering the Caribbean, is prone to hurricanes. These are violent, devastating weather systems that come through this region with regularity, every year, sometimes multiple times during a season.

Hey, Plaid Avenger, does that have anything to do with this region's poverty problem? Hell yes it does! How many financial investors think it's a good idea to build a multimillion dollar hotel or factory that may be completely destroyed in a hurricane or earthquake? Not too many. Nobody is that rich, or nobody who's that rich is that dumb. Very few companies would even try to go there. The outside world does not regularly invest anywhere in Central America precisely because of the physical world. Pretty much only fruit production companies are heavily invested here, because how much damage can your banana trees sustain during an earthquake? It's a pretty safe bet. The physical world complicates life here, and it will continue to do so.

VIOLENCE IN THE SOCIAL SPHERE

Central America is also a very violent arena from the standpoint of the people. Central America shares its ancient history with Mexico, so we won't go into that too much. It was part of Mexico during the colonial period through when Mexico became independent in 1821. In 1823, Central America seceded from Mexico and formed a union of independent states. By 1838, even their union started falling apart and the devolution doesn't stop until they end up as seven dinky independent territories. They are all very small countries now. And as the Plaid Avenger always says, "Size *does* matter!" Since they are small they don't really have any sort of big world role, nor do they have a lot of resources, individually.

Their experimental Central American "Republic" lasted from 1823 to 1838, when it began to disintegrate due to civil wars. Apparently, they had so much fun with their early civil wars, that they continued to have more of them for the next 150 years! Born in wars, grown up in wars, and still living with the aftermath of wars . . . just not the best real estate in the Americas. They just couldn't seem to hold a union together. Too bad; to be a singular political entity may have helped them a lot in the long run. Instead, they ended up being a bunch of small bananas, with limited resources and political power, in a much bigger world. Pun intended. What pun you ask? Just this:

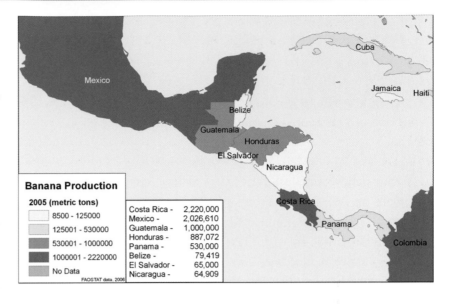

Banana Production

2005 (metric tons)

☐ 8500 - 125000	
☐ 125001 - 530000	
☐ 530001 - 1000000	
☐ 1000001 - 2220000	
☐ No Data	

Costa Rica -	2,220,000
Mexico -	2,026,610
Guatemala -	1,000,000
Honduras -	887,072
Panama -	530,000
Belize -	79,419
El Salvador -	65,000
Nicaragua -	64,909

FAOSTAT data, 2006

Bananas, fruit in general, became the main source for revenue (and not much at that) as well as conflict (much more than revenue). There were several attempts in the 1800s to unionize Central American fruit labor; it all pretty much ended with the union dudes dying in battle or getting executed later for political reasons. The region became synonymous with a political term, as well . . . **banana republics.** Hit up the box below for the full story.

What's the Deal with Banana Republics?

A "banana republic" is a small nation south of the border that is plagued by political corruption and is economically dependent on basic agricultural exports. The term was coined in reference to Honduras, which at the time, was basically owned by US multinational fruit companies. Although the terminology sounds cute, it is also highly disparaging—implying a backwardness that can only lend itself to producing fruit for rich Americans. Leadership typically consisted of a very small, wealthy, corrupt elite invariably topped off by an overbearing generalissimo type in a uniform covered with medals and badges. Even worse than being under the domination of such an oligarchy, "banana republics" were/are typically under the domination of US multinational organizations.

ECONOMIC VIOLENCE

In these places, and this even goes back into the 1820s when these guys were declaring independence, there were foreign multinational companies doing business there. It's not just a current phenomenon. A lot of the folks who still own the resources in Central America aren't even citizens of the countries themselves but are these exact same multinational companies. Gee, I wonder where these companies are from . . . You guessed right! Predominately the good ol' US of A. You may be asking yourself, "What do these people make down in Central America that anybody wants?" Well, the bananas you had for breakfast probably came from there. Coconuts, starfruit, chocolate, most tropical fruits . . . all this is from somewhere south of the US-Mexican border, and a lot of it comes from Central America. This has been the case for several hundred years. Who brings all of these goods to America? The US companies that established the markets.

Some of our favorite tropical commodities.

When impoverished countries start to have leftward leanings—leaning towards socialism or communism—one of the first things the people start asking themselves is, "Why does this American company own 100 percent of the banana market in our country? We produce all the bananas, and we don't get squat for them. This company takes them from here, where they were grown with our cheap labor, pays us a penny and gets a dollar for them in the US. We're getting screwed!" Case in point: United Fruit Company was so huge they controlled virtually all the fruit in Central America for about a hundred years. Check out the box about this on the bottom of this page.

There is a big part of the history of this region involving the US protecting its own economic interests. In many of these countries, when they have a significant leftward lean and appear to be heading towards a socialist or communist revolution, one of the first things that the new socialist leaders will do is **nationalize** the industries. As I said before, this is essentially taking an asset that was held by a private multinational company, and saying, "Hey, we've

What's the Deal with The United Fruit Company?

The United Fruit Company (UFCO) was an American corporation founded in 1899 that was dedicated to providing the American consumer with delicious and affordable bananas and pineapples. The United Fruit Company is also one of the best examples of capitalism gone awry. Throughout the 20th century, the United Fruit Company maintained a virtual monopoly on banana exportation to the United States. UFCO owned huge plantations in Columbia, Costa Rica, Cuba, Jamaica, Guatemala, Nicaragua, Panama, and Santo Domingo. They also owned 11 ships named "The Great White Fleet" and miles of railroads. United Fruit was the unofficial king of Latin America. Like most kings, United Fruit was a giant ass to its subjects.

The worst offenses by United Fruit occurred in Guatemala. As in many other countries, United Fruit owned or leased much of the farmable land in Guatemala. They also left a significant portion of their land barren (not producing fruit) just in case something happened to their good land. All this wasted farmable land started pissing off hungry people in Guatemala. In 1951, Guatemalans elected, in their first ever election with universal suffrage, Jacobo Árbenz Guzmán, who pledged land reform. Árbenz proposed redistributing some of the unused land to the large percentage of the population that was landless.

The United Fruit Company was royally miffed about Árbenz, so it launched a campaign to convince its friends in the US Government (Dwight Eisenhower, John Foster Dulles, etc.) that Árbenz was aligned with the Soviet Union. UFCO even went so far as to produce a video titled, "Why the Kremlin Hates Bananas," documenting UFCO's fight against Árbenz. The result of UFCO's propaganda and influence was Operation PBSUCCESS: a CIA covert operation designed to overthrow Guatemalan president Árbenz. The CIA trained and armed an ad-hoc "liberation army" and organized "strategic" air strikes on Guatemala City. The result of CIA action was years of oppression for Guatemalan citizens under a right-wing dictatorship that "saved the day" from the communist threat. On the bright side, Americans can, to this day, buy bananas for less than $0.50 a pound—thanks partially to Chiquita Brands International, which took over United Fruit in 1970. Thanks guys! You wacky bunch of bananas!

been doing all the work, and you pay us jack and make a ton of profit. But this is *our* land! We're taking it back and we're going to nationalize it. Thanks for setting up shop, for setting up this oil platform, or copper mines, or whatever, thanks; we're going to take it from here and make more money for ourselves. You may now leave." This is nationalization. Corporations do not dig it.

Multinational companies live in mortal fear of this, since basically they get their stuff taken from them. As you can imagine, they have a point. They spent money on the investments there, they have stockholders, and they don't want their livelihoods taken away. They get bothered by this. History shows us that when a company fears that this may happen to them, or if it actually happens to them (and it has happened plenty), they go to the US government and say, "Hey, we're US citizens. Those are US investment dollars down there; that's US *property* down there! You need to help protect US property!" By and large, over the last 150 years, that's exactly what the US government has done, especially in Central America. When a government like Nicaragua is taken over by popular uprising, and they want to nationalize the banana industry, suddenly, the US marines show up to save the day! Saved for who? The US corporation is saved and the poor people who slave for it get to work another day for the man.

"Help US Army! Save the banana train!"

Some of you may stop reading this right now because you think I'm just talking communist gibberish. That's fine. I can't please everybody, and I'm not going to lie. The Plaid Avenger won't just pretend things like this never happened. They are all part of the public record. Just because the history books you read back in the day didn't teach you this stuff doesn't mean it never happened. There were several instances when the US military went down to quash uprisings and attempts at nationalization, dating back to the 1850s when it looked like some Panamanians would endanger the railroad down there, and maybe nationalize it. The US did not want this because that railroad was a critical part of a much bigger shipping network between the east and west coasts of the US. The US sent troops several more times to protect the railroad and the Panama Canal.

You typically think of US military services as guarding the US, as protecting US citizens. But by and large, in this part of the world, they have done none of that. They have protected the private interests of US businessmen. A lot of folks, including the Plaid Avenger, speak out against this because it's basically whoring out the Army to protect some rich guy's stuff. That bothers me a little bit. It bothers people in Central America even more because they are the ones who catch the bullets from the US military when these sorts of shenanigans go down.

There's a history of violence since their independence based on the physical world and even the economic world. But that was then. This is now. Even more modern events were not much kinder because Cold War commie influence served to create more friction, even in the 20th century.

Whew! Low banana prices are saved again! Circa 1930s Nicaragua.

UNDER THE INFLUENCE

We know that when people are "under the influence" they should be having a good time. Unfortunately for Central America, their time "under the influence" has been a little destructive. Understatement alert! It has been *incredibly* destructive to Central America, which has recently awoken from its haze thinking, "What the hell happened?

How did I get so jacked up? I was just hanging out in the backyard, and all of a sudden, I'm awake and have got a royal hangover!" That's almost exactly what happened to Central America.

We already discussed the **US's Backyard** principle in the introduction to Latin America; indeed, the US has been *the* major influence in Central America's recent history. It has been under the US's influence technically since the **Monroe Doctrine** and **Roosevelt Corollary** days, but didn't really get messed with too much until a bunch of lefties got together down there during the Cold War years. So a bunch of lefties were hanging out in the backyard and ended up under the influence. Now they're emerging from it with some serious boo-boos.

In the Latin America overview, I touched on this a little. The US hates commies. The Cold War clearly shows that they just can't stand the commies. The US and Soviet Union were vying for influence all over the world, willing to sell arms or intervene covertly to get more people on their team. That's always part of the Cold War game, but perhaps no other region in the world has been so negatively affected by this face-off of ideologies than Central America.

How negative could it be? Central America saw some pretty nasty nuggets during the Cold War. Some of the political parties and presidents in Central America acquired leftward-leaning administrations or liberalizing policies to try to pull their people out of poverty in the 1950s and 1960s. A lot of talk about nationalization of industries—and sometimes direct action—incited serious suspicion from big brother in the north. The US interpreted and treated all leftward-leaning governments as the first step of an all-out communist invasion, and spent most of the Cold War years of 1950–1990 facilitating the interior destruction of many of these countries by any means necessary. Virtually all of Central America has been racked by civil war that has been promoted, if not initiated, by outside US forces that thought the leftward lean was just a little too commie for their backyard.

For those of you who are going to stop reading this because you think the Plaid Avenger is bashing the US, maybe you should. Maybe you do need to stop reading this. I am not going to pull any punches here. This is not a liberal rant. It's not a pro-communist rant. This is a matter of public record. The recent history of Central America has been well documented, and even more information has been released as a result of the Freedom of Information Act. In various countries there was unabashed CIA involvement, primarily to incite civil war. Covert operations were employed to destabilize the countries the US perceived as potential communist threats. The US is responsible for the funding, fueling, and arming of extreme-right rebel groups all over

Central America whose sole purpose was to topple legitimately elected governments and keep certain US-approved military dictators in power. A fairly current example should help illustrate this point . . .

There was some heavy-handed US activity in Nicaragua as a manifestation of the fear of commie takeover and because of the American perspective of this area as US backyard territory. In places like Nicaragua, your tax dollars are still infused to help defeat the Sandinistas. Daniel Ortega led this popular Communist Party that the Reagan administration tried to defeat with millions of US dollars. Reagan's tactics eventually worked, and the Sandinistas lost. By the way, I also brought this up because the same dude, Daniel Ortega, after 20 years, just won back the presidency again. Today. Now. Your US tax dollars are already hard at work funding his opponent to make sure this doesn't happen again next election. And maybe you know enough to have heard about . . .

Ortega back in the socialist saddle in Nicaragua.

THE IRAN-CONTRA SCANDAL

Even though Nicaraguan dictator Anastasio Somoza had been in control of Nicaragua for 50 years and had been a staunch ally of America, a leftist rebel group called the Sandinistas overthrew him in 1979 and established a new government headed by Daniel Ortega. Protecting its old friends, America helped Somoza and his generals escape Nicaragua safely. Since the Sandinistas were beginning to drift towards the Soviet Union and Cuba and were Marxist-Leninists, America started organizing old Somoza National Guardsmen, disaffected peasants and others who didn't support the Sandinistas, into an army called the Contras. The Contras were armed and trained by Americans, and they operated in Honduras. Since the Sandinistas had a huge army, the Contras could not fight them in a head-on war, so they focused on attacking soft targets like schools, factories, etc. to make people realize that supporting the Sandinistas would only cause disaster.

Ollie sez: "I was just following orders!"

By 1986, Americans were sick of supporting the Contras, so Congress passed a law prohibiting aid to the Contras. Since people in the Reagan administration were bent on destroying communists, they hatched up a plan where they would illegally sell arms (specifically anti-tank missiles) to Iran and use that money to illegally fund the Contras. This plan was known as the Iran-Contra scandal, which became the biggest political scandal of the 1980s. Iran was desperate for weapons because it was fighting Iraq in the Iran-Iraq war, and Americans thought that if we sold the Iranians arms, they would release American hostages in Lebanon held by Hezbollah. The problem was that Iran was an avowed enemy of the United States, and its government was the largest state sponsor of terrorism in the world. Furthermore, America was already selling arms to Iraq to use on Iran. Both sides of the plan were illegal, and the plan was exposed in 1986. Some members of the Reagan administration were indicted, but nobody went to jail.

Fast forward to 2008. Iran is now building nuclear weapons and perhaps becoming a menace to the world. Just like then, Iran is run by religious fanatics. The Contras and the Sandinistas signed a peace treaty in the 1980s and Daniel Ortega won back the presidency last year. He is president of Nicaragua again, after serving from 1979 to 1990. Iran is back in the spotlight as well, and lo and behold, the president of Iran has already met with Ortega a couple of times in order to beef up their relationship. The US is not a happy boy right now.

Fun fact: A member of the Reagan administration named Oliver North (America's favorite traitor) was indicted for the Iran-Contra scandal and also for lying about it. Ollie claimed that he had only been following orders, but according to the Uniform Code of Military Justice, it is a soldier's duty to disobey illegal orders.

UNENVIABLE INTERVENTIONS

This outside intervention from the US has really "been unhelpful" in Central American society, from the inside out, multiple times. This happened in Guatemala, Nicaragua, Honduras, and El Salvador. Those countries in particular have destroyed themselves twenty times over in the last forty years. They have been totally racked by civil war. There are always exceptions, of course, and Costa Rica is considered the most stable country in this region. I wonder why that is? Here's why: they got rid of their military 50 years ago! They saw the writing on the wall in all the other countries around them, and they actually disbanded their own military.

Panama also looks semi-stable now. It avoided having civil wars due to a string of military dictatorships that ended up running the show for most of the violent Cold War period.

Where Is Manuel Now? A Brief History of Manuel Noriega

A former CIA spook, a former leader of Panama, a former prisoner in Miami, Florida—but where is Manuel now? Okay, so he's in a hospital, but it is still a pretty nutzo story . . .

Manuel Noriega was a career soldier—having received training in Panama and at the School of the Americas in the United States. By 1983, Noriega was the de facto ruler of Panama. Noriega may have played a role in the 1968 military coup in Panama, but the details are uncertain. What is fairly clear is that Manuel Noriega was on the CIA payroll from the early 1970s to 1988. During this time, Noriega was a favorite of US diplomats. When the Shah of Iran—Mohammad Reza Pahlavi—was overthrown in the Islamic Revolution, the United States convinced Noriega to offer him amnesty in Panama. He even helped the United States funnel money to right-wing guerilla movements in El Salvador and Nicaragua.

And Manuel: the US imprisoned him.

Over the years, the United States began to see through Noriega's kleptocratic and narcotic ways. By 1989, official Panama/United States relations were at a low. US diplomats and soldiers were being harassed by Panamanian officials. After one US soldier was killed leaving a restaurant, President George H. W. Bush launched Operation Just Cause—a military invasion of Panama. During the invasion, Noriega fled but was eventually captured in the Vatican embassy in Panama. Noriega was brought back to the United States and tried on drug and racketeering charges. In 1992, Noriega was sentenced to 40 years in US prison. In 2004. In April 2010, he was extradited to France in order to face up to even more criminal charges!

What a resume: Military. CIA. President of a country. Drug Trafficker. US prisoner.

The US government propped up one dictator there named Manuel Noriega, a drug lord and former CIA employee. See inset box for Manuel's awesome rap sheet!

While we have this overall leftward lean in Central America, it was countered by US support for extreme rightist politicians and outright military dictatorships. This set the precedent for this region's continual violence. The people have been politically divided and usually brutally suppressed in terms of human rights, individual rights, and other political freedoms that are commonplace in civilized societies. The current effects of this turbulent and violent past cannot be understated.

Some of you readers and Americans in general may have no problemos with this approach. After all, American intervention may possibly have averted Soviet takeover. Umm . . . maybe, I guess, if you were really worried about a Honduran commie invasion of Texas. Ha! But American support for US business interest and right-wing dictators has with no reservations been responsible for the price of bananas staying at 50 cents a pound for 100 years straight! Might makes right! Or is it the right makes might? I always get it confused in this region.

CONTINUED CYCLE OF VIOLENCE

What is still fueling this violence if the Cold War is over? Well, it's not so easy to just set up shop again when such harsh dividing lines were drawn for so long. There was so much human suffering and loss of life and so much political division that recovery will be equally long and hard. For at least 100 years, poverty has been endemic to this region. It's a poor place—the poorest region in the western hemisphere, actually. With the possible exception of Costa Rica, there is anywhere from 60 to 80 percent of the population below poverty level. That's A LOT. There is a huge, intense wealth disparity in this region. Many of these states have assessed that it's gotten worse, even since the end of most of their civil wars in the last decade. Even though the violence has toned itself down, it's still hard to get the countries going economically. The people are putting together new governments and are trying to get things back on track. Like we said before, these governments tend to lean to the left.

Why do Central American countries have leftward leanings in the first place? This is something we talked about that applies to all of Latin America. Remember? Any place on the planet where you have endemic poverty, where most people are ridiculously poor, they tend to gravitate towards leftist political and economic systems. Why is that? Because it makes complete common sense. Socialism and die-hard communism are based on the redistribution of wealth. Pretty much everywhere in the world, there are at least some socially influenced national programs like welfare and such that come from taxing the population and then redistributing additional benefits to people in need. Then you have full-on communism, which ideally takes all the wealth and distributes it equally. Most places on the planet are someplace in between.

In places where most people have nothing, which system are they going to choose? Free-market capitalism, where it's every man for himself, or communism, where everybody gets a share of the total? Obviously, if you have nothing, you'd support a system that can give you something. That's why there is a leftward leaning in Central America. It's the 60 to 80 percent poverty rate! Of course the majority of voters there will lean way left, and favor socialism or communism!

Am I defending these people? Not really. I'm not really interested in promoting communism or any other—ism. I just want you to understand the mindset in impoverished countries. When you don't have anything, you want to get something. Plus if you are politically oppressed and have no political voice, what are you supposed to do about it? Eventually, this type of situation caps itself in some sort of revolution or outright civil war. Indeed, that's what has happened and continues to happen. Leftward leaning politicians and parties gained popular support. In a region where 2–5 percent of the people own everything, and the other 95–98 percent split up whatever's left, it's no wonder that social programs are widely supported. For the most part, people have no title to land, no real home, no nothing, and they vote left because they can't possibly get poorer.

This is part of the history of Central America, but it's not over. There are many companies in the region, and not all are owned by the US anymore, that have inordinate amounts of rights beyond what even humans have. By that, I mean that there are some plantation-style economic establishments where people are essentially slaves. Where the people who own the banana companies have hired men with rifles standing by to make sure workers are picking bananas fast enough. This sounds incredible, but it has become the way it is. There are no labor unions, no real labor rights. Protection of companies' interests over those of the individual people—with an infusion of US interest usually to support rightist regimes—conflict continues to this day in Central America.

We usually think of the US as the good guys who go out and fight for peoples' human rights and individual rights, for democracy all over the world. Unfortunately, we don't really have any of that on our track record where Central America is concerned. Quite frankly, the US has been more interested in supporting strong, right-wing leaders who will maintain economic stability at any cost; the hope is that they will make sure that stuff will not be nationalized, so the private investments aren't compromised. As such, they will even support military dictatorships that will suppress the local population who may be trying to rise up and fight for a revolution. Probably a damn commie revolution—yet another reason to squash it.

But the times are a-changing. The Cold War is indeed over, and fighting the communist threat in Central America doesn't hold a lot of water. The United States now has a new tactic in order to ensure economic growth and stability for itself—and the region as well. That tactic is free trade blocks. As we previously discussed, the FTAA is a US-supported attempt at a hemispheric-wide trade block. One that has fizzled as of late. But things are still going forward on this front in Central America. Thank CAFTA/DR-CAFTA for that. (See box on right.)

To be fair, many politicians and businessmen truly believe that free trade is the real solution to poverty in Central America. Who the hell am I to claim righteousness? Perhaps they are right. Former US President George W. Bush said that free trade "will advance peace and prosperity" in the region. In this vein of thinking, free trade = movement of capital = more businesses = more jobs = more money to these depressed economies. Also, creation of jobs in the poor places means people won't have to emigrate to the US to get a job. Sure, that might work. However, most people believe it will just help them get ripped off more: just more crappy jobs not worth much money, which is not real economic development and diversity. Free trade

What's the Deal with . . . CAFTA?

CAFTA stands for Central America Free Trade Agreement (DR-CAFTA is the same thing, but includes the DR for Dominican Republic) and is an international treaty to increase free trade. It was ratified by the United States Senate in 2005. Like NAFTA, its goal is to privatize public services, eliminate barriers to investment, protect intellectual property rights, and eliminate tariffs between the participating nations. Many people see DR-CAFTA as a stepping stone to the larger, more ambitious, FTAA (Free Trade Agreement of the Americas).

The controversy regarding DR-CAFTA is very much like the controversy regarding NAFTA. Many people are concerned about America losing jobs to poorer countries where the minimum wage is lower and environmental laws are more lax. Also, some people are concerned that regional trade blocs like DR-CAFTA undermine the project of creating a worldwide free trade zone using organizations like the WTO.

CAFTA members

is not widely supported in these countries by the general population, but widely supported by their administrations—as witnessed by CAFTA being signed.

LEGACY OF THE CIVIL WARS

What Central America is known for now, aside from Costa Rica being a major destination for ecotourism, is narcotics production, its transfer and trafficking. A lot of crack, dope, smack, amphetamines, and whatever else is produced in South and Central America, have to go through Central America to get to their ultimate destination: the US. What is a by-product of this? GANGS! Some really vicious ones, too! This ties into the growth of power and geographic scope of those Mexican cartels discussed last chapter. Those cartels now increasingly use Central American gangs as hired muscle on the streets of the US. Groups like MS-13 now have a presence in all major American cities. Yikes! (See box below.)

Currently, several Central American countries, along with Mexico, have actually signed a pact and accord to combat gang violence. What is that all about? Independent sovereign states have to form a coalition to fight organized gang crime? YES! This is a big deal. Why is this? Gosh, I don't know . . . long history of civil war, divided society, oppressed societies, tremendous wealth disparity, people who are freakin' poor as dirt, poor governments, corrupt governments, and drugs, which are everywhere. Put that all together in a stew, and what do you come up with? GANG CONTROL!

During the civil wars in Guatemala, Honduras, Nicaragua, and especially El Salvador, lots of people fled the place, as you might imagine. This resulted in an enormous refugee population that emigrated to the US. There were also tremendous amounts of people that tried to get out of Central America to the US just to find work. During all the years of oppression, violence, and civil war, lots of folks who made it to places like Los Angeles, Santa Fe, even as far north as San Francisco, were poor and uneducated. This lovely combo makes some people gravitate towards crime. Over the years, this has evolved into a syndicate of criminal activities, with ties back to Central America, and now they are importing people just for this criminal activity. It's a mafia now.

Central American gangs are a problem all across North America, from Central America into the US. They have gained a lot of strength. Since they have no options, the poor kids gravitate toward gang membership—the same reasons people join gangs in inner cities in the US. This same phenomenon is happening in Central America, so the popularity of being in a gang and joining this organized crime movement has gotten so out of control that the governments can't even handle things in their own countries. That's why you have this effort now, signed by Mexico, Guatemala, and Belize, to basically work together to combat organized crime in and among their countries, as well as to combat movement to the US.

On the same lines, Mexico is under a big squeeze because so many people, not just gangs, want to get to the US. Work immigrants want to as well. They aren't really refugees anymore; they just want to emigrate from a hellhole to the

Maras are gangs originally from Central America, including MS-13 and Sombra Negra.

What's the Deal with MS-13 and Maras?

How did they get here? People from El Salvador, Honduras and other Central American countries escaped during the 1970s to the United States of America. These people were running away from the civil wars that struck the countries of Central America, particularly El Salvador. Disaffected and disenfranchised refugee youth in the LA area gravitated toward gang life. Almost all maras members display radical tattoos on their bodies as a sign of their affiliation to their gang.

MS-13 is a gang based in Los Angeles with roots in El Salvador and operations throughout Central America. Many experts believe MS-13 and other maras have spread and benefited from the US policy of deporting criminals to their country of origin, allowing maras members to recruit new members abroad. MS-13 has recently been in the news for activities in Northern Virginia and Maryland. Maras are involved with everything from drug trafficking to petty crimes.

land of milk and honey. How are they going to do that? They aren't swimming, so they have to go on foot across borders. The same way that Mexicans get across the border into the US, Central Americans have to go all the way through Mexico to get to the US. Mexico has become a funnel; it's even funnel shaped, a throughway to the US. It has to deal with all these people who are even poorer than its own people coming through its territory, sometimes not making it to the US and staying in Mexico, putting even more stress on the ailing Mexican economy.

Now there are organized criminals and gangs running drugs through Mexican territory. Mexico's in a real pinch because the US wants to build a larger fence, to fortify the borders even more to keep immigrants out, and more are still coming in from Central America. One side of Mexico is being dammed up and the other is still open for the free movement of people. The US has put pressure on Mexico to stop anybody from coming to the US, but its population is growing from people just trying to pass through its territory.

IS THERE A LIGHT AT THE END OF THIS TUNNEL?

I'm looking, but it's such a faint glimmer. So many factors are working together to keep this place hurting.

At least the civil wars are officially over, but Central America remains replete with latent violence. This is a violent arena due to tremendous wealth disparity perpetuated, and in some cases accelerated, by the US's role. In our Central American backyard, US intervention has typically been a negative thing.

Economically, all of the countries we're talking about are highly dependent on the US economy. What is it that they produce there that is shipped to the US? Primary goods. Products that aren't worth much. Pretty much all they have to offer is worth nothing. Absolutely nothing in terms of big business, and the businesses that are there are typically owned by foreign companies anyway. That's why poverty is endemic to this region.

The price of bananas hasn't changed in 100 years. It has only crept up because of standard inflation/cost of living. Adjusted for cost of living, bananas cost the exact same as they did 100 years ago. You can go into the grocery store and buy them for *50 cents a pound*. That's after they have been cultivated, fertilized, pruned, picked, packaged, and then delivered a few *thousand* miles to get to you. How is that even possible? What are the people getting per pound in Nicaragua? Approximately jack is the Avenger's calculation!

Politically, the civil wars of the 1960s, fueled by wealth disparity and anticommunist fervor, have yet to stop damaging these societies. Re-leaning to the left for many of the countries in Central America will certainly cause more friction with the US. Immigration is also a hot button issue between the US and all of Latin America; an issue that Central America will probably not come out winning, no matter what the eventual solution may be. Growth of the **maras** is another current event that will not be going away anytime soon and is radically affecting the region, the US, and everyone in between: the reach of these Central American maras is now up to Seattle in the west and Baltimore on the east coast.

This cycle of violence and the endemic poverty, which has propagated even more violence due to gangs, is why the Plaid Avenger calls this a really violent arena. Central America has been a place of open warfare within and between states, it has been a Cold War battlefield, a corporate battlefield, and now that the gang violence is skyrocketing, it's a drug and crime battlefield. This is not likely to go away anytime soon.

But don't get me wrong. It's an awesome place to party. The people in Central America are incredibly resilient, and continue to push forward in spite of all the chips being stacked against them. Get down there. Check it out. But please remember this Plaid Avenger Tip: Just say "no" to gang tattoos.

CENTRAL AMERICA RUNDOWN & RESOURCES

View additional Plaid Avenger resources for this region at http://plaid.at/camer

 BIG PLUSES

→ Hmmmm . . . . hold on. I'm thinking. Nope, got nothing. It's a tough place.

→ Oh wait! I got one! Costa Rica is totally stable and an awesome destination for eco-tourism and tasty waves to surf!

BIG PROBLEMS

→ Hurricanes, earthquakes, volcanos

→ Gangs; some of which are becoming more powerful than local governments

→ Serious wealth disparity and landlessness remain chronic political issues

→ Significant transportation corridor of illegal narcotics; gangs help with that

→ Political instability the standard, not the exception (except for Costa Rica)

DEAD DUDES OF NOTE:

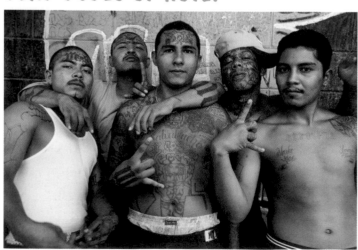
Anyone on the bad side of MS-13.

PLAID CINEMA SELECTION:

Sin Nombre (2009) Damn, this movie is hard core, gritty, gang activity stuff. And it actually mostly takes place in Mexico, but given its themes of migration from Central America and gang influence, I felt it fit in even better for this region. Honduran family trying to migrate to US gets caught up in a internal gang dispute. Great scenery of the region, great depiction of how migration actually happens, realistic gang life, extremely topical.

Agua Fria de Mar (2009) Thrilling story of a rich couple who take a vacation at the beach and come across a little girl who has terrible stories to tell, which sets off a crisis of meaning in the woman who begins to rethink all of the privileges of her life in the upper middle class. Spectacular Costa Rican landscape almost distracts from the action.

Under Fire (1983) A Hollywood presentation of the very real conflict that plagued Nicaragua during the late 1970s. Follows a photographer and a couple of his journalist friends who are covering the civil war against president Somoza.

El Norte (1983) A touching coming-of-age film that follows the fictional journey of two young indigenous Guatemalans as they attempt to free themselves of ethnic and political persecution. Covers the journey starting in the small rural town of San Pedro in Guatemala through Mexico and eventually to Los Angeles. Selected for preservation by the Library of Congress because it is "culturally, historically, or aesthetically significant." But don't expect a happy ending.

Romero (1989) True story of the catholic priest Archbishop Oscar Romero who lived in El Salvador during the political unrest in the 1970–80s. The government launched a "terror campaign" against leftist guerillas in an attempt to crush them. Archbishop Romero's protests against governments' actions is perceived as disloyalty. and the government begins to destroy churches and murder priests. Yeah, and then they assassinated him. Look into "liberation theology" before or after viewing this one.

Salvador (1986) James Woods stars as a journalist, down on his luck in the US, drives to El Salvador to chronicle the events of the 1980 military dictatorship, including the assasination of Archbishop Oscar Romero. He forms an uneasy alliance with both guerillas in the countryside who want him to get pictures out to the US press, and the right-wing military, who want him to bring them photographs of the rebels.

LIVE LEADERS YOU SHOULD KNOW:

Manuel Noriega: A "CIA asset" and double agent that eventually became President/Dictator of Panama from 1983-89 until the US invaded the country to remove him from power for drug trafficking, racketeering, and money laundering. An object lesson on why the US should never support genuinely bad people, even when those bad peoples' objectives temporarily coincide with your own.

Daniel Ortega: Current President of Nicaragua, a post he first held back in 1985-90 as the leader of the leftist Sandinista movement which overthrew an US-backed dictator (Somoza). Carried out controversial land reform and wealth redistribution (that is, communism), which brought the wrath of Uncle Sam against him. That is why the Reagan administration illegally funded and armed the US-backed Contras to take him out. Like Fidel Castro, the US still hates Ortega after all these years.

CHAPTER OUTLINE

The Caribbean

16

REGGAE and calypso music. Voodoo religion and Carnival. Rum. Pirates. Banana daiquiris on sunny beaches washed by that beautiful blue Caribbean Sea. A tropical paradise for those that visit; a tropical hellhole for those washing the dishes in the hotel where you stay. Caribbean color, Caribbean music, Caribbean-style shrimp platter at Red Lobster. The Caribbean is just too distinct to be included as part of any other region in Latin America. Yes, it is also considered a "US backyard." Yes, it is also endemically poor. However, the culture, history, and current events of the Caribbean all combine to make this place different.

PHYSICAL

Like Central America, the Caribbean is a violent arena from a climatic and geological standpoint. The islands of the Caribbean, as you can see from this plate tectonic map, are on the edge of a trench between two plates that are being pushed together. A lot of the islands are volcanic in origin, but not all of them. The big islands are also referred to as the **Greater Antilles:** the islands of Cuba, Jamaica, Haiti/Dominican Republic, and Puerto Rico. They are not volcanic in origin, but are old parts of the larger plates and are quite stable, geologically speaking. However, the arc of smaller islands that form the chain known as the **Lesser Antilles** are the result of contact at plate boundaries, which in this circumstance, results in volcanic activity. Some are still active, volcanically and seismically.

Though the larger islands are more stable geologically, they and the smaller islands both have to deal with the climatic instability of the region. *The Caribbean is the hurricane zone of all hurricane zones!* There may be big typhoons in the Pacific, and the US may get hit by a few big-ass hurricanes every now and then, but no place has them like the Caribbean. No matter where hurricanes end up in the regions near the Atlantic, most of them go through this region first. And due to the small size of the islands, hurricanes have a devastating impact almost every time. We are talking about storm systems that can completely cover an entire country. In places like the US and Mexico, the hurricanes may hit the coast or travel a little bit into the mainland, but they are not destroying all areas of the country simultaneously. The Caribbean is a place that is, physically speaking, an incredibly violent arena.

Caribbean plate tectonics: active arena.

Another consideration is that it is a tropical region. It is a very hot and humid place. However, large bodies of water always act as moderators of temperature, and thus it's always a little nicer right along the coast, where everybody lives, and where everybody visits. Which ties into another distinct quality of the Caribbean: tourism is the biggest GDP earner on pretty much every single island nation. That's why everybody comes here to party. Everyone flocks to the nice tropical beaches for the nice warm water. The entire region is tropical—it's located in the tropics! The tropical temperatures also play a part in warming the water of an important Atlantic physical feature, the Gulf Stream—a warm ocean current originating here and flowing as far north as Russia, moderating climate its entire journey. Ever wonder why it never snows in England, even though it is very far north? Gulf Stream effect is the answer. It originates in these parts.

WHAT ELSE IS GOING ON THERE?

The simplest way to highlight the cultural distinctness of this region, Plaid Avenger style, is by talking about the five S's: Sun, Sand, Sex, Sin . . . which is why people come here. The Bahamas, Jamaica, the Virgin Islands, Barbados . . . what comes to mind? Party! You know that's right! Let's get it on, Caribbean-style! Bronzed bodies basking on baked beaches. Their economy is largely based on tourism. What's the fifth S? SUGAR, which we'll get to shortly.

Tourism is a main component, if not the major component of the Caribbean's GDP. In some Caribbean islands, tourism accounts for more than half of the entire GDP each year—in some places it's even higher than that! Half of the entire state's economy is due to one single industry. That's a lot. As such, so much of the wealth of the region is dependent on other people from other countries hanging out there and spending their money. This of course sounds good—bring them on!—but there are some negatives, maybe more than the positives.

SUN, SAND, SEX, SIN: TOURISM IN THE CARIBBEAN

We can start out by asking: what is tourism really worth to the Caribbean? The Plaid Avenger's take is that it's a **primary economic activity.** You are essentially just selling the land as a resource, not unlike drilling for oil in it or cutting trees off of it. All you are doing is letting people come look at the land. As a primary commodity, it's not really worth that much, economically speaking.

Fun, fun . . .

fun . . .

and rum!

On top of that, there is quite a bit of variability in tourism. If there is a bad economic year somewhere else, it can affect how much money the Caribbean nations make from tourists. A bad hurricane can affect tourism negatively, as well. People won't come from all over to hang out on an utterly devastated beach. Tourism fluctuates to both extremes very quickly. It is very unstable; it's definitely not something that you would want as your economy's anchor. But it unfortunately is for many nations in the Caribbean region, which you'll see in the box to the right.

What do the locals actually get out of selling their beach? Do they line up and have all the tourists give them a dollar each? Not hardly. Typically what happens is a multinational corporation from somewhere else, like the US, Great Britain, or Germany, comes and builds a big-ass hotel on a nice stretch of beach. Those corporations are also the ones getting the $300 a night for the tourists to stay there. They also get the $8 that a tourist pays for a mai tai at the hotel bar. The McDonald's and T.G.I. Friday's and Olive Garden restaurants that spring up around the hotels are also foreign-owned.

For the people actually living there—the locals in Jamaica or Grenada or the Virgin Islands—tourism equates to low-paying, minimum wage jobs. The local is the guy who serves the $8 mai tai, the guy who opens the door, does the dishes, changes the sheets, and flips the burgers at Mickey D's. Those aren't really the most enviable jobs, and we all know inherently what those jobs are worth. It can be argued that tourism is a complete sham for the locals, and

Country/Territory	Contribution of Tourism Economy to GDP (2002)
	Percent of GDP
Anguilla	58
Antigua and Barbuda	72
Aruba	47
Bahamas	46
Barbados	37
Bermuda	26
British Virgin Islands	85
Cayman Islands	31
Cuba	11
Dominica	22
Dominican Republic	18
Grenada	23
Guadeloupe	33
Jamaica	27
Martinique	10
St. Kitts and Nevis	25
St. Lucia	51
St. Vincent and the Grenadines	29
Virgin Islands (U.S.)	42

Tourism: major big deal to this region.

that all the money made there doesn't stay in the country to do any good. The locals are working the crappy jobs while all the money being made there is exported to another country via the multinational company that owns the hotel or casino or swanky bar there. I've seen statistics indicating that for every dollar spent in the Caribbean, less than a dime actually stays in the country. I can't prove it, but I believe it.

Others would argue that those may be shit jobs, but they are jobs, period. What would the locals do without those jobs? Wouldn't they be poorer than they are now? Both are valid points, but just remember next time you visit the multi-million dollar hotels, the locals are not the ones partying and having a good time. They're mopping up because you drank too much.

For the most part, it is Awesome Vacation Land for us, where we can party, do whatever we want to do, hang out in the sun, walk on the sand, have lots of great sex, and live in sin. The sin part is one to pay attention to as we later consider Cuba. One of the reasons that Cuba went communist when they had their revolution was because of the sin part. People saw Cuba as a tropical island paradise that became infiltrated by American mafia and became a playground for other rich and famous Americans from the late 1800s all the way up to the 1950s. It was essentially the Sodom and Gomorrah of the tropics. People would flock down there for their vacations and take advantage of all the legal drugs, gambling, prostitution, and alcohol, whatever. Just thinking about it, the Plaid Avenger salivates, anxiously awaiting the return of those good old days . . .

Though that sounds absurd, this is actually how much of the Caribbean region is viewed, as a place for sin and all around partying. This is one of the reasons why Fidel and his boys kicked everybody out of there. Tourism is a double-edged sword that, overall, may not have the greatest of impacts on the Caribbean.

WHEN THE US GETS A SNIFFLE, THE CARIBBEAN GETS A COLD

"Welcome back to the islands, Mr. Avenger. Can I get you the usual?"

What does this post-nasal drip reference mean? Since we are considering the economic make-up of the region, it's important to point out this economic relationship. This saying has way more than a grain of truth in it; it is a fact. And what it's saying is this: If anything bad happens in the economic colossus of the US, there is a ripple effect that gets magnified down south. The Caribbean gets it first and worst. No matter how small the fluctuation is in the US, it can heavily influence the entire economy of this region.

The tourism industry is a perfect example of this, since it relies heavily on people traveling to spend time and money there. When there is a bad economic year in the US, people are less likely to go on vacation because they can't afford it. If you need to make money, you're not going to take off from work and spend thousands of dollars on a Caribbean vacation. If there is an economic depression in the US, the Caribbean is trashed. Economically devastated immediately. This ripple effect reaches into all aspects of life down there. Even the 9/11 terrorist attacks precipitated a drastic reduction in Caribbean tourism. People were afraid to fly on planes, and overnight, the Caribbean economy got dumped. Into the next year, there were still repercussions from the decrease in tourism due to 9/11. This single event, that didn't even affect the American economy that much, *destroyed* the Caribbean economy. Even something as trivial as an increase in airfare to these places can affect the economy negatively.

Another way that the Caribbean is reliant on our economy is through something called **remittances.** This term can be applied not only in the Caribbean, but across Latin America as a whole. Many people come from other countries—like Mexico and virtually every Caribbean country—to the US to work. These people work primarily in the agricultural sector, but there are also people who move to cities like New York and work low-paying jobs there. Some even start their own businesses. New York is a good example, because there is a huge Jamaican population there. These people are not necessarily immigrants, though some of them are. Many come here just to work,

Not likely to be visiting the resorts anytime soon.

since the job outlook might not be very good in their respective countries.

What does that have to do with this term, remittance? A remittance refers to money sent back home to the families of those people who have come to the US to work. Jamaicans, or Puerto Ricans, or Barbadians come here to work and send part or most of their paychecks back home to support their families.

Why bring this up while talking about the Caribbean region? Remittances comprise a significant component of the GDP of many Caribbean countries. Think about that. In 2004, the remittance market for Latin America as a whole exceeded $40 billion. In some Caribbean countries, 5–10% of the economy may

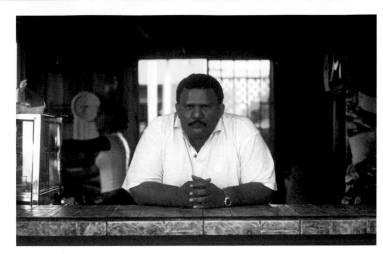

"I've got something you can remit!"

depend on getting money sent from people, working in the US and other places. If this activity were stopped, if guest workers could no longer send money home to their families, there would be an immediate economic impact on the economies of this region. The Plaid Avenger is not being a bleeding heart here—these are just the facts. To stop guest workers would mean immediate, instantaneous negative repercussions south of our borders. The sniffle becomes the cold—perhaps pneumonia for some of these small states.

THE FIFTH "S": SUGAR

The role of sugar in the Caribbean cannot be understated. When the New World was being settled by the colonial powers, primarily the Spanish and even the British, there was one single commodity that had an enormous impact on the historical development of the Caribbean. This, of course, is the processing of sugar.

Sugar's an interesting tale that not many people know about, for whatever reason. By the 20th century, sugar had become so entrenched in the Western diet that it's no wonder the average person nowadays really doesn't know how or when sugar became popular. We only know that sugar is a huge, prominent part of our diets. We think it has been around forever. Everybody since the beginning of time has consumed an average of 152 pounds of sugar per year just like we do now, right? Hell no.

This consumption of sugar is a new phenomenon. Sugar was originally from Southeast Asia. It is a type of grass, never planted and processed in volume anywhere. It moved from Asia to India to Africa, but not until it got to the Caribbean did it become a mass-produced cash crop. The Spanish had

Sugar is still big business.

small sugar plantations on the Madeira Islands, which were a way station between Spain and the New World. As they were looking for gold and silver in the New World, they also looked into what crops could be grown there.

When they brought sugar to the New World, it exploded. Sugarcane was brought into an environment in which it goes gangbusters. It could be grown so fast, sometimes two or three harvests a year, so cheaply and in such abundance that it caught the eye of those Spaniards. Up until this point in history, the "sweet tooth" was pretty much unheard of. Sugar was a scarce commodity. Nobody in Europe had sugar. Cane sugar in tea, cookies, and crumpets crumpets was unheard of 500 years ago. Nobody knew what the hell it even was; it was only a plaything of the rich and famous. Its appeal then is analogous to that of

Sugar as high as an elephant's eye.

cocaine now: An incredibly valuable commodity imported from a far away tropical location. But the Caribbean changed all that. By providing this commodity en masse, the Caribbean was the single region that changed the dietary consumption throughout the entire planet for the next 500 years. But it also changed the Caribbean quite a bit.

Sugar is an extremely labor-intensive commodity. Today, it is still mostly done by hand, planted and harvested by hand with knives and baskets. During the colonial era, people couldn't get enough of it. That's the case even today. It was processed a variety of ways, like the table sugar with which we are familiar, but that also led to by-products like molasses, which can be made into rum. Even by-products and leftovers from the sugar-making process were used to make other products. This essentially diversified sugar into a ton of different commodities, all of which made good money.

Rum was almost as big a hit as sugar was. It was gangbusters part two in the colonies and in Europe, so much so that British sailors even got a rum ration during much of this era. They were paid in rum . . . the Plaid Avenger should really have been an old scallywag. Yo ho ho and a bottle of rum.

MO' MONEY

Sugar was a big business, a big deal. The point I am trying to make about sugar's impact on the Caribbean is this: When it became popular, everyone wanted to plant it everywhere; it was the crack cocaine of its day. It's awesome; it gets great prices. People will pay anything for it. You can make buckets of money on it. However, as I suggested, it is very labor-intensive. The plantation owners need lots of labor, and cheap labor is preferable. Cheap labor? How about free labor?

Guess what that means? That's right: slaves. "Hey guys, let's enslave the local population! It's the perfect solution!" They tried. But most of the natives, as I pointed out in the Mexican section, died of European imported disease. It virtually wiped out everyone in the Caribbean before they even saw white dudes. The few that were left over got worked to death in very short order. Basically, the colonizers virtually wiped out the native populations of the Caribbean islands.

So the colonizers were on the lookout. "We need more labor. Where are we going to get them?" You already know the story. They found out that they could bring people over from Africa. This set up what is called the **Triangle Trade.** There are several different routes one can take on the Triangle Trade, but the bottom line is: if you're going to sail about

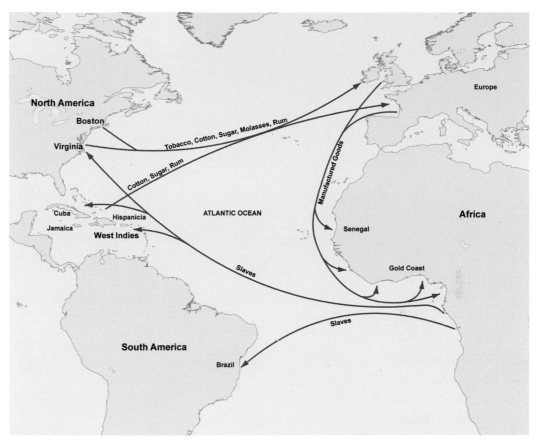

Triangle trade.

from one place to the other, you never want to sail the ship empty. It's a waste of time and a waste of resources. You always want to have something in your boat that you will trade or sell at the next place before picking up another load to take somewhere else. And the first leg of the triangle trade . . .

Let's say you're a British trader. What do you have in Great Britain? Well, you have finished goods. You've got guns, knives, swords, cigarettes, alcohol, woodworks, woven fabrics, and a cute accent. See, all the places in the New World, they just have raw commodities that must be brought back and processed. You can process tobacco, process wood, process cane sugar, or take sugar and do something else with it. Turn that into rum, actually, just add value to it in any way you can so you can charge premium prices and keep yourself in business.

So you're in Britain and you load up your ship with finished goods; in this case, alcohol and guns—what a fantastic combination. You take your alcohol and guns, and you float down to Africa. This is the first side of your triangle. What are you going to get in Africa? You're going to offload the liquor and guns and sell them to the local chiefs in exchange for what? Slaves. Fill the ship that you just emptied, fill every last nook and crevice with slaves. What are you going to do with those? Take them on the next leg of the trip to the Caribbean.

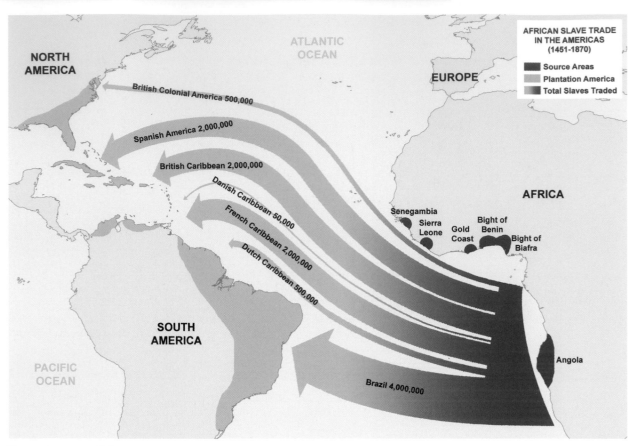

Massive human trafficking.

Now I am getting ahead of my story, because not all of the slaves went to the Caribbean. Some of these slaves went directly to the east coast of South America, and very few went to North America, proportionally speaking. However, millions went to the Caribbean. Millions and millions of black African slaves ended up in the Caribbean. Why so many? Well, the Caribbean's population was not that big at the time, and there were a lot of sugar plantations that needed to be worked. Once millions of slaves had moved to these very small islands, why did the slave trade continue over such a long time? Why so long? Why didn't the slave traders or owners have the slaves propagate themselves?

Because sugar production is an extremely labor-intensive industry in a tropical location. It's HOT. It is hotter than hell in the Caribbean during the summertime. It is hot in those fields. It sucks. Not only that, but there's malaria. People died like there was no tomorrow. People were basically worked to death. A huge percentage of the slaves brought to the New World to work died within two to three years of their arrival. As you can see, this caused the need for continual replenishment. More slaves. Every year the traders needed more because the slaves kept dying off. I don't mean to underestimate figures; there were certainly large numbers of slaves brought to the United States. A significant proportion of today's US population is of African-American descent. However, the numbers that went to the Caribbean dwarfed the total that came to North America proper. This is all solely because of the economic engine built around the sugar industry. The Plaid Avenger can't stress the impact of this trade enough.

Once you offload your slaves in the Caribbean or North America, what do you pick up then to take back home? All those raw commodities. Fill your ships with sugar, tobacco, rum, and wool. Take all that stuff back home and process it. That's all the things that people want, and it's cheap as hell. You've made money on every single leg of the journey.

That's the Triangle Trade, which lasted for several hundred years. Lots of folks got really, really rich from it, at a terrible cost in human lives, primarily African lives. Sugar can't be underestimated, or undervalued, in terms of its contributions to human suffering, economic growth, and its worldwide dietary impacts.

Am I telling you this long tale just so you can understand why people eat so much sugar in the world today? In part. But also think about the face of the Caribbean today. How would you describe Bob Marley? More generally, what does your average Jamaican look like? Even broader, why are many faces black in the Caribbean? Think of Jamaica. Think of Haiti. They aren't white, and they aren't Chinese; they are black, as are most of the populations of the Caribbean islands. Why? Because of the Triangle/Slave trade, which significantly impacted the demographics of this region.

Many slaves also ended up in what is now Brazil, on the eastern coast of South America, which was another sugar production center in the New World. You can look at many countries in Latin America today, and you can see in the reflection exactly how much sugar they grew. The more sugar was grown in the country, the larger the black population presently is. When we think of the Caribbean, we think of its population as mostly from African descent. That's absolutely true, and it's all because of sugar.

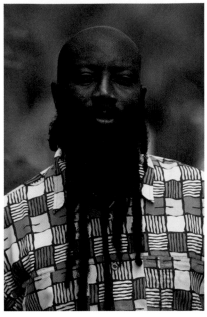

The hell with sugar, I make reggae.

THE MELTING POT

The Caribbean is also a place that I consider to be a great melting pot. We often think of the US as a melting pot, but the Caribbean is even better. There is such a unique culture that emerges, on the individual islands and as a whole, from the numerous colonial powers that had colonies in the Caribbean.

As you can see from the figure on the right, the Spanish, the British, the French, and the Dutch had colonies here. These colonial powers were in control of these islands. Some of the islands changed hands between these countries multiple times. This equates to European cultural influence on top of the indigenous culture of the surviving natives, infused with the African culture brought along during the days of the Triangle Trade. Over time, this has created a unique place on the planet, culturally speaking.

Three continents have come together in the Caribbean and crystallized in several ways. The first obvious fusion that we already talked about is race. Many different ethnicities have been combined to come up with several unique ethnic cultures. Languages have also changed in the Caribbean. The way people talk is a mixture of colonial, native, and African influences, resulting in Creole languages, which are formed by infusing

What Is the Deal with Voodoo?

Voodoo (which can be spelled many different ways, including Vudu, Voudun, Vodun, etc.) is an animistic religion that began in West Africa many years ago and was transplanted to Haiti by way of slaves. Animism is a philosophy that believes that everything, even regular objects, has a soul and a spirit. Most Vodouisants believe in a single God that created the world. However, this God is distant and detached from the world, so Vodouisants must turn to "mysteries," "saints," or "spirits" for help. Voodoo has many different traditions, and these different traditions have slightly varying beliefs and worship different spirits. But on the whole, most Vodouisants believe in personal spirits, harmony with nature and the world, and the importance of family. Western pop-culture sometimes depicts voodoo as a bizarre religion that is all about zombies and sticking pins in dolls. In reality, these elements are very small and insignificant portions of the religion.

Fun Plaid Fact: Harvard ethnobotanist Wade Davis went to Haiti in 1982 and claimed the zombie tradition actually had some real basis in fact. Years ago, when voodoo priests had determined that somebody deserved to be punished, they would feed them pufferfish, whose toxic glands put people in a paralytic coma. After burying this person, they would dig them up a couple days later, and give them another dose of hallucinogenic drugs. This entire experience, including the drugs, the burial, and people's religious beliefs, were enough to actually convince people that they were really will-less zombies. Obviously, Davis's research has been questioned. Check out the film *The Serpent and the Rainbow* (1988) for Davis' screen adaptation. Pretty spooky!

terms from several different languages into one type of speech. For example, the official language of Haiti is Haitian Creole, a combination of French and several West African dialects. There are also the several music styles of the Caribbean. The biggest one we can think of is Reggae, which is a distinctly Caribbean style that has roots in other regional styles, such as Calypso. And voodoo—what the hell is that? (See the box above.)

The Caribbean is a combination of a whole smorgasbord of stuff, from three different continents.

SMALL ISLANDS; BIG POLITICAL PROBLEMS

We already talked about Central America, and the Caribbean shares the common feature of being in the **US's backyard.** Since the Monroe Doctrine, no foreign powers will mess around here; the US won't allow it. Especially today. These countries don't need to spend money on a military or any other form of national defense, and many of them don't. This is definitely a good thing, because they are damn poor. Their biggest concern should be avoiding widespread devastation by hurricanes, not getting invaded by anybody, because they are under the protective umbrella of the US.

But that's a double-edged sword, as I have said before, because being under the umbrella means more US intervention. Haiti, in particular, has been controlled by

To hell with reggae, I grow ganja.

the US several times in the last 100 years. The US military occupied Haiti from 1915 to 1934. Why did the US military occupy Haiti? Once fighting ended after the long Haitian Revolution period, they did fairly well until their national debt started to get out of control. This was fine for the American banks they owed until Haiti became unstable and had another revolutionary movement. Scared that they wouldn't make any of their money back, the banks pressured Woodrow Wilson, who sent in the troops. The occupying US forces improved Haiti's infrastructure while they were there, mostly by supervising forced labor chain gangs to improve old roads and build new ones.

We've supported some fairly brutal leaders in Haiti, as well as in the Dominican Republic, which was taken over by the US in 1965 after a rightist coup (whose connections to the US are unclear) had trouble completely overthrowing the leftist government there. The US went in to make sure that the leftists wouldn't regain control and turn it into "a second Cuba." Which gets us to the biggest intervention that the US has had in the Caribbean, if not the world . . .

CUBA

A fifty-year-old economic and diplomatic embargo. Refusal to allow US citizens to visit the country. CIA sanctioned assassination attempts on the leader of the state—Fidel Castro. Why does the US hate Cuba so much?

Historically, the United States and Cuba have had a very close relationship, especially because Cuba is only 90 miles away from Key West, Florida. The United States has dominated Cuban politics, intervening whenever it wasn't happy with the leadership, and basically treating Cuba like a vassal state. This relationship changed in 1959, when Fidel Castro and a band of revolutionaries seized power in Cuba and installed a communist regime. Since then, Cuba and America have had absolutely no diplomatic contact or official trade.

In the 1950s, Cuba, especially the capital city of Havana, was a playground for rich Americans. Flights left Miami every hour on the hour for an orgy of drugs, prostitution, and gambling for which Havana had become famous. Havana became a hangout for American mafiosos, and many believed that Havana was going to become bigger than Las Vegas. (Check out *The Godfather, Part II* (1974) for insight.) Some Cubans were becoming rich, but a vast majority of them were still desperately poor and living in the countryside, and these peasants became distrustful of their corrupt government. To make matters worse, Cuba was controlled by an unelected dictator named Fulgencio Batista, who had somehow managed to anger everybody in Cuba from the landless poor to the middle and upper classes of society. Every time people tried to revolt against Batista's government, he responded violently and brutally, often executing those who were responsible. The time was ripe for somebody like Fidel Castro to come and seize power in Cuba.

The Cuban Revolution was an intense struggle. Castro and his army of around 100 men—including 20th century badass Che Guevara—sailed to Cuba on a rickety yacht named the Granma. Things turned sour when they landed, and the Batista army quickly killed most of them. The remaining dozen or so soldiers went and hid out in the Sierra Maestra mountains, beginning a long guerrilla war that quickly gained supporters around Cuba. After defeating Batista's forces several times, Batista left Cuba on January 1, 1959, and the rebels took power.

Cuban "liberator" . . . or "dictator"?

At first, the United States supported the Cuban revolution because they thought that Castro was a liberal constitutionalist and nationalist and that he was good for Cuba. He ended corruption, gambling, prostitution, and he expelled the American mafia who were living in Cuba. However, Castro quickly turned communist and took some steps that angered American officials. He began seeking ties with the Soviet Union (remember, this was during the Cold War!) and purging anti-communist people from his administration. He nationalized all foreign-owned property and even nationalized the land and property of most Cubans, both wealthy and poor ones. For this reason, many rich Cubans, extremely angry at Castro, left Cuba and went to America. The largest exile group formed in Miami, which has become a famous base for anti-Castro activity.

Why does the United States hate Cuba? During the Cold War, it was a no-brainer. Cuba was a satellite state for Soviet Russia, and America was fighting a war against communism. In 1962, Americans became very uneasy when Castro let the Soviet Union point nuclear missiles at America from Cuban soil during the Cuban Missile Crisis, which you can read more about in the box to the right. During this time, the United States made several attempts to assassinate Castro, even hiring Mafia members to do the job. It never worked. After the Soviet Union collapsed, Cuba became much poorer and desperate because its main supporter was gone. Many people thought that the time had come for America and Cuba to begin re-establishing relations.

Yet, the Cuban and US governments stayed enemies, mainly because of Cuban exiles living in Miami. Remember we talked about these guys before? The rich guys who got their land taken away by Castro's communist cartographic changes? More than one million Cuban exiles now live around Miami, and these people hate Fidel Castro with a flaming passion. They had been living rich, comfortable lives in Cuba before the revolution, and the communist regime took everything they had away from them. In America, they have become a huge lobbying force that is very influential in American politics; their goal is to do everything they can to hurt the Cuban government and take Castro from power.

What's the Deal with the Cuban Missile Crisis?

Many people consider the Cuban Missile Crisis as the closest America—and the world—has ever come to nuclear war. In 1962, during the Cold War, the Soviet Union deployed nuclear missiles in Cuba that were aimed at the United States. Part of the reason the Soviet Union wanted nuclear missiles so close to America was because America had deployed similar nuclear missiles in Turkey aimed at Soviet cities. After American spy airplanes revealed the existence of the missile sites in Cuba, there was an intense debate in the White House about what America should do. Some people in the Kennedy administration favored a naval blockade, of Cuba, while others insisted that America invade Cuba. The Kennedy administration decided on a blockade, and it was later revealed that the Russians had short-range nuclear missiles that would have probably been used on American troops had they invaded.

For several days, the situation was very tense between the United States and Russia. An American U-2 spy airplane was shot down over Cuba and another was shot down over Russia. After 12 days, Soviet Premier Nikita Khrushchev eventually decided to remove the missiles from Cuba, and in return, America promised not to invade Cuba and also to remove the American missiles that were in Turkey. This crisis was widely seen as an embarrassment for the Soviet Union, and the Cubans felt betrayed because the situation was resolved between America and Russia, with Fidel Castro playing no part in the negotiations.

Fun Plaid Fact: The Cuban Missile Crisis led to the development of the "hotline," or the famous red telephone that Moscow and Washington could use to have direct communication in the case of another crisis.

The bat-phone to Moscow.

This is a goal they don't have to work at quite so hard now, since Fidel Castro's health has been declining steadily for the past few years. It's gotten so bad, in fact, that his brother Raul had to take over as president of Cuba for him. Politically and diplomatically, this hasn't amounted to much change so far. Raul is maintaining the old ways for now, though some people speculate that this won't last forever. Raul is not quite as extreme as Fidel, which means he might start making moves to liberalize the economy or even normalize relations with the United States. That's a big change!

But what about us? It doesn't mean jack if the president of Cuba wants to improve US relations if the US isn't on board. Cuba has been left-leaning for decades and they redistributed land, resources, and wealth through nationalization—and the

What Is the Deal with Che Guevara?

Why is Che the baddest ass revolutionary in the 20th century?

Che Guevara has become a symbol of youth rebellion for generations, but most have no idea who he was or what he did. He has become a wildly popular pop-culture icon and a symbol for alternative culture and also for communism and socialism. His images have been reproduced on a vast array of merchandise, such as T-shirts, posters, coffee mugs, and baseball caps. In Cuba, his face adorns billboards and the sides of government buildings.

Ernesto Guevara (Che is a nickname that means "buddy" or "pal") was born in Argentina and studied to become a physician. However, he took a year off of school and traveled around Latin America on a motorcycle to witness first-hand the crushing poverty that many Latin Americans were enduring. These experiences helped turn him into a revolutionary and a Marxist. He believed that revolution was the only way to obtain equality for the people, so he began traveling to Latin American countries and helping out with Marxist revolutions, first in Guatemala and later in Cuba.

Around 1955, Che met Fidel Castro and agreed to join him in this battle against the Cuban dictator Fulgencio Batista. They sailed to Cuba in 1956 on a rickety yacht named the Granma, and after a two-year war, took over Cuba. Since Che was a Marxist, he was instrumental in persuading Castro to become communist. For his work in the revolution, Che was awarded some important positions in the Cuban government and wrote some books about guerrilla warfare right after the revolution. However, he could not sit still long. He soon left Cuba to encourage revolutions in other parts of the world, including Congo and Bolivia. Che was eventually caught and assassinated by Bolivian forces, assisted by the American CIA. They chopped off his hand so they could prove it was him.

While many people admired Che, others saw him as a dangerous lunatic. He has been accused of murdering and torturing thousands of people in Cuban prisons, as well as murdering peasants in guerrilla areas where he was fighting. Che has also been called an idiot and has been accused of being single-handedly responsible for the collapse of the Cuban economy, which had been one of the strongest in Latin America up to that point.

Che is famous for many reasons. For one, he was good-looking, charming, and got laid a lot, as opposed to most world leaders. Secondly, he was killed in the prime of his life fighting for his cause, so he has that whole Bob Marley/Jimi Hendrix/Buddy Holly dead rock star thing going. Thirdly, even though he came from a rich family and was trained as a physician, he dedicated his life to helping poor people around the world and often put his life on the line for his beliefs. For this reason, many people who disagreed with his communist beliefs still admired him for his self-sacrifice. Lastly, an important reason Che has become so famous is because of a really cool-looking photograph of him taken by Albert Korda in 1960 that has become a symbol for counterculture youth around the world.

US can't stand that. Cuba also had missiles pointed at us. That didn't help much either. Taking the world to the brink of nuclear war probably caused some of the animosity that has kept that archaic embargo in place against them to this day.

However! Unlike President Bush, who was not open to negotiating with current Cuban President Raul Castro, US President Obama has already shown signs that he's not ascribing to many of Bush's policies, particularly as far as diplomatic relations go. Obama said from the start that he was willing to have open discussions with Cuba, and much to everyone's surprise, Raul said, "Yeah, okay. Let's do this." They have already allowed remittances to resume, which as we said earlier, hugely impacts these volatile Caribbean economies. They have also agreed to allow family members to travel between the countries. Things are practically back to normal! Well, maybe not so much. Historically, liberal US presidents have done everything they could to open relations with Cuba, and then the next conservative presidents have closed everything up again. But things might be different now.

Obama is wildly popular the world over, and there aren't ANY world leaders competing to be at the top of his hate list—not even Hugo Chavez! Even these leftward-leaning Latin leaders are trying to abate the hate. Positive US-Cuban relations could definitely affect other Latin leaders' attitude toward the US. We're talking regime shifts, more open economic discussions, perhaps new thoughts about the FTAA . . . but nothing is certain yet. Now it's up to us world-watchers to pay attention and see what happens!

THE CARIBBEAN TODAY

This brings us to the two issues that do show how the Caribbean is trying to diversify their economy and bring in higher paying jobs: offshore banking and drug trafficking. Wow. I guess that's one way to diversify. Let's elaborate.

Perhaps due to their endemic poverty, or due to the fact that they are close to the US, two lucrative industries have popped up in the Caribbean. One of them is **narcotics trafficking,** and perhaps this also applies to other places in Central and Latin America, but it's definitely big in the Caribbean as well. They don't actually produce a lot of illegal narcotics there, but traffickers fly it there and end up launching from their small islands in little clipper planes, or cigarette boats, and dumping the stuff off around the US coasts. Once it's on the coast, it can go anywhere else in the US, and you've got a large-scale trafficking operation on your hands.

The US is, of course, not happy about this. Unfortunately for them, it's simple market forces at work. Capitalism at its fine-tuned best. Dig the facts: The US is the end-consumer of virtually all narcotics made in Latin America (okay, some of our European crack head friends get some too, but not that much). The Caribbean is very close to the US, and has lots of poor people in it willing to do anything to make ends meet. The ocean is a hard entity to control and monitor all the time. End result: the Caribbean is an excellent launching pad for drug-runners to get to the US. Always has been. Always will be. It's a growing sector in the region.

The second industry that has popped up is **offshore banking.** Lots of people now do offshore banking through an account in the Bahamas. Which is great! I guess. Isn't it? Why wouldn't people just put their money in a US bank?

If you have millions of dollars in the United States, you have to pay taxes on it. And if you happen to be doing anything that happens to be, say, slightly illegal, then you might get punished for that. One good way to avoid being caught evading taxes, or dealing drugs or whatever, is to take your money outside the US. Banks are increasingly opening up in the Caribbean, and they're operated essentially like Swiss bank accounts. There is a high degree of privacy, and since these are sovereign states, they don't have to reveal bank records if the United States asks for them: "We're a private bank in a sovereign state, and we don't have to show you our customers' records, thank you very much."

This happens even though the FBI, the CIA, or the IRS may know that the people who are putting their money in the bank are big drug dealers, or crooked businessmen in the US who are either scamming or just evading taxes, or they are mafia types trying to launder money. Places like the Bahamas—because they are more stable economically than the others and not entirely poverty stricken—have become the Swiss of the Caribbean. Since it's not too far offshore, banking in the Caribbean is becoming much more popular. The bank is close enough to easily do business, but just far enough to get away from those annoying taxes and laws in the US. Today the Caribbean is still under the US umbrella of defense, except for Cuba, which we would like to un-defend, a.k.a. attack. As I already suggested, the region is also heavily reliant on the US economy. This makes them particularly susceptible to economic fluctuations, which means they are unstable. Like all other places in Latin America, they have, as a general rule, a tremendous wealth disparity and poverty. Because what do they produce? Tourism, which isn't worth a lot, and sugar, which is worth even less. Also, drugs and offshore banking activities which are illegal or unsavory. We all think that hanging out on a Caribbean island is a slice of heaven on Earth; it more often than not is a hard-scrabble slice of Hell for the economically and politically challenged folks who live there.

Let's not end on a negative note. Let's end with someone we can all rally around:

What's the Deal with . . . Bob Marley?

Bob Marley, famous reggae singer and song-writer, was the ambassador of the Rastafari Movement to the Western world. Marley lived his life and created his music in the Rasta tradition. Rastafarianism is a religion that developed in Jamaica in the 1930s. Rastafarianism has also come to embody a cultural movement of racial equality and African heritage. Central to Rastafarianism is the belief that Haile Selassie I—former emperor of Ethiopia—is a reincarnate of God (or "Jah" in Rasta terminology). Rastas cite Old Testament prophecies to justify this belief. In fact—like Judaism, Islam, and Christianity—Rastafarianism is an Abrahamic religion. Many Rastas see themselves as true Israelites—the descendents of the 12 tribes of Israel.

Rastafarianism is a diverse religion. In fact, most Rastas reject the term Rastafarianism ("-isms create schisms") and prefer to call the Rastafari movement a "way of life."

However, there are several near universal symbols and traditions in Rastafarianism including:

→ The lion—the proud and noble ruler of the African savannas
→ Ethiopia—the home of Selassie I and a country that fiercely resisted European colonialism
→ Dreadlocks—a natural hairstyle at odds with European fashion, and
→ Ganja—the stuff they smoke.

There are over one million Rastas in the world today, including approximately ten percent of the Jamaican population.

CARIBBEAN RUNDOWN & RESOURCES

View additional Plaid Avenger resources for this region at http://plaid.at/carib

 BIG PLUSES

→ Awesome group of semi-tropical islands; a tourism mecca
→ Just off the coast of the largest economy on earth . . . the US!
→ Have no need to waste money on militaries; the US would protect them from foreign attacks without even thinking about it

 BIG PROBLEMS

→ Hurricanes, earthquakes, pirates (specifically, Johnny Depp)
→ Smallness:small islands, small economies, small amounts of resources
→ Have no real economic engine or even valuable resource to export; sugar used to be king, but is now so cheap as to be worthless
→ Significant transportation corridor of illegal narcotics and zone for money laundering and tax evasion
→ Highly, highly dependent on US economy; when it stinks, they stink

DEAD DUDES OF NOTE:

Bob Marley: Jamaican singer-songwriter and musician who is the most widely known and revered performer of reggae music, and is credited for helping spread both Jamaican music and the Rastafari movement to a world-wide audience

Ernesto "Che" Guevara: Major figure in the Cuban Revo-lution, a devout marxist, intellectual, guerilla leader, doctor, diplomat, etc. etc. whose face is now iconic for reasons that most T-shirt wearers don't understand. Had a falling out with Castro after the Revolution, and went on to incite other social uprisings in Africa and Latin America until the CIA iced him in 1967.

PLAID CINEMA SELECTION:

The Harder They Come (1972) A poor Jamaican, a 1970s anti-hero, tries to make it with a hit record but breaks bad when he refused to sign away his rights, starts dealing marijuana and becomes an underground fugitive and political hero. This no-budget, ghetto film was the first to bring this music called "reggae" to the big screen and subsequently the American mainstream and made Jimmy Cliff a star. Great look at poverty in Jamaica and gangsta' life before it became hip. And you will hear the the theme song played about ten million times. Great period piece.

Extraordinary Women (2009) A moving documentary that captures the lives of six of the most influential women from the Dominican Republic. The women in the film all lead very contrasting lives from a woman who lead the way in healthcare to women that were very influential in the politics of Latin America. Creates an excellent view of the culture of the Dominican Republic.

Havana Blues (2005) The story of two young musicians in Cuba who make music that combines the traditional aspects of Cuban music with more modern types like rap. Takes a look at the struggle to keep their sound while facing the monetary restraints of the music industry. Film contains criticisms of life in Cuba including poverty and Nationalism among other things.

Life and Debt (2001) An intense documentary that examines the economic and social situation in Jamaica. The film provides a harsh view of the World Bank, whose policies forced the Jamaican government to enact strict economic reform, which left the country nearly $5 billion in debt. While not a happy look at Jamaica, opens an interesting window into how life really is for some people.

Burn! (1969) A British agent, Sir William Walker, sent to the island of Queimada (a fictional Portuguese colony) to organize an uprising of black slaves to overthrow the Portuguese regime. Great Britain wants to get economic control of the island, because it is an important sugar cane producer. Interesting historical, albeit fictional, look at 1800's Caribbean economy and great-power-politics in the region.

Pirates of the Caribbean (2003, 2006, 2007, 2011*) Q: What kind of list would this be if we didn't mention a trilogy, and soon to be quartet, of films that have grossed nearly $3 billion with the name "Caribbean" in it? A: A better one.

LIVE LEADERS YOU SHOULD KNOW:

Fidel Castro: The un-killable king of communism in the Western Hemisphere, leader of the Cuban Revolution of 1959, provoker of the Cuban Missile Crisis of 1962, grand poobah of Cuba from 1959 to 2008, and sole reason for the 50 year old US embargo against Cuba. He is revered in leftists circles as a demi-god, and his death (coming soon!) will transform the US/Cuban relationship overnight.

Raul Castro: Current President of Cuba, much quieter older brother of Fidel who is continuing to carry on the wanna-be communist legacy. But, many analyst assume that Raul is already making slow moves to open up the island's economy and politics in preparations for his brother's death, at which time Cuba will change dramatically. Maybe.

Maracaibo
Caracas
VENEZUELA
Georgetown
Medellín
GUYANA
Paramaribo
Bogotá
Cayenne
SURINAME
COLOMBIA
French Guiana
Cali
(FRANCE)
Quito
ECUADOR
Belém
Guayaquil
Manaus
Fortaleza

PERU
BRAZIL
A
N
Lima
D
E
S
Salvador
La Paz
Brasília
BOLIVIA
Belo
Horizonte
A
T
PARAGUAY
Rio de Janeiro
of Capricorn
A
C
A
M
A
Asunción
São Paulo
D
E
S
E
R
T
Porto
Alegre
South
CHILE
Córdiba
Pacific
URUGUAY
South
Santigo
Ocean
Buenos Aires
Atlantic
Montevideo
A
N
D
ARGENTINA
Ocean
E
S

Falkland Islands
(Islas Malvinas)
(administered by UK
claimed by ARGENTINA)

Stanley

Punta
Arenas

South America

17

ALRIGHT Plaid fans, it's time to get to our last sub-region of Latin America, the region/continent of South America. Makes it nice and tidy. South America is the fourth largest continent on the planet. A continent comprised of 12 countries, and fairly good-sized countries for the most part, which distinguishes them from the other subregions in Latin America, particularly in the Caribbean. Middle America is mostly dinky states, but there are full-grown countries in South America—including Brazil, which is the fifth largest country on the planet. So The Plaid Avenger always wants to ask the question: you have the United States of America up there in North America, why don't we have a United States of South America down here? Why are these distinct countries in South America not unified? The answer is, I'm not sure. From all practical standpoints, we should be looking at a much more unified entity down south of the border. Maybe that's where they are heading.

Why isn't there a US of South America? Many people would answer, "There are all these differences from country to country! Bolivia's got nothing in common with Peru or Chile or Argentina!" Many people would be wrong. What is it that's the same about these places? We already talked about a lot of these similarities back in the Latin America chapter. There's a common history here, a common colonial presence. Lots of commonalities with very few differences. Looking across the entire continent, there are only a couple major languages spoken. You really can't say that about any other continent besides North America (okay, maybe Australia . . . but isn't it more like an island anyway?). Portuguese spoken in Brazil, and Spanish spoken in the rest of South America along the western seaboard. There's not even a major difference in language. How about major differences in religion? Nope, they are all die-hard staunch Catholics, which we talked about in the Latin America chapter. Where are these differences? What's different here?

Machu Picchu Mucho!

We have to look a little bit deeper into the histories of these places to find any differences whatsoever. Let's look at a couple of major entities. In precolonial history there's the **Inca Empire** down here, as opposed to the Aztec up in Mexico, but like the Aztec up in Mexico, the indigenous cultures were largely wiped out, or denigrated fairly rapidly, after the introduction of the European colonial masters. Even that's not a separating factor; that's not why there is no United States of South America. How about independence movements? Did they all get up and run with different independence movements led by different folks in different places? No—in fact one guy led the independence movement all across South America, the George Washington of South America, **Simón Bolívar.** During the 1810s and the 1820s, he played a direct role in most of the independence movements in South America, and an indirect role in all the rest. So what is the difference? Why is this not the United States of South America?

The main man of South America.

PHYSICAL

Perhaps the main reason why we don't have a singular state in South America is because of the physical factors, specifically the terrain. If you look at the Rocky Mountain system up in North America, that's a pretty high range (highest peak at 14,000 ft., averaging in at about 10,000 ft.) but not enough to really separate things from east to west in the United States of America. It's a divider, but not a permanent divider. However, when we get down to South America, the Andes system running through the spine of South America is indeed a true divider, both culturally and physically. At roughly (highest 23,000 ft., 13,000 ft. average) 13,000 thousand feet high, it's a big divider. The Andes separate Chile, Ecuador, Peru, and Colombia from everywhere else, so there is not a lot of east-west movement or cultural interaction across the continent. We just talked about all these similarities that exist between these countries, and then there is this physical factor, which keeps things fairly divided.

The Andes: major continental divider.

On top of that there are a couple of other physical factors to consider, one being a physical term I want you to know: **escarpment.** What is an escarpment? An escarpment is a very abrupt change in elevation right off the coast. It's a common physical feature in South America and also Africa. Some of the best examples of this are the Brazilian Highlands and the Guyana Highlands up north. The Brazilian Highlands are in the southeastern quadrant of Brazil, but they lead all the way down to Argentina. The Guyana Highlands go all the way through into Colombia, Venezuela, Guyana, and the northern part of Brazil. This kind of abrupt change as you get off the coast means there's not a lot of coastal margin. A few miles inland, although it's not the Andes or high mountains or anything, there's a little jump of maybe a few hundred feet up to an elevated plateau.

Throughout history, this has kept the interior hard to get to because explorers or traders traditionally traveled on rivers through waterways to get into the interior of a continent. That's not the case in South America. Most of the places that have escarpments cause rivers to turn into waterfalls. Boats and waterfalls don't mix, so you'll have to figure out a new way in, conquistador! Unfortunately, your journey to the waterfall didn't really bring you in too far from the coast either. It's been historically hard to enter and traverse the continent. The Andes on one side of South America and the highlands or escarpments on the other side of South America give travelers a double whammy of difficulty. And that's just the terrain!

Remotely sensed Amazon—sweetness!

There's another difficult double whammy for any travelers, traders, and explorers, which is the climate and vegetation combo. When thinking of South America, the gut reaction that people have is rainforest, big rainforest, a bunch of damn monkeys running around in the rainforest! In large part, that is true. The

only river system that allows you to penetrate the continent at all is the Amazon River system. However, it's the one that coincides with the Amazon rainforest basin, meaning it's a damn jungle out there: the biggest continuous jungle in the world; the single largest acreage of rainforest on the planet. It's mostly throughout the northern part of the continent in Venezuela, Colombia, and Guyana. Brazil holds the biggest chunk of the rainforest, about 60 percent of the total. There's also some in Bolivia, some in Ecuador, some in Suriname, and some in Peru. But watch out; don't make the common mistake of thinking that all of South America is rainforest.

Keep in mind that South America is the 4th largest continent. The equator goes through the northern part of Brazil in the true tropical region. But South America spans all the way down to the tip of Tierra del Fuego, which is closing in on the Antarctic Circle. And there's almost every possible climate in between. In Argentina and Chile, you will find midlatitude climates like humid continental, humid subtropical, with temperate forests very much like the eastern seaboard of the United States. The Pampas, the grasslands of Argentina, are very much like the Midwestern United States. You've got the Atacama—it hasn't rained there in a hundred years—Desert in Peru and Chile. Over in Chile, there is even an area or two with a Mediterranean-style climate. This huge latitudinal range means South America has got a bit of everything, a huge diversity of vegetation and climate. It's not all rainforest.

It's a combination of the tough terrain: the Andes and the escarpments—manifesting themselves as the Brazilian Highlands and the Guyana Highlands—combined with thick jungle vegetation of the rainforest has served for centuries to keep people out of the interior, making it very hard to traverse the continent. The interior is sparsely populated, as you can see from our favorite Lights at Night image. Additionally, there is not a lot of communication and interaction from east to west, which is probably the main reason why there is not a United States of South America.

SOCIALLY SPEAKING

We have already talked about a lot of social factors across Latin America. Problems like poverty, wealth disparity, high urbanization rates, and landlessness all appear in South America, as well, and some of them manifest themselves in extreme ways. Is there anything different about South America? What's perhaps a little more unique about South American society in contrast to other places in Latin America?

Glad you asked! South America is a true melting pot, and Brazil is really the centerpiece of this. What's the Plaid Avenger talking about here? Well, like the Caribbean during the colonial period, there was a huge infusion of folks from Africa, who were slaves at the time. Brazil and the Caribbean were the two main destinations of African slaves back in the day. Between three and four million Africans ended up in Brazil, and five to eight million more in the Caribbean, in contrast to the half a million that went to all of the United States. We are talking about exponentially larger numbers of Africans, and it shows in the face of Brazil as well as in the culture.

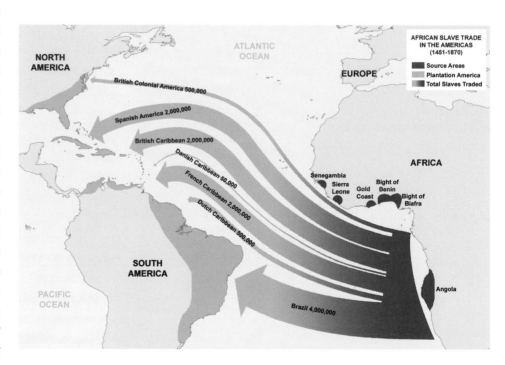

What does that equate to in today's world? There is a currently a significant African component in Brazil's culture as well as the rest of South America. Cultural input from the African continent added to the cultural fray in South America. What other continents are represented? We have the colonial masters themselves, the Portuguese and the Spanish. They have infused their culture into South America as well, through years of conquest and rule. Like the African flavor of Brazil, the European background is also very apparent in the way people look and speak, the music they create, and holidays they observe. You can see extreme manifestations of the European influence in places like Argentina and Chile.

This is not widely known here in the US, but during the 19th and early 20th centuries, there were huge infusions of Europeans to South America. We Americans tend to think of our country as the immigrant country, but not all of them came to the United States of North America. A bunch of them went down to South America. In places like Argentina and Chile, we see that there were significant numbers of Italian and German immigrants during this period of mass European movement. Even in the 21st century, you can run into the unusual phenomenon where entire villages speak only Italian or German.

The extreme manifestation of the Portuguese colonial heritage in Brazil is why their official language is Portuguese. The Spanish were everywhere else, and that's why they speak Spanish in the rest of South America. We have the African influence and we have the European influence. But there's one more: the indigenous influence. There were people hanging out in South America before the Spaniards and Portuguese got there. The Inca Empire was kicking ass down there for a while, and so were some other small native groups that were spread all over, similar in structure to Amerindians in North America, but also distinct jungle-dwelling native cultures as well. Indigenous peoples still make up a significant portion of South America's population today, as opposed to some other places in Latin America.

Hernán Cortés and Francisco Pizarro: Conquistadors of Chaos.

What am I talking about? South America being a big place and the Inca having a big Empire meant there were lots of folks already there. As we already pointed out, when the conquistadors got here, not only did they take over the hierarchical structure of the Inca Empire and the Aztec Empire of Mexico, but they also brought with them diseases that pretty much wiped out a huge component of the native populations all across Latin America, and across South America, in particular. Most natives of South America died long before they saw a white Spanish or Portuguese dude. However, there are still a lot of descendants of the indigenous peoples here, particularly in Peru, which had the highest concentration of indigenous peoples when the conquistadors arrived. That brings us to three main ethnic groups in the South American social mix, from three continents.

THE DARK SIDE

A theme that I didn't elaborate on in great detail in the Latin America chapter is the concept of racism, because it manifests itself in a greater extreme in South America than it does in other places. Racism is a very real part of South American society, where it's worse than anywhere else in the Americas. How is it more extreme here than everywhere else?

There is a direct correlation between how light your skin is and how well you are going to do in life, how easy life is going to be for you, how many times you might be arrested, or if you are going to get a bank loan. The lighter your skin is, the more doors are open to you. If you go into a bank to get a loan, you will probably get it if you have light skin. If your skin is very dark, then you probably won't. If you're walking down a street somewhere in a bad part of town and the cops roll by, they are probably not going to bother you light-skinned folk, but if you have dark skin, you're more likely to get harassed. It's true that we have racism in the United States, as there is some amount of racism in every society across the planet; but it's nowhere near as ingrained as it is in South America. The Plaid Avenger will put money on that. You can ask folks on the street there all day long and nobody will disagree with that statement. It is a very real and very visible part of life. Of course it's been outlawed; it's not legal at all, but it still exists. It's still the way it is.

The only exception to the very strict hierarchy of color is the indigenous population. They are at the bottom rung, even though it's not a direct skin correlation. You can clearly see that the indigenous folks are not as dark-skinned as say, someone with an obvious African heritage. Even though they aren't as dark, they have fewer rights and are looked upon as the lowest tier of society virtually everywhere in South America. If you look at a list of classes that are most impoverished, the indigenous will always be there at the top of that list. It's a hot button issue across all South America, and it's important because this manifests itself in today's world. Lots of these indigenous groups are fighting back for their rights. There was even a dude named Evo Morales of indigenous descent who just got elected to the presidency of Bolivia, the first indigenous president in South America since the Inca Empire. This is a very big step forward for the indigenous population.

These are very real factors that I want you to be aware of in order to comprehend what's going on and how the social world is slightly different in South America. But wait a minute! We're not done yet, because there is actually a fourth main ethnic group in South America. Along with the indigenous, the European, and the African influence, there's a visible Asian influence. Similar to the United States, there are folks that came across from Asia in the last 100 years. Perhaps not in numbers as large as those in the United States, but still significant and continuing to grow. I pointed out that the current president of Bolivia is of indigenous decent, but check out this recent president of Peru.

Evo Morales: "I used to grow cocaine. Now I'm President. Go figure!"

Alberto Fujimori demonstrates this other element of the diversity in South American society. Here is a guy of direct Asian persuasion who ends up being the president of a South American country. We'll see later on that Asia is playing a larger role in South America: China being the forerunner of all this. Chinese influence is permeating the continent as more and more Asian and Chinese folks come in. The situation looks much like what is happening in the United States. South America is a very diverse place with a lot going on, making it socially different; however, some aspects of its social hierarchy are not particularly nice.

"I used to be President. Now I'm under house arrest. Go figure!"

THE MAKING . . . AND UNMAKING . . . AND NOW REMAKING OF MERCOSUR

MERCOSUR (MERCOSUL)

▢ Member states
▢ Associate members

What do people do in South America for money? What's their GDP? What's hot and happening? They've got themselves a trade bloc just like we have NAFTA up here. We need to talk about trade blocs for a little while. This is perhaps one of the reasons that most of the countries in this region are not in the fully developed category. What comes out of South America? What do they do down there?

They are all about primary products, as you might imagine. They're just like the rest of Latin America in that respect. We get a lot of raw materials from South America like copper, iron, and tin. We already talked a lot throughout this book about what that means in terms of value. It doesn't equate to a whole lot. There is some industrialization there, but what cars have you gotten from South America? What computers? Do you know of any corporations that were founded in South America? It is increasing in today's world to be sure, but they certainly have not developed any fully industrialized societies for the last 100 years like Western Europe or the United States, and therefore, they are still seen as a provider of raw materials. Again, that's changing, but it's one of the reasons that they are not as rich as other parts of the world. What does any of this have to do with MERCOSUR?

MERCOSUR is the local trading bloc of South America. You see that the current MERCOSUR states are Brazil, Paraguay, Uruguay, and Argentina, with Chile as an associate member. The newest inductee was Venezuela, and perhaps others will follow. Why just these states for now, and why isn't there a United States of South America? We can't we even have a single trade bloc of South America like NAFTA?

We have talked a little bit about the physical differences, and those remanifest themselves here. Chile and Argentina are a classic example. Why are two countries that are next-door neighbors not big trading partners? The answer is the Andes. Why is Chile only an associate member of MERCOSUR? Because it actually trades more with the United States—it's too hard to transport stuff over to Argentina, but it's quite easy to put stuff on a boat and float it up to the United States, which has more money to spend anyway. That's one issue; the physical obstacles of the world do play a part in why this map looks the way it does.

Why are only the southern states of South America in this trading bloc? Physical barriers are one reason, but reality is the other. If you look at South America as a whole, as a pretty picture, it looks kind of like an ice cream cone. The Plaid Avenger wants you to remember that. South America is an ice cream cone, and if you were actually holding that ice cream cone, the cone part is Chile, Argentina, Paraguay, Uruguay, and southern Brazil. That's the cone; the ice cream is all up on top. Here's a term I want you to remember that will help you to understand what's going on in South America in terms of economic clout: **the southern cone.**

The reality of the South American continent is that most of the money is in the south. That's where the action is, where the economies are most developed. They're the places that are most industrialized, so they've got more to trade with each other; they have more in common. If you had to pick some place to go to in South America that was most like the United States, then you would probably pick Chile, Argentina, Paraguay, Uruguay, or Southern Brazil. Not northern Brazil, unless you want to take a ride on the gigantic mosquitoes and live in mortal fear of panther attacks. Southern Brazil is where you get that rich southern cone action.

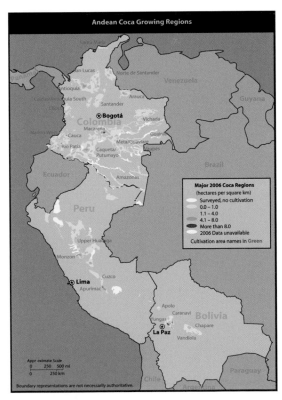

The ice cream up top isn't even ice cream, really. It's just a big ball of cocaine. As you see in this graphic, there is an inverse relationship in which the biggest cocaine-producing countries on the planet are the exact opposite of the MERCOSUR countries.

Coincidence? Probably not. It is a big deal. Why are these guys cocaine producers? Well, because the whole continent produces primary products, and one of the most profitable primary products to produce is something with a guaranteed market, with customers willing to pay whatever necessary. In short, cocaine or any other kind of drug is the way to profit from a primary product. Bananas don't get much money on the market, but cocaine gets a ton. Here's a fun fact: the street value of cocaine sold every year in America is somewhere around 35 billion dollars. You do the math and figure out why people make cocaine in South America. Colombia is the biggest cocaine state on the planet, but Peru, Bolivia, and Ecuador are not too far behind. It makes for a nice dividing line on the continent. We already said there's a physical dividing line, but this is kind of an economic dividing line as well. It has a lot to do with the current issues in South America—why things are the way they are.

Let's get back on point. MERCOSUR, like so many other trading blocs around the planet, is set up to encourage trade between the countries so their economies will grow and propel them further. There's also a point of pride here. This is something the Plaid Avenger wants you to know about as far as what's happening in South America: the real leader of MERCOSUR, if not South America as a whole, is Brazil. Brazil is a big proponent of MERCOSUR. Why is this? Brazil sees itself largely as the United States sees itself in NAFTA: as The Man.

Andean Coca Cultivation
Source: State Department International Narcotics Control Strategy Reports, 1996-2005

There is really no questioning that the United States is the real nucleus of trade with Canada and Mexico. Likewise, Brazil sees itself as the real regional leader in South America. It is the biggest country, the most populous, and has the biggest GDP. In the self-defining role of regional leader, they really want to perpetuate MERCOSUR and make it successful. MERCOSUR's growth makes Brazil grow as well, making its role in the world bigger, making South America a bigger and more prosperous, industrializing place.

Lots of countries in South America, particularly Brazil, are really keen on making MERCOSUR work. There has really been a rallying effect around the group in the last several years, especially since Hugo Chavez has been beating the drum for his continent-wide "socialist revolution" and economic independence from the US. Ten years ago, I would have said, "It's doing okay, but it's starting to go downhill." Five years ago, I would have said, "MERCOSUR is pretty much done, you can stick a fork in it." But my, my, my, how times change. What is the Plaid Avenger talking about here? They were done, but perhaps they are getting resurrected. How? About ten years ago, some new idea called the FTAA sprouted up.

FTAA. ¿QUE? THE BATTLE OF TRADE BLOCKS IN SOUTH AMERICA?

What the heck is the FTAA? The FTAA stands for the **Free Trade Area of the Americas.** I really want you to know this stuff and understand it because it plays a big part in what's happening in South America right now. The FTAA is something that has changed radically and flip-flopped completely in the last decade. Over ten years ago, the United States dreamt this up: a free trade area of all the Americas. This would be a free trade bloc like NAFTA, but for the entire Western hemisphere. How fantastic would that be? They held a meeting in 1994 in Miami. The heads of states for 34 democracies in the region, excluding Cuba, all got together and decided to do a NAFTA sort of thing. "This would make a free trade area, lower tariffs, and eliminate subsidies to protect our own industries. This will be great, and it will encourage trade across the whole hemisphere. We will kick ass in the rest of the world!"

Why would the United States lead this off? They are already the richest in the world, why would they care? Much like the little lesson we learned back in Western Europe, the EU wants to expand to include more member states and to include more economic activity to make themselves bigger on the world stage in order to be a real competitor. With this logic, the United States thinks ahead (something they don't do very often) and says, "Hey, we are the biggest economy in the world, but that EU is growing over there, and look at China! We should probably grow as well. Let's do this FTAA thing. We will make the largest free-trade bloc on the planet, and we will continue to lead the pack."

Not a bad idea. Ten years ago, all countries were at least partially on board, and many were avidly on board saying, "That's awesome, let's do it!" Several countries were more hesitant, but everybody said that free trade sounded like a good idea. Free trade typically means investment, which typically means increasing industrialization and all of the rest of the good things

The Three Amigos: socialists smacking down the FTAA.

NAFTA members   **CAFTA members**   **Proposed FTAA members**

that encompass growth. Everybody was at least a little onboard, if not fully. Eight years ago, President Bush was really hot on this and was pushing hard, saying, "Let's get ahead of schedule and start inking some of these trade agreements right now." In other words, "Let's get it on!" They set a target of 2010 for everybody to sign up.

Again, this is basically like NAFTA, but for everybody. Unfortunately for the Bush administration and the FTAA as a whole, other cards entered the picture here, one of them being Hugo Chavez of Venezuela. Hugo, as you might imagine, is an ally of Fidel. When their powers combine, they are two leftists who consider the United States an imperial power and look at the proposed free-trade areas as a vehicle for the United States to get more of what it wants while screwing over more poor people in Latin America. That's not a Plaid Avenger call, just what Hugo and Fidel were thinking. And then Evo Morales, another hard-core leftist, just joined their ranks when he became President of Bolivia, so the leftist socialist, anti-free trade, anti-FTAA ranks have been swelling. This movement has now attracted more than just the extremists.

Because more and more governments in Latin America are going to the left, this whole FTAA process has really been derailed. More and more folks have said that they are more hesitant about this now, and Brazil has already said, "Wait a minute, we have MERCOSUR already, let's grow this more." Brazil was opposed to FTAA from the get-go because it saw itself being removed from its role as the leader of South America. Brazil would just be another subservient state to the United States powerhouse in the FTAA schemata. Then we had Venezuela come onboard fully against it, and Fidel was already against it. In the last five years they have really turned this thing back around to the point that a few years ago Washington backed off on its push and said, "Okay, we will give up on the whole FTAA thing for right this second. We are not going to try and shoot for the deadline that we were originally shooting for. Let's just do free-trade agreements with individual countries, and then make it an official group later."

This has manifested itself *just in the last few years* as something called CAFTA. We already have NAFTA, which is the North American Free Trade Agreement. Now we have CAFTA, which is the Caribbean Area Free Trade Agreement that involves five different countries in Central America and the Caribbean. We already talked about this in the Caribbean section, but basically CAFTA is somewhere between NAFTA and the FTAA. It is the United States saying, "We are encountering too much opposition with the whole big deal right now, so we will start doing smaller deals and eventually conglomerate them all into a big group." This is the deal with FTAA; this is where it stands right this second. It has fully reversed itself in the last ten years—the momentum it had back then is all but gone right now, but we can only wait and see where it goes.

I am not jumping on the communist bandwagon with the lefties down there and saying that the FTAA is all doom and gloom and that it's horrible. Most people from the North American standpoint (and many business leaders in South America and Latin America as a whole) would say, "Hey, come on. The way out of poverty and the way to get richer is to encourage trade, which encourages business, which encourages job creation. What you guys should do, all you poor saps down in South America, is support this. This is going to be good for you!" It is very pro-business, but the conservative take is that pro-business plans will equate to better stuff for all of you once you get a job. This is one avenue towards growth.

The leftists on the other side of the political and economic spectrum approach the argument differently. They say, "No, we've been doing that for years. We've been trading and we've been selling our cheap commodities to the United States, and we're still poor as hell! We've got the greatest wealth disparity on the damn planet! Why are you suggesting that continuing this is going to help us?"

The Plaid Avenger's not telling you which side is right; there's never any right and wrong on stuff like this. You can't really prove either side. These are two options up for debate that are causing some friction. That's the battle currently happening within the FTAA that I want you to know about because this may swing back and forth over the next few years. Individual leaders of countries, some of them even leftists, have said, "Well, we're not sure that the FTAA as a whole is great or that the United States as a whole is a great entity for us personally, but certainly we would like to trade with them. We'll certainly sign a one-on-one free trade agreement with America." This is something that is not black and white. It is with Fidel and it is with Hugo, but it's not with most other countries. This whole story about FTAA ties to . . .

LEFTWARD SWEEP

This is the real deal of what's happening in South America right now, and it will have huge effects on how things down there in the future. We've referred to politics across the region in the Latin America chapter and every chapter since, and it's the same deal here. There is indeed a movement towards left-leaning governments. Not communist governments, because nobody is going to call themselves a Communist besides good ol' Fidel, but they are governments that are openly embracing and encouraging socialist ideologies. It is a more proactive socialism than anywhere else, even in Europe or the United States. We've talked about this before in various points in this book, this manual to understanding the world.

Pretty much every government is somewhere in the socialist category, even though we in the United States say we are hardcore capitalists. We say free trade is what we are all about. Yeah, that's true; it's all good, but don't we have welfare systems and unemployment benefits? Sure, we have all those things. We look out for members of our society on some basic levels. The Latin American governments, particularly here in South America, are now saying, "Yes, we are going even further down that road. We want to nationalize industries, like Venezuela, which controls their oil industry." It's not a private affair; the state runs it, and they are saying that their interpretation of socialism is they can use that money to build better schools and roads and hospitals. Private investment may come and build a business, but the state is going to be very proactive in helping people more rather than less. I am not going to lie: it's happening. Bolivia just nationalized their natural gas industry in May 2006.

The Plaid Avenger calls it like he sees it. This movement is gaining real momentum because of Chavez's success in Venezuela. His success has fueled his self-defined 21st century "revolution" in South America. What revolution?

Chavez is a guy who has totally embraced socialism. How has he been able to pull this off? The socialism thing is only working so well because his country produces massive amounts of oil, which we know is the crucial resource in today's world. The price of oil continues to go up, so every time you put five-dollar-a-gallon gasoline in your SUV, Hugo Chavez is being empowered. I am not making fun of the guy; I am not even making fun of oil companies. I don't give a damn. I just want you to understand what is going on.

In fact, I'm not so sure that we can say that his movement is even that successful there in Venezuela. Their economy outside of oil is pretty flimsy, and they have yet to make any big strides in infrastructure development or poverty eradication. Thus far, Hugo's bark is much louder than his bite, but boy, oh boy, can that dog bark. He has most successfully used all that oil wealth to make himself a loud voice on the global stage, making pledges of foreign aid to other countries and making speeches bashing the US, when perhaps his time would be better spent tending to business back home.

The main reason Hugo has been able to launch this socialist experiment is because his country was making shale-loads of money off of oil. Not all South American governments are in that category. His country is getting rich, and he was investing a lot of that money in schools, satellite communications to make his country's communications independent, building roads, building hospitals, and training medical folks. This is the fringe, the far leftist fringe of socialism. The state was doing all of this. Those are things that private businesses do in our country. He has been afforded the luxury of meeting some of those needs because of oil revenues.

But hold the phone, Hugo! Oil prices have taken a huge dump in the last year, which means Venezuela is not basking in the shade of hefty profits. Oops. That hurts Hugo's state-run plans, and Venezuela as a whole. Hugo's popularity is on the wane here in 2010. Too much rhetoric, not enough results, and it has become unpopular to bash the US as well since Obama's star power out-shines the Hugo hate. Hugo's time in the sun may be running out, but the movements towards a more united South America will probably continue, as we can see by the region-wide shift to the political/economic left here recently.

What's the Deal with the Bolivarian Revolution?

The **Bolivarian Revolution** is an ongoing mass social movement and political process started in Venezuela and is closely linked to its rabid leader, Hugo Chavez. Proponents of Bolivarianism trace its roots to an avowedly democratic socialist interpretation of the ideals of Simón Bolívar, an early 19th century Venezuelan and Latin American revolutionary leader (you know, the George Washington of Latin America) prominent in the South American Wars of Independence. He was the man. One of the main ideals of "Bolivarianism" is promoting the unification of Latin America into one country.

Simón in space?

This push for MERCOSUR could be interpreted as a true beginning stage of perhaps an entire South American trade bloc, which is what Hugo Chavez and his Bolivarian revolution is all about. Simón Bolívar wanted a United States of South America. Hugo Chavez is using all of his power and oil money to try to reestablish this whole movement of a United States of South America, and the movements toward the unifying trade bloc seem to be working. And the satellite?

The Simón Bolívar satellite, so dubbed by Hugo, was launched into

Keeping the revolution alive.

space in October 2008. The satellite provides broadcasts of Latin America news and entertainment, and is accessible to all in Latin America. Pretty interesting stuff. One last point of interest: Guess who helped build the satellite and launched it into space for the Venezuelans? If you said "the Chinese," proceed directly to GO and collect $200 from the bank.

The ideological sweep that's been occurring for the last decade has seen virtually all the governments of South America now going towards the left, more openly embracing the socialist take on how the world should work. Places like Argentina, which elected two consecutive left-leaning presidents, the Kirchners, which are actually a husband/wife tag team! Chile just elected their first female President, Michelle Bachelet, who is left-center. Peru, Ecuador, Uruguay, and Paraguay all now have leaders of the liberal left stripe. Brazil's Lula da Silva has just been put in for another term as well, a staunch man of the people, even though his economic and trade policies are nowhere near as hard core as his neighbors. Which neighbors? The aforementioned Chavez of Venezuela and Evo Morales of Bolivia as about as left as you can go without falling off the hacienda. We already talked about other places across all of Latin America, but this is a big trend and a new trend specifically for the big states of South America; this is a big deal.

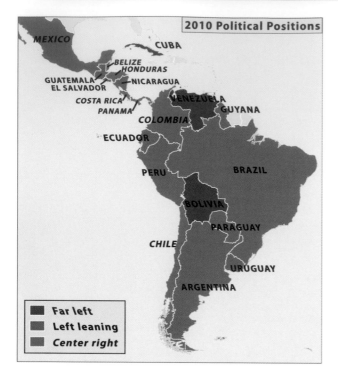

2010 Political Positions

Far left
Left leaning
Center right

It's such a big deal that a lot of folks around the planet, including world watchers like the Plaid Avenger, are starting to see South America really gaining its own identity on the planet, maybe for the first time. The region is doing something unique, and it is presenting an alternative to the traditional systems here in the 21st century. In the old world, you are either communist or capitalist, and everybody sided up. Everybody left in the middle was polarized to one side or the other. You had one or the other, and that's why you had a lot of US intervention and even Soviet intervention and influence in much of the world, including South America, Sub-Saharan Africa, and Southeast Asia. That's why the US fought the Korean and Vietnam Wars, over a battle of ideologies between communism and capitalism. It's why the US has also supported shady right-wing dictators in this part of the world.

That world is gone now, and Latin America, particularly South America, is filling the void with a new option. It is a region, with the voice of a singular entity, that is taking this socialist approach openly and more extremely than any other place on the planet right this second. A lot of folks around the world are looking at it and saying, "Hmmm . . . that's interesting. It is a new axis of power, so to speak, this leftward socialist axis of states." If MERCOSUR continues to strengthen, it will become the world's only "socialist" trade block! Interesting indeed! It's important to know about this if you're going to understand what's happening in the world.

Make no bones about it; Washington is not thrilled with this development. As has been pointed out already in the previous four chapters, Latin America as a whole has been historically viewed as the **backyard** of the United States. The backyard is increasingly slipping away from US control. Even the phrase "under US control" is completely inaccurate because it is not even "under US influence" anymore. Washington will not encourage all those policies of blatant socialist origin; it is not in the US's economic or political self-interest. There is a lot of concern and a lot of debate in American politics about "losing Latin America." The US has been focused on other parts of the world like the Middle East, and lo and behold, what used to be the US's subservient little stepchild of the south is now staunchly not.

That's a big deal. That is why we are talking about world regions. This is a place that's drastically different then it was fifty, twenty even ten years ago. It is a very different place that the US now has to deal with on entirely different terms. The leftward sweep can't be denied. Will it last? Nothing ever lasts, but it is here to stay for a little while at least. All of these leaders are new, and they are getting elected in some cases by radically popular consensus. This movement is not to be underestimated. This movement is sometimes referenced in the United States as the **pink tide.** Pink referring to pinko commie.

EL EXTREMO

That brings us to the end of this chapter and to a few closing comments about South America as a whole. The leftward sweep: can't be denied, it's making a big impact. New axis of power? You decide. Loss of the United States' backyard? If not a full loss, certainly trouble that the US is not prepared to deal with right now, manifesting itself in the leftward sweep and also in the derailment of the FTAA. Finally, we've got one thing left to discuss about South America, and it's got the US all hot and bothered: the influence of China.

China, as we will see when we talk about it several chapters from now, has a very savvy foreign policy in the world right now, as the Plaid Avenger sees it. Some would say they are very strategic in dealing with countries on a one-to-one basis to win them over, or as the US likes to say, "to win over their hearts and minds." China is doing it perhaps better

What's the Deal with Left vs. Right in South America?
A Summary:

1. Extreme left
2. US hates him
3. Democratically elected; won 60 percent of vote
4. US claims he is a threat to democracy and stability of the continent
5. US funds opposition parties to him, zero dollars given to government
6. Undeclared "leader" of leftist movement in South America
7. Country is massive oil producer; US buys most of the product

Hugo Chavez of Venezuela.

1. Extreme right
2. US loves him
3. Democratically elected; won 70 percent of the vote
4. US supports him as a close ally and a model of democracy
5. Through Plan Colombia, US has sent over 6 billion dollars to government
6. The only rightist leader in South America
7. Country is massive cocaine producer; US buys all of the product

Alvaro Uribe of Colombia.

than the United States right now. China is certainly more successful at winning the hearts and minds of the people in Latin America. What am I talking about? China is increasing its presence in South America. It is a minimal presence compared to the United States, as is their foreign investment in South America when compared to US investment. But it's a presence that is strategically increasing, day to day.

President Hu Jintao of China and his Premier Wen Jiabao have paid official state visits to every South American country, some of them multiple times in the last decade. President Hu has signed multiple trade and aid deals with everyone on the continent, particularly with Venezuela, for oil and energy resources, but also for agriculture commodities. The Chinese have an unquenchable thirst for raw materials, and they are doing their best to get the hookup from the Latin Americans. They really are on kind of a goodwill tour with South American

Hu's on first? Maybe heading for second base in South America . . .

countries; a lot of their investment comes with no strings attached, unlike the United States, who usually hands them a whole ball of string. Additionally, in 2009 China officially became a board member of the Inter-American Development Bank (the IDB is the biggest source of lending for development projects across all of Latin America) and contributed $350 million to bank programs. Very interesting development . . . oh, that pun is too good!

This Chinese influence is currently nowhere near US levels of involvement, investment, or trade, but the Chinese are gaining ground fast—leaving the US a little worried, and rightly so. Perhaps even more so because people like Hugo Chavez are encouraging it and saying they want to sell *all* their oil to China and not the United States. This is yet another thing to consider when you're trying to figure out what's happening in the world. There is Chinese influence, the FTAA, the BRIC, and the leftward sweep; consider what all this stuff means for South America and the world as a whole.

How far will the Bolivarian Revolution reach? I wouldn't start buying ammunition to repel the pinko-commie horde just yet. It appears that current US President Obama is moving quickly to reset relations and open new doors of dialogue with South America in an effort to establish goodwill and hemispheric harmony. He may have the goods to pull it off: after his keynote address at the OAS meeting in April 2009, he was roundly praised and backslapped by South American leaders, and even a Cheshire cat smiling Chavez ponied up to shake his hand! It will certainly be an interesting time ahead for our hemisphere.

SOUTH AMERICA RUNDOWN & RESOURCES

View additional Plaid Avenger resources for this region at http://plaid.at/s_amer

➕ BIG PLUSES

→ Huge continent absolutely packed with natural resources

→ World powers (China, Russia, US) are now courting the region big time to form economic and political collaboration. It's good to be wanted!

→ The region is increasingly defining itself on its own terms (as a center of alternative socialism, or as having their own foreign policy direction, or as distancing itself from the US) and doing so confidently

→ In particular, Brazil is becoming is an up-and-coming major world power player. Remember BRIC?

➖ BIG PROBLEMS

→ Internal economic integration, while growing, is still weak

→ Environmental degradation, particularly the of rainforest, continues to increase as the region industrializes and develop

→ Wealth disparity, endemic poverty (especially among indigenous groups), and landlessness still pervasive issues across the entire region

→ Despite billions of dollars from the US, the region (mostly Colombia) is still the largest producer and mover of cocaine

→ Political polarization across much of the region between leftist and conservative rightist elements always has potential to become flashpoint of violence; especially in Venezuela & Bolivia

DEAD DUDES OF NOTE:

Simón Bolívar: The "George Washington of South America": hero, visionary, revolutionary and liberator. He led Bolivia, Colombia, Ecuador, Panama, Peru and Venezuela to independence and instilled democracy as the foundations of all Latin American ideology.

Hernándo Cortés: The white dude that led the Spanish conquistadors into Mexico in 1519 to level the Aztec Empire in just a couple of years, and was the first wave of colonizers to lay claim to vast areas of the entire hemisphere in the name of the Spanish crown.

Francisco Pizarro: The other famous Spanish conquistador who (in the 1520s–30s) conquered and completely destroyed the other major civilization in the New World: the Incan Empire of South America.

LIVE LEADERS YOU SHOULD KNOW:

Hugo Chavez: President of Venezuela and self-proclaimed leader of the leftist Bolivarian Revolution of Latin America. Pushing hard for socialism, deeper integration of Latin American economies with each other, and pushing out US influence. Appropriately, he is despised by US.

Evo Morales: President of Bolivia, first indigenous dude to become so. Staunch member of the leftist/Chavez team, has nationalized lots of industries in his country, and also used to be a coca farmer!

Rafael Correa: President of Ecuador, highly educated economist and linguist who is also pushing hard for socialist reform and even an overhaul of how his country deals with international financial institutions too. Also on the Bolivarian Revolution train.

Lula da Silva: President of Brazil, the largest Latin American state by size, population, and economy too which is 8th biggest in world. Has overseen Brazil starting to gain a serious international political power position; a BRIC state that is increasingly speaking with an independent mind on many foreign policy issues, including Iran, who they support. Lula is definitely center-left, but not really on-board for the extremes advocated by Chavez, et al.

Cristina Kirchner: First female President of Argentina, a top 30 world economy, and, along with Chile, one of the most fully developed states in South America. Has attempted socialist reform in her country, and is a strong ally of leftist/Chavez team, although she maintains good relations with US and Team West.

Alvaro Uribe: center-right President of Colombia. Distinct in the region for being an open, 100% committed, ally of the US and no fan whatsoever of leftist policies of his neighbors. Gets billions form US to fight drugs and has semi-successfully "cleaned up" crime and corruption in his state, for which he has wide public support.

PLAID CINEMA SELECTION:

Cidade de Deus aka *City of God* (2002) HUGELY popular street crime in the slums of Rio De Janeiro that spans decades. Based on real events and real people. Great for showing life in the favelas and the evolution of Rio society, and try to remember this when watching: the primary 'hood location is the same throughout the film, but watch how it changes over time as Rio grows to envelope it.

Central do Brasil aka *Central Station* (1998) An emotive journey of a former school teacher in Rio, who write letters for illiterate people, and a young boy, whose mother has just died, in search for the father he never knew in Brazil's remote northeast. Fanstastic landscape/cultural shots show diversity of place as well as the diversity of Brazil's peoples and its social classes. A sentimental piece, but a crowd pleaser nonetheless.

American Visa (2005) Similar to many Latin American films, this film focuses on the idea of the American Dream. The film was set in La Paz, Bolivia and features many shots in and around the city. In attempting to gain an American visa and consequently falling in love, the film demonstrates the irony of looking on the outside for what can only be found inside.

Crónicas (2004) Murder/thriller/detective story starring John Leguizamo. Plot follows a journalist who attempts to uncover a murderer and a rapist, despite the potential danger. Set in rural Ecuador, film presents a great view of the local landscape.

Machucha (2004) Set in 1973, the film centers around a military of coup of the socialist government in Chile. Although not the central theme, film focuses on the oppression of the poor in Chilean slums through the filter of a rich kid. Successfully demonstrates how the monetary oppression of the masses makes other Chileans wealthy.

The Motorcycle Diaries (2004) Based on Ernesto "Che" Guevara's memoir, the film follows a 23 year old Che as he journeyed around South America. Throughout the film, the viewer is presented with real life landscapes, and paints a true portrait of Latin America. Interesting view of one of the world's most well known revolutionaries and the experiences that shaped him. Easily one of the best road trip movies of all time, and its based on real events.

Maria Full of Grace (2004) Wow. Insanely realistic and good. A pregnant Colombian teenager becomes a drug mule to make some desperately needed money for her family. Shows life/landscapes of Colombia and the inside guts of how the drug trade works . . . and more importantly, how good people get coerced into doing it.

Ônibus 174 aka *Bus 174* (2002) Documentary about a June 2000 bus hijacking in Rio de Janiero, Brazil that brings up disturbing issues about crime, drugs, violence, social justice, violence, and media ethics and responsibilities, just to name a few. Incredible aerial shot in the opening scene shows the staggering breadth of class disparity between the city's wealthy and impoverished areas.

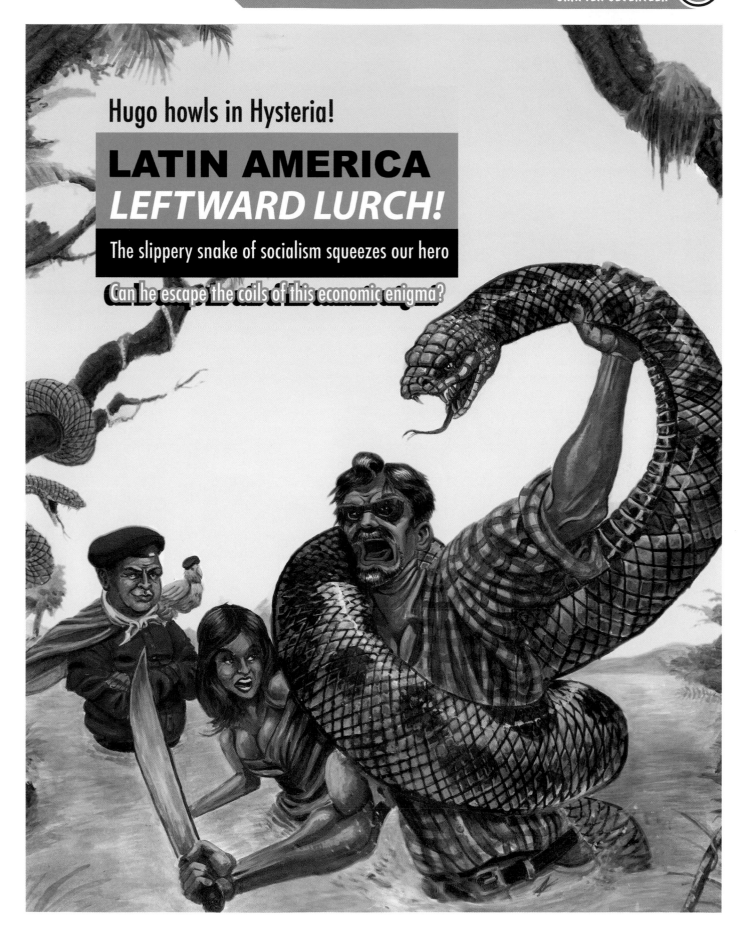

Hugo howls in Hysteria!

LATIN AMERICA
LEFTWARD LURCH!

The slippery snake of socialism squeezes our hero

Can he escape the coils of this economic enigma?

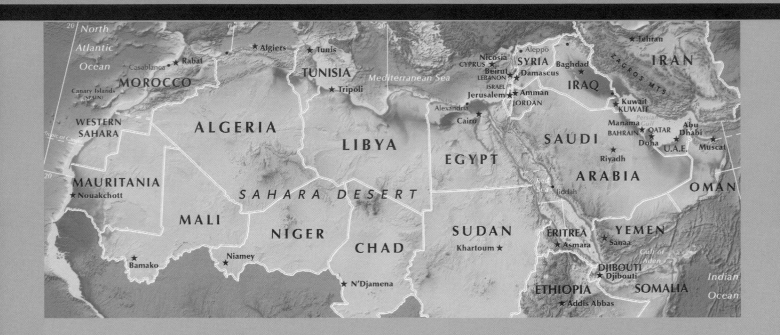

CHAPTER OUTLINE

Middle East and North Africa

18

THE Middle East is the hot spot of the globe and the thorn in the US's giant side. Everybody's watching the Middle East. Will there ever be peace in the Middle East? Hell no, there won't be peace in the Middle East. How did it get to be such a pain in the ass anyway?

WHERE IS THE MIDDLE EAST?

"Hello again, Mr. Avenger. Can I get you the usual?

I'm confused. Is the Middle East the center of the planet, the point from which everything emanates? Obviously not. So what's the Middle East in the middle of? Western Europeans defined the region with this term, as you might expect, during the Western European colonial era. The Western Europeans, of course, are in the west and all of Asia is to their east. China is as far east of Europe as you can get—thus the phrase "Far East." In between Europe and the Far East becomes, you guessed it, the Middle East. It's a term everybody in the world recognizes today that is just a historic artifact from a bygone era. So there you go, students of global history and current events, that's where the Middle East is—it's the middle of the old British Empire's known and controlled world at the time, several hundred years ago.

Where's the Middle East in the terms of the Plaid Avenger's world regions? There's a classic section of the middle of the Middle East, and that is the Arabian Peninsula, consisting of Saudi Arabia, Yemen, Oman, United Arab Emirates, Qatar, Kuwait, and Bahrain. We also add to this core area by including Jordan, Syria, Iraq, Iran, Lebanon, and Israel. These places

we would all definitely agree are in the center—indeed, the middle—of the Middle East. Everybody accepts that; it's the Middle East. However, we are going to expand the region for our definition to include most of North Africa as well. Places like Egypt, Libya, Tunisia, Algeria, Morocco, are all obvious players in the Middle East which share some homogenous traits, but also places like the Western Sahara, Mauritania, Mali, Niger, Chad, part of Sudan, Ethiopia, Somalia . . . now we're starting to split hairs. There's kind of a fuzzy line somewhere in the middle of these countries. Everything north of and including the Sahara Desert in Africa is kind of the Middle East as well. In addition, we could go into places like Turkmenistan, maybe Afghanistan.

We are in the "Middle"—but middle of what?

For the Plaid Avenger's book, we're going to put those in other regions. They have typically been included here, but we're going to hold off for now. Turkey has also been defined as part of the Middle East, but not in my world. So that's the core: North Africa and Southwestern Asia, from Iran in the east all the way to Morocco and Mauritania in the west, and everything in between. What's homogenous about all these places? What are the four big factors that are the same across all these territories? Are there some major exceptions to them?

There are four big factors that often come to mind when we think of the term "Middle East": desert, oil, Islam, and conflict. We're going to look at those four characteristics. We're also going to look at the history of the Middle East, to see how it got to be the way it is, why it's so far behind, and its explosive potential in the very near future.

FOUR FAMILIAR FACES OF THE REGION

Over 3000 miles of beautiful sun-baked sand.

As always, we will start with some physical attributes of this place, and then get to some cultural factors.

NUMBER ONE: IT IS DRY IN THE MIDDLE EAST

The physical world of the Middle East is obviously a very nice homogeneous trait to pick out. What is the first thing that pops in your head when asked, "Hey what's the climate like in the Middle East?" It's *dry*. Indeed it is. It is mostly desert; the big Sahara Desert is plopped down in North Africa. It is the largest hot desert on the planet. The United States would fit nicely into the Sahara, as you can see.

But, even outside of there, the Arabian Peninsula is mostly desert. When we get into Iraq, we think of desert in the southern parts of that country as well. Outside of the true desert regions, we have a lot of steppe. Steppe is just like adding a little bit

Rain in the Middle East occurs primarily during winter months; summers are so hot and dry, except in some northern and highland areas, that irrigation is necessary for most summer crops even where rainfall totals 20 to 40 inches.

Mean Annual Rainfall

Inches		
Under 10		Nomadic herding; no cultivation possible without heavy irrigation
10 to 20		Wheat, barley, sorghums, dry beans, olives, almonds
20 to 40		Winter vegetables, maximum grain yields
Over 40		Corn, tobacco

The mean annual rainfall for Washington, D.C. is 40 inches.

Most of the Middle East measuring in at much less than 10 inches—of rain, that is.

of water to the desert; there is some scrub vegetation, and that extends this dry region all the way to the borders that we have just defined. This is a dry place, though there are some exceptions.

These exceptions are along the Mediterranean fringe, where there is a Mediterranean style climate. There are some narrow bands of nice climate around the Mediterranean that are well-watered enough for agriculture. You also have the Fertile Crescent, a classic area of Biblical lore. The Fertile Crescent includes the Tigris and Euphrates river valleys, all the way over the Levant, which is now part of Syria, Lebanon, and Israel. It's a fertile, well-hydrated place. The Tigris and Euphrates rivers make up the old Mesopotamia river valley where western civilization actually started, and you can't have that without enough water. Let's add one more exception: Northern Iran. A lot of people don't know it, but believe it or not, up around the Caspian Sea, there are big plains of well-watered area. There are big grasslands that look like the Midwestern United States and can produce quite a bit of food. Even though Iran is mostly an elevated plateau and mostly dry, it has big areas that are well-watered. Those are the exceptions to the rule, but by and large, this is a huge area, and very much of it is very dry.

NUMBER TWO: THEY GOT OIL

The second homogeneous trait we think of when we consider the Middle East is *oil*. Indeed, this place does have some oil. If we look at proven reserves of oil on the planet, the Middle East has the lion's share. This is an equation that seems to be changing daily in the Plaid Avenger's world. As technology increases, the amount of extractable oil from dif-

ferent types of shales and tar sands changes according to extraction technology, and it is getting better and more efficient every day. As a result, it appears that other countries have more oil than the Middle East right now. Places like Venezuela, Canada, and Russia hold a lot in nontraditional oil reserves.

But for the sake of argument, let's just say for right now, in today's world, Saudi Arabia is the giant in proven oil reserves. That means they could stick a straw in the ground and oil

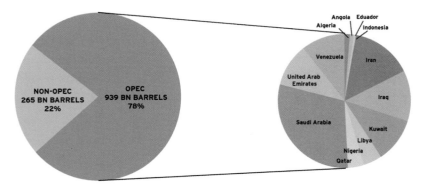

Wow! The Middle East gots the goods!

will come up—loads of it. Iran, Iraq, Kuwait, and the UAE have tons of oil as well. Here's the exception: As you get farther and farther away from the Persian Gulf Basin, which is the singular geological structure that all of these oil wells are tied into, the likelihood that you have lots of oil diminishes. As you go to the other side of Iran, into Central Asia, there's not a lot of oil there. As you go north out of Syria, into Turkey, there's not much there. South of Saudi Arabia, the far end of the peninsula, not much down in Yemen, and indeed, when you cross into Africa, Egypt's got some, Libya's got some, Algeria some as well, but nowhere near the levels of what the Persian Gulf Basin does. As a general rule, the further from the Persian Gulf you are, the less oil you have.

Oil plays such a tremendous role in the world now, and the Middle East has so much of it. That's why this region is such a focal point of global events. As the Plaid Avenger's writing this in May of 2009, the price of oil has plummeted from its all-time-high of $130 a barrel in July 2008 to just under $70 now . . . but it remains the cornerstone of world energy use, and therefore the engine of the world economy, so we need to talk about oil a little bit more.

Petroleum use can be traced back to at least the 4th century CE when the Chinese literally began drilling for oil with bamboo pipes. The Chinese used this oil to light lamps and to produce salt by evaporating seawater. Petroleum was also utilized early in history by the Persian Empire (now Iran). However, petroleum use was slow to spread to the West. Instead of crude oil, most Western street lamps were lit using whale oil—which, as the name suggests, is harvested by dudes in boats with spears. Whale oil was the primary source of artificial illumination and lubrication until American Edward Drake "discovered" oil in 1859 (sorry, China!).

The petroleum industry in the West began as a means to produce kerosene, which was used to fuel lamps. Enter the automobile. Once the automobile came on the scene, gasoline became the most popular petroleum derivative. Gasoline was abundant and cheap for almost a hundred years. For much of this time, the United States was self-sufficient in oil production. Slowly though, America evolved into a car culture; advanced interstates were developed and everyone rich moved to the suburbs. The United States became highly dependent on foreign imports of oil. Even this wasn't that big of a problem, because the United States propped up dictators in almost every major oil exporting country. This all changed in 1973.

In 1973, the US and Western Europe supported Israel in a war (explained below) against other Arab states. The

Oil: source of world energy, world conflict, and world lubrication!

result: the Arab states got all pissed off. One country that was definitely pissed off was Iran. Iran and several Arab states decided to have an oil embargo. They understood their position of oil supremacy and they said, "Okay, since you helped out Israel, we're not going to sell you any more oil. How about them apples?" Indeed, in a matter of days, and certainly the course of a few weeks, the price of oil went up from $3 to $12 a barrel. It may not seem like much, but that's an instantaneous quadruple in price. Ask your parents or your grandparents about this deal—they probably remember. The result of this in the United States was gas rationing. You could only go to the gas station to fill up your car on even or odd numbered days, depending on the last digit of your license plate number. This was a big deal—it caused serious economic ripples around the world, damaging the economy of the US and elsewhere. This was something that people remembered.

Even after the 1973 oil embargo ended, oil prices continued to climb. People realized that petroleum was a finite resource and that one day, it would run out. The future of petroleum production is open to debate. Most agree that the production capability has peaked in almost all non-OPEC nations (except Russia). Experts have continued to warn about the imminent peak in global oil production. However, the oil industry has such shady accounting practices that no one really knows how much anyone else has, much less how much is left globally. There are also other methods to produce gasoline if crude prices become exorbitant. These include the gasification of coal or natural gas and extraction of tar or other impurities. The Plaid Avenger endorses ethanol as an alternative fuel, mainly because it makes a great cocktail.

Technology will increase in order to find new ways to get to other sources of oil, and get it out of the ground cheaper. I'm telling you this story, in summary, because this is why OPEC's best interest is typically to keep oil prices very stable. Just the same way a crack dealer is with their product: keep it steady, keep it stable, so you can keep them coming back. You don't want people to overdose and you don't want them to go dry and get cured of their addiction. You don't want to price yourself out of the market, and you don't want people to die. To keep the oil price stable is in OPEC's best interest; and that's exactly what they've been doing for years.

Not all OPEC countries are in the Middle East. As you can see from the map above, places like Nigeria, Venezuela, and Indonesia

OPEC NET OIL EXPORT REVENUES AT A GLANCE

| Country | Nominal Dollars (Billions) | | |
	2006E	2007E	2008E
Algeria	$45.1	$51.6	$70.4
Iran	$54.8	$58	$82.5
Iraq	$32	$37.7	$59.8
Kuwait	$50.9	$55.3	$80.2
Libya	$36.1	$41.3	$56.1
Nigeria	$53.2	$56.6	$69.8
Qatar	$24.6	$26	$38.1
Saudi Arabia	$184.2	$196.7	$285.5
UAE	$56.7	$62.4	$89.1
Venezuela	$42.3	$45	$58.7
All OPEC total	$618.6	$682.2	$968

Source: Energy Information Administration

High gas prices for you equals money in the bank for them.
E = earned, F = forecast.

are OPEC members. They are all making serious jack, as you can see on this chart—about 522 *billion* US dollars in 2006 alone. Just on oil.

When we think of oil in the Middle East, we invariably think of another thing, and that's OPEC. As you can see from the box, OPEC is a cartel whose sole reason for existence is to stabilize and control the price of oil. Many in the United States and the world abroad would say, "Oh, they are going to use that as a tool against us." By and large, OPEC has been a stabilization force for the price of world oil. It is in their best interest in Saudi Arabia, and every other oil producing country, to keep the price stable, and they know it. Here's why:

What's the Deal with OPEC?

The Organization of the Petroleum Exporting Countries (OPEC) is an oil cartel designed to regulate the supply and, therefore, the price of crude oil in the global market. In the United States, cartels are prohibited by antitrust laws and are often called "monopolies." However, international cartels such as OPEC are both legal and successful. The goal of any cartel is to regulate the supply of a commodity (for OPEC, this is oil). By restricting the supply, a cartel is able to control the price of the commodity (again, for OPEC, this is oil). Cartels prevent the biggest producers from attempting to out-produce each other. If too much oil is being produced, prices drop and all oil producing countries are hurt. Oil is a finite commodity; OPEC sees its role as rationing the reserves to ensure constant supply for consumers and maximum profits for producers.

OPEC was founded in 1960 by the big five—Iraq, Iran, Kuwait, Saudi Arabia, and Venezuela—to protest against lowering prices. At this time, foreign owned oil companies such as British Petroleum and Dutch Shell were taking the lion's share of profits from oil production in the soon-to-be OPEC nations. Over the years, OPEC became more powerful and more unified (even playing a critical role in the 1973 US oil embargo). Currently, OPEC nations possess approximately 66 percent of the world's proven oil reserves and supply about 40 percent of the total oil production, including half of all the global oil exports. In other words, OPEC has the power to COMPLETELY shut down the global economy, although this would also clearly hurt the member nations.

	Top World Oil Producers, 2007* (*OPEC members in italics*)	
	Country	Total Oil Production** (million barrels per day)
1)	*Saudi Arabia*	10.22
2)	Russia	9.87
3)	United States	8.46
4)	*Iran*	4.03
5)	China	3.91
6)	Mexico	3.50
7)	Canada	3.42
8)	*United Arab Emirates*	2.95
9)	*Venezuela*	2.67
10)	*Kuwait*	2.62
11)	Norway	2.57
12)	*Nigeria*	2.35
13)	Brazil	2.25
14)	*Algeria*	2.17
15)	*Iraq*	2.10

Table includes all countries total oil production exceeding two million barrels per day in 2007.
**Total Oil Production includes crude oil, natural gas liquids, condensate, refinery gain, and other liquids.*

However, there are several major oil producers who are not in OPEC. These suppliers—notably Russia, Canada, the United States, Mexico, China, and Norway—are able to fluctuate their production with increasing or decreasing demand. So, when oil prices are high, Russia (for example) cranks on the spigot and starts selling more oil at the inflated prices. When oil prices drop back down, Russia turns production back down. By doing this, Russia is able to capitalize on the market fluctuations of oil. OPEC countries, since they agree to limit their production, do not get to sell more oil when prices are high. This again, however, is the purpose of OPEC. If all oil producers could crank up production when prices were high, they all would. This would create a huge market surplus in crude oil and prices would instantly plummet. In this sense, Russia and other non-OPEC nations are free-riders on the OPEC regulatory system.

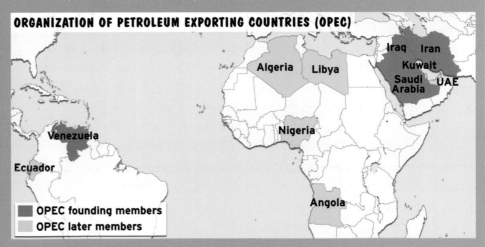

ORGANIZATION OF PETROLEUM EXPORTING COUNTRIES (OPEC)

Age of the Caliphs

■ Expansion under the Prophet Mohammad, 622-632

■ Additions during the Patriarchal Caliphate, 632-661

□ Additions during the Umayyad Caliphate, 661-750

Avars Peripheral peoples

— Present international boundary

From 600 AD onwards, Islam sweeps the region!

NUMBER THREE: THE MIDDLE EAST IS ISLAMIC

What else do we think of when we think of homogeneous traits of the Middle East? Perhaps this should be number one, but we definitely know that in the Middle East, they're overwhelmingly *Muslim*. Indeed, the predominant religion is Islam across all of the countries that I've thrown into this region. We could push it on further and could say Central Asia is predominantly Muslim and Afghanistan and Pakistan, but those are different cultures. They are so culturally different from the Middle East that not even the fact that they're Muslim can make us include them in this chapter. How Islamic is the Middle East, and how'd they get to be that way?

Here's a quick summary. The movement of Islam started in this region, right in the middle of the Middle East, on the Arabian Peninsula. There you have Medina and Mecca, the two holiest cities of Islam, where the prophet Muhammad transcribed the holy book from Allah (Allah = God). Islam then expanded outward from this core in Saudi Arabia, in what can only be defined as an Arab/Islamic Empire. You may have never heard of that term before, but take it from the Plaid Avenger, it's a good way to put it. Saudi Arabia, as you might expect is Arab, and because this is also an Islamic movement, I think it's a fair assessment to call the expansion of this political/religious entity the Arab/Islamic Empire.

After the death of the prophet Muhammad in 632 AD, you can see that they expanded outward across all of what's now North Africa, into what's modern day Turkey, Central Asia, and South Asia in very short order, in a matter of a few hundred years. That's how the empire grew.

Was everybody happy within the empire? Not exactly. There was some disagreement amongst Muslims about the faith, resulting in some subdivisions of Islam, the two main ones being Sunni and Shi'a. There's a third that not many know about called Sufi. Definitely check out where the major groups of Islam are located—especially the Shi'ites, as they are the minority sect of the religion. Most Muslims from virtually all parts of the world outside of Iran and Iraq are of the Sunni sect. Sunni is the vast majority.

The superfluous Sunni–Shi'a schism.

SUNNISM, SHI'ISM, AND WHY IRAQ IS SCREWED

When the prophet Muhammad died, Islam as a movement was left without a clearly identified successor/leader. The two major branches of Islam—Sunni and Shi'a—were formed in response to this dilemma. Sunni Muslims believe that Muhammad died with no intention of appointing a successor. Because of this, Sunni elites chose Muhammad's councilor and father-in-law Abu Bakr as the first Caliph (leader of Islam). There was a steady stream of Caliphs until the collapse of the Ottoman Empire in 1923 and there haven't been any since. Conversely, Shi'a Muslims believe that a dude named Ali, who was also Muhammad's cousin, was chosen by Muhammad (before his death) to lead Islam. Ali became the First Imam—roughly translated as "leader." Besides this, the differences between Shi'ism and Sunnism are minor.

Today, Sunnis make up approximately 85 percent of the world's Islamic population. Shi'as make up only 15 percent and are concentrated mainly in Iran (90 percent of population), Azerbaijan (75 percent of population), and Iraq (70 percent of population). This is highly important in Iraq today because the Sunni minority was in power under Saddam Hussein, even though his reign was highly secular. Since the United States crushed Saddam, the Shi'ites have a clear advantage in democratic politics. Much of the violence today in Iraq can be attributed to sectarian violence (i.e., Sunnis fighting Shi'ites) and is concentrated in the "Sunni Triangle" (where the minority Sunni population lives). Sunnis are afraid that if they lose power entirely, then the Shi'ites and Kurds (Kurds are typically Sunni, but represent an ethnic minority) will marginalize and/or discriminate against them.

Geographically, Iraq can be viewed as a tub of Neapolitan ice cream. The chocolate-flavored Kurds live up north, the strawberry-flavored Shi'ites live down south, and the vanilla-flavored Sunnis live in between; also, there is a lot of unin-

The Iraq Sundae

habitable desert—or dessert!—that doesn't neatly fit the Neapolitan ice cream model. Why doesn't the country just split up into three smaller countries, or at least into self-governing districts? Oil, oil, oil—and power politics. Most of the oil is in the Shi'a south, so if the country broke apart, the Sunnis and Kurds would be instantly poor. The international community is also afraid that Iran (Shi'a) and Saudi Arabia (Sunni), the strong neighbors of Iraq, would support their respective religious factions and cause a Balkans-style bloody war. Also, there are Kurds in Turkey who want an independent state of Kurdistan. Basically, Iraq is a mess.

Iraq isn't the only place that has some Sunni-Shi'a friction, it is just the hotspot of current conflict which reflects this friction. In fact, we can back up and examine the entire region as having a bit of cultural clash based loosely on opposing teams of which can be defined, in part, by their Islamic sect differences. More on that later. First, let's get back to school, because school is cool!

Here is a better map of the mess.

OLD SCHOOL OR NEW SCHOOL ISLAM?

The other thing to consider: most of the Middle East is Islamic, but how conservatively or how liberally do they interpret Islam? With any religion on the face of the planet, you can have people who are real reactionaries, ultraconservative, or you can have people who are a little more, oh, how should I put it, free thinking, a little more open to change in the modern world. Of course, most people are usually somewhere in between. I'm pointing this out because it makes a tremendous amount of difference in daily life, country to country. Even if the whole region is Islamic, there's extreme variation from one state to the next. Let me give you an example.

In Saudi Arabia, perhaps *the* most conservative state in terms of Islamic interpretation, there are lots of things that are completely accepted as part of common Islamic life which are different in other places. They strictly follow Sharia: the old-school Islamic code of law. They enforce legal and social restrictions for women, meaning women have to typically ask for permission to marry, travel, to drive, to leave the country, get a job, and go out in public. In Saudi Arabia, there is also a strong tradition of capital and corporal punishment, meaning if you get convicted of a crime, you can be killed, have your hands or feet amputated with a huge sword, or get whipped, depending on your crime. That's a pretty conservative interpretation.

In other parts of the Middle East like Tunisia, none of those things really apply. There may be some elements of Islamic law that you can see, like the Islamic dress code. Every place else is someplace in between. It's like labeling them all Christian, or all Catholic. Not all Catholics in the world are the same. Go look at some Catholics in Haiti who are doing voodoo, versus Catholics in Italy who are really uptight. There's a lot of variation in how liberal or conservative countries are within the Middle East.

Most of the Middle East is Islamic, and that's the end of that story . . . oh okay, you got me; there are substantial Christian minorities in some countries such as Egypt, Syria, and Ethiopia in particular. But that's about it . . . right? Oh hell no! Wait a minute! There's one other exception of note, and it is a big, big, exception indeed. Every place in the Middle East is Islamic except Israel: the Jewish state of Israel. Boy is this a convoluted mess, and the Plaid Avenger's going to have to give this one a full page! But we will wait for the Team Play section in chapter 18A, Addendum to get to that. First, let's have a little fun identifying our Middle East Muslim leaders in a little game I like to call Sunni, Shi'a, or Sikh?

SUNNI, SHI'A OR SIKH?

Instructions: Of the following world figures, tell me what state/group they lead and what type of Muslim they are. But watch out! A wild card Sikh has been thrown in to increase the challenge, and fun, of this game that is sweeping the nation!

Mahmoud Ahmadinejad
President of

_____

Sunni, Shi'a or Sikh

Hamid Karzai
President of

_____

Sunni, Shi'a or Sikh

Susilo Bambang
President of

_____

Sunni, Shi'a or Sikh

Muammar Qaddafi
Colonel & Honorable
Leader of _____

Sunni, Shi'a or Sikh

Hosni Mubarak
President of

_____

Sunni, Shi'a or Sikh

Saddam Hussein
Ex-President of

_____

Sunni, Shi'a or Sikh

Recep Tayyip Erdoğan
Prime Minister of

_____

Sunni, Shi'a or Sikh

Asif Ali Zardari
President of

_____

Sunni, Shi'a or Sikh

Osama bin Laden
Leader of

_____

Sunni, Shi'a or Sikh

Manmohan Singh
Prime Minister of

_____

Sunni, Shi'a or Sikh

Abdullah Al Saud
King of

_____

Sunni, Shi'a or Sikh

Ali Khamenei
Ayatollah & Supreme
Leader of _____

Sunni, Shi'a or Sikh

NUMBER FOUR: PEACE IN THE MIDDLE EAST

Which leads us to the last homogenous trait which defines the Middle East and that fourth factor is CONFLICT. The Middle East is a region defined by conflict. I've already said this about Central America, a pretty small region in between North and South America, and that does apply. Central America is a violent arena, but perhaps no other place on the planet right now has so many current active conflicts: interstate conflicts (countries fighting countries), intrastate conflicts (people within a state fighting each other), and maybe the worst, foreign sponsored conflicts (US war in Iraq). This place is a mess, and here's the worst part: They aren't out of the woods yet. They've got a long 21st century of conflict ahead of them.

Old School Ottoman.

"Gosh, Plaid Avenger, how could you make a projection like that? Aren't you just being negative? Couldn't things get better?" Quick answer: NO! They're not going to get any better anytime soon! Not in my lifetime. Things may simmer down in a couple of places, but the region as a whole will be mired in conflict for some time to come and it could get fairly nasty before it's done, as if it's that clean right now. What are we talking about here? Let's back up the oil tanker and start at the beginning. Why is this place mired with conflict? We just talked about Israel; let's take it further back than that, all the way back to WWI.

World War I saw the demise of the Ottoman Empire. We'll look into more detail of the Ottomans in the next regional chapter of Turkey. For now, just know this: The Ottoman Empire controlled what is now the classic Middle East, the Balkan Peninsula in Europe, and expanded over a lot of North Africa, and even controlled territory in what's now Iran. However, they were an empire in decline coming into the modern area. The Ottomans were an old-school style state going into the 20th century. They were way behind the technological times, their economy sucked, and they still had a sultan on the throne. People in Europe really looked at the whole Ottoman Empire as a redheaded bastard stepchild that none of them wanted to deal with. Nobody wanted to take the time to whip them, much less do anything else with them. The Ottomans looked around for an ally, and leading into World War I, they said, "Hey, Britain, would

Ottomans: the last big Muslim Empire to dominate the Middle East.

you be our friend? Hey, France, would you be our friend? Somebody be our friend, because we're worried Russia's going to invade us!" The Ottomans had several incursions with Russia at this point in history. Finally, somebody said, "Sure, Junior, we'll be your friend," and that was the Germans.

Long story short, the Germans lost World War I and their ally, the Ottoman Empire, lost with them. Something happened here, which many historians would say is the critical reason why you have such tremendous conflict in the Middle East today. A guy wrote a book about it called *The Peace To End All Peace: The Fall of the Ottoman Empire and the Creation of the Modern Middle East* (David Fromkin, 1989). Although a fairly dry read, if you can get through it you'll understand why. The title says it all; the peace process at the end of World War I subdivided the Ottoman Empire and drew arbitrary boundaries in such a way as to basically *ensure* that everybody would be pissed off at everybody else *forever!* Wow. I know it seems impossible, since we're talking about something that happened ninety years ago.

Let's fast-forward to today's world. "Still looks pretty good, Jim. What do you think from your angle?" "Yep, they're still pretty pissed off at each other!" Again, it's not the entire reason; it's not the only thing going on here, but it is the start of the problems in the Middle East. What do I mean by arbitrary boundaries? Look at Iraq, that's a great one, someone drew the damn country with a T-square—they're not based on any natural or ethnic divisions. Somebody *drew* them. That somebody was the winning powers at the end of World War I, mostly the British and the French. They subdivided up the old Ottoman Empire, saying, "You lost, you suck, and we want to make sure you don't come back and start a fight with us again, so we're going to parcel you out into smaller pieces. So let's see. Somebody get out a ruler. Okay, there's Iraq, good straight lines. Jordan, that's some good straight lines. Syria, yeah. Saudi Arabia, kind of an ethnic group there, we'll give you guys Saudi Arabia. Egypt, there's the T-square."

What you had at the end of this process was Turkey; in today's world, the remnants of the core of the Ottoman Empire, which was technically left intact, and all the other countries were divided up as I explained. Most of these countries were not given outright independence. Some, like Saudi Arabia, were semi-independent even under the Ottomans. But most of them were put in a situation where they were called **mandates.** Primarily the British and the French, and some other players in there as well, weren't so much overlords, but more like the big brothers of the new Middle Eastern countries. Egypt and Iraq

Europeans take over from the Ottomans; use of T-square is evident.

were mandates of the British, as were trickier territories like Palestine and Transjordan. Syria and Lebanon were mandates of the French.

In those cases, Big Brother basically said, "Here's what you need to do; we're going to put people in charge. We'll protect you militarily, but we'll also basically run the show." I can tell you with certainty, after reading that book and others, that a lot of people in the Middle East were immediately incensed, and outright pissed off, about this. In fact, places like Syria, a place that the US would like to bomb right now in today's world, *asked* the United States to take over their territory as a mandate. They *wanted* to be a mandate of the US. Wow, how bizarre is that. The United States, which participated in World War I, said, "We don't want anything to do with that mess over there." Boy, don't they long for the good old days of the Middle East

Watch out for the pyramids!

when the US didn't want to get involved. World War I is the launching pad for dissent in the Middle East. Let's take it up to World War II, shall we? The fun's not over yet!

Not only do we start with foreign influence and foreign dominance by the British and the French, we also have these artificial borders. It's incredibly similar to European colonialism, but not quite the same. In World War II, the Middle East as a whole does not get very involved. There is some fighting on their soil, but by and large, they stay out of it. The Germans did have their North African campaign—go look up The Desert Fox, what a bad-ass—so things got a little messy, but it was more of an influence thing and no one really sided up. The Allies said, "Hey, don't side up with the Germans, and we won't invade you." By and large, that's the way it went down.

However, it's when we get to the Cold War where things start to get tricky. The Cold War came to the Middle East like every place else on the planet, with the US and the Soviets vying for influence. The Soviets were pushing for influence in places like Iran and Turkey for years at this point. It became a Cold War battleground for influence, which set people against other people. The US supported questionable characters in any effort to make sure they didn't have Soviet influence. One place in particular that springs to mind is Saudi Arabia, which is an entrenched monarchy. Totally not democratic, totally the antithesis of everything United States stands for, but that's the effect of Cold War; support anyone as long as they don't go commie. Saddam Hussein is another classic example of western forces supporting a total dictator simply so he wouldn't turn to the Russians. Boy oh boy, did we pick a winner on that one. Another one of particular note is some guy called the Shah of Iran, who was basically a dictator who the US supported for quite some time, again, just to counter Soviet influence. You can read about him a little later in the Team Persia section.

We're still under this banner of conflict, still in the Cold War era, but there were also internal wars in Sudan, Yemen, Lebanon, and Chad, interstate wars between Sudan/Libya, Iraq/Kuwait, Eritrea/Ethiopia, and Iran/Iraq, and even international interventions into Somalia, Iraq, and Lebanon. Let's not forget the multiple Arab-Israel conflicts, which we'll get to momentarily.

You've got religious strife, ethnic strife, territorial border wars, and ideological wars all happening here in the last fifty years. Wars between states, wars within states, wars involving troops from outside the region altogether. What a mess. This really gets at the heart of the world's perception of conflict in a lot of these countries. Western support of

Israel, including its attempts to establish a peace process, manifestations of Islamic extremism, factional infighting between Sunni and Shi'ite, the war on terrorism; all these have now involved the outside world even more. The issue of Israel and the War on Terror in particular make this region unique on the planet because the globe is a player whether it wants to be or not. Conflict is endemic; it has been and will be a defining feature of the Middle East.

WHY ARE THESE GUYS SO FAR BEHIND?

Now that we've looked at a bunch of homogeneous traits of why we define this area as a region (and some major exceptions), the Plaid Avenger wants to take a little step back in time again, but for a different reason. I'm not just going to look at conflict. Why is it that the Middle East is behind in the world? Yes, there are *some* countries that have *some* money. There are even some countries that look kind of rich, but let's call a spade a spade. There are a few countries that have a ton of oil and really not much else going on. Looking at these countries demographically and economically in terms of economic diversity and standards of living for the average man, you will find that they are far behind on the development path. Like South America, this is a place of wealth disparity, where very few people own an excessive amount of resources. In this case, the rich people own oil resources, but the vast majority of folks have virtually nothing. This is compounded by the physical world, which makes it very hard to just go out and be a laborer or farmer. It's a desert! What are you going to do, farm sand? It's a pretty extreme environment and a place that's fairly far behind by any standards.

The Plaid Avenger's question is: Why is that? What has happened here? How is a region that is right beside the fully developed Europe so far behind? If we go back and look in our own neighborhood, we see that the United States is a fully developed country, and Mexico is not quite as developed. We already pointed that out, and it's absolutely true, but they're not as far behind as the Middle East. How can a neighbor of a fully developed region be so far behind? In other words, how did the Middle East get left behind? Here's a brief run through of history that makes a whole lot of sense out of this region's condition.

It's a combination of several factors, which come together about 500 years ago. Up until this point in history, the Ottomans were a pretty kick-ass empire. They were a powerhouse. The Ottomans took over and ran with the Arab/Islamic Empire and continued the expansion. They were actually beating down Europe's door. The Ottoman Empire attacked Vienna, Austria on multiple occasions; that's how far they encroached into Europe. They were large and in charge. At this point in history, it was the Ottomans and the Middle East that had the highest centers of learning, some of the oldest universities. Most of the true breakthroughs in scientific technology, from the 1100's to the the 1400s, were in the Middle East, not Europe. This is where we reach a critical phase, because at the exact time that Europe was entering its Renaissance, when it started to blossom around the 1500s, the Middle East started to fall behind. Why is that? There are several main reasons.

REASON NUMBER ONE: PHYSICAL OVERLOAD

We've already defined the Middle East as a physically challenging place. It's dry, and as such, it's very easy to overfarm, overgraze, use too much water, and make even drier. Unlike Europe, where people had not been hanging out there for very long, in the Middle East, you've had people hanging out forever! The Middle East is the birthplace of western civilization. You've heard of Mesopotamia? All the Biblical stuff you've ever heard of, you can look at the Jewish Torah, the Christian Bible, and the Islamic Koran. It's all in the Middle East. People have been here for a long time. Western Civilization, that is people building cities, towns, craftsmen, agriculture, all of that happened in the Middle East, not Europe. It spread to Europe much, much later.

The reason I'm telling you this is because civilizations amount to thousands of years of people using stuff. From around 6,000 or 5,000 BCE, people have used trees, grown crops, mined minerals, and used water and other resources. For thousands of years! Dry climates are easy to abuse, so by 1500 CE, the land is exhausted. Thousands of years of resource depletion take its toll, and the Middle East has simply run out of stuff, just as Europe *starts* to use its stuff. Also, there are critical resources that this region never had in the first place: coal, for instance. Coal, steel, and water were the engine for industrial growth elsewhere, and these guys don't got none of that from the get go. Think back to our North America chapter. One of the reasons that North America kicked so much ass is that Europe started running out of stuff when America opened up and started to use its stuff. There is a clear distinction between where people have hung out for thousands of years, and places that are untouched. It has a lot to do with who's rich in the world today.

REASON NUMBER TWO: THE GOLDEN AGE OF ISLAM COMES TO AN END

Staring in 700 CE, there was this Golden Age where everything was awesome in the Middle East. There was continuous expansion of territory and wealth; they had centers of higher learning, but it came to a crashing halt in 1258 CE. How can we attach things to such a specific date? It's the date that another Empire intrudes into this one, and made sure that everything came to a screeching halt. The intruders were the Mongols from Central Asia. The rise of the mighty Mongol Empire, out of what is modern day Mongolia, spread across China into Northern India, all through Central Asia, and all the way into the Middle East. This date is significant because 1258 is the year that the Mongols sacked Baghdad, a center of Middle Eastern power, and *razed*, or *totally freakin' demolished*, it to the ground. It's partly due to the rise of another

The party is over.

region during world history that this one started to get behind. I've prepped you that the Ottomans took over shortly and rose back up again, but this was a big blow to Middle Eastern expansion. The Mongols really knocked things out.

REASON NUMBER THREE: BYPASS

No, not heart surgery. They were physically bypassed on the planet. What am I talking about here? I've already told you that this place doesn't grow a lot of stuff. It's dry; it's not an agricultural epicenter, and nobody was really industrialized at this point in history, so what is it that these guys did? What big riches did they have? Gold? Copper? Anything? I've already given you the answer; it was dry and they depleted all their resources. They didn't have much.

What kept the Middle East going up until this point? The answer: trade. When you think of the Middle East, think of the term "Middle Man." What does a middle man

Da Gama & Columbus: bypassers extraordinaire!

do? He buys something on one end, moves it to some place that needs it, and sells it for a profit. The Middle East has been classically "The Middle Man" of Eurasia, moving stuff from China and India to Europe and vice versa. Making money going both ways, they've been doing this for a good long time. Think about things like, I don't know, the Silk Road out of China. That stuff went through the Middle East. All the carpets, the fine silks, the whole spice trade—people think that the Plaid Avenger's joking them, but spices back in the day are like crack now. No price was too high and people would snort them up their nose and they could never get enough. Black pepper was the crack of its day, back in the 15th century; people loved it, and the Middle East was the dude that brought it to you.

What's that convoluted long story got to do with the Middle East getting left behind? It just so happens in the 1400s and 1500s that they got bypassed. Bypassed by whom? A couple of surly European lads, maybe you've heard of them. Christopher Columbus, who was trying to find a sea route to India. Gosh, why was Chris doing that? That's right, I remember! Here's the impact for those of you who think this has nothing to do with the Middle East today. The combination of Christopher Columbus trying to head to India and accidentally bumping into the

huge New World (1492), and Vasco da Gama, who indeed found a way to India by passing the Middle East and going around Africa (1498), was a one-two punch. It essentially eliminated the need for the Middle East in the span of a *decade*. These guys figured out how to get what the Europeans want without paying "The Middle Man." Think about it. Overnight, your business is out of business.

This was compounded by the fact that Columbus didn't find India; he found North *and* South America, and everything in between. He hits the jackpot, a literal goldmine. He wasn't getting the same old stuff from India or China or Indonesia; he bumped into a whole new source of stuff, and this stuff started flowing back to the Old World in tremendous volume. I don't even have to tell you about *all* the things they shipped back, only two things: silver and gold. Think about all the silver and gold that the Spaniards pulled out of Mexico and South America. They had huge mines and a tremendous amount of wealth was pulled back into Europe. Europe became richer and richer and richer, pulling new stuff in from the Americas and going straight to India, bypassing the Middle East. Getting bypassed, in combination with the general physical overload and the invasion of my main man Genghis from Central Asia, really took its toll on the Middle East.

Bringin' in the booty!

REASON NUMBER FOUR: OTTOMAN STAGNATION

Wait a minute. How can we say that this was a period of decline in the Middle East when it coincided with the rise of the mighty Ottoman Empire? You're going to see this when you get to Turkey in the next chapter, but you can sum it up all in one word: booty. That's a word the Plaid Avenger never minds throwing out. The Ottoman Empire's economy was largely based on expansion by acquiring wealth from areas taken over. It's one of the reasons they were knocking on the door of Vienna, because under such an economic system, you have to continue to expand and take new areas over in order to get their wealth. This means that the Middle Eastern/Ottoman economy was fairly stagnant. That type of economy is artificial; it's not based on producing anything. This was ultimately their undoing. The Ottoman Empire: successful in appearance, bankrupt at the infrastructure level. There territorial expansion ceased by the 16th century, and from then forward the economy stagnated, and the Ottomans were in a perpetual state of defense in order to hold their

Middle East governments usually to the right—but rarely in the right!

THEIR RULERS

Let's compound the situation further, shall we, because it doesn't seem complicated enough. Let's look at some government types. What's a typical government type in the Middle East? That's right! Theocracies, autocracies, monarchies, dictatorships: damn, all the rightist regime types are here! Power to the government! No power to the people!

Let's mix all these fun facts up in a bowl. Limited resources that are getting scarcer, undiversified economy, limited jobs becoming scarcer, way more people, and then top it all off with a nice layer of rightist regimes, which typically limit human rights and/or freedoms. Let's complicate it even further. Places like Saudi Arabia, that have a lot of money and see the explosion coming, are actually trying to appease their population by investing in education and welfare programs, but even that may be harmful.

What happens in a country like Saudi Arabia with a repressive regime and a bunch of people who are unemployed and highly educated? How about extremism and terrorism? Saudi Arabia is the true fighter of terrorism on the planet right now. We might be fighting a war on terrorism over there, but Saudi Arabia is the hardest working fighter of terrorism on the planet. No doubt in the Plaid Avenger's mind. Those guys are going to work every day, taking out suspected cells and arresting extremist whack-jobs. There are lots of folks with nasty intentions in Saudi Arabia, mostly directed at their own government, not America or any place else. Saudi Arabia is the hardest working antiterrorist group on the planet because of all those factors we just mixed together to make that big beautiful bomb-shaped cake. Also in the antiterrorism league are states like Egypt and Pakistan, who have the same conditions that are ripe for extremist activity.

We can add in one more fun fact: foreign influence. We've already talked about foreign influence in history, but it doesn't seem like we've got enough going for this region yet to really, really and genuinely, piss people off, so let's bring in people from the other side of the planet, loaded to the teeth with guns. The Middle East doesn't seem like the vacation spot for the rich and famous right this second. But things may change. Wait a minute—no, I don't think so. Things will only get worse, and probably fast.

HOLY HOOKAH, ARE WE DONE YET?

Yes. Well, for now. Of course, I haven't really even touched upon the hotbed of current conflict that defines this region, and this is conflict that, while actually being played out within the region, has global repercussions that affect us all. The Israeli/Palestinian issue is a world issue. The US War on Terror is a global phenomenon. The competition for the region's resources has planetary scope. That's why I decided to add a special section to this chapter just to tackle the thorny issues of exactly what forces are shaping and defining this region, and thus the world. It is an addendum of sorts. How quaint! An addendum! What supposedly scholarly book would be complete without an addendum?

DEAD DUDES OF NOTE:

Napoleon Bonaparte: The short dead dude from your history review, he was the French general and emperor that rolled over Europe back in the 19th century. For this chapter, his importance lies in his 1798 invasion of Egypt just for kicks, which opened the floodgates for increasing European control of the perceived weak Middle East.

Saddam Hussein: The not so short dead dude from your Iraq War history review. Former President/dictator of Iraq that first inflamed the Shia and Kurds in his own country, then inflamed Iran by invading them in 1980, then inflamed Kuwait by invading them in 1990, then inflamed the US by simply existing, which the US proceeded to remedy. Now he is in-flamed in hell. Or is that in-flames?

MIDDLE EAST RUNDOWN & RESOURCES

View additional Plaid Avenger resources for this region at http://plaid.at/mid_e

⊕ BIG PLUSES

→ Hugest producer and supplier of oil to the planet; big bucks

→ Some states like UAE are leading the way to using oil wealth diversity their economy into banking, service sector, and computer engineering

→ Center of Islam: one of the world's major religions, and one that is growing fast; this provides at least a little cultural homogeneity across most of the region, and links to Muslims across the world

⊖ BIG PROBLEMS

→ Exploding populations which are already taxing scarce critical resources like water

→ Undiversified economies based almost exclusively on primary products (namely oil)

→ Great wealth disparity within states, and across the region as a whole

→ Government types across region are almost exclusively rightist regimes with power consolidation in the hands of few

→ Many states/power centers within the region hate each other, and this is one of the few regions on earth where interstate conflict will likely increase

→ Radicalized elements of society popping up all over region; existing "terrorist" groups like Hamas, Hezbollah, Al-Qeada, et al, are holding their own or increasing

→ Significant dissatisfaction and discontent among large segments of society in Saudi Arabia, Egypt, Lebanon, Iraq, Iran, Somalia, Sudan, Algeria, Palestine, Yemen

→ Current chronic conflicts: Israel/Palestine; Iraq War; coming soon: Iran

LIVE LEADERS YOU SHOULD KNOW:

King Abdullah: Monarch/leader of Saudi Arabia, the birthplace and holy center of Islam. Arab, Sunni, Saudi, center-right, conservative, massively wealthy, and a huge US ally.

Ayatollah Khamenei: Religious/ Spiritual leader and ultimate wielder of political power in Iran, since it is a theocracy. Persian, Shia, ultra-right, conservative, and totally hates the US. A lot.

Hosni Mubarak: President of Egypt (a one-party state), a position he has held for 30 years. Arab, Sunni, Egyptian, center-right, conservative, and a huge US ally.

Mahmoud Ahmadinejad: Current President of Iran, and great agitator to make the entire world hate his country by continuing to flaunt uranium enrichment. Persian, Shia, ultra-right, conservative, and totally hates the US. A lot. Like a lot, lot.

PLAID CINEMA SELECTION:

Marmoulak aka *The Lizard* (2004) Believe it or not, this is an Iranian comedy! Yes, they like to laugh! But is also a scathing look at the Islamic Republic's experiment with theocracy, through the eyes of a common thief caught-up in a case of mistaken identity when he poses as a mullah religious leader.

Paradise Now (2005) Follows Palestinian childhood friends Said and Khaled who live in Nablus and have been recruited for suicide attacks in Tel Aviv. Filmed on location in Nablus, West Bank and in Tel Aviv, this film is fantastic insight into realistic Palestinian life, but, more importantly, the whole thought process behind what brings people to such an extreme act.

Waltz with Bashir (2008) Now I'm not pushing cartoons because I am one, but this is easily the best, most intense animated film I have ever seen. Based on absolutely real events. An Israeli film director interviews fellow veterans of the 1982 invasion of Lebanon to reconstruct his own memories of his term of service in that conflict. Kick ass intense. A crowd-stunner every time I have shown it.

The Kingdom (2007) Okay, at least one fun action adventure film: A team of U.S. government agents is sent to investigate the bombing of an American facility in the Saudi Arabia. Interesting insight into Saudi culture and their anti-terrorism campaign, which in real life is one of the best in the world. The intro title graphics are the the best part.

Persepolis (2007) Another animated experiment. Poignant coming-of-age story of a precocious and outspoken young Iranian girl that begins during the Islamic Revolution of 1979. Great for showing how the society changed over the last several decades.

A Time for Drunken Horses (2000) Set in a Kurdish village in snow-capped Zagros mountains on the border of Iran and Iraq, this pathetic tale of hard life as a Kurdish teenage boy struggles to hold his family together and care for his severely disabled brother after their father dies. Will assuredly make you appreciate your life more, or commit suicide, or both.

The Battle of Algiers (1966) A totally intense war film based on occurrences during the Algerian War (1954–62) against French colonial rule in North Africa. So gritty and well made that it looks like a documentary that is just recording the events. Grating tense soundtrack and lots of symbolism make this film not for the weak of constitution. The fact that it depicts urban guerrilla warfare, suicide bombings, and sleeper cells long before the "modern era" should give one pause for thought.

Lawrence of Arabia (1962) Epic desert movie portraying the real life adventures of T.E. Lawrence who served in British Army during World War I. He helped organize Arab resistance to the Ottoman Turk Empire. Is great insight in Arab Bedouin culture and the historic events of the fall of the Ottomans, which established modern day countries of the region.

The Ten Commandments (1956) Got to give a shout out to all my Hebrew friends on this one, and for everyone else, you should watch this cinematic masterpiece to better understand how the whole creation of Israel thing went down back in the day. Like Old Testament back in the day, that is.

Bab el shams (2004) Roughly translated meaning "the gate of sun," this 4.5 hour epic faithfully depicts the birth of the nation of Israel. Shows the relations between Zionists and Palestinians both before and after the formation of Israel in 1948. Considered by some to be one of the greatest Arabic films of all time and potentially one of the greatest films of all time in general.

Ekhrajiha (2007) Made by a ultra-conservative right-wing dude, a controversial look at the final days of the Iran-Iraq War. Unlike other Iranian films depicting this strife, the director paints the heroes as fundamentally flawed, often acting in ways that would be considered by some to be immoral. Filmed in and around Tehran, depicts real life living conditions in modern day Iran.

Lost Boys of Sudan (2003) A feature length documentary that highlights the cultural differences that two Sudanese children experience when they are brought to America. Orphaned by one of the most brutal civil wars in Africa, the two boys survived lion attacks as well as militia gunfire before being chosen to come to America.

The Jacoubian Building (2006) The highest budgeted Egyptian film of all time, bears its plot from a novel of the same name. Set around the time of the first Gulf War, is a biting view of Egyptian society in the years since the 1952 coup d'état. Set in downtown Cairo, the film plays wonderfully with metaphors and is a great representation of the book.

LIVE LEADERS YOU SHOULD KNOW:

Benjamin Netanyahu: Current Prime Minister of Israel, and a conservative, center-right, hawkish fellow. Don't look for any Palestinian "peace process" to go forward on his watch. Is a US ally, even if relations are strained with the Obama administration right now.

Colonel Muammar Gaddafi: the leader/dictator of Libya since 1969. Semi-insane, used to sponsor terrorism and nuclear weapons development until he renounced all and became a good boy in 2006. He is Arab, Sunni, conservative right, but has in times past renounced his "Arab-ness" in favor of his "African-ness."

Mahmoud Abbas: President of the Palestinian National Authority, and the "head" of Palestine, with which Israel, the US and the West all deal with. He is Arab, Sunni, Palestinian, centrist, and effective head of the West Bank . . . not so much of the Gaza Strip anymore though.

Omar al-Bashir: President of Sudan since a 1989 coup, and the first sitting leader in history to be indicted for war crimes and genocide for the Darfur deal. There was great outcry by Arab states when this arrest warrant was issued. Why? Bashir is ethnically Arab, a Sunni Muslim, center-right, and holds all power . . . just like the other Arab leaders!

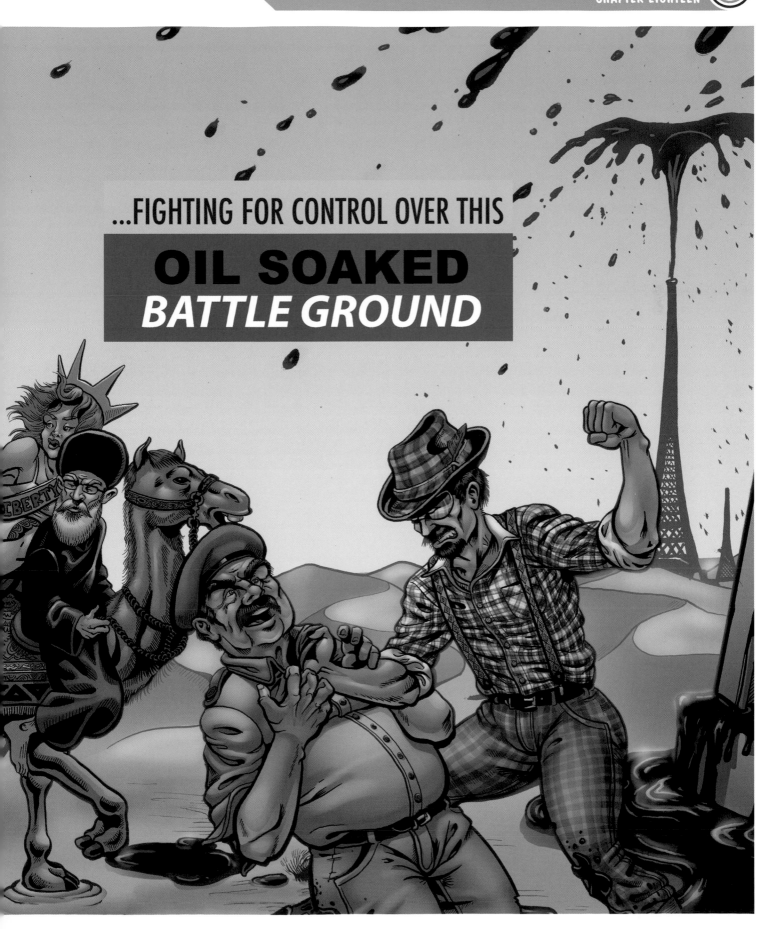

...FIGHTING FOR CONTROL OVER THIS

OIL SOAKED
BATTLE GROUND

Ethnic Breakdown of the Middle East
Percent

- Arab 45 [a]
- Turk 19
- Persian 12
- Kurd 8
- Azeri 6
- Other 10

Major Ethnic Group

- Arab [b]
- Turk
- Persian
- Kurd
- Azeri

Other Ethnic Group

BALUCH

CHAPTER OUTLINE

Addendum: The Competition for Control

18

NOW for the last, and most complicated, component of understanding the Middle East mess in the modern context. Many, if not all, of the conflicts, trials, and tribulations that have been described so far in this chapter can be related to a much bigger competition that is occurring across this region, and that is a competition among big powers for influence, if not outright control, of the destiny of this troubled chunk of land.

This is a total Plaid Avenger assessment, and would be labeled by experts as completely unorthodox and overly-simplistic in its approach, which means it's probably exactly right! I admit right from the get-go that this approach does not do a thorough analysis of all the details and all of the complex inter-relationships that exist between these groups; if you want to understand them better, then by all means use this text as a launching point for further research into this tangled web of geopolitical skullduggery. Wow! How often do you see the word skullduggery in a textbook? But I digress.

Here is what you need to know to know your Middle Eastern mess: there are many ethnic and religious and political differences among people in this region which cause fractures and frictions, and almost all of these things are totally unrelated to input from the outside world. In other words, many players are vying for influence and control from within the Middle East itself. Moves from outside forces like the US, the EU, Russia, or even al-Qaeda simply accentuate, benefit or stymie the game being played internally. You dig what I'm saying so far?

Before you go any further, go back to the addendum opening page and examine the map for major ethnic distinctions within the Middle East, as they are the primary basis for the Team divisions.

The following is a list of distinct teams that the Plaid Avenger feels are currently in this competition. Again, some of these teams are vying for influence, some are vying to control resources, some are vying to control major events, some are trying to outright control territory, and some are just trying to disrupt the other teams from winning. I will point out what makes each team distinct from the others, their motives, who they like, and who they hate. I will start with the easiest ones and continue to get further complicated as we go. You ready for this reality? Then let's do this!

TEAM TURK

We start with the easiest and least complicated: the Turks. First and foremost, this team's distinctive characteristic is its ethnicity. Turkey is full of Turks. Go figure. But Turks are not Arabs, nor Persians, nor Middle Easterners, whatever that means. The next chapter of this book deals with Turkey in much more detail, so I will keep it brief for now. As you will find out soon enough in the following pages, I do not count Turkey as a part of the Middle East region at all. In a sense, it's a bit of an outside entity itself.

Turks takin' it to the streets!

Having said that, Turkey is in a very unique position to influence affairs in the Middle East in multiple ways. First, unlike any other outside entities, Turkey is overwhelmingly Muslim, which makes it more culturally sensitive and sympathetic to all its Muslim Middle Eastern neighbors. But that is about where the similarities end.

Unlike its regional neighbors to the south, Turkey is a staunchly secular society that maintains a strict separation between Islam and the state. Turkey is also a well-established democracy, a founding member of the UN, one of the earliest inductees into NATO, a possible future member of the EU, and has a well-established and strong, modern military. All those factors together make it much more Western in outlook, and indeed, Turkey is an ingrained part of most Western institutions, especially that NATO one; all operations in the Middle East utilize the Turkish corridor as an operating platform. Most NATO and UN operations in the region would be screwed without Turkish support. That gives Turkey a loud voice on all Middle Eastern matters.

That's why Team Turk is in a strong position to influence some Middle Eastern policies, especially ones that are advantageous to itself. Since the Turks are US/NATO allies, they typically work toward the goals agreed upon by those entities—to a point. Turkey openly refused to support the current US invasion of Iraq on the grounds that it could not be party to an illegal invasion of a fellow Muslim state. Recently, Turkey actually invaded Iraq itself to go after Kurdish terrorists, much to the chagrin of the US. That is important to note: Turkey has a large population of Kurds in its own territory, and thus has a vested interest in any/all Kurdish developments in the region. Stability of Iran and Iraq play prominently into the Kurd situation, and thus the Turkish response.

Other important considerations: Turkey controls the all-important headwaters to the Tigris and Euphrates river systems, which supply the critical resource to many countries to the south, meaning they have a very effective control measure should they ever decide to use it. In addition, Turkey has quietly and methodically been increasing its role as a mediator and host between sparring Middle Eastern parties. Most recently, Turkey has overseen talks between Syria and Israel, and is likely to be a key moderator in the inevitable Palestinian/Israeli peace talks. Look for their role as moderate Muslims paving the way to peace to expand in the future. As a stable, successful, Muslim state in the neighborhood, Turkey is uniquely fit for such a role.

Turkey: the last remaining remnant of the Ottoman Turk Empire.

TEAM HEBREW

Onto the next team, and what a doozy this one has become! Team Hebrew represents one state and one state only, the state that may be a central issue for tons of regional friction: Israel. Now I know what you may be thinking already: "What? How can this be the next easiest team to comprehend when it is the source of so much animosity and conflict?" I'm glad you asked. While many folks believe the Israeli-Palestinian issue may be the source of all conflict across this region, their team's motives and motivations are actually quite easy to identify and understand.

Before you read any further, you must understand the basics of how this state came to be and what that has meant for the modern world. Check out the "What's the Deal with Israel" box on the next page.

The Kosher Club. On unleavened bread.

Okay, now that you are back, we can make some generalizations. All the neighboring Arab states have attacked Israel on multiple occasions ever since its inception, and Israel has pretty much won each of these wars, resulting in increased territory for Israel and control of other areas that are not even part of the state. It also has resulted in the displacement of most of the ethnically Arab Palestinians, who are without a state of their own. Many of these Palestinian refugees are located in the surrounding Arab states. For these reasons and perhaps many others, Team Arab really hates Team Hebrew. Team Persia hates Team Hebrew as well, even though they have never openly engaged each other, militarily or otherwise.

Let's call out some other characteristics of Team Hebrew. Obviously, they are Jewish, and as such, the only non-Muslim actors within this region vying for influence and/or control. Team Hebrew is also a strong, secular, well-established democracy as well as a fully developed country with extremely high standards of living. All of those factors make it quite unique within the Middle East region. Team Hebrew is indeed a fully Western country in every sense of the word when it comes to development, economic and political systems, and even religious and cultural values.

Most importantly, Israel also has high levels of technology, especially military technology, and is an undeclared nuclear power. That is crucial. Team Hebrew is the only entity in the Middle East that has nuclear weapons. They are an undeclared nuclear power because the US and others insist that they do not openly declare this fact, otherwise everyone in the neighborhood will want a nuclear weapon, thus launching a regional arms race. Nobody wants that right now, or ever.

Speaking of the US, it should also be evident to you that Team Hebrew is a staunch ally of the US, the EU, and all western institutions in general, with the possible exception of the UN, since UN members often give Israel the smackdown in that forum. The inverse holds true as well: the US has supported Israel openly and covertly for decades. Israel is regularly the top recipient of US foreign aid, even though they are a rich country in their own right, and have a powerful and well-trained military. The US has regularly shared/sold weapons, weapons technology, and military intelligence with Israel. You can go ahead and make the assumption that this relationship pisses off all the other teams in this regional competition.

Why would I suggest that Team Hebrew motives are easy to explain? Because they are fairly well defined and there aren't that many of them. Their primary objective? Maintain their territorial integrity. Keep the boundaries of their 60-year-old state intact at all costs. Second objective: have national security—that is, to be secure in their state by not having terrorist attacks or open declarations of war against them. Third objective: get all other neighboring states to recognize their right to exist, which, of course, helps out with the first two objectives.

BACK IN THE BIBLICAL DAY: CIRCA 1000 BCE

David's Kingdom (c.970 B.C.)
Solomon's Kingdom (c.930 B.C.)

PALESTINE British Mandate (1920-1948)

Jewish settlements, 1947

PALESTINE U.N. Partition Plan (1947)

Jewish state
Arab state

What's the Deal with Israel?

Israel is the loaded topic of all loaded topics. There are so many emotions surrounding the forma- tion and history of Israel, it is hard to be completely unbiased about the issue. If you lean too far in either direction, you can be quickly charged with anti-Semitism or, conversely, Zionism. But, by the mercy of Elijah, here is the deal with Israel.

I won't get into Biblical history too much, but will make mention of this: This area was the historic home- land of the Jews, "The Promised Land" that Moses brought them to many millennia ago. Fast forward to the Roman Empire, which persecuted the Jews (one in particular you may have heard of: Jesus Christ) and even- tually totally kicked the vast majority of them out of the area in the second century AD. Since then, locals have been living there, hanging out for a couple thousand years.

The modern history of Israel begins around 1900, when Theodor Herzl, among others, began pressing for the creation of a national Jewish state—this movement became known as the Zionist movement. Jews began buying property in Palestine and forming small Jewish communities. In 1917, the British government issued the **Balfour Declaration,** which endorsed the establishment of a Jewish homeland in Palestine. Shortly after, Pales- tine became a *protectorate* of the British government because of dismemberment of Ottoman Empire after WWI (see next chapter).

This caused a surge of Jewish immigration that continued until 1939, when the British government issued the **White Paper,** which limited, but did not stop, Jewish immigration to Palestine. This pissed off the Jewish community, who viewed the White Paper as a rejection of Zionism, and also pissed off the Arabs in Palestine, who wanted Jewish immigration to stop completely.

After World War II, when the horrors of the Holocaust were revealed, there was a giant uprising of sympathy for Jews and for the Zionist movement in general. Simultaneously, Jewish armed forces in Palestine became more aggressively defensive of Jewish territory, attacking both British and Arab forces. The British decided that keeping Palestine as a protectorate was no longer in their interest, so they ceded control to the UN. The UN

That's it. That's all. Pretty easy to digest. Now I am not saying its right or wrong, or good or bad, or that it will ever even happen. I'm just saying their objectives are pretty easy to identify and understand. All of Team Hebrew's foreign policies, international alliances, and strategic actions serve to accomplish one or more of those very simple objectives.

Israel's occupation of the West Bank, of the Gaza Strip, and even areas within Syria referred to as the Golan Heights, is maintained to achieve their national security goal. Israeli development of a strong military and nuclear weapons was done to ensure its existence by discouraging any more open attacks across its borders. Israel usually sides up with Team West (particularly the US) when it serves their purposes to achieve those objectives. Usually, but not always. Israel sometimes goes against US foreign policy by negotiating with neighboring states that the US hates to achieve the "recognition" goal. That is currently happening right now: Israel is meeting with Syria, much to the chagrin of the US, and for sure the issue of Syria recognizing Israel's right to exist is on the negotiating table. We better get to the next, more complicated force affecting this region.

accelerated the development of a plan to partition Palestine into separate Jewish and Arab states. This formed the Jewish State of Israel, which was quickly recognized by the United States and eventually by most everyone else, but not any of the surrounding Arab countries. This established the 1947 UN partition borders (see map insert).

Violence erupted soon after the partition. Armies from Egypt, Syria, Jordan, Iraq, and Lebanon all clashed with Israeli forces. Jordan gained a foothold in the West Bank and Egypt gained a similar foothold in the Gaza Strip. This is important to note because these are still disputed areas today. A ceasefire was finally brokered in 1949, creating a new set of de-facto borders now known as the green line (see map insert).

Israel frequently sparred with its Arab neighbors throughout the 1950s and 1960s. The culmination of this aggression was the 1967 Six-Day War, where Israel, using advanced weaponry from the US, went gangbusters and conquered the West Bank (including East Jerusalem), Gaza Strip, Sinai Peninsula, and Golan Heights (see map insert). Egypt and Syria were highly pissed about this, and attempted to regain their lost territory in the 1973 Yom Kippur War. This war was more of a stalemate—little territory changed hands—but the Yom Kippur War was significant because the United States sided with Israel, pissing off EVERY Arab nation and inciting the 1973 oil embargo.

The last major shift in Israel's borders was peaceful. In 1979, President Jimmy Carter invited Egyptian leader Anwar Sadat and Israeli Prime Minister Menachem Begin to the United States and helped negotiate the Camp David Accords. This treaty returned the Sinai Peninsula to Egypt and granted more autonomy to Palestinians residing in occupied territory. Since 1979, most violence associated with Israel has been within its borders. The Palestinians living within Israeli-controlled territory have garnered significant international support for statehood. Recently, Israel has begun taking steps that seem to suggest that the formation of a sovereign Palestine is imminent. However, Israel is not prepared to cede the amount of territory that the Palestinians believe they deserve, and has even started construction of a wall encircling much of the disputed area in East Jerusalem.

TEAM ARAB

Now we are onto the real cultural anchor of the Middle East, and here's where it starts to get really messy. Team Arab refers to an ethnic group, just like Turks or Persians. However, this ethnic group happens to be the majority within the Middle East as an entire region, and many of the states/groups of this region are overwhelmingly Arab in descent. Maybe you've heard of Saudi **Arab**ia or the **Arab**ian Peninsula or perhaps even Aladdin and other tales of "The **Arab**ian Nights"?

Before the advent of Islam, the Arabic ethnic group was centered in the Arabian peninsula, natch. Although the Arabs were originally primarily a nomadic people with an itinerant lifestyle centered around the use of the camel and an extensive network of desert oases,

Is that you, Aladdin?

TEAM PERSIA

Never should have took on the Spartans . . .

Onto the next, and final, of the major teams in our Middle East round-up. For this one, we have to go back even further in time to tell their tale. Further back than the Ottoman Empire, further back than the Arab Empire, and, indeed, even further back than the advent of Islam itself. Team Persia's story goes back several thousand years, but we will just hit the highlights here so that you can understand how very different and distinct this team is from all of its neighbors. Never heard of Persia? In today's world, we call it Iran. While Iran is the core of this Team, there are other players on their side as well. But let's start at the beginning.

Persia can track its origins back to 1500 BCE when Aryan tribes—namely, the Medes and the Persians—settled the Iranian Plateau. Power went back and forth between these groups until the Persians came out on top in 558 BCE when Cyrus the Great beat out the competition and then went on to consolidate the peoples of the plateau and expand the empire outward into Lydia and Babylonia and eventually Egypt and beyond, making it the most powerful political entity of the time.

Later, Darius the Great tried and failed to incorporate the Greeks into the Persian fold. Look up the epic Battle of Marathon as to how that went down. Also, watch **The 300** to see an excellent, but not terribly accurate, depiction of this Greek/Persian face-off period—Iran actually protested the release of the film as being racist and inflammatory. Next

The 300 stopped them, and then Alexander whipped them.

name of note: Alexander the Great united the Greek city-states and led his famous campaign across Asia primarily to squash the power of the Persians for good; he was fairly successful in this endeavor, as Darius III was killed (and the empire with him) in 330 BC. While the entity lasted a bit longer off and on, it never regained its past power or glory. Persians have a long, proud history that is still looked back upon with reverence and distinction. Thus, their ire at the negative depiction of their forefathers in ***The 300***.

Let's now fast forward. The Arab/Muslim conquest of Persia in the 640s BCE was to forever change their destiny. Not only did this convert the Persians to Islam, but it set the stage for the current Islamic sect differences that are still very much alive today. As referenced earlier in this text, after the death of Muhammad, the religion gets split into two main branches: Sunni and Shi'a.

Now, the liturgical and ritual differences between Sunnis and Shi'as, or Shi'ites are minimal and mostly unimportant. The branching off of the Shi'a (literally, partisans) of Ali

Iran: the core of the Persian power, Shi'a power, and a whole lot more!

occurred when certain members of the early Islamic community disputed the line of succession following Muhammad's death. Most folks supported one of Muhammad's top men Abu Bakr, but others backed Ali, who was Muhammad's son-in-law. In this contest for power, Ali and then his son Husayn ibn Ali were killed and these early partisans were dispersed throughout the Islamic realms. The death of Husayn ibn Ali particularly became a focal point for the community, especially in modern times, with open manifestations of "passion plays" mourning him and his followers' deaths in the desert near present-day Karbala.

What's all that ancient history have to do with modern day Iran? Just this: Iran became the haven for the supporters of Ali, and over time evolved into the core of Shi'a Islam. While Shi'a is the minority sect worldwide (world = 85% Sunni, 15% = Shi'a), it is the majority of followers in modern day Iran (Iran = 90% Shi'a, 10% Sunni) and that makes all the difference for our team competition.

Let's make another jump forward. Persia was picked on and beat up on by Russia and Britain during the European powers' imperial battles for world control. However, it always managed to maintain its independence and was never colonized. By 1906, they instituted a constitutional monarchy and by 1941 a dude named Reza Shah was on the throne and increasingly ruling with an autocratic iron fist. It should be noted that this dude came to power with the assistance of the US and the UK who had forced Reza's father to abdicate the throne for his supposed Nazi-sympathizing behavior. Later in 1953, the US and UK coordinated a secret plot responsible for deposing the popular Iranian Prime Minister Dr. Mohammad Mossadeq because he had nationalized the Iranian oil industry, much to the chagrin of western countries. That left the bumbling puppet King Reza Shah in charge of Iran via his western allies. It was not to last.

Foreign powers had to get involved in the Middle East to "protect" their oil industries. (Hmmm, what is that old saying about history repeating itself?) This Shah guy was a little too over the top and pissed off too many Iranians, and the shit soon hits the fan. Or should I say Shi'ite hits the fan? Time for the Iranian Revolution! Check the box for details:

What's the Deal with the Iranian Revolution?

Up until 1979, Shah Mohammad Reza Pahlavi was the constitutional monarch of Iran; he was happy exporting oil, quashing dissent, and resisting Soviet influence. The US and the Shah were the best of friends because he was basically a US puppet. He liked playing with big guns, and we liked supplying him with just such toys, just to make sure the Soviets wouldn't. Unfortunately for the United States, most people in Iran were very unhappy with the Shah. It seems that Iranians did not like living under a dictatorship.

The Shah and the Ayatollah.

Open protests of the Shah's government began to occur in January 1978, and the Shah ordered the military to shut them down. Hundreds of demonstrators, including students, were killed. This happened several times, and popular support against the Shah really took hold. A populist coalition of liberals, students, leftists, and Islamists escalated the protests to the point of revolution and ousted the Shah in January of 1979. We call this the 1979 Iranian Revolution or Islamic Revolution.

The primary political figure during the revolution was the Ayatollah Khomeini, a Muslim cleric who encouraged demonstrations against the US and Israel, whom he declared "enemies of Islam." During the final chaotic days in November of 1979, a group of young radical Muslim students took over the US Embassy and held 52 Americans hostage for 444 days.

The Ayatollah Khomeini was the most popular figure in Iran because of its strong Muslim background, but there was also a powerful secular movement. A power sharing system of government was attempted, but eventually Iran became a true Islamic Republic, with all of the power vested in the religious elite led by Ayatollah Khomeini. The United States became even more enraged, especially since it was unable to rescue the hostages, and thus cut all diplomatic ties with Iran.

To this day, there is no official US presence in Iran—no diplomats, no troops, nothing. This is one of the reasons there is currently so much animosity between the United States and Iran. Many US leaders see Iran as a threat to Western stability in general, *especially* if they become a nuclear power. This is a critical issue in today's world, as Iran continues to be in the spotlight by developing nuclear technology—which they say will be used for peaceful purposes, but the West is convinced will be used to build a bomb. The rhetoric is running full steam on both sides right now.

Just know this: the US is all about shutting Iran down, either diplomatically or ultimately by force. The EU wants to shut them down, but only diplomatically. Russia is kind of an ally, and wants to help them develop their nuclear program for energy production, and China wants to do nothing about the Iranian situation because they are all about the sovereignty. Whatever goes down, don't look for it to be dealt with at the UN Security Council, which is already deadlocked before the process even begins.

Now we arrive at the present. The Iranian Revolution has been called the last great revolution of the 20th century, and for good reason. It is a grand experiment of Islamic theocracy with limited democratic elements, but it is, in essence, a blending of church and state into one big ruling system. It's really the first of its kind, and one of the reasons that other Middle Eastern countries are terrified of Iran is the fear that this type of revolution could spread, meaning that Iranian-style theocracy could sweep into Egypt or Jordan or Algeria and displace the systems/leaders that currently have the power. And no one wants to lose the power!

Let's get to the meat and potatoes: Team Persia is doing quite a bit to assert its power and influence across the Middle East, which severely pisses off Team Arab. These two teams HATE each other, and as I have alluded to earlier, are the biggest forces facing off within the region. This hate started in earnest when Saddam Hussein, with backing from other Arab states, the US, Russia, and Europe, invaded them, thus starting the decade long Iran-Iraq War which ended with about a million casualties. The hate between Arab and Persia exists to this day. Why so much hate? Dig this:

HATE number 1: As just mentioned, Team Persia has no problem exporting the ideals of its revolution to other places. Iran increasingly sees itself as the only true Islamic country of the region, the only real and true purveyor of the faith. It mocks the Arab countries for their morally corrupt leadership as well as for being stooges of US foreign policy. Iran is trying to assume a moral and ethical leadership role on issues like the Palestinian debacle, the existence of Israel, and any foreign intervention into Middle Eastern affairs.

Since Team Persia is the only fully Shi'a state, we have come to define Team Persia in this religious sense as well, but they are not totally alone. I want you to be aware of a new entity that is named the **Shi'a Crescent**. It is based on a projection of Iranian influence and power to other Shi'a groups across the wider region, but please don't mistake this Persia/Arab animosity as a religious war of any sort. The Shi'a Crescent is simply a nice way to highlight areas in which Team Persia has increasing influence. Take a look at the map.

Shi'a Crescent: this ain't no Lucky Charm for the Arabs or the US.

The map shows you the percentages of Shi'a folks in selective states, and we should note a few choice groups that make daily news and effect events. Iran is the core of this crescent, but its effective reach spans from the Persian Gulf countries all the way through Iraq, which has a majority of Shi'a and is why Iran is helping fund and arm Shi'a militant groups in the current Iraq civil war. The Shi'a vein also runs thru Syria, a country whose leadership belongs to a sub-sect of Shi'a, and therefore malleable to Iranian Shi'a influences. To continue on the road, you get to southern Lebanon, where Shi'as also have a slight majority, and also where a radical Shi'a terrorist group named Hezbollah hangs out. Iran funnels money and guns through Syria to Hezbollah to help them fight against Team Hebrew. You starting to get a sense of the Iranian deal here?

"Israel? I do not recognize. Does not compute."

HATE number 2: Team Persia still openly utterly and completely hates Team Hebrew, and the current, ultra-conservative President Ahmadinejad actually called for the destruction of Israel. We've already pointed out that Team Arab hates Israel, but some Arab leaders have recognized Israel, while still others have been softening their rhetoric about the Jewish state over the years. Meanwhile, Team Persia leaders have held the hardliner attitude of refusal to recognize, but also calling for its destruction. Hardcore! That's why Iran supports Hezbollah, but it also supports Hamas down in the Gaza Strip, just to keep jabbing a sharp stick into the Israel flank at every available opportunity,

This also puts Iran in the position of appearing to be a true helper and defender of the Palestinians, reinforcing the idea that the Arabs are just a bunch of losers that can't look out after their own. It makes them appear to be the only country in the region able and willing to stand up not only to Israel, but also to other outside forces.

HATE number 3: Team Persia is developing a nuclear industry. Hold on! I didn't say nuclear weapons! But that is what all the other Teams think is going on. Iran has been pissing off its neighbors and world powers by its persistence in developing fuel to be able to develop a nuclear power industry, and this is the issue that is really causing the most consternation across the region, and outside the region as well. As of this writing, Iran has not broken any international law in its nuclear pursuit—it is not illegal to produce nuclear energy.

However, virtually all Western nations, including the US and the EU, all Arab nations, and the UN as a whole, have condemned the move harshly and are busy setting up international sanctions to stop the Iranians. For their part, Iran has claimed they have a God-given right for nuclear energy, and nothing will stop them in their quest. Iran's open defiance sets them apart from all the other states in the region, and is seemingly a point of pride with Iranian leadership. Great. Like we needed another problem in this region.

Here's why it is a problem: Iran getting the tools to create a nuclear bomb tips the balance of power in the region radically. No one else has the bomb—except Israel, who won't admit it. While most folks assume that Israel would be the country most frightened of a nuclear-armed Iran, in fact that's probably not quite true. Israel has the bomb as well, making for an effective deterrent to an Iranian attack. Why would Iran nuke Israel, knowing that 100 nukes would be sent back in response? The folks who are really worried are Team Arab, because they don't have a bomb! A nuclear Iran would be stronger than any Arab country, and would contain the most powerful deterrent to prevent any attacks against their Persian motherland, including any attacks potentially from the US or others!

Sum up: Team Persia hates Team Arab. Team Persia hates Team Hebrew. Team Persia hates Team Foreigner. In return, all those teams hate Team Persia right back, and may be working with each other in order to stop any further rise of Persian power. You dig? Arab states might work with the US, and maybe even Israel, to make sure the Persians get sidelined.

Interesting. Or should I say, interesting Shi'ite?

TEAM FOREIGNER

Now our job starts getting way easier. The major forces have been outlined in perhaps too much detail, but we still have some other characters in this Middle Eastern drama that are powerful players affecting events. I don't have to spend as much time with these, because they are in the news on an hourly basis and if you don't know these cats yet, then you must be living under a rock. Team Foreigner consists of those states not actually from the region, but somehow find themselves here anyway.

With no reservation, the US is the primary outside entity that has dramatically altered events of the past decades. The US has supported kings, monarchs, dictators and dirtbags aplenty in its quest to influence events and resources in the Middle East that are of strategic interest. Well, I guess all countries do that, but the US is the most powerful at this game. The Saudi royal family, the Shah of Iran, Saddam Hussein, and Hosni Mubarak all quickly spring to mind.

It also should be noted that Israel and Egypt are the number 1 and number 2 recipients of US foreign aid, and have been for decades. Simultaneously, US companies have sold tens of billions of dollars worth of arms to Saudi Arabia. But the US is also a staunch ally and

Foreigners love to party in the Middle East!

weapons supplier to Israel. Damn! The weapons business must be good! Uncle Sam has now invaded Iraq not once but twice, and the US maintains a troop presence in multiple states of the region; a visible sign of its presence can be seen almost everywhere. The US-led War on Terror is actively engaged across the entire region, both overtly and covertly, to root out rebel/terrorist groups whose ideology conflicts with the US world view. Of course, there are also diplomatic interjections: the US is typically the sponsor of most Israeli/Palestinian peace talks; the US is leading the trade embargo against Iran; the US is a builder of democracy in Iraq, or at least they are trying. The list could go on.

Of course, they are not totally alone. The US does have its "Coalition of the Willing" in Iraq which includes its typical lapdogs, the UK and Australia, along with 49 other countries—well, it had 49 originally, but that number has been dwindling fast as of late. The UN is, of course, intimately involved in trying to help stem the tide of conflict in the region, albeit with not much results. Now there is something called the Quartet on the Middle East: a foursome of entities collectively working together to mediate the peace process in the Israeli-Palestinian conflict. The Quartet consists of the US, Russia, the EU, and the UN, and former UK Prime Minister Tony Blair is the group's current Special Envoy. Go get 'em, Tony!

Special Envoy Blair. Oh, Tony, you are always special in my book!

Let's cut to the chase on this Team Foreigner. Team Persia hates 'em, especially the US. In return, Team Foreigner really hates Team Persia, especially the US. Did you know that the US and Iran don't like each other? Well, now you do. The US typically supports and sides up with Team Arab on a whole host of issues, but mostly on the hating Iran one. Unfortunately, the US position with Arab states gets extremely complicated because it is best friends with Team Hebrew. Let's rank the Teams in order of how much the US likes them:

1. Team Hebrew comes out on top.

2. Team Turk is close behind. Remember, they are a NATO member!

3. Team Arab is supported by US on some issues, but not all.

4. Team Persia comes dead last. Perhaps that's exactly how the US wants it right now. Dead. Last.

Starting to make sense? I doubt it. Let me add in one last complicating clause of this foreign influence. While many Arab state leaders' support the US, and vice-versa, most people in those Arab states are increasingly pissed about US presence and their leaders' support of US policies. This is making the water even hotter for a lot of these folks, as they become increasingly unpopular with their own people. One need only point out that Osama bin Laden's original mission was to drive the US out of the Saudi holy land. Not accomplishing that, he then turned to start attacking the Saudi government themselves for being corrupt stooges of the US. And the Saudis aren't alone, as there are other groups within the region expressing their displeasure in any number of violent ways.

ADDITIONAL NON-STATE ACTORS

Now for the last. I won't go into great detail on these groups, but I did want you to be aware that there are other entities that are affecting the flow of events within the region, much smaller entities that are not states or governments. Therefore, these groups do not behave like states or governments, cannot be coerced the same way as states or governments, and cannot be effectively attacked or punished like states or governments can. That makes them very sticky entities indeed, and they are often thorns in the sides of the bigger Teams we have already talked about. But, they can also be used as tools by the big Teams to attack or influence one another as well. Hmmmm, tricky, tricky, sticky, sticky.

I know that terrorist groups are probably the first things that come to mind, but there is actually a much bigger and more important one to tackle first: the Kurds. The Kurds are an ethnic group (check back to map on opening page again) that are located in the mountainous areas of Iran, Iraq, Turkey and Syria. They are a nation of people without a state, and they very much would like to have one. For over a century, the Kurds have dreamt of and petitioned big powers to have a Kurdistan country of their own. They have been used, abused and betrayed by virtually every regional and world power in this quest. The Kurds are seemingly a damned bunch of people, and I mean damned in terms of doomed.

They have been sporadically beaten down by the governments of all the states that they occupy, mostly because no government wants to see a free Kurdistan. That would entail the loss of some of their own territory, and therefore no one is going for it. Team Turkey, Team Persia as well as components of Team Arab, mainly Syria and Iraq, actively work against any Kurd movement toward independence. You may remember that Saddam Hussein used biological weapons on these people multiple times to keep them in their place. You may not have known that Turkey has also been fairly oppressive in keeping the Turkish Kurds down.

I bring up Team Turk in particular because they invaded Iraq back in February 2008, much to the ire of the US, who is trying desperately to keep a lid on the Iraq mess. Why did the Turks invade? To root out a radical pro-independence Kurdish terrorist group named the PKK that has been responsible for multiple attacks within Turkey. Just so you can see how convoluted alliances can become in the Middle East, Team Turk is actually getting help from Team Persia in this effort, while the normally pro-Turk US is trying to stymie the effort. Geez! How confusing!

ADDENDUM! IT'S EXTRA! SO HAVE SOME MORE STUFF!

View additional Plaid Avenger resources for this region at http://plaid.at/mid_e

DEAD DUDES OF NOTE:

Mohammad Mosaddegh: Democratically elected Prime Minister of Iran from 1951 to 1953, until he was overthrown in a coup d'état backed by the US CIA. Was an ardent nationalist with a passionate opposition to foreign intervention in Iran. He nationalized Iranian oil, which so infuriated the UK and US that they labeled him as a dangerous commie and got him jacked out of power, which is one of the reason Iranians hate the US and UK.

Mohammad Rezā Shāh Pahlavi: The Shah of Iran from 1941 to his overthrow in 1979; only actually held all the real power from 1953 onward, after the US CIA had chucked out Mosaddegh (see above). The Shah did industrialize and modernize Iran, but unfortunately he was a typical corrupt and clueless monarch, as well as an US/Western stooge, who increasingly pissed off his people until they had a revolution to throw him out.

Ayatollah Khomeini: Fiery Shi'a orator and holy man, he inspired and led the Iranian Revolution of 1979 that deposed the Shah and created the first Islamic Republic of Iran, of which he then became the Supreme Leader. Has god-like status to millions of Iranians, and a demon-like status to millions more Westerners due to his condoning the Iranian Hostage Crisis of 1979–1980 and his extremist view of the US as "the Great Satan."

Saddam Hussein: Him again? Yep. In this context, know that Saddam was supported, funded and armed by the US, Western powers, and even other Arab states in the 1980's for his willingness to declare war on Iran, the country that Team West and Team Arab started despising after the Iranian Revolution. Saddam was seen as an Arab fist that would smash this Shi'a/Persian theocracy threat. Good call on that one, everybody.

LIVE LEADERS YOU SHOULD KNOW:

TEAM ARAB:

King Abdullah: Monarch/leader of Saudi Arabia, the birthplace and holy center of Islam. Arab, Sunni, Saudi, center-right, conservative, massively wealthy, and a huge US ally.

Hosni Mubarak: President of Egypt (a one-party state), a position he has held for 30 years. Arab, Sunni, Egyptian, center-right, conservative, and a huge US ally.

TEAM PERSIA:

Ayatollah Khamenei: Religious/Spiritual leader and ultimate wielder of political power in Iran, since it is a theocracy. Persian, Shia, ultra-right, conservative, and totally hates the US. A lot.

Mahmoud Ahmadinejad: Current President of Iran, and great agitator to make the entire world hate his country by continuing to flaunt uranium enrichment. Persian, Shia, ultra-right, conservative, and totally hates the US. A lot. Like a lot, lot.

TEAM HEBREW:

Benjamin Netanyahu: Current Prime Minister of Israel, and a conservative, center-right, hawkish fellow. Don't look for any Palestinian "peace process" to go forward on his watch. Is a US ally, even if relations are strained with the Obama administration right now.

TEAM TURK:

Recep Erdoğan: The kick-ass Prime Minister of Turkey and chairman of the Justice and Development Party (AK Party). Despite internal friction due to his association with the religious-based AK Party, he has overseen an era of economic prosperity and democratization, and Turkey's rise as a serious regional power and trusted mediator of Middle Eastern conflicts.

Abdullah Gül: President of Turkey and first former-Islamist party President in the modern history of Turkey. His AK political party is accused of being too religiously inspired by staunch secularists. He mostly deals with domestic affairs while Erdogan is really the head cheese in charge.

PLAID CINEMA SELECTION:

Take a Middle Eastern Team Tour via Cinema! In the interest of saving space, I won't describe all these in detail, and many are repeats from the previous chapter, but check out these team lists of films to watch to get a fuller sense of the cultures and backgrounds of each team. Total TV team party!

TEAM ARAB:

The Battle of Algiers (1966)
Gaza Strip (2002)
The Kingdom (2007)
Lawrence of Arabia (1962)
Paradise Now (2005)
The Yacoubian Building (2006)

TEAM PERSIA:

About Elly (2009)
Bashu, the Little Stranger (1986)
Dayereh aka *The Circle* (2000)
Ekhrajiha (2007)
Marmoulak aka *The Lizard* (2004)
Persepolis (2007)
300 (2006)
Two Women (1999)

TEAM TURK:

Eskiya (1996)
Günese yolculuk (1999)
Propaganda (1999)
Uzak aka *Distant* (2002)
Yol (1982)

TEAM HEBREW:

Ajami (2009)
Bab el shams (2004)
Sallah Shabati (1964)
The Ten Commandments (1956)
Walk on Water (2004)
Waltz with Bashir (2008)

TEAM KURD:

Günese yolculuk (1999)
Marooned in Iraq (2002)
A Time for Drunken Horses (2000)
Turtles Can Fly (2004)

CHAPTER OUTLINE

Turkey

19

TURKEY IS A:

(a) Country

(b) State

(c) Nation

(d) Nation-state

(e) Region

(f) All of the above

F you! I mean, it's F to you. Turkey is like Japan and Russia, in that it is a sovereign state in its own right, with enough distinctions about it to set it apart from all of the places nearby, which makes it a Plaid Avenger world region. What is the deal with Turkey? What's going on here? Why is it different enough to be apart from the Middle East—the region with which it has classically been associated? Anybody from the Middle East, and particularly from Turkey itself, would say, "No way! We don't have anything in common with each other!" Here in the West, we just see Turkey and the Middle East as kind of a common whole. That is all changing, though. There is a lot about Turkey historically, presently, and in the future, that distinguishes it from all other Middle Eastern countries. Does that mean it's more like Europe? Nope, it's quite distinct from Europe as well. A lot of people in Europe want to distance themselves from Turkey, while some want to embrace it. Turkey is in a strange place in the world right now; it has its own thing going on, while at the same time acting as a bridge between two cultures and regions. That's the Plaid Avenger keyword for Turkey: **the Bridge.**

As we discussed in the Middle Eastern region, there are lots of different ethnic groups in what is collectively referred to as the Middle East, and one of those is Turkic. Turkic is also a distinct linguistic group. Where are the Turkic people? Oddly enough, many people say, "Turkey, they've always been in Turkey." Not necessarily. In modern day Turkey, they refer to themselves ethnically and linguistically as Turkic or Turks; however, this group is originally from Central Asia. They have not been in charge of what is now the present state of Turkey for very long in history,

Turkish Delight: aka lokum or rahat, is a 15th century tasty confection made from starch and sugar, with a soft, jelly-like consistency. It is often cut into small cubes and dusted with powdered sugar before serving. It is sometimes flavored with cinnamon, mint, lemon, or rosewater . . . that last one giving the candy its characteristic pink hue. I always wondered what the heck it was since the White Witch fed some to Edmund in *The Lion, the Witch, & the Wardrobe*. Oh Edmund, you little traitorous scumbucket.

maybe only about 800 years. The folks who would become the Turks came from Central Asia, across what is now Iran, through Iraq, and into modern day Turkey about 1000 years ago. After several hundred years, they took over, their culture took hold, and they made it their own. Perhaps we get ahead of ourselves, but that's what makes them distinct: a different ethnicity and linguistic group from all the surrounding countries. Why and how is Turkey so different from every place around it?

Turkey is more western than virtually every other Middle Eastern country in terms of economic development and government. At the same time, they are not as Western as European countries. This is the first of

Islamic people, but not Islamic state.

many things that pitches Turkey out as a sort of no-man's land, somewhere in the middle. They have a capitalist system that is fully integrated into world economic dynamics. Nobody would disagree with that. They are the strongest fully established, democratic Muslim country.

That's important enough to pause and restate: democratic, fully Muslim country. Perhaps the main reason why they are typically classified as Middle Eastern is their single commonality, which is Islam. Turkey's population is almost 100 percent Islamic. However, it is *not* an **Islamic state,** and that makes all the difference. Turkey has religious ties to its Middle Eastern brothers, but all other aspects of their society, like democracy and capitalism, make them very European. This duality reinforces the idea that Turkey is a bridge. Before we get to a more cultural background, let's talk Turkey physically.

PHYSICALLY . . .

It's pretty easy since Turkey is a single country. If we were to compare Turkey to the US, and overlay it with latitude consistent, we see that it stretches from Washington D.C. to Kansas City, Missouri. It's about the same latitude, and covers West Virginia, Virginia, parts of North Carolina, Tennessee, Kentucky, Indiana, Illinois, and parts of Missouri. It's a decently sized country. Given that its latitude is roughly the same as the states I just mentioned, Turkey has a pretty similar climate. It is humid continental, with some humid subtropical, in the southern parts. However, given that it borders the Mediterranean Sea, we know it must have some Mediterranean climate. Indeed, it does around its coastal fringes. Turkey has four distinguishable seasons, just like we get here in this part of our country.

The only other major physical factor to consider is that the terrain is quite different from here in the eastern United States. Turkey, as a whole, is a pretty mountainous country. It has an uplifted plateau in the middle, with some high mountains, particularly on its eastern borders, where you can find Mt. Ararat (16,000+ ft.) as you go into the Caucasus Mountains. Even over in the western part, the elevated plateau is on average over 6000 feet in elevation.

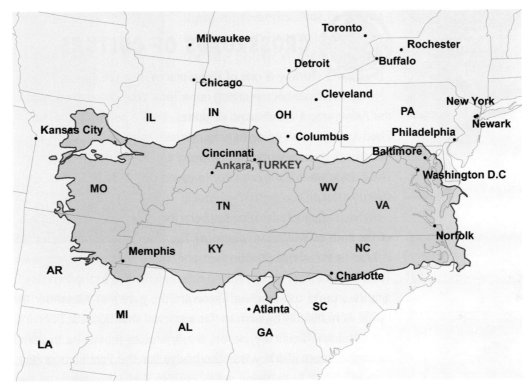

Size comparison.

This is an **escarpment,** as we talked about in South America and will again in sub-Saharan Africa. There are not a lot of coastal plains or flat areas in Turkey, so as soon as you leave those nice, sunny Mediterranean shores, the terrain and the elevation make it much cooler, much faster. As you get to the far eastern side of Turkey, there can be fairly tough winters. It does have some Mediterranean and Black Sea frontage, which moderates things a bit, but it still is a fairly cooler place than eastern North America at similar latitudes.

Turkey is such a mountainous country because it is on the border of several different tectonic plates. It is at the confluence of the Eurasian, African, and Arabian plates, very much like we had several plates coming together in Japan. As with all geologically active mountain-building scenarios, it's an active earthquake region. In the last five or six years, Turkey experienced some serious earthquakes, having tremendous impact in terms of human lives and property damage. That about wraps up the physical traits of Turkey—let's get back to the cultural. Why is Turkey a crossroads of culture?

This is an extremist group that is actually considered a terrorist organization by Turkey, the US and the EU. They have undertaken a campaign since the 1970s of blowing up Turkish stuff and Turkish people in order to fight for their rights, with an ultimate goal of gaining independent territory and national autonomy. This has been a main sticking point for Turkey, as I've already referred to earlier, in that the European Union says, "You guys are picking on those Kurds too much. That's not good." At the same time, Turkey says, "Hey, wait a minute! These guys are terrorists, just like you guys are dealing with terrorists!"

This was a big sticking point for the Turks for decades, but it actually had begun to settle out in the last six or seven years. The Turkish military captured Abdullah Öcalan, the head of the PKK, in 1999 and made plans for his execution, but in an obvious show that they were trying to be conciliatory to the EU, they said, "Okay, we won't kill him. We'll keep him alive in jail and, even though he's a terrorist, we're not going to kill him." He's still in a Turkish jail, and if you know anything about Turkish prisons, you understand that Öcalan is probably begging to be put to death.

Kurdish refugees.

Since Öcalan's arrest, the conflict died down, the number of terrorist attacks diminished, and the Turkish parliament passed lots of laws to try to equalize human rights and give these guys a little more power. Things in Turkey had been getting much better for the Kurds, but then the American invasion of Iraq stirred the pot again. The PKK regrouped in northern Iraq and has carried out several attacks on Turkish soil in the last several years. This led to renewed trouble for everyone here in 2008 and 2009.

Remember I told you that Turkey has a strong and proud military? Well, the Turks got pissed at these PKK attacks, and decided to act. Much to the displeasure of the United States, Turkey conducted several bombing raids and mobilized ground troops to go into Iraq and destroy the PKK forces. The US is not happy, mostly because the northern part of Iraq is the only peaceful part of the country right now, and no one wants to see more people with guns getting into this mess. But those Turks are not sitting still for the fight, and future movements are probably inevitable. Keep an eye on that one, my friends.

TURKS TRANSITIONED

Another big reason that Turkey deserves to be teased out as an independent region from its Middle Eastern and Eastern European neighbors is the situation of its people and economy.

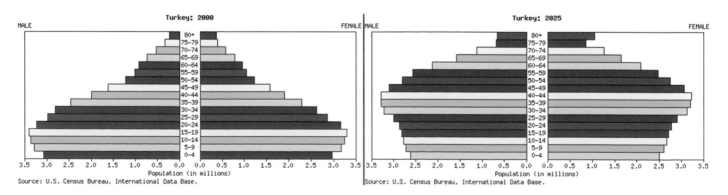

As you can see from the population pyramid here, Turkey, even just thirty years ago, was considered developing because of its explosive population. But look how much has changed in the last thirty years. Their pyramid has basically rounded out, tapered off, and as you can project ahead by 2025, will become completely stable and even slightly shrinking. It would be exactly what we would consider a fully developed nation. Its population is pretty stabilized, and getting even better.

And the cash? Economically speaking, they're not the richest place in the world. They're not even rich by Eastern European standards. However, they're doing pretty well. They have a diversified economy—10 percent of an agricultural sector, and 30 or 40 percent of what we'd call an industrialized sector, which isn't too bad. It has an almost 60 percent service sector, and that's the type of thing recognize as an economy of a developed country. It's yet another example that they are quite different from all the places around them, just for their modern situation if nothing else. They are still on track to become part of the EU. As we've already suggested, the EU is running out of excuses to resist their admittance. The final assault of paperwork to become a full fledged member is supposed to be processed by 2015. This almost imminent EU membership puts Turkey in the catbird seat to expand economically.

With no reservations, I say that from just about any measure you want to examine, Turkey will certainly be considered a fully developed country within the next decade or two.

Turkish President Abdullah Gul: perhaps not so secular.

Let's end this modern assessment with the strife over secularism. While you now understand that the secular nature of Turkey is what sets it apart from its Middle East neighbors, I should warn you that this status is still heavily debated in their society. The country is almost exactly split on the extreme nature of their secularism. The more western, urban populations favor the staunch separation of Islam from politics, but the rural populations are much more conservative in thought and perhaps want to change things to incorporate religion into the state a little more.

You know what? It's about exactly how the US is right now—think about it. Red states with big rural populations vote Republican, while blue states with big urban centers generally vote Democrat, an almost even split in the last several elections.

Prime Minister Recep Erdoğan also accused of not being secular enough.

Republicans would vote for school prayer, Democrats for getting rid of a nativity scene in a government building. That about exactly outlines the Turkish situation as well, only with Islam instead of Christianity. Damn, am I good or what?

Back to Turkey: the current president and prime minister are from a political party that is more conservative and religious (The Justice and Development Party, or AK Party for short.). Many people from the other big political party are staunch secularists, and distrust the President greatly, fearing that his party is changing laws and possibly amending the constitution to allow for more religious stuff in the government. Some opposition leaders have recently called for the president and prime minister to be fired and their entire political party to be banned on constitutional grounds that they are threatening the republic's very existence. As absurd as that sounds, the case has been cleared to be heard by the Supreme Court. This is serious business, serious enough for the head generals to issue some veiled threats to government leaders to check themselves before they wreck themselves, as a house cleaning may be in order if the pendulum starts to swing too far away from the secular roots of the nation. 2010 Update: The court case to ban the AK Party and therefore toss out both the President and Prime Minister was narrowly defeated. Everything is cool again for now, but do note, it was *narrowly* defeated! This fight ain't over yet.

FINISH UP YOUR PLATE OF TURKEY

Unlike most states in this neighborhood, national pride abounds.

If Turkey is admitted to the EU, which still seems likely at this point, their economy will grow. They will become even more incorporated as a member of Europe. They will perhaps become even more incorporated as a Western ally in this new war on terrorism in the Middle East. They will be distancing themselves from all of the radical elements that people in the West are frightened of in the Middle East, which will be to their great benefit. The Plaid Avenger is not making fun of anybody in the Middle East. I'm just saying what's going to happen to Turkey if they get into the EU.

If they *don't* get into the EU, things are going to swing the exact opposite way, and that's what's so fascinating about Turkey's position in the world today. They really are in the catbird seat, as the Plaid Avenger has mentioned several times now. If they go the EU route, they will become more Western, there's no doubt. If the EU turns their back on Turkey, Turkey is independent enough and economically strong enough, and it's certainly militarily strong and competent enough that it will say, "Fine. The hell with the CU (Christian Union). We'll C U later!" They will turn right around and become a leader within the Middle East. There's no doubt in the Plaid Avenger's mind.

That does not mean Turkey's government will become Islamic, but it will turn around and become a regional leader in the opposite direction. If it turns its back on Europe and embraces the Middle East, it would become, instantaneously, one of the wealthiest countries in the region. It would easily be one of the most diversified economic countries, and probably the one with the most ties to different parts of the world—and one that is not reliant on a single commodity for its wealth, like so many countries nearby are dependent on oil. That gives Turkey a lot more power. **The bridge** of Turkey is actually strengthening. The Turks are gaining more power in today's world because they are becoming what the Plaid Avenger calls a *pivotal historic player.*

THE PLAYER

How are they a player? Turkey is a player because they've got two different directions they can. Just like we've talked about with Russia already—they can go China, or they can go Europe. Turkey can go Europe, or Turkey can go Middle East. They're a strong NATO member, but they actually refused to help the US movement in Iraq. This actually came as a great surprise to the United States. The US said, "Hey, NATO member since 1952! Turkey, you're our boy! Sweet! We're going to launch our Iraq invasion from your soil!" Turkey said, "No way in hell. It's not going to happen. We don't like Saddam either, but those are Islamic people about to get bombed. We don't support this war. You're not going to bomb people from our soil. It's not going to happen." What was the direct result of this? The challenge of, dare I say, *smacking down* the world's military and economic superpower's request? What were the repercussions? What happened? Not a damn thing is what happened.

Erdoğan: in a powerful position.

Turkey is *that* strong now; it is a pivotal historic player on the world stage, and we know that because nothing happened to them. The US even threatened to cut off international aid, saying, "You're going to do what we want or we're not going to give you money anymore!" and Turkey said, "Fine. Don't." US Secretary of State Colin Powell was really pissed off about that, and nothing happened. The threat of pulling aid was all smoke and mirrors; the US was powerless and totally knew it. In fact, the exact same scenario played out again when Turkey sent troops into northern Iraq to get the PKK in 2008. The US begged them not to do it, but Turkey went ahead anyway; the US was forced to support their old ally, even though they weren't happy about it.

Turkey: the other, other, other white meat.

Evidence of Turkey's increasing independence and regional leadership abilities continue to grow here in 2009. Not only has Turkish public opinion about EU membership waned, but increasingly they could care less, moves have been made to secure economic relationships with more Middle Eastern AND Central Asian countries, and the idea of a Mediterranean Union is also starting to look more promising. Why? Well, mostly because the Western European economies are all in the toilet right now thanks to bad management and the recession; many think it's a one-two punch that Europe is not likely to recover from as fast as the rest of the world will. Why should Turkey throw in their lot with a geriatric basket-case at this point? A lot of Turks think the EU option is not smelling so sweet.

Politically, Turkey is increasingly shaping up to be a major player in Middle Eastern affairs, perhaps the only party with enough street cred to pull it off. The Turks have been the host for multiple talks between Israel and Syria, and will soon have a chair at the table for any Arab-Israeli peace settlements as well. The US is also hoping the the Turks will take on even more responsibility in Afghanistan, and maybe even Iraq. Why? Turkey is stable, a democracy, Muslim, moderate, and part of the neighborhood . . . but with no inherent conflicts of interest in the Middle East messes. That makes them quite unique, and uniquely positioned to help.

Add to that a strong sense of nationalistic pride, a strong and independent military, a strong and functioning democracy, and strong political leaders, and you have one hell of a world region. We'll have to watch them quite closely to see in which other regions they end up becoming a major power. It could be one, or it could be several, because **the bridge** Turkey is strengthening, is a pivotal power player, is a region of its own with balls of its own, and therefore be a regional leader. I consider Turkey already to be a second-tier world power; that is, a major regional power on the world stage, just underneath the big boys like the US, China, et al.

TURKEY RUNDOWN & RESOURCES

View additional Plaid Avenger resources for this region at http://plaid.at/turk

 ## BIG PLUSES

→ 100% Muslim, secular, fully functioning democracy: the only one of its kind

→ NATO member and huge political/military ally of the US

→ Strong and modern military in its own right

→ Diversified economy that is growing

→ Slow-growing and therefore stable population

→ Modernized state that is fast becoming a most significant regional power; I predict it will soon join the BRIC

→ Muslim culture AND pro-Western relation-ships make Turkey the most awesome mediator of conflict for Middle Eastern affairs; trusted ally of the US, Israel, Syria, Palestine, Iran . . . . hell, that's everyone!

BIG PROBLEMS

→ Due to its "Muslim-ness" and current cultural/economic attitude of Europe they are not likely to get into the EU

→ While gains have been made in the last decade, the Kurdish situation and problems with the PKK still remain and could get hot again

→ The secular vs. religious "crisis of character" that the Turkish state is dealing with is far from over, is very divisive to the general population, and may result in political gridlock of epic proportions at some point; I sure hope it doesn't come to that, but it might

DEAD DUDES OF NOTE:

Mustafa Keaml aka Atatürk: "The George Washington of Turkey." Turkish army officer, revolutionary statesman, writer, and founder of the Republic of Turkey as well as its first president. Staved off attacks from the Allied powers and held together the core of the Turkish homeland after the defeat and collapse of the Ottoman Empire in WWI. Once in office, embarked upon a program of political, economic, and cultural reforms and entrenched Turkey as a modern, secular state.

LIVE LEADERS YOU SHOULD KNOW:

Recep Erdoğan: The kick-ass Prime Minister of Turkey and chairman of the Justice and Development Party (AK Party). Despite internal friction due to his association with the religious-based AK Party, he has overseen an era of economic prosperity and democratization, and Turkey's rise as a serious regional power and trusted mediator of Middle Eastern conflicts.

Abdullah Gül: President of Turkey and first former-Islamist party President in the modern history of Turkey. His AK political party is accused of being too religiously inspired by staunch secularists. He mostly deals with domestic affairs while Erdogan is really the head cheese in charge.

PLAID CINEMA SELECTION:

Hokkabaz aka *The Magician* (2006) A Turkish comedy-drama that is also a road-trip movie. A magician/juggler tours around Turkey with his father and best friend so that he can make enough money for laser eye surgery. Ha!

Takva aka *A Man's Fear of God* (2006) Drama following a devout Muslim man's internal search for the right path. In the film, the man works at a seminary that exposes him to the temptations of the modern world, and causes him to have a major crisis of faith. Movie has garnered many awards, in large part for one of the best and most fitting conclusions to a film this century.

Eskiya aka *The Bandit* (1996) After serving a 35-year jail sentence, Baran, a bandit, is released from prison in a city in Eastern Turkey and heads to his ancestral home . . . which is now underwater. He then heads to Istanbul to enact revenge on the rat that put him in prison and manic adventures ensue.

Uzak aka *Distant* (2002) Story of Yusuf, a young uneducated factory worker from western Turkey who loses his job and travels to Istanbul to stay with his wealthy and intellectual photographer cousin. Aimlessness and loneliness ensue.

Propaganda (1999) Based on a true story set in 1948, customs officer Mehti is faced with the duty of formally setting up the border between Turkey and Syria, dividing his hometown. He is unaware of the pain that will eminently unfold, as families, languages, cultures and lovers are both ripped apart and clash head on in a village once united.

Yol (1982) Winner of the Cannes film festival highest honor, this film has been banned in Turkey until 1999. The film paints an accurate picture of Turkey after the 1980 Turkish coup d'état through the eyes of five prisoners given a week's home leave.

Güneşe yolculuk (1999) Mehmet, a young Turkish man newly migrated from the village Tire, takes a job searching for water leaks below the surface of the streets of Istanbul. Due to a strange set of events, he is mistaken for a Kurd, imprisoned, and brutally beaten. Great film depicting the Kurdish tension within modern Turkey.

Vizontele (2001) The story of a small town called Hakkari in Turkey at the beginning of the 1970's that gets its first television. Chaos and hilarity ensue.

Crossing the Bridge: The Sound of Istanbul (2005) A documentary that takes an in depth look at the music scene in modern Istabul. Takes an interesting look at a variety of musical genres while simultaneously providing interesting commentary on the culture of Istanbul. Lovers of music will thoroughly enjoy this film.

CHAPTER OUTLINE

Sub-Saharan Africa

LET'S move south from the Middle East into Sub-Saharan Africa, a place the Plaid Avenger could perhaps call the "Basket Case Region of the World." Does that sound too harsh? Am I too cruel? I don't think so. By any measure, any standard to which we compare human life on this planet, the states of Sub-Saharan Africa fall to the bottom of the list. What am I talking about? Things like life expectancy—some Sub-Saharan African countries give you 29, 30, 31 years until you die. Also, Sub-Saharan Africa has some of the lowest literacy rates in the world, some of the highest infant mortality rates in the world, and pretty much the lowest GDP figures you can find anywhere on the planet. Many people are living on less than a dollar a day here. By all accounts—and not just those defined by the West—Sub-Saharan Africa seems to fall in last place in the world race at this juncture in history. Why is that? Why is this the face of Africa? Let's find out.

Why this?

GIRAFFE HAIR

Africa is the second largest continent on the planet, dominated only by the monster continent of Asia. This is a really big place that has a lot going on. Any place that has a lot of size comes with a lot of good stuff. Not only do you have really large tracts of land, those tracts of land have huge mineral resources of all different varieties; crazy things like uranium, which is hardly used on the continent. Africa also has lots of diamonds—as you probably already know—copper, manganese, and all kinds of mineral resources. There are some tremendous patches of oil, though not widespread. Overall, there are a whole lot of resources. But wait a minute! This doesn't explain why Sub-Saharan Africa is poor. Hang on! We'll get to the poor part in a bit. This is a really huge place, so huge, in fact, that a lot of the regions we have talked about would fit easily inside the continent.

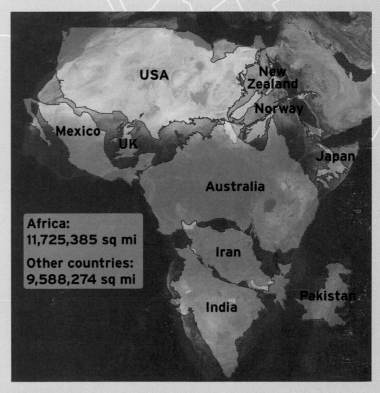

USA
New Zealand
Norway
Mexico
UK
Japan
Australia
Iran
India
Pakistan

Africa: 11,725,385 sq mi

Other countries: 9,588,274 sq mi

A big ass place.

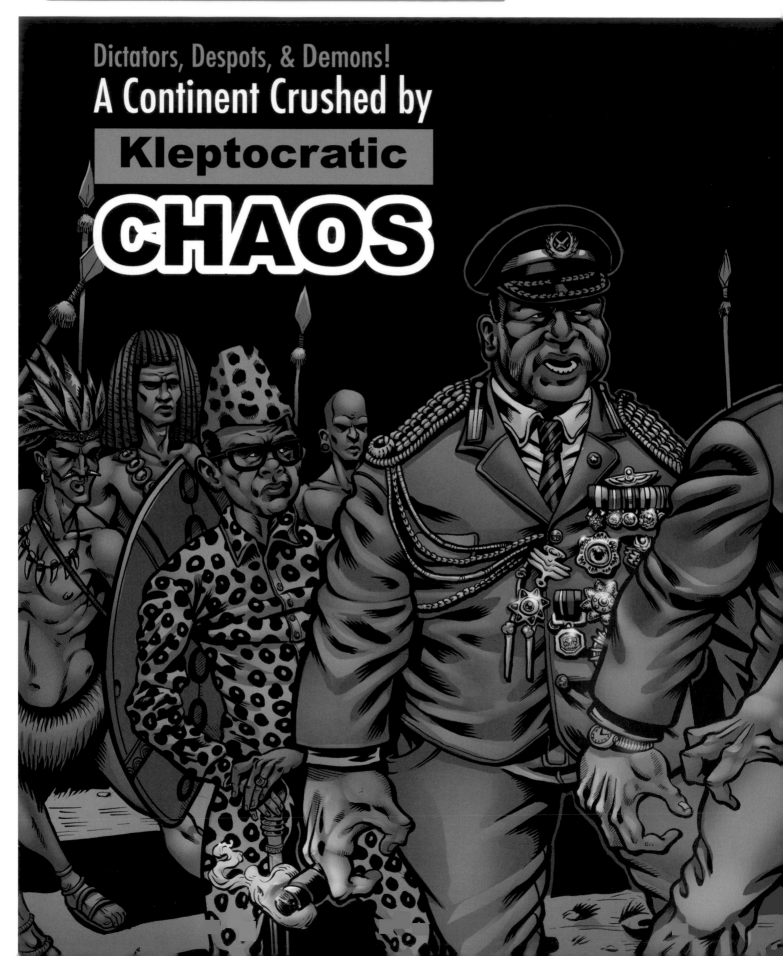

Dictators, Despots, & Demons!
A Continent Crushed by
Kleptocratic
CHAOS

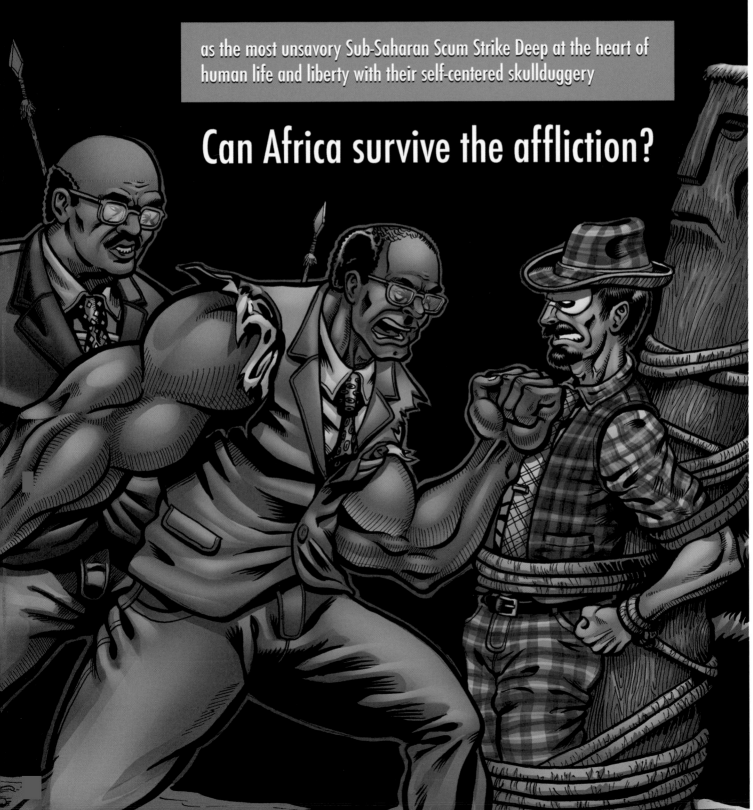

WATCH

as the most unsavory Sub-Saharan Scum Strike Deep at the heart of human life and liberty with their self-centered skullduggery

Can Africa survive the affliction?

Islamabad

Lahore

PAKISTAN

New Delhi ★

HIMALAYAS

NEPAL   BHUTAN
Katmandu   ★ Thimphu

Lucknow
Jaipur   Kanpur

BANGLADESH
★

Karachi
Tropic of Cancer

Ahmadabad

Kolkata
(Calcutta)   Chittagong

Nagpur

INDIA

Arabian

Mumbai
(Bombay)
Pune

Sea

5

Hyderabad

Bangalore

Chennai
(Madras)

Bay of

Bengal

Kochi

Jaffna

SRI
LANKA

Colombo ★

Indian Ocean

75   90

CHAPTER OUTLINE

South Asia

SOUTH ASIA is often referred to as "the subcontinent" because geologically and plate tectonically, it is. A few million years ago, it was a separate land mass and has been slammed into the continent of Asia ever since. I point this out just so you can see physically what is going on here. We have the Himalayan Range, the highest range on the planet, because this little region is *still* actively being slammed into the rest of Asia. But South Asia is a subcontinent in more ways than mere geology.

Indeed, if we looked around the rest of Asia proper, we would see that we can distinguish people we call Indians from India quite easily from the Chinese, or the Burmese, or the Vietnamese, and definitely the Japanese. These folks are different and it's obvious in the way people look, in the way they dress, the way they behave, and in the religions they have. How is South Asia separated from the rest of Asia?

First, what is South Asia? It is the big three: India, Pakistan, and Bangladesh, and the small three: Nepal, Bhutan, and Sri Lanka. We could also throw the small island nation of Maldives in there, but I won't say much about them. Thanks to the rising sea level due to global warming, the entire country will be underwater soon. Sorry, guys!

India, Pakistan, and Bangladesh are the big three not only because they dwarf the other countries in this region in size, but also because they are in the top ten most populated countries on the planet. South Asia may not be a big place geographically, but it is certainly a very populated place.

EURASIAN PLATE

INDIA
Today

10 million
years ago

SRI LANKA

38 million
years ago

Equator

55 million
years ago

INDIAN OCEAN

71 million
years ago

"INDIA"
Land mass

SRI LANKA

LET'S GET PHYSICAL

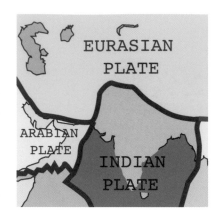

One of the reasons why we have this distinction of culture in South Asia is based somewhat on the physical world; South Asia as a subcontinent has been kind of isolated from the rest of Asia. Isolated how? If we refer back to our opening map, we can see that it is isolated in several ways, mainly by terrain and climate. It is isolated terrain-wise by the Himalayan Range, the mightiest, most powerful range on the planet. The highest mountain in this range is Mount Everest, standing at 29,028 feet. All the other peaks that make up the range are in excess of 20,000 feet, in fact, the top ten highest peaks on the planet are all here.

The Himalayan Range is important because it serves as a barrier. It is difficult for people from our part of the world to differentiate between people from Vietnam and China, for example, but to distinguish any of them from an Indian is pretty easy. The Himalayan Range is just too tall to transit. Do some people get through it? On pack mules, yes, but a very few; there has never been a lot of economic or human transaction across this barrier. Like the Andes, the Himalayan Range is one of the major barriers to human movement on the planet. The Himalayas are even bigger than the Andes and have kept things quite separate as cultures evolved in terms of religious systems, diets, languages, and ethnicities. It is all quite distinct from one side of the Himalayan Range to the other.

Even though we often only think about the Himalayas, if you follow the border of this region you get to the Hindu Kush, the Pamir Knot, and the Karakoram Ranges. All of these are really huge mountain systems on par with the Himalayans themselves. These latter ranges wrap around Pakistan, separating it from Afghanistan. If we go to the other side, the Himalayan Range wraps down in between what is now India and Burma. The Himalayas are the biggie, but it is a continuous system of hills that very nicely isolates this part of the world from the rest of Asia.

Climate starts to play a role as you progress westward out of this region; some pretty severe rainforest and jungle vegetation lies on the Burmese border. If you go in the opposite direction, you run into the Thar Desert and into more deserts as you go into Iran—so dry on one side and wet on the other. Sounds like a good martini!

Climate, vegetation, and terrain have really kept this place isolated from the rest of Asia. Having said that, I want to make a quick point that while South Asia has been *isolated* throughout history, it is not *isolationist*. This is an important point to consider. China, our friend to the north, has been an isolated country by design for many millennia. By that, I mean they are distinctly different, want to keep foreign influence out, and are only concerned about what is happening in their own country; they make a conscious effort not to be part of the wider world. India, Pakistan, and Bangladesh have been isolated physically, but not by choice. They have been open free traders with the rest of the planet for a good long time, mostly by sea via the Indian Ocean.

SLIPPERY WHEN WET

A final, distinct climate factor in South Asia is the **monsoon.** The monsoonal system was first identified and characterized in India. In winter, cool dry air moves from across the continent, flows outward over the ocean and keeps the climate dry. During the spring and early summer, this system completely reverses. The winds change and start moving toward the land. They move from the warm wet waters of the Indian Ocean, bringing warm wet air masses over the Indian subcontinent, and start to produce huge amounts of rainfall once the wet air masses slam into the mountains. The first terrain that they hit is the **Western Ghats.** The Western Ghats is just a small mountain range that floats down the western fringe of India. It doesn't take much; these mountains are maybe two to three thousand feet high, but it just enough to force up the air masses and drop tremendous amounts of rainfall on the west coast of India creating a classic

Monsoon mania: the shifty air system switch-a-roo!

monsoonal system, dropping in excess of 80 to 90 inches of rain per year. As the rest of the air mass progresses inward, it eventually bumps into the Himalayan Range; as that warm wet air is pushed upwards, it has the same effect again, resulting in heavy rain on the fringe of the Himalayas and in Bangladesh.

This system has really become a life cycle in South Asia. Grain harvests, movements of people, and whole economies are based on this, and when the monsoon rains are too early or too late, it can spell disaster. There is really a pulse to the South Asian way of life that moves around this whole monsoon system. However, not all places in India get torrential rain during one time of the year and not the rest. It is really subtle, and it is different depending upon where you are in this part of the world.

Parts of the subcontinent get tremendous amounts of rain, while other places like New Delhi, the capital, are not so much different than Washington, D.C. They are in the midlatitudes and have a seasonal change, but it is a bit warmer and drier throughout the year. They don't get torrential rains, but there is a strong rainy season. It gets dry in the winter, really dry into the spring, and then the rains come. The rains tend to concentrate in late spring and early summer, not much different from parts of the United States. Just to give you an idea and make sure that the Plaid Avenger is not steering you wrong, we hear about monsoon Asia and monsoon India, and it is a factor in the physical world there, but it's not uniformly distributed. There aren't tremendous amounts of rainfall in all places at once with dry seasons in between. It is quite a dynamic system, actually.

PEOPLE POWER

We've discussed the physical components of South Asia, but what about the people? Where are the people? In South Asia, there are loads of people. India's population alone has topped 1 billion. If we look at Pakistan, their population is over 165 million; Bangladesh, over 147 million. All three of those countries are in the top ten of the most populated countries on the planet. Taken as a singular region, it is well over a billion and a half people. Someone do the math for me, what's a billion and a half of six billion? Isn't that closing in on 20 percent of the world's

Undercover agents at work.

population in this one region? This is of serious consequence when trying to figure out what is happening in the world.

Where are these people? Are they concentrated in coastal margins? Are they in big cities? Small villages? Are they in the mountains or the river valleys? The answer is yes! They are everywhere and live all over this place. In fact, to go out on a limb here, the Plaid Avenger spent quite a bit of time in India undercover for various missions, and there really is no place you can go in India that you can't find people at all hours of the day and night. This is a region that does not sleep. This is a busy place all the time with people everywhere. This place is bustling, it's happening, and it's happening nonstop. If we just look at a handful of countries like Bangladesh, India, and Pakistan, throw in China, Indonesia and Japan, we are looking at maybe 12 percent of the world's land area. On that 12 percent of the world's land area, 52 percent of its population lives.

Let's describe some of these people packed in all over the place in a little more detail. Why are South Asians different from other Asians? When we think of India, we typically think of Hindus. Is that a religion, a language, or an ethnic group? Let's sort some of these terms out.

HINDU OR HINDI?

Hindi is a language; therefore, we think that's the main language of India. We are wrong already. Hindi is a language, one of maybe fifteen or twenty major languages spoken in just this one region. Those are just the major languages; there are several hundred dialects and mixed languages through South Asia. This is very confusing for people from other parts of the world who live in primarily single language societies. We assume there must be some linguistic commonality in this region. There is no majority language at the moment in India. In fact, if you want to cite a lingua franca of this region, that would be English. That's got something to do with India's English colonial period. English is spoken by a lot of people, but perhaps only by fifteen to twenty percent of the population. Hindi is just another language of many spoken here; indeed, if you talk to people from India, Bangladesh, or Pakistan, you will find that many of them speak several languages.

One of the first languages South Asians learn is their local dialect. That can be one of several hundred dialects and mixed languages. The second one they learn is often some-

Major Religions

- Hindu
- Muslim
- Christian
- Tribal / Animist
- Buddhist
- Sikh

Hindu, Muslim, and Buddhism abound . . .

thing like Hindi, which can be used as a kind of lingua franca inside India. The third one is typically English, for perhaps obvious reasons of economic advantage. There are a variety of languages spoken and they exist in a kind of hierarchy of how they are learned. English usually wins out in today's world, Hindi is a far distant second, and a local dialect would be third.

Not all South Asians are Hindi, not even close. They are not all speaking *Hindi,* but are they all *Hindu?* **Hindu** is a religious system, and we tend to think of Hinduism as a description of the religious lifestyle of people in India. When you are around Indian people, they now recognize the term Hinduism as describing their religion, but it does not really mean anything to them. It is not a self-defined term, like Christianity being based on the life and teachings of Christ. Hinduism is a conglomeration of cultural beliefs that someone from the outside world said, "Well, you guys speak Hindi . . . how about we call this Hindu?"

When we think of India, we think the majority of people follow Hinduism. However, the majority of people in Pakistan are Muslim. The majority of people in Bangladesh are Muslim. The majority of people in Sri Lanka are neither of the two. They are Buddhist instead. We have a nice little mix of some Western and Eastern religions dancing around this place. Bhutan is primarily Buddhist with some Hindu, and Nepal is mostly Hindu with some Buddhist. We have a confusing mix of things going on here, but the two major power players, of course, are Hinduism and Islam.

Buddha sez: Talk to the hand.

VISHNU VS. MUHAMMAD VS. BUDDHA

How did this get to be? What is the deal with this religion stuff? Buddhism is primarily in Sri Lanka, Bhutan, and the Tibetan plateau just north of this region. The Buddha, Siddhartha, the main man in the Buddhist lifestyle, was actually a Hindu born in India. (In a similar vein, Jesus Christ was actually Jewish.) He eventually thought, "Hey, I dig Hinduism; I dig the lifestyle, except this whole life cycle and being reborn again and again, and always suffering and being reborn sucks!" He invented his little reform movement to change things, think of things in a different way and be removed from the endless cycle of rebirth. Buddhism is a universalizing religion and as such, he wanted to spread it to other places. It spread itself right out of India. It had

its heyday from about 300 BCE to 300 or 400 CE. It was in vogue. Everybody dug it for a while, but Hinduism eventually displaced it in India once again, and it largely disappeared. When we think of Buddhist areas, we have Sri Lanka and Bhutan, but we also think of Tibet, China, even Mongolia and Japan as having a huge Buddhist influence. Buddhism moved on beyond India.

Where did the Muslims come from, then? Well, it's the same deal if we think religiously. Muslims didn't come around until about 600 or 700 CE, after the death of the prophet Muhammad. The empire, what I call the Arab-Islamic empire, expanded out from the Middle East all the way over to the northern fringes of South Asia. For the next thousand years, they heavily influenced South Asia. There has historically been some friction between the Muslims and Hindus, and it's still not over. Muslim-Hindu friction is far from a historical remnant. It is still a very real issue, typically where the majorities of each belief meet: on the Pakistan-India border. Pakistan is predominately Islamic; India is predominately Hindu. Tensions primarily arise in the western states of India and sometimes manifest themselves in violence.

Hinduism: multi-faceted, and multi-faced, culture of most Indians.

CULTURAL HEARTHINESS

Like China, Mesopotamia, and the ancient civilizations in Middle America, the Indus River valley, where we find India and Pakistan, is an ancient cultural hearth. A civilization cropped up on its own, with big cities and architecture, mathematics, and unique cultural ideas. South Asian culture was perpetuated throughout the millennia in its isolated environment, allowing it to remain quite different from China, or even closer next door, Mesopotamia. These are very different places because of their spontaneous creation and uninhibited growth for extended periods of time. I am not going to bore you with a lot of details about ancient history in this part of the world because it is too rich, and like China, there is too damn much. I just want you to know that, throughout history in this part of the world, there were multiple episodes of different empires and kingdoms, and also formations of some of the big time players in philosophy. Some classics of world religion started out here. Hinduism started here and gave rise to the evolution of Buddhism. Islam was infused later to combine a unique cultural dynamic in this region.

HISTORICAL HAPPENINGS

Let's get back to the period that I was talking about earlier, the period of Muslim dominance. We had Hinduism and Buddhism, but eventually the Muslims came to town around 1000 CE. This was a continuation of the expansion of the Arab-Islamic Empire, which began to spread after the death of the prophet in 632 CE. Islam made its way into Afghanistan and, with the help of the Mughal Conquest and a little bit later, ended up taking over virtually all of what is Pakistan and India in today's world. They created the Mughal Empire.

MUGHAL MANIA

The Mughal Empire dominated South Asia for about 800 years from 1000CE to about 1757 CE. It was basically a hierarchy of Muslim rulers, a thin veneer of Islamic influence over the millions of Hindus that lived there. The ruling class was Islamic, but the majority of the population remained Hindu. I want to make sure you understand that because,

MUGHAL EMPIRE 1526 - 1707
Extent of Mughal Empire in 1530
Expansion of Mughal Empire to 1605
Expansion of Mughal Empire to 1707
Mughal expansion into Babur's Afgan kingdom
Modern Political Boundaries

The Muslim Mughal period . . .

when we look at today's India, there are a huge number of Muslims in India today—around 150 million. That population of Muslims in Hindu-dominated India is actually larger than the population of Muslims in Saudi Arabia, Iraq, Iran, or just about any country. The Muslim minority in India is bigger than the Muslim majority in most other Islamic countries. This is a significant demographic to consider, and it has its roots in this period of Muslim influence during the Mughal Empire.

The dominance after 1757 soon shifted. Small kingdoms and fiefdoms comprised this period of the Mughal Empire, like European feudalism or Japanese Shogunates, with princes and royal courts. There is kind of a main king, but there were also sub-princes and sub-dukes under those guys that controlled smaller and smaller territories. The beginning of the end of this was around 1700, as foreign intervention started to creep in. Surprise! Who was responsible for this foreign intervention? Who sent out fleets of ships to establish in-roads in other parts of the world?

ENTER THE EUROPEANS

That's right, our old friends in Western Europe, and one up-and-coming colonial power in particular: the British. Actually, the Portuguese also established a small trade province on the west coast of India, called Goa. These two European powers made inroads into South Asia for the main purpose of trading. You may have even heard of the British East India Trading Company, for instance. It was a company sponsored by the British government. They worked out a deal with the company by saying, "Here is your charter, go out and establish trade with South Asia. We will insure the boats and we get a cut of your business."

Why did they want to do this? You should know very well by now. They wanted to get raw commodities—the good stuff, such as spices, silks, and ceramics. The East India Trading Company, sponsored by the British, wanted to

Can you spot the European establishing trade links in this picture?

get in here and score first pick on all the best stuff. They turned out to be very good at this.

These guys were not just partially successful; they were radically successful at establishing trade with South Asia because the Mughal Empire was winding down a little, and did not have a very firm grip on things. There were only a small veneer of Mughals in control of that vast majority of Hindus in India, so their control weakened and it became fairly easy to get in and establish port cities and trading colonies. These cities started to grow into territories that the trading company controlled. They essentially went into the next fiefdom or dukedom over and chatted with the prince saying, "Hey, we're going to give you loads of money to trade some stuff with us. It's going to be good for you!" Plenty of princes said, "Yeah, it looks good to me. I'll sign a trade deal, no problem!" Through diplomatic relations and strategic ties, the British made their way in and were more successful than they ever dreamed. They ended up controlling huge chunks of land.

Eventually, disputes arose between princes who had some previous friction between their kingdoms. This trading company was so successful that, though it was set up exclusively for trade, it found itself acting as a diplomatic entity between these feuding kingdoms. These disputes could potentially turn into violent conflict, and that would ruin trade completely. The higher-ups at the trading post glanced at their royal charter, and got Britain on the horn to let them know that things may be getting out of hand.

Great Britain looked at this mess and says, "Whoa, this is not your charter! What the hell is going on here? Sit tight, we're taking this party over." A trading company was not fully equipped to handle colonization. The British crown sent in the warships and court jesters and everything in between and fully colonized India. From then forward—we are talking about 1800—this whole territory of what is now India, Pakistan, and Bangladesh, was under the umbrella known as **British India.** It was an official British colony. There were some independent kingdoms left over that held out and had diplomatic relations, places like Bhutan, the kingdom of Nepal, and Ceylon, which is now Sri Lanka. These guys held out as independent territories and avoided the burden of colonialism. All the rest of it, the big three, became one big land conglomeration called British India.

British India 1800
- British Adminstered States
- British Protectorates
- Semi-Autonomus Princely Fiefdoms

. . . followed by the British colonial period . . .

India is the biggest country (I keep referring only to India because India is the power player—the Plaid Avenger calls it like it is); it has the biggest population, the biggest economy, and the biggest military. When we think of India and South Asia as a whole, it is not completely developed, but it is certainly not in last place. It is much better off than other places like Africa, or even closer places in Central Asia or Southeast Asia. What different about South Asia that has kept it ahead of the pack when it comes to developing countries or regions? It has a lot to do with its colonial experience. Some things happened in British India that gave it its strategic advantage. Before I piss off my Indian friends, let me state for the record: Colonialism sucks! The fact that the British were controlling your people probably sucked for a couple hundred years. However, there were some distinct advantages that have put India in the catbird seat today.

DROP THE WICKET, JAMES, IT'S TEATIME: ADVANTAGES OF BRITISH COLONIALISM

My Indian friends, you're not so bad off. *Number one:* it was a singular European entity that took you over. As such, there wasn't internal fracturing like in Africa or even to a lesser degree in South America or Southeast Asia. That's kind of a plus. At least you know exactly who to blame. *Number two:* the colonizer was Britain, which means you spoke the Queen's English. While at the time it may have been revolting to your great granddad, it has benefited you greatly in today's world. English is the lingua franca of business, travel, airlines, the international space station, and technology. Everybody speaks English when they deal with that stuff, and that has put you, Indians, on a strategic fast track. It is a great advantage to speak English; that's part of your colonial heritage.

There's a good chap. Now fetch us a spot of tea!

What else did Britain do differently here than in other places that were colonized on the planet? *Number three:* Internal investment. That's a biggie. In Africa, we pointed out that most investment was simply to extract the resources. We could even say that about the New World. When they got to the New World, or even to Africa or Australia, the British and other colonial masters didn't really add too much in the way of infrastructure. When the British arrived in India in the 1800s, this was a huge place with a long history, big cities, and millions of people, more people than were in Europe at that time. The British couldn't just wipe India clean and start again by building new industries, nor could they merely focus on extracting stuff. There was already stuff going on, preexisting economies and cul-

---

WTH

What's the Deal with the Great Mutiny?

Why two different names for the same thing? It depends on who's telling the story. "Mutiny" has the connotation of something bad that needed to be suppressed. "War for Independence" has a more positive connotation: "We are trying to be free." Try and figure out which group called it what. What was the Great Mutiny all about? It was obviously about independence, but amazingly enough, it came to a head because of fat—animal fat to be exact. Pig fat, cow fat, lard, all kinds of yummy animal fat, put together in a big stew. Why would the British care about fat? They didn't. However, during their colonial days, the British were pretty savvy about controlling the local populations. One of the more savvy ways they did this was by employing locals in the army and the police force. Why would they do that, Plaid Avenger?

Here's why: When you are from a different part of the world and your skin color, your religion, and your language are obviously different, people are immediately on guard if you boss them around and tell them what to do. That sort of thing causes resentment issues to crop up among the locals: "This bastard thinks that he's better than me! I don't like being bossed around by an outsider. What the hell does he know?" The British were familiar with this human tendency. They knew that they could alleviate this problem by getting local people who looked, talked, and understood the problems and issues of the people there, and training *them* to beat down the locals! It was a brilliant system, and also easy to implement; the British did it all over the place, and it worked magically in India.

Back to the fat: Nobody was eating it. They were using it to grease the cartridges for their guns. That's not a big deal—how could that cause a mutiny? People in India at the time were of what two religions? That's tural systems. The British focus in British India was updating the infrastructure, improving it, modernizing, and building railroads and communication systems across the colony, some of which are still in use today.

I cannot stress enough that colonialism sucks. I am sure South Asians would have preferred being on their own, but the British brought in a lot of perks. If you look at colonial experiences around the world, British India's was not too bad in comparison. In addition, the introduction of the Europeans in the Americas decimated local populations; that didn't happen here. The colonial story is radically different in South Asia.

ADVANTAGES, SCHMADVANTAGES

Having talked about the advantages, it still sucked. The Indians were ruled and controlled by a different people, with a different culture. British dudes dress funny and talk even funnier, and play games like cricket, and dance around playing croquet—pretty strange stuff. Who wants to be ruled by guys like that? Indeed, internal unrest developed fairly early on. Many Indian folks weren't too keen on this from the get-go. They weren't so keen on the Mughals, and they were less keen on the British and wanted to get them the hell out of there. This came to a head for the first time in 1857, when something called the **Great Mutiny** occurred. You might also see this referenced in India as the "First War for Independence."

MY MAIN MAN MAHATMA

Enter Mahatma Gandhi. Everybody knows Gandhi. He's one of the coolest dudes in world history. Everybody loves Gandhi, kind of, so what's his deal? Gandhi was an Indian guy, trained as a lawyer in Great Britain, who spent some time in South Africa peddling his craft. He was a British citizen because all people in the colonial system were citizens of the mother country. When he lived in South Africa, he became incensed because he realized that, though he was a British citizen, he was still considered second-class by "true" British people (a.k.a. white British people). Gandhi had an awakening at this point and realized, "This sucks. I am not really a British person, even though I went to school in Britain, talk like a British person, and work with British people. The British don't think I'm British."

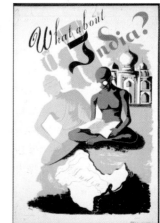

Most famous "little brown man."

right, Hinduism and Islam. What people would have problems handling cow fat and pig fat to grease the cartridges of their guns? That's right, Hindus and Muslims. Cows are sacred in Hinduism, while pork is unclean to Islamic folks. In all of their wisdom, the British soldiers said, "Here's the grease for your guns, chaps. Cheerio!" The local soldiers said, "We hear it's made of pig and cow fat. We're not touching it." The British, in all of their worldly wisdom, said, "Do it or die." And the Great Mutiny began.

It was quelled fairly quickly and didn't become a very big uprising, but it is still remembered in popular culture. This was the first attempt to throw off the yoke of British Imperialism. The Great Mutiny, as coined by the British, and the War for Independence as coined by the locals—those being the Indian guys. Obviously, the British were going to be ejected at some point, because they aren't there now. How did British colonialism end if it didn't end with the Great Mutiny? Where did they go from there?

Oh! A circus! No wonder they mutinied.

Bothered by this, he went back to the motherland, where he realized the British sucked. (Okay, excluding Monty Python.) He was Indian and wanted India to be run by Indians.

Gandhi started a peaceful movement to kick the British out. In other words, he started the movement by saying, "You are going to leave. We're not going to shoot at you. We are not going to fight you, we are not going to beat you down with clubs and physically kick you out. We are going to make you leave without even raising a fist. With no violence."

How did he do this? He did a variety of things. Of course, he didn't do it by himself, but he was the driving force and most popular leader of this nonviolent movement. He not only ended colonialism in British India, he simultaneously, and much more importantly, ended **neocolonialism.** He realized the two things were inherently tied together.

Gandhi G is money! Literally!

What is neocolonialism? Neocolonialism is when a foreign entity controls your country, not politically, not physically, but economically. It owns a lot of the business and controls the flow of goods and services, and sets up things that are an advantage to their country and not yours. One of the reasons India is doing really well in the world today, while places in Africa aren't, is because neocolonialism is still happening in Africa and it was stopped in India.

When the British came into India, it was during Britain's industrial era, and they needed raw commodities. They had weaving mills and industrial stuff and the industrial capacity to make things, but they needed raw materials. They then processed the cheap raw materials into things that sold for more money. The best example of this neocolonial economic system in India was the wool the Indians had been spinning into their own cloth for 5,000 years. The British bought the wool from them for virtually nothing, processed it into nice crisp linens in factories back home, which employed their own people. British workers made a good wage, and then Britain brought back the cloth to sell to the Indians at a huge markup. This was really a fantastic, sweet deal. How could the Indians say no? They really couldn't because the British were in control of the country.

Gandhi was aware of this system when he started this nonviolent movement. He told everyone, "We need to kick these guys out of here. We could physically take up arms and kick these guys out, but the system is so skewed, we'd still be screwed. We need to fix it from the inside out. We need to end this neocolonialism crap along with the political colonialism. Hey! Why are you dudes buying this British cloth? What in the hell are you thinking about?" I am paraphrasing; Gandhi probably never said "hell" or "dudes." Back to Gandhi: "We are Indians; we have been making cloth since before there even was a Great Britain. Why are we buying cloth from these guys? Can someone explain this to me? It makes no sense whatsoever! Stop buying British cloth and start weaving your own again." Gandhi only wore homespun cloth he made himself for the entire second half of his life. His kind of skimpy toga was a symbolic gesture saying, "Look, this is all you need. You don't need any of that fancy stuff." If you ever see pictures, a documentary, or even the movie *Gandhi*, you will see that he is often around a spinning wheel. The spinning wheel was a symbol for the peaceful independence movement: "Do it yourself; let's break from this economic cycle. Free yourself from this slavery and make your own cloth!"

Once people heard of this practical way to gain independence, the movement started to gain speed. Around the late 1930s and into the early 1940s, it was not yet a nationwide deal. More people were talking about independence, but most folks were still talking about nothing. This little nonviolent movement was kind of a mosquito bite to the British, no big deal. As the movement progressed, the British started to pay attention: "We might want to start dealing with this Gandhi guy and figure out how to shut him down." What did they do? They made the cloth cheaper. They made it so cheap that people couldn't afford not to buy it.

When Gandhi saw this, he said, "Well, that got their attention! I have another idea. We are currently buying salt from the British. Hello, can I have everyone's attention? We have a ton of coastline where there is this substance called *salt-water*. It becomes salt when the water evaporates. Salt is free, why are we paying for it?" He got the word out and, in 1930, organized a Salt March to the sea, like a common strike, where everybody went to the coast and made salt. The movement grew in popularity; Indians set up salt producing shops on the coastline. Gandhi himself worked at them between speaking engagements and rallying the people. This became a big deal; the British were starting to get pissed off because their profits were being cut in two by this salt boycott.

These things culminated in British discussions with Gandhi: "Hey Gandhi, lets work things out; we are your buddies." Gandhi refused: "It's time for you limeys to get the hell out." The British still did not think that it was too big of a deal. Gandhi tried a different tactic. By now he was massively popular, and he encouraged everybody in India, which at this time was probably half a billion people, to not go to work the next day: "Everybody skip work; we're having a general strike." The British, being very much in touch with the common people—can you smell the sarcasm?—had no idea this was happening. It was a smashing success. The whole country just stopped for one day.

The British really saw the writing on the wall and realized that the Indian people had the real power here. They called a general strike, they ceased all economic activity, and they shut down the country. They were willing to make it incredibly unprofitable for the British to be there. At the same time this was happening, World War II broke out. If you know anything about World War II or read any of the chapters thus far in this book, you realize that it was kind of a big deal in Europe, and that kept the British quite busy.

We know that Europe was essentially destroyed at the end of World War II. The British were spent physically, mentally, and economically, and all these protests were occurring in India at the same time. It just became too much. They dragged India along to support them in World War II, but the common perception on the street was, "It's not our war. We are not getting involved. We are trying to kick you out of here. We are not coming to Europe to spill blood for you, ours or anyone else's." By 1945, the British had to throw in the towel; they just couldn't hold onto India anymore. They didn't have the resources to keep it under control, by force or otherwise. They had to rebuild at home. They started concession talks for India to become independent; in 1947, that is exactly what happened. In 1947, they drew it up on the conference table and handed over control to the locals.

Ali Jinnah, Father of Pakistan.

PAKIN' OUR BAGS FOR THE PARTITION PARTY

Now the story gets complicated. A bunch of other people in the country wanted another kind of independence: "We want an India as well, but not Gandhi's India. We aren't Hindus like Gandhi; we're Muslims." This brings us back full circle on the topic of religion. There was still a huge minority of Muslims in this country. Their basic platform was, "The British suck, but here is the deal. We are a minority, and if the British walk out of here, the Hindu majority will dominate us. The only reason they haven't yet was because the British have been in control for a few hundred years. If we don't get our own place, if we can't subdivide British India and get our own country, then we don't want the British to leave."

Here is where we have to introduce a new character in our play, a guy called Muhammad Ali Jinnah. Gandhi is often credited with being the father of India, and Jinnah is often credited with being the father of Pakistan. He was a Muslim in British India and led the fight for the formation of a distinct and separate sovereign state for Muslims. He was also British trained and schooled, a lawyer just like Gandhi, and a savvy politician. Gandhi was vehemently opposed to this, as were many others in India. However, when all was said and done, that's how it had to go down. It got tense once Jinnah told Gandhi that he didn't want the British to leave. Gandhi didn't want that; he had been fighting for years to be free of the British, so he considered it the lesser of two evils. He and his party capitulated and said, "We want a unified state, but we'll settle for the split." On a side note here, there was a minority of people in India who actually hated Gandhi. They blamed him for the country split.

In 1947, Britain packed up shop, redrew the map, set up partitions, and sailed off. What we see here in this map is something similar to today's map. We've got Pakistan, India, and another place called Bangladesh, but back then it was called East Pakistan. The agreement set in place two separate homelands, areas for the Muslims in British India. East

Pakistan and West Pakistan, which were two different territories that, at the same time, were a singular sovereign state. It was Pakistan, but with an eastern and western side. India was for the Hindus, and Pakistan was for the Muslims. This is all fine and dandy on a map, but the reality was that Muslims and Hindus were living all over the place. It came to a fever pitch on the day of independence in 1947, when there was a mass migration of people. Tens of millions of people found themselves on the wrong side of the border and suddenly needed to move.

The Muslims in India said, "We better get over to East or West Pakistan or we are going to get the crap beat out of us!" The Hindus in East and West Pakistan said, "We're on the wrong side; we need to get over to India." This was a very turbulent time, a bloody day in India's history. As you might expect, people were being

Independence! With partition and relocation!

uprooted from their homelands, places where their families may have been forever, and were now on the wrong side because of the new lines on the map. They ripped up all their material possessions, all their family, and moved. They were instantaneous refugees. The friction and the tension grew between these massive movements of people who were not necessarily enemies but certainly not friends, their differences accentuated by going in two different directions down the highway. This ended in violence and massive rioting. It was a nasty day in history, and set the stage for future tensions between India and Pakistan.

This gets back to what I was talking about with issues between Muslims and Hindus in today's world. This is still hot. In the last five years, there have been three different massive rioting incidents. Unknown things spark the unrest and massive slaughters of Muslims, which then spark slaughters of Hindus, which are then avenged in mass slaughters of Muslims. This is nasty business, and has escalated to full-fledged international warfare three different times since 1947.

The only date I want you to remember is the one in 1971, when it wasn't so much based on religious conflict as it was a political maneuver by East Pakistan. They weren't happy. They felt that West Pakistan was too far away to properly understand their needs. India helped fuel this internal dissent, which turned into outright warfare between West Pakistan and India, during which India helped convince East Pakistan to declare independence and became Bangladesh. Now we have three countries, and now you understand why Pakistan is almost 100 percent Muslim, why Bangladesh is almost 100 percent Muslim, and why India is somewhere in between with a vast Hindu majority. Occasionally, riots still occur, mostly along the Pakistan/India border. I remember a few years ago when a trainload of about forty Muslims burned to death after some Hindus barred the entrances and exits and caught the thing on fire. This sparked about two months of retribution riots. This problem is a historical relic of the tension from long ago, still active in today's South Asia.

South Asia now . . . well, at least for now.

TIME FOR TODAY'S SOUTH ASIA

This is a mixed bag of states, an assortment of cookies. Are these places developed, or are they developing? Who's got the money? Who's doing well? Who's not? When we look at South Asia, India is the premier powerhouse player with the most people and the biggest economy—one that is really exploding right now. Exploding like China? Not quite that hot, but it is developing fast. They are developing a middle class as well, so the developed/developing question is a tough call. Let's look at some issues to help us define their status.

THE LITTLE COUNTRIES

We have mostly talked about the three big boys in this region: India being the giant, and Pakistan and Bangladesh being the other two. What about the other countries, the three smaller guys, Bhutan, Nepal, and Sri Lanka?

Bhutan is easy. The whole country is like a Buddhist monastery. They have been hosting their refugee brothers from Tibet for quite some time. It is a home away from home for the Tibetan monks, including the Dalai Lama. Bhutan is a curious place in that it is trying to preserve its 11th century standards in the face of

Bhutan house party!.

21st century advancements. Until 1999, there was a nationwide ban on television and the Internet. Though the ban has been lifted, there are still active movements to prevent popular culture from the rest of the world intervening in their culture that is still an old school monarchy. Bhutan has held its own throughout the centuries. If you want to time travel, go there. Via the Internet and telecommunications, this tough nut is starting to be cracked, so hurry and check it out before it becomes totally globalized!

Nepal is perhaps even more fascinating, because it would be similar to Bhutan twenty years ago, but now it is utter chaos. I want to end this little section talking about two poles of conflict on either side of this South Asian region. The active conflict bookends: Nepal in the north, Sri Lanka in the south. Both countries are on the brink of civil war/collapse/insurgency where people are going to get killed en masse. In the last few years, Nepal has had an increasingly bigger problem with a Maoist insurgency that wants to totally eject the ruling monarchy. Their primary mission is to change the government from a constitutional monarchy to perhaps communism, or maybe socialism. It's not very clear. What is clear in Nepal is that there is fighting, and over 11,000 people have died since 1996. A rebel group scattered throughout the country has been fairly effective in striking targets and generally causing chaos.

On top of that, in June 2001, the heir to the Nepalese throne went postal and massacred most of the royal family over a reported dispute about his choice of potential bride. He then shot himself, but lived for a little while longer. He was crowned king while he was comatose. That event fueled the fire for the Maoist rebels; they loved the idea of having a comatose king. They thought it was great and that they may be able to get control of the state by causing more chaos with no king to rule the country. When the comatose king died two days later, a lesser-known uncle became king and began pulling power away from more democratic institutions to himself, under the guise of needing more power to fight the rebel insurgency.

In April 2006, in the government's effort to crack down on the Maoists, they pissed off the pro-democracy movement in the country resulting in a bizarre triangle of folks: the Maoists are teamed up with the pro-democracy people to overthrow the monarchy all together. They pretty much accomplished this by 2008; the monarchy was sidelined, elections were held and the place settled down quite a bit. It is still a very new democratic experiment for these folks, so future instability is entirely possible, and probable, as they figure out how to go forward. Need proof of the bizarreness? The monarchy was fully abolished in 2008, and the first full democratic election resulted in their current (and first) President who is a centrist Hindu, with a Prime Minister who is a Communist atheist. Party on! Most Nepalese folks live on less than a dollar a day, adding to the fray of instability.

Let's go to the other side of the South Asian region for the other still quite active conflict in *Sri Lanka*. We will talk more about Sri Lanka in the Plaid Avenger hotspots chapter, but let's introduce the situation here: Sri Lanka is a coun-

What's the Deal with the Tamil Tigers?

In Sri Lanka, the rebel insurgents/terrorists had a killer mascot . . . literally. The dudes called themselves the Tamil Tigers. That's their political party. These guys were fairly vicious and by all standards they would be in the top tier of terrorist organizations for their practices. The Tigers have been blowing up people via human suicide bombs for quite some time now, a technique they mastered in the 1970s. In fact, they were even responsible for the assassination of Indian Prime Minister Rajiv Gandhi in 1991. They were well equipped and organized, had uniforms, boats and even a few aircraft, but most importantly actually controlled territory in the northern part of Sri Lanka. That all came to an end in summer 2009 as the government made an all-out effort to smash the entire organization. Even though it caused massive civilian casualties, it appears the civil war is over and the back of the Tigers has been broken. For now.

try that has been struggling with a full-on on civil war. They have been off and on for about twenty to thirty years now, all based on an ethnic division. In an ethnic enclave on the northern fringe of the island, there are people called the Tamils. It's an ethnic group that actually came from India, and they had what was easily the most organized and outfitted rebel group on the planet. See box on the previous page on the "Tamil Tigers" for titillating details. The Sinhalese Sri Lankans, the people on the rest of the island, are the ones that run the government and have the real power. This has been a face off for several decades now in terms of the Tamils either wanting an independent homeland, a sovereign state, or more autonomy and more power. This civil war came to a bloody conclusion in 2009, with the almost total destruction of the Tamil rebel/terrorist force, and horrific civilian casualties. However, the thing about rebel/terrorist groups is that it only takes a handful of survivors to re-establish operations, so I'm not sure we have heard the last of this conflict. It will certainly be much quieter in the near future as the government rebuilds the society and strengthens the state.

This is a summary of the two poles of South Asia outside the realm of the three giants. We have some conflict that is quite active, and may get much hotter. But back to the giants . . .

Ethnic communities and religions

The Plaid Avenger seeking out Singh . . .

ENERGETIC INDIA

World power position, here we come! India is hustling and bustling right now, my plaid friends, and shaping up to be an Asian titan on the world stage. India has the distinction of being the absolute largest multi-ethnic, multi-linguistic, multi-religious full fledged democracy on Earth! On top of that, they have been steadily growing their economy at a respectable 5% to 8% GDP growth rate for over a decade. Those numbers are overshadowed by China's huge double-digit growth, but they are nonetheless quite respectable for a country of 1.3 billion people. More to the point, India's growth is much more diverse and sustainable in the long term than China's, which means that the Hindus are here for the long haul. How is the India model so different than the Chinese? I'm glad you asked . . .

For most of its modern history since independence in 1947, India has followed a government-heavy-handed approach to regulating and controlling the economy . . . you know, it's called social-ism. It was never full-on communism like the Chinese model, but the Indian state did produce a massive, bloated bureaucracy in order to outright control some sectors of the economy, protect other sectors from competition, and in general regulate the hell out of everything else. All this was done to redistribute some of the resources of the states via services like education, infrastructure, and employment in general. After decades of stagnation and inefficiency, in 1991 India put into play a crucial reform package which restructured the entire government/economy relationship, resulting in tons of privatization, slashing of bureaucratic red tape, and promotion of entrepreneurship. All this set India on a path for sustained economic growth and true integration into the global economy, for the first time ever!

Our man man Manmohan.

In other words, India started the conversion from a heavy socialist state to one based more on capitalist principles of free trade and less governmental control. Wow! Who was the genius that thought all that up? The main brain behind this plan in the early 1990s was the finance minister Dr. Manmohan Singh—hey, wait a minute! I know that dude! He is currently the Prime Minister, isn't he? You know this! And Prime Minister Singh was so successful in his first term, that he has just been re-elected for another four years. The man is unstoppable! Singh has been a big force behind the country's successful economic conversion. Successful in strange and sustainable ways as well.

How so? Well, India is very unique in that it has kind of "jumped" stages of the natural economic evolution pattern. Namely, it has yet to fully and thoroughly industrialize like most other rich countries. It has gone from a largely agricultural and primary products based economy straight to a service and information economy. How bizarre! To compare, China used to be mostly ag-based, and then industrialized to become a mega-manufacturing giant, producing everything from toys to tubas to Toyotas, and now it is diversifying into services and higher-end technologies. India, on the other hand, jumped straight to the top: service sector jobs have the highest growth rate, with high-tech manufacturing and research/development industries also exploding quickly. Money! 150 of the Fortune 500 companies traded on the US stock market currently have research and development bases in India. It's blowing up! Combine that with a rapidly growing small-business class, and now you have the recipe for India's current success. The place is hustling and bustling right now; go watch *Slumdog Millionaire* again, and pay attention to how much change occurs in Mumbai during the course of the film to get a sense of what I'm talking about here.

Why else is India bustling right now? They have several distinct advantages from British influence; one we already pointed out is that they speak English. India is well-equipped to embrace the world economically, and they are doing just that. Indeed, when your computer breaks and you get on the phone to have someone help you fix it, who are you talking to? You are probably talking to someone from India. Again, think about *Slumdog Millionaire*: what was Jamal's occupation when he got on the gameshow? They are big into telecommunications, high technology, and the service sector. It is actually quite fascinating because they have whole divisions of technical support and telemarketers there that specifically train people to not just speak English, but how to speak certain regional dialects of English. If you go into a technical support center outside of New Delhi, the huge room with 500 to 600 people in it will be subdivided into what region of the United States from which they are receiving calls. There is a Midwestern section, perhaps a Californian section where they talk surfer dude language, or a northeastern section where they talk real fast with those Boston accents, or a southeastern quadrant where they talk with a long drawl, Southern belle style.

We also talked about how the British invested heavily in their infrastructure, and that has benefited them in today's world as well. Another thing that India is famous for is something called **back offices.** The hot word in today's world is **outsourcing.** What's that? It means there is cheaper labor there and more people to do it, so jobs move there because companies can save money. Unlike other places in the world, say China or other developing countries, these folks speak English, and most working age Indians are fairly well-educated. This is a huge advantage to India in terms of this outsourcing, but also something called back offices.

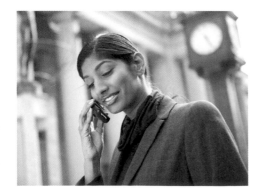

"Yes, Plaid Avenger, my back office is always open for you . . ."

Back offices are companies that set up in India decades ago. When you go to the doctor, for example, he scribbles out your symptoms as you tell him you have herpes, or hemorrhoids, or ingrown hairs, or whatever it is that is ailing you. The doctor writes all this down, at the end of the day, he hands it to his secretary to transcribe into a digital file. What has been happening in the US is that, after the doctor's office closes down, the secretaries fax the notes to India. People who speak and read English transcribe the notes into a digital file, and then send them back. What's this back office got to do with it? Why was this whole system possible? Think about what I just said, as the doctor's office is closing in America, what is happening in India? That's right! They are waking up. It is a complementary business arrangement, so doctors can get work done more efficiently.

But that's not all! India is fast becoming a center for information technology development, not just basic manufacturing and low-level service sector stuff. Call centers combined with software development centers—now that's a combo that everyone can rally around! India has an extremely large pool of highly educated and skilled engineers, programmers, and entrepreneurs that are making it a desirable location for technology-oriented companies across the board. We are talking quaternary level stuff here, brothers and sisters! Every country wants those jobs! India is doing a great job becoming a real global center for emerging technologies, perhaps even better than China, and increasingly competitive with the US and EU.

Things are looking up for India; they were never looking down too much to begin with, but this is a place that is bustling right now. You've got democracy, capitalism, international investment, and jobs here getting outsourced to our Indian friends. The result of all these things taken collectively is that you also have a burgeoning middle class in India as well, and that is a true marker of success in today's world. Obviously, it must be a developed region, right? That's still a tricky call.

Why does the Avenger have trouble calling India a fully developed state even after I've talked up all its awesomeness for three pages straight? For starters, take a look at its population pyramid. Dudes! This place has serious dudes! Even as the population growth rate stabilizes (which it has been doing for years), India is still destined to become the most populous place on the planet due to the principle of population momentum that we discussed way back in Chapter 2. So many people; so many more to come. While their economy has been growing, as has their middle class, you still have hundreds

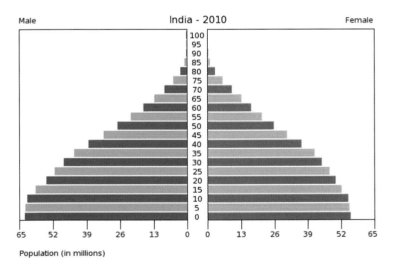

Male   India - 2010   Female

Population (in millions)

of millions of people living in abject poverty. I'm talking dirt poor. Heck, I'm talking so poor they can't even afford to pay attention.

This is India's biggest challenge, and why it is hard to qualify them as a fully developed state. A big economy, yes; high levels of technology, yes; a world power, yes! But a full-fledged, fully-developed state . . . hmmm . . . not yet. The average Joe on the streets is still living on a dollar a day or less. Part of that may have to do with the leap-frogging economic situation I referred to earlier: India has never fully industrialized, which means they don't have millions of factories creating tens of millions of jobs. A lot of people are getting left behind, and population momentum ensures that whatever economic growth they do have in the future will be offset by the increase in peoples. Lots of challenges ahead for Singh and his successors, for sure.

One last thing about India's position in the world today is a reiteration of the fact that the whole South Asian region is physically isolated, though not isolationist. India has been an independent player for the last fifty years; they are very careful about the countries with whom they make allegiances. India's independence from Britain coincides with the beginning of the Cold War. I point this out because India never sided up during the Cold War. In fact, they are one of the few countries in the so-called Third World category that said, "No, we are not going to choose a side." Remember, First World was the capitalist democracy, the Second World was the Commie Soviets, and the Third World referred to everybody who wasn't on team one or two. The term is a Cold War relic that had nothing to do with whether you were poor or rich, but whether or not you sided up.

The Indians are independently minded. I have been fascinated for a long time about why the US has not established stronger trading and strategic ties with India. Why would they? Well, India has a huge population and a huge potential market for businesses, and the people even speak English! India is also a democracy, just like the US. They have all kinds of traditions that are just like ours, so why have we not had a closer relationship with them? One of the answers is because of its independent status; they never got on our side during the Cold War or embraced our ideals, and never helped combat the evils of communism. That's just a Plaid Avenger speculation, but it has some weight when we look to the other power player in the region and that is Pakistan.

PLAID AVENGER INSIDER TIP: Know this, world-watchers. The US-India relationship is changing fast. The US is increasingly seeing India as not only a strategic business partner, but also as a partner in balancing the power of rising China. And don't forget terror! India is also seen as a partner in the War on Terror, as it is a great example of a multi-cultural, democratic state that other states should follow. In 2008 alone, the US has done a decade's worth of courting the Indian government, not the least of which was a US-sponsored deal to help them out with their nuclear power industry, even though India has not signed the Non-Proliferation Treaty. We shall see how this proposed marriage works out.

PAKISTAN IS PAKIN' THE HEAT

The US on the job, helping beef up the Pakistani military.

Pakistan did side up in the Cold War with—guess who—the US. While India was independent, Pakistan needed a strong ally because they didn't have anywhere near the economy, money, or manpower of India. They received tremendous amounts of foreign aid from the United States during the Cold War in order to keep them on the US team, and help fight commies, especially when those Russian commies took over Afghanistan. Go check out *Charlie Wilson's War* to see a great film rendition of those events. Pakistan still receives vast amounts of aid from the US today, but for different reasons: the War on Terror. Unfortunately, this presents a major problem for Pakistan: the US-led war is almost exclusively against Muslim extremists, and Pakistan is almost exclusively Muslim. The average dude on the street in Lahore is not a fan of the US.

However, Pakistan's administration has always been a staunch US ally, even though the people have not been. Pakistan is currently fronting the war on terror for the United States in its fight to find Osama bin Laden and other Taliban rebels and extremists on its border with Afghanistan. This active role has earned it the number three spot for US foreign aid recipients. Unless you have been hiding under a rock for the last two years, you probably know that this fight has not been going well. The Taliban have been winning in Afghanistan, and have even taken over parts of Pakistan itself! The areas highlighted in blue in the map on the next page represent areas of both countries which are primarily controlled by ethnic/tribal groups who don't recognize any international borders, and who also don't give two shakes of salt about the Afghan or Pakistani governments either. Al-Qaeda and the Taliban have both gained in strength in these areas, despite the best efforts of the US and NATO and less than a best effort from the Pakistani military. But the US funds still flow to Pakistan in order to keep them fighting the good fight.

Afghanistan-Pakistan Border

The blue areas are not exactly fully controlled by either states' governments, if at all.

Too bad all that great US foreign aid has been only directed at beefing up Pakistan's military capabilities to fight terrorism, because the country has quite a few other problems which are just as pressing, if not much worse. Its economy can be described as weak, at best. Its democratic institutions: weak, at best. Its political stability: tenuous, at best. Its potential for further extremism, more terrorism, and perhaps open revolution: HUGE!

There's no sense in getting into great political detail here, because the events are changing too rapidly and whatever I write will probably be out of date by the time this book gets into your hands, but we can say a few things that will stick.

The current President, Asif Zardari, and the whole Pakistani government are trying to pacify the wants and desires of its 170 million citizens—that's the 6th biggest population in the world. It's also a devoutly Islamic society, including the whole spectrum of religious views from the mainstream to the seriously extreme. It's a society that has attempted to be a democracy since its inception back in 1947, with less than desirable results—multiple military coups have occurred, mostly to wipe the slate clean of massively corrupt administrations. The current state of politics in the country is totally grid-locked and corrupt, and essentially useless to the vast majority of its citizens. And Pakistan is a nuclear power, with nuclear missiles that need to be controlled. To fight terrorism, they have had to crack down on civil liberties in the country, which pisses off the locals. To keep getting international aid, they have to suck up to the western powers, which pisses off the locals more. All these things have further radicalized lots of folks, some of whom would not mind the entire overthrow of the government. And, and, and . . . this country is screwed!

Just in the last year, the Pakistani military and the government have officially gotten serious about trying to reign in the terrorist elements in their western fringes, finally succumbing to US pressure and the cold reality that their entire country may be lost in its entirety! The military has made huge, albeit bloody, gains in their untamed western regions against the Pakistani Taliban and al-Qaeda. Zardari has done his damnedest to restore civil liberties and even went so far to relinquish emergency powers back to the Congress, and even gave up sole power of the nuclear arsenal to Congress as well, all in an effort to assure the people that democracy is back to stay. But . . . .

Virtually every political event that happens causes widespread protests by folks who are either pro-democracy, or pro-Islamist, or pro-independence, or anti-US, or just anti-Pakistan. This is a society on the brink of collapse, which is a situation that absolutely no one in the world wants. They got lots of Islamists, jihadists, "terrorists," separatists, extremists, and they also have a nuclear arsenal! Not good!

But all that internal turmoil and international pressure and the War on Terror is still not the whole story with Pakistan. We haven't even gotten to the Indian side of the country yet.

Paki Prez Zardari: toughest job on the planet.

India and Pakistan are two quite different tales altogether. We need to define the difference between India and Pakistan a little more, because there is still potential for some serious conflict. We have the independent India—though it could be argued that they are not completely independent after buying arms from Russia at one point, making the US a little leery—and the US-funded and militarily-supplied Pakistan. About thirty years ago, India entered the nuclear club after testing a bomb they called "Smiling Buddha." Pakistan immediately said, "Crap! We have been at war with that country a few times; we need nuclear bombs!" The United States discouraged them big time from doing this, but they went ahead and covertly ran a nuclear development program throughout the 1980s and 1990s, confirming their nuclear capacity by testing their first nuclear bomb in 1998. This development, two countries that essentially hate each other's guts both going nuclear, is cause for alarm for everybody outside this region. Things are stable right now, but people know that at any time some serious nuclear business could go down. It's not probable, but still possible. Kashmir has been a long-standing flashpoint between these two South Asian titans that we have all feared may be the spark that starts a nuclear throw down. What's that? You don't know Kashmir? Well, check out the box below then!

What's the Deal with Kashmir?

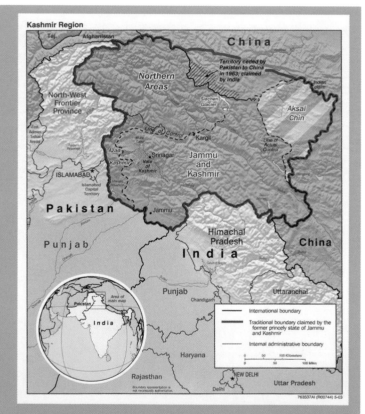

The hottest example of continuing conflict between India and Pakistan is the instance of Kashmir. It's not a goat-wool sweater; it's a disputed territory. What's the deal? You already know about the partition in 1947. When the British were there with Gandhi and the leaders of the future Pakistan, they were saying, "Where do you guys want to draw a line? Who wants to be Muslim and who wants to be Hindu? Who wants to be India and who wants to be Pakistan?" They went region to region and asked regional leaders what side they wanted to be on. States said, "I am Hindu, I want to be in India," or "We are predominately Muslim and want to be in Pakistan." When it came to Kashmir—the proper name is Jammu and Kashmir—a little region nestled in the foothills of the Himalayan system, a mountainous, beautiful, rugged place where you could get killed if you visit, the people were mostly Muslim while the government was Hindu. The Hindu governors wanted to be in India, and the Islamic people wanted to be part of Pakistan, but the governors were the only ones the British heard. It was immediately contested before the British even got on the damn boat to leave.

This is still the situation. It is still a very much disputed territory. The Indians say, "Hey, sorry! Kashmir is part of India." Pakistan says, "Come on, that's crap! It's a bunch of Muslims who didn't get a voice, and you guys screwed us!" As of right now, this is a fairly stable situation. Violence has flared up and there are extremist groups on both sides of this border who want to either make sure it stays in Indian hands or see it reverted to Pakistan. Everyone remains slightly worried that this region will inevitably spark another major conflict between these two nuclear powers. For the sake of South Asia, and the world, let's hope that never happens. Pakistan kind of has its hands full with self-implosion right now, so the Kashmir deal is not an active hotspot for now. Emphasis on "for now."

A typical freakin' flood in beautiful Bangladesh.

BANGIN' BANGLADESH

I would be remiss in my regional duties if I did not at least mention the other giant of South Asia, even if it's not a major player in the neighborhood, nor the world. Sorry to my Bengali brothers out there, but we all know it's true. Bangladesh may not have a lot of regional or global power, but it still carries the titan status because of its huge population packed into a small little area: over 160 million folks, ranking 7th in terms of most populated countries, squeezed into a state about the size of Iowa. Damn!

As you know from earlier in the chapter, Bangladesh started its life as the overwhelmingly Muslim East Pakistan; due to linguistic and racial discrimination, along with lack of proper representation, the Bengalis declared and gained independence, with the help of India, in 1971. They have had a pretty rough road ever since.

Famines, natural disasters, droughts, floods, and widespread poverty have defined life in Bangladesh for its entire existence. Just about every year, monsoonal rain systems totally trounce the area with floodwaters, which isn't hard to do since almost all of the land is a flat alluvial plain that sits just slightly above sea level. Death and destruction seems to be a way of life, but that is only the beginning of the fun for this place! Bangladesh has been plagued by a weak economy, political instability, and internal corruption, which has regularly resulted in coups and rapid administration turnover.

Hmmmm . . . I guess they still have a little in common with their Pakistani brothers after all.

 ## MOMMY WOW! I'M A BIG KID NOW!

Now I'm not making fun of these countries here, but please do consider that they are all fairly young states, having achieved independence in 1947. They just celebrated their 60th anniversaries, but while these states may be youngsters in the modern world, they have grown up fast and are global players already. In conclusion, when we think about South Asia, we do have to consider that India is the big power player. They are big into industry and technology. India is becoming a centerpiece for software creation and programming. In fact, there are now whole cities built up as IT centers, and a lot of computer programmers and technology companies from the United States are relo-

India's gonna get one!

cating there. Several years ago, California chip maker AMD said it was moving to India, causing a lot of US senators to blow steam about taking away American jobs. AMD moved their *design center* to India. They didn't just outsource the low-paying jobs! They are moving the high-paying design work! That's a big deal! AMD said, "There are more highly educated, skilled programmers in India than in the US. All the people coming to this country that are being trained in computer programming are Indians and they are going back to India. There are more computer programmers in India capable of this kind of work."

This is a major event. It is one thing to move cheap factory assembly jobs where people put TVs together for a nickel an hour. That kind of work is not going to be missed, but moving a computer chip design center is a big deal. AMD is not alone. A lot of global firms are hastening to India's back offices. India are happening and companies want in on the big action. In addition, India is now an associate member, along with China, of **ASEAN,** the **Association of Southeast Asian Nations.** Let's not forget my other favorite acronym: India puts the I in **BRIC**! Hopefully you remember that the BRIC group is the new up-and-coming economic and political power block on the planet. South Asia is on the fast track to roll— with all the powerhouse trading blocs of the planet in the next hundred years, and there is speculation that India may become a member of the UN Permanent Security Council as well. I mean, why not? They have 1/5th of humanity and nuclear weapons. What more of a resumé does one need?

In 2005, India started constructing its own aircraft carrier. They bought some others from Russia and Britain in recent years, but they are building a gigantic custom one. Lots of folks who aren't military people, including the Plaid Avenger, are about love, not war. They say, "Who cares? What's the big deal?" An aircraft carrier is quite different from any other military hardware because it can be used as a projection of power anywhere on the planet. You are not to be messed with if you have an aircraft carrier. You don't just have armies of people, you don't only have tanks, you have some planes with rockets that will go to other countries. But now you can put all of that on a big platform that floats and take it anywhere on the planet you want. It is a true projection of power and only the big time countries have that. India also has a vibrant and growing space program, a burgeoning middle class, a hot economy, a stable democracy, and thanks in part to the US, a growing nuclear energy industry. India is hip and happening.

Pakistan is slightly different from India. It is a big country with lots of people and problems, not the least of which is its relationship with the US, which the people in charge really like, but, is very unpopular with the masses. This type of internal dissent is not something that goes away without a fight, so this is a big problem for Pakistan. On top of that, their economy is not in great shape. Pakistan is not growing nearly as fast as India. For those of you curious about military affairs, I should also tell you that India out-competes their Pakistan neighbors on all things military, and by an exponent. Indian army, aircraft counts, tanks, missiles, and even nukes are about ten times that of what Pakistan possesses. We are not talking about evenly matched entities if a war were to ever break out. Of course, nuclear weapons even the score fairly quickly, in that pretty much everyone in the entire region would die if it ever comes to that . . . but let's hope they don't!

Now I must finish this South Asian round-up with the most important regional development of them all: a major alliance shift is underway! Who? The US! The shift? From Pakistan to India! Big time! Why? Dig this:

While relations between India and the US were chilly during the Cold War, they have thawed amazingly fast in the last decade. Like the US, India has a stable democracy, a vibrant economy, a capitalist outlook, a multi-ethnic society with an emphasis on individual liberties and human rights. The US is helping India develop its nuclear energy program and is also sharing intelligence with them on a variety of national security initiatives. Most importantly, India is solidly on board with the US in its War on Terror, especially since the Mumbai attacks of 2008. And where were the Mumbai terrorists from? That would be Pakistan, as were some of the terrorist in the Kashmir attacks, and in attacks on Britain, and in attacks on NATO forces in Afghanistan. Oops.

Yes, the old alliance between the US and Pakistan has now fallen on hard times, as that state struggles just to hold itself together. They have a weak central government, a fragile democracy, political gridlock, and a military that has been so focused on fighting India that it can't seem to restructure itself in order to beat the extremists and separatists inside their own state! That's why the US has lost confidence in them, and started conducting attacks on terrorists camps within Pakistan itself—and Pakistan is their ally!

In conclusion, India/US relations are now stronger than ever before in history, and Pakistani problems are destroying the state, and its relationship with the US and Team West as a whole. But let's leave it there for now.

Now it's time to relax, have some chai, and get ready to rock and roll into Central Asia.

SOUTH ASIA RUNDOWN & RESOURCES

View additional Plaid Avenger resources for this region at http://plaid.at/s_asia

➕ BIG PLUSES

(these pertain mostly to India)

→ Enormous Indian economy that is just getting warmed up for the 21st century

→ Indian economy is interestingly diversified; focusing more on services and high-tech stuff over basic manufactures

→ Both India, and, to a lesser extent, Pakistan are functioning democracies and allies with western powers, although both keep their options open.

→ India is a associate member of ASEAN and full partner of BRIC and a possible future member of UN Permanent Security Council; they will be a world power of note this century

➖ BIG PROBLEMS

→ Pakistan. There, I said it . . . I love the Pakistanis, but their state is in trouble; stagnant and small economy, besieged internally by terrorists, pressured externally by US and India, weak government, and exploding populations

→ Population, population, population; this region has 3 of the biggest populations on the planet and they are growing. Will there be enough resources to go around indefinitely? The biggest challenge for the region, and India in particular

→ While countries are developing fast (esp. India) the poverty level are still exceptionally high; most people of this region live on about a dollar a day

→ Pakistan and India have significant issues internally with terrorism and separatism; Taliban and al-Qaeda in Pakistan and the Naxalites in India

→ India and Pakistan hate each other's guts, and both are nuclear powers; that can't end well

→ On-and-off again open conflict between India and Pakistan over Kashmir; a festering hotspot

→ On-and-off again open conflict between Hindus and Muslims, especially in border areas

DEAD DUDES OF NOTE:

Mahatma Gandhi: The "Father of India" who pioneered the concept and practice of non-violent civil disobedience to achieve political change. Led India to independence from the UK and inspired movements for civil rights and freedom across the world, including Martin Luther King Jr.'s approach to the US Civil Rights Movement.

Ali Jinnah: The "Father of Pakistan" and its first president/governor-general in 1947. During the Indian independence movement, he became the main advocate for a separate Muslim state in order to protect the rights and liberties of India's massive Muslim population. In other words, no Jinnah = no Pakistan.

LIVE LEADERS YOU SHOULD KNOW:

Manmohan Singh: Popular Prime Minister of India, the first Sikh to hold the office, and an all-around smart cookie. Singh was formerly the Finance Minister from 1991–96 and is widely credited for carrying out reforms resulting in the restructuring and opening of the Indian economy . . . which is why it is kicking ass today.

Asif Zardari: President of Pakistan, which is possibly one of the worst jobs on the planet. Has to be a stooge to US demands to crack down on terrorism, which pisses off his people. He is a shady character in his own right anyway, having dozens of corruption charges levied against him in the past, and really only got the position by sympathy vote after his popular wife (who would have won the office) was assassinated.

PLAID CINEMA SELECTION:

Gandhi (1982) Huge award winning film on the life of Mahatma Gandhi, who led the nonviolent resistance movement against British colonial rule in India during the first half of the 20th century. Yes, it's three hours long, but you owe it to yourself to be smart, so do it. Great depiction of the independence movement and philosophy behind the man, as well as fantastic scenery/culture of India.

Lagaan (2001) Alright already! Every South Asian student I've ever taught cites this film as the best thing to ever come out of the subcontinent! Set in 19th century British India, it is an epic cricket match movie, pitting the Brits against the locals in a high stakes showdown. It is a Bollywood production, which means there is random song and dance numbers crammed into the film, and contains great story/scenery even despite those MTV interludes. Like most real life cricket matches, I think the film is about four days long.

Monsoon Wedding (2001) Wildly popular and entertaining story depicts romantic entanglements during a traditional Punjabi wedding in Delhi. Even better, shows insight into modern Indian lifestyles/cultures of both the upper and lower classes, with many of the same family/wedding issues that people deal with here in the US! Go figure!

A Train to Pakistan (1998) Tensions run high near the border of British India, which is about to be partitioned with a new country called Pakistan. Sikhs living in this border town have heard numerous stories of Muslims killing, raping, and looting other Sikhs, Hindus, and Christians, and many of whom are their friends and relatives. Enraged at the loss of law and order, they plan their own attack on a train full of Muslims leaving British India. Great depiction of South Asia's darkest days after independence.

Junoon (1978), WIth a love story as the backdrop, chronicles the period of 1857 to 1858 when the soldiers of the East India Company mutinied and many smaller kingdoms joined the soldiers in the hope of regaining their territories from the English . That would be the "Great Mutiny" referenced in this chapter.

Bhutto (2010) A fantastic documentary on one of the most polarizing figures in the Arab world, Benazir Bhutto. Follows the events of her life, leading up to the 2008 election that she was expected to dominate, and her assassination which resulted in her husband (Asif Zardari) becoming the current Prime Minister by default. Considered by some to be a martyr or a messiah for the common man.

The Clay Bird (2002) A masterful piece of Bangladeshi cinema, film was banned in Bangladesh for three years because of issues of religion. Set in the late 1960s, focuses on the increasing tensions in East Pakistan that lead up to the Bangladesh War of Liberation. Film was shot almost entirely in the streets of Bangladesh, creating a sort of rustic appeal with the cinematography.

Nayagan (1987) A sort of *Godfather*-esque movie set in India, and typically called one of the country's best films ever. Based on true to life don in the underworld of Bombay, takes a sympathetic look at the struggles of South Indians in what is now Mumbai. Depending on who you ask, a better film than *The Godfather*.

Slumdog Millionaire (2008) Kid who grew up in the "slums" of India that makes it big on a game show, arousing the suspicion of the authorities. One of the most internationally acclaimed films set in India, also depicts life in the poorer areas of India fairly accurately and a great travel flick through northeast India.

Sulanga Enu Pinisa (2005) Roughly translated meaning "the Forsaken Land," is a highlight of film in Sri Lanka, which does not have the richest history of film. Winner of one of the Cannes Film Festival's highest honors, the Camera d'Or, the film is a masterful take on the effects of decades of civil war on the land. Stunning landscapes and images of people make the lack of a plot less obvious.

CHAPTER OUTLINE

Central Asia

LET'S move to the center of the Eurasian continent. This is a place mired in turmoil and the centerpiece of world history for quite some time, but suddenly found itself left behind. Central Asia is kind of a vacuum in the heart of Asia that, as opposed to going through, people go out of their way to avoid. Times are changing fast, my friends, and Central Asia may have found a new home as the delicious meat center of a Russia-China sandwich, but I am getting ahead of the story.

What is it about Central Asia that makes it a region? Is it a region? A lot of people may say that it's not a separate region, but it is to the Plaid Avenger and here is how I'm going to define it.

THE GAME PIECES

Central Asia consists of a core of countries that everyone might agree upon: the "-stan" countries that no one knows how to locate or pronounce. Kazakhstan is the big one, and then Uzbekistan, Turkmenistan, Afghanistan (I know you've heard of that one), Tajikistan, and Kyrgyzstan. Everybody would say, "Yeah, we think that's Central Asia, or at least we know where you're talking about—all those places we can't pronounce."

Kazakh Hotties!

This may be the trickiest region to define because we have to take parts of another country in order to do it. We are going to take the western parts of China, including Xinjiang, one of the biggest, most significant westernmost provinces of said country. We must also take two other Chinese provinces, Tibet and Inner Mongolia, as well as the independent sovereign state of Mongolia. The Plaid Avenger calls all of these places Central Asia. It's a little tricky because you will say, "Wait, you just took parts of China and China is its own country. It's a sovereign state." We're going to talk a lot about China in the next chapter, but what you'll find is that China has a very distinct east/west divide. Virtually all the people and businesses are in the east. All economic activity is on the eastern side closer to the coast. You can't consider the country divided down the middle; most inhabitants are as close to the coast as possible. Most of the transportation, communication, and government are there as well.

China as it has been known throughout the centuries, is the eastern side of the country, but not the west. The west is quite different in terms of its population. It is sparsely populated and contains ethnic groups that are not historically Chinese. Consequently, religions there are very different from those in the east.

All the reasons eastern China has *little* to do with western China are the same reasons that western China has *a lot* to do with Central Asia. The dissimilar groups in parts of Mongolia and the "-stan" countries are thrown into this region called Central Asia. Why is it a region? What's homogeneous about the disparate group of countries, states, and Chinese substates? Let's get to work.

Central Asia: formidable, inhospitable, and largely un-livable.

THE GAME BOARD

The most obvious similarities between all of the countries in this region lie in the physical attributes. Unlike other regions that contain a variety of climates and terrains, like South America or North America, Central Asia is relatively standard throughout. Like the Middle East, it is mostly desert and steppe, making it homogeneously dry across the board. There is really nothing else, no other climate to speak of. You definitely won't find any big forests. There are patches of growth, but this region is mostly either grassland or desert, which has had a definite impact on how people have settled and survived for the last several thousand years.

Grand Canyon? Nah, these things are a dime a dozen in this region.

Before we get too deep into dryness, let's look at the terrain factor. This is one of the highest and toughest terrains on Earth. We already referenced the Himalayas when discussing the division of South Asia from the rest of Asia, and they play a big part here as well. It's not just the range itself—it's the whole Tibetan Plateau, which sits over 12,000 feet above sea level. It has extremely high mountains. The **Hindu Kush Mountains** run through Afghanistan; the **Tien Shan** run through Kyrgyzstan and Tajikistan. These mountains seem wimpy in comparison to the Himalayas, but what they lack in physical harshness, they make up for in another kind of tactical danger; just ask the US military in Afghanistan. This is not a fun part of the world. It is very difficult to get around, through, or across the plateau.

In addition to the Tien Shan, the Hindu Kush, and the Himalayas, we have the Altai Mountains in Mongolia. Although there are a few basins where things level out a bit, it boasts some of the toughest terrain on the planet.

The terrain and dryness go hand in hand. For the same reason that there are monsoons in South Asia, Central Asia is nearly all dry. All the water that would float up north drops from the sky as the air is pushed higher by the Himalayas. This causes the monsoons, and makes for only dry air to make its way up the mountains and into Central Asia.

The dryness doesn't support much vegetation. A lot of Central Asia is what we would distinguish as grasslands. We think, "Oh, grasslands are good for things like wheat and barley." No, those are long grasses. Central Asia can't even sustain most of that stuff. There is only enough water in this ecosystem to support shorter grasses. Since the land cannot support any type of large-scale food crops, in turn, it cannot support huge populations. Much

Central Asian rush hour here at the airport.

of the food that the locals eat has to be imported. This is a fairly stark environment.

Throughout the centuries, one of the main perceptions we hold of Central Asians is that they are horse people. Why don't they raise cattle or something else? The environment will not allow it. It cannot be done because the vegetation is not there for farmers to raise large amounts of cattle in one place, year after year. But short grasses can sustain animals that move around a lot, like horses, which is why the region's inhabitants are known for having them.

LANDLOCKED

What is the most unique feature of this region? It's landlocked, which is another condition that makes it a homogeneous whole. In fact, some of these places are doubly landlocked. What is "landlocked" and why is it significant? What does this mean for the place as a whole? **Landlocked** means you have no tie to the oceans. Not even a river system that goes to a place that can indirectly get

States locked out of ocean access, thus global access, thus economic access.

you to an ocean. What's the big deal about that? In the good old days, when people used to travel across the continent on trade routes, Central Asia's location in the middle of things was a bonus. Those days were good, but they are long gone, my friends.

In today's world, virtually all the world's traffic and economic activity happens via the oceans. If you do not have access to the oceans, then you are not part of the world economy. Therefore, Central Asia is not part of the world economy today. It is what The Plaid Avenger calls a **marooned region.** It is not attached to what's going on around the rest of the planet, and the region is economically isolated and therefore stagnant.

As I mentioned before, some of these places are **doubly landlocked,** which means they are landlocked by other landlocked countries. That means that their economy is internal and they are not doing squat, with the possible exception of something like drilling for oil and making pipelines to places that are not cut out of the world economy. A few of these places have that advantage, but places like Kyrgyzstan are so far from anything that they cannot possibly foster any meaningful movement of goods or services across the Asian continent. It's just not going to happen. Being land-locked is a physical condition that has an enormous influence on what's going on internally and externally for Central Asia.

A Yurt: Central Asian party hut!

CULTURE CENTRAL

Let's look at some cultural traits that permeate Central Asia, the main one being religion. We look at Central Asia and typically think Islam, which is a good place to start. All of the "-stan" countries and the western provinces of China are Islamic. Islam spread there from the Middle East during the big growth of the Arab-Islamic Empire. These countries have been staunchly Islamic ever since. However, there are some exceptions in the region, such as the Tibetan Plateau and Mongolia. These are a couple of core

Who is in the white areas? Answer: Nobody.

areas for the purest kind of Buddhism in the world. When we talk about China, the Koreas, Japan, and South East Asia, Buddhism is there, but it is usually incorporated into lots of local beliefs.

While this region is primarily Islamic like the Middle East, it is still different enough to be teased out of the Middle East. One of those differences is Western China. A lot of people don't know this about Western China, but it is predominantly Muslim and comprised of an ethnic group that is not Chinese, but **Uyghur** (pronounced Weeger, like Weezer). This Turkic ethnic group has been hanging out for several thousand years in what is now known as Western China, and they have embraced Islam.

They are quite different from everybody else in China; you don't hear a lot about them because they are kind of being repressed right now by the Chinese government. Lots of people in the Uyghur community have been fighting for some sort of autonomous state or perhaps even a fully sovereign state. At this point, China has deemed these guys Muslim terrorists. Go figure. This issue will come back into our story in just a little bit, but that is why we tease out part of China to put with Central Asia. These guys in this part of China have way more in common with Central Asia than with their own country.

PRANCING AROUND THE CONTINENT

We talked about the physical features of the region being dry and landlocked. What has this landlocked dry, arid, short grass steppe meant culturally to this region over the centuries? It means that they are not a big agricultural region. They are mostly **nomadic;** that is, they pick up their Yurts (those big white tents that you see) and move on a moment's notice to find better grasslands for their horses. Some people native to this region are not sedentary and noncentralized, consisting mostly of small tribes of folks on the move. There have never been huge populations in this region. These guys have been forever focused on the horse, not just as a main means of locomotion, but also as a way of life. I'm thinking specifically of the Mongols. Mongol domination at one point in history is one of the other unifying cultural factors of this entire region. The value of the horse in Central Asia can't be understated, especially for this group we call the Mongols.

Uzbeki Zorro!

The Mongols were the most kick-ass group of horse warriors that the world has ever seen. The Plaid Avenger would put money on these guys in today's world. Even now they would be a serious bunch of ass-kickers. What was so cool about them? What did they do that was so unique?

Don't mess with the Mongols!

MONGOL MANIA

The Mongols were a small group of ragtag horsemen who rallied under **Genghis Khan** and started a campaign to conquer the whole planet right around 1200 CE. Genghis is the one dude who got fairly close. Lots of people have had that ideal such as, I don't know, Hitler and Mussolini? But this was a guy who actually came fairly close to conquering the whole world at the time.

A couple of unique things about the Mongol Empire: It crossed the Eurasian continent for the first and perhaps only time in history, maybe even in today's world. They created a single empire that tied together the peoples of Europe and the peoples of the rest of Asia under a single umbrella. To my knowledge, this has not been done since. We could

look at the modern world and say, "Oh yeah, people have interactions now," but not on this scale. This is a singular empire that placed white Europeans and Chinese people in the same state. What's so important about that? Perhaps nothing, except that this cultural interchange was all under a singular empire.

The Mongols set up this system where they were bad asses; under their rule, it was said that a virgin with a pot of gold on her head could travel from one side of the empire to

Genghis got game: the largest land empire of its time . . . perhaps ever.

another unmolested and untouched. That may or may not actually be true, but it gets at the idea of Mongol citizens' safety. They had a good legal system that was strictly enforced. What that type of safety infrastructure creates is a lot of trade and cultural interchange. You had this mass movement of goods, services, materials, and technologies across the Eurasian continent like never before, and perhaps not since. The Mongol Empire was very unique in world history; it encompassed all of what is now China, parts of Southeast Asia, and parts of India, as well as big chunks of the Middle East that stretched all the way into parts of Europe. They sacked Baghdad in 1258, which marked the end of Middle Eastern expansion—remember that from a few chapters ago?

Gengis Khan—but not really because they didn't have cameras 800 years ago, but this guy is funny as hell as a replacement.

How did they unify all of these lands under one common empire? They were ruthless conquerors. Their environment propelled them into this rough way of life where they were simply bad-ass warrior dudes who could ride horses for days. These guys were totally brutal. One of Genghis Khan's sayings was, "Submit or die." He didn't negotiate with anybody, period. Typical Mongol foreign policy would be going to a town and telling the inhabitants, "Here's the deal; you guys get down on your hands and knees and start begging for mercy right now. We'll circle around you, slowly making our way toward your homes, and decide if we'll kill you. But if anybody takes up arms against us, we will kill every freakin' one of you down to the last man, woman and child. Blood will flow in the streets and we'll burn the town to the ground."

That was how they were successful in storming across the continent. Perhaps even more important to their success were their fighting tactics. They could cover HUGE amounts of territory in a day. They would ride horses continuously and would have stations set up so that whole cavalry units could get new horses and essentially ride nonstop for 72 to 96 hours. That is an amazing feat in today's world, much less a thousand years ago. The Mongols were so tough they trained their ponies so they didn't have to get out of the saddle to eat; they made cuts on the ponies' necks and drank their blood for nourishment. Drinking blood is not only a fun fact; it also accentuates this tough environment. What did their diet consist of? Mare's milk and blood. Protein rich! I think somebody should invent the Mongol diet because these guys were lean, mean fighting machines.

If you go to Mongolia today, you'll see a lot of people doing these same things. Not in terms of raping and pillaging, but what they eat and what they do for a living has not changed much. They still herd goats, still drink funky milk, and generally are chillin' out on the central Asian plains.

The Mongols ended up ruling much of the Eurasian continent, but their empire was not a superpower for very long. Their glorious reign was pretty short after Genghis Khan died. After that, they stopped conquering, and eventually the Mongol Empire broke apart into separate kingdoms that affected world history in lots of different places: Kublai Khan ruled China; Tamerlane was in Central Asia; descendants of the Mongols end up as the Mughal Empire in India, and even the Cossacks of Russia are lineage of the Mongols. But for a while, under the main man Genghis, the Mongols whipped ass and took names, making a pretty huge mark on history, especially military history.

PARKER BROTHERS INSPIRED

There's one thing the Plaid Avenger wants you to know about in Central Asia because it is still kind of happening; it's called **The Great Game.** The Great Game, coined by some British guys as so many things on our planet have been, describes the major world power players' attitudes toward Central Asia in the last few hundred years. That attitude has resulted in Central Asia becoming very much like the game of *Risk*. It's a platform or playing field for different countries to vie for influence. No one really wants it. No one wants to actually control it. They just want to make sure they have their fingers in there to ensure that other people do not control it. This was a scenario that arose during European imperialism, and in the build up to WWI and beyond.

THE CLASSIC ORIGINAL BOARD GAME

Basically, it's the Russians vs. the British vs. The Persians/Iranians vs. the French vs. the locals. All these colonial powers and others who are in the neighborhood, such as the Chinese and the Persians, all jockeyed around Central Asia to make sure that no one else got in. Everybody protected their own backyard. It's mostly the Russians who started up this game because they had been expanding their territory for hundreds of years, perhaps in a bid to expand their coastline. Among other things, they increased their influence by pushing into Central Asia. Many would say they wanted to push down into Iran to gain access to the Indian Ocean, which is one reason that the Persians did not want the Russians there.

Main Central Asian currency unit: force.

As the Russians were coming down from the North, the British, who controlled British India at the time, were pushing up from the South, effectively buffering against Russian influence in the region. The Chinese did not want anyone in there, so they were vying for influence to make sure that no one encroached on their territory. This became a big game where rulers were moving soldiers around on this very real chessboard. That is why it's funny in today's world to see the United States vying for influence in Afghanistan by pushing US ideals and working against Muslim influence—same story, different century.

Afghanistan is a good country to discuss for just a second. The Russians and the British found this out a long time ago; you just don't mess around in Afghanistan. Everybody, all these world powers, have tried very hard in the past, and let me tell you what the historical scoreboard reads: Afghanistan: 1000, Outsiders: zero. No one from Europe or anywhere else has successfully occupied or influenced Afghanistan to do a damn thing, and it remains to be seen if the US/NATO is going to have much impact either. These groups of folks throughout Central Asia, particularly Afghanistan, have a fierce independent spirit. They understand that they are pawns in the game and they will have none of it. When the British went into Afghanistan to thwart the Russians, the Afghans kicked the hell out of them. Then when the Russians came in fifty years later, they kicked the hell out of them as well. These dudes are tough; they have serious balls.

Not even a century later, the Soviet Union invaded Afghanistan in their bid to expand the communist sphere of influence even further. This time a new player joined the game: the US. The United States armed and trained a bunch of locals—let's call them the mujahideen to really stick it to the Ruskies in order to stymie the Soviet advance. It worked great! That 1979 to 1989 Afghan campaign proved absolutely disastrous for the Soviets, and has been credited as part of the reason for their eventual collapse just two years later. Of course, those CIA trained mujahideen then ended up becoming the Taliban and members of al-Qaeda, which the US now finds itself fighting, but that is a different round of this unfolding drama. Isn't this region just a pack of fun? Kind of like playing nude lawn darts.

THE 21ST CENTURY EDITION

Lots of the parties who were vying for influence in the last couple hundred years are some of the same players in today's world, with a few new entries—like the United States, the Taliban, al-Qaeda and a country that didn't even exist back then, now called Pakistan. As in the past, no one really wants Central Asia, but everybody is trying to expel other influences and powers. The Game is back on. For your own note, most of the powers originally got involved to curb the power and growth of pre-Soviet Russia. The British, in particular, didn't really want to get into the northern parts of India, but felt compelled to in order to stop the Russian advance. The game to stop Russia is over, but there are three new reasons that the game started back up.

1. THE VACUUM CREATED BY MOVING THE SOVIETS OUT

Russians, under the Soviet umbrella, gained control of all of Central Asia, except Afghanistan, by the 1940s. All of those "-stan" countries became Soviet republics—you know, the R in the USSR. Afghanistan was never brought into the fray; that's why the Russians invaded them in 1979, much to their own chagrin for the next decade. Since the fall of the Soviet Empire in 1989, all of those former Soviet SSR's declared independence and became sovereign states again. Who is in charge now? For most of the "-stan" countries, this has resulted in authoritarian dictators/one-party states that are extremely open to outside influences, especially when there is money involved. How refreshing. Oops, I mean, how exactly the same as always.

2. BECAUSE OF INCREASING FINDS OF PETROLEUM AND NATURAL GAS

These natural resources are items with which the world cannot live without, as evidenced by the fact that people were still willing to pay 130 dollars a barrel for oil back in June 2008. Oil and natural gas, and the pipelines that carry it, are popping up all over the region. Every day, it seems, they increase their findings of potential natural reserves. Kazakhstan is the leader of this. It is the biggest country with the largest amount in reserves.

Where is this stuff going? Everywhere. This game is back on because everybody wants that stuff. No one wants to control the places, but they want the influence inside the region in order to get a piece of the oil action. As described by the US's Energy Information Administration: "*Central Asia has large reserves of natural gas but its development as a major natural gas exporter is constrained because of a lack of pipeline infrastructure.*" Everyone wants a piece of the infrastructure-building action.

Who are they supplying? Kazakhstan's and Uzbekistan's stuff has mostly moved west into Russia and then on into Europe. Turkmenistan and Uzbekistan supply the Ukraine and other Eastern and Western European countries, as well as Iran. Some of it floats south to or through Iran. Increasingly, even Tajikistan, Turkmenistan, and Kazakhstan are building pipelines into China. Why would China want that stuff? Their population is exploding and they cannot ever possibly have enough oil and natural gas. These historically landlocked economies of Central Asia are in a prime position now. The one thing that they could move out of their countries in order to make money is being discovered in large amounts.

Source: Energy Information Administration

3. TERRORISM AND DRUGS

Why would anybody from the outside world be interested in vying for influence of drugs and terrorism? Ask the US government! That's the precise reason that the United States is there, quite frankly. The current US-led war in Afghanistan is to try and stop the Taliban, al-Qaeda, and any other radical extremist groups which may be there training, setting up shop, or otherwise trying to control the area. I do want to be quick to point out that this is a US-*led* effort; the Afghan campaign is actually a NATO mission, of which the US is the biggest player. Why is that important? Because it shows that all other NATO members, namely all of Team West, are involved because they all believe that the anti-terrorism fight is a worthy cause that they will continue to pursue.

Do not lose sight of the irony that the US and NATO are currently fighting against forces that they helped train to fight the Soviets back in the 1970s. Ah, the game continues. Of course, drugs are a bad thing; Central Asia is historically one of the largest producers of opium, so lots of developed countries around the world in their **War on Drugs** have had their fingers in Central Asia long before the current conflict in Afghanistan. Unfortunately, in a war-wrecked country, drug production is one of the few, if not only, economic opportunities for these folks to embrace. It has been further complicated by the Taliban and al-Qaeda now using the drug trade money to help re-arm and re-equip themselves to do further battle against Team West. Damn, could this mess get worse? It sure can! While virtually all this product used to be shipped abroad to the rich, bored citizens of Europe and America, it has been increasingly used at home. Drug consumption and addiction has soared in Central Asia, Russia, and East Asia.

Terrorism, drugs and petroleum products are the main reasons that Central Asia has become an area of much interest for people around the globe who otherwise would not care about this economically marooned region. There is not much else to this place to interest the outsiders. What's made this even more important in today's world is the **War on Terror.** It is the reason why the US is in Afghanistan, supposedly the reason they are in Iraq, and a reason why there are US military bases that had cropped up all throughout Central Asia—because of the fear that terrorism and extremism will be on the increase, particularly in this region. The United States is vying for influence here not to control the place, but to control the extreme elements within the place. The United States is worried about terrorists in this Central Asian society, but they're not the only ones.

The Russians are also worried because they have lost a lot of territory since the implosion of the USSR, so they are continuing activities in the region. Their long history of influence in the region, desire to maintain their status as a world power, and close ties between Russian and Central Asian economies give them more reason to stick around. They have their terrorist problems as well, mostly with Muslim extremists over in Chechnya, but also here in Central Asia.

And then there's China. Here is a theme that's perfect for identifying western China as part of Central Asia and not as China proper. It is a little known fact, that when the United States declared war on terrorism after 9/11, there were two countries that IMMEDIATELY jumped on board and said, "Yeah, we'll help! We agree that terrorism should be fought on all fronts!" Those two countries are probably not ones you would think of as the first in line: Russia and China. Russia said, "We've been fighting Muslim extremists for years. We call them Chechens and we are going to continue to beat the hell out of them in our war on terrorism." China said, "We have Muslim extremist terrorists as well. The Uyghurs out in the western states have been blowing stuff up and making attempts at independence movements. We're going to fight the War on Terror by continuing to beat the hell out of the Uyghur separatists in our country."

Terrorist hunters have their work cut out for them in this neck of the woods.

The terrorism thing is a rallying cry for a lot of countries to continue to be involved in Central Asia. This is a theme that is probably not going away any time soon. We've got Russia, China, and the United States in there vying for influence for oil, trying to control terrorism, and lots of other things. Who else may be involved in The New Great Game? For starters: the Pakistanis, who are huge US allies and the ones fighting the truly active War on Terror on their own border. Pakistan's largest border is shared with Afghanistan; that border is a real hotspot for active conflict. People are shooting at each other there all the time. That is where everyone thinks Osama bin Laden is currently hiding. The US is moving money and guns around and sending soldiers to the area, but in Pakistan, they are actually shooting people and making the kills.

Iran, which also fronts this region, is increasing its power on the planet by building nuclear facilities and playing up its role as a leader of Muslim culture. It is also a major mover of natural gas and oil out of Central Asia to the rest of the world. They want to join the power players and are vying for influence as well. They have the advantage of being Islamic like all their Central Asian brothers. 2010 Update: Kazakhstan just inked a deal with Iran to build a major pipeline from Central Asia to their "Muslims brothers in Iran," as spoken by Kazakh President Nursultan Nazarbayev. Game on! Because of this, Iran may end up being a major political player in this region in the very near future—or perhaps the US will invade them first, but I kind of doubt it right now.

THE GAME CONTINUES TO EVOLVE WITH NEW PLAYERS

To summarize: Central Asia is an isolated region both physically and economically—a culturally and economically marooned region—which has been suddenly thrust back into prominence in the new version of The Great Game. Why? It's mostly for resources, such as oil and natural gas, but also for the fight against terrorism and the drug trade. We also see some of the old school elements of The Great Game here, in terms of Russia not wanting to completely lose all of its influence in the region. The US military presence is actually seen as a direct threat to this historic Russian influence. Vladimir "The Man" Putin is not too happy about it.

What's the Deal with Drug Production?

Hey man, want some heroin? If you want to get it cheap, why not go right to the source? In that case, you'd probably take a trip—no pun intended—to Afghanistan. Afghanistan is the largest producer of opium in the world, weighing in at almost 5,000 metric tons/year. That's 87 percent of the opium supply of the entire world. Quite impressive.

The funny thing is that under Taliban rule, opium production was much, much lower. Once the US intervened and knocked the Taliban out, with an almost audible "smack" heard round the world, opium production nearly doubled each year after 2001. 2009 was a world record breaker for most opium produced in the country. Nice job, guys! Here's a hint for you: most of that isn't going to the pharmaceutical companies that turn opium into legitimately consumed pain killers. This is hardcore stuff getting released into the streets, mostly in Europe and Southeast Asia, in larger and larger quantities because that's where the money can be made. It's untaxed, uncut, and a hell of a cash crop for this economically landlocked region. Production is only increasing, despite US occupation.

What a pretty poppy garden these boys are tending—of opium poppies, that is!

Luckily for him, his country is currently winning the fight. Some countries have requested the US troops to leave as soon as possible, and Uzbekistan recently just blatantly kicked them out. Many of the "-stan" countries are already reestablishing their old ties with Russia for security purposes, but they are also increasingly looking to Russia for leadership in the oil and natural gas industries. Putin is happy again! The vehicle for this renewed Russian leadership is a supranationalist organization named the SCO. You heard it here first: this group has huge potential to become a major global force in the coming decades. Best to know a bit more about it right now.

YOU GOTTA KNOW THE SCO

Comrade Russia iz still vatching Central Asia.

Watch out! This coalition could be hot! The Shanghai Cooperation Organization (SCO) is an intergovernmental organization founded on June 14, 2001, by leaders of the People's Republic of China, Russia, Kazakhstan, Kyrgyzstan, Tajikistan and Uzbekistan.

The SCO facilitates cooperation and organization on issues like natural resource extraction, counterterrorism, extremism, and separatism. They are now holding joint military exercises and also thinking about a free trade pact. Though the declaration on the establishment of the SCO contained a statement that it "is not an alliance directed against other states and regions and it adheres to the principle of openness," most observers believe that one of the original purposes of the SCO was to serve as a counterbalance to the US, and particularly to avoid conflicts that would allow the US to intervene in areas near both Russia and China.

How are they pulling this off? In lots of curious ways that have tremendous potential for the future of these states and also the world. First, there have been very secretive discussions about these countries creating a common cartel

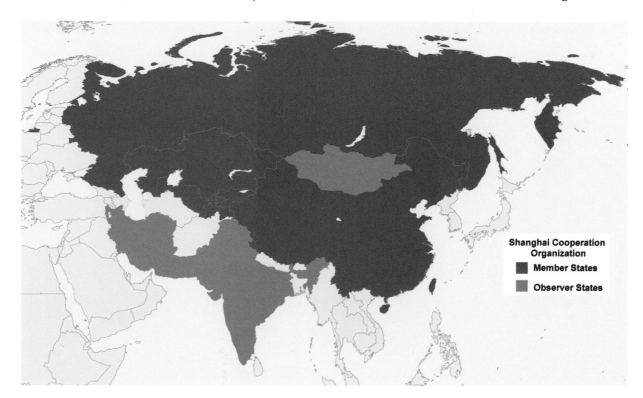

Shanghai Cooperation Organization
Member States
Observer States

A hot ass trade block to watch.

based on their exports of natural gas—basically, an Asian version of OPEC. Just as OPEC countries control the lion's share of exported oil and, therefore, control the supply and price, the combined SCO countries control a significant amount of global reserves of natural gas. It is not a stretch of the imagination to see them pooling their resources together under a single umbrella of control, which would make them all even richer.

Second, the SCO states are strengthening their defense pacts with each other to ensure that no interference or invasion will be allowed from outsiders. In essence, they have formed an Asian version of NATO. The movement in this direction is why most US military bases have now been kicked out of SCO states, and also why America's request to become an observer state has been declined every single year. It's also why the SCO has started doing the joint military exercises. By the way, don't start digging your backyard bunker in preparations for WWIII anytime soon; militarily, these guys are still pretty clueless—okay, they outright suck. The main point is that they are just beginning to do these exercises, thus setting the trend for the future.

Let's get you even smarter. What current observer state in the map above do you think is desperate to become a full member of the SCO? If you said Iran, then give yourself a cookie and a barrel of oil. If Iran joined this Asian NATO club, then the prospects of US/UN actions to prevent Iran from going nuclear would instantaneously become a world crisis. Dig what I'm saying here? It's a really big deal.

But hang on! Don't let me paint a picture that makes the SCO look like an enemy of the US or Team West in general! They are not! The SCO met in April 2009 specifically to try and find "an Asian solution" to the complete War of Terror debacle going down in both Afghanistan and Pakistan. The US/NATO/Team West is losing this battle, and the SCO club knows it, and are NOT happy about it! See, China, Russia, and India are all states that have active Islamic extremist/terrorist problems too, and they DO NOT want to see the Afghan/Pakistani area continue to melt down, mostly because the impacts to them will be much, much, much greater than any real impact to the US. Think about it: the SCO (plus observers) surround this troubled area, and trouble has a way of spreading like a cancer. On multiple fronts like terrorism and drugs, the SCO shares strategic interest with the US and the West. Hopefully, they can think up a better solution than the West has been trying, 'cuz it can't get worse!

Organizing pipeline construction, conducting military exercises, trying to come up with Asian solutions to Asian problems, and refusing to grant the US observer status. Ouch! This thing is on fire, and no one in our country has probably even heard of it, but I think you should.

THE GAME IS ON

Terrorism is a problem which, despite US influence, is not going away; it's actually increasing. To be completely frank, Afghanistan is the only real hotspot and haven for most of the terrorism in the region right now, mostly related to the US/NATO war and the lack of any strong and stable government functionality. When you look at the rest of the "-stan" countries in this region, they are all strong-arm authoritarian types, being influenced mostly by the biggest strong-arm of them all,

Vladimir Putin in Russia, and also the fairly assertive commie crew over in China. As such, those states are extremely successful at repressing and/or eliminating terrorist elements. Unfortunately, they are also good at repressing any democratic and human rights elements. I don't want to paint this region in an entirely negative light, because they do have some positive things coming with some of the wealth accumulation due to their increasing natural gas and oil exports. One of the things I like people to remember is when we say, "Damn it, this sucks. Gas is going to be five dollars a gallon this summer. This is terrible. Oil is 130 dollars a barrel, this sucks!" It may suck for you, but it actually means great things for Central Asia and any other oil and gas producing region. That means their revenues are expanding, and they have a little more wealth, hopefully to spread around to their citizens.

Things may be looking up for the "-stans." Economic integration in Central Asia has risen to an all time high for the last 500 years. States are figuring out that they must work together in order to effectively build the infrastructure to get

We ain't doing so bad . . . for a bunch of bad-asses!

their petroleum products exported out to the rest of the world. With that type of cooperation comes increased trade and communications. That is why the Plaid Avenger really wants you to know all about that SCO, because it is becoming the most effective organizational superstructure to accelerate this process. Look for the SCO to not only become an OPEC-style cartel of natural gas in Asia, but also a NATO-style defense structure with which many Asian nations might be keen to get involved. Trade and economic integration will follow.

Still, this is a place of fairly extreme economic disparity and massive challenges in terms of infrastructure creation, but at the same time, due to its Soviet influence, this is a region that is fairly literate. People are fairly well-educated and the illiteracy rates are some of the lowest in the world (except Afghanistan, of course). If you look at how much money they make, it looks like they are impoverished like a lot of Sub-Saharan African countries. In terms of standards of living, access to health care and literacy rates, they are not doing too badly (except Afghanistan, of course). With Russia and China as powerful bookends, a new Asian OPEC and an Asian NATO, things are not completely dire and could be looking up, although the authoritarian structure in the governments of most of these places may still keep the people down for a some time to come. But that is a story for another time and another place.

Let's get to the next superpower on the planet . . .

CENTRAL ASIA RUNDOWN & RESOURCES

View additional Plaid Avenger resources for this region at http://plaid.at/c_asia

 BIG PLUSES

→ Huge reserves of oil and natural gas, with more being discovered every year

→ Region now being courted heavily by Russia and China and Iran, with even a distant Uncle Sam trying to exert some influence (albeit mostly unsuccessfully)

→ The SCO is a major unifying entity of the region that is just getting warmed up here in the 21st century

→ Region is surrounded by great powers (Russia, China, India) who all have a sound and stable Central Asia as their best interests; that was not so 100 years ago

 BIG PROBLEMS

→ Landlocked and largely isolated from world economy (although this is changing)

→ Tough terrain and climate make inter-regional connections challenging or impossible

→ Ummm . . . . Afghanistan? Enough said

→ Drug production and distribution (primarily of heroine) is widespread, and drug addiction is actually increasing within the region as well

→ Overwhelmingly reliant on oil and natural gas exports; not economically diversified

→ Supposedly a great area for terrorists, separatists, and other rabble rousers . . . although this seems to me to be skewed reality as government/SCO crackdowns in the region have crushed much dissent, both of terrorists but also of political activists. (except Afghanistan)

→ Almost all governments of region are one-party states/dictatorships, with political power consolidated in the hands of few

DEAD DUDES OF NOTE:

Genghis Khan: The total bad ass founder and Khan (ruler) of the Mongol Empire, which became the largest contiguous empire in history after his death. After uniting the horse-warrior, nomadic tribes of northeast Asia in 1200 AD, went on a world tour of whoop-ass, invading and destroying political entities in China, India, Iran, Iraq, Egypt, Russia, and Eastern Europe. And totally ravaged Oshman's Sporting Goods in *Bill & Ted's Excellent Adventure.*

LIVE LEADERS YOU SHOULD KNOW:

Nursultan Nazarbayev: President of Kazakhstan since the Fall of the USSR and the nation's independence in 1991. Pretty much in charge for life in this one-party state bordering on dictatorship . . . but he is actually very popular and well-liked, so its a tough call. Kazakhstan is fast becoming a regional powerhouse and serious economy, and is invited to SCO, G-20, Nuclear Summits, NATO meetings and other important international gatherings. Watch this guy; he is important.

Hamid Karzai: President of Afghanistan since 2004, and pretty much the US-sponsored head cheese since the fall of the Taliban in 2001. Has been accused of wild corruption, cronyism, and vote-rigging, and he certainly isn't making anyone's list of top 100 leaders in the world. But, the US is trying to stick with him a little bit longer in the hopes that he can hold the country together and get the government's act together. Don't hold your breath on this one.

PLAID CINEMA SELECTION:

Charlie Wilson's War (2007) AWESOME! A dramatic biographical film, documents the efforts of Texas senator Charlie Wilson, who passed away in 2010, in his efforts to help Afghanistan fight Soviet occupation. While certain elements of the plot are fictional, the film does a great job of laying the basic details of the actual event on the table for this generation to understand.

Beshkempir (1998) A Kyrgyz film, shot and produced entirely in Kyrgyzstan, is a prime example of the new wave of films produced after the country gained independence from the Soviet Union. Film follows an adopted child growing up in rural Kyrgyzstan. Demonstrates several Kyrgyz traditions, including funeral and engagement ceremonies.

Seven Years in Tibet (1997) Based on real events of Austrian mountaineer Heinrich Harrer on his experiences in Tibet between 1944 and 1951 during the Second World War, the interim period, and the Chinese People's Liberation Army's invasion of Tibet in 1950. Features the Dalai Lama is is pretty historically accurate on the timeline and events, despite the presence of a young Brad Pitt.

True Noon (2009) An absurdist film made by filmmakers in Tajikistan about a change in the border between Tajikistan and Uzbekistan. The film centers around two villages that are very close that get separated by the new divide with barbed wire fence, all while a marriage is about to occur between two people, one from each town.

Kandahar (2001) Depressing film is based on a story (partly true, partly fictionalized) of a successful Afghan-Canadian who returns to Taliban-led Afghanistan after receiving a suicidal letter from her sister.

Osama (2003) Depressing story of a girl in Taliban-led Afghanistan who disguises herself as a boy in order to support her family. It was the first film to be shot entirely in Afghanistan since 1996, when the Taliban régime banned the creation of all film.

The Kite Runner (2007) Depressing tale of abandonment set against a backdrop of tumultuous events, from the fall of the monarchy in Afghanistan through the Soviet invasion, the mass exodus of Afghan refugees to Pakistan and the United States, and the Taliban regime.

Mountain Patrol (2004) Shot on location in extreme awe-inspiring landscapes, depicts the struggle between vigilante rangers and bands of poachers in the remote Tibetan region of Kekexili (Hoh Xil). It was inspired by the documentary *Balance* by Peng Hui.

Story of Weeping Camel (2003) The most exciting film you will ever see about camel weaning! A family of nomadic shepherds in the Gobi desert of Mongolia try to save the life of a rare white Bactrian camel calf after it was rejected by its mother. Great scenery and unique insight into the culture, and if you don't like reading subtitles, don't worry; I'm not sure they speak more than five minutes during the course of the entire 87 minute film.

Mongol (2007) The first installment of what I heard is to be a three-part series on Genghis Khan. This film is slow, quiet, long and chronicles the rise of the man in his early years before he got to the world conquering stuff. That sounds boring, right? But man, the scenery is totally epic, the battles are bloody, and the pacing and feel so real as that you would swear you are actually there watching the man live. Actually shot in Kazakhstan.

CHAPTER OUTLINE

East Asia

THE BEAST IN THE EAST

This region is the big bad boy on planet Earth right now, and perhaps the next superpower. A lot of people are scared that they're going to be *the* superpower and take over the Earth. I'm scared! They certainly are going to be *a* superpower. They are not going to be the sole superpower, but perhaps they are going to become the balance for US power on the planet. They are going to be the yin to the US's yang. My God, that is good! Isn't that good? The main country we are talking about here is China, the main master-blaster for the 21st century. We are going to talk about why it is the powerhouse of this region, and the wider world. Also in this region, we are going to take on North Korea and South Korea. For those that aren't sure where it's supposed to go, Taiwan falls in this region as well.

China and most of the planet consider Taiwan to be China's renegade province, but a lot of folks in Taiwan think they are independent. About twenty five countries in the world recognize it as an independent sovereign state; that number is dwindling fast, so no one really cares. Taiwan counts as part of China because I live in the real world, not Taiwan's pretend one.

Before we go any further, let's make sure we identify the specifics of our region from the map on this page. China is divided in half, and we have taken out Western China and put it in Central Asia for lots of reasons that you have already read about. The region we are going to call East Asia is made up of East China—the core of the Chinese Empire for centuries—Taiwan, South Korea, and North Korea.

China and US: roughly same size, same latitudes.

PANDA FUR: THE PHYSICAL WORLD

As you see in the graphic on the previous page, China and the United States have some similarities. Which one is bigger? Which one is smaller? I don't know. It depends on which sources you are using. Some say China is the third largest country on earth and the US is number four, some reverse that; doesn't matter to me, it's pretty darn close either way. What you see in the chart on the next page is that latitude is held constant, so it's near the exact same size as the US, but the latitudinal range is a bit larger, i.e. it goes a little bit further pole-ward than the continuous United States and stretches further south of the tropics. Hainan Island, in the southern part of China, would be about where Cuba is in our hemisphere. What does this equate to climate-wise? Latitude being held constant, you know what climate is like on the east coast of the United States and that's about what the east coast of China is like as well. From north to south on the eastern seaboards of both countries, the climate regimes are identical.

What's different? Here's the difference. The United States has an east coast like China, and a west coast unlike China. China's western fringe is buried in the continent. Continentality has a different effect on the climate than coastal regions, as we already know. The Plaid Avenger wants you to know that when you travel from the coast to the western part of China, several things happen. The west gets cooler in the winter and oftentimes hotter in the summer. Elevation increases and terrain gets rougher and rockier as you move west. You have the Tibetan Plateau in Western China, as well as the Taklimakan Basin. These are areas that are way above sea level, particularly the Tibetan Plateau propping up the Himalayan Range, the largest mountain range on the planet.

As you progress off the coast, you will go upward in elevation and the temperature disparity will increase. That means it will get hotter in the summer and cooler in the winter. **Continentality** means it will also get drier, as there is less contact with large bodies of water. Temperatures get more extreme as you progress westward from the coast, getting drier and higher. This lovely clothing chart pretty much sums it all up.

Clothing Recommendations for Travel in China

Winter
- North, Northeast, Northwest, and Southwest: heavy, warm clothing, coat, hat, gloves, boots
- South, Yungui, and Sichuan: mediumweight, warm clothing, light coat, rainwear in Sichuan
- Southeast: lightweight, warm clothing, sweater

Summer
- Northeast, Northwest, and Southwest: summer clothing, light coat or sweater in the evenings, rainwear in the Northeast for occasional rains
- North, South, Yungui, Sichuan, and Southeast: light, loose tropical clothing, sunglasses, rainwear

Spring/Autumn
- North, Northeast, Northwest, and Southwest: mediumweight clothing, light coat, hat
- South, Yungui, Sichuan, and Southeast: lightweight clothing, sweater, light coat, rainwear

PANDA PEEPS

Ethnically, I want to consider why we subdivide China into separate regions. As we pointed out in the Central Asia chapter, we have a lot of different ethnic groups in China. In Mongolia, of course, there are Mongols. They also live in Inner Mongolia, a province of China. In the Tibetan Plateau, there are Tibetan folks, and of great importance in the northwestern quadrant, we have some Cossacks and some Uyghurs (pronounced Weegers). This is the exact reason why we classify most of Western China as part of Central Asia. Those are the ethnic groups that are not Chinese.

As you can see, the vast majority of people in China are on the eastern side, particularly along the eastern seaboard. The vast majority of those same people are what we call **Han Chinese,** named for an ancient dynasty. The Han dynasty's rule spanned from 200 BCE to about 200 CE. They were a very popular dynasty, so popular that people started calling themselves by the dynastic name. They're still known today as Han Chinese. Which brings up the question, where are people in China?

We pointed out that most of the Chinese population is on the eastern side of the country. That is another reason for this east-west divide within China. The eastern side is where all the people are and where the ethnically Han Chinese people are located. It also has a more moderate climate with more moisture, which is essential for food growth. Where most of the food is

China: Ethnolinguistic Groups

grown is where most of the industry is happening, most of the cities are located. This is not a coincidence. This eastern scenario is quite different from the situation for the western people who are not distinctly Han Chinese. In the western countryside, it is more sparsely populated, there is a much more rural base, and it is cooler, higher, and drier. That's your East Asia roundup of climate, terrain, and ethnicity.

PANDA OF CHRISTMAS PAST

Why do we call it the powerhouse? Several things make China quite distinct in today's world—and I'm going to get to Korea, just be patient. China is by definition the world's oldest continuous state. Was it a state 4,000 years ago? I don't know, but it was something pretty damn close. We already talked about what a sovereign state is, but here I think the term that better applies is **nation-state,** a culturally distinct group of people with a common culture that they all recognize and perpetuate in their defined area. That's what China has been for a long time. Have there been states as old, or older? Perhaps. Mesopotamia was right up there, but it's gone now. Ancient Egypt was there, but it's gone now. China has been there for about 5,000 years, and they're still here.

In order to understand China's history and current state, we need know that they have been **isolationist** by design. This has been facilitated by the physical world. How so? Let's look at China and some of the physical factors that we just talked about. It has been coined "the Far East" by Europeans, which just means it was on the other side of the planet from everything with which Western societies were familiar. Just by physical distance, China has been far away from a lot of history. It has the Pacific Ocean, the world's largest ocean, on one side of the country, putting some serious distance between it and everything else. Progress around to the north of China, and one will find big deserts, like the Gobi. To the northwest are more big deserts, like the Taklimakan Basin. These are some dry places, and people tend to like water for some reason, so

China: Population Density

Agricultural Regions

China: Industry

Can you detect an east/west pattern?

nobody's there. Keep going around to Central Asia and one will find steppe and desert climates intermingled with some tough terrain. Let's keep the tough terrain going in the southwest. We have the Himalayan Range, the largest on the planet, keeping things isolated. To the south, we have a thick rainforest and jungle environment in Burma, Thailand, and Vietnam. The physical conditions of China alone kept things isolated. On top of that, they wanted to be isolated. Their physical environment provided everything they needed to thrive.

The last big theme I want you to think about when you go through this chapter: China has historically been based on authoritarian regimes, centralized power in the hands of the few. Their 5,000-year history has been dominated by what we call an imperial period. That is an empire. All the big names you have heard, like the Han dynasty, are **dynastic successions** of centralized power. Also consider that, throughout most of history, China has been one of the most populous states, if not *the* most populous state, and it still is today.

CHINA IN WORLD HISTORY

Date	Status
1000 BCE	China is "the bomb"
500 BCE	China is "the bomb"
100 BCE	China is "the bomb"
YEAR 0	Jesus is born; China is "the bomb"
100 CE	China is "the bomb"
500 CE	China is "the bomb"
1000 CE	China is "the bomb"
1300 CE	Mongols invade; despite this, China is "the bomb"
1500 CE	Age of European Colonialsim kicks off; China is still "the bomb"
1600 CE	China is "the bomb"; Manchu Dynasty reaches largest extent ever
1800 CE	Things start to change; China is no longer "the bomb," it starts getting bombed!

What you see in the table above is the only real ancient history that I want you to understand about China. China, as both a distinct culture and a distinct state, has been the bomb for most of human history. What do I mean by "most of human history"? Pretty much from around 2000 BCE right on up to 1800—that's right, only 200 years ago. If you had been anywhere in the world and you said, "Hey, what country has the most going on, what country has the most thriving economy, who's making the most money, who has the highest level of technology, where is it happening, where should we go to invest?" The answer for all these things, throughout all of human history, would have been China. They have been a powerhouse of economic activity and population forever. Western history books are too wrapped up in their own issues to recognize this fully, but the Plaid Avenger will help you see. Learn this the first time and never forget it: Although we see modern China growing and we say, "Wow, look at them go! Isn't this great?" just keep it in perspective. They have been at the top for most of history. The United States has only been in existence as long as China has stumbled and fallen down, but now they are reasserting themselves. This is a theme I will get back to by chapter's end.

PANDA EXPANSION

As you can see throughout the historical expansion of China, the core of China has always been the eastern seaboard. While the empire has fluctuated and its borders have grown (sometimes retracted, but mostly grown), the core has always been maintained. I said earlier that the Chinese have been isolationists by design. Throughout most of history they know they're the bomb; it's not as if they don't know the rest of the planet exists. They just aren't interested. People came to them for education, and came to their cities because they were the most cosmopolitan and happening places. People came to trade with China because they wanted all of that cool stuff China made. China has historically been the center for tea production, ceramics, and porcelain—what do you call the stuff that your mom breaks out for fancy occasions like Thanksgiving? That's right! China! It's not called china because it's small and breakable, but because it's from China! The spice trade was also a huge market based out of China.

All of the stuff that the Europeans and the Middle-Easterners and lots of other folks around the planet wanted throughout history was produced in China. Trade was mostly one way: going out. As you know, this is something that is true still today, but on top of that one-way trading, the cultural interaction was also mostly one way. Yes, sometimes things come into China that are adopted and adapted into their culture. Sometimes even foreign invaders come into China and take over. But the one thing at which China has been exceptionally good throughout all of its history is maintaining its distinct sense of culture.

Even when invaded and taken over by other groups of people, like Mongols or the Manchus, China assimilated the foreigners very rapidly. It's like an old out-of-hand saying: "Anybody can go to China and do anything he wants, but they are going to be Chinese in the end." Everything gets **Chinafied** once it gets in there. This is because the Chinese have this isolationist design, very inward-looking and self-preserving. Take the Great Wall of China, for example. This is one of the major features of China that is a direct material manifestation of its isolationist design: a big wall built to keep people out. The basic Chinese self image: "We are China on this side. Keep the hell out. We don't need your stuff. We don't need your culture. We don't need anything from you. We are the bomb. We are the center of the universe!" They really said that last part; there is a place you can go in Beijing called the center of the universe. That's pretty much the way they've seen themselves throughout history.

Does that mean that they never had interaction with anybody else on the planet, and that they were always alone? Absolutely not. There has been trade throughout the centuries. The **Silk Road** provided exterior trade and contact with regions as far away as Europe. Why'd they call it the Silk Road? Like the fine china for

Hmmm . . . Chinese silk. I should investigate.

which China was named, it wasn't self-applied; that's just what European traders called it. The Silk Road's purpose was for people to move silks out of China to trade to the Middle East and Europe. The point is that China knows there is a world going on outside its borders. They had contact with the other regions, but mostly kept to themselves. Not many records of Chinese exploration, economic entities expanding trade, or world conquests are to be found in their history.

They remained quite isolated and that was fine and dandy for the past 4,000 years. When we get to the modern era, China met its undoing. This is what we mostly want to spend our time on when we talk about more current history and where China is today. Isolationism, while very successful for virtually all of Chinese history, unravelled in the past 300 years in a massively bad way. What are we talking about here? Up to the 1700s, global interaction and trade was there, but it was controlled by the state, and was mostly one way. China sold you all the crap you wanted to buy, but they didn't need any of your stuff. They said, "Keep all that. We don't need any of the goods you produce. Keep your culture as well. We don't need that. We've got our own culture already."

Once the Europeans got to the age of worldwide exploration and colonization, China was one of the last places they arrived. Trade was eventually established. Maybe you've heard of a couple of these distinctly European trade entities, like the Dutch East India Trading Company and British East India Trading Company. The British are the ones we already talked about back in South Asia; they ended up taking over all of what is now India, Pakistan, and Bangladesh. These were economic entities sponsored by Western European countries, but became a lot more. They took over large sections of South Asia and Southeast Asia, and then they started working on China. This was a slow process staved off consistently by the Manchus for as long as they could hold out.

1800 is a critical date to remember. This is the swing date. China was big and bad up until this point in history, then things started to go downhill, and the sliding board is steep, my friends. By the 1800s, trade companies had made inroads into China. At the same time, the Industrial Revolution changed the whole world in radical ways. Machines made stuff in much greater volumes, which meant for the first time, Europe could produce things like silk, maybe even pottery, for as cheap as China could. This shifted the balance of power away from China.

STONED PANDA

On top of that, there was a big push for capitalism and free trade in the world, sponsored by the British. Adam Smith published the *Wealth of Nations* in 1776, an important red letter date for lots of different reasons, but this was the kick-off for the whole concept of free trade. The basic premise of **free trade** is that all countries and all businesses ought to have a right to trade with anyone they want. The British primarily sponsored free trade in the beginning because they had been trying to make inroads into China and get some trade action for years. China was very conservative in their dealings. The Chinese said, "You guys can buy all the stuff you want here, just leave us the money. You bring all your silver and you can have all of the pottery, silk, and spices that you want."

Lots of money had been flowing into China for a while and this was pissing off the Europeans, who said, "Hey, China has all the bank money. All of our money goes there, and then they don't buy any of our stuff." The British were looking around and said, "What can we do? How can we break into this market? They don't want any of our stuff like the textiles we are producing via the Industrial Revolution. What could we sell them? Damn, we can't think of anything. Wait, I've got it: Opium! That's awesome, what a fantastic idea!" That is exactly what the British did. You'd think they were joking, but the new plan was to get everyone addicted to drugs and sell it to them like gangbusters to reverse the flow of silver back to Europe. It worked perfectly. Once this influx of drugs was established, it was unstoppable. By the mid-1800s, the British, the French, the Germans, Dutch, and Russians all had established trading ports, and the Manchu Dynasty started to weaken.

Opium War: the British win the right to sell crack.

Why did I bring up the whole story of opium? As the Chinese weakened, they said, "Whoa, what the hell is going on here? All of our people are addicted to opium. We can't have this. Yo, British dudes, back the hell up with that drug boat. You can't sell that here. We refuse to let your ship dock up with all that opium." The British replied, "Oh, then we declare war on you." Thus, from 1839 to 1842, the British and Chinese fought the aptly named **Opium Wars.** The British were fighting for the right to peddle drugs to the Chinese. If you look back at British historical documents, they say the whole fight was over free trade. They gauged it all on something that made them sound like sincere and honest brokers, when in fact, they were drug dealers. Millions of Chinese people were addicted to opium and it was disintegrating the social fabric of the nation. Meanwhile, the British fought a war and won the right to distribute opium to the Chinese population.

How did this happen? How did this mighty, mighty nation, that had been around so long, lose a war over drugs to the British? Isolation is a double-edged sword. Through most of history it kept China distinct, and for most of history they were ahead. But the other edge of the sword is that, because they weren't paying attention to what was going on in Europe, they missed the Industrial Revolution. The Industrial Revolution, which goes hand in hand with military revolution, ended up giving the British a technological advantage. By the time the British showed up with their gunboats and drug boats, they were militarily superior to the Chinese. This three-year war shouldn't have even lasted that long; it was a duck shoot. How do you say "quack" in Chinese?

ANGRY PANDA

This ended in 1842 and was a stunning defeat for the Chinese. Yes, empires have come and gone, and people have beaten each other up, and they've had some wars—but they have never had a foreign body of people from somewhere on the other side of the planet invade their soil, and whip their ass completely. They received such a sound thumping in the Opium Wars that they were forced to basically cede all control of territory over to the Brits. The British forced China to open up all trade to all states in the world. In fact, they had this hilarious thing that was called "no favored nation status." We think of that in today's world as the MOST favored nation status, but the British said, "You are going to have a *no favored nation status*, which means you have to trade with everybody, and any rights you give to one country you have to give to us all." They completely liberated the Chinese economy for every other country's taking overnight. This was a titanic blow to the Chinese culture, to the Chinese way of life, and to the Chinese economy. In this same peace treaty, concessions of the Opium War included the British picking up a fairly significant territory that you have probably heard played out for the next twenty years, well into the 1930s.

This left people in China looking for some answers. "What should we do? What type of system should we implement? The imperial system is gone and we're not going to do that again." Some said, "Let's embrace the US model, or the French model, or the UK model," and others said, "Hey, what about that Soviet model? That looks pretty good." This started the face-off of ideologies within China. In 1928, the **Nationalists,** under a guy named **Chiang Kai-Shek,** were fighting for a republic. They defeated the folks

fighting for a Communist state. The Nationalists also defeated, allied with or outright paid off all those warlord guys remaining in

Chiang Kai-Shek

the northern states, uniting the country. But this was tenuous. Why was it tenuous? Because of another incursion I haven't mentioned yet.

Look back to the spheres of influence in China map. Look at what the Japanese were doing. Japan's empire was expanding. I already pointed out they took over the Korean Peninsula back in 1895, but they didn't stop there. The Japanese also staked out some

How Now Chairman Mao? Who the Hell Is Mao?

Mao Zedong (Mao was his last name) became the leader of the Communist party in China in 1927 when he formed the People's Liberation Army. The Communist Party and Mao were largely seen as folk heroes and true Chinese nationalists during the Japanese occupation, as they conducted a guerrilla war against the Japanese aggressors throughout the entire conflict. It should be noted that the Nationalist Party, led by Chiang Kai-Shek, did little to nothing during the occupation, choosing instead to hoard weapons and money given to them by the US—given for the sole purpose of fighting the Japanese.

After WWII and the brutal Chinese civil war against the Nationalist/Kuomintang party, the Communists took over mainland China in 1949 and declared the People's Republic of China. You can like him or you can hate him, but Mao was largely seen as "the George Washington of China" at this moment in history, because he declared that "the Chinese people have stood back up." Meaning: the two centuries of foreign occupation and humiliation were over.

Mao became the leader of China and was known as the "Four Greats": "Great Teacher, Great Leader, Great Supreme Commander, Great Helmsman." He became the supreme dictator of China; every Chinese person was required to have a book of Chairman Mao's quotations. He has been praised by many for unifying China and making it free of foreign domination for the first time since the Opium Wars.

However, Mao is sometimes credited as a lethal dictator. Because of some of his projects—such as the Anti-Rightist Campaign, the Great Leap Forward, and the Cultural Revolution—over 80 million Chinese people died. Part of the reason so many people died was that Chinese officials were so afraid of criticizing Mao that they told him that everything was going fine. Also for this reason, China did not start implementing capitalist reforms until after Mao died in 1976.

Fun Commie Fact: Mao started his own kind of communism, called Maoism, that stated that communist revolution needed to come from rural peasants. Marxist communism was designed for industrialized countries, like the ones in Europe.

claims of ownership of Chinese lands after they helped squash the Boxer Rebellion. They made further incursions into what is now Manchuria, and started to take control of some port cities. The Europeans were already doing it, so the Japanese wanted to play ball as well. Japan largely stayed out of the whole WWI conflict, because they were busy securing more empire for themselves over in East Asia. By the time chaos happened in China, when there was no real leadership and no one knew what the hell was going on, Japan had seriously invaded them.

This was the point—in between World War I and World War II—when the Japanese secured real control over all the major facilities in China. This Japanese invasion only perpetuated the chaotic state in China, and a civil war broke out amongst the Communist and Nationalist forces again. During this civil war, something called the **Long March** occurred; **Mao Zedong** led the

Chinese Communists in a retreat through Northern China after a defeat by the Nationalist forces. The fight should have been over after that initial battle, but somehow this guy named Mao pulled off a last-second, fourth-quarter win. This leads us to the question: who is this Mao guy? See insert box on page 484.

In 1937, the Japanese army attacked China outright. This was the buildup to World War II. By the following year, Japan controlled most of eastern China. Remember, that's where the most people, the most businesses, and where the most of everything is located.

Japanese plans for the mainland. China was not happy.

WWII was disastrous for the Chinese. Recall from way back in the Russian chapter that the Russian losses were something along the lines of 10–20 million people during World War II. It's a lesser-known fact that the Japanese did one hell of a job slaughtering the Chinese at the same time. This mass slaughter has been barely acknowledged by Western historians and people like you. The losses in China may have been upwards of 20–30 million people, and possibly could have been 40 million. It's almost impossible to tell in hindsight due to record-keeping issues. Somewhere between 20 and 40 *million* Chinese were killed during the Japanese occupation in the buildup before and during the war. Very, very few of those millions were actually combatants. In other words, they were unarmed civilians.

Many were innocent women and children who were slaughtered in nasty ways by the Japanese. I guess it was just another way they were trying to embrace the West. Japan tried the first kind of modern biological testing and warfare during World War II. Some of their experiments included dropping rats infected with bubonic plague from bombers over heavily populated cities to see how fast people would get the disease; they also poisoned water supplies in major cities to see how fast people would die. We also talked about the **Rape of Nanking** in which millions of people were slaughtered in the streets. The Japanese didn't want to set up internment camps. I am reiterating this again in this chapter because it's just that important.

When we think of the horrors of World War II, we usually think of the German atrocities against the Jews—and those were horrible, make no bones about it. But when China thinks of World War II, they recall the horrible atrocities which left a body count probably eight or ten times higher in their country at the hands of the Japanese. This makes for bad blood, my friends. It's still there today. Also remember that the Japanese have occupied the Korean Peninsula since 1895, an even longer time, under the exact same kind of brutal regime. The Koreans haven't forgotten either. All of Korea ended up being a work camp for the Japanese to get resources out of mines. All the resource extraction from the Korean Peninsula was shipped back to Japan. Why would Japan be building this empire, taking all these resources, enslaving the population of Korea, and taking over places in China? For the reasons we have already

This really sucked for China.

What the Hell is the Story Behind Taiwan?

For most of its history, Taiwan was an island territory off the coast of China that was of no great consequence. (Sorry my Taiwanese friends! You know it's true!) However, Taiwan immediately became a Cold War hotspot when Chiang Kai-Shek and the Chinese Nationalists (Kuomintang), after losing the Chinese Civil War, retreated to Taiwan and set up a government called the Republic of China (ROC). Meanwhile, Mao and the Communists controlled mainland China and called themselves the People's Republic of China (PRC).

FORMOSA
FROM THE LATEST AUTHORITIES
Revised by Rev. W. Campbell

The leaders of both countries long subscribed to the one-China policy—that there is only one China and Taiwan is part of China—each insisting on their own government's legitimacy. Of course, during the Cold War, capitalist countries recognized the ROC as the legitimate government of China and communist countries recognized the PRC as the legitimate government of China.

Today, the Taiwan situation is starting to settle out, perhaps closing the chapter on China's last disputed territory (forget about Tibet). Most countries do not have relations with the ROC and the Taiwanese position has eroded over the past few decades as the PRC has gained international prominence. Because of its one-China policy, the PRC only participates in international organizations where the ROC is not recognized as a state. The United Nations, for example, expelled the ROC in 1971 when the PRC was admitted. Just so you understand what I'm saying here, let me reiterate that last point: prior to 1971, Taiwan actually sat in the China chair at the UN, including in the Permanent Security Council seat. After 1971, both the UN and the US recognized mainland China as the true leaders of that place we call "China," and therefore the UN seat reverted to the commies, and Taiwan was no longer considered a sovereign state. To make matters even more complicated, while most countries do not have official relations with the ROC (to not make the PRC mad), they do have informal relations with the Taiwan government. For example, the United States operates the American Institute in Taiwan, which is like an embassy. However, it is not officially called an embassy because America is not allowed to have diplomatic relations with Taiwan.

The Taiwan situation was really tricky for the last decade, because the Kuomintang lost control of Taiwan in elections in 2000 to President Chen Shui-bian, who was from a staunchly pro-independence party that regularly pissed off China by making moves to secure said independence. However, things have settled down considerably just this year as the KMT won the presidency back, and the new President Ma (that's right, just Ma—like your mother) has made great strides to mend ties with China.

Fun Fact: While the US officially adheres to the one-China policy, in reality, it practices a two-China policy. Under the 1979 Taiwan Relations Act, the US sells Taiwan military weapons, and the language of the act warns the People's Republic that any coercive unification efforts would be "of grave concern to the United States."

pointed out in the Japan chapter: They don't have any resources on their island, and to expand and get richer, they've got to take stuff from other places. That's why they became an imperial regime.

The Japanese occupation was so horrifically bad that the Nationalists and Communists even teamed up at one point. They said, "This sucks so bad, there is no point in us fighting each other right now; we have to get these invaders out of here first!" They teamed up and kicked out the Japanese. Of course, it was the United States' involvement in the war against Japan in the Pacific that did most of the job, but the Chinese were doing some fighting on their soil as well, making life for the Japanese difficult. Finally, in 1945, it was lights out for Japan, literally and figuratively.

In 1946, after WWII was over, the civil war was back on again. The Nationalists and Communists said, "Cool, the Japanese are gone. Yeah, the war is over, so let's hurry up and rebuild so we can get back to fighting each other to see who controls this place." Long story short: after this stretch of 150 years where China was completely dominated, the end result was that, in 1949, the Communists won the civil war. Mao was a long-shot to win at several different points, but the Commies pulled it out. The Communists won, and the People's Republic of China was established in 1949.

What happened to the Nationalist party that had a lot of supporters that fought the civil war? Most of them withdrew to the island of Taiwan. Taiwan? I've heard of that place. (See inset box on opposite page.)

The Commies took charge, and started to pull the country up by the bootstraps. They had an agricultural revolution, and began industrialization. The Communists started to make strides to rebuild their society, their country. But this isolationist vein, this antiforeign vein, so prevalent in Chinese history popped back up again in 1966–1969. This is what some call the Cultural Revolution; at least, that's what it says in Mao's little red book.

The **Cultural Revolution** was very much like the Boxer Rebellion in that the sentiment was basically, "We don't like any of these foreigners. We don't like foreign influence, so let's purge it all. Destroy all Western instruments, destroy Western literature, banish people that are from the West, persecute, imprison, or kill people who speak English or people who were Western educated." A real social upheaval and purge occurred within China. China regained a little sanity after World War II and the civil war, but it's not out of the woods yet. The last bad event for them that I'm going to talk about occurred in 1989, when hundreds of students were massacred during the pro-democracy protest in **Tiananmen Square.**

This event puts us up into what I think most of you readers here will know about . . .

THE DRAGON AWAKENS: CHINA IN THE MODERN ERA

This is stuff you probably remember, or have at least heard referenced. This is the end result of the Chinese communist experiment: They made some progress since the wars ended, but they also had internal purges and internal problems—and they were not really that rich yet. China was still kind of backwards and behind. To top it all off, they were persecuting democracy movements. How crappy is that? But this is where China began to reevaluate some of its actions, because the world watched the Tiananmen Square massacre and said, "How horrific, how terrible! What's the deal with these guys? They are bastards!" Strangely enough, this was when everything started to turn around for China.

ECONOMIC EXPLOSION

After Mao Zedong died in 1976, his subsequent successors in the Chinese government started to liberate the economy and adopt capitalist reform—something which Mao absolutely raged against his entire life. The first guy who took the country in this new direction was a cat named Deng Xiaoping. If we are going to credit Mao with bringing China out of its "period of sorrow," then we really have to credit Deng with truly bringing China back to its restored position of wealth and power in today's world. It was Deng who pushed for capitalist economic reforms, put the country on the path of modernization, and pretty much gave up on the commie experiment thing that Mao had attempted.

As we already suggested many times in this book, Communism has never worked anywhere. It is a political and economic system that is just too complicated, and not one single manifestation of it anywhere has ever managed to work. It didn't work in Russia, didn't work in Vietnam (mostly because the US ruined its chances from

Deng and Carter in 1979. Well, at least one of them was a successful leader.

the get-go), hasn't really worked in Cuba, and didn't work in China.

Here is the big difference: in Soviet Russia, the USSR, in one fell swoop overnight, said, "Okay, we are going to get rid of this. Anybody that wants to be out of the USSR, go ahead and vote yourself out." Then the Berlin Wall fell and the whole damn Russian economy fell with it. The Chinese were watching those events extremely closely. This is one reason why the Chinese are liberalizing very carefully, very slowly, which they've been doing for the last forty years. They have opened their markets, but slowly. They've allowed foreign capital investment, but slowly. They have privatized some industries, but slowly. Because when did Tiananmen Square happen? 1989.

Tiananmen Square: where all the action happens.

That's exactly when the whole kit-n-caboodle came crashing down for the Soviets. Mikhail Gorbachev, the leader of the Soviet Union, was actually visiting Deng in China during that incident. Chinese leaders rightly surmised that the reason the pro-democracy movement popped up at that time and that place was because people were supporting Gorbachev. Some college kids said, "Yeah, Birthmark-head is opening up and liberalizing and making democracy in Russia. Let's all have a big protest here to support that!" The Chinese government said, "No! Look what's happening there; those guys suck! They're falling down and eating crap. We are not going to do that again."

Thus, the massacre. The Tiananmen massacre was terrible. The Plaid Avenger doesn't want any college kids killed, because hey, college kids are cool, but it was a very intentional move by the Chinese government. They said, "We can not allow this to happen because we can not allow our society to spiral out of control like the Soviet one did." If you think about it in hindsight, it was a calculated, conservative move. China is bustling in today's world while Russia is struggling to catch up. The Chinese have had infinite patience. Since Deng Xiaoping took over as head of state after Mao died, they started to liberalize and open up, but at their own pace, a pace that was massively accelerating right at that point in time.

TIANANMEN TURNAROUND: 21ST CENTURY SUCCESSES

The point of entry is the Tiananmen Massacre of 1989. It got a bunch of bad press for China, but I'm putting it back in here as a turning point, because it doesn't happen again, and it won't ever happen again. They may very well have done it again, but they figured it out: "Oh, we don't want bad press. We want people to invest here. We want to become part of the world economy. We want to have influence in the world. We want to have the Olympics here. We want to have the Miss Universe Pageant." You can't have any of that if you are killing your own citizens. This is a great place to start in terms of the 21st-century turn-around for China, because it is the last time you are going to see a tremendous and bloody crackdown of that magnitude. The Chinese government learned its lesson well—bad press equals bad investment strategy.

The government is still run by the Communist Party, but this is not a communist state as we suggested way back in the *Know Your Heads of State* chapter. True, communism is economics and politics put together, but there isn't a damn thing about this society that's economically communist. This is the wild west of free-market capitalism, my friends. Since the Communist Party is still part of the government, it's better to term the government a **one-party state.** True, communism is gone. Nobody is paying attention to that nonsense anymore. By the way, only about two percent of the entire Chinese population is a card-carrying commie. That's two percent of a billion and a half people. What does that equate to? A decent sized number, but still almost nobody. This is not a communist economy, and it is not necessarily a communist country; it is a one-party state.

Let's get to the entire decade right after the Tiananmen massacre, when China enjoyed massive economic growth. There were huge influxes of foreign capital in the form of investments by multinational corporations. The Chinese were very particular about how this happened and controlled things very stringently. They said, "Okay, Microsoft, Boeing, Exxon, you guys can come over here and start a company if you like, as long as you give us all the technology we want. In other words, we are going to get something out of this; we're not just going to open our markets and let you come do what you want."

"Plaid Avenger, I have the secret formula for Chinese economic growth . . . but I think I'm being followed . . ."

They certainly got something out of their international relationships, but why would they want to be so anal about everything? Look where it got them. In a single decade, they pretty much caught up. Granted, they were not on the technological level of the West yet, but they were catching up fast. 1990 was the kickoff of massive economic growth, large amounts of foreign capital, investment, and business. Why would foreign business want to be in China? Oh, I don't know. Would you like to be in a place to sell your product to a billion and a half people? Yeah, I thought so.

This 1990s economic growth was due not only to foreign investment, but also to private enterprise within China. Liberalization of government control led to growth in **entrepreneurs**—Chinese people starting Chinese businesses. And there are a billion and a half people there, man! They were emerging from a communist economic system where no matter how hard you work—or don't work—you are going to get paid the same. What incentive is that to work hard? There are no incentives. But put them in a capitalist environment and see what happens then: "Hey dudes, if you work harder you get more money. You get more money, you get more stuff, your life can be better." If you get a billion and a half people who desperately want more stuff and offer said stuff to them, man, watch out! This place was blowing up, due mostly to entrepreneurial growth of private business within China. This economic explosion can also be linked to the growth of the Tigers, the thing we talked about way back in the World Econ chapter. Other countries in the vicinity were gaining in all these categories as well: international investment, international business, etc.

The reason companies were going to Indonesia, Taiwan, or South Korea was that they had cheaper labor. China is the cheap labor pool of the planet. Businesses were flocking to it to take advantage of that. Every major business on the planet now has a presence in China. This has all happened in the last fifteen years. This is an economy that is so damn hot that they typically have what we call double-digit growth. If they say the GDP growth is 11 percent or 12 percent or 13 percent, that means the GDP next year will be 11 percent bigger than it is right now. Take what we have right now and multiply it by 11 percent and add it on next year. In countries like the United States and most of Western Europe, 3 percent or 4 percent growth is fantastic. In China, 10 percent, 12 percent, 14 percent growth is titanic, but they are consistently

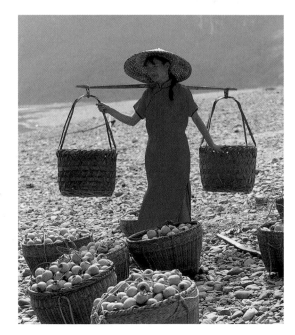

achieving it. The Chinese government's main problem right now is not how to make their economy grow—they are trying to figure out how to put the brakes on it: "We're going too fast; things are getting out of control. Let's cool it down, cool it down!" It is a situation of which every country in the world is envious. Who wouldn't like to be in a situation of growing too fast as opposed to slow or no growth?

THE PANDA TAKES BACK ITS CUBS

In 1997, China conducted training off the coast of Taiwan. This consisted of firing gunboats and some missiles over Taiwan's airspace. It was a very specific move at a very specific time to symbolize that China was ready to reassert itself. There was rhetoric and talk before, but now that the Chinese economy and military had caught up enough, they said, "Okay, we're telling you what's going to go on. Taiwan is our territory. We are going to do something and see what happens." It was a symbolic gesture, I think, and marked a turning point where China was ready to reassert itself militarily, if necessary.

In 1997, Hong Kong was returned to China. The British packed up everything that they claimed from the Opium Wars and sailed out. The Chinese weren't really waving goodbye, either. They just went to work pulling Hong Kong and its mighty capitalist economy back to the motherland. That same year, six months later, the Portuguese returned Macau to China. Taiwan is now the final piece of the lost Chinese empire, which is soon to be put back into its strategic place.

The new leader of Taiwan, President Ma, has made every indication thus far that he will be working to smooth out the relationship with China. In the first month he was in office, there were high level meetings between Chinese President Hu Jintao and major Taiwanese leaders. They agreed to resume commercial flights between the countries on weekends, and also agreed to triple the amount of tourist allowed to visit the island every day to 3000. This is the most open that communications and travel have been between these two entities since before 1949. That is big news, and please keep in mind that all of this has occurred just in the first month that Ma was in office. I predict significant changes in his four-year term in office. You know what? I'm just crazy enough to make a grander prediction: I believe we are seeing the beginning of the end of the historic dispute between China and Taiwan. Look for Taiwan to be firmly back in the Chinese fold within a decade.

WORLD TRADE ORGANIZATION
ORGANISATION MONDIALE DU COMMERCE
ORGANIZACIÓN MUNDIAL DEL COMERCIO

But onto other issues. In the year 2000, the United States established **favored nation status** and traded with China. In 2001, China joined the World Trade Organization (WTO). This is a society on fire. We can add a few other things here, such as: China is now an associate member of ASEAN, a core member of the SCO, a core member of the BRIC, a member of APEC, and hosted the 2008 Olympics. And they won the games to boot! China is all over the damn place.

Here is a quote from the chief Chinese negotiator, Long Yongtu, regarding China's entry into the WTO: "The fifteen-year process is a blink of an eye in the 5,000-year history of China." That resonates with the Plaid Avenger. Awesome, awesome quote to get you to understand what is going on in this society. They're telling the world, "We are here for the long haul, friends. We are reasserting ourselves. We are going to reclaim our proper position in the world economy and the world politic. And fifteen years, you think that's a long time? Whatevs. We will sit here for 100 damn years, if that's what it takes. We are China. We have the patience of a rock. We will get it done." If it sounds like I'm getting too fired up about China, it's because this is *the* vibrant place right now. It's really happening.

To finish off our categorized date list of Chinese achievements in the 21st century, we have to include outer space. In 2005, China put a man in space. China joined the most exclusive country club on the planet. It's a short list. Do you know it? It's the US, Russia, and China. Not even Japan has done it, the mighty, mighty wonder to the east of China and the number two economy on the planet. How about Germany, the number three economy? No! They've never done it, either. To up the ante, in September 2008 China conducted its first "space walk," further underscoring China's technological prowess and determination to go where no man has gone before. Call in Captain Kirk for back-up! The Chinese are setting the stage. This is again like so many of these other things I've mentioned: it is a symbol. China said, "We are in the big boy club now. We are the bomb. We have got it going ON!" Think about it. There is no reason to put a man in space. It's all about prestige. They are reclaiming their world role. The 21st century is a whole different world for the Chinese.

They aren't even satisfied with just putting a Chinese citizen in orbit for a few days. The Chinese have every intention on putting a man on the moon, and they have already announced tentative plans to build a permanent moon base! Holy green cheese! A freakin' moon base! Not even the US pulled that one off! Just to give you an idea of how serious this is, China was actually six months ahead of schedule when they succeeded in the manned orbit plan. They then busted a move right after the 2008 Olympics by having the first Chinese space walk . . . and the panda pride is showing! Now they are slated to get to the moon by 2012, and appear to be on track. In what is assuredly a total random coincidence, the US upped NASA's budget times ten, and NASA then announced that they were now planning to build a moon base first. Space race is back on, my friends!

I actually hope the Chinese base gets built first. That way, once the US base is being worked on, the Americans will have a place from which to order take-out.

Danger Will Robinson! China is here!

BIG PLACE, BIG ECONOMY, BIG MILITARY—BIG PROBLEMS!

I know I have stressed this a million times, but let me stress it one million and one times: China is reassuming its place on the world stage. It is almost impossible for the United States to understand this scenario, because think about the timeline. The entire time the US has been rising in the world is the exact same time period China spent falling. Throughout all of US history, China sucked. But that's not looking at the big picture. They've been on top for 5,000 years. China is not saying, "Hey, we are growing and we're finally going to be a part of the world economy." They are saying, "We are taking back our place at the top." That is a much better way to phrase it, and a much better way for you to understand what's going on. In the same light, China is increasingly becoming a model to follow for other states all over Asia.

During the entire Cold War, we lived in a bipolar world. The US was one big power, and the USSR was the other. All the states in the world could choose one side or the other. Some, a scant few, chose neither. Nowadays, we are getting back to a bipolar world again. The US had a good run there for ten to fifteen years as the sole superpower in the world, but China is rising to meet it (not overtake it). Some countries in South America are now making strategic ties to China. In Africa, a lot of nations are making strategic ties to China. Certainly, Southeast Asia is making strategic ties to China. It's just the way things are going down right now; China is the other option in a newly bipolar world.

How is China doing this? Their explosive economy is a big part of it—double digit growth now for a decade and a half. Part of that is entrepreneurship, which leads to a growing middle class. That's what you have to have if you are going to have an internal economic engine that keeps going. You've got to have that middle class that likes to buy a lot of stuff, and China is growing a big fat middle class right now. Here's some other cool stuff that makes them appealing: China is on the permanent UN Security Council, which means, since World War II, they have had a world political voice. They are in the WTO. They are a member of ASEAN and APEC and SCO. They are pretty much in all the power player clubs. They are in the space club! On top of that, they have what the Plaid Avenger has got to refer to as one suave-ass foreign policy.

SUAVE-ASS FOREIGN POLICY?

There are two parts to this. *One:* For the last twenty years, China has been working to resolve all of its border disputes. Thirty years ago, China disputed all its borders with everybody. In today's world, that is going away. They have peacefully reabsorbed Hong Kong and Macau, and as I suggested earlier, Taiwan is slowly coming back into the fold as well. They are cementing ties with all their land neighbors, a pretty suave move if I do

President Hu Jintao

Prime Minister Wen Jiabao

say so myself. *Two:* They are setting up strategic ties with countries all over the planet, sometimes with no strings attached. It's a very odd thing. In the US, this no strings attached business is looked upon with suspicion. China lends money to countries with no motive? We find this hard to believe. We always have a motive behind everything we do. We say, "Oh, we will lend you some money if we get something in return." But China just lent half a million dollars to Palau, some Pacific nation no one has even heard of before. They build bridges and stuff in Africa. Throughout Latin America, Africa, Southeast Asia, and even India, they are setting up economic ties, buying different resources and setting up free-trade options.

This is done primarily with an eye for **resource acquisition.** As China's economy continues to explode, they need more energy, like all big economies do. What types of energy? Coal, which they have in abundance, and oil, which they don't. You often see **President Hu Jintao** of China making his rounds. In 2006, he visited all of South America and came to the United States to visit President George W. Bush. He went to Saudi Arabia, and then toured all of the African nations. This guy gets around. His premier, **Wen Jiabao,** gets around even more. These guys are hustling around the planet right now.

DETRIMENTAL DIPLOMACY

One of the problems is this same suave-ass foreign policy. For those who are ultraconservative out there, and you think the Plaid Avenger is some liberal commie who is supporting China no matter what, just hold on, you'll see. I said their policy was SUAVE. Suave doesn't mean morally or ethically good; I didn't even say it was good, period, but it is very freakin' suave.

How is this suave-ass foreign policy detrimental for the Chinese? China does business for business' sake. They don't really worry about the details too much. Throughout this book, we talk about the UN's Permanent Security Council and China's role in it, and the issues of sovereignty. China is one of the strictest adherents to the ideas of sovereignty. They are all about it. They don't want to intervene anywhere. Actually, the Chinese have no troops in any country and they like it that way. They say, "Sovereignty is sovereignty. Whatever you do to your people, it's not our business." The reason they do that is they don't want anybody messing in their backyard anymore. They respect sovereignty because, ultimately, they want everyone to respect theirs. They don't want anyone messing around in their country because of what they are doing to the Uyghur people over in the western part of China. This means they will do business with states no matter what those countries may be doing to their own people.

I am thinking particularly of Sudan in today's world, Burma, and even Zimbabwe. Most of the world does not like, does not support, and does not want to trade with these countries because they have fairly brutal records of persecuting their citizens. The morally and ethically right thing to do is to refuse to support those states in any capacity. But China says, "We don't give a crap. We will trade with you. Hey, can we buy oil from you, Sudan? Thanks, buddy!" Perhaps their open policy is not such a great thing. This causes friction between China and other rich countries around the world. Developed countries say, "You can't do that." China says, "Hell yeah we can. We are a sovereign state." The issue is a source of friction for a lot of the Western countries.

I should tell you that even this attitude has been changing fast in China just in the last few years. China was very keen to make a good, if not great, impression on the world with the Olympic Games they hosted in 2008. But the world was not going to let them achieve this so easily. Growing attention to the Sudan situation in particular cast such a negative light on China's dealings there were calls for an Olympic boycott of at least the opening ceremonies, if not the whole affair. This spooked China enough for them to allow the UN to move on the Sudanese situation without stopping it; remember, as a member of the UN Permanent Security Council, China had, up to this point, used its veto power to prevent anything from happening to its Sudanese buddies. That situation has now changed due to international pressure. Most of us are eagerly awaiting similar Chinese capitulations when it comes to doing something about Burma . . . but that may still be a pipe dream at best for now. See the international friction that is caused by the Chinese foreign policy? But we don't even have to travel outside of the borders of China to see this international tension . . . how about . . .

TUMULTUOUS TIBET

Speaking of frictional Chinese policies, there is the small matter of Tibet. Or should I say, huge matter of Tibet. The area we refer to as Tibet has been various things at various times in the last thousand years: it was an independent kingdom, a vassal state, an autonomous region, a semi-autonomous region, a colonial holding, and a fully absorbed territory into a state we call China. For purposes of understanding today's world, we need only concern ourselves with that last description—as part of Chinese territory.

During the heyday of the Manchu Empire in China, well over 300 years ago, Tibet increasingly came under the influence of the Chinese. But Chinese power was destroyed by internal factors and civil war, combined with Western and Japanese imperialism in the 1800s. As China was falling apart, Tibet first became a pawn between Western powers (mostly Russian and British), and later began

Tibet: an autonomous province of China. Probably forever.

asserting its outright independence—and to keep the record straight for you, their independence was proclaimed while China was self-destructing and the West was preoccupied with World War 1. Basically, Tibet was largely left to its own devices while all the other world powers were busy.

Long story short, once China got their act together after WWII and their Civil War, they immediately starting re-establishing their presence in Tibet, and in fact had never renounced their claim of sovereignty on the area. The Dalai Lama continued to partially rule in Tibet with, to some extent, autonomous power given by contemporary Chinese governments, until the People's Republic of China invaded the region in 1949, taking full control in 1959. The Dalai Lama then hauled ass to India and has since ceded temporal power to an elected government-in-exile. Which brings us up to date enough to understand today's world . . .

The current 14th Dalai Lama seeks greater autonomy for Tibet. Not outright independence, but greater self-rule autonomy. The Chinese have interpreted this as a threat to their sovereignty—and they hate the guy! They hate that he is so popular. They hate that he is well respected, and even venerated, as a world figure. They probably even hate his sweet flowing robes. And they really hate it when any world leaders meet with the Dalai Lama. The Chinese think that the more recognition the guy gets, the more the world will demand that China give Tibet back to him. It is a similar issue to their Taiwan situation—the Chinese do not want any country to officially recognize the guy, for fear that Tibet will someday claim independence.

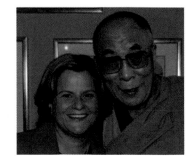

What is the Dalai Lama really up to? The dude now tours the world—and he is the first Dalai Lama to go abroad—spreading the Buddhist message and preserving Tibetan culture. He officially leads the government in exile from Dharamsala, India. He is a fantastic speaker, promotes world peace, wildlife conservation, and a host of other awe-

Lama popular with the ladies

some stuff that has won him great respect, acclaim, and even a Nobel Peace Prize. Let's face it: the dude is the Buddhist shizzle. How about we call him the Budd-izzle?

"Let's go get those commies! I'm ready to invade the North!"

Super-economy in the South; lights out in the North. Yep, that's Korea.

PLAID AVENGER INSIDE TIP: How come it's not just one Korea? What does that have to do with Hawkeye Pierce? A really cheesy TV show named *M*A*S*H* depicted the Korean War for the prime-time enjoyment of US viewers. The funny part? The Korean War lasted three years, from 1950–53. The TV show lasted 12 years. That war was just so damn funny we had to watch it four times longer!
You should also know this: the Korean War was the first UN military action. That's right: it was not a US war, even though it looks that way on TV. A UN resolution was passed to stop the North Korean invasion, and this UN force was, of course, led by the US, but there were also soldiers from other UN member states. That's why when you watch *M*A*S*H* you will see the random British or Australian dude hitting on Hot Lips Houlihan.

whole peninsula. To this day, over 30,000 American troops are stationed in South Korea in case North Korea attacks again. This conflict became the first hot spot of the Cold War.

Since then, North Korea and South Korea have gone radically separate ways. South Korea is a capitalist democracy with the world's tenth largest economy, while North Korea is still a communist dictatorship whose population is starving. However, there is a Korean reunification movement, and the two Koreas are trying to reestablish relations with each other. A unified Korean team has marched in the opening ceremonies of the past several Olympic Games. However, reunification will be difficult because the Koreas have been apart for so long and their economies and governments are very different. Also, many observers think that both China and the United States prefer that Korea be divided for geopolitical reasons.

N. Korean Dear Leader
Kim:I'm crazy!

S. Korean President Lee:
I'm rich!

The North-South Korea thing is a relic of the Cold War. It is one of the hot spots that flared up during the Cold War, where fighting actually occurred. What's going on in today's world with this battle of ideologies? A telling illustration can be seen in the map of lights at night in the Koreas on the previous page. South Korea: bright lights, big city. North Korea: lights out. This really underlines what's going on within these two countries, and really shows who won the ideology battle of the Cold War. The Koreas sum it up so perfectly, so beautifully, that we have to point it out here. North Korea went down the communist path, the radical communist path. Now they are radically freakin' broke! They've got nothing. It is a society that is about to disintegrate under our good friend Kim Jong-Il.

The opposite is South Korea, which embraced the democratic capitalist West and is now the number ten economy on the planet. We have three of the top ten economies right there in a nice little grouping of China, South Korea, and Japan. South Korea is a bustling and happening place. North Korea can't pay the light bill, but South Korea is going gangbusters.

It is funny that you don't know as much about South Korea, or hear about it that much in the news. Here is why: South Korea is a country wedged between the giants. Japan is the number two economy to its east and China the number four economy to its west. To the north is the nutso nuclear-armed North Korea that catches lots of headlines as well. South Korea looks like a little place, but it's not. It is big. China, South Korea, and Japan, to a lesser extent, are going to be the technological centers of the planet in the next 100 years.

These three countries have made that their mission, their goal. In fact, the South Koreans vowed in 2006 to put a robot in every home by 2020. This is not science fiction. It's not even fiction fiction. They actually said it! I believe they will do it, too. They already have the fastest Internet connections on the planet, and have made Internet accessibility available to every single one of its citizens. They are not playing around, man! South Korea is the most connected country on the planet per capita. All of the countries in this neighborhood have societies that are embracing technology with a vengeance. This is going to affect what's going on in the Web-world in the very near future. Soon you will see how these countries' technological expertise will impact the entire planet. Let it be known that these guys are hot and heavy with the technology sector, and they are transforming the playing field every single day.

I shouldn't end this little discussion without giving at least a little positive press to our North Korean friends. Actually, who gives a hell about those wackos, but you should know the reference to their "PARTY."

What's the Deal with the Six-Party Talks?

Those crazy Koreans do love to party! As long as it's with six! The six-party talks is the name given to a series of meetings with six states—China, North Korea, South Korea, Russia, Japan, and the United States—to deal with North Korea's nuclear ambitions. These talks were a result of North Korea withdrawing from the Nuclear Non-Proliferation Treaty in 2003. The aim of these talks was to find a peaceful resolution to the security concerns raised by the North Korean nuclear weapons program. Five rounds of talks resulted in nothing actually happening and little headway made in disarming North Korea.

Why no movement towards a solution? Ummm . . . I think mainly because the leadership of North Korea is utterly and completely in freakin' la-la land. It should be noted that pretty much everyone agrees that North Korea is getting close to collapse, and bordering on completely hopeless. Their number one GDP earner is counterfeiting US currency. Does that count as sustainable development? What a joke!

Basically, the only thing this "country" has to its name is supposed nuclear weapons. That is the only bargaining chip they have to be taken seriously by the outside world. Patience from the outside world is growing thin. Of course, Japan and South Korea don't want them to melt down completely, which could result in a nuclear weapon being launched. China and the US are fairly secure that no one in North Korea would be dumb enough to launch a missile in either of their directions, but all bets are off here in 2010. North Korea has walked away from the talks, re-started its nuclear program, tested at least one nuclear device, and shot off several missiles as a test/warning to the neighborhood. This situation grows grimmer by the day, and it's entirely possible that the entire state may have collapsed or been invaded by the time this book makes it to print. More on this in the hot-spots chapter.

Party?

ENOUGH ALREADY ON EAST ASIA

I think you have got the picture now, and I'm probably going to repeat some things for the fifth time, but let's do it again anyway. When we think about China, we think about one of the world's largest states, maybe the third largest state in the world. We also think of the world's largest military. Am I saying it's the best military in the world? No, the US has the best military in the world, but China has the largest free-standing army on the planet.

New China sez: "I see China moon colony from here. We're so rich. This is fun."

China also now has the number three economy on the planet, having just surpassed Germany in 2009. China will probably overtake Japan this decade, and even the mighty US by 2050!. But hey! China isn't alone in this region of big money: both Taiwan and South Korea are bangin' out the bucks as well, and all three of these entities are busting out with the newest and best technological sector development to boot. South Korea in particular has the highest level of high speed Internet access in the world, and has also vowed to have a robot in every household by 2020. No, seriously . . . like I could make this stuff up? Now, I don't know about the robots, but it is a safe prediction to say that within the next decade, three of the top ten world economies will be located here in this East Asian region. No doubts. That's a lot of bank!

But back to the big boy: China is now also a member of all the world's most progressive and fastest growing trade blocs. Their middle class is growing just as fast as their prestige. They are doing all the things the power player countries do, like the Miss World Pageant, like the Olympics, like the space programs. This is a place that is really on fire. Yes, it's got problems, but there are a lot of things going on in China that are right on target. China is back, and it is once again a world power to be reckoned with.

Along with the Taiwanese and South Korean titans, this region promises to be an epicenter of activity and excitement of all types in the coming century. If only Kim Jong-Il and his funky bunch can be coerced out of declaring war on the entire world, this region will totally be rocking out the 21st century.

PLAID AVENGER INSIDE TIP: Want to double your salary as soon as you walk out of school, regardless of your major or your GPA? Then do this: LEARN CHINESE! Anyone who is bilingual in English and Chinese can pretty much write their own ticket in the 21st century, as a business/political/cultural middleman between the two hugest world powers. Learn Chinese. Do it!

CHAPTER OUTLINE

Southeast Asia

24

CROSSROADS, CONFLICT, AND CUBS

Let's get it on! I am talking about the Thundercats, my friends, because this is where it's all going down: Southeast Asia, the "Archipelago Region," a collection of peninsulas and islands on the southeastern quadrant of the Eurasian landmass. It's been a mover and shaker throughout the years, but it's one of those places we don't really know a whole lot about. A lot of big events have happened there in the last 100 years. Even in the last fifty years, the Archipelago Region has been a place of crazy genocide, insane outbreaks of war, and massive movements of refugees into and out of the region. The last few years have been interesting for the region: a lot of economic growth, a little political turmoil, and—oh yeah—two big-time natural disasters. So, what's going on in Southeast Asia?

PHYSICALLY ON FIRE

Southeast Asia is rugged and looks complicated, but it's actually quite simple to understand. The variation in terrain predominately runs north to south in this region. We have rugged mountains that run down as a continuation of the Himalayan Range, and turn due south through Burma and Thailand. There is another chain that runs down the Vietnamese coast called the Chaine Annamitique. Damn the French and their language. The Northern parts of Vietnam, Laos, and Burma are mountainous along the Chinese border. Most of the Indonesian Archipelago has at least some mountainous terrain as a result of volcanic activity. It is yet another geologic hot

The Ring: Areas of greatest volcanic and seismic activity.

spot in terms of plate tectonic activity. The convergence of some pretty major plates makes this one of the most volcanically and seismically active regions on the planet. It is a definite centerpiece of **The Ring of Fire.**

You may have heard of Krakatoa, a volcanic island that exploded into oblivion in 1883. The blast was so enormous that the dust, ash, and smoke which entered the atmosphere created a haze that partially blocked out enough sun to cool world temperatures for about a decade. In addition to some volcanic activity, there is also seismic activity. This fosters the development of **tsunamis,** giant waves resulting from offshore earthquakes. I bring this up because, unless you've been hiding under a rock, you've heard of the massive tsunami that occurred in the Indian Ocean on December 26, 2004, claiming more than 200,000 lives. Southeast Asia is geologically active and has some fairly tough terrain, but nothing like the Andes or the

Himalayas that keep people from moving around. Because of the seismic activity, Southeast Asia is a fairly dangerous place, particularly in Indonesia and most coastal areas, which just so happens to be where most Southeast Asians live. As if tsunamis and volcanoes weren't enough, Southeast Asia also occasionally gets hit by tropical cyclones (a.k.a. typhoons). On

May 2, 2008, Cyclone Nargis made landfall in Burma and killed *at least* 50,000 people. Why did I just emphasis *at least*? Because the Burmese governing junta spent 90% of their collective effort trying to hide the damage. What did they do with the other 10%? Answer: they tried to keep international aid workers out. More on this later . . .

The final factor for physical geography is climate. Almost every country falls below the Tropic of Cancer. Indonesia straddles the Equator. All of the countries in this region have what we would call tropical climates. We can visibly see all three subdivisions of tropical climates in Southeast Asia. There's a whole lot of **tropical rainforest.** Indonesia is primarily rainforest, the biggest

Tsunamis: Great for surfers, bad for Southeast Asia.

chunks of rainforest left on the planet aside from the Amazon. There's some **tropical savanna** in and around Thailand, Burma, and Cambodia. All along the coastal areas of Vietnam and Cambodia, you can get a taste of **tropical monsoon** climate as well.

If anyone remembers Forrest Gump during his little Vietnam adventure, he talked about the rain that started one day and kept going for six months. Forrest was right; it is a true monsoonal climate. Perhaps the second best example of true, big-time tropical monsoon outside of India would be here in Southeast Asia.

There's some fairly decent terrain north and south in the Burma to the Vietnam area. There is some tectonic activity with implications for disaster in Indonesia and around the coastal areas, and the region is home to a nice blending of the tropical climates. That's your physical roundup for Southeast Asia.

WHO'S THERE?

This is pretty easy. It's just a few handfuls of countries, so we'll go ahead and fire them off for you: Burma (there is a new name, Myanmar, established by the military junta there which I refuse to recognize, so we're going to go with Burma), Laos, Thailand, Vietnam, Cambodia, Singapore, Malaysia, Indonesia, the Philippines, and the Sultanate of Brunei. And, introducing the newest sovereign state on Earth, East Timor! Congratulations, East Timor. Our plaid-thoughts are with you on this special day!

What is it that we want to know about this region? The subtitle of this chapter mentioned that this region was a crossroads. What is it about Southeast Asia that has made it a crossroads? Historically, it has always been and still is considered a crossroads of all types of Asian culture. It has been the true melting pot of Asia. Influences from all over have made their way here and dropped off a lot of their cultural baggage, which has been picked up by the locals who were already there. This amalgamation of different things from different places in Southeast Asia makes it quite unique, but you can still pick out where a lot of these influences came from. What am I talking about?

BACK UP FOR BACKGROUND

What's the story on this part of the world, anyway? Americans know that we fought a war here that we lost, and that all our Nike shoes and clothing are increasingly made in this place. Let's back up the refugee boat for a minute and take a look at just a few historical and cultural artifacts that will help us understand the region.

CHINESE INFLUENCE

Since forever, Southeast Asia has been a subsidiary vassal state of the Chinese. We've just finished talking about how the Chinese have been around for 5,000 years and for much of that time, border states have always been kind of "semi-China." China has been the big dog, the one everybody looks up to, or at least respects. Everybody on this part of the planet has known forever that the Chinese are the real power. This leads to pervasive Chinese historical influence, so much so that a lot of the folks currently in Southeast Asia (Thais and Vietnamese) were once in China. The Han Chinese influence kept pushing people further and further south until they were completely out of China's current borders. The Thais re-established themselves in what is now—that's right—Thailand!

Chinese influence is a dominant force throughout history, and we will see at the end of this chapter that it still is today. Southeast Asia has been in the Chinese cultural sphere of influence for a very long time. Chinese philosophy, Chinese religion, the Chinese way of life, Chinese governmental standards, and political philosophies have rubbed off in this region.

It is not just the Chinese that have influenced the culture. Southeast Asia is an archipelago with small islands and big islands. In fact, Indonesia has 14,000 islands. These are coastal peoples, maritime peoples. What do maritime people do? A lot of them end up trading.

SEE YOU AT THE CROSSROADS

Southeast Asia has been an epicenter of global trade for quite some time. I know this isn't something we often think about, but what was it that Columbus was trying to reach? He was trying to get to the East Indies, **The Spice Islands.** Why there? To get all the good stuff for which all the Europeans of the time would pay an arm and a leg. "The Spice Islands" and "the East Indies" are just European synonyms for Southeast Asia, predominantly Indonesia, which was the destination to get all the goods. For a very long time, even before the Europeans came around, people from South Asia (India) and China were trading stuff back and forth between each other, and a lot of the times, it was through maritime routes. As you might expect, all those maritime routes go through Southeast Asia. The people of the Southeast Asian islands became integral to this trade system very early on. There were Hindu traders from India who established trading posts in this area while they were trading with the Chinese, who also had a presence there. In time, there were Muslim traders as well. The Europeans arrived fairly late to this ballgame, but they showed up and participate in the trade game.

Why am I telling you all about this ancient trade? Why is it important for today's Southeast Asia? Well, it's this crossroads idea, not just a physical crossroads of traders and goods, but a crossroads of all of the traders' cultures. When you go to Southeast Asia, you will see cultural influences that are obviously not local. Let's pick religion. You can pretty much find all world religions in Southeast Asia. Even the Christians made their way to this part of the world via European

traders. In places like Burma, Thailand, Laos, Vietnam, and Cambodia, you will see old-school Buddhism in practice. In fact, some of
the biggest Buddhist monuments and temples on the planet are
located in this place. Buddhism came from India. What else came
from India? Hinduism. You'll see a big Hindu component in all those
countries as well.

But wait a minute! We aren't finished yet. There are some other
religions like Islam, for instance. Islam is predominant in Indonesia,
Brunei—the fact that Brunei has a sultan might tip you off there—and
Malaysia. Malaysia, Indonesia, and Brunei are predominantly and
overwhelmingly Islamic, with Indonesia being the largest Islamic
country on the planet. Then we go to a place like the Philippines. The
Philippines, eastern parts of Indonesia and even East Timor, the
region's newborn, are all predominantly Christian. The concept that
there are both Muslims and Christians in Indonesia warrants pause
for thought, because while most of the Eastern religions and Eastern
philosophies get along with each other, typically those Western ones
don't. If you want to find religious violence in Southeast Asia, go
straight to Indonesia, where the Muslims and the Christians both
cohabitate, though not very well.

You will see Hindu temples, Islamic mosques, Christian
churches, and Buddhist temples all over this region. You can say
that about every part of the world; everybody is mixed up a little
bit, but here you can see some very ancient places that really

Spices: the crack-cocaine of the 16th century.

A little bit Hindu, a little bit Buddhist.

Singapore for Dummies

Calm down, my Singaporean friends—I mean no disrespect. "Singapore
for Dummies" only implies that your average American could find his or
her way around the island. If you happen to be the average—or even
slightly below average—American, this is the Asian country for you! Singapore is a global city, like London, Paris, or Tokyo. English is an official
language; everyone speaks it. Singaporeans, in general, still like Americans—this is a disappearing quality in the world, enjoy it here while it
lasts! Oh, and they also have couture shopping, and five star hotels, and great food. Did I mention it's cheap—
again, enjoy it while it lasts. The exchange rate, even as of 2010, is still pretty damn good! You can even walk
across the whole island in one day! It's a damn nation-city. How cool is that? They've got a semi-official
national beverage called the Singapore Sling that is one part gin, one part cherry brandy, and one part pure
delicious! And their national symbol? A MERLION! Half mermaid, half lion. Who wouldn't want to crawl into
the sack with that! Especially after a couple of Singapore Slings! Rawwwwrrrr!

Why is Singapore so Western? One answer is British colonization, but there is also a more complicated
picture that goes back to the trading. Being a primary shipping and trading hub, Singapore acquired aspects
of many cultures, including Chinese, Malay, and Indian. Through the years, Singapore recognized the value in
being international and has focused on projecting a positive global image. Singapore is still one of the world's
leading trading ports—over 1 billion tons of cargo flows through every year. It is also home to some of the
most elite universities in Asia.

One final word of caution to all my plaid traveling friends: DO NOT BRING DRUGS INTO SINGAPORE. They
will execute you for it. I am not making this up.

reflect how long this melting-pot idea has been going on in Southeast Asia. As you might expect, I'm just using the example of religion, but language is also very diverse here as well. Ethnic groups are very diverse, as there's a huge presence of the Chinese, which we will get back to in just a little bit. This is a place that has been truly a crossroads for a long time and, I might point out, still is in the present.

CONFLICT

The last historical section of the cultural crossroads has to do with European colonization. The development of Southeast Asia has been impacted heavily by outsiders. That may be something that the locals don't want to admit, but it's a fact. All of those religions and a lot of the languages spoken here were imported from other places. A lot of the development in Southeast Asia, including the way the governments work, is imported or at least heavily influenced by other places as well. The last big wave of influence came from the European colonizers, who made their way through Siam, Indochina, and the Dutch East Indies.

Where do all these terms come from? These are terms that were invented by the European colonial masters who established trade and, ultimately, political control of this region. This group of masters included a little bit of everybody, similar to Africa where we have a whole bunch of countries represented. The British had possessions here, the French had a huge chunk of it, and the US even controlled the Philippines for a time after taking it from the Spanish. The Dutch controlled all of what is now Indonesia. The Portuguese had a colony named Timor, which is now East Timor, which is why it was separate from the rest of Dutch-controlled Indonesia. Even the Japanese had a hand in this part of the world, particularly during World War II.

Siam? Indochina? British India? Where is SE Asia?

When did all this come about? Same old, same old. When you get into the 1700s and 1800s, the Europeans started coming in and made themselves at home. It was not really a land grab, but it started off just like it did in South Asia and in British India, where people set up ports of trade. As we've already suggested, Southeast Asia had been the center of trade for 1,000, maybe 2,000 years already, so the Europeans just wanted to get in the game. Quite frankly, they were shut out for a good long time because trade had already been established. But inevitably, the British and Portuguese wore them down and started to make inroads. One thing led to another over the course of several hundred years and they ended up controlling the territories outright.

I'll give you a rundown here just to make it completely clear. The British controlled British India. At the time, British India consisted of Myanmar and Burma. The French controlled a part of this region as well, named French Indochina. The Brits also controlled Malaysia and Singapore, which is really just a tiny island adjacent to Malaysia. The Spanish initially controlled the Philippines until 1898, when the US assumed control of the island nation. The Dutch controlled all of Indonesia and the Portuguese controlled what is now East Timor.

Everybody had a hand in this region, though strangely enough, one country remained unoccupied. That was Siam, or modern day Thailand. This is a great piece of trivia, placed on government tests for employees trying to get into foreign service. The question is, "Which country was never colonized by a foreign nation?" The answer is Thailand. If you ask "Hey, what is the richest nation in Southeast Asia today? What's the most stable nation in Southeast Asia today?" you'll be directed to Thailand, more often than not. Coincidence? Probably not. But we're talking about this foreign influence and where it is going to go.

What's the Deal with French Indochina?

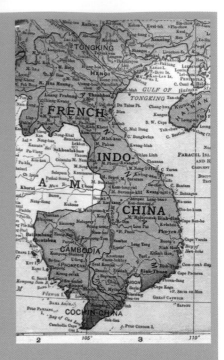

French Indochina was a group of French colonial possessions in Southeast Asia including modern day Vietnam, Laos, and Cambodia. France acquired these colonies in the late 1800s and held them until World War II, at which point Japan kicked them out and took Indochina for themselves. Japanese rule, however, lasted only until the United States dropped atomic bombs on two of Japan's most populated cities. With Japan's withdrawal, Indochina was theoretically free from colonialism. That is, for the three seconds before France attempted to colonize them again.

France found it impossible to regain control over Vietnam. This is partially because of a homegrown Vietnamese insurgent group of communist nationalists led by Ho Chi Minh. This group, the Viet Minh, had been fighting for independence even before WWII, then fought against the Japanese, and then quickly shifted their efforts to fight against the French once the Japanese were ejected. After years of devastating war, the Viet Minh had gained decisive control of northern Vietnam, declaring independence as the Democratic Republic of Vietnam in 1954. At the Battle of Dien Bien Phu, the French were forced to surrender. As part of the cease-fire peace agreement, Southern Vietnam (the State of Vietnam) was officially brokered by world powers, namely the US, until elections which were to be held the following year. It didn't go down that way, but that is a story for another box.

Poor Frenchies. Germany spanked them in Europe. The Japanese spanked them in Indochina. Then the Vietnamese spanked them again in Vietnam. No more French Indochina after that last spanking.

MORE CONFLICT

In 20th century events, it got very interesting in Southeast Asia, the location of some of the nastiest throw-downs in the last fifty years. Since the Europeans had their fun time with World War I and then World War II, because obviously they didn't get enough the first time around, the world has largely been devoid of huge conflicts with massive death tolls—that is, everywhere in the world except Southeast Asia. While we in the West were having our Cold War, where Team USA faced off with Team USSR, we never engaged in active conflict. The guns remained cold, hence the name "Cold War." But there were several flare-ups, several hot spots, where people shot each other and where this ideological war reared its ugly head in active conflict. The Korean War we mentioned already. The other major flare-ups are here in Southeast Asia.

Before we can get to the tale of that aggression and transgression, we have to set up the scenario, because some more violence occurred on the soil here during World War II. During the buildup of Japanese power, Southeast Asia and Southern China became a battleground for World War II, mainly because of the Japanese occupation. Some fairly nasty Japanese war crimes took place in these regions, as I've alluded to before.

How did this go down and why is this of particular significance? Southeast Asia has been a crossroads of trade and culture, and became a crossroads of occupation. Unlike any part of the planet, this is a very unique trait of Southeast Asia: it was taken over by the West and subsequently taken over by the East. This is the only place the Plaid Avenger has ever heard of that had European colonization that was then supplanted by Japanese occupation. Southeast Asia got it from both ends. That will probably leave a mark in the morning, and it certainly did at the end of the 20th century.

SMART GODZIRRA!

As you know, Japan built up its empire in the early part of the 20th century. Then in 1931, they started intruding into northeastern China and took over the Chinese coast. They were still invading, fighting, and conquering into the 1940s. They started taking over the Philippines and before World War II broke out officially, they had a presence in all Southeast Asian nations. How did they get away with this, and more importantly, how did they get away with this without firing too many bullets? Every country we have just discussed was controlled and occupied by the Japanese, but you don't really hear that much about fighting there.

The reason why it wasn't a big shoot-out for the Japanese to take over this place was because of, if you remember back to our lecture on Japan, the **Greater East Asia Co-Prosperity Sphere** that was established in 1938. To reiterate what that was about: the Japanese used a savvy piece of foreign policy, although they were

The busy Japanese.

holding guns at the time. They went to all these places like French Indochina, the Philippines, and Indonesia and said, "Hey, look dudes. Look at our skins. We're Asians. We are all yellow here, we're brothers. You've got a huge bunch of foreign white dogs on your soil that are controlling you. You're just their puppets. You're letting them treat you like punks! Come on, let's all get together as Asians and expel all the Yankee scum-dog pigs!" Many saw the Japanese as liberators at the time, so they were able to waltz through Southeast Asia without firing too many shots. Were the Japanese telling the truth? I think we all know the answer to this question: hell no! They were actually just planning to supplant the European colonizers, which is exactly what they did, in a fairly brutal manner. Work camps, death camps, and prisoner of war camps were set up all over Southeast Asia.

BATAAN DEATH MARCH

The Plaid Avenger is giving you examples of some incredible atrocities perpetrated by the Japanese in Southeast Asia. We talked about them in China, about the death there, and we know about Japanese history against the United States in WWII, but a lot of people don't know about Southeast Asia. It's some fairly nasty business, as evidenced by the Bataan Death March, where more than 10,000 US and Filipino soldiers were marched about 100 miles from one camp to another across the Philippines. Many were not fed, and those who began to fall behind were executed or tortured.

Rounding up people and slaughtering them was a common occurrence all over Southeast Asia. A lot of this has not been forgotten by the Southeast Asian nations, but they are not as hardcore as the Chinese and the Koreans about it. The Chinese and the Koreans still really hate the Japanese. The Southeast Asians harbor some resentment, but it is not as strong or as big of a deal to them. But it is a big of enough deal to talk about for a little bit.

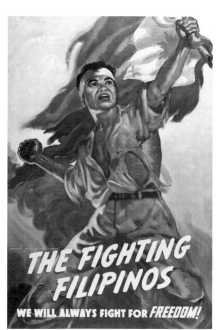

THE FIGHTING FILIPINOS
WE WILL ALWAYS FIGHT FOR *FREEDOM!*

Don't mess!

POL POT PIE

Vietnam is not the only place for strange violence in Southeast Asia. Indonesia, in its movement into the modern era, has been run by dictators who were supported by the United States. Burma is currently run by an outright military junta. Lots of the other countries, however, are leaning toward democracies—places like Singapore, Indonesia, and the Philippines. You have some holdouts from the Communist era, such as Vietnam. But even Vietnam is softening that commie stuff and reintegrating quickly into the world economy. Besides the brutality of the Burmese leadership which is still happening, most places have gotten past their violent past . . . but one country barely survived its violent past: Cambodia. Cambodia is the scene of one of the most horrific cases of post–World War II genocide, under our good friend Pol Pot. Pot who? Ah! Read the box below!

What's the Deal with Pol Pot?

As one of the most egregious violators of human rights in recent memory, Pol Pot easily earned the Plaid Avenger title of "Ass-munch of the Decade" for the 1970s. Pol Pot was the leader of Cambodia, or as he called it "Democratic Kampuchea," from 1975 to 1979. The revolutionary movement that brought Pol Pot to power is largely considered the most murderous of the 20th century. Around 3 million Cambodians died from overwork, malnutrition, and state-sponsored executions. This equated to approximately 35 percent of the Cambodian population at the time.

Pol Pot's politics were a brutal offshoot of Maoist Communism. He attempted to tear down Cambodia's old political structure, which was in part established by French colonialism, to make way for an agrarian communist utopia. His tactics included suppressing religion and intellectualism. Citizens were executed if they failed to meet production quotas and also for more trivial matters like wearing glasses, being a monk, being intelligent, speaking a foreign language, being an ethnic minority, etc. Many of those executed were forced to dig their own graves and were then buried alive; many speculate this was done to conserve bullets. Although technically removed from power in 1979, Pol Pot continued to exert brutal influence on Cambodian politics, in one way or another, until his death in 1998.

See a depiction of this regime by watching the really historically accurate film *The Killing Fields*. Whew! Talk about a place that *should* have been invaded!

But enough of the death and destruction, let's get to why these places are hot in today's world. I'm not talkin' tropical heat here, I'm talkin' cash money!

CUBS IN THE CATBIRD SEAT

Cubs? What? What are you talking about? I'm talking about the cats. The tigers. Let's do Southeast Asia. What is happening in today's Southeast Asia?

This has a lot to do with things we have already referenced. There is Chinese influence, which is still big and may be growing as China's influence expands in the world. Lots of people emigrate from China to Southeast Asia, set up businesses, and bring their families along. Is this good? It can be good. The Chinese often bring a lot of capital and set up businesses, but the negative is that it's the stuff the locals were probably going to do.

Indeed, there is some friction between ethnically Chinese people and all the other ethnicities within Southeast Asia. The Chinese are a major component of all the populations within Southeast Asia we talked about. Cause for concern? I

NUMBERS OF ETHNIC CHINESE IN SOUTHEAST ASIAN COUNTRIES

Country	Ethnic Chinese	% of Local Population
Thailand	9 million	14%
Indonesia	7.5 million	3.1%
Malaysia	7 million	25%
Singapore	2.8 million	76%
Vietnam	2.5 million	4%
Philippines	1.5 million	2%
Burma	1.5 million	3%
Cambodia	200,000	1.3%
Brunei	60,000	15%
Laos	50,000	1%

don't know, but certainly cause for friction. Indeed, when the economies go south, say if Indonesia goes into a depression, one of the first things all you news watchers will see are Chinese businesses being attacked. Chinese individuals become kind of a whipping post of anger that people rally around: "The damn Chinese, they're here taking our jobs!" The Chinese typically don't assimilate themselves into the culture of the countries to which they emigrate. Throughout Southeast Asia, there are visible pockets of Chinese influence and businesses all over the place.

What else is going on in Southeast Asia today? Economically, it is a bustling and booming place, which is where the *Cubs* come in. You might have heard of something called the **Asian Tigers,** or **The Economic Tigers** in reference to Hong Kong, Taiwan, South Korea, and Singapore, which have been exploding economically since the 1970s and 1980s. Growth rates have been astronomical in these places, making them very rich. The expansive growth rates are beginning to spread to places like Thailand, Vietnam, Malaysia to a certain extent, the Philippines, and Indonesia. That's why I'm calling them the *Cubs*. They are on their way to becoming tigers themselves, but they're just getting started.

Why are these places in Southeast Asia picking up economically right now? One of the reasons is cheap labor. Most businesses go to China for this reason, but if they don't go to China, they go to Indonesia, Thailand, or the Philippines. Because of this cheap labor, a lot of businesses and multinational corporations are relocating to Southeast Asia, if not outright starting whole new businesses there. I'll go out on a limb and say that all car manufacturers have a plant or two in one or more of the countries in Southeast Asia.

Why else are more businesses moving there? Lax environmental laws. Nike has been in Indonesia for a decade or two now. Apparently, it makes more economic sense to ship leather from Brazil, cloth from China, rubber from Vietnam, and then manufacture it using cheap labor in the Nike plant in Indonesia, before shipping it to the United States, where you can still sell the shoes for $20 and still make a profit—but you charge $150 and make more profit. That's the way the economic world is working right now, much to the advantage of multinational corporations, and the Southeast Asian nations, to some extent. Some of the losers in this process are places like Mexico. Some places in South America used to be cheap suppliers of labor, but they have gotten a little bit more expensive, so labor is moving over to Asia. Companies go wherever the labor cost is the lowest. How low can you go? Southeast Asia and China are winning the limbo right now.

The other factor in this is that Southeast Asia is a massive supplier of raw materials to the world. Where are the places that want raw materials more and more? We say, "Oh! The US and Western Europe, the advanced countries. We use all that stuff." Wrong! Think again. The world is changing. Japan is a huge importer of raw materials. When I say raw materials, I mean everything from oil to rubber to trees to tin to bauxite, everything. Southeast Asia has a lot of this stuff, and even the stuff it doesn't have goes through their waterways and shipping channels.

Lots of stuff has gone to Japan, and as a result, the Tigers, like Taiwan, have become big processing centers. Wait a minute, who is the new big tiger? Who is the 800 pound tiger? Who is the 800 pound gorilla on top of the 800 pound tiger? That's China. China is now pulling in resources from all across the planet with an unquenchable thirst, and a lot of those things are coming from Southeast Asia, which is right next door. If they have something, China will use it. It's very similar to the situation between the US and Mexico. Mexico can't possibly produce enough to feed the US market.

Gorillas and Tigers: these guys are all kicking ass!

Southeast Asia is exactly like this right now and they don't have enough wood, enough rubber, enough aluminum, or enough vegetables. They can't possibly have enough. China will import it all. It is a phenomenal place for them to be, and it's one of the reasons why their economy is starting to climb out of the gutter and one of the other reasons why I'm saying this litter of cubs will soon be tigers. Claws up! RAWWWRRR!

This region is growing, but before I go any further—is this place bustling to the point that everybody is getting wheelbarrows full of gold and becoming fat-belly rich? Of course not. One of the reasons why these countries are getting rich is because of cheap labor, typically meaning a lot of the wealth isn't filtering down to the lowest classes. There is endemic poverty here, lots and lots of poverty. But economically speaking, looking at GDP and foreign investment, they are starting to do pretty well. That doesn't mean they are out of the hole yet, they still have a long way to go. One of the things that may help them go a long way is the Association of Southeast Asian Nations (ASEAN).

ASEAN

I can't get enough of ASEAN because it is setting up—and this is a Plaid Avenger insider tip—to be one of the most successful trade blocs on the planet. It's hard to imagine how they aren't going to be at this point. One of the things that may take them to the level of development, and I'm talking about the region, is that ASEAN may become more than just a trade bloc. This is speculative of course, at best. What is **ASEAN?** ASEAN is a trade bloc, a free-trade zone that consists of all of the countries in Southeast Asia. Here's the kicker: it's becoming so popular as a free-trade zone and is starting to incite so much economic activity that other countries want to get in the club. Yes, there are still some countries that want to get into the EU, but it's getting close to the end of its growth as a trade bloc. Let's not even mention the FTAA, because that idea is played out and probably won't happen. All the other trade blocs are approaching their limits, but ASEAN is in position to keep expanding. How about China? Big plus. How about India? Another big plus. They are two associate members, with a combined population of almost three billion people, who want to be in this free-trade zone with Southeast Asia. How can this be a bad thing for them? Another associate member who wants to do more business is Japan, the number two economy on the planet. Any country in ASEAN is really sitting pretty. This is a trade bloc that is happening. I can't see how anything but good can come of it for the member countries.

BUMP IT TO THE NEXT LEVEL, BABY

If you poke in and see what's going on within ASEAN, you'll find out pretty quickly that it's becoming much more than a trade bloc. They are starting to turn into something similar to the EU. It's only in the early stages of this, mind you, but it is becoming apparent already. Visit the ASEAN web site to see what I'm talking about. You'll see plans for hydroelectric power as part of a proposed ASEAN-wide power grid. Let me say that again: a joint electric grid for the entire region! That is crazy! Europe doesn't even have that, to my knowledge. If you are going so far as to do that, then you have to think that, if they are already talking about infrastructure in terms of roads and bridges and ports, they might simultaneously raise the standards of living for every country, which might mean an integrated healthcare system across the region. It's hard to tell where they are going with this, but certainly they are already integrated in economic terms, and they don't have any qualms about free movement of people.

ASEAN is setting itself up to be something a whole lot more like the EU with maybe even less friction between the countries involved. This will, dare I say, be a stabilizing force within a region with a track record for serious conflicts. ASEAN has become a savior to these countries. It's hard to see any intraregional conflict cropping up here in the future, because once these countries become integrated in every way that they've proposed, conflict will be quickly resolved and made nearly impossible. Soon, nobody will be able to dredge up a reason to fight. Are there people who are unhappy in these countries? I'm sure there are unhappy people all over the place, but there are no unhappy governments in this deal.

We talked about power grids, hydroelectric systems, and possible healthcare systems. I'll go out on a limb and say that the regional stability that ASEAN provides may indeed be the impetus for a common military. No one has talked about that yet, but the Plaid Avenger is going to say it. I don't care what other people may be saying. All I know is that it is a very likely possibility in the years to come. Here is a little quote for you: "Today, ASEAN is not only a well functioning indispensable reality in the region, it is a real force to be reckoned with far beyond the region. It is also a trusted partner of the United Nations in the field of development." Who said it? Kofi Annan said it, former Secretary General of the United Nations, on February 16, 2000. A thumbs-up from Kofi can only mean good things. How awesome is Kofi! I love Kofi.

I love Aung San Suu Kyi as well. I feel a Plaid Avenger mission to free this babe is imminent. What? You don't know Aung San Suu Kyi? Well, she is only the finest democracy-promoting babe in the Asian archipelago, fighting for freedom and liberty and justice for all in her home state of Burma. Speaking of which, there is only one cause of friction within the ASEAN countries, and that is Burma. Let's find out a little more about the situation there . . .

BURMESE BASTARDS

Burma is the redheaded stepchild right now that everyone else keeps in the closet because the world has put pressure on Aung San Suu Kyi's situation.

In 2007, political tensions once again flared and all international, humanitarian eyes were on Burma. The junta, in an unexceptional move, raised prices on fuel and other basic necessities. This time, it was the straw that broke the camel's back.

What's the Deal with Aung San Suu Kyi?

NATIONAL LEAGUE FOR DEMOCRACY

Suu Kyi is a prominent pro-democracy advocate in Southeast Asia. In 1988, she founded the National League for Democracy in Burma, after many pro-democracy demonstrators were killed and radically repressed on the infamous day of August 8th, 1988, a day now referred to as the 8-8-88 uprisings. The military junta that was in power at the time had a pretty terrible track record as far as human rights were concerned. A general election was held there in 1990 as a result of the uprisings for democratization. Aung San Suu Kyi's non-violent democracy party won 90 percent of the vote. The junta immediately nullified the results and is still in power.

In 1990, her cumulative work and nonviolent tactics won her both the Rafto Prize and the Sakharov Prize for Freedom of Thought. A year later, she was awarded the Nobel Peace Prize. What's this hero of democracy doing today? Funny you should ask! She is currently sitting in a dark, damp prison cell in Burma. Why? Because Burma is ruled by a corrupt military dictatorship and her speaking out about human rights pissed them off.

What is the international community doing to help Suu Kyi out? The other members of ASEAN (Myanmar joined in 1997) are sufficiently embarrassed and have pressed Myanmar to reform politically. The West has cut off almost all relations with Myanmar. The United States won't even officially call them Myanmar; they're still on the books as Burma. How will this help Suu Kyi? It probably won't. She's pretty much screwed, as are the rest of the people. Too bad they don't have a ton of oil there, or we'd go and "free" them.

But I won't end by slamming Uncle Sam; the US is actually doing the most to help her and her country out. We have a 100 percent trade embargo against the country, and encourage everyone else in the world to follow. Unfortunately, our European friends and most of the world have not yet followed suit. In particular, both China and India continue to trade with Burma, because their thriving economies have an insatiable need for all the raw resources that Burma possesses. Of course all of the money from this trade further strengthens the junta, which then smashes the people even harder under their iron boot. Sucks all the way around for Suu Kyi, and the fighters for democracy everywhere.

Activists started to protest, the government broke them up, but then the monks started to protest. Thousands and thousands of monks donned saffron colored robes and marched through Rangoon (Yangon if you prefer the Myanmarification) protesting against the junta. The world watched—thanks largely to mobile phones and other digital cameras, as no official reporters are allowed in the country—as the government debated whether to forcefully put down the giant protests. In a particularly moving moment, the monks marched to Aung San Suu Kyi's house, where she was under house arrest, and she came out to receive them—in a sense, blessing the revolution and thanking the monks for their courage. Fortunately, although the junta did use some force, there was no massive slaughtering. Unfortunately, the protest failed to accomplish much other than to raise awareness. In fact, on May 29, 2008, the junta decided to add another year on Suu Kyi's house arrest sentence.

As mentioned earlier, Burma just got slammed by one of the most deadly cyclones ever in 2008. Guess what: the first thing the junta did was deny anything was wrong! Seriously! The global community was poised to help and the Burmese government basically came out and said, "We don't need foreign aid. Everything's under control. Trust us. We're cool." Meanwhile, their population was totally ravaged and in ABSOLUTE need of foreign aid. Get this: eight days after the cyclone, the government conducted a previously scheduled nationwide vote! Don't mind the water, just proceed to the polls! The whole time, the entire world was flipping out just trying to send in aid. Damn sovereignty—the main rule is that you can only come in if asked. Long story short, the Burmese government didn't allow in foreign aid workers for two weeks after the disaster and even then, it was only aid workers from ASEAN member nations. They waited another week before they allowed in aid workers from the rest of the world. Lots and lots of people died. Many may have been saved if Burma had a government that was interested in the well being of its citizens. In 2009, the junta once again put Aung San Suu Kyi on trial for crimes against the state; for reasons which elude everyone, the junta continues to allow her to live, but go out of their way to make her life insufferable. What great guys. Enough with the heartless bastards in the Burmese junta, let's go back to ASEAN.

TERRIBLE TERROR POTENTIAL

We'll end on a negative note here, unfortunately. Terrorism is a real force to be reckoned with right now, as the US-led War on Terror is quite active around the planet. This War on Terror is definitely not a Cold War. It's quite hot at the moment. One of the regions that experts worry about, but you don't seem to hear about, is Southeast Asia. Why would you have a War on Terror here? Indonesia is the largest Muslim state in the world, and as such, is considered a hotbed of extremist activity. For those of you not in the know, several Western hotels and buildings have been blown up just in the past few years here. A bunch of Australian tourists were killed in a fairly nasty blast at a tourist hotel not long ago as well. There are quite active terrorist groups in the southern Philippines, Malaysia and lots of other places in Southeast Asia.

It has to do with physical geography as well, because these very separate islands provide cover for lots of secret stuff to go on. There are a lot of terrorist cells within Southeast Asia; because they can get on small islands and operate fairly independently without anybody checking them out, they are completely under the radar. I can tell you without reservation that Australia has been very worried about this for a while. They are probably the next country that will be outright attacked. They spend a lot of money and time trying to figure out where terrorists are; in case it's not clear by now, they're looking at Southeast Asia. They aren't looking in the Middle East, that's for sure. None of the terrorists there are a threat to Australia. However, there are some radical groups within Indonesia and in the southern Philippines. There is a rebel/terrorist group that has been kidnapping tourists for quite some time. Check out the news; you don't have to look too hard to find them. They are called **Abu Sayyaf.**

You can rest assured that Uncle Sam has been checking this out. The United States and everyone involved in the War on Terror has operatives checking out movements. Another reason for worry is clashes between Christians and Muslims, which happened notably in the small island group called the Maluku Islands in Indonesia.

Southeast Asia has some negative things to deal with nowadays, terrorism being the big one. Australia, being a power player in the region, has taken on most of the workload for the anti-terrorism movement and is supported by the United States and Europe. This offends some countries in Southeast Asia, namely Indonesia and Malaysia. Those countries get really hot and bothered about foreign influence, even if it's on issues concerning terrorism.

ROUND-UP

Terrorism: bad. ASEAN: good. Southeast Asia: rockin'. Thundercats: Ho! This region has tremendous potential for economic growth as it becomes the newest workshop of Asia producing tons of manufactured goods. Its placement between India and China makes it well suited for both production and distribution of a variety of goods and services to Asia as a whole. The ASEAN grouping is set to explode into the 21st century, having put its century of conflict well in the rear view mirror.

Unfortunately, the region also has explosive potential of other kinds. Volcanic, earthquake, tsunami, typhoon, and monsoonal activity are a very real part of life for Southeast Asians, and one that will never go away. In fact, it seems to be increasing lately! This region continues to get pummeled with the most horrific natural disasters year after year. Coupled with Mother Nature's ire is the terrorist potential which seems to permeate many areas in this widely dispersed, and hard to effectively control, archipelago arena.

The upcoming century will still be hot and active for Southeast Asia and ASEAN. Let's hope it's hot babes and hot economic growth versus hot lava and hot spots of conflict. Shout out to Aung San Suu Kyi: I love you!

Level Blue
Status No active shooting. Arms build-up may be happening, but discreetly. However, political ideological differences on site make conflicts possible, and perhaps inevitable.

Level Yellow
Status Active violence by individuals or small groups is happening, or getting very close to erupting. Arms build-up and other preparations are happening, and not discreetly. Political or ideological differences getting hot enough for active, organized forces to be on the move. Could go down any moment.

Level Red
Status GAME ON! Active violence by individuals, small groups, and/or large organized forces like a state military are happening. Nothing is discreet, and open war may have been declared. People are shooting other people, and you can watch it all on CNN, Facebook, and also read tweets about it from the front lines.

CHAPTER OUTLINE

Plaid Avenger's Hotspots of Conflict

25

WHAT CAUSES HUMANS TO KILL EACH OTHER?

Since the end of the Second World War in 1945, there have been over 250 major wars in which over 23 million people have been killed, tens of millions made homeless, and countless millions injured and bereaved. In the history of warfare, the 20th century stands out as the bloodiest and most brutal—three times as many people have been killed in wars in the last 90 years than in the previous 500.

> One from the west: "And there went out another horse that was red: and power was given to him that sat thereon to take peace from the earth, and that they should kill one another: and there was given unto him a great sword."
>
> —*The Revelation of St. John the Divine*: 6:4

The nature of warfare has also changed. From the set-piece battles of the earlier centuries, the blood and mud of the trenches in the First World War, and the fast-moving mechanized battlefields of World War II, to the high-tech "surgical" computer-guided action in Iraq and Afganistan,

> And one from the east: "Now I am become Death, the destroyer of worlds."
>
> —from *The Bhagavad-Gita*

war as seen through our television screens appears to have become a well-ordered, almost bloodless, affair. Nothing could be further from the truth. During the 20th century, the proportion of civilian casualties has risen steadily. In World War II, two-thirds of those killed were civilians; by the beginning of the 1990s, civilian deaths approached a horrifying 90 percent.

This is partly the result of technological developments, but there is another major reason. Many modern armed conflicts are not between states but within them: struggles between soldiers and civilians, or between competing civilian groups. Such conflicts are likely to be fought out in country villages and urban streets. In such wars, the "enemy" camp is everywhere, and the distinctions between combatant and noncombatant melt away into the fear, suspicion and confusion of civilian life under fire.

Also, people kill each other because of ethnic differences, religious differences, cultural differences, and any other difference that distinguishes groups of humans. Wars are also fought over resources, land, and political control of areas—particularly where states or empires have dissolved into multiple entities, such as British India, or Yugoslavia. Now we have new wars with new dimensions the likes of which the world has not seen before: Battles of ideologies that span the entire planet.

Perhaps you are thinking the Cold War was just such a conflict—and you would be right. But it was cold, as its name suggests. Here in the 21st century, we have the War on Terror, the War on Western Imperialism, and the War on Drugs, which are global ideological battles—but damned hot

Go ahead; make my millennium.

523

ones! People are actively shooting at each other in these wars, wherever they are sponsored, all over the planet. That's the new part.

Conflict within or between states, and ideological conflicts in which the entire globe is the battlefield: we've got it all in our day and age, but we can't possibly cover all the active conflicts happening. The Plaid Avenger wants to pick out just a few situations that have global implications, as well as a few more than may be heating up in the coming year.

DEMOCRATIC REPUBLIC OF CONGO (DRC)

HOT SPOT: EASTERN CONGO

The history of the Democratic Republic of the Congo has been a complicated one, full of instability, coups d'etat, violence, and name changes. When the Republic of the Congo gained independence from Belgium in 1960, a guy named Patrice Lumumba was elected president, but was overthrown in a coup d'etat in 1965 by Mobutu Sese Seko. Sese Seko, a dictator, was supported by the United States and Belgium, and controlled every aspect of life in the country. He even changed the name of the country to Zaire in 1971. After the Cold War was over, the United States did not think it was necessary to support Mobutu anymore, so he was overthrown by Laurent Kabila in 1997, who renamed the country back to Democratic Republic of The Congo-Kinshasa. The name of the capital city is added to the name of the country to distinguish it from the Republic of the Congo-Brazzaville which is a different country that is next door to Democratic Republic of the Congo. Get it? Good. Someone explain this stuff back to me.

This new Kabila government immediately came under fire by rebel groups and has yet to establish any sort of stability. Kabila quickly lost control of parts of eastern Congo to Ugandan, Rwandan, and Burundian backed rebels while still receiving support from Angolan, Zimbabwean, and Namibian troops. The organization Human Rights Watch wrote that Congo is a human rights disaster area and "soldiers of the national army and combatants of armed groups continue to target civilians, killing, raping, and otherwise injuring them, carrying out arbitrary arrests and torture, and destroying or pillaging their property. Tens of thousands of persons have fled their homes, several thousand of them across international borders." In fact, the DRC conflict is

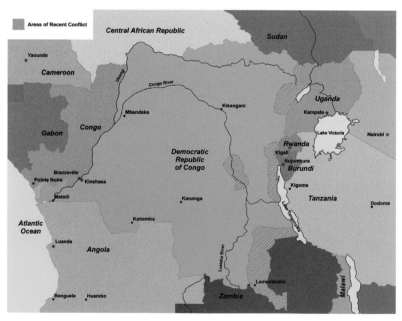

responsible for the establishment of a new category of war crime: institutionalized rape. Roaming groups of soldiers raping women with total disregard for laws or morals has left an entire generation of women physically and psychologically wounded and another generation fatherless. In fact, the conflict in the Democratic Republic of the Congo has been called "Africa's World War" and 3.8 million people have died as a result of it. A peace treaty was signed in 2003, but the situation remains unstable and could devolve back into war at any time. In a few years, you could be watching "Hotel Congo."

Why the fighting? Quite simply: money. This area is huge, massively huge, and filled with gold, diamonds, uranium and practically every commodity the developed world wants. Also, there is no sense of nationhood and the leaders of the different factions are war criminals and thieves who are only looking to line their own pockets. The natural wealth of the

Congo is taken out of the country, leaving a poor, uneducated population embroiled in turmoil. Things here are really bad and the near future holds few foreseeable good changes.

Some areas of the country are effectively controlled by the armies of other neighboring states, rebel, or terrorist groups from neighboring states, or local rebel groups, or local warlords, or . . . I think you are starting to get the point.

To sum up the DRC: huge country with a weak central government; a valuable and tempting resource base; a hideout for rebel groups of all sorts; a place where perhaps seven different states have forces in and out of the territory. What a mess, and it could implode soon, turning into an all-out territorial grab by all the involved parties: The DRC, Uganda, Rwanda, Burundi, Angola, etc. This DRC mess has the distinction of having the largest UN peace-keeping force stationed in it already. However, given the huge size of the country, the small size of the UN force, and the general warlord-driven politics of the region, don't think for one minute that the UN or anyone else is really in control of this part of the planet.

SUDAN

HOT SPOT: DARFUR

Often the conflict in Darfur, which is a province in western Sudan, is painted as a war between the Arab government and the black African commoners. But if you go to Darfur, everybody looks black. What's the deal? Well, as Arabs began to dominate the government in the past century and gave jobs to members of Arab tribes, being Arab became a political advantage and some tribes adopted that label regardless of their ethnic affiliation. Nowadays, each tribe gives itself the label of "African" or "Arab" based on what language its members speak and whether they work the soil or herd livestock. The true division in Darfur is between ethnic groups, split between herders and farmers, who are fighting over the region's scarce resources.

The Darfur conflict started in 2003 when two non-Arab groups, the Sudan Liberation Army and the Justice and Equality Movement, took up arms against the Sudanese government, alleging mistreatment by the Arab regime in Khartoum. In response, a government-backed paramilitary group called the Janjaweed began pillaging towns and villages inhabited by members of the African tribes from which the rebel armies recruit members. Janjaweed literally means "armed men on horseback" in Arabic and is not a Rastafarian pot-smoking army. The Janjaweed militia supported by the government in Khartoum are tasked with the job of removing all inhabitants who might make resource extraction difficult, or demand compensation. What resource extraction? Oil, of course! Southern Sudan is awash with oil and the revenues it brings—which is perhaps the main reason that the government does not want any independence movements cropping up in these areas. Send in the Janjaweed!

Of course, the Sudanese government has denied helping the Janjaweed, especially because the Janjaweed have been accused of genocide and ethnic cleansing of Arabs. Together with government troops, the armed Arab militia is responsible for the deaths of up to 50,000 African villagers and the displacement of another million from their homes in Darfur. It should be noted that both sides are accused of serious human rights violations, including mass killing, looting, and rape of the civilian population. However, since the Janjaweed are better armed and funded, they are doing a better job of it.

Why isn't the world stepping in to stop it? Mostly because China is a veto-wielding member of the UN Permanent Security

On February 17, 2008, Kosovo formally declared independence from Serbia. Serbia rejected this notion and upheld that it was illegal under U.N charter; Albania, who strongly supported the KLA (Kosovo Liberation Army) who fought guerillas wars against Serbia, was the first to support Kosovo.

Are you ready, 'cause here's where it gets interesting. Technically speaking, Kosovo is a region within Serbia, which is an internationally recognized state by the U.N., which then gives Serbia the right to preserve its territorial integrity. The wrong words and the wrong moves could push this region over the edge and start a war. No biggie, right? Well, except for the fact that this is the same region that sparked WWI.

Dig this: The US and a dozen other EU countries, including the UK and France, recognized the Kosovo independence claim. Unfortunately for Kosovo, both Russia and China, which are both veto-wielding members of the UN Security Council, side with Serbia on this question of sovereignty. I'm starting to see a larger world showdown over this tiny little province. Which ties directly to our next section on a couple of other tiny little provinces causing calamity over similar claims of independence, but these two are backed by the Russians!

RUSSIA-GEORGIA WAR

Let's get to that rascally Ruskie move right now! The 2008 Russia–Georgia War was an armed conflict in August 2008, between Georgia on one side, and Russia together with most ethnic Ossetians and ethnic Abkhazians on the other.

See, this whole area used to be a part of the mighty USSR, but once it crumbled in 1991, Georgia claimed independence and claimed these two ethnic enclaves as part of their territory. To be fair, it historically had been counted as part of Georgia for a long time. However, many ethnic Ossetians (with a smattering of Russians in the area) actually fought a war for their own independence from Georgia in 1991–1992 which left most of South Ossetia under control of a Russian-backed internationally unrecognized regional government. Some Georgian-inhabited parts remained under the control of Georgia. This was pretty much the exact same situation in Abkhazia after the War in Abkhazia (1992–1993).

With the story so far? These two dinky provinces were technically part of Georgia, but were "protected" or "administered" by Russians. By the way, in what is a richly ironic claim, the Russians always said that they were there simply to "protect" these locals from genocidal tendencies of the Georgian government . . . much the same way the US and NATO was protecting the Kosovars from the Serbian government. Ah! Starting to see the connections here?

The newly independent states of Abkhazia and South Ossetia???

Let's pile kindling onto this pre-fire: the Georgian President Mikheil Saakashvili is a hugely pro-western, pro-US leader who has been petitioning for EU and NATO membership for years, mostly to shield his country from Russian influence. Of course, this is the rub that really pisses off the Russians. That Georgia might join NATO was an option utterly unacceptable to Russia, and they have been very vocal about this, so tensions were rising even further. Then US President Bush gave a speech at a NATO conference where he openly pushed for member states to put Georgia on a fast track for NATO membership. Pressure built more.

For reasons which continue to elude the entire planet, on August 8, 2008, Georgia launched a large-scale military attack against the self-proclaimed Republic of South Ossetia. Within hours, Russia reacted and deployed combat troops in South Ossetia and launched bombing raids farther into Georgia. Yeah, if you haven't picked up on this yet, be sure to take note: the Russians were totally prepared for this attack to happen. Russians landed support craft in Abkhazia and opened up a second front there.

Long story short: After five days of heavy fighting, Georgian forces were totally ejected from South Ossetia and Abkhazia. Russian troops entered Georgia, easily kicking the crap out any resistance. Fighting ended and in the subsequent peace agreement Russians withdrew from Georgia, but remained as guardians in the two small enclaves. Oh but here's the fun part: On August 26, 2008, Russia recognized the independence of South Ossetia and Abkhazia. The US and Team West said, "Hey! You guys can't just invade a small ethnic province, help them secede, and then recognize their independence! That's not cool!" To which Russia responded: "Oh really? You mean like what you guys did in Kosovo?" Ouch! That stings!

Now this international fracas is not settled yet, and it certainly is calling the whole perceived concept of sovereignty into question, but I want you to know this for now as we watch the future events of this area: Russia is back! This invasion has announced the return of Russia not just as a military power re-establishing control over its neighborhood, but also as a military power that is not afraid to use force to stop what it perceives as threats to its security, and by threats I am going to specifically call one by name: NATO. This Georgian debacle could well have been started by President Saakashvili because he truly believed that NATO would come save him, and that is why it's an international hotspot, even though based on local factors. Georgia is not the only place that Russia may be facing off with NATO and the West, which brings us to . . .

RUSSIA-UKRAINE: TERRIBLE INTERNAL TENSIONS

As elaborated on back in chapter 8: Eastern Europe, Ukraine has now become the center stage for the ideological battle for control between Team West and Russia. The Plaid Avenger believes that to deter-

mine which world power has the upper hand in this part of the world, simply keep your eye on the events in Ukraine.

Like Georgia, Ukraine used to be part of the USSR, with Russia as the supreme overseer. Like Georgia, Ukraine declared independence when the USSR collapsed. Like Georgia, Ukraine had a mini-revolution that put pro-democracy, pro-Western leaders into power. Like Georgia, Ukraine petitioned for EU and NATO membership. And like Georgia, former President Bush lobbied to get NATO to accept the Ukraine.

Unlike Georgia, Ukraine has yet to be invaded by Russia. Yet.

istani politics are hopelessly corrupt and gridlocked, with politicians bickering about judicial control and foreign policy while their state is imploding around them.

What's worse, the Pakistani military has been fighting what can at best be described as a totally half-hearted campaign against these insurgents. Why would they do that? Because the military and intelligence communities are the ones who actively built and helped the Taliban come to power in the first place, so now they have found it difficult to go out and kill the guys that used to be their allies. On top of that, the whole Pakistani military structure has been so focused on an eventual war with India, that they can not seem to re-adjust their priorities to accept the fact that they are losing the whole country from the inside out! They have more of their military stationed on the border with India than actually out fighting the dudes who are ripping their country apart!

2010 Update: Pakistan's military finally got serious in late 2009 about holding their country together and organized a massive redeployment of troops to fight the Taliban and reclaim control over the western half of their country. They wrestled back control of the Swat Valley, and have made significant gains in the hottest spots of the FATA. Of course, the US had been putting tremendous pressure on them to make this move, supplying billions in aid and logistics, but also intelligence sharing has increased greatly. Pakistani Taliban and some al-Qaeda terrorist attacks continue to plague the state, but as of this writing, the military is still making strides to contain these dangerous entities within their borders. The US is a proud papa for sure.

US IN AFGHANISTAN

Well hell, let's just stay in the neighborhood, shall we? U.S. involvement in Afghanistan is still fresh in our memories—oh right, because we're still there. The story, however, is a long one. In 1996, the Taliban, a fanatic Islamic extremist group, took control of Afghanistan, which had before then been a mishmash of warlords fighting for power. On October 7, 2001 NATO (led primarily by the US) began a military campaign against Afghanistan known as *Operation Enduring Freedom.* The invasion was in direct response to the 9/11 terrorist's attacks and under the belief that Afghanistan was harboring the same terrorists that planned the attacks. With the help of a rebel group called the Northern Alliance (which gains much of its funding through opium sales), America and its allies established a new, secular government in Afghanistan. This invasion kicked off what is now known as the Global War on Terror.

The main problem in Afghanistan has been the unsuccessful implementation of its established government. Afghanis are arguing that the ruling government is comprised of ethnic Tajiks, while the majority of Afghanistan is Pashtun. The Pashtuns are freaking out cause they think the Tajiks are too Westernized with their skintight jeans and pink Armani t-shirts, creating a secular government. The Pashtuns would prefer a Pashtun-dominated Islamic based government, which is strongly supported by its neighbor to the south, Pakistan. A reoccurring problem the U.S. is seeing is the failure of its exported form of democracy in the Middle East (*See: U.S. in Iraq*).

A recent surge in Taliban activity has many speculating that the U.S. and its NATO allies are failing in reconstructing Afghanistan. A clear example of that was on April 2008, when Afghan President Hamad Karzai survived a failed assassination attempt. Even though the attempt failed, it was a victory for the insurgents, as they were at least capable of getting close to Karzai. This puts immense pressure on Karzai's administration to successfully establish and proclaim an effective government.

A particular problem posing itself against the Afghan government is the sharp increase in production of opium, which can be processed into heroin. Can't be that big of a problem, right? Afghanistan is a war torn country; when are you ever going to have time to grow opium? Apparently there's something in the air, because Afghanistan produces 92% of the world's opium and 80% of the world's heroin. Let's get down and dirty with the problem itself. The Taliban and al-Qaeda have used the opium trade to re-equip, re-supply, and re-organize themselves, and have turned the tide of the battle back in their favor.

Yes, you are reading this correctly: the Taliban is currently gaining ground and beating the NATO coalition. Damn! The US has been outright begging other countries to contribute more to the cause, but unfortunately, more folks are pulling out than putting in: Australia is out, and Canada and UK have been downsizing troop numbers as well, preparing for an eventual total withdrawal. As just expressed in the last section on Pakistan, this whole area on both sides of the border is a no-man's land for control, from either government. NATO is losing just as bad on the Afghan side as the Pakistani military is losing on the Paki side. It's all one big interconnected mess that no one in the world wants to see disintegrate further, but no one in the world wants to send more troops or get involved with at all. Geez! Why does the US have to do every damn thing?

We call Afghanistan a country because it occupies a space on the map of the world, but it isn't really one. For years, Afghanistan has been a battlefield for rival warlords and ethnic groups. Every time somebody has tried to set up a strong central government, such as the Soviet Union in the 1980s, war has broken out. People in Afghanistan are used to war and are good at defending their homeland. America better take some lessons in history before it tries to impose a government that people do not want. I almost hesitate to call this place a failed state, only because I'm not really sure it's ever been a state to begin with!

US IN IRAQ

Ever since Saddam Hussein invaded Kuwait in 1991, he has been one of America's worst enemies. In the first Gulf War, American forces drove Hussein out of Kuwait and destroyed much of Iraq's army. When asked why he didn't pursue Hussein to Baghdad to finish the job and remove him from power, former President George H.W. Bush told a group of Gulf War veterans, "Whose life would be on my hands as the commander-in-chief because I, unilaterally, went beyond the international law, went beyond the stated mission, and said we're going to show our macho? We're going into Baghdad. We're going to be an occupying power—America in an Arab land—with no allies at our side. It would have been disastrous. We're American soldiers; we don't do business that way."

After George W. Bush was elected president in 2000, he decided that American soldiers **did** do business that way. America unilaterally attacked Iraq, went into Baghdad, and occupied the country—

Iraq: Military Conflict and Aftermath 2003 - 2005

- Areas of primary insurgency
- British Troop Advances
- U.S. Troop Advances

man's-land issue, Somalia's pirate issue, even Zimbabwe's AIDS/cholera issue are all bound by one common theme: all these problems were spawned in areas that the world gave up on, and now the world has to deal with the consequences. Because AIDS spreads. Because extremist militants attack. Because nuclear bombs can be launched. And yes, because pirates will climb out of the hole that the world left them in, and come and steal your booty.

The point of this rant at the end of our hot-spots chapter? Heck, I don't know. Maybe it's to keep you engaged in what's happening in the world so that the next hot-spot can be avoided. But for sure it is to alert you to a stone cold fact of life in our times: world ignorance may be bliss, but it won't stop world problems from reaching your shore. Even when it comes ashore dressed as a pirate. Speaking of the next imminent hot-spot, let's finish the chapter with a current conflagration that may end up re-defining our times and the world order if/when it goes down. Let's head back to Persia . . . .

IRAN VS. THE US, OR THE WORLD IF NECESSARY

Iran and the United States have been enemies since the 1979 Iranian Revolution, when Islamic extremists overthrew the US-backed Shah, and took control of the government. When the fanatics took over, one of the first things they did was raid the American embassy in Tehran and take 52 Americans hostage for 444 days. The images of American hostages on American TV made Americans furious at Iran. Iran has also funded terrorist groups worldwide, including Hezbollah, which was responsible for bombing a Marine barracks in Lebanon in 1983 and killing 241 American marines.

Iran has the dubious distinction as being listed by the State Department as the top state sponsor of terror worldwide, making it a natural target in the war on terror. To make things worse, Iranian officials are hostile to America's main ally in the Middle East, Israel. The current President of Iran, Mahmoud Ahmadinejad, has even said that Israel should be wiped off the map, and other clerics are famous for their anti-Semitic rhetoric about Israel. No wonder George W. Bush called Iran part of the "axis of evil" in 2002.

Despite years of talking shit, the US may finally have an excuse to attack Iran . . . . and others have been getting on board for the action as well. In 2006, Iran admitted that it was enriching uranium to build nuclear power plants. Iranian officials claim that they are just doing this for nuclear power, but some American officials are concerned that this is just the first step in developing a nuclear bomb. Game on.

Obviously, American policy-makers are scared to death of Islamic extremists, known for supporting terror and threatening Israel, having nuclear weapons. There has been speculative debate for years now about a possible US invasion or a US air-strike to shut down this nuclear nonsense. Before that happens, the US has been pushing hard for crippling UN economic sanctions against the regime. Both avenues of punishment have been resisted big-time by China and

Russia, both of which are doing big deals with Iran for energy importing and exporting, so this situation has some beyond-the-Middle-East, whole world repercussions as well.

However, even China and Russia have been rethinking their protection of Iran as Iran has become even more ballsy with their nuclear ambitions in the last two years: they failed to allow IAEA inspectors full access to crucial areas, were busted with a secret underground uranium processing base, and even made proud claims that they are enriching uranium fuel to levels higher than needed for nuclear energy, but not quite high enough to be used for bombs. They continue to intentionally stay in this murky middle ground, as if they actually are daring outsiders to attack.

Think I'm exaggerating? Both the Ayatollah and Ahmadenijad have made fiery speeches about how it is Iran's "god-given right" to have a nuclear industry, and that nothing on the planet will stop them. (I forget what part of the Bible God specifically addresses fissile material in, but I'm sure it's in there.) No amount of wheeling and dealing seems to be able to push Iran off of this path, which is why they may be bombed off it instead.

Iran's air force and navy is shaky at best, and the US could take it in a couple hours with some surgical bombing. A ground war is another story. Unlike Arab Muslims, who usually consider themselves more Muslim than nationalistic, Iranian people are very nationalistic and would resist an attack violently. I cannot conceive of anybody in the US government being dumb enough to attempt a ground war in Iran, but we should never underestimate the capacity for ignorance, I suppose.

I believe the worst case scenario that we might see would involve surgical bombing of the nuclear production facilities, and the US probably won't even be the ones to do it! Israel has publicly stated many times now that a nuclear Iran is unacceptable and that they will not let it happen. The Iranian situation is now the #1 most worried about foreign policy issue to nearly every single Israelite.

It will probably be Israel that conducts a bombing campaign, unless some diplomatic breakthrough occurs. The US, the EU, most of Team West and, strangely enough, most Arab states will secretly support such a strike, while publicly distancing themselves from it. This will serve to infuriate the Iranians, and piss off the Russians and Chinese as well. The Iranian government has also said that it will step up terrorist attacks, especially in US occupied Iraq, if force is used against them.

Do you think that's all the Iranians can do if they get pissed off? Consider this: Iran could, in less than a day, drop sea mines into, or start picking off ships in, the critical Straights of Hormuz, where a huge daily dose of the world's oil supply passes through. In effect, they could halt the entire world economy by clogging up this small artery of oil flow, which would spike oil prices exponentially and instantaneously. This one could get ugly, quickly—and everyone is going to be involved one way or another.

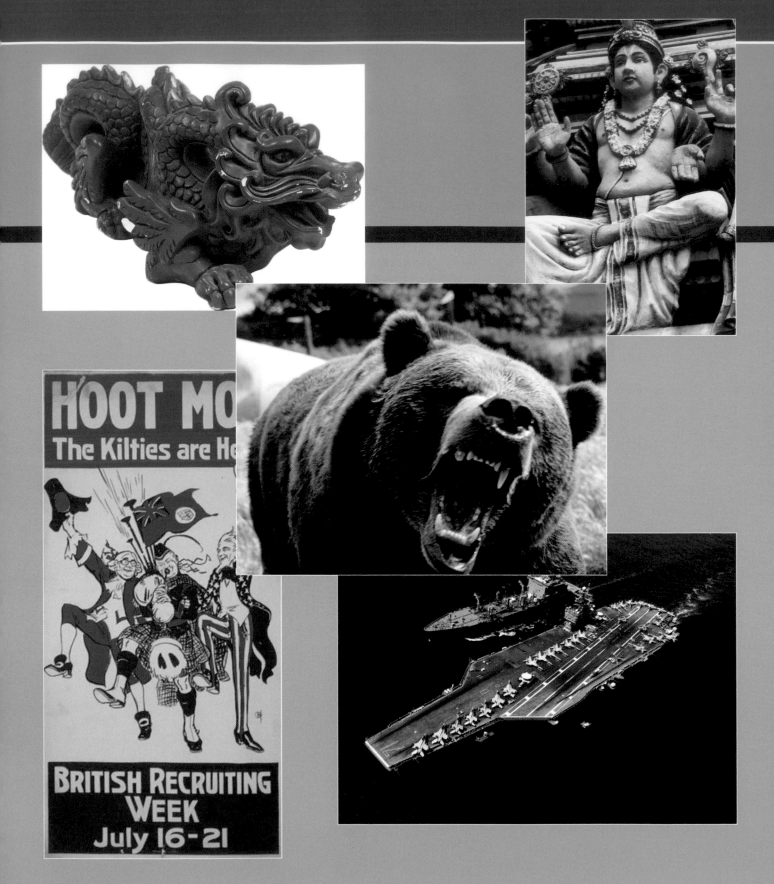

CHAPTER OUTLINE

1. Political Teams
2. Military Teams
3. Economic Teams
4. The Final Final

Team Play: Evolving Power Centers of the 21st Century

26

MY friends, it's long past due to wrap up this blundering batch of buffoonery I call a book. What better way to round up a world regions textbook than to back up from the entire planet and assess exactly how these world regions are interacting with each other—either working with each other, against each other, or forming up teams to cancel each other out. It's such a delicious stew of international intrigue! Think of it as high school, except these states have nuclear weapons and control the planet. Other than that, it's the same old same old human nature. But I digress.

Let's once again look at the major players that are affecting the course of events on our planet strategically, politically and economically. Then we'll call it a day.

LET'S MEET THE POLITICAL POWER PLAYERS

No sense trying to pretend otherwise: the United States is still the undisputed heavyweight when it comes to a single entity with the absolute most political power. To put it simply, what the US wants, the US gets. An example: There was never any credible threat that any other country was going to attack the US because of its recent invasion of Iraq. Most countries, institutions, and people on the planet may have been staunchly opposed to the US move, but no one was actually going to do anything about it. That is raw political power, and the US is the only state that has been able to wield that sword solo for a couple of decades.

But the world is changing fast, my friends. The US still has the power, but other states and groups are rising fast to match their diplomatic skills with Uncle Sam. With no reservations, I tell you that we are moving from a uni-polar world (only one power, namely the US) to a multi-polar world (with many major powers). This is the setting of transformation that we find ourselves in here at the beginning of the 21st century. Politically speaking, let's take a look at the major forces that shape decision-making across the globe, and who teams up with who in order to get their agendas pushed. I will identify the major players, their motivations, their agendas, who they like and who they hate, and see how that is translating into current events that are going down around the globe.

SAMMY SOLO

America has long been a team of one. Its physical isolation far from the rest of the world has forever insulated it from the global events in which it participates, or in which it declines to participate. Its entire history could be viewed as a wavering cycle of either isolation (in which it does not get involved in global events) or full-on engagement (in which it is full-on the predominate player.) Take a wild stab which side of the spectrum it is on right now.

When Uncle Sammy decides to go for the global gusto, he has seemingly unlimited energy, money, military, and ambition to get the job done, regardless of world opinion. For the last hundred years, the US usually had a global coalition of participants that backed it up. Let's call them Team West for right now. In WWI, WWII, the Korean War, the Cold War, the first Iraq War and countless others, the US served as a team leader that rallied the world to victory, or at least something close to it. Point is, that mostly the US didn't have to stand alone, because the UK or the EU or NATO or the UN or Team West was there to back them up.

However, since the end of the Cold War—circa 1990—Sammy has increasingly worked on his own to achieve his agenda. Why? During most of the last fifty years, it was the US and the USSR in a bi-polar world of competition, giving the world at least two options to choose from. But now it has been a couple of decades that the US has stood completely alone at the top of the heap, alone at the top of this uni-polar world. In this time, the US quickly grew accustomed to the role of sole political power. Therefore, it has increasingly acted alone whenever it really wanted something that the rest of the players would not support.

I'm not just picking on the former Bush administration, either; the Clinton administration acted unilaterally on several different occasions as well, either to stop perceived terrorism in Africa or perceived genocide in the Balkans. The dynamic duo of Dick Cheney and Donald Rumsfeld just took the US even exponentially further down this unilateral path (willing to act alone), with the most extreme example being the aforementioned current Iraq War. Beyond even a willingness to act alone, the US for over a decade has actually preferred to act alone, so it does not have to waste time with negotiation and organization and cooperation that is required by international diplomacy.

The times are a-changing, though. Under the new US President Barack Obama administration, the US is already rapidly leaning back to diplomacy and coalition-building as the most effective tool for international action. We can see this unfolding currently as the US is working exceptionally hard to rally world support on the growing threats of both the North Korean and the Iranian nuclear industry, and it is having much success. The entire EU backs them on it, and even Russia and China are starting to come around to the US point of view after lots of wrangling and back-room debates. The NATO-led Afghan mission has also been recast as needing more international support, as opposed to being primarily a US military force.

Uncle Sam had a solo run in the sun for some time, but it appears that in this newly forming multi-polar world, his future role may be as primary leader of Team West. Okay, who the hell are they?

TEAM WEST

Throughout this text, I have thrown around the concept of a core world culture that is primarily steeped in western traditions and values. It's finally time to identify just exactly who is on Team West. Obviously, the core of the team is Western Europe, the place where Western Civilization was born and evolved, thus the team name. *"Western civilization"* encompasses the big ideas on which our lives are based. I'm talking about the big things here: things like philosophies, legal systems, economic systems, medical practices, writing systems, and particularly religions like Christianity and all its sub-sects.

However, the true adhesive of this team is based on common ideologies. All the members of Team West also share particular values such as liberal democratic governance, emphasis on individual human liberties and rights, and the free market/capitalist system. These are more important to consider than the other stuff, since there are some non-European actors on this team; while they are not Christian or European or even white, they are staunch believers in the team's principle values. That's why they are on the team. Okay, so who?

Joining Western Europe, we have Eastern Europe, and let's just go ahead and refer to the team elements of both regions as the EU. The EU countries may have been the historic core of Team West, but the all-star quarterback of the squad is now the US. But there are even more players on the team! Canada and Australia always show up to the game, as does Japan. That's right, Japan is definitely part of Team West even though it is in the east, and Asian to boot! It shares all the West's values and has staunchly supported the US and the team ever since the end of WWII. One other surprise entry: Turkey. As a staunch secular democracy, capitalist country, and NATO member, Turkey also primarily sides up with Team West, even though it is Muslim. Primarily, but not always. We could even count Israel on Team West, although for various reasons, it does not usually openly participate in most of the Team's competitions.

How does it work in today's world? Well, when the Team comes up with a desired policy or goal—say, the War on Terror, the US usually leads the charge, and will often be supported on the UN Permanent Security Council by having the UK and France back them up. The EU as a whole typically is on board as well. Then when it is time for the real action to go down, Canada, Australia and Turkey will jump in to join with the EU and US troops, and Japan will voice its support for the endeavor, and perhaps even supply money or materials to aid the effort, since Japan does not have offensive military capacity. Then the team hits the field and tries to score the goal. Got it? Good.

Team West is a potent force today, mostly because it consists of most of the planet's richest countries, some of the most powerful and technologically advanced militaries, as well as having three out of the five nuclear powers. Can you feel the power yet? No? Consider this: all NATO countries are on Team West, which essentially means that NATO itself is a tool of Team West's arsenal. And NATO kicks ass.

An example as referenced above, the team's quarterback, Uncle Sam, is currently leading the charge against Iran to embargo the state and possibly have eventual military strikes against them. The EU is already on board, as is Canada, Japan, Australia, and even perhaps Israel, which has been conducting military exercises as part of the propaganda campaign designed to scare the Iranians. See how it all works, my friends?

But I must give you this 2009 update, my friends: Team West, and the US in particular, have really taken it on the chin since this whole global economic meltdown started. Most places on planet Earth now squarely put the blame on the capitalist excesses of Team West. This has started a whole re-think in terms of following the capitalist path of the West, with some folks suggesting that capitalism as a whole is on the way down. Couple the economic crap with what is now seen by many as over-extension of political and military power in the Middle East, Central Asia, and Eastern Europe, and you have the makings of a good old fashioned smear campaign against the West. I can't lie: they are taking a hit right now in the global scheme of things and will lose some power. But the Team is resilient, and rich, so they are still a global playa' for some time to come. Had enough of the West yet? Then let's get on to some other entities which are not part of this team.

THE BEAR

We already had a whole chapter on Russia, so I can keep it brief here. It was largely assumed that Russia would inevitably join Team West after the collapse of the Soviet Union in the early 1990s. It does share most of the common cultural characteristics of Western Civilization, but somehow it has always remained just on the fringe of that grouping, always slightly different, with a distinct "not European" component. After the demise of the USSR, Russia was a second rate power, with even less prestige, that was really at the mercy of international business and banking and stronger world powers like the US, the EU, and NATO. Russia pretty much just had to go with the flow, even when events were inherently against its own national interests, like the growth of NATO, for example. But all that has reversed in the last eight years under the long judo-chopping arm of Vladimir Putin. He, along with tons of revenue from the Russian oil industry, has brought the Bear politically back to a position of strength. He plays hardball in international affairs now, and has reinvigorated a Russian national pride that has long laid dormant. In short: the Bear is back. Grrrr! As I have suggested to you last chapter, Russia's full-frontal invasion of Georgia last year was essentially a calling card that they are back, ready to wrestle, and more than willing to engage militarily if pushed on issues of their national security.

Now that the Bear is strong again, it has been re-thinking the whole joining Team West business, and it appears it is declining the invitation. Russia prefers to be an independent player in order to be a global power again, as well as to achieve its own unique foreign policy goals, and it is in a prime position to do this.

Since the Russians supply one-third of European energy demand, this gives them all sorts of economic and political leverage over their Eurasian neighbors. Get Russia upset at you, and you might not have heating oil next winter. But the Europeans aren't the only ones who need oil. Look eastward and you see Japan and China both vying for petroleum resources as well, so Russia is really sitting pretty right now. The Russians are forging economic and strategic political ties to their east as well, mostly with China. They are at a historical east/west pivot point and they are straddling the fence about which relationships to make or break. I think they're being extremely savvy and are going to avoid taking sides in anything.

We can see this rift between the Bear and Team West in a variety of ways in today's world. The US and many Europeans express concern or outright criticize Russia for becoming too authoritarian under Putin, thus detracting from their democracy and human liberties, which is, of course, one of the foundations of Team West. The US and EU also accuse Russia of using oil as a political weapon to get its way; a not entirely false charge, but is that illegal?

In return, Russia usually counters most US movements at the UN Permanent Security Council, where it holds veto power. One need look no further than the current Iranian issue, where the Russians have been quick to dismiss Team West's fears of Iran's nuclear ambitions, has promised to veto any severe embargoes or military action against Iran, and is even helping the Iranians build their nuclear power industry. Russia is increasingly working together with China economically, diplomatically, and militarily, which is perhaps unsettling to the other world teams.

The Bear is a center of political power not to be taken lightly, but is there really ever a situation that a bear would be taken lightly? While I would never brawl with a bear, I would be even less likely to disagree with a dragon . . .

ENTER: THE DRAGON

Just as with the Bear, the Dragon has been resurrected as of late and is on the fast track to becoming a major world political power. As you undoubtedly deduced from the chapter on China, the state had a rough go of things for most of the 20th century, from internal destruction to civil wars to colonialization to wartime atrocities to counter-productive communist policies. Since the capitalist reforms of the 1970s, China has really turned things around and become an economic powerhouse of the globe. Remember, it jumped two whole slots just last year to become the 4th largest economy on the planet.

With that economic clout has come global political power. The Dragon has been very focused on rebuilding itself for the last few decades and therefore was not that interested in exerting itself in the global political structure, except of course when it was in its own interest to do so; think of any issue dealing with the status of Taiwan. China also is the staunchest supporter of sovereignty in the world, so its attitude towards global issues and conflicts outside of its own territory has typically been "live and let live," although "live and let die" may be a more appropriate descriptor. China does not like to get involved in the affairs of other states, no matter how horrific the situation, and in return wants no one poking their noses into Chinese business. You dig?

Now this would all be just an asinine academic excursion but for one thing: China is one of the veto-wielding members of the UN Permanent Security Council. When international action is called for by Team West to punish Iraq or Burma, the Chinese position is usually to play the spoiler and veto any actions by the UN, or at least dumb-down the UN action to the point that it is ineffective or useless. Need an example?

Take Sudan, Zimbabwe, and Burma. Most of the world does not like, does not support, and does not want to trade with these countries because they have fairly brutal records of persecuting their own people. The morally and ethically right thing to do is to refuse to support that state in any capacity. But China says, "We don't care. We will trade with you. Can we buy oil from you, Sudan? Thanks, buddy!" Perhaps their open policy is not such a great thing. This causes friction between China and other rich countries around the world, especially "Team West" countries. Developed countries say, "You can't do that," and then China says, "Hell yeah we can. We are a sovereign state." The issue is a source of friction for a lot of the Team West countries. Both China and Russia are very good at this game. Speaking of which . . .

I just can't help myself but to over-exaggerate a subtle theme that has been forming globally for some time now, and has burst into full flower just this year: China and Russia are totally in love, dudes! These two titans have pretty much agreed on every single global item of consequence in the last year, and have met more times than I can even count anymore. From heads of state meetings on trade and security, to a joint space program, to meetings of the SCO and the BRIC; China and Russia have pretty much thrown down the gauntlet and created a new power block for the planet.

What do I mean by this? Well, in addition to all the joint stuff they are doing, both Prime Minister Putin and Premier Wen Jaibao have openly body-slammed Team West for causing the current financial meltdown. They both are also pushing for way more security and cooperation via the SCO structure . . . not through the UN or any other Western device. These guys recently made a joint declaration after their SCO meeting in June 2009 that they favoring scrapping the US dollar as the world standard. Damn! This is total cage-match smack-down. But back to China now . . .

With the number four economy on the planet and increasing international pressure to pony up and accept some global responsibilities, China's star is on the rise politically. China's steadfast respect for the power of sovereignty still trumps all, and thus, the Dragon will be very hesitant to throw its weight around in the international arena. China still does not commit very many troops to UN functions, and will hesitate from any unilateral action on its own part, and also mostly stalls multilateral actions even when sponsored by the UN. While the Dragon does in theory support the US-led War on Terror, it will continue to stymie any major efforts by Team West to transform other countries, either by invasion or persuasion. With its UN veto-wielding power, it more often than not will be siding with Russia to counter major moves by Team West, while strengthening its hand at home and in its immediate neighborhood. That is done with an eye towards countering another global power in the Dragon's 'hood: India.

TEAM HINDU

I would be remiss to not include the other significant growing power center on our planet, and that would be our Indian friends. Like China, Team Hindu is a burgeoning economy here in the 21st century and that economic power will increasingly be translated into political power. That's right, India will soon be another major axis of planetary political power. But I don't want to exaggerate the circumstances! India is on the rise for sure, but currently is nowhere near the economic, political, or military power of a Russia or China—yet. Stress on the "yet."

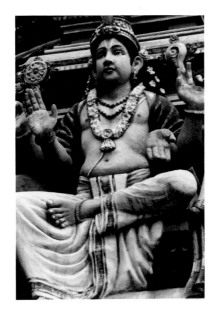

India is soon to be a major power player because it has a whole lot of unique attributes which will soon force it to be a player. Let's quickly list them: India will soon be the most populous state on the planet; China is now, but not for too much longer. India has a vibrant and growing economy, and it is simultaneously diversifying nicely. It is a nuclear power, and, yes, it has nuclear weapons. India has a significant military, certainly the strongest in the region. As part of that, India has an aircraft carrier. That means it has a means of projecting power abroad. The only other countries in the neighborhood that fit that description are China and Russia, who are both power players already.

However, unlike their Chinese and Russian counterparts, Team Hindu actually shares a lot of attributes, ideals, and goals with Team West. India is a strong, established democracy—the biggest in the world, actually—and a supporter of free market principles and global trade. India, like Team West, has human rights and individual liberties as a foundation stone of its society. India is an avid supporter of the War on Terror and, as such, does quite a bit at home to thwart extremism of all sorts. They even speak English, for Pete's sake . . . how much more Western could they get?

Well, I'm pushing it a bit far now—they are not Western, and do maintain their own distinct culture, as well as their own distinct take on foreign policy and global affairs. But look for them to become a stronger and stronger voice in the near future. Former President Bush met with Indian Prime Minister Manmohan Singh multiple times during his presidency in an effort to warm relations between the two titans. The US was actually working very hard to get a deal signed with India in order to help them out with their nuclear power industry, and that deal finally went through here in 2009. It's a really big deal, too! The US and India are now the best of buddies, in a friendship that is just now starting to blossom, all because of nukes!

Why do I keep bringing up the nuclear issue? The US and Team West want to legitimize the Indian nuclear position—India never signed the nuclear non-proliferation treaty—so as to further isolate and de-legitimize the future Iranian one. See how this works?

Team Hindu may still be a minor world player right now, but that status won't last for too much longer. They are one of the five potential additions to the UN Permanent Security Council, and given their western tendencies, I would look for their membership to be supported by Team West. I would also speculate that Team Hindu will likely be increasingly siding with Team West on global issues of the future, albeit with a more reserved tendency to use force. Gandhi taught them way too well.

POLITICAL TEAM SUMMARY

Uncle Sam has been the sole political superpower on the world stage, but that brief era is coming to a close. The rise of China, India, and the rebirth of a strong Russia preclude the US from acting unilaterally in the future. The likely US response is to rebuild its base of allies and become a stronger leader of Team West. And Team West will be strong.

China, and increasingly Russia, has a tendency towards authoritarianism and an emphasis on the trump card of sovereignty; therefore, they do not completely share in the value systems of Team West. As such, these two power players are a likely alliance that will balance/counteract the Team West influence on global affairs. Team Hindu does actually have much more in common with Team West, and will likely be an ally of the West in future global issues.

This section has merely been a summary of the **MAJOR** power players on the planet. Of course, there are other states and entities that will affect global events and influence the direction of the planet in a myriad of ways. Brazil, South Africa, Islam, and ASEAN all spring to mind. We simply focused on the most powerful, most organized, and most influential teams that are or will be the major shapers of global political policy for the near future. These are the teams that will decide how to conduct the War on Terror and the global War on Drugs. These are the teams that will decide all major UN actions, including the possible expansion of the UN Security Council. These are the teams that will shape all major policies on global warming, fighting global crime, and conducting global war.

They are the majors of political power. But what about other types of power?

MILITARY MACHINATIONS

You might think that political power immediately equals military power, and you might be right. Might does sometimes make right. There are many individual powerful states on the planet right now. However, the alliances of military power that have occurred between states has been accelerating greatly in the last decade, and these military power centers have themselves become an important component of under-standing how the planet works. Let's briefly look over the major military entities on the planet and how they interact with one another.

THE BIG BOYS WITH THE BIG TOYS

The United States is the undisputed heavyweight of military power, technology, and spending. Look back at the table in chapter 6 to check out military expenditures for 2009 and you can quickly calculate that the US alone accounts for half of the total world spending on all things military. Damn! That's some power! However, China actually has the largest standing army, and is spending fast to catch up with the US. Even they are not alone.

Let's just call a spade a spade here. The most powerful state military entities in terms of global reach are the US, the UK, France, Russia, China, and India. Why those? Those are all the states with mostly modern mili-taries, the money to make them stronger and keep them up-to-date, the ability to project that power outside of their own countries, and they all have nuclear weaponry to boot. Places like Israel and Pakistan may have many of those qualities, but not all. Certainly Israel, Pakistan, Turkey and Brazil are powerful regional entities, but I would not necessarily call them powerful global ones. That make sense?

All the power players, except India, are also on the UN Permanent Security Council, which means they all have a big voice in how that organization is run. For this section, just know this: these are all countries that have, or could, act uni-laterally from a military standpoint. But that's not really the way things go down anymore.

ARMED ALLIANCES

Mostly, use of military force in global conflicts occurs as a coordinated effort between states as part of a bigger institution or entity. Most of these groups have already been discussed throughout this text, but let's hit them up one last time and make some predictions on not only future use of military power across the globe, but also how these entities will be working with, or against, each other in shaping global events.

THE UN

Most member states contribute troops, supplies, or money to the United Nations for its active military missions. Since any active mission must clear the UN Security Coun-cil, the countries described above get to decide where those missions will be allowed to happen. Have you figured out where virtually all UN missions have occurred? If you said "Africa," then give yourself a gold star! Why there? Because it's the only place that all the major powers can agree on with regard to having a UN presence. China would never allow a UN military mission to Burma (their ally), Russia would never allow a UN mission to Kazakhstan (their ally), and the US would never allow a UN mis-sion to Canada—okay, maybe that one would fly, but you get the picture.

The only places that UN troops end up in are typically poor, developing coun-tries in which no major power has a vested interest, and therefore no one on the Security Council will veto. The Democratic Republic of the Congo, Liberia, Haiti,

UN Secretary General Ban Ki-Moon.

Lebanon, Côte d'Ivoire, Chad, Ethiopia, East Timor and Kosovo are all excellent examples of current UN deployments that lack vested interest of major power players. However, Kosovo should throw up a red flag to you, as I have explained earlier in this text how it has become a hot-button issue between world powers.

Dig this: that mission was agreed upon by Russia back in the late 1990s when it was in a significantly weakened state. Russia would never let something like that go down now! Same thing goes in reverse though: the UN mission to poor, undeveloped Sudan has been held up by China for years, because it formed a vested interest in the place when Chinese companies started developing Sudan's oil fields. Only increased international pressure has forced the Chinese to allow a mission to happen, but in a much more limited capacity; that is, a smaller force with more constraints on what it can do.

That brings us to the last point about military maneuvers of the UN: they are largely weak and ineffectual. The big powers can never all agree on any single issue, and therefore any mission which gets passed is typically watered down to the point of nothingness, if there is any action taken at all. Remember the Rwandan genocide? What a freakin' debacle! The major powers couldn't even form a plan of action on that huge mess, even though no one had a vested interest in the place. The entanglements of getting military missions passed through the UN system is the major reason that the US typically bypasses the UN altogether and goes straight for NATO.

NATO

NATO is easily the most powerful and effective military arrangement on the planet right now, and the preferred choice of the US, since the US is the primary player and most influential member in the club. In other words, the US has a much easier time getting actions sanctioned by NATO than by the UN. You know all about Article 5 and how the group works, so let's cut to the chase.

NATO is essentially the military arm of Team West—yes, the whole Team, not just the US. Think about it. Makes sense, doesn't it? All members of NATO are part of Team West, and even Japan and Australia (non-NATO members) often help out NATO missions with supply and support services. This is what makes Team West so potent: a combination of common ideologies with an organized and powerful military structure. They can get the job done, and more often than not, can agree about what the job is.

This is significant in today's world because NATO has done a major mission shift to now incorporate the War on Terror. As you know, after 9/11, the US invoked NATO Article 5 in order to get the club to help out with the Afghanistan mission, which they did. The current war in that state is a NATO war, not a US one. That sets the stage for many more NATO engagements in this global war on terrorism in the future. Granted, NATO will not dive head first into every US anti-terror effort; it is important to note that NATO did not support the current US war in Iraq. However, they may eventually come to the US's assistance in this situation as well. NATO has become stronger over the years and has increased its mission to a global reach, which is fitting

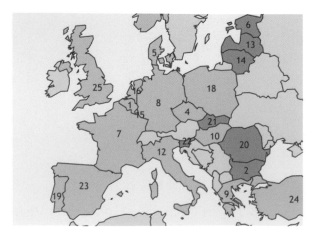

since they are the most effective global military in the world. Look for India to start helping with any future NATO endeavors.

What's not to love about NATO? If you don't necessarily agree with all the foundations of Team West, then you might be a bit leery of NATO's power. Russia is the obvious antagonist of NATO, and this has been in the news big time in 2008. Vladimir Putin openly threatened to target missiles at the Ukraine if they attempted to join NATO, and also to more generally target the nuclear arsenal at Europe as a whole if NATO proceeded with its missile-defense systems being built in Eastern Europe. Then there was that small matter of Russia invading Georgia before it could become a NATO member. In fact, the Avenger is just going to level with you here: NATO is done. Not in terms of its power or position, but in terms of expansion. Because Russia now has demonstrated its resolve to keep Georgia and Ukraine out of the NATO alliance, I would not look for NATO to be doing any more growing anytime soon. Or ever. No one wants to risk a land war with Russia just to increase NATO membership. Russia is invited to most high-level NATO meetings in an effort to placate the Bear, but it appears that Russia has other things in mind. It is not looking to ever join NATO, because perhaps it has an alternative . . .

SCO: SHANGHAI COOPERATION ORGANIZATION

Of course! From chapter 22! Russia + China + all of Central Asia. That's the SCO: the anti-NATO! Okay, that is a bit too strong of a descriptor, but the Plaid Avenger wants you to be smart about the world, not politically correct. The hell with that! Let's get to the goods.

Though the declaration on the establishment of the Shanghai Cooperation Organization contained a statement that it "is not an alliance directed against other states and regions and it adheres to the principle of openness," most observers believe that one of the original purposes of the SCO was to serve as a counterbalance to the US and NATO, and, in particular, to avoid conflicts that would allow the US to intervene in areas near both Russia and China. How are they pulling that off?

SCO states are strengthening their defense pacts with each other to ensure that no interference or invasion will be allowed from outsiders. In essence, they have formed an Asian version of NATO. The movement in this direction is why most US military bases have now been kicked out of SCO states, and also why the US request to become an observer state of the SCO has been declined every single year. It's also why the SCO has started doing the joint military exercises.

However, it is a very young organization, so I wouldn't call them a military powerhouse on par with NATO just yet. But the alliance does consist of two nuclear powers, Russia does have the second largest nuclear arsenal on the planet, and China does have the largest standing army. While I do not predict this entity doing anything aggressive anytime soon, I also do not think it's a stretch of the imagination that the US and/or NATO would be extremely hesitant to ever attack any of the SCO members, even the dinky ones, for fear that the defense alliance might strike back. I mean, that is the whole point of a defense alliance after all.

Let's pretend the US/NATO strikes a terrorist cell in Uzbekistan, which then forces the SCO to counter-attack. Sounds like a WWIII scenario to me! Don't get too worked up yet, though; these guys are still organizationally pretty weak, and their mettle is untested. Would Russia and China really counter a US attack? Only time will tell. Actually, let's hope we never have to find out.

SHANGHAI COOPERATION ORGANISATION

■ Member States　■ Observer States　■ Dialogue Partners

The more important issues have to do with those observer states of the SCO, particularly Iran. As suggested in Chapter 22, Iran would just love to be a full-fledged SCO member so that it could have an insurance policy against western aggression. Iran thinks that the SCO membership will somehow shield it from any UN or NATO or US attack. But it's not a full member yet, and Russia and China are not likely to grant it that status, because no one involved wants to get into a global power battle over the antics of Ahmadinejad. Again, let's hope that is the case.

The SCO is a fascinating study on the future of Eurasia, and the world. Be sure to keep up with them as the entity continues to evolve. We already have two major power players in the club, as well as the entire region of Central Asia. India is also an observer member: a position which sets it up as a future power player on the globe. Iran really wants to be part of the club, which effectively moves SCO power and influence into the Middle East as well. These guys are just all over the place!

OUT OF AMMO

Summary: the UN is weak, NATO is strong, and the SCO is evolving. All three will be the primary military alliances which shape future conflicts around the globe, both the small ones and the big ones. The UN is likely to expand the Permanent Security Council, which will make them even weaker from a military standpoint; more voices at the table means less things that can be agreed upon by all. NATO is nearing the end of its expansion period, having pulled in most of Eastern Europe, and stands more powerful than ever given its new global objectives. The SCO is young and ineffectual so far, but that means it has the most growing to do, and possibly the greatest future potential of them all.

Of course, each individual state has its own military might, and the power players will continue to dominate the game in the global competitions. Smaller powers like Israel, Brazil, Pakistan, Saudi Arabia, and Iran will continue to build up their military might and will affect regional politics in their prospective neighborhoods, but won't have global reach. I suppose I should also throw in smaller and smaller military entities like rebel and terrorist groups, which can shape regional or even global policy in general by their actions. I know they are the ones that seem to be the big deal every single day when you read news headlines, but the reality is that they are, militarily, just a pin-prick on world affairs. Many pin-pricks can add up though.

I did want to give a final shout-out to my AU military brothers as an up-and-coming force for regional power as well. The African Union as a whole may be largely ineffective in terms of economics or politics, but the AU military is starting to gain some steam. It is increasingly being used for peace-keeping efforts all around Africa—it is a critical part of the UN mission in Sudan—and is getting a lot of support from the big power players to keep on getting bigger and better. Indeed, perhaps it will be a strong and professional pan-African army that will help the region as a whole put itself back together, fight corruption, and build a stability that will allow for economic investment and growth. Wouldn't that be grand? Speaking of economics . . .

ECONOMIC POWER PLAYERS

Another facet of global competition is the quest for more dollars—more dollars for your country, more dollars for your country's businesses, more dollars for your country's citizens. Mo' money, mo' money, mo' money! Do we have Team play at the global scale for economics? Sure we do!

To be sure, economies are made up of businesses, which are made up of people, and all people have different personal incentives and goals and ambitions and opportunities to make money. I'm not going to get down to the abstract, philosophical reasons for why people do what they do, or even why countries do what they do. When the rubber hits the road, it's really every man for himself, or in this case, every state for itself, since states are first and foremost beholden to their citizens to make sure that their economy is as strong and rich as possible. Some states are obviously way better at this than others, sometimes at the expense of other states. But that is the way the proverbial cookie crumbles.

However, even though every state looks out after itself first, some states have figured out that they get richer when working with other states. The economic centers of the planet do shift according to who is doing the best, producing the best, or growing the fastest. We can look at what entities and Teams are major forces for economic activity in the world, how they compete with each other, and what the future might bring in terms of cooperation or collision. Sounds like fun, huh? Then let's expound about some economies!

BIG BOYS WITH BIG TOYS: PART DEUX

Why not stick with the pattern? We can identify the individual states with the biggest economies, for starters. The US is by far and away the biggest economy in the world, larger than the next three economies combined. You know the next three: Japan, Germany, and China. The rest of the top ten is rounded out with other rich European countries, but watch out! A simmering South Korea is making its way up the ranks and soon will break into the top ten. Why should we care about these economies with big numbers?

Because money is power! Rich societies are typically stable and happy societies—typically. Who doesn't want to be in a rich society? Levels of richness effects all sorts of things like political power, military might, standards of living, but also global patterns like commodity chains, trade routes, distribution of economic activities, and even immigration/emigration patterns. I know, big shock: people migrate from poor states to rich ones. Go figure.

Where these super-economies are located also has a lot to do with how economic alliances go down, how competitive these states are with each other, and how powerful they can become. Don't believe me? Then let's revisit the EU.

EUROPEAN UNION

The EU has a dozen of the top world economies within its ranks, but individually, none of them can compete effectively with the US economically. But hold the phone! Take all of the EU states together as a single entity, and you are suddenly looking at the richest organization on the planet, even richer than the US in terms of GDP and GDP per capita. The EU as a singular entity has increased trade among its member states, increased trade abroad, and become much more effective at attracting international investment. That's what everybody wants to do! Which is why these supranational organizations based on trade have become so popular lately—and rich.

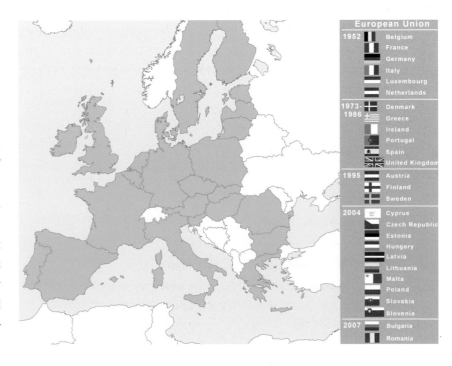

Before we get to that, a few more points on the EU. Like NATO, the EU seems to be at the end of its expansion streak. It has pretty much absorbed all of Eastern Europe, and the only likely future members are the states that were formerly Yugoslavia (no real economic gain for the EU here), the Ukraine (big potential gain here) and finally Turkey (big gain with some big risks here). The former Yugoslavian states are economically weak and have little to offer even when strong. The Ukraine is an agricultural and manufacturing powerhouse with a huge land area and population that would radically affect the EU. Turkey is almost exactly like Ukraine for all the reasons just listed, but promises to be divisive within Europe as a whole because of its Islamic culture. Look back to chapters on Western Europe and Turkey for more details.

The EU is at a breaking point where lots of people think they can simply not get any bigger and maintain any sort of effective control and economic cohesion, but they do have a lot to work with already. Creating this union has been the only thing not just keeping Europe afloat, but making it a global powerhouse to compete with the US and a rising China. The EU will continue to bust ass to fine tune its EU program—because it knows it has to in order to continue to compete with the economic prowess of Asia as a whole.

I'm not just talking about China here. All of Asia is on fire with economic growth, from Korea to Indonesia to India. The center of the economic game is shifting. For hundreds of years, the Europeans were the center of the global economy, eventually forfeiting their top slot to the powerhouse Americans who have held onto it for about a century. But nothing ever stays the same forever, and the 21st century promises to be the Asian century in terms of becoming the economic center of the universe.

This transition is already well underway, and the Europeans do not want to get left totally behind as the Asians start kicking economic ass and taking names. In the 1990s, when the USSR folded up shop and the EU expansion began in earnest, there was even talk of eventually incorporating Russia into the EU. What a continental powerhouse that would have been! Russia is such an important part of the EU economy that it is already invited to major summits and consultations on EU policy, even though it is not a member. Right this second it doesn't appear that it will ever be, by choice, because the Bear is straddling the fence, already looking to the other side of the continent for alternative companionship, which brings us . . .

BACK TO THE SCO

What? Back to the SCO! Remember them? I've already told you that this group may eventually be an anti-NATO, but they also started the organization to be a regional trade block. With the Eurasian titans of Russia and China as the bookends, this is increasingly looking like the team to beat.

As you already know, the SCO is building infrastructure like roads and pipelines across the member states, mostly to facilitate natural resource extraction. Remember I told you about the possibility of them becoming a natural gas cartel akin to OPEC? That may very well be the building block that turns into increased trade among the nations, but more importantly will facilitate trade to other parts of the world. Central Asia has done well to throw in its chips with the SCO. Otherwise, they would be marooned in the middle of the continent fending for themselves. That trade block stuff really works for some states! Instead of being on their own, those states are now a central hub of export supplying petroleum products to the eastern and western sides of the Eurasian continent. Damn! Silk Road back in action!

More important than salvaging Central Asia is the blossoming relationship between Russia and China. You know from the political power players section above that both Team Bear and Team Dragon typically find themselves as the opposing end of a lot of Team West initiatives, so they have a common alliance of sorts already. Both states are avid supporters of sovereignty, and don't want anyone messing in their backyards. The evolution of a friendship between the two, and then the creation of the SCO, is a predictable development. Team West and the EU were hopeful that Russia was going to join their squads eventually, but it doesn't look like that is going to happen, perhaps ever.

Russia is strong again, but it's no powerhouse economy on its own. Hanging out with China certainly is beneficial to Russia, especially since the Chinese demand for natural resources and energy supplies is insatiable. The Russians find themselves in the enviable position of supplying energy to the powerhouse EU and also the powerhouses China and Japan. Their economy is thriving, life is good, and it probably will be getting a lot better, because as that world economic focus shifts to Asia, Russia stands to continue to benefit even more. The Bear will be increasingly dining on Moo Goo Gai Pan and sake shots as it rolls over to economically embrace the Dragon.

THE DRAGON AS ASIAN LEADER

I've been stressing that Asia as a whole is on fire with economic activity, and with no doubts you know that China is the main engine for all this explosive exponential economic energy. Team Dragon has been cranking out double digits in terms of increases in GDP growth year after year for over a decade. That is crazy talk growth! Their manufacturing, industrial and service sectors have been blowing up as they produce everything from toothpaste to Nike shoes to rocket parts for NASA spacecraft. They have become the workshop of the world.

Why am I bothering to repeat this? Because with no reservations, I tell you that China will become the world's largest economy in the next fifty years. It will displace the US from the top slot, although you have learned enough from this book already to know that this shift does not equate to China being truly richer or better off than the US. They will have the biggest economy, and more importantly, will continue to be a focus for international investment, as well as increasingly a center for evolution of new technologies.

Here is the real deal about being a world economic power player and the focus of world economic energies: more things happen in your neighborhood. Huh? You know what I'm sayin'! With this increase in economic energy comes an increase in interest, an increase in investment, an increase in education, and an increase in technologies. The best and smartest people are attracted to where the flame is burning the brightest. The newest innovations in all sorts of technologies almost invariably occur in hot, happening societies where the action is, and that center of action is increasingly Asia!

Team Dragon is being looked upon as not only a very desirable trading partner among other Asian states, but as a model of success to be duplicated. Most Southeast Asian economies are now tied into China, as are the Koreas, and even the Central Asian countries via the SCO as described above. China is truly regaining its historical legacy as the center of the Asian universe.

Asian countries are not alone. Japan (okay, they are Asian too, but very western!) is turning more to trade, invest, and compete with China, as is Russia, Australia, and the US. Japan and Australia in particular have publicly pronounced that they know they must work together more economically with China if they are to continue to thrive; both countries' foreign policy initiatives have shifted immensely to suck up to China more, even though both are still part of Team West.

Hey man, money talks!

I call it Team Dragon because I want you to know that it really has become more of a team affair. Yes, China is the center of the action—but remember, there are other economic powerhouses in this 'hood. Taiwan, South Korea, Singapore, and Hong Kong were once titled the "Asian Tigers" because they underwent decades of phenomenal industrialization and economic growth. Those tigers have now come home to roost under mother Dragon. This place is a veritable smorgasbord of animated animals, and they are getting rich! Throw Japan into the lot, and you have a whole cluster of top world economies here—with one big difference:

Tigers back with the Dragon!

Most top twenty economies are in Europe, and Europe is about played out. The rest of the top twenty world economies are Asian, and they are just getting warmed up! Damn! Look for Asian states to totally dominate the world economic measures of wealth in the coming decades. For sure, China will soon be number two, Japan will be number three, and South Korea will be number ten. And they are all next door neighbors! Are you starting to get a fever for the flava' of East Asia?

To sum up: there will be major growth, competition, and shifts in economic focus and economic policy around the world as Asia rises. Don't get all sad on me—your region is still good! The US and Europe will still be rich, don't worry about that! There are just a few other entities I want mention before escaping this escapade.

SOME OTHER ECONOMIC ENTITIES OF NOTE

I've mentioned ASEAN back in the chapter on Southeast Asia; it is a supranationalist organization with more potential for economic growth than I can imagine right now. Smack dab in the middle of the powerhouse China and Japan to the north and growing power India to its west, all of which are associate members, the ASEAN core might well become the epicenter of an Asian EU. Wow. That would be insane. It's still some ways off, but the point is that this group is in a position of it being almost impossible for them to NOT grow economically right now. Southeast Asia is starting to absorb a lot of manufacturing jobs not just from abroad, but also directly from China. It's good to be close to the top dogs. Speaking of Asian top dogs . . .

As with the rise in political clout, Team Hindu stands to become an economic powerhouse in its own right, although it is going to take a bit longer than their Asian brothers. It's that damn big population that makes things problematic for them to advance as fast! But advance they will nonetheless, but for different reasons than others. Namely, India is fast becoming a high-end technological center for growth in Asia and the world.

China and other Asian nations have focused first on becoming agricultural and manufacturing giants, then incorporating more and more service sector and quaternary activities as they get richer. India is on rather the reverse course: it focuses heavily on increasing its service sector, and especially on new technology stuff. Computer programming, information technology, and engineering applications are fields that India is specializing in immediately. While international business may be attracted to China or Indonesia for their low wages, international business is attracted to India for their lower wages AND highly educated and skilled service sectors. Why pay a European programmer when you can pay an Indian programmer half as much? Look for Team Hindu's star to rise fast in our technologically-focused world.

Finally, I will reference the Latin Lefties. Team Lefty if you like. You can love him, you can hate him, or you can depose him in an illegal coup, but Hugo Chavez represents this Latin America shift to the left that has taken on a bit of a revolutionary flavor. While the leftward swing is a political thing, it also heavily incorporates an economic component,

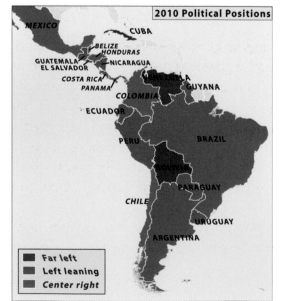

Just look at all that leaning!

which is why I include it here in this section. I won't go so far as to suggest that Team Latin Left is an economic power of global significance, but it is one of global interest, since it represents a significant shift in thinking and strategic economic alliances.

What am I talking about? Team Lefties have a common denominator: a desire for greater social services and wealth redistribution via the state structure. They aren't communist, but they are pretty far to the left side of the Socialist spectrum we discussed in chapter 4. The so-called Bolivarian Revolution has resulted in a couple of things I want you to note: a movement away from outside free trade unions, namely the FTAA, which is currently dead in the water. That is related to the second big thing: a Team Lefty shift away from the US as its sole economic influence, and shifting toward China, but also the Middle East and Sub-Saharan Africa.

Interesting turn of events. Need proof? In May 2008, China joined the board of the Inter-American Development Bank, which is a major source of funds for Latin American countries to finance projects for the social and economic development for the region. Damn. First Asian member of that group. Uncle Sammy ain't happy about losing influence in his backyard, and Team Dragon doesn't mind spreading its love around.

FINALLY THE FINAL FINAL FINAL SUMMARY

We have identified the major forces that shape the future of our planet by battling it out every day politically, militarily, and economically, or sometimes cooperating with each other. Either on their own or within international organizations, the most powerful sovereign states plan, buy, sell, trade, agree, disagree, fight, make peace, plot, unify, embargo, or bitchslap each other in various ways to achieve their objectives. It's not a pretty process, but it's the only one we have until smarter folks like you make it better.

Does it appear that I have forgotten large parts of the globe? Oh no, my friends, I have not forgotten anyone! This chapter was about major movers and shakers, and that list is not all inclusive. Sub-Saharan Africa is at the whim of the international system until they straighten themselves out internally. The Middle East as a region is doomed for eternal conflict and a variety of debilitating internal problems until they get their business straight as well. Most of the sub-regions of Latin America are doing okay, but do not impact world events in a major way. Eastern Europe has effectively become part of Western Europe. Regions like Turkey, Japan and Australia play more of a role within the ranks of Team West than they do on their own.

But history is not done, my friends! Unpredictable events can shake things up quickly in today's world and change the course of states, or regions, or the whole planet. Even with my super-human powers of insight and alcohol absorption, I could not have predicted the attacks of 9/11, the massive Asian tsunami of 2004, or the horrible outcome of the final Indiana Jones movie release. Events like these have huge repercussions for the regions in which they take place, but are also felt throughout the world in the form of global policies and actions that are implemented due to the event itself.

That's why it is important to keep up with your planet. You have taken a very large step in the right direction by reading this book. Congratulations on that feat of endurance and patience. But the game is far from over. Stay involved and educated about is going on in the world, so that when the time comes, you can make the biggest impact for positive change, no matter what it is you decide to do in life.

Lots of people ask me how I keep up with the events and actions of the planet. Well, I do a lot of on-the-spot super hero action within these regions on a daily basis, but when I'm at home in the underground lair, here are a few of the Web sites I keep up with, so that I can keep up with the world:

· http://news.bbc.co.uk/ for daily lightweight international news
· http://www.iht.com/ for more in-depth daily international news

- http://www.worldpress.org/ for deep in-depth weekly assessments of major news events. On this site, you will also find links to every single digital newspaper on the planet from every single country that has them.

You can tune in to CNN, MSNBC, and Fox News Channel anytime to check out the daily arcane domestic political party finger pointing nonsense, and up to the minute status on what-ever celebrity drama is making headlines that day. Mainstream American news sources are not really worth much else.

Always read at least two different news sources for every story you are learning about; make sure one news source is from inside the country where the news happens, and one is outside the country where the news happens. It's the only way to get a balanced view of what's actually happening on the planet.

For those of you who want to do more, here are some ideas and things you can do.

Ever heard of micro-finance? It is an awe-some and easy way to help the poor for those of you who may not have time to volunteer. Some-times charities and organizations get so big and wrapped up in politics that the money never actually gets to those who really need it. What microfinance does, is supplies small loans (sometimes it's even as little an amount as $25) to individuals (usually women, 'cause let's face it guys, when it comes right down to it, women do tend to be the most responsible sex) to help them start small businesses. For example, a source close to the Plaid Avenger was working with a group of Haitian women in the Dominican Republic who were trying to support themselves by making and selling candles. These women were making candles one at a time and it was taking them forever. But, if they had someone who could loan them the money to buy a candle mold, they could make a lot more candles in a lot less time and increase the revenue as a result. Get it? With microloans, a small amount of money can go a long way in helping change and improve lives but with dignity—because it's not a handout, the recipient has to pay the loan back. What my friend in the DR did, was have them pay the loan back to a community account, so that money could stay within the community and be there for the next person needing a loan—recycling money for good—I love it!

If you are interested in micro-lending, check out this site—you can even donate under Team Plaid!

- http://www.kiva.org/team/team_plaid

Not into micro-lending and want to choose a cause instead? Here's another cool website that allows you to give to a grassroots project of your choice.

- http://www.globalgiving.org/dy/fundraiser/helpaddfund/gg.html?projid=4185

If you want to do actual service work (you know you do!), friends of the Plaid Avenger work very closely with this organization and—bonus! It was even started by two college students. See, one or two people can make a difference! Now it's your turn. Now get your asses out there and start changing the world—it's up to YOU!

- http://www.esperanzameanshope.org/

To be unaware and ill-informed about the world around you is to be a passive player in the game of life. Keep your head in the game. Stay informed. Read. Pay attention. Write a letter. Protest. Help someone in need. Start a revolution. Hell, just make the world a better damn place. Peace.

And party on!

GO TO THE WEBSITE...
OR PUTIN WILL HAVE TO
PAY YOU A VISIT.

LOG ON TO
WWW.PLAIDAVENGER.COM
FOR UP TO DATE INFORMATION AROUND THE WORLD AS WELL AS PLAID MERCHANDISE.

Image Credits

Part 1 Opener: map courtesy of Katie Pritchard

CHAPTER 1

Page 4: © 2010 JupiterImages Corporation; **Page 5:** courtesy of Katie Pritchard; **Page 6: top:** courtesy of Katie Pritchard; **bottom:** © brave rabbit, 2010. Used under license from Shutterstock, Inc.; **Page 7:** © 2010 JupiterImages Corporation; **Page 8:** © 2007 JupiterImages Corporation; **Page 13: a.** © 2009 JupiterImages Corporation, **b.** © 2009 JupiterImages Corporation, **c.** © 2009 JupiterImages Corporation, **d.** © 2009 JupiterImages Corporation, **e.** © 2009 JupiterImages Corporation, **f.** Royalty-Free/CORBIS

CHAPTER 2

Page 14: © 2010 JupiterImages Corporation; **Page 17, fig. 2.2:** map source: US Dept. of Agriculture; **Page 27, fig. 2.14:** courtesy of Katie Pritchard

CHAPTER 3

Page 31, fig. 3.1: courtesy of Katie Pritchard; **Page 34: top:** official White House portrait; **bottom:** photo by SSgt. Lance Cheung, U.S. Air Force, from Defense Visual Information Center; **Page 36:** © 2003 by Damon Clark. Used with permission; **Page 37: left:** © 2007 JupiterImages Corporation; **center:** © 2007 JupiterImages Corporation; **right:** © 2007 JupiterImages Corporation; **fig. 3.2:** map source: *The World Factbook*; **Page 38: fig. 3.3:** map source: *The CIA World Factbook*; **bottom:** White House photo by Eric Draper; **Page 39: top:** U.S. Air Force photo by Tech. Sgt. Craig Clapper; **bottom:** map source: *The CIA World Factbook*; **Page 40: top:** map source: University of Texas Libraries; **middle:** © 2007 JupiterImages Corporation; **bottom left:** New York City Police Department; **bottom left center:** photo by Joseph Randall Blanchard (ca. 1898), from Library of Congress; **bottom center:** Swiss Federal Council of the year 2007 from The Federal Authorities of the Swiss Confederation; **bottom right center:** official White House portrait; **bottom right:** Dept. of Defense photo by William M. Firaneck; **Page 41: bottom left center** Saudi Information Office; **bottom right center:** Dept. of Defense photo; **bottom right:** National Archives & Records Administration photo; **Page 42: top:** New York City Police Dept.; **bottom left:** © 2007 JupiterImages Corporation; **bottom right:** © Hulton-Deutsch Collection/CORBIS; **Page 44: left:** photo by Joseph Randall Blanchard (ca. 1898), from Library of Congress; **right:** official White House portrait; **Page 45: top left:** photo by AIC William M. Firaneck, U.S. Air Force, from Defense Visual Information Center; **top right:** White House photo by Eric Draper; **bottom left:** U.S. Air Force photo by Tech. Sgt. Craig Clapper; **Page 46: left:** from Defense Visual Information Center, photographer unknown; **right:** Dept. of Defense photo by Helene C. Stikkel; **Page 47: top:** caricature by Edmund S. Valtman, from Library of Congress; **bottom left:** photo from Iraqi Freedom II CD Collection by Joint Combat Camera composed of Army, Navy, Marine, and Air Force photographers; **bottom right:** Dept. of Defense photo; **Page 48: top:** National Archives & Records Administration photo; **bottom:** National Archives & Records Administration; **Page 49: fig. 3.4:** courtesy of Katie Pritchard; **Page 52: top left:** Bundesregierung/Laurence Chaperon; **top left center:** Dept. of Defense photo; **top right center:** Dept. of Defense photo by William M. Firaneck; **top right:** © European Community, 2008; **middle left:** Turkish Embassy; **middle left center:** official White House photo; **middle right center:** Prime Minister's Office, Government of India; **middle right:** Saudi Information Office; **bottom left:** Brazilian Embassy; **bottom left center:** Government of Argentina; **bottom right center:** © Robert Gilhooly/epa/Corbis; **bottom right:** Government of Argentina; **Page 53: top left center:** U.S. Air Force photo by Tech. Sgt. Craig Clapper; **top right center:** © European Communities, 2006; **top right:** © Anindito Mukherjee/epa/Corbis; **middle left:** © Daniella Zalcman; **middle left center:** © NATO; **middle right center:** © European Community, 2009; **middle right:** official White House Photo by Pete Souza; **bottom left:** Government of Argentina; **bottom left center:** official White House photo by Pete Souza; **bottom right center:** Dept. of Defense photo; **bottom right:** © NATO

CHAPTER 4

Page 54: All images © 2007 JupiterImages Corporation; **Page 55: left:** photo by unknown (ca. 1920), from Library of Congress; **center:** White House photo of Paul Morse; **right:** stipple engraving by MacKenzie (ca. 1805), from Library of Congress; **Page 56: top:** photo by unknown (ca. 1920), from Library of Congress; **bottom:** stipple engraving by MacKenzie (ca. 1805), from Library of Congress; **Page 58: left:** photo by unknown (ca. 1920), from Library of Congress; **left center:** photo by Warren K. Leffler, from Library of Congress; **center:** White House photo by David Bohrer; **right center:** photo by PHI (AW/NAC) Martin Maddock, U.S. Navy, from Defense Visual Information Center; **right:** www.g8russia.ru/; **Page 59: left:** photo from Official Russian Presidential Press and Information Office; **center:** Government of Argentina; **right center:** official White House portrait; **right:** stipple engraving by MacKenzie (ca. 1805), from Library of Congress; **Page 60: top:** photo by Jack Delano (ca. 1940), from Library of Congress; **bottom left:** Dept. of Defense photo by SSGT David Nolan; **bottom center:** U.S. Air Force photo by Airman Ryan Ivacic; **bottom right:** U.S. Air Force photo by Staff Sgt. Vincent Mouzon; **Page 61:** © 2007 JupiterImages Corporation; **Page 63: left:** © 2007 JupiterImages Corporation; **right:** © 2007 JupiterImages Corporation; **Page 64: top left:** © 2007 JupiterImages Corporation; **top right:** © 2007 JupiterImages Corporation; **bottom left:** © 2007 JupiterImages Corporation; **bottom right:** © 2007 JupiterImages Corporation; **Page 65: top right:** © 2007 JupiterImages Corporation; **middle left:** © 2007 JupiterImages Corporation; **middle right:** © 2007 JupiterImages Corporation; **bottom left:** © 2007 JupiterImages Corporation; **Page 67:** National Archives & Records Administration photo; **Page 68:** map courtesy of Katie Pritchard; **Page 70:** map courtesy of Katie Pritchard; **Page 71:** © 2009 JupiterImages Corporation; **Page 73:** From *The Silent War* by John Ames Mitchell, Illustrations by William Balfour Ker (New York: Life Publishing Co, 1906). Courtesy of Library of Congress.

CHAPTER 5

Page 74: Dept. of Defense photos; **Page 76: left:** Courtesy of Library of Congress; **right:** © 2009 JupiterImages Corporation; **Page 73: top:** Photo by Walter P. Miller (1929), Courtesy of Library of Congress; **bottom:** Courtesy of Library of Congress; **Page 78:** © 2009 JupiterImages Corporation; **Page 79:** © 2009 JupiterImages Corporation; **Page 80: top:** © 2009 JupiterImages Corporation; **bottom:** © 2007 JupiterImages Corporation; **Page 81:** © 2009 JupiterImages Corporation; **Page 83:** © 2007 JupiterImages Corporation; **Page 84:** all photos © 2007 JupiterImages Corporation; **Page 85:** © 2009 JupiterImages Corporation; **Page 87: fig. 5.1:** courtesy of Katie Pritchard; **Page 88 & 89:** NASA/Goddard Space Flight Center Scientific Visualization Studio; **Page 90:** map courtesy of Katie Pritchard

CHAPTER 6

Page 94: top left: © 2007 JupiterImages Corporation; **top right:** Frank and Frances Carpenter Collection, from Library of Congress; **middle:** © Royalty-free/CORBIS; **bottom left:** © NATO; **bottom**

right: Copyright © African Union, 2003. All rights reserved. Used by permission; **Page 95:** © 2007 JupiterImages Corporation; **Page 96:** flags: *The World Factbook*; **Page 97: top:** map courtesy of Katie Pritchard; **bottom:** map courtesy of Katie Pritchard; **Page 98:** map courtesy of Katie Pritchard; **Page 99:** map courtesy of Katie Pritchard; **Page 100: top:** map courtesy of Katie Pritchard; **Page 101: top:** OECD logo used by permission; **middle:** © 2007 JupiterImages Corporation; **Page 102: top:** © NATO; **bottom:** © Royalty-free/CORBIS; **Page 103:** NATO logo used by permission of NATO; **bottom:** © NATO; **Page 104:** map courtesy of Katie Pritchard; **Page 105:** courtesy of Katie Pritchard; **Page 106:** *The World Factbook*; **Page 107: top right:** Frank and Frances Carpenter Collection, from Library of Congress; **middle:** Organization of American States; **Page 108: top left & right:** Copyright © African Union, 2003. All rights reserved. Used by permission; **middle right:** U.S. Air Force photo by Tech. Sgt. Jeremy T. Lock; **Page 109: top:** flags: *The World Factbook*; **middle:** flags: *The World Factbook*; **bottom:** © European Communities, 2009; Page 100: top: © European Communities, 2009; **bottom:** photo from Official Russian Presidential Press and Information Office; **Page 111:** WTO logo used with permission; **Page 113:** map courtesy of Katie Pritchard; **Page 115:** Government of Argentina

Part 2 opener: map courtesy of Katie Pritchard

CHAPTER 7

Page 120: Page 164: map courtesy of Katie Pritchard and NOAA; **Page 121:** © NATO; **Page 122:** NASA/Goddard Space Flight Center Scientific Visualization Center; **Page 123:** map source: *The Cambridge Modern History Atlas 1912*, courtesy of the University of Texas Libraries, Perry-Castaneda Library Map Collection; **Page 124:** U.S. Marine Corps photo by Lance Cpl. Kelly R. Chase; **Page 125: top:** map courtesy of Katie Pritchard; **bottom:** all images © 2007 JupiterImages Corporation; **Page 126: top:** photo by M.B. Marcell (ca. 1911), from Library of Congress; **bottom:** U.S. Air Force photo by SSGT Jacob N. Bailey; **Page 127: top:** Dept. of Defense photo by U.S. Navy; **bottom:** U.S. Navy photo by Mass Communication Specialist 3rd Class Kathleen Gorby; **Page 128:** U.S. Navy photo by Mass Communication Specialist 3rd Class Geoffrey Lewis; **Page 129:** Library of Congress; **Page 130:** art by John C. McRae (ca. 1620), from Library of Congress; **Page 131:** U.S. Navy photo by Chief Warrant Officer 4 Seth Rossman; **Page 132: middle:** photo by The New York Times (ca. 1954), from Library of Congress; **bottom:** map courtesy of Katie Pritchard; **Page 134:** U.S. Dept of Agriculture, from Library of Congress; **Page 135:** © 2007 JupiterImages Corporation; **Page 136:** map courtesy of Katie Pritchard & US Dept of Defense; **Page 137: middle:** U.S. Air Force photo by SSGT William Greer; **bottom:** U.S. Air Force photo by A1C Tanya M. Harms; **Page 138: top:** created by Acme Litho. Co., New York (ca. 1910), from Library of Congress; **bottom:** created by Leslie-Judge Co., New York (1917), from Library of Congress; **Page 139:** created by United Cigar Stores Company (1918), from Library of Congress; **Page 140: top:** U.S. Government Printing Office (1943), from Library of Congress; **bottom:** created by American Lithographic Co., New York, from Library of Congress; **Page 141: top:** Illinois Co., Chicago (1917), from Library of Congress; **middle:** American Lithographic Co., New York (1918), from

Library of Congress; **bottom:** official White House photo by Pete Souza; **Page 142: left:** Library of Congress; **middle:** Brady-Handy Photograph Collection, Library of Congress; **right:** official White House photo; **Page 143: left:** official White House photo; **left center:** © European Community; **right center:** official White House photo; **right:** office White House photo

CHAPTER 8

Page 144: map courtesy of Katie Pritchard and NOAA; **Page 146: left:** originally published by Thomas B Noonan, from Library of Congress; **left center:** Library of Congress; **right center:** Library of Congress; **right:** Engraving by W. Holl after painting by Franz Hals, from Library of Congress; **Page 149: top:** *Blue Marble: Next Generation* image produced by Reto Stockli, NASA Earth Observatory (NASA Goddard Space Flight Center); **Page 151: left:** National Archives & Records Administration; **right:** National Archives & Records Administration; **Page 152: top:** Farm Security Administration, Office of War Information Collection 12002-27, from Library of Congress; **bottom:** maps courtesy of Katie Pritchard; **Page 153:** maps courtesy of Katie Pritchard; **Page 155:** created by James Montgomery Flagg (1918), from Library of Congress; **Page 157:** Library of Congress; **Page 158:** map by Katie Pritchard; **Page 159: top:** Library of Congress; **bottom:** © European Communities, 2006; **Page 160: top:** Government of Argentina; **bottom:** Bundesregierung/Laurence Chaperon; **Page 161:** © JupiterImages Corporation; **Page 162: left:** Farm Security Administration—Office of War Information Photograph Collection, from Library of Congress; **left center:** Library of Congress; **right center:** National Archives & Records Administration; **right:** Dept. of Defense photo; **Page 163: left:** © European Communities, 2009; **left center:** © European Communities, 2009; **center:** © European Communities, 2006; **right center:** © European Communities, 2010; **right:** © European Communities, 2003

CHAPTER 9

Page 164: map courtesy of Katie Pritchard and NOAA; **Page 167: top:** © 2008 JupiterImages Corporation; **bottom:** map source: *The World Factbook*; **Page 168:** map source: *The World Factbook*; **Page 169: top:** map source: *The World Factbook*; **bottom:** map source: *The World Factbook*; **Page 171: top:** phioto © 1941 by J. Russell & Sons, from Library of Congress; **bottom:** map source: *The World Factbook*; **Page 172: top:** map source: *The World Factbook*; **bottom:** map source: *The World Factbook*; **Page 173:** source: *Nuclear Weapons and NATO: Analytical Survey of Literature* by U.S. Dept. of the Army, courtesy of University of Texas Libraries Perry-Castaneda Map Collection; **Page 174: top:** map source: *The World Factbook*; **bottom:** map source: *The World Factbook*; **Page 175:** map courtesy of Katie Pritchard; **Page 176: bottom left:** map by U.S. Central Intelligence Agency, courtesy of University of Texas Libraries, Perry-Castaneda Map Collection; **bottom right:** map by Katie Pritchard; **Page 177: left:** Dept. of Defense photo by Tech. Sgt. Cedric H. Rudisill, US. Air Force; **left center:** © NATO; **right center:** © NATO; **right:** photo from Official Russian Presidential Press and Information Office; **Page 179: top:** © NATO; **bottom:** © 2008 JupiterImages Corporation; **Page 180:** © 2008 JupiterImages

Corporation; **Page 181: top:** © 2008 JupiterImages Corporation; **bottom:** from *Former Yugoslavia: A Map Folio* (1992) by CIA, courtesy of University of Texas Libraries; **Page 182: left:** White House Photo Office Collection (1971), from Library of Congress; **center:** © Lucas Jackson/Reuters/Corbis; **right:** © Herbert P. Oczeret/epa/Corbis; **Page 183:** CIA map, courtesy of University of Texas Libraries; **Page 184:** map by Katie Pritchard; **Page 186: left:** George Grantham Bain Collection, Library of Congress; **center:** National Archives & Records Administration; **right:** © NATO; **Page 187: left:** Dept of Defense photo by Robert D. Ward; **left center:** © NATO; **right center:** © European Communities, 2007; **right:** © NATO

CHAPTER 10

Page 188: top: map courtesy of Katie Pritchard and NOAA; **bottom:** created by Strobridge Lithography Co. (1895), from Library of Congress; **Page 189: top:** © 2007 JupiterImages Corporation; **bottom:** adapted from *Blue Marble: Next Generation* image produced by Reto Stockli, NASA Earth Observatory (NASA Goddard Space Flight Center); **Page 190: top:** created by Strobridge Lithography Co. (ca. 1898), from Library of Congress; **bottom:** created by Strobridge Lithography Co. (ca. 1896), from Library of Congress; **Page 191:** map source: *The World Factbook*; **Page 192: top:** created by W. Holland (1803), from Library of Congress; **bottom:** map source: *The World Factbook*; **Page 193: top:** scanned from Helmolt, J.F. ed. *History of the World* (New York, Dodd, Mead & Co., 1902); **top middle:** from *Harpers Monthly 1883, vol. 67* (page 99), Library of Congress; **bottom middle:** engraving by A. Muller (1879), Library of Congress; **bottom:** scanned from Helmolt, J.F. ed. *History of the World* (New York, Dodd, Mead & Co., 1902); **Page 194:** from the George Grantham Bain Collection, Library of Congress; **Page 195: top:** lithography by M.A. Striel'tsova (ca. 1918), from Library of Congress; **bottom left:** *New York Times*, 1919, Library of Congress; **left center:** *Tsar Nicholas II* (1915) by Boris Kustodiyev; **right center:** Library of Congress; **right:** photo ca. 1909; **Page 196: left:** Library of Congress; **right:** photo from *Liberty's Victorious Conflict: A Photographic History of the World War* by The Magazine Circulation Co., Chicago, 1918; **Page 197:** map source: *The World Factbook*; **Page 198:** from New York World-Telegram & the Sun Newspaper Photograph Collection, Library of Congress; **Page 199:** U.S. Signal Corps photo, from Library of Congress; **Page 200: top:** photo by U.S. Office of War Information Overseas Picture Division, Library of Congress; **bottom:** map source: *The World Factbook*; **Page 201:** photo by U.S. Office of War Information Overseas Picture Division, Library of Congress; **Page 203:** © 2007 JupiterImages Corporation; **Page 204:** official White House portrait; **Page 205: top left:** Library of Congress; **top center:** U.S. Signal Corps photo, from Library of Congress; **top right:** photo from Franklin D. Roosevelt Library, Library of Congress; **bottom left:** White House Photo Collection, Library of Congress; **bottom left center:** © Bettmann/Corbis; **bottom right center:** © Bettmann/Corbis; **bottom right:** White House Photo Collection, Library of Congress; **Page 206:** White House Photo Collection, Library of Congress; **Page 207:** photo by Earle D. Akin Co, 1909, from Library of Congress; **Page 210:** map courtesy of Katie Pritchard; **bottom:** photo from Official Russian Press and Information Office; ; **Page 211: top:** © NATO; **middle left:** © NATO; **middle right:** photo from Official

Russian Press and Information Office; **bottom:** photo from Official Russian Press and Information Office; **Page 212:** map from U.S. Dept. of Energy; **Page 213:** © NATO; **Page 214:** Produced by the Office of The Geographer and Global Issues, Bureau of Intelligence and Research, US Dept. of State, courtesy of University of Texas Libraries; **Page 215:** cover of *The Great Train Robbery* by Scott Marble, 1896, from Library of Congress; **Page 216: left:** George Grantham Bain Collection, Library of Congress; **right center:** U.S. Signal Corps photo, from Library of Congress; **right:** © NATO; **Page 217: left:** © European Communities, 2009; **left center:** © European Communities, 2009; **right center:** © NATO; **right:** © NATO

CHAPTER 11

Page 219: map courtesy of Katie Pritchard and NOAA; **Page 220: top:** Dept. of Defense photo by Mass Communication Specialist Seaman Bryan Reckard, U.S. Navy; **middle:** Dept. of Defense photo by Tech. Sgt. Rob Marshall; **bottom:** Blue Marble: next Generation image produced by Reto Stockli, NASA Earth Observatory (NASA Goddard Space Flight Center); **Page 221: top:** Tsuta-ya Kichizo (1858), from Library of Congress; **bottom:** U.S. Navy photo by Photographer's Mate 2nd Class Nathanael T. Miller; **Page 222: top:** Library of Congress; **bottom:** Library of Congress; **Page 223: left:** Dept. of Defense photo by PHI (AW) M. Clayton Farrington, U.S. Navy; **right:** photo by Mathew B. Brady, from Library of Congress; **Page 224: left:** Heinoya (1870), from Library of Congress; **right:** Dept. of Defense photo; **Page 225:** art by Rivinger (1860), from Library of Congress; **Page 226:** map source: *The World Factbook*; **Page 227:** photo by U.S. War Department Signal Cops, from Library of Congress; **Page 228:** Office for Emergency Management, Office of War Information; **Page 229: top:** image created by James Montgomery Flagg for Office of War Information Domestic Operations Branch, from National Archives & Records Administration; **bottom:** from the George Frantham Bain Collection, Library of Congress; **Page 230: top left:** photo by Office of War Information Overseas Operations Branch (August 9, 1945), from National Archives & Records Administration; **top right:** Dept. of Defense photo, Dept. of the Navy, U.S. Marine Corps; **bottom right:** photo by U.S. Army, from Library of Congress; **Page 231: top left:** photo from NASA; **top left center:** photo ca. 1918, from Library of Congress; **top right center:** © European Communities, 2006; **top right:** © Robert Gilhooly/epa/Corbis; **bottom:** all photos © 2007 JupiterImages Corporation; **Page 233: top left:** © 2008 JupiterImages Corporation; **middle right:** Dept of Defense photo; **bottom left:** Dept. of Defense photo; **Page 234:** Dept. of Defense photo; **Page 235: left:** Dept. of Defense photo by Helen C. Stikkel; **right:** © Robert Gilhooly/epa/Corbis; **Page 236:** all photos © 2008 JupiterImages Corporation; **Page 237:** Library of Congress; **Page 238: left:** Harris & Ewing Collection, Library of Congress; **left center:** Library of Congress; **right:** Dept. of Defense photo; **Page 239: left:** © European Communities, 2004; **right:** © Robert Gilhooly/epa/Corbis;

CHAPTER 12

Page 220: map courtesy of Katie Pritchard and NOAA; **Page 241: left:** *Blue Marble: Next Generation* image produced by Reto Stockli, NASA

Earth Observatory (NASA Goddard Space Flight Center); **right:** NASA/Goddard Space Flight Center Scientific Visualization Studio; **Page 242:** all images: © 2007 JupiterImages Corporation; **Page 244:** all images: © 2007 JupiterImages Corporation; **Page 245:** ca. 1915, Library of Congress; **Page 246: top:** Dept. of Defense photo by Tech. Sgt. Jerry Morrison, U.S. Air Force; **bottom:** © 2007 JupiterImages Corporation; **Page 247:** © 2007 JupiterImages Corporation; **Page 248: top:** Dept. of Defense photo by R.D. Ward; bottom; © 2007 JupiterImages Corporation; **Page 249: left:** stereograph (1919), from Library of Congress; **right:** poster by Farmer's (1915), from Library of Congress; **Page 250:** lithography by Cincinnati Lithography Co., from Library of Congress; **Page 251:** Courtesy of Foster's Americas; **Page 252: left:** Dept. of Defense photo by Robert D. Ward; **center:** Dept. of Defense photo by Cherie Cullen; **right:** © Anindito Mukherjee/epa/Corbis

CHAPTER 13

Page 254: map courtesy of Katie Pritchard and NOAA; **Page 255: top:** photo ca. 1867, gift of Oliver Wendell Homes, from Library of Congress; **bottom:** photo by William Henry Jackson (ca. 1885), from Library of Congress; **Page 256:** map by CIA, courtesy of University of Texas Libraries; **Page 257:** all maps: from CIA, courtesy of University of Texas Libraries; ; **Page 258: top:** map courtesy of Katie Pritchard; **bottom:** Library of Congress; **Page 259: top:** map source: *The World Factbook*; **bottom:** photo from the Frank & Frances Carpenter Collection, Library of Congress; **Page 260:** © 2008 JupiterImages Corporation; **Page 261: bottom:** Library of Congress; **Page 262: top:** scanned from Helmolt, J.F. ed. *History of the World* (New York, Dodd, Mead & Co., 1902); **bottom:** courtesy of Brazilian Embassy; **Page 263: top left:** Library of Congress; **top left center:** Government of Argentina; **top center:** courtesy of Brazilian Embassy; **top right center:** photo by Warren K. Leffler, from Library of Congress; **top right:** Government of Argentina; **bottom:** photo ca. 1900, from Library of Congress; **Page 264: top:** from *Judge, February 15, 1896*, Library of Congress; **bottom:** photo ca. 1900, from Library of Congress; **Page 265: top:** photo by Elias Goldensky (1933), from Library of Congress; **bottom:** photo by Warren K. Leffler, from Library of Congress; **Page 267:** both photos by U.S. Drug Enforcement Administration; **Page 269:** map courtesy of Katie Pritchard; **Page 270:** Government of Argentina; **Page 272:** maps courtesy of Katie Pritchard; **Page 273:** © 2007 JupiterImages Corporation; **Page 274: left:** painting by Ricardo Acevedo Bernal; **left center:** The White House Historical Association (White House Collection); **right center:** National Archives & Records Administration; **right:** Library of Congress

CHAPTER 14

Page 276: map courtesy of Katie Pritchard and NOAA; **Page 278: top:** from *Historical Atlas* (1911) by William Shepherd (pp. 186-187), courtesy of University of Texas Libraries; **bottom:** map source: *The World Factbook*; **Page 279:** from *Historical Atlas* (1911) by William Shepherd (p. 106), courtesy of University of Texas Libraries; **Page 280:** all maps: *The World Factbook*; **Page 281:** all maps: The *World Factbook*; **top right:** © 2007 JupiterImages Corporation; **Page 282:** all images © 2007

JupiterImages Corporation; **Page 283:** © 2007 JupiterImages Corporation; **Page 284: top:** © 2007 JupiterImages Corporation; **bottom:** all maps: *The World Factbook*; **Page 285:** map source: *The World Factbook*; **Page 287: top:** from George Grantham Bain Collection, Library of Congress; **bottom:** from George Grantham Bain Collection; **Page 289: top:** map source: U.S. Drug Enforcement Administration; **bottom:** Government of Argentina; **Page 290: left:** Library of Congress; **left center:** engraving by W. Holl, Library of Congress; **right center:** Library of Congress; **right:** George Grantham Bain Collection, Library of Congress; **Page 291:** © European Communities, 2007

CHAPTER 15

Page 292: map courtesy of Katie Pritchard and NOAA; **Page 293: top:** from *This Dynamic Earth: The Story of Plate Tectonics* (online edition) by W. Jacquelyne Kious and Robert I. Tilling, prepared by U.S. Geological Survey; **bottom:** © 2007 JupiterImages Corporation; **Page 294: top:** © 2007 JupiterImages Corporation; **bottom:** from *Historical Atlas* (1911) by William Shepherd (p. 213), courtesy of University of Texas Libraries; **Page 295:** map courtesy of Katie Pritchard; **Page 296: top: left, left center, center right center:** all images © 2007 JupiterImages Corporation; **top right:** photo by U.S. Drug Enforcement Administration; **bottom:** UnifruitCo Magazine, October 1948, from Library of Congress; **Page 297: top:** photo by Capt. Charles Davis, U.S. Marine Corps, from National Archives & Records Administration; **bottom:** ca. 1920, from Library of Congress; **Page 298:** U.S. Air Force photo by Tech. Sgt. Sonny Cohrs; **Page 299: top:** official U.S. Marine Corps photo; **bottom:** Dept. of Defense photo; **Page 301:** map courtesy of Katie Pritchard; **Page 302:** © Christian Poveda/Corbis; **Page 303:** © 2007 JupiterImages Corporation; **Page 304:** © Christian Poveda/Corbis; **Page 305: left:** U.S. Marshals Service; **right:** U.S. Air Force photo by Tech. Sgt. Sonny Cohrs

CHAPTER 16

Page 306: map courtesy of Katie Pritchard and NOAA; **Page 307:** from *This Dynamic Earth: The Story of Plate Tectonics* (online edition) by W. Jacquelyne Kious and Robert I. Tilling, prepared by U.S. Geological Survey; **Page 308:** all images © 2007 JupiterImages Corporation; **Page 310: top:** © 2007 JupiterImages Corporation; **bottom:** photo by Jack Delano, from Farm Securities Administration Collection, Library of Congress; **Page 311: top:** © 2007 JupiterImages Corporation; **bottom:** Library of Congress; **Page 312:** photo by C.B. Waite, from Frank and Frances Carpenter Collection, Library of Congress; **Page 313: top:** map source: *The World Factbook*; **bottom:** created ca. 1830, from Library of Congress; **Page 314:** map source: *The World Factbook*; **Page 315: top:** © 2007 JupiterImages Corporation; **bottom:** map source: *The World Factbook*; **Page 316: top:** © 2009 JupiterImages Corporation; **bottom:** © 2007 JupiterImages Corporation; **Page 317:** photo by Warren K. Leffler, from Library of Congress; **Page 318: top:** Dept. of Defense photo; **bottom:** © 2007 JupiterImages Corporation; **Page 319: top:** © 2009 JupiterImages Corporation; **Page 320: top:** photo by U.S. Drug Enforcement Agency; **middle and bottom:** © 2007 JupiterImages

Corporation; **Page 321: top:** © David Brooks/Corbis; **bottom:** photo by U.S. Drug Enforcement Administration; **Page 322: left:** © David Brooks/Corbis; **right:** Photo by Alberto Korda; Page 323: left: © European Communities, 2005; right: Government of Argentina

CHAPTER 17

Page 324: map courtesy of Katie Pritchard and NOAA; **Page 325: top:** *Blue Marble: Next Generation* image by Reto Stockli, NASA Earth Observatory (NASA Goddard Space Flight Center); **bottom:** © 2007 JupiterImages Corporation; **Page 326: top:** scanned from Helmolt, J.F. ed. *History of the World* (New York, Dodd, Mead & Co., 1902); **bottom:** *Blue Marble: Next Generation* image by Reto Stockli, NASA Earth Observatory (NASA Goddard Space Flight Center); **Page 327: top left & right:** *Blue Marble: Next Generation* image by Reto Stockli, NASA Earth Observatory (NASA Goddard Space Flight Center); **middle left & right:** © 2007 JupiterImages Corporation; **bottom:** NASA/Goddard Space Flight Center Scientific Visualization Studio; **Page 328:** map source: *The World Factbook*; **Page 329: left:** photogravure by G. Garrie, 1903, from Library of Congress; **right:** etching by Max Rosenthal, 1902, from Library of Congress; **Page 330: top:** Government of Argentina; **middle:** U.S. Air Force photo by SSGT Karen L. Sanders; **bottom:** map courtesy of Katie Pritchard; **Page 331:** map source: Office of National Drug Control Policy; **Page 332: bottom left:** U.S. News & World Report Magazine Photograph Collection, from Library of Congress; **bottom center:** Government of Argentina; **bottom right:** Government of Argentina; **Page 333:** map courtesy of Katie Pritchard; **Page 335: top:** © 2007 JupiterImages Corporation; **bottom:** scanned from Helmolt, J.F. ed. *History of the World* (New York, Dodd, Mead & Co., 1902); **Page 336:** map courtesy of Katie Pritchard; **Page 337: left:** photo by PHI (AW.NAC) Martin Maddock, U.S. Navy, from Defense Visual Information Center; **right:** Dept. of Defense photo by Helene C. Stikkel; **bottom:** www.g8russia.ru/; **Page 338: left:** Painting by Ricardo Acevedo Bermal; **center:** Library of Congress; **right:** Painting by Ölgemälde von einem unbekannten Maler; **Page 339: top left:** Government of Argentina; **top center:** Government of Argentina; **top right:** Government of Argentina; **bottom left:** © European Communities, 2009; **bottom center:** Government of Argentina; **bottom right:** Government of Argentina

CHAPTER 18

Page 342: map courtesy of Katie Pritchard and NOAA; **Page 343: top:** photo by PHAN Christopher B. Stoltz, U.S. Navy, from Defense Visual Information Center; **bottom:** U.S. Marine Corps photo by Sgt. David J. Murphy; **Page 344: top:** *Blue Marble: Next Generation* image by Reto Stockli, NASA Earth Observatory (NASA Goddard Space Flight Center); **bottom:** map source: CIA map courtesy of University of Texas Libraries; **Page 345:** Oil & Gas Journal; **Page 346: left & right:** © 2007 JupiterImages Corporation; ; **Page 347:** map courtesy of Katie Pritchard; **Page 348:** map scanned from *Atlas of the Middle East* (CIA, 1993), courtesy of University of Texas Libraries; **Page 349:** map source: CIA map courtesy of University of Texas Libraries; **Page 350:** map from *Iraq: A Map Folio* (CIA, 1992), courtesy of University of Texas Libraries;

Page 351: top left: © Daniella Zalcman; **top left center:** Dept. of Defense photo by Tech. Sgt. Jerry Morrison, U.S. Air Force; **top right center:** Dept of Defense photo by Tech. Sgt. Jerry Morrison, U.S. Air Force; **top right:** © European Community, 2008; **middle left:** Dept. of Defense photo by R.D. Ward; **middle left center:** Dept. of Defense photo; **middle right center:** © European Community, 2008; **middle right:** © T. Mughal/epa/Corbis; **bottom left:** Dept. of Defense photo; **bottom left center:** www.g8russia.ru/; **bottom right center:** Saudi Information Office; **Page 352: top:** from George Grantham Bain Collection, Library of Congress; **bottom:** map scanned from *Atlas of the Middle East* (CIA, 1993), courtesy of University of Texas Libraries; **Page 353:** map scanned from *Atlas of the Middle East* (CIA, 1993), courtesy of University of Texas Libraries; **Page 354:** photo from National Archives & Records Administration; **Page 356: top:** from Library of Congress; **bottom left:** Girsch & Roehsler (1892), from Library of Congress; **bottom right:** photogravure by G. Barrie after P. Baretto (1902), from Library of Congress; **Page 357: top & bottom:** © 2007 JupiterImages Corporation; **Page 358: top:** map from *Historical Atlas* (1923) by William Shepherd, courtesy of University of Texas Libraries; **middle:** created by Jacques Louis David, from Library of Congress; **bottom:** © JupiterImages Corporation; **Page 360: left:** © 2007 JupiterImages Corporation; **right:** from George Grantham Bain Collection, Library of Congress; **Page 362: left:** White House photo; **right center:** Dept. of Defense photo; **right:** Dept. of Defense photo by R.D. Ward; **Page 363: top left:** Dept. of Defense photo by Staff Sgt. Shane A. Cuomo, U.S. Air Force; **top middle:** Dept. of Defense photo by Spc. Katherine M. Roth, U.S. Army; **top right:** Dept. of Defense photo by Lance Cpl. Samantha L. Jones, U.S. Marine Corps; **bottom left:** Library of Congress; **bottom right:** Dept. of Defense photo; **Page 364: top left:** Saudi Information Office; **top right:** © Mohsen Shandiz/Corbis; **bottom left:** Dept of Defense photo by Mass Communication Specialist 1st Class Chad J. McNeeley, U.S. Navy; **bottom right:** photo from Official Russian Presidential Press and Information Office; **Page 365: top left:** © European Communities, 2010; **top right:** U.S. Navy photo by Mass Communication Specialist 2nd Class Jesse B. Awalt; **bottom left:** © European Communities, 2005; **bottom right:** U.S. Navy photo by Mass Communication Specialist 2nd Class Jesse B. Awalt

CHAPTER 18 ADDENDUM

Page 368: map scanned from *Atlas of the Middle East* (CIA, 1993), courtesy of University of Texas Libraries; **Page 369:** Dept. of Defense photo by TSGT Jim Varhegyi; **Page 370:** map scanned from *Atlas of the Middle East* (CIA, 1993), courtesy of University of Texas Libraries; **Page 371:** photo from the George Grantham Bain Collection, Library of Congress; **Page 372:** maps from *The World Factbook*; **Page 373:** maps from *The World Factbook*; **bottom:** photo from Frank & Frances Carpenter Collection, Library of Congress; **Page 374:** map courtesy of Katie Pritchard; **Page 375:** White House photo; **Page 376: top:** photo from George Grantham Bain Collection, Library of Congress; **bottom:** map from *Historical Atlas* (1911) by William Shepherd, courtesy of University of Texas Libraries; **Page 377:** CIA map, courtesy of University of Texas Libraries; **Page 378: left:** © Bettmann/Corbis;

right: © Bettmann/Corbis; **Page 379: top:** CIA map adapted by Katie Pritchard, courtesy of University of Texas Libraries; **bottom:** © Daniella Zalcman; **Page 380: top:** ca. 1917, from Library of Congress; **bottom:** Dept. of Defense photo; **Page 382:** CIA map, courtesy of University of Texas Libraries; **Page 383:** Dept. of Defense photo; **Page 384: top left:** National Archives & Records Administration; **top left center:** Dept. of Defense photo; **top right center:** © Bettmann/Corbis; **top right:** Dept of Defense photo; **middle left:** Saudi Information Office; **middle left center:** © Mohsen Shandiz/Corbis; **middle right center:** © European Communities, 2010; **middle right:** © European Communities, 2004; **bottom left:** Dept. of Defense photo by R.D. Ward; **bottom middle:** photo from Official Russian Presidential Press and Information Office; **bottom right:** © European Communities, 2009

CHAPTER 19

Page 386: map courtesy of Katie Pritchard and NOAA; **Page 387:** © 2009 JupiterImages Corporation; **Page 388: top:** © 2007 JupiterImages Corporation; **bottom:** © JupiterImages Corporation; **Page 389: top:** map courtesy of Katie Pritchard; **bottom:** CIA map, courtesy of University of Texas Libraries; **Page 390: left:** maps from *The World Factbook*; **right:** by Elihu Vedder, 1896, Library of Congress; **Page 391: left:** stereo by Underwood & Underwood, 1907, Library of Congress; **right:** maps from *The World Factbook*; **Page 392:** map from *The Cambridge Modern History Atlas*, 1912, courtesy of University of Texas Libraries; **bottom:** © 2007 JupiterImages Corporation; **Page 393: top:** from George Grantham Bain Collection, Library of Congress; **bottom:** from George Grantham Bain Collection, Library of Congress; **Page 394:** map source: *The World Factbook*; **Page 395:** from George Grantham Bain Collection, Library of Congress; **Page 396: top:** © JupiterImages Corporation; **bottom:** Dept. of Defense photo by R.D. Ward; **Page 397:** Dept. of Defense photo by Tech Sgt. Jim Varhegyi; **Page 398:** map courtesy of Katie Pritchard; **Page 399: top:** Government of Argentina; **bottom:** CIA map, courtesy of University of Texas Libraries; **Page 400:** Dept. of Defense photo by PH2 (AC) Mark Kettenhofen, U.S. Navy; **Page 401: top:** © NATO; **bottom:** © NATO; **Page 402:** Dept. of Defense photo by SSgt. Jeremy T. Lock, U.S. Air Force; **Page 403: top:** © NATO; **bottom:** © 2007 JupiterImages Corporation; **Page 404: left:** from George Grantham Bain Collection, Library of Congress; **center:** © European Communities, 2004; **right:** © European Communities, 2009

CHAPTER 20

Page 406: map courtesy of Katie Pritchard and NOAA; **Page 407: top:** CDC photo by Dr. Lyle Conrad; **bottom:** adapted from *Blue Marble: Next Generation* image produced by Reto Stockli, NASA Earth Observatory (NASA Goddard Space Flight Center); **Page 408: top:** *Blue Marble: Next Generation* image produced by Reto Stockli, NASA Earth Observatory (NASA Goddard Space Flight Center); **bottom:** from *This Dynamic Earth: The Story of Plate Tectonics* (online edition) by W. Jacquelyne Kious and Robert I. Tilling, prepared by U.S. Geological Survey; **Page 409:** NASA/Goddard Space Flight Center Scientific Visualization Studio; **Page 410:** map from *Literary and Historical*

Atlas of Africa and Australasia by J.G. Bartholomew (1913), courtesy of University of Texas Libraries; **Page 411:** map source: *The World Factbook*; **Page 412: top:** map from *The Struggle for Colonial Dominion*, courtesy of University of Texas Libraries; **bottom:** photo by Sophus Williams (1884), Library of Congress; **Page 413:** map source: *The World Factbook*; **Page 414:** map source: *The World Factbook*; **Page 415:** map courtesy of Katie Pritchard; **Page 417: top:** caricature by Edmund S. Valtman, from Library of Congress; **top middle:** Dept. of Defense photo by Frank Hall; **bottom middle:** Dept. of Defense photo; **bottom:** © European Community, 2008; **Page 419:** CIA map, courtesy of University of Texas Libraries; **Page 420: top:** © JupiterImages Corporation; **bottom:** USDA map; **Page 421: top:** photo ca. 1911, from Library of Congress; **bottom:** © JupiterImages Corporation; **Page 422:** © JupiterImages Corporation; **Page 423:** map courtesy of Katie Pritchard; **Page 426: top:** © JupiterImages Corporation; **bottom:** Dept. of Defense photo by Airman 1st Class Marc I. Lane, U.S. Air Force; **Page 427: bottom:** © 2009 JupiterImages Corporation; **Page 428: left:** caricature by Edmund S. Valtman, from Library of Congress; **center:** Dept of Defense photo by Frank Hall; **right:** USSR stamp; **bottom left:** © European Communities, 2009; **bottom right:** U.S. Navy photo by Mass Communication Specialist 2nd Class Jesse B. Awalt; **Page 429: left:** © European Communities, 2004; **center:** Official White House Photo by Lawrence Jackson; **right:** © Afolabi Sotunde/Corbis

CHAPTER 21

Page 432: map courtesy of Katie Pritchard and NOAA; **Page 433:** map from U.S. Geological Survey; **Page 434: top:** from *This Dynamic Earth: The Story of Plate Tectonics* (online edition) by W. Jacquelyne Kious and Robert I. Tilling, prepared by U.S. Geological Survey; **middle:** © JupiterImages Corporation; **bottom:** *Blue Marble: Next Generation* image produced by Reto Stockli, NASA Earth Observatory (NASA Goddard Space Flight Center); **Page 435:** map courtesy of Katie Pritchard; **Page 436: bottom:** map source: *The World Factbook*; **Page 438:** map courtesy of Katie Pritchard; **Page 439: top:** photo by Underwood & Underwood (1903), from Library of Congress; **bottom:** map courtesy of Katie Pritchard; **Page 440:** U.S. Army Air Forces photo (ca. 1942), from Library of Congress; **Page 441: top:** created by Maurice Merlin for Works Project Administration, from Library of Congress; **bottom:** created by Courier Lithography Co. (1899), from Library of Congress; **Page 442:** © 2009 JupiterImages Corporation; **Page 443:** © Bettmann/Corbis; **Page 444:** map courtesy of Katie Pritchard; **Page 445: top:** map source: *The World Factbook*; **bottom:** Dept. of Defense photo; **Page 446:** © 2007 JupiterImages Corporation; **Page 447:** CIA map, courtesy of University of Texas Libraries; **Page 448: top:** © European Community, 2009; **bottom:** © 2007 JupiterImages Corporation; **Page 450:** Dept. of Defense photo; **Page 451: top:** CIA map, courtesy of University of Texas Libraries; **bottom:** © T. Mughal/ epa/Corbis; **Page 452:** CIA map, courtesy of University of Texas Libraries; **Page 453: top:** Dept. of Defense photo by Staff Sgt Val Gempis; **bottom:** Dept. of Defense photo; **Page 456: left center:** Ministry of Information & Broadcasting, Government of Pakistan; **right center:** © European Communities, 2008; **right:** © European Communities, 2008

CHAPTER 22

Page 458: map courtesy of Katie Pritchard and NOAA; **Page 459:** Dept. of Defense photo by SSgt. Jeremy T. Lock, U.S. Air Force; **Page 460: top:** *Blue Marble: Next Generation* image produced by Reto Stockli, NASA Earth Observatory (NASA Goddard Space Flight Center); **middle:** Dept. of Defense photo by SSgt. Cherie A. Thurlby, U.S. Air Force; **bottom:** Dept. of Defense photo by Sgt. Michael A. Abney, U.S. Army; **Page 461: top:** Dept. of Defense photo by SSgt. Joseph P. Collins, Jr., U.S. Army; **bottom:** map courtesy of Katie Pritchard; **Page 462: top:** photo ca. 1915 from Sergei Mikhailovich Prokdi-Gorskii Collection, Library of Congress: **bottom:** CIA map, courtesy of University of Texas Library; **Page 463: top:** Dept. of Defense photo by SSgt. Jeremy T. Lock, U.S. Air Force; **middle:** photo ca. 1915 from Sergei Mikhailovich Prokdi-Gorskii Collection, Library of Congress: **bottom:** map source: *The World Factbook*; **Page 464:** photo from Sergei Mikhailovich Prokdi-Gorskii Collection, Library of Congress; **Page 465:** Dept. of Defense photo by Spc. Jerry T. Combes, U.S. Army; **Page 466:** map source: U.S. Energy Information Administration; **Page 467: top:** photo from Enduring Freedom CD Collection by Joint Combat Camera composed by Army, Navy, Marine, and Air Force photographers, from Defense Visual Information Center; **bottom:** Dept. of Defense photo by Cpl. Justin L. Schaeffer, U.S. Marine Corps; **Page 468:** Dept. of Defense photo by SSgt. Jeremy T. Lock, U.S. Air Force; **Page 469: top:** Dept. of Defense photo by SSgt. Jeremy T. Lock, U.S. Air Force; **bottom:** map courtesy of Katie Pritchard; **Page 471:** Dept. of Defense photo by SSgt. Jeffrey Allen, U.S. Air Force; **Page 472: left:** National Palace Museum in Taipei; **center:** Official White House Photo by Pete Souza; **right:** Official White House Photo by Pete Souza

CHAPTER 23

Page 474: map courtesy of Katie Pritchard and NOAA; **Page 475:** *Blue Marble: Next Generation* image produced by Reto Stockli, NASA Earth Observatory (NASA Goddard Space Flight Center); **Page 476:** CIA map, courtesy of University of Texas Library; **Page 477: top:** CIA map, courtesy of University of Texas Libraries; **bottom:** © 2007 JupiterImages Corporation; **Page 478:** CIA maps, courtesy of University of Texas Libraries; **Page 479:** maps courtesy of Katie Pritchard; **Page 480:** © 2007 JupiterImages Corporation; **Page 481:** wood engraving in *The Illustrated London News* (1858 March 6, p. 233), from Library of Congress; **Page 482: top:** © 2007 JupiterImages Corporation; **bottom:** map source: *The World Factbook*; **Page 483: top:** stereograph by Underwood & Underwood (1901), from Library of Congress; **middle** lithography by Joseph Keppler (1900), from Library of Congress; **bottom:** from George Grantham Bain Collection (1902), Library of Congress; **Page 484: left:** photo ca. 1945, from Library of Congress; **right:** © 2007 JupiterImages Corporation; **Page 485: left:** map by Mark D. Sherry from *The China Defensive Campaign* brochure, courtesy of University of Texas Libraries; **right:** stereograph by Underwood & Underwood (1901), from Library of Congress; **Page 486:** map from *The Scottish Geographical Magazine* (Volume XII: 1896), courtesy of University of Texas Libraries; **Page 487:** photo from U.S. News & World Report Magazine Photograph Collection (1979), Library of Congress;

Page 489: top: © 2007 JupiterImages Corporation; **bottom:** © 2008 JupiterImages Corporation; **Page 490:** WTO logo used with permission; **Page 491:** © 2007 JupiterImages Corporation; **Page 492: left:** www.g8russia.ru/; **right:** © European Community, 2008; **Page 493: top:** map source: *The World Factbook*; **bottom:** photo from House Committee on Foreign Affairs; **Page 494:** both © 2007 JupiterImages Corporation; **Page 495:** CIA map, courtesy of University of Texas Libraries; **Page 496: top left:** photo by U.S. Information Agency Press and Publications Service Visual Services Branch, from National Archives & Records Administration; **top right:** photo by U.S. Information Agency Press and Publications Service Visual Services Branch, from National Archives & Records Administration; **bottom:** NASA/Goddard Space Flight Center Scientific Visualization Studio; **Page 497: left:** © Toshiyuki Aizawa/Reuters/Corbis; **right:** © European Community, 2009; **Page 498:** National Archives & Records Administration; **Page 499:** © 2007 JupiterImages Corporation; **Page 500: left:** Library of Congress; **center:** National Archives & Records Administration; **right:** National Archives & Records Administration; **Page 501: left to right:** © European Communities, 2009; © European Communities, 2009; © Richard Chung/Corbis; © European Communities, 2006; Official White House Photo by Pete Souza; photo from Official Russian Presidential Press and Information Office

CHAPTER 24

Page 502: map courtesy of Katie Pritchard and NOAA; **Page 503:** U.S. Geological Survey map; **Page 504: bottom:** © 2008 JupiterImages Corporation; **Page 505:** © 2007 JupiterImages Corporation; **Page 506: top:** © 2007 JupiterImages Corporation; **bottom:** © 2008 JupiterImages Corporation; **Page 507:** map from *Cambridge Modern History Atlas*, edited by Sir Adolphus Ward et al (London; Cambridge University Press, 1912), courtesy of University of Texas Libraries; **Page 508:** map from *Historical Atlas* (1923) by William Shepherd (pp. 186-187), courtesy of University of Texas Libraries; **Page 509: top:** map by Jennifer L. Bailey from *Philippines Campaign* brochure, courtesy of University of Texas Libraries; **bottom:** poster by Office for Emergency Management War Production Board, from National Archives & Records Administration; **Page 511: top:** © 2007 JupiterImages Corporation; **bottom:** Dept. of Defense photo by SSgt. Herman Kokojan, U.S. Air Force; **Page 512: top:** © Bettmann/Corbis; **Page 514: top left & right:** © 2007 JupiterImages Corporation; **bottom:** map courtesy of Katie Pritchard; **Page 518: left:** © Bettmann/Corbis; **left center:** © Bettmann/Corbis; **center:** © Adrees Latif/Reuters/Corbis; **right center:** © Alison Wright/Corbis; **right:** Dept of Defense photo by Tech. Sgt. Jerry Morrison, U.S. Air Force

CHAPTER 25

Page 423: © 2007 JupiterImages Corporation; **Page 524:** map courtesy of Katie Pritchard; **Page 525:** map courtesy of Katie Pritchard; **Page 527: top:** map courtesy of Katie Pritchard; **bottom:** map source: Former Yugoslavia: A Map Folio, 1992 (CIA), courtesy of University of Texas Libraries; **Page 528:** Produced by the Office of The Geographer and Global Issues, Bureau of Intelligence and Research, US Dept. of State, courtesy of University of Texas Libraries; **Page 529:** CIA map (1994), courtesy of University of Texas Libraries; **Page 531:** CIA map (1988), courtesy of University of Texas Libraries; **Page 532:** CIA map, courtesy of University of Texas Libraries; **Page 533:** from *Global Trends 2015: A Dialogue About the Future With Nongovernment Experts* [page 73], National Intelligence Council, 2000, courtesy of University of Texas Libraries; **Page 534: top:** CIA map (2003), courtesy of University of Texas Libraries; **bottom:** CIA map (1988), courtesy of University of Texas Libraries; **Page 535:** CIA map (2008), courtesy of University of Texas Libraries; **Page 536:** map courtesy of Katie Pritchard; **Page 537:** map courtesy of Katie Pritchard; **Page 538:** map courtesy of Katie Pritchard; **Page 540:** Somalia and Djibouti Map, CIA 1977, courtesy of University of Texas Libraries; **Page 541: top:** CIA map, courtesy of University of Texas Libraries; **bottom:** CIA map, courtesy of University of Texas Libraries

CHAPTER 26

Page 542: bottom left: from Library of Congress; **all others** © 2008 JupiterImages Corporation; **Page 544: top:** lithograph by Illinois Co., Chicago (1917), from Library of Congress; **bottom:** ca. 1917, from Library of Congress; **Page 545:** © 2008 JupiterImages Corporation; **Page 546:** © 2008 JupiterImages Corporation; **Page 547:** © 2008 JupiterImages Corporation; **Page 549: top:** Dept. of Defense photo; **middle:** © 2008 JupiterImages Corporation; **bottom:** © NATO; **Page 550: top:** NATO logo used by permission of NATO; **bottom:** map source: *The World Factbook*; **Page 551:** courtesy of Katie Pritchard; **Page 553: top:** © 2007 JupiterImages Corporation; **bottom:** map courtesy of Katie Pritchard; **Page 555: top:** © 2008 JupiterImages Corporation; **bottom:** © 2007 JupiterImages Corporation; **Page 556:** maps courtesy of Katie Pritchard